South of France

Marseille to Monte-Carlo

Penguin Books

PENGUIN BOOKS

Published by the Penguin Group
Penguin Books Ltd, 27 Wrights Lane, London W8 5TZ, England
Penguin Books USA Inc., 375 Hudson Street, New York, New York 10014, USA
Penguin Books Australia Ltd, Ringwood, Victoria, Australia
Penguin Books Canada Ltd, 10 Alcorn Avenue, Toronto, Ontario, Canada M4V 3B2
Penguin Books (NZ) Ltd, 182-190 Wairau Road, Auckland 10, New Zealand

Penguin Books Ltd, Registered Offices: Harmondsworth, Middlesex, England

First published 2000
10 9 8 7 6 5 4 3 2 1

Colour reprographics by Westside Digital Media, 9 Bridle Lane, London W1
and Precise Litho, 34-35 Great Sutton Street, London EC1
Printed and bound by Cayfosa-Quebecor, Ctra. de Caldes, Km 3 08 130 Sta, Perpètua de Mogoda, Barcelona, Spain

Edited and designed by
Time Out Guides Limited
Universal House
251 Tottenham Court Road
London W1P 0AB
Tel + 44 (0)20 7813 3000
Fax + 44 (0)20 7813 6001
Email guides@timeout.com
www.timeout.com

Editorial

Editor Lee Marshall
Deputy Editor Ruth Jarvis
Consultant Editor Natasha Edwards
Listings Editor Rosemary Bailey
Copy editors Sophie Blacksell, Anne Hanley,
Cath Phillips, Ros Sayles
Proofreader Tamsin Shelton
Indexer Marion Moisy

Editorial Director Peter Fiennes

Series Editors Ruth Jarvis, Caroline Taverne
Deputy Series Editor Jonathan Cox

Design

Art Director John Oakey
Art Editor Mandy Martin
Senior Designer Scott Moore
Designers Benjamin de Lotz, Lucy Grant
Picture Editor Kerri Miles
Deputy Picture Editor Olivia Duncan-Jones
Picture Admin Kit Burnet
Scanning & Imaging Chris Quinn

Advertising

Group Advertisement Director Lesley Gill
Sales Director Mark Phillips
International Sales Manager Mary L Rega
Advertisement Sales (France) Clare Sibley

Administration

Publisher Tony Elliott
Managing Director Mike Hardwick
Financial Director Kevin Ellis
Marketing Director Gillian Auld
General Manager Nichola Coulthard
Production Manager Mark Lamond
Production Controller Samantha Furniss
Accountant Catherine Bowen

Features in this guide were written and researched by: **Introduction** Lee Marshall. **History** Lee Marshall. **Le Midi Today** Kate Chambers. **Art & Modernism in the South** Natasha Edwards. **Emigrés** Rosemary Bailey. **Arts & Entertainment:** **Contemporary Art** Natasha Edwards; **Film** Toby Rose; **Music: Classical & Opera** Stephen Mudge; **Music: Rock, Roots & Jazz** Lee Marshall; **Theatre** Annie Sparks; **Dance** Carol Pratl (*Tu tires, ou tu pointes?* Lee Marshall). **Provençal Food & Drink** Alec Lobrano, Margaret Kemp (*The Ducasse Empire* Alec Lobrano, Lanie Goodman). **Nîmes** Rosemary Bailey. **North of Nîmes** Rosemary Bailey. **Around the Alpilles** Rosemary Bailey. **Arles** Rosemary Bailey. **The Camargue** Rosemary Bailey. **Avignon** Rosemary Bailey. **Orange & Around** Stephen Mudge. **Carpentras & Around** Stephen Mudge. **The Luberon** Natasha Edwards. **Marseille & Around** Alec Lobrano (*The Olympique spirit* Kate Chambers). **Aix-en-Provence & Around** Natasha Edwards. **Cassis to Toulon** Inger Holland. **Hyères to the Maures** Toby Rose, Anne Hanley. **St-Tropez & Around** Toby Rose, Anne Hanley. **St-Raphaël & Around** Toby Rose, Anne Hanley. **Western Var** Inger Holland. **Central & Eastern Var** Inger Holland. **Gorges du Verdon** Deirdre Mooney, Anne Hanley. **Cannes** Toby Rose (**Mougins, Vallauris** Margaret Kemp). **Antibes to Cagnes** Jane McFadyen (**Biot** Margaret Kemp). **Nice** Lanie Goodman (*Rosbif rock* Lee Marshall). **The Corniches** Lanie Goodman. **Monaco & Monte-Carlo** Lanie Goodman. **Menton & Around** Lanie Goodman. **Grasse & Around** Margaret Kemp, Anne Hanley. **Vence & Around** Margaret Kemp, Anne Hanley. **The Arrière-pays & the Var Valley** Lanie Goodman, Lee Marshall. **Into the Alps: Vallées de la Roya & de la Bévéra** Lanie Goodman (*La Vallée des Merveilles, Parc National du Mercantour* Lee Marshall); **Vallée de la Vésubie, Vallée de la Tinée** Lee Marshall. **Directory** Rosemary Bailey; **The South by Season** Natasha Edwards; **Gay** Toby Rose.

The Editor would like to thank the following: Sarah Guy, Nicholas Royle, Polly Timberlake, Rosalind Sykes, Kate Fisher, Karen Albrecht, Anne Hanley, Richard Lines, Clara Marshall.

Maps by JS Graphics, 17 Beadles Lane, Old Oxted, Surrey RH8 9JG.
Street plans are based on material supplied by Thomas Cook Publishers.

Photography by Adam Eastland except: page 12, 13, 19, 21, 30, 33 AKG; page 26 Clews Foundation; page 31 All Action; page 34 Abel/Orange; page 36 Boisnard; pages 94, 95 J L Seille; page 186 Ville de Saint-Tropez; page 245 Empics; pages 272, 273, 275, 276, 278 Anne Hanley. The following photographs were supplied by the featured establishments: pages 14, 37.

Contents

Introduction   vi

In Context

History   4
Le Midi Today   15
Art & Modernism
  in the South   19
Emigrés   24
Arts & Entertainment   29
Provençal Food & Drink   38

The Rhône Delta

Nîmes   56
North of Nîmes   65
Around the Alpilles   68
Arles   75
The Camargue   83

Avignon & the Vaucluse

Avignon   88
Orange & Around   102
Carpentras & Around   108
The Luberon   114

Marseille & Aix-en-Provence

Marseille & Around   124
Aix-en-Provence   139

The Western Côte

Cassis to Toulon   152
Hyères to the Maures   161
St-Tropez & Around   168
St-Raphaël & Around   175

Inland Var

Western Var   182
Central & Eastern Var   187
Les Gorges du Verdon   193

The Riviera

Cannes & Around   198
Antibes to Cagnes   210
Nice   218
The Corniches   235

Monaco & Monte-Carlo   242
Menton & Around   250

Inland Alpes-Maritimes

Grasse & Around   256
Vence & Around   263
The Arrière-pays & the Var Valley   268
Into the Alps   271

Directory

Getting There   282
Getting Around   283
Accommodation   286
The South by Season   288
Resources A-Z   292
Essential Vocabulary   306
Further Reading   307
Index   308
Advertisers' Index   315

Maps

The South of France   318
The Rhône Delta   320
Avignon & the Vaucluse   322
Marseille & Aix-en-Provence   324
Inland Var & the Western Côte   326
Inland Alpes-Maritimes   328
The Riviera   330

Introduction

The South of France is more a mindset than a place. As with the equally evocative 'Provence', the borders of what English-speakers think of as 'the South of France' – or what the French refer to as Le Midi – are determined by visions and clichés rather than lines on a map. Palm trees on a promenade, backed by cream-coloured *belle époque* hotels; a lazy lunch under the lime trees in the square of a honey-coloured hill village; Roman aqueducts and galloping white horses; a screen diva with Hermès scarf and Gucci shades on the Corniche.

For many, the South of France is synonymous with the Côte d'Azur – a term invented by French writer Stéphen Liégeard in 1887. Once again, the geographical boundaries of the term are vague – some take it only as far west as Cannes, others push it all the way to Cassis. The real Côte is wherever enough people participate in the ritual of beaches, bronzed bodies and conspicuous wealth: Monte-Carlo, Juan-les-Pins, St-Tropez. Summer traffic congestion can take some of the shine off the glamour, but once you're ensconced at a café table overlooking the Mediterranean, there's no getting away from the Riviera's effortless, innate sense of style. As one of the first areas to discover summer beach tourism, the Côte d'Azur has had plenty of time to get it right; there is rarely anything brash about its come-ons.

Variety, though, is the spice of Provence. If palm trees and shaken-not-stirred dry martinis don't do it for you, there's the back country to discover. Inland from Menton, Nice and the Var resorts is a landscape of *villages perchés*, vineyards, lavender fields, abbeys and ruined chateaux where life really does move at a more relaxed pace. To the west, around the lower reaches of the Rhône, vine-laden hills alternate with towns bloated with history: Roman Arles, Vaison-la-Romaine and Orange, papal Avignon and the rocky medieval fiefs of the Alpilles and the Luberon. For some of the urbane elegance of Paris in a Provençal setting, head for Aix-en-Provence, with its café culture and *hôtels particuliers*. And finally, if the postcard perfection gets too much to bear, Marseille makes the perfect antidote: a sprawling, vibrant, multicultural port city with a legendary football team.

Add some of the best food to be had in France – bought fresh from the local market or sampled in one of the region's temples of gastronomy – and a lively summer festival scene, and you begin to wonder why anyone would ever want to go anywhere else. Denizens of the cold, grey north tend to agree with Vincent Van Gogh, who wrote to his brother Theo from Arles: 'I think I'll go further south... I need the warmth too much: it helps the blood flow properly.'

ABOUT TIME OUT GUIDES

The *Time Out South of France Guide* is one of the expanding series of *Time Out* guides produced by the people behind London and New York's definitive listings magazines. For the first time, the *Time Out South of France Guide* applies the dynamic, critical approach of *Time Out*'s successful city guide series to a whole region. While most general guides to the South concentrate on sightseeing, the *Time Out South of France Guide* has a distinctively cultural slant and includes a full selection of the best places to stay, eat and unwind, from the glitziest Riviera hotel to the humblest village brasserie, all with extensive listings information.

THE LIE OF THE LAND

For most people, the borders of that nebulous entity 'the South of France' are those of the southern portion of the modern French region of Provence-Alpes-Côte d'Azur, which includes the *départements* of Bouches-du-Rhône, Vaucluse, Var and Alpes-Maritimes. These are also the confines of the area covered by this guide, with a couple of exceptions: Nîmes and Uzès are included because their Roman and medieval legacies link them with the adjacent Rhône Delta; while further east, the spectacular Gorges du Verdon area lies at least partly in the remote *département* of Alpes-de-Haute-Provence. Our regional sections are arranged roughly in a west-east order.

All areas covered, from big cities to rural backwaters, follow a similar format, starting with background and sightseeing information and ending with where to eat, where to stay and

> There is an online version of this guide, as well as weekly events listings for over 30 international cities, at **www.timeout.com**.

transport and visitor information, including the relevant tourist offices. If you are interested in activities or themes that span the whole region, such as wine-touring or pottery museums, consult the index.

ESSENTIAL INFORMATION

For all the practical information you might need for visiting the area – including disabled access, emergency numbers and a list of useful websites – turn to the Directory chapter at the back of this guide. It starts on page 292.

THE LOWDOWN ON THE LISTINGS

Above all, we've tried to make this book as useful as possible. Addresses, phone numbers, transport information, opening times and admission prices are all included. However, owners and managers can change their arrangements at any time. Note particularly that seasonal closed periods for restaurants and hotels can vary from year to year. Before you go out of your way, we'd strongly advise you to phone ahead to check opening times and other particulars. While every effort and care has been made to ensure the accuracy of the information contained in this guide, the publishers cannot accept responsibility for any errors it may contain.

PRICES & PAYMENT

In the listings given for venues, we have noted which credit cards are accepted out of American Express (**AmEx**), Diners Club (**DC**), MasterCard (**MC**) and Visa (**V**). Other cards may also be taken. We have not given credit information for museums or churches, as cards are seldom accepted and prices usually low.

For every restaurant we have given the price range for set menus offered. Note that the lowest-priced menu is often only available at lunch. Where no set menus are served, we have instead given an average, which covers a three-course meal, not including drink, for one person.

The prices we've supplied should be treated as guidelines, not gospel. Fluctuating exchange rates and inflation can cause charges, in shops and restaurants particularly, to change rapidly. If prices vary wildly from those we've quoted, ask whether there's a good reason. If not, go elsewhere. Then please let us know. We aim to give the best and most up-to-date advice, so we always want to know if you've been badly treated or overcharged.

TELEPHONE NUMBERS

The area code for the whole area covered in the guide – with the exception of Monaco – is 04. If calling from abroad, the code for France is 33, then 4 (drop the zero). Numbers prefixed by an 06 code are mobile phones, 08.36 numbers

premium-rate (usually 2.23F a minute) and 08.00 numbers free of charge (sometimes available from outside France at usual international rates). The Monaco code is 00 377.

MAPS

At the back of the book you'll find a series of colour-coded maps of the areas dealt with in each regional section. In addition, the historic centres of the nine most important cities in the South are plotted in easy-to-use maps within the relevant chapters.

LET US KNOW WHAT YOU THINK

We hope you enjoy the *Time Out South of France Guide*, and we'd like to know what you think of it. We welcome your tips for places to include in future editions and take notice of your criticism of our choices. There's a reader's reply card at the back of this book – or you can email us on southoffranceguide@timeout.com.

Money From Home In Minutes.

If you're stuck for cash on your travels, don't panic. Millions of people trust Western Union to transfer money in minutes to 176 countries and over 78,000 locations worldwide. Our record of safety and reliability is second to none. For more information, call Western Union: USA 1-800-325-6000, Canada 1-800-235-0000. Wherever you are, you're never far from home.

www.westernunion.com

WESTERN UNION | MONEY TRANSFER

The fastest way to send money worldwide.

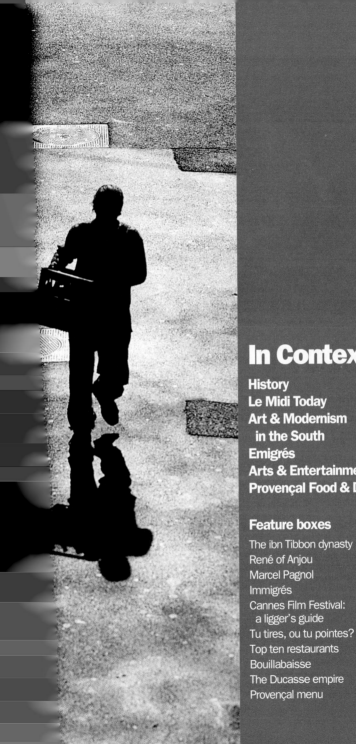

In Context

History	4
Le Midi Today	15
Art & Modernism in the South	19
Emigrés	24
Arts & Entertainment	29
Provençal Food & Drink	38

Feature boxes

The ibn Tibbon dynasty	5
René of Anjou	6
Marcel Pagnol	14
Immigrés	25
Cannes Film Festival: a ligger's guide	30
Tu tires, ou tu pointes?	35
Top ten restaurants	39
Bouillabaisse	43
The Ducasse empire	44
Provençal menu	50

The **Village des Bories** in Gordes, Luberon. *See page 121.*

History

Roman market garden, land of the troubadours and religious battleground – Provence and its neighbours have been around a bit.

Though Occitan autonomists have attempted to provide the South of France with a unified history to complement its supposedly unified language and culture, the truth is more complex. Only under Roman occupation, briefly in the Middle Ages and to some extent in more recent times has the territory known loosely as 'the South of France' or 'Le Midi' had any real regional cohesion.

Even the narrower term 'Provence' is volatile. It originated in 'Provincia' – the Romans' unimaginative term for their first transalpine province. But it did not enter common use until the ninth century, was more a title than a cohesive territory under the medieval Counts of Provence, and became an official entity only in 1956, with the creation of the region of Provence-Alpes-Côte d'Azur.

The only permanent and uncontroversial boundary of Provence was the southern one – fixed by the Mediterranean coastline. To the west, the Rhône became a frontier with the Treaty of Verdun in 843, a short-term partition that had lasting consequences, as it later came to define the respective spheres of influence of the Holy Roman Emperor and the papacy – east of the river – and the French kingdom to the west. Though the Alps would seem to be the logical eastern limit of the region, the territory around Nice was Italian (or at least Savoyard) for six centuries until ceded to France by Italy in 1860, too late to qualify for inclusion in anyone's mental Provence; the term Côte d'Azur later stepped in to fill the terminology gap. To the north, where the land was more rugged and less covetable, the border was even more nebulous.

EARLY DAYS

Evidence from sites near Nice and Monaco show that our ancestors lived here half a million years ago, perhaps earlier. Even before the last ice age, hunter societies had left propitiatory animal paintings on the walls of caves such as the Grotte Cosquer near Cassis, and after the last ice age, neolithic man took up residence in this fertile region.

Around 1200 BC, the Gauls – a Celtic people – began to migrate south and west from the Rhine valley into France and Italy. The southernmost front of this advance developed into the Ligurian culture, which stretched from Spain into Italy. Skilled metalworkers and stone carvers, the Ligurians lived in *oppidiums* – fortified villages such as that at Entremont (*see page 141*).

Western civilisation first came to Provence in the form of the Greeks from the Ionian city of Phocaea, who founded the colony of Massalia (modern-day Marseille) in around 600 BC. By the beginning of the fifth century BC, Massalia had become so powerful that it was coining its own money and had begun to plant other colonies along the coast, at Nice, Hyères and Agde, and inland at Arles. The Greek innovations of wine, olive oil and other goods traded around the Mediterranean soon filtered through to neighbouring Celtic areas.

ROMAN PROVENCE

Marseille took the Roman side during the Carthaginian Wars, a smart move that stood it in good stead when Rome went annexing beyond the Alps towards the end of the second century BC. The main reason for expansion into the south of France was the need to secure the land route to Spain, parts of which had been in Roman control since the end of the third century. Called in by Marseille to help the city repulse a Celtic attack, the Romans stayed on, destroying the Celto-Ligurian *oppidium* of Entremont and founding the city of Aquae Sextiae (Aix) in 122 BC. In recognition of its support, Marseille was allowed to stay an independent state within Roman territory. By 118 BC Rome controlled the whole coast westwards to the Pyrénées and a large swathe of the hinterland. In time-honoured fashion, the Romans subdued by colonisation: vast numbers of settlers, many of them army veterans, were attracted by a promise of free land. Narbonne, in the south-west, became the capital of Gallia Narbonensis, also known, more simply, by its former name of 'Provincia'.

Without firm borders to the north, Roman Provence was difficult to defend, and the Celts had not yet conceded defeat. After 115 BC, the northern Celtic tribes of the Cimbri and the Teutones mounted a series of raids on Provence, culminating in a humiliating defeat for the Romans at Orange in 105 BC. The

Provençal lives 1:
The ibn Tibbon dynasty

The high summer of Provençal culture in the twelfth and thirteenth centuries is testified to not only by the poetry of the troubadours but by a new interest in science, philosophy and the cabbala. Briefly, the Rhône delta area, from Marseille west to Montpellier (where a school of medicine was founded in 1220), became an enlightened crucible of learning, where Arab and Jewish scholars worked side by side with their Catholic colleagues. Exemplary in this respect were the three generations of the ibn Tibbon family. The patriarch, Judah ibn Tibbon (1120-90), was a Jewish doctor and translator who fled from Granada in 1150 to escape persecution. Settling in Lunel, south-west of Nîmes, he dedicated himself to translations of important rabbinic texts written by Arabic-speaking Jews. His son, Samuel ibn Tibbon (1150-1230), followed on in the same vein, making a living by practising as a doctor but channelling his intellectual energies into translations from Arabic into Hebrew, above

all of the philosopher Maimonides, who proposed a fusion of holy scripture and Aristotelean philosophy. Samuel's work was carried on by his own son, Moses ibn Tibbon (c1220-83), who helped to further disseminate Maimonides' works, and also translated Averroes' commentaries on Aristotle. But it was Moses' nephew, Jacob ben Machir ibn Tibbon (1236-1312) – also known as Don Profiat or Prophatius – who was to have the most lasting influence on European scholarship. Born in Marseille, Jacob set up as a doctor, and became so successful that he was invited to head the faculty of medicine at the University of Montpellier. Medicine and translation were a family tradition, and Jacob excelled at both – but he also had a keen interest in science and astronomy, designing a quadrant that was later adopted by mariners, and drawing up a table of fixed stars, the Luhot, that helped Dante to get his cosmography right in the *Divine Comedy*.

Augustus's **Trophée les Alpes** at La Turbie. *See page 241.*

Roman general Marius went in to repair the damage in 102 BC.

Under the *pax romana*, Gallia Narbonensis became a model province. Even after Julius Caesar had subdued the rest of Gaul in the Gallic Wars (58-51 BC), this remained the most Roman of the empire's transalpine possessions. The lower Rhône valley, in particular, bristled with fine cities: Aix, Arles, Nîmes, Orange and the major port of Fréjus, probable birthplace of the historian Tacitus. Marseille was eclipsed after it chose the wrong horse, supporting Pompey against Caesar in the Civil Wars. Besieged by Caesar's troops in 49 BC, it lost its independence, and its possessions were transferred to Arles, Narbonne and Fréjus – though it continued to be

Provençal lives 2: René of Anjou

Otherwise known as Good King René – a sobriquet he earned by not being excessively cruel, encouraging the arts and putting in some quality time with his Provençal subjects, unlike previous absentee Anjou rulers. A dynastic blend – his father was an Anjou, his mother an Aragon – René (1409-80) further extended the family territory when he was betrothed to Isabella of Lorraine in 1420. By the time he was 20, he had four children, and he could concentrate on amassing titles: duke of Anjou and of Bar, duke consort of Lorraine, count of Piedmont and Provence and titular king of Naples – though it was the loss of the latter territory to Alfonso V of Aragon in 1442 that prompted René to settle down and indulge his literary and chivalric streak. He delighted in organising tournaments, and wrote a treatise on the knightly rules of battle. He also composed a 10,000-line ode for his second wife, Jeanne de Laval, in the form of a debate between a shepherd and a shepherdess on the nature of love. Poet François Villon, who

read René's effort, is reported to have said that the shepherdesses he knew took far less persuading. It was around this time, in the 1450s, that René established a court at Aix and began to give some thought to administrative and legal reforms. Like Cosimo de' Medici, René believed that the enlightened ruler had a duty to generate culture as well as income, and he surrounded himself with local, Flemish-influenced artists such as Nicolas Froment and the anonymous Master of the Aix Annunciation (Froment painted the king and his queen into the wings of his curious, symbolically loaded Mary in the Burning Bush, now in Aix cathedral). René continued to add to his string of essentially meaningless titles (which included the honorific 'king of Jerusalem') in 1466, when Catalan rebels proclaimed him king of Aragon and count of Barcelona. But his almost continuous deferrals to Paris made René increasingly dependent on the French crown, and ensured that the kingdom of Provence's finest moment was also its last.

a centre of scholarship, the last outpost of Greek culture in the west.

Provence became an important supplier of grain, olive oil and ships for the ever-hungry empire. In return, it was treated more as an extension of the motherland than a colonial outpost. The aqueducts, baths, amphitheatres and temples that serviced the citizenry of burgeoning centres such as Arles and Nîmes often surpassed those of similar-sized Italian cities. The Rhône became the trading river par excellence, with Arles acting as the northern European port of entry for goods from Spain, Africa and Arabia; it was often quicker and cheaper to trade even with Britain via the Rhône and the Seine rather than on the dangerous Atlantic route. The imperial connection with Provence was reinforced under Antoninus Pius (emperor from AD 138 to 161), whose family came from Nîmes; and with Constantine, the first Christian emperor, Arles became a favoured imperial residence in the early fourth century.

MONKS & INVADERS

After its clandestine beginnings in the second century BC, the Christian community came into the open with the foundation of the monasteries of St-Honorat on the Iles des Lérins and St-Victor in Marseille in the early fifth century.

The latter was the centre of a monastic diaspora that gave the South a generous sprinkling of abbeys, ensuring the land was worked even in times of crisis – though the monks could be as tyrannical in exploiting the peasantry as any feudal landlord.

When the Roman empire finally fell apart in 476, the bishoprics maintained some semblance of order in the face of successive invasions by Visigoths and Ostrogoths. It was the Franks – who originally came from the west bank of the Rhine – who eventually gained the upper hand, after a period of anarchy during which Roman embellishments such as aqueducts, bridges and theatres fell into ruin and drained fields returned to swampland. In addition, the new rulers looked north rather than south, and the Mediterranean trade that had provided a living for cities like Arles or Marseille gradually dried up.

At the beginning of the eighth century the Moors spilled over the Pyrénées from Spain into Aquitaine, the south-western portion of modern-day France, before being defeated at Poitiers by Frankish generalissimo Charles Martel. The invasion was not unwelcome to all; the local rulers of Provence even petitioned the Cordoba caliphate to help them fight off the pesky Franks. But Frankish rule was reasserted under Pepin the Short and his son, Charlemagne.

Roman engineering at the **Pont du Gard**, a three-storey aqueduct. *See page 67.*

Yo, brother: the medieval cool of **St Trophime** in Arles. *See page 79.*

The three-way partition of the Carolingian empire in the Treaty of Verdun in 843 made the Rhône a frontier and provided the basis for the later division between Provence and Languedoc. Over the next couple of centuries, imperial rule gave way to out and out feudalism, with a succession of local lords using brute force and taxes to subdue the territory around their castle strongholds. In the eighth and ninth centuries, the Saracens terrorised the coast and launched raids on the surrounding countryside from their base at La Garde-Freinet in the Massif des Maures.

CATALANS & TROUBADOURS

In around 931 the kingdom of Provence – one of the increasingly small fragments of Charlemagne's former empire – was allied with Burgundy, and a century later, as the kingdom of Arles, it became part of the Holy Roman Empire, which thus established the Rhône as its westward limit.

The Church's influence was stronger than ever before, and towards the end of the eleventh century more efficient agriculture, the revival of trade and the rise of the guilds provided the money for the construction of new religious foundations such as the magnificent abbey of

St-Gilles on the edge of the Camargue (*see page 84*) and the restoration and embellishment of pre-existing ones like St-Trophime in Arles.

Sometime in the eleventh century, a small local dynasty had felt confident enough to award itself the title of Counts of Provence. When the line died out in 1113, the title passed to the House of Barcelona, which became the nominal ruler of the area. However, the larger cities were soon asserting their independence, setting up governments known as consulates, and in the country, local bosses like the lords of Baux reigned supreme in their own fiefdoms and put up fierce resistance to those claiming higher authority.

> **'A distinctive local culture was being formed, which reached its fullest expression in the poetry of the troubadours.'**

The Catalan sway over Mediterranean France was helped along by language. Occitan, or Provençal, the dialect that had developed in the south-west and east into Provence, was very different from French but a close cousin of

The Gothic **Palais des Papes** in Avignon. *See page 11.*

Catalan. Out of the apparent anarchy and the frequent shifts in the balance of power among the warring seigneuries, a distinctive local culture was being formed, which reached its fullest expression in the poetry of the troubadours.

These itinerant love poets – refined and occasionally high-born descendants of the *jongleurs*, or court entertainers – emerged with a distinct voice and style at the beginning of the twelfth century, composing and singing not only short lyrics to their chosen fair one but also heroic ballads and mock-erudite debates on the nature of love. As later in Renaissance Italy, the existence of a number of strong but powerful fiefdoms in a culturally unified area encouraged the emergence of a class of wandering artistic freelancers.

ANJOU COUNTS, BABYLONIAN POPES

Provence was spared the destruction and slaughter visited upon south-western France during the Albigensian Crusade between 1209 and 1229, as the Cathar heresy had never really caught on east of the Rhône. But the crusade altered the balance of power in the south – indeed, this had been one of its main ulterior motives all along. The Counts of Toulouse – who had tolerated and even encouraged the Cathars – were crushed, and the whole of Languedoc passed to the French crown in 1271.

The Counts of Provence emerged as sole rulers of the land between the Rhône and the Alps, though their links with their cultural base of Barcelona were cut by the French wedge of Languedoc (it was this, as well as the disappearance of the flourishing small courts, that caused the demise of the troubadours). The last of the Provençal counts, Raymond Berenger V, was also one of the shrewdest and most cultured. He gave his territories an efficient administration and appeased the increasingly muscular power of France by marrying his daughter Béatrice to Charles d'Anjou, brother of Louis IX, in 1246.

Angevin rule lasted two and a half centuries, bringing a great deal of stability, though the Anjou princes at first preferred to reside in Palermo or Naples, the other poles of their Mediterranean empire. The administrative reforms introduced by the last Count of Provence were continued with the establishment of the States General, a sort of regional assembly that had the power to raise taxes and take over the reins of government in times of crisis. The last of the local warlords, the Baux family, retreated to Orange, setting off the dynastic daisy chain that would lead to this becoming a corner of Protestant Holland in the sixteenth century.

Other interlopers were of a very different stamp. The Comtat Venaissin around Carpentras, Avignon and the Luberon was a territorial overspill of the Counts of Toulouse east of the Rhône. In 1274, three years after the Counts' main territory was annexed to the French crown, this enclave – whose borders had the shape, and the territorial logic, of an inkblot – was given to the papacy by Philippe III (the Bold). At the beginning of the fourteenth century, the French pope Clement V would make good use of this bolthole, transferring his whole court first to Carpentras and then to Avignon, and ushering in the papacy's 70-year 'Babylonian captivity' (*see box page 91*).

The Black Death hit Provence in 1348, entering through the port of Marseille, which had regained its maritime power thanks to the Crusades and the revival of Mediterranean trade. In 1282, the Angevin kings had been chased out of Sicily and thus had a little more time to devote to Provence. But after centuries of absentee rulers, the South had learned to get along without them. Trade had picked up; exemplary in this respect was Montpellier, a town that was founded only in 985 as a farm estate but that by the end of the thirteenth century had become a thriving mercantile and university city – though for most of this time it was a possession of the unlikely-sounding kingdom of Majorca, which had its capital in Perpignan. This brief medieval renaissance, with its multicultural exchange of people and ideas, provided fertile ground for Jewish scholars like the ibn Tibbon family (*see box page 5*).

After 1377, when the popes returned to Rome, Provence went through a new period of instability, with local warlords like Raymond de Turenne once again terrorising the region. Though it started unpromisingly with the loss of the Anjous' last Italian possession of Naples, the reign of Good King René (1434-80) was longer and more stable than most, and the king, himself a poet, encouraged a minor artistic revival from his court in Aix (*see box page 6*). By and large, though, the major currents of international art bypassed the South of France. Significantly, it was in the field of ecclesiastical architecture that the most confident and original work was being done, from the twelfth-century Romanesque of buildings such as the Abbey of Montmajour (*see page 73*) to the flamboyant fourteenth-century Gothic of the Palais des Papes in Avignon (*see page 93*). Painting was dominated by Italian artists in the fourteenth century; only in the fifteenth did artists such as Enguerrand Quarton (*see page 101*) and Nicolas Froment, King René's court painter, develop a more local, Flemish-influenced style of crystalline painterly detail. To the east, in the territory of Nice (grabbed by the House of Savoy in 1388) – and especially its mountainous hinterland – Niçois painter Ludovico Bréa and Piedmontese imports Giovanni Canavesio and Jean Baleison would found a distinctive school in the mid-fifteenth century.

UNION WITH FRANCE & THE WARS OF RELIGION

When it came, the inevitable union was almost accidental. Charles du Maine, René's nephew, survived his uncle by only a year. Dying without an heir in 1481, he bequeathed the territory of Provence (excluding Savoy, Monaco and the Comtat Venaissin) to portly King Louis XI of France. Not only Provence but Roussillon, Burgundy, Lorraine and even parts of northern Italy came under the sway of this fat controller, who probably did more than any other king to fix the borders and form the institutions of modern France.

After trying strong-arm tactics for the first three years, France decided to allow Provence at least the illusion of independence for the time being, with the Act of Union (1486) granting the region substantial autonomy within the French state. A *parlement* was established at Aix in 1501, but within the region it was supposed to govern there were still several pockets of autonomy – notably Marseille, which stoutly defended its republican traditions, though its shipyards were at the mercy of the prevailing overlord. François Ier used them in his Italian wars against his arch-enemy, the Holy Roman Emperor Charles V; the latter replied by besieging the city in 1523.

But on the ground the dominant issue became that of religious difference. Protestantism had achieved a firm foothold in Provence and in eastern Languedoc, especially among the rural poor. Even before Luther, the Waldensian sect – whose tweaking of Catholic doctrine was more than enough to have it branded heretical – had put down roots in the South, especially in the Luberon. In April 1545, with the connivance of the parliament in Aix, a series of massacres decimated the Waldensian population of the Petit Luberon: 3,000 people were killed and Waldensian strongholds such as Mérindol and Lourmarin (*see page 114*) were put to the torch.

This, though, was only the opening salvo of the Wars of Religion, which really kicked in when French Calvinism – or Huguenotism – spread throughout France in the 1550s. Settlers from the Dauphiné and Piedmont brought Protestantism to Orange, Haute Provence and the Luberon, but the main seedbed of the new faith was in the areas west of the Rhône: in Nîmes, three-quarters of the population became Huguenot. In 1560, a wave of factional violence spread through the region, with atrocities on both sides. Most of the Huguenot population of Orange was massacred in 1563; in reprisal, the notorious Baron des Adrets, who had converted from Catholicism only the year before to settle a few personal scores, went on the rampage; he specialised in throwing Catholic prisoners from the top of the nearest castle (two years later he converted back, and retired to the family estate).

> ## 'Le Midi was drained of funds and, at the same time, kept in line by an increasingly centralised state.'

Henri IV's Edict of Nantes (1598), guaranteeing Protestants civil and religious liberties, and effective political control of certain areas, marked the formal end of hostilities. In the South its main effect was to reconfirm the Rhône split – this time as a religious rather than political frontier. To the east, Provence had demonstrated its essential loyalty to France and the French crown; the French language, too, was becoming more dominant in the region, with Occitan resisting mainly west of the Rhône or in the more remote Alpine valleys. When Louis XIV revoked the Edict of Nantes in 1685, the main effect was to deprive Montpellier, Nîmes, Uzès and other eastern towns of their industrious Huguenot manufacturers, who were forced to emigrate in their thousands (though a few stayed on to make silk and the blue linen 'de Nîmes' that English merchants referred to as 'denim').

REVOLUTION & DICTATORSHIP

By the seventeenth century, the history of the South had become bound up with the history of France. Of use to Paris mainly as a source of fruit, sugar cane, olive oil, wine, textiles and taxes, and as a builder and launcher of ships for royal wars, Le Midi was drained of funds and, at the same time, kept firmly in line by an increasingly centralised state. When restless Marseille dared to set up a rebel council in 1658, Louis XIV turned the town's cannons on itself and built two forts designed above all to keep an eye on the unruly citizens. At the same time, the port of Toulon was expanded and turned into the main base of the Mediterranean fleet. Marseille took a further body blow in 1720, when a visiting Syrian ship caused one of the last big outbreaks of plague in the West, which killed 50,000 people in the city alone.

But the eighteenth century was also a time of increasing prosperity, when the South – especially the fertile, mercantile western part of Provence between Arles, Avignon and Aix – benefited from being largely left to its own devices. A prosperous bourgeoisie developed around the main industries – textiles in the Gard (around Nîmes), salt and trade on the coast, furniture in the lower Rhône valley, pottery in a number of centres, especially around Marseille and Aubagne. In the two 'parliamentary' cities – Aix and Montpellier (capitals, respectively, of the States General administrative areas of Provence and Languedoc), a wealthy caste of politicians with plenty of time on their hands built themselves sumptuous townhouses – known as the *hôtels particuliers*.

Religious piety still dominated the lives of the lower orders. This was the golden age of the penitent orders, lay confraternities that vied with each other to build churches, hold processions and collect funds for charitable works – providing the area with its first, rudimentary form of social security.

Nevertheless, resentment of distant, uncaring Paris continued to simmer, and when the Revolution broke out in 1789, the South joined in enthusiastically, its appetite for change whetted by a couple of bad harvests and rising urban unemployment. The dockers of Marseille were particularly active – though the battle-hymn of the republic, the *Marseillaise*, was in fact written by an Alsatian captain in Strasbourg as a marching song and only

David's *Napoléon Crossing the Alps*.

associated with Marseille when adopted by the city's Jacobin national guard (*les Féderés*) on their march to Paris in July 1792. A big hit in the capital, it was adopted as the national anthem in 1795, and once more – after an enforced retirement – in 1879.

The papal enclave of the Comtat Venaissin had been reincorporated into France in 1791, and in 1792 Revolutionary forces took Nice, which was handed back to Italy only in 1814. But anarchy soon set in all over France, with counter-revolutionary uprisings and the White Terror of 1795 setting faction against faction. The British took advantage of the confusion to occupy Toulon in 1793; they were sent packing by artillery troops commanded by a rising military star, the 24-year-old Napoléon Bonaparte.

Though he hailed from Corsica and had served his military apprenticeship in Antibes and Toulon, Bonaparte had little affection for Provence, and the feeling was mutual. His return from exile on Elba and flight north to Paris in 1815 are today commemorated by the Route Napoléon, a scenic drive promoted by local tourist boards (*see page 258*). But at the time, this roundabout mountain road via Grasse and Sisteron was chosen as the safest and quickest way out of a potentially hostile area.

FROM RESTORATION TO REPUBLIC
Perhaps the main legacy of the Revolution was a further weakening of regional autonomy with the abolition of the States General and the carve-up of France into centrally administrated *départements*. But while most Southerners now thought of themselves as French, this did not mean that Paris was the unavoidable point of reference. Provençal radicalism, nurtured in the shipyards of Toulon and Marseille, re-emerged in force, and most of the South threw its weight behind the 1848 revolution.

At the same time, though, an ever-present current of Catholic fundamentalism, at its strongest in rural areas, created a reactionary minority that would take different forms in coming years, from the revival of the Occitan language and traditions promoted by Frédéric Mistral (*see box page 72*) to the proto-Fascist Action Française movement founded in Paris in 1899 by Southerner Charles Maurras. Even the later success of the Front National in the region (*see chapter* **Le Midi Today**) may at least partly be explained by this strong Provençal undercurrent in which wounded pride mingles with nostalgia for a mythical purity of language or race.

The last of the major territorial reshuffles took place in 1860, when Napoléon III received Nice and its mountainous hinterland from the House of Savoy in return for his diplomatic

Provençal revivalist **Frédéric Mistral**.

THE TWENTIETH CENTURY

After years as the poor and untrustworthy rump of France, Le Midi was slowly becoming fashionable. The first to discover the charms of the warm south were *les anglais* – the local catch-all term for the British, Germans, Russians and other beau-monde foreigners who came with their parasols, portmanteaus and lapdogs to take the air. Nice had been discovered as early as the 1750s by intrepid English travellers prepared to brave the two-week journey down from Calais, Hyères loomed into fashion in the early nineteenth-century and Cannes followed soon after (*see chapter* **Emigrés**).

The turn of the century was the era of the great waterfront hotels, built in response to a surge in tourism: between 1890 and 1910 the number of foreigners visiting Nice grew almost sixfold to over 150,000 (*see chapter* **Emigrés**). Amused by these eccentric milords, the French bourgeoisie continued to winter in the country, and it was not until the 1920s – when the summer season was invented – that French artists, fashion designers and socialites began to descend on Le Midi in any great numbers, preferring chic coves like St Tropez to the promenades of Nice or Cannes (*see chapter* **Art & Modernism in the South**).

The two world wars took their toll on generations of Provençal conscripts. While the first was a distant, rain-soaked northern affair, the second came visiting when the Germans occupied the South after the collapse of Vichy France in the autumn of 1942. Hardest hit were the strategic naval ports of Marseille and Toulon, ravaged both by Allied bombing raids and by the retreating Germans in 1944; in Marseille a year previously, the Germans had dynamited the entire *quartier* of Le Panier, considered to be a dangerous lair of anarchists and reprobates. 1947 saw the last of the border tweakings, when the French-speaking upper Roya valley – which had remained Italian in 1860 at the insistence of King Vittorio Emanuele, who liked to go hunting there – was handed over to France.

> ## 'There has been an enthusiastic rediscovery of regional identity and regional dialects.'

Post-war reconstruction was responsible for some of the architectural horrors that dog the South; lax or corrupt planning departments did the rest, suffocating the Côte in concrete.

Heavy industry, too, has done its share of environmental damage, especially west of Marseille where the bird-filled salt marsh of the

neutrality during the unification of Italy. Monaco was now a one-town state, having lost Roquebrune and Menton in 1848 when the inhabitants revolted against the Grimaldis' exorbitant taxes; after a period as independent republics, the towns were formally transferred to France in 1860. Ironically, it was his principality's increasing isolation and threatened bankruptcy that spurred Charles III to reinvent Monaco as the gambling capital of Europe – so successfully that by 1870 he was able to abolish taxes for residents.

Meanwhile, industrialisation was transforming the region. The opening of the Suez Canal in 1869 and the spread of colonial France quadrupled Marseille's port traffic, and the coastal railway, an engineering feat with its many tunnels and viaducts, had reached Nice by 1865 and Monaco by 1868. Development of the coast and the Rhône estuary proceeded apace, to the detriment of the mountainous hinterland, which went into a slow decline that was not reversed until the modern era of second homes and bijou restaurants. Agriculture was an unreliable source of income: phylloxera struck the vines in 1875, and although the industry recovered, overseas competition caused a huge price slump in the early twentieth century.

Provençal lives 3: Marcel Pagnol

For generations of Frenchmen, Pagnol (1895-1974) embodied Provençal culture. Frédéric Mistral's attempt to salvage and refound the language and literature of the South (*see box page 72*) alienated many outside the region – as was no doubt intended – with its militant brandishing of folklore and funny costumes. Pagnol, in contrast, charmed an entire nation with his novels, plays and films, with their humorous but indulgent take on the stubborn, resilient Provençal character. Born in the workaday provincial town of Aubagne, east of Marseille, Pagnol began his working life as an English teacher in Marseille, but soon moved to Paris and began writing plays, hitting the big time with *Topaze* (1928). Three of his plays about the 'little people' of Marseille were made into films – *Marius* (1931), *Fanny* (1932) and *César* (1936), known collectively as the 'Pagnol trilogy'. Pagnol moved into the film business with his usual energy, not only directing, but producing films by other directors through his own Marseille-based studio. His unashamedly populist, theatrical films (almost all of which began life as stage plays) helped to mould an abiding modern vision of Provence as a place of struggling workers and dour peasants, buffetted by misfortune and the uncertainties of life on the land, surviving through a mixture of cunning and fatalistic irony. This was fully in the spirit of rural novelist Jean Giono from Manosque, three of whose works – among them *La Femme du boulanger* (1938) – were made into films by Pagnol. After the war, Pagnol continued to work with unabated energy, preparing his autobiography and continuing to

Manon des Sources.

write and direct. But it was the work of another director that gave Pagnol's Provence an international resonance: Claude Berri, whose four-hour cinematic adaptation of Pagnol's novel *L'Eau des collines* was released in 1986 as two separate films: *Jean de Florette* and *Manon des sources*. For many, this tale of the slow erosion of a city dweller's rural idyll, set in the hills behind Aubagne, is as Provençal as they come – up there with lavender, aïoli and the warm stone of a rural *mas* at sunset.

Etang de Berre became a huge oil dump, or in the valleys of the Durance and Verdon rivers, bloated into a series of lakes by overambitious hydro-electric projects. The proud radicalism of the port towns (Marseille had elected France's first socialist mayor, in 1892) was becoming tinged by corruption and by a new kind of reactionary radicalism, reflecting the poor white workers' fears of the new immigrants from North Africa who began to pour in after 1945 (*see page 15* **Le Midi Today**).

It was only in the 1980s – when Mitterrand granted the regions a limited form of autonomy – that the centralising impetus of the previous two centuries began to be reversed. There has been an enthusiastic rediscovery of regional identity and regional dialects, with school courses in Occitan and the appearance of dual language French/Occitan road signs. A new kingdom of Provence is still a long way off, but at last, after centuries of being told how ugly it is and only a few decades of admiring glances, the Cinderella of the French state has begun to put its broom away and think about the ball.

> ► For events since the 1980s, *see chapter* **Le Midi Today**.
> ► For the history of the Riviera as a holiday destination, *see chapter* **Emigrés**.

Gene Hackman goes fishing in *French Connection II*.

Le Midi Today

The idyllic identity of Le Midi as perceived by outsiders has little in common with a reality fraught with corruption, economic struggle and racism.

Step off the plane at Nice's Côte d'Azur airport into a taxi bound for the town centre and you're straight into the French Riviera as it should be – blue sea to your right, beaches dotted with well-oiled bodies and, in the distance, the wedding-cake outline of the Hôtel Negresco.

You could be forgiven for not noticing a crop of peach-coloured towers on your left as you pull out of the airport. Topped with a giant Mercedes logo, symbol of wealth and glamour, the Les Moulins council estate is an early introduction to Nice's – and the South's – less photogenic side. With its boarded-up shopfronts, small-time dealers and petty criminals, Les Moulins has much in common with more famous suburban trouble spots around Paris. Along with the notorious Ariane estate to the north of the city, where a policeman was killed during violent clashes with residents in 1995, Les Moulins is a reminder that life in Mediterranean holiday-land isn't all luxury.

Luxury is what the place is supposed to be about. Take a walk along the main streets of Cannes or Monaco. What counts here is what you see. Jewels, designer labels, cars, blonde women – if you've got it, flaunt it. *La frime*, the French call it – showing off. *La frime* characterises life in France's south-eastern corner, or at least, the tourist part of it. But once you step off the seafront and into the backstreets, a different South emerges, in which corruption, racism, unemployment and the unmistakeable whiff of the Mafia all rear their heads.

STRONG MEDECIN

'A sunny place for shady people' was how Somerset Maugham described the Riviera. And the last two decades have been peppered with corruption scandals, prison sentences for top politicians, not to mention an unexplained murder (or three). All of which locals have taken with a shrug, firmly persuaded as they are that Paris has a downer on the PACA (Provence-Alpes-Côte d'Azur) region.

Pick your resort – there's a scandal in every one. Cannes? The mayor, Michel Mouillot, was arrested on corruption charges in 1996 after allegations that a local casino had financed his election campaign. Sleepy old Hyères? The site of one of modern France's rare political assassinations, in 1994, when rightist female deputy and anti-corruption campaigner Yann Piat was gunned down. A local bar owner and the hit squad he hired went to prison for her murder in 1998, but a question mark still hangs over the real hand behind the killing. Two journalists wrote a book alleging Piat was the victim of a political plot laid in Paris, but they and their publisher were heavily fined.

Even Monaco, where security and discretion are the local gods, has had its share of scandal – most recently the surprise death-by-suffocation of billionaire banker Edmond Safra, in December 1999. Le Rocher was rocked by the tale of mystery armed and masked attackers who set fire to Safra's penthouse, killing the tycoon, who had barricaded himself into the bathroom. The culprit was quickly revealed to be a nurse who wanted his boss to notice him – though it has yet to be explained why Safra took on a former soldier with no formal health qualifications for the job.

Le foot is still a religion in Marseille.

And then, of course, there was the granddaddy of them all: Jacques Médecin, former mayor of Nice: a convicted criminal for the French legal system, but no worse than a loveable rogue for most Niçois. Médecin took over the mayorship of Nice's fifth largest city from his father in 1965 and remained in power until 1990. He was a flamboyant bon vivant who went through three glamorous wives and even found time to write a cookery book. Locals adored him, and Jacquou returned the favour. He loved going on walkabouts around the market on the cours Saleya, basking in the adulation of flower sellers on first-name terms who were straining to shake his hand.

'The rise and fall of Bernard Tapie brings together many strands in the south-eastern identity.'

But suspicions that he was involved in money-laundering and had links with the local property-speculation and casino-controlling Mafia began to be aired more and more openly. In 1982, British author Graham Greene, a long-time resident of Nice, published the pamphlet *J'Accuse: the dark side of Nice* – ostensibly about a divorce and child custody case, but really an attempt to debunk the image of sunny, laid-back Mediterranean bonhomie that the city likes to project by showing that it was 'the preserve of some of the most criminal organisations in the South of France', organisations that, Greene claimed, had 'the connivance of high authorities'.

Jacques Médecin fled to Uruguay in 1990 when things got a little too warm: he was facing criminal charges and owed income tax of around 20 million francs. He was extradited in 1994, tried, and given a 21-month prison sentence. On his release, as even more serious charges were pending, he fled back to Punte del Este. But when he died in November 1998, the Niçois gave him a hero's burial.

Like the Médecin saga, the rise and (at least temporary) fall of Bernard Tapie brings together many strands in the south-eastern identity – cash, corruption and the conviction that Paris has it in for PACA. Tapie was a poor lad who came south and struck rich. His speciality was to take over failing firms, revamp them and make millions. In the 1980s, with Président Mitterrand bewitched, Tapie became a local MP and Euro MP and (briefly) held a cabinet post. He presented a few TV programmes as well.

Monaco: high-rise condos for the absent rich.

But it was football that brought him true adulation – and proved his undoing. Tapie took over in April 1986 as president of Marseille's first division team, l'Olympique de Marseille (*see box page 133*). For a while the shaggy-suited businessman's magic seemed to be working for the club, and he was idolised by its fiercely loyal supporters. As Tapie dug into seemingly bottomless pockets to ship in new players, the team went from strength to strength, winning four league titles and two European semi-finals. Just one thing was lacking to make his – and Marseille's – happiness complete: the European Cup. Tapie was determined to get it and, in May 1993, he did, when OM beat AC Milan in the final.

But the sweet taste of victory was short-lived. The very next day, news broke that the team's previous league match against Valenciennes had been fixed. It was alleged that money had changed hands to buy a win, with Tapie's connivance. He vigorously protested his innocence, but his team was plunged into ignominy: stripped of its league title and relegated to the depths of the second division. In 1998, Tapie was eventually convicted of match-fixing and embezzling team funds and sent to prison. But the spell wasn't fully broken. Marseille still had, and has, a place in its heart for old Bernard. He had been fighting on their side, after all. He just got caught out by Paris.

POLITICS IN THE SOUTH

There's little history of safe centrists in the South; instead, PACA seems to have swung from one extreme to the next. If today the

region has gained notoriety as a hotbed for the far-right Front National (FN), the days when the far left ruled Provençal hearts and minds are less than two decades ago.

With its armies of underpaid dockers, Marseille proved a fertile hunting ground for the CGT, the Communist-linked trade union, in its 1970s heyday. Business at the port has waned now and so – not just in Marseille – has CGT membership. But reminders of leftist hearts live on, mostly in street names. Vitrolles, an industrial satellite of Marseille, boasted an avenue Salvador Allende, an avenue Nelson Mandela and a place Olof Palme – at least, it did until the Front muscled its way in.

PACA now has the highest percentage of anti-immigrant Front National voters in France, along with Alsace in the north. In the 1998 regional elections, 27 per cent of the region's electors voted FN. Part of the reason for the Front's popularity lies in the region's gloriously corrupt past – its Médecins and its Mouillots. The Front has trumpeted itself as a down-to-earth 'clean' party of the people. Some of it also has to do with the region's high percentage of *pieds noirs* – the French from Algeria who refuse to forget the estates and businesses they were forced to flee when the Front de Libération National came to power there in 1962. And the high rate of unemployment in PACA – 14.5 per cent compared to a national average of 11.5 – has also contributed; Le Front knows how to beat the 'jobs for the French first' drum.

It's proved a winning ticket in four towns: Toulon, the Roman city of Orange and two communes just north of Marseille, Marignane

Philippe Starck bus stop in Nîmes.

made to keep the Provençal dialect alive: students at Nice university will find Provençal included on the list of foreign language options they can choose from.

SUN, SEA AND SECOND HOMES

Ask the average Niçois, Marseillais, Cannois or Monégasque what's wrong with the place and they'll look at you aghast as they squint into the sun. Move north? Never. Not even for a job? Now there's a question…

Forty per cent of jobs in PACA are in the tourism industry. Which means that 64,000 people do often-seasonal, poorly paid work in hotels, restaurants and beaches, catering for the nine million visitors who come here each year. But, by and large, it's not the French who are staying in the hotels. The rest of France just doesn't buy that Mediterranean mystique any more – they find it too expensive. They still come down to the Riviera all right, but they stay with friends, or in second homes that have been in the family for years; two-thirds of households here put up a friend or family member during the summer months.

'In Orange, the FN mayor Jacques Bompard banned African traders from the outdoor market.'

and Vitrolles. In Orange, the FN mayor Jacques Bompard banned African traders from the outdoor market and replaced some African books with FN authors in the municipal library. But it is in once-Red Vitrolles, where unemployment stands at 20 per cent, that the most blatant racist policies have been adopted.

The Front came to power here in a disputed poll in 1997. Bruno Megret, then party deputy, now leader of a breakaway faction, wanted to stand but was disbarred for campaign overspending. So his wife, Cathérine, stepped in. Once elected she promptly renamed place Nelson Mandela 'place de Provence', banned café performances by rap singers and tried to set up a system of cash grants to parents of new babies – if they were French citizens; to her chagrin, the measure was judged illegal.

While the Front may seek to win voters here by reminding them of their Provençal identities, you'd be hard-pressed to find someone here who will tell you, when asked where they come from: 'Je suis Provençal.' There's no strong sense of regional identity to match that of the Basques or the Bretons, though half-hearted attempts are sometimes

And they don't go to the top resorts, considered too flash and showy. If the French come south – and many more of them are now heading for the western Atlantic coast, or Brittany – they go to the 'unfashionable' beaches between Marseille and Toulon, which are judged – with some justification – to be less polluted, less *frimeur* and less of a rip-off.

But for the Italians, Brits, Germans and Americans who flock here (in that order) in the summer, the film stars, the glitz and the Mediterranean warmth still seem to work the old magic. Since 1994, the number of foreigners holidaying in the region has increased steadily by ten per cent or more each year. Some of these come to stay in the 140,000 second homes dotted around the coast and hinterland, some on cruise ships that bring 300,000 visitors to the Riviera each year. For les Anglais, at least, it'll take more than the odd backhander, race riot or overpriced, uninspiring meal to destroy the myth.

► For more on immigration, *see page 25.*
► For Olympic Marseille after Tapie, *see box page 133.*

Paul Cézanne's *La Montagne Sainte-Victoire* (1902-6).

Art & Modernism in the South

The dramatic light and colour of the South – along with its more sybaritic natural charms – attracted a steady stream of ground-breaking artists from Van Gogh to Picasso.

For a crucial period in the first half of the twentieth century, the South of France became a pivot of the art world. The discovery of the Riviera as a summer resort coincided with the modern artist's discovery of strong light, strong colours and a strongly physical approach to paint, charcoal and clay.

Provençal landscapes had often featured in the background of paintings, but it was only towards the end of the nineteenth century, after the painters *en plein air* and the Impressionists, that landscapes became acceptable subjects in their own right. The Impressionists, however, were more interested in capturing the shifting, watery light of northern France, and in the urban scene, with its steam trains and buses, busy boulevards, cafés and fêtes. It took Paul

Cézanne, a native of Aix-en-Provence, to show how the South could become an inspiration and an abiding artistic presence.

RED ROOFS ON A BLUE SEA

Cézanne sought the permanent truth behind the landscape, as opposed to the transient impressions of the Impressionists. In 1871, escaping the Franco-Prussian war, he painted the fishing village and the coast at L'Estaque, near Marseille, returning frequently in the 1870s and 1880s. It was the 'red roofs on a blue sea' that drew him here; but he was put off by the arrival of 'progress', when first gas and then electric lights were installed along the quays. From the 1880s, Cézanne turned increasingly to the area around Aix and above all to the unspoiled savagery of Montagne Ste-Victoire (*see box page 142*), which he painted over and over again, searching for the key to its structure: 'to paint a landscape well', he wrote, 'I must first discover its geological characteristics'. Influenced by the rationality of Poussin, his ordering of nature on canvas – 'Nature must be treated by the cylinder, the sphere, the cone…' – led towards a new conception of perspective.

WILD THINGS

In February 1888, Vincent Van Gogh arrived in Arles, where he painted many of his most celebrated works, staying first in a hotel, then renting a room at the house depicted in *The Bedroom at Arles* and *The Yellow House* (*see box page 81*). His relationship with the South was far more visceral than Cézanne's; he wanted to understand not the underlying structure but the underlying emotion of these glaring Provençal landscapes: describing *The Night Café*, one of his Arles canvases, he wrote: 'I have tried to express the terrible passions of humanity by means of red and green'.

Van Gogh failed to establish the school he had hoped for, but his Arles period influenced Matisse and André Derain, who discovered his works at a Paris exhibition in 1901. Using colour, like Van Gogh, for its expressive value, they found inspiration in the fishing boats and village houses of Collioure, on the south-western coast near the Spanish border, and around Marseille, where Derain painted in 1906. Their unnatural use of colour caused a scandal at the 1905 Salon d'Automne and led to these painters being dubbed *Fauves* (savage).

In 1906, Georges Braque visited L'Estaque, a fishing village west of Marseille, in what proved to be a crucial moment in the transition between his Fauvist and Cubist periods. His Fauvist paintings of the port are a rhythm of waves of pink; but by 1908, when he again spent the summer in L'Estaque, this time joined by Othon Friesz and Raoul Dufy, Braque had seen the light, in the form of Picasso's revolutionary (and as yet unexhibited) painting *Les Demoiselles d'Avignon*. Braque's works of this summer show a new concern with structural planes, and a more sober palette dominated by greens and ochres. In this Braque was influenced not only by Picasso but by Cézanne, the original Cubist.

Further along the coast, keen yachtsman Paul Signac had discovered St-Tropez, then a simple fishing village as early as the 1890s. His paintings of the port seem infected by the wildness of the coast: Seurat's tiny, demure pointillist dots were no longer adequate, and Signac began to play with larger blocks of colour. In 1904, he was joined by Marquet, Manguin, Henri-Edmond Cross – a fellow disciple of Seurat – and Matisse (*see below*), whose canvas *Luxe, Calme et Volupté* is clearly influenced by Signac's divisionism and reveals part of his continuing attempt to resolve the relationship between line and colour. The works of many of these painters can be seen in the Musée de l'Annonciade in St-Tropez.

In 1907, the ageing, rheumatic Auguste Renoir bought the Domaine des Collettes in Cagnes-sur-Mer, where he built himself a house and studio (now the Musée Renoir, *see page 214*). Although he painted his late, garish *Les Grandes Baigneuses* here, he complained of the sun as too dazzling and turned to sculpture in his final years. For Pierre Bonnard, the '*affolant*' (maddening) southern light pushed art further towards chromatic patterns in which the solidity of outlines and perspective are broken down. In 1926, he bought a house at Le Cannet, on the outskirts of Cannes, where his large canvases of the garden and intimate domestic interiors are marked by the vibrant dematerialisation of form.

BOHEMIAN RHAPSODY

The inter-war period heralded a new age of sun worship and a new cult of the body. As the avant-garde mixed with the jet set, the Riviera – in constant dialogue with Paris as artists moved between the two – became a meeting place for artists, writers and photographers such as Man Ray, Paul Eluard, Roland Penrose, Lee Miller, Pablo Picasso, Dora Maar, Robert Capa and Marcel Duchamp, who drew inspirations from the Mediterranean light, the still-uncommercialised Provençal culture and the Riviera set's lack of restraint and unconventional behaviour. Society playboy and photographer Jacques-Henri Lartigue snapped fast cars and the rich at play. Francis Picabia was both a satirist of the jet set and a part of it, with his passion for cars (he owned 127) and the extravagant fancy-dress balls that he organised in the casino at Cannes. A move in his art from Dadaist machines to more dreamy, mythological canvases was reflected in the design of the Château de Mai, the house Picabia built for himself at Mougins, which was in a constant state of flux as he added more terraces, a swimming pool, turrets and an atelier.

In 1917, Henri Matisse paid his first visit to Nice; from 1919 on he spent half the year there, finding in the South and its light a feeling of calm, but also, in this increasingly cosmopolitan city, a spur to his interest in oriental, Greek and African art. Despite his long friendship and frequent contact with Bonnard and Picasso, Matisse essentially remained isolated on the hill

Van Gogh's *Le Café le soir* (1888).

Robert Mallet-Stevens & Modernist architecture

In the 1920s, while sumptuous art deco palace hotels like the Majestic and Martinez were going up in Cannes and private clients were indulging their rather limited fantasies in a range of neo-Grecian, neo-Provençal, neo-Tuscan or neo-oriental villas, the Riviera also saw some more interesting architectural experiments.

The advent of Modernist architecture on the Côte can be dated to 1923-4, when glamorous Robert Mallet-Stevens built the Villa Noailles at Hyères for the high-society patrons Charles and Marie-Laure de Noailles on the site of a medieval castle. Its Cubist form was influenced by the Dutch De Stijl movement, with a complex arrangement of spaces following the terrain and roof terraces overlooking the bay. Originally intended as a winter residence, the design evolved during construction to meet the new demands of summer hospitality, with a swimming pool and gym. Eileen Gray, François Jourdain and Théo Van Doesburg were among those involved in the decoration and guests soon included such figures as Poulenc, Buñuel, Giacometti, Stravinsky and Man Ray, who made his Surrealist film *Les Mystères du Château du Dé* here in 1929. The villa was recently saved from ruin by the municipality and is now used for exhibitions (*see page 161*).

Others followed suit. At Beauvallon, between St-Tropez and Ste-Maxime, Pierre Chareau built the Club-House du Golf-Hôtel and the Villa Vent d'Aval, both more Cubist in style than his later and more famous work, the glass and steel Maison de Verre in Paris. In 1927-9, Georges-Henri Pingusson designed the highly sculptural Villa Romée on avenue de la Plage at Cannes, with its drum-like rotunda and floating, suspended dining room, but his most radical work was the Latitude 43 hotel at St-Tropez. This vast, linear building, with its curved prow and central mast, was intended to welcome artists and intellectuals, although the hotel soon went bust and was later converted into apartments. Some of the most ostentatious villas went up on Cap d'Antibes, where in 1938 US architect Barry Dierks built the Villa Aujourd'hui, with geometrical seaside façade and curvaceous street side, which almost seems to prefigure the '50s streamlining of designer Raymond Loewy.

Oddly, though, it was the conservative, easternmost strip of the Riviera around Menton that saw the most radical projects. Irish-born designer and interior decorator Eileen Gray conceived E-1027, a house built in 1926-9 on stilts against the rock of Cap-Martin. With a radical new disposition of space, the building is dominated by a gigantic salon whose sea-facing wall consists almost entirely of windows. Gray also designed the furniture, including the Transat chair and

of Cimiez (now the site of the Musée Matisse – *see page 223*) from the frivolity going down on the beaches below, developing in his interiors, still lifes and Odalisques an interest in blocks of colour and stark patterns and in the simplification of forms marked by the arabesque line of his *La Danse* murals. The Chapelle du Rosaire in Vence (*see page 265*), designed in 1948-51 by the elderly Matisse, is in a sense the ultimate expression of these dual impulses, where simplified line drawings in black on white-tiled walls are juxtaposed with the lucent yellows, greens and blues of the stained glass.

PICASSO'S PEOPLE

Pablo Picasso was less interested in the light of the South – he was a Spaniard, after all – than in its people. Bathers and the human body became a recurrent subject, from simple oil

sketches on cardboard and oils to the elongated bronze sculptures and tin cut-outs of the 1950s and 1960s. His *Baigneuses regardent un avion,* painted in 1920 at Juan-les-Pins, and his curious, sand-covered tableaux-reliefs of the 1930s (made at much the same time as André Masson's automatic sand paintings, produced in Antibes) show his affinity with the Surrealists. Other works celebrate the Mediterranean as a place of myths and archetypes, in which Pan, centaurs and the Minotaur appear alongside local fishermen.

In 1946, Picasso moved down south with his new love, Françoise Gilot. They spent four months at the Château Grimaldi at Antibes (where a museum is now dedicated to him; *see page 213*), where the artist was given a studio, before moving along the coast to Vallauris, just outside Cannes. It was here, at the Atelier

Villa Noailles.

tubular steel and glass table, seminal examples of Modern Movement functionalism that contrasted with the luxurious art deco decoration of the lacquered screens for which she was famed. A couple of years later, north of Menton at Castellar near the Italian border, she designed her second and last house, the much smaller Tempe a Pailla (subsequently bought by Graham Sutherland), in an idiom pared down to its most elemental and minimalist.

In 1952, also on the headland of Cap-Martin, Le Corbusier built himself Le Cabanon (*see page 253*), a study in the idea of housing at its most basic. The tiny rectangular building was clad in pine logs. Inside, he painted murals and squeezed two beds, a table, fitted shelves, a washbasin and a toilet, each carefully positioned to make the most of the space and the viewpoints. This glorified beach hut is a soothing return to nature, light years from the same architect's early villas, mass housing projects or even his late organic style – and equally distant from the modern loads-of-money estates that cover the Cap.

Madoura, that Picasso discovered pottery; he also painted the allegorical panels of *La Guerre et La Paix* for the chateau's deconsecrated chapel. But perhaps the most important works of these years were the '*assemblages*', made with found objects: the *Petite fille sautant à la corde* (*Little Girl Skipping*) of 1950 was cast from a basket.

During World War II, numerous artists, many of foreign birth, had gravitated south; at least until November 1942, this was France Libre. Some, like Jean Arp, Alberto Magnelli and Sonia Delaunay, were based around Grasse. The Surrealists mostly went to Marseille, congregating at the house of young American Varian Fry, who had been sent by the Emergency Rescue Committee to help artists and intellectuals leave the country. While they were waiting for their ticket to freedom, André Breton, Max Ernst, Victor Brauner, Marcel

Duchamp, André Masson, Tristan Tzara and others devised a card game, Le Jeu de Marseille, and drew *cadavres exquis* – a sort of pictorial Surrealist version of the game of consequences.

Other artists returned to the South of France after the war: Jean Cocteau painted the Salle des Fêtes in the town hall at Menton; Marc Chagall took up residence in Vence, encouraged by his dealer Aimé Maeght; the Nouveau Réalistes and Support-Surface groups had their offshoots in Nice. But the focus of art had shifted increasingly across the Atlantic, and the Southern scene began to seem curiously passé.

▶ For more on the contemporary art scene in the South, *see chapter* **Arts & Entertainment**.

Nice's **Promenade des Anglais**.

Emigrés

From British literati to Hollywood glitterati, it was a bunch of foreigners who created the cachet of the Côte.

Foreigners created the South of France. Before it was flooded with tubercular English, eccentric White Russians and ponderous German archdukes, it was merely another poor Mediterranean region growing olives, vines, citrus fruit and flowers. Then *'les anglais'* arrived – as the locals called all foreigners, whatever their nationality. They included politicians, European aristocrats and crowned heads, doctors and cure-seeking invalids, and writers and artists by the carriage-load.

Everyone agrees the British started it all. Scottish writer, doctor and seasoned complainer Tobias Smollett first went to Nice in 1763, when it took at least two weeks by bone-shaking coach. While finding time to upbraid the Niçois for their religious bigotry and tendency to charge rich foreigners like himself as much as 30 per cent more than the locals, he found the climate and views 'inchanting', and helped to popularise the idea of sea bathing as a health cure. A trip to the Riviera soon became a regular prescription for wealthy invalids. But it

was the mild winter climate that attracted them, not the summer sun: the first hotels were built facing away from the sea, and everything closed down between May and September.

By the beginning of the nineteenth century, Nice had a distinct English colony, in a quarter called La Croix de Marbre – which they rechristened 'Newborough'. They brought their culture with them, establishing English churches, libraries, charities, boarding schools, even bandstands. English food was readily available (boiled senseless, with no oil and not a whiff of garlic) along with 'le butler' to serve it, and hotels reassuringly advertised 'drainage executed by English engineers'.

Les anglais became famous for their eccentric habits: taking long country walks, botanising and painting watercolours. They planted gardens all along the coast, introducing the idea of landscaping and importing many plants now considered typical of the Riviera, including mimosa, palms and eucalyptus. Their lawns caused particular

Immigrés

Odd, really, that two words for the same thing seen from different angles should have such different connotations. Emigrés are those who have left their homeland – intellectuals, anarchists, artists and eccentrics – impelled sometimes by a desire for new experience, sometimes by politics, sometimes by necessity. But the French extreme right prefers to view the phenomenon through the other end of the telescope, talking of *immigrés* rather than *émigrés* as it peddles the spectre of an unstoppable wave of destitute North Africans swamping Le Midi.

With its major ports, the region has always been home to a broad mix of nationalities – especially from the other shores of the Mediterranean. In the twentieth century alone, Marseille has accommodated economic and political refugees from Italy, Greece, Armenia, and Spain, as well as white *pieds noirs* returning from former French colonies of North Africa. When Algeria won independence from France in 1962, 800,000 French *pieds noirs* returned to France, many of them settling in Provence.

By the mid-1980s, Provence had become a stronghold of Jean-Marie Le Pen's Front National. In time-honoured fashion, it was often the descendants of earlier waves of immigrants – such as the Babbis (late-nineteenth century Italian settlers) of Marseille – who were most vocal in their xenophobia. Rising unemployment and illegal immigration fuelled the fire, and by the mid-1990s the Front had made substantial gains. In 1995, it took control of town councils in Orange, Marignane and Toulon; the new mayor of Toulon, Jean-Marie le Chevallier, boasted that he would refuse all requests for immigrants to settle in the town. In the 1998 regional elections, the Front National attracted 27 per cent of the vote in the Provence-Alpes-Côte d'Azur region.

Although the Front National has since been split by internal wrangling, there is no doubt about the current level of racism in southern France; local newspapers carry frequent reports of racially motivated beatings and even killings. And social integration has made slow progress: a 1998 government report showed that 42 per cent of children of Algerians who had moved to France were out of work, compared to 11 per cent in the rest of the population.

While the first generation of immigrants were often single men recruited to work in ports, mines and factories, who always intended to return home, later waves have put down roots. And the extreme right's contention that they have muscled their way in through the back door is a falsehood: in the boom years of the 1960s, thousands of Algerians were brought in to provide manpower for the steelworks of Fos, west of Marseille.

The children of these post-war migrants are French-born, and few have any desire to return to the lands of their parents. But neither are they fully integrated, and within the banlieues of Marseille and Nice an ethnic street culture reigns, thriving on its separateness. Until recently, such places really were unknown territory for outsiders, but Marseille rap groups like IAM (*see page 34*) and writers such as Jean-Claude Izzo, whose hard-boiled thrillers are set in the city's ethnic underbelly, have begun to make them public property.

Perhaps the greatest blow to Le Pen's tired Gallic rhetoric has come from the world of sport. When Zinedine Zidane held aloft the Jules Rimet trophy at the end of France's victorious World Cup Final match against Brazil on 12 July 1998, it was a sign that multicultural France was here to stay. Zidane was born in Marseille in 1972 to Berber parents from Algeria, but none of those who celebrated on the Champs-Elysées that night, beneath an Arc de Triomphe decorated with the illuminated message 'Merci Zizou', thought of him as anything less than an all-French hero.

astonishment to the natives: those who could afford it shipped turf from England. In 1822, Nice's grand, Brighton-like esplanade, the Promenade des Anglais, was constructed at the suggestion of an Anglican vicar, to satisfy the English demand for restorative sea air.

In 1834, Lord Brougham, former Lord Chancellor of England, escaped 'fog-land' and arrived in Cannes, where he was held up because cholera quarantine prevented him crossing the Var river from France into the Savoy territory of Nice. He took a fancy to the tiny fishing village and built himself a villa, transforming its fortunes forever. He was followed in 1837 by Thomas Robinson Woolfield, a canny property developer who began buying up land. Woolfield's gardener founded the first estate agency, John Taylor & Son. Now under Monegasque control, it is still the biggest real estate operation on the Riviera.

It didn't take long before Beaulieu and Antibes were also colonised, and the mild climate of Menton made it especially favoured as an open-air sanatorium. Distinguished corpses in its cemeteries include Aubrey Beardsley and Prince Feliks Yusupov – famous for poisoning, shooting and finally drowning Rasputin. 'Cannes for living, Monte Carlo for gambling and Menton for dying,' so the saying went.

THE BOOM YEARS

A critical factor in the development of the coast was the railway, which was extended from Marseille to Nice in 1864. By 1874, the colony of

Henry and Marie Clews dress up. *See p28.*

expats in Nice had grown to 25,000, and it had the highest growth rate of any city in Europe during the latter half of the nineteenth century. A tradition of despots-in-residence was begun by Leopold II of Belgium, notorious for his spectacularly cruel treatment of the Congo.

By the 1880s, Queen Victoria had become a regular visitor to the Riviera – first Hyères and later Nice, where she wintered in the elegant quarter of Cimiez. It was relatively easy for her to keep an eye on the family firm from here, as so many British politicians also liked to winter on the Riviera, Gladstone in particular finding it most refreshing. The Queen also liked to entertain European royalty with proper English food like mutton chops, Irish stew and tapioca. Her favourite occupation, though, was visiting cemeteries. She refused to set foot in the 'moral cesspit' of Monaco – unlike her son, the roué Prince of Wales and future Edward VII, who was perfectly at home in the casino.

> ## 'The Côte d'Azur was rapidly losing its healthy image and becoming 'a sunny place for shady people'.'

Monaco discovered the gambling industry in 1856, but it was not until 1863 that a French entrepreneur called François Blanc founded the Société des Bains de Mer to give the casino the administration and infrastructure it needed, and turned the poorest state in Europe into one of its richest. Royals and unemployed aristocrats from all over Europe and even as far as India flocked to gamble in Monte Carlo. The Côte d'Azur was rapidly losing its outdoor, healthy image and becoming 'a sunny place for shady people', in Somerset Maugham's classic description.

The railways also brought Russian tsars and grand dukes escaping Russian winters along with recalcitrant serfs, who established almost as big a colony as the British, building lavish villas, churches, even a Russian cathedral in Nice (*see page 220*). They arrived with a retinue of servants and samovars, and were so imperious that the trains were obliged to go more slowly so they could sleep. The Russians were enthusiastic gamblers, drinkers and party-goers, and certainly among the Riviera's more eccentric visitors. Admiral Popov tried to buy Monaco outright, and a certain Count Apraxin was famous for being so suicidal he needed a group of cellists to play night and day to soothe him; his servant had to stand behind his chair to prevent him topping himself in a melancholy moment.

Nice on the Volga: the Russian Orthodox **Cathédrale St-Nicolas**.

Soon to join the party were American tycoons like J Pierpont Morgan, Vanderbilt and James Gordon Bennett. Bennett, proprietor of the *New York Herald*, was once so enraged at having to wait for dinner that he bought the entire restaurant and gave it as a tip to the waiter, Ciro, who went on to found a dining empire. Exotic courtesans – known as *les horizontales* – added spice to the mix. One of the most celebrated was La Belle Otéro, whose breasts were the models for the cupolas of Cannes' Carlton hotel.

PARTY ARTY

While the Russians partied and defenestrated themselves in Monte Carlo and the English swam sedately with their hats on, a revolution was under way in Antibes, spearheaded by the 'lost generation' of Americans, escaping prohibition and spending a strong dollar. Socialites Sara and Gerald Murphy, who built the Villa America on Cap d'Antibes, were the inspiration for the central characters of F Scott Fitzgerald's novel *Tender is the Night*: 'One could get away with more on the summer Riviera and whatever happened seemed to have something to do with art.' For the first time, Riviera hedonism was identified not with diamonds, champagne and gambling, but with nature-worship and peasant chic: the Murphys and their guests (who included Cole Porter, Pablo Picasso, Rudolf Valentino, Ernest Hemingway, Gertrude Stein and Dorothy Parker) wore espadrilles and stripy fishermen's sweaters, swam in the sea and sunbathed with religious dedication.

American railroad baron Frank Jay Gould and his socialite wife Florence were largely responsible for developing the long sandy beach of Juan-les-Pins, creating a new level of tacky glamour. In 1927, Rex Ingram took over the Victorine film studios in Nice, and though they failed to become the Hollywood of France, plenty of celebrities turned up for a while, from Charlie Chaplin, Mary Pickford and Douglas Fairbanks to Harpo Marx and George Bernard Shaw. Cagnes-sur-Mer, meanwhile, had become a sort of Greenwich-Village-by-Sea, its louche bohemian atmosphere captured perfectly in Cyril Connolly's mannered novel *The Rock Pool*.

Two of the most eccentric émigrés were Henry and Marie Clews, a rich American couple – he a failed Wall Street banker turned symbolic sculptor, she a society heiress – who lived out a fantasy lifestyle in a faux-medieval castle in La Napoule, near Cannes. They entertained lavishly, dressing their servants in Provençal costume and themselves in a kind of neo-Arthurian costume of their own invention. Their peacocks were famous for straying on to the train line.

Writers always found the Côte d'Azur a pleasant retreat. Somerset Maugham lived in great style in Leopold II's old place, the Villa Mauresque on Cap Ferrat. Aldous Huxley lived in Sanary with his wife Maria and her red Bugatti; Thomas Mann and Sybille Bedford were neighbours. Katherine Mansfield sought repose in Menton, and DH Lawrence died in Vence. HG Wells built a villa near Grasse, and Graham Greene lived in Nice, finding time towards the end of his life to denounce the city's underlying climate of corruption in his 1982 pamphlet *J'Accuse: the dark side of Nice*.

THE GLOW FADES

By 1931, a few years after the Hôtel du Cap in Antibes (*see box page 210*) had pioneered the summer season, all hotels on the Côte d'Azur were staying open in July and August. Summer holidays on the Riviera soon caught on, and when paid vacations for French workers arrived in 1936, the Côte's days of exclusivity were over. The Train Bleu – which began its Paris-Nice run in 1922 as the last word in luxury travel – added second-and third-class sleeper cabins. By 1929, observed Fitzgerald in *The Crack-Up*, the glow had faded: no one swam in the Eden Roc pool any more, except as a hangover cure before lunch.

But, as often happens, the dream became common currency just as it was vanishing. Society hostesses like Florence Gould and Maxine Elliott ticked off long, star-studded guest lists. Elsa Maxwell, a gossip columnist and party organiser from Iowa, was paid $20,000 to promote Monte Carlo. The Duke and Duchess of Windsor found the Côte d'Azur a perfect lotus-eating escape. When war was declared in 1939, they were about to go swimming in their rented château. On hearing the news, the Duke simply dived into the pool.

The glamorous image persisted, despite the rigours of German occupation. When the liberating US troops landed on the beach in St-Tropez in 1944, they brought guidebooks with them. Although many of *les anglais* returned after the war, it wasn't the same. Somerset Maugham reduced his staff to five, and many of the Belle Epoque villas were sliced up into apartments. Winston Churchill still visited, but switched from the Windsors' pad to Aristotle Onassis's yacht. The newly established Cannes Film Festival attracted Hollywood aristos instead of the princely variety, and film stars joined the Riviera real-estate rush. And in 1956, a screen princess became a real princess. Grace Kelly's marriage to Prince Rainier of Monaco was definitive proof that the fantasy potential of this overdeveloped stretch of coast was as strong as ever. As Mary Blume puts it in her definitive account of the period, *Côte d'Azur – Inventing the French Riviera*: 'The Riviera was still a place where you could invent yourself.'

> ## 'The Russians are back, some in Prada jackets and convertible Mercedes, but more on cheap coach tours.'

It still is, though today the performance goes on behind high security fences or aboard luxury private yachts. Ringo Starr has a house on Cap Ferrat, as do Joan Collins and Josephine Hart. Cannes stars still bask in the luxury of the Hôtel du Cap, and Monaco remains the world's leading tax haven. (Columnist Taki observed that one does not choose one's friends in Monte Carlo: 'It's a bit like being in prison. You talk to the people you are thrown in with.'). But the Côte d'Azur today also attracts émigrés with jobs, especially those working in the high-tech industries of Sophia Antipolis (*see box page 262*).

There are still plenty of writers, artists and potters holed up in over-restored village houses or hill-side villas, and the English presence endures with nanny agencies, English churches, radio stations, rock groups (*see box page 228*) and charity sales. The Russians are back, too, some in Prada jackets and convertible Mercedes, but many more on cheap coach tours, enticed by the potent Riviera legend, which struggles gamely on in the face of concrete suffocation, corruption scandals, traffic jams and overcrowded beaches.

Arts & Entertainment

Marseille raps, Avignon emotes and Cannes turns on the glam – so who needs Paris?

CONTEMPORARY ART

The South of France is associated above all with the Modern Movement in art, from forefathers like Cézanne to Modernist icons like Picasso (*see chapter* **Art & Modernism in the South**). But contemporary artists down South don't let this weighty legacy get to them; the Provence-Alpes-Côte d'Azur region today has a thriving and highly international art scene, with a large number of institutions from museums and private galleries to artist-run associations and studio schemes. While every *village perché* seems to have its dabbling daubers and pottering potters, the main art

> ▶ For all festivals and venues mentioned in this chapter, *see* **Index**.

hubs are Marseille and to a lesser extent Nice, where young artists deal with issues such as the everyday, the body, sexuality, consumer society and art about art.

Several young artists from the region have recently emerged at the forefront of the current French scene, including Gilles Barbier, whose work treats technology and genetics, photographer Valérie Jouve, who is more concerned with housing estates and Marseille's multiracial population than with beaches or the Southern light, and Stéphane Magnin, whose paintings using industrial materials embrace and reflect techno culture.

Beyond the contemporary art museums in Nice and Marseille, the principal body in the region is the FRAC (Fonds Régional d'Art Contemporain), which runs as an extremely active programme of exhibitions in museums, chateaux and schools across the region and develops external projects with young local artists. Marseille's specialist contemporary art museum, the **MAC**, in a hangar-like space on the eastern hills, has a wide-ranging international collection that includes Rauschenberg, César, Roth, Balkenhol, Absalon and Laffont, and varied exhibitions.

But the South's most dynamic city also has several artist-run associations. The first stopping-off point for those keen to catch up on the more alternative scene has to be **La**

Friche la Belle de Mai, a disused industrial complex up in the scruffy Belle de Mai quarter west of the centre. First an artists' squat, now home to numerous artistic, musical and theatrical groups, its gallery is used both for exhibitions put on by its resident artists and associations, and for shows organised by the FRAC.

Among the commercial galleries, the one that has long set the agenda with its international roster of artists is the **Galerie Roger Pailhas**. Much of the Marseille art buzz is word of

Cannes Film Festival: a ligger's guide

1967, and Cannes was already clothing-optional.

mouth, but some events are listed in the weekly freebie publication *Taktik*.

In the 1960s, Nice was a satellite of the Nouveau Réalistes, the French version of Pop Art – leading members Yves Klein, Martial Raysse and Arman were all born in the Riviera city. In the 1970s, the Support-Surface group also had its Nice outpost with Viallat, Pagès and Toni Grand. Both movements feature strongly in the collection of the city's **Musée d'Art Moderne et d'Art Contemporain**, which also stages temporary exhibitions. **Villa**

Arson, home to both an art school and a contemporary art centre, has a more adventurous conceptual bent, with exhibitions that reflect the latest international trends. Nice also has its own contemporary art fair in May, **Art Jonction**.

A survivor of the 1960s scene who has become a local institution in his own right is Fluxus artist Ben, whose instantly recognisable script statements adorn everything from socks to babies' bottles. His art actions included swimming across the port in 1963, while the

In the late 1930s, French authorities noticed that Italy's Fascists were hogging the cinematic limelight with their Venice Film Festival, and decided to retaliate with a similar gig in Cannes. A world war put paid to the Fascists, and put the French film fest on hold. When the show finally got on the road in 1946, facilities were few; during the 1947 event, rain was still coming through the unfinished roof of the old Palais des Festivals. In 1948 and 1950, money was so tight that the ever-more prestigious event had to be cancelled. But by the 1950s, things were definitely looking up.

When an ambitious, topless starlet threw herself at Robert Mitchum in 1954, the Cannes Film Festival entered the paparazzi age. The glam and tack factors mushroomed: Prince Rainier wooing actress Grace Kelly; high-speed boat chases well within telephoto-lens distance of the Croisette; Charlotte Rampling meeting Jean-Michel Jarre; Tom Jones crooning at sex-and-sand beach parties.

Competition film screenings are strictly for the professionals – filmmakers, film writers, film critics – or at least, that's the idea. In fact, invites galore are handed out to dignitaries and local personalities: who knows, your humble butcher may have a couple. It doesn't hurt to ask. And though the films shown in the non-competitive Directors' Fortnight and Critics' Week are similarly off-limits for the person on the street, wring a hack-friend's arm and they might be able to procure you one. The festival's website (*see below*) gives full details of accreditation procedures, plus a history of the festival and festival personality profiles.

Failing this, it's the street where you'll have to look for your action. If you're a serious Cannes junkie, it pays to approach the job with a real sense of mission. Word of mouth is the key. Middle-aged Frenchmen with cameras wearing the Riviera equivalent of an anorak – a T-shirt from the 1980

festival – are sure to be in the know. Even if you're pointed to what look like off-circuit events, don't despair: you'll be surprised at your A-list haul.

To get up close and personal make for the big hotels: the Carlton, Martinez and Majestic. Don't join the unimaginative crowd round the entrance: get to the hotel bar. OK, so £4 is a lot for a Perrier, but it's a small price to pay for prime people-spotting. If you're really determined to spot the stars, try hotel hairdressers, especially before the nightly gala screening.

Work the same circuit for an invite back to a villa or hotel for an 'After Party'. Dance till breakfast, then book on to a beach lounger and crash. Who knows, you may wake up from oblivion to see Jodie Foster chatting about her latest oeuvre with the world's press on the deckchair next door. Don't go straight back to sleep, you might not be dreaming. After all, this is Cannes.

Cannes Festival International de Cinéma

99 bd Malesherbes, 75008 Paris (01.45.61.66.00/fax 01.45.61.97.60/ festival@festival-cannes.fr). **Press office** *(01.45.61.66.08/fax 01.45.61.97.61/presse@festival-cannes.fr).* Website: www.festival-cannes.fr

Magasin de Ben, originally his bookshop, became an artwork that was later bought up by the Centre Pompidou. Ben regularly sends out his own idiosyncratic newsletter, and his **Le Centre du Monde** boutique (*see page 227*) doubles as a meeting place and a gallery. One other essential Nice address for contemporary art buffs is the **Hôtel Windsor** (*see page 229*), a genuine hotel where for the past 15 years owner Bernard Redolfi-Strizzoli has taken art out of the museum and given contemporary artists, including Ben, Jean Le Gac, Gottfried Honegger, Lawrence Weiner and Glen Baxter, the freedom to decorate a bedroom as they wish.

In Nîmes, the **Musée d'Art Contemporain** in the minimalist high-tech glass Carré d'Art, designed by Norman Foster, has a permanent collection that is strong on New Realism, Support-Surface, *figuration libre* and Italian Arte Povera. Arles becomes a centre of pilgrimage for creative and contemporary photographers each summer during the **Rencontres Internationales de la Photographie**. In Avignon, the big art date has long been the major themed exhibition put on to coincide with the summer theatre festival – but the opening in July 2000 of the **Collection Lambert** has at last given the city a year-round place on the French contemporary art map.

'Roger Vadim made St-Tropez the topless capital of the world as early as 1956.'

As so often in France, funding comes from an enormous number of public sources, from national to local level, and many regional arts boards have their own galleries – a good example being the **Espace 13** gallery in Aix-en-Provence, run by the Conseil Régional du Bouches du Rhône. There is some action outside the major towns, too. The **Musée Picasso** in Antibes alternates classic modern art with contemporary exhibitions, as does the **Hôtel Donadeï de Campredon** in L'Isle-sur-la-Sorgue.

Vence and its pretty satellite, St-Paul-de-Vence, have more modern art per square metre than any other Provençal towns, with an army of private art galleries of varying quality. The **Fondation Maeght** museum is the powerhouse, focusing on the modern greats, but the permanent collection of the **Galerie Beaubourg**, which moved south from Paris in the mid '90s, is also worth a visit. In Mouans-Sartoux, north-west of Cannes, the **Espace de l'Art Concret** centres on a core collection of geometrical abstraction and minimalism (Albers, Honegger, Bill, Twombly, Judd, etc) donated by Swiss painter Gottfried Honegger

and the widow of artist Josef Albers. It also puts on three themed exhibitions a year that make imaginative links between historic greats and young artists or new media.

FILM

The seaboard from Marseille to Monaco – and the lavender-covered *arrière-pays* behind – is a location scout's heaven. *The French Connection* was made here, a thousand interior design trends were launched by *Jean de Florette* and *Manon des sources*, and James Bond – in his Sean Connery incarnation – made the obligatory casino stopover in *Never Say Never Again*.

Much of the glamour Bond traded on came from Cinemascope Hollywood, notably 1950s films like Hitchcock's *To Catch a Thief* starring Cary Grant and Grace Kelly – famous for its cross-cutting of foreplay and fireworks. Ten years later the Riviera was the destination of the lovers in Stanley Donen's *Two for the Road*, a sophisticated tale of marital crisis starring Albert Finney and Audrey Hepburn. Dirk Bogarde came to the South for one of his last films, Bertrand Tavernier's *These Foolish Things* (French title *Daddy Nostalgie*).

Roger Vadim made St-Tropez the topless capital of the world as early as 1956 when he launched a scantily clad teenage Brigitte Bardot in *And God Created Woman* (*Et Dieu créa la femme*). Since then the sun-and-sex angle has been worked into the ground by countless imitators, including the soft-focus schmaltz of David Hamilton in *A Summer in St-Tropez*.

Thirty years later the fantasy landscape moved inland, with the release of Claude Berri's *Jean de Florette* and *Manon des sources*, based on Marcel Pagnol's novel *L'Eau des collines*. The fragrance of Provençal mimosas and lavender wafted into suburban cinemas around the world, creating the basis for the runaway success of Peter Mayle's escapist travel book *A Year in Provence* and launching a thousand estate agencies.

Pagnol himself had a hand in getting his Marseille trilogy of the 1930s on to the screen. Set in the city's *vieux port*, the films *Marius*, *Fanny* and *César* (this last not only scripted but also directed by Pagnol) are warm, sentimental homages to the characters, traditions and accents of France's second city.

An altogether less idyllic portrayal of Marseille was offered in John Frankenheimer's *French Connection II* (1975), which showed the city's grimy, drug-ridden underbelly. Luc Besson continued to plug the Marseille-Chicago comparisons in 1998 with his instant cult movie *Taxi*. A more sensitive, affectionate portrait of the city – or rather of one of its run-down

Et Dieu créa la femme: **Brigitte Bardot** at Cannes.

western suburbs, L'Estaque – was given in local director Robert Guédiguian's delicate *Marius et Jeanette*, a story of working-class friendship released to critical acclaim in 1997.

MUSIC: CLASSICAL & OPERA

Classical music in the South of France benefited greatly from Mitterand's policy of decentralisation, and both orchestras and festivals can count on a level of subsidy that most European musical directors would give their batons for. Despite this, orchestral standards can be variable, and poor preparation can sometimes let down a promising performance. But the major opera houses make up for any shortfall: casts and stagings often rival the Bastille or the Garnier in Paris. In the best Mediterranean tradition, they tend to be at the centre of the city's music scene, and also the best places to collect information about local one-off concerts.

The region's leading temples of opera are Marseille, with its vociferous Italophile public, Nice and Monte-Carlo. Monte-Carlo's **Palais Garnier** is a shimmering jewel of a venue, and the principality also boasts the best orchestra in the South, the **Orchestre Philharmonique de Monte-Carlo**, which once had the great conductor Marek Janowski as musical director. The other orchestras of the region are kept fairly busy in the opera pit, and their symphonic success is very much dependent on the quality of the visiting maestri; don't, in any case, expect the Vienna Philharmonic.

The major trend in the last ten years has been for summer festivals, which crop up everywhere. Sometimes these are just simple marketing exercises: two or three concerts in a pretty *village perché* become the excuse for an 'International Arts Festival', without the

Storming *Norma* at the **Chorégies d'Orange** opera festival.

funding or organisation to make it work. But many young and promising European musicians are to be found in chamber music events across the region; often the backdrop – whether natural or architectural – itself justifies the price of the ticket. Of the established major festivals, the **Chorégies d'Orange** (*see box page 104*) continues to provide a small number of Verona-style performances of Romantic opera with international casts, in the spectacular setting of the world's best-preserved Roman theatre, as well as a couple of symphonic concerts. A similar amphitheatre setting is home to the less prestigious **L'Eté de Vaison** festival at Vaison-la-Romaine, while both Nîmes and Arles also put on occasional shows in their own Roman arenas.

But the doyen of Southern classical music festivals is the **Festival International d'Art Lyrique** in Aix-en-Provence in July (*see box page 146*), featuring operas, orchestral concerts and recitals by top international artists. Recently, Early Music has become something of a speciality. The Avignon festival is perhaps better known for its theatrical presentations, but there are also occasional concerts, and the atmosphere is unrivalled. Nearby Carpentras also has a summer festival, **Les Estivales**, but here budgetary constraints impose a more modest level of performance – unlike the rather ritzy little **Musiques au Coeur** opera festival that has recently sprung up in Antibes.

MUSIC: ROCK, ROOTS & JAZZ

Until the 1980s, it was almost impossible to make it in the modern French music industry without putting in time in Paris; rockers, ragamuffins, punks and African groups all gravitated towards the capital. The regional resurgence came not so much with folk – which has always bubbled under in the provinces – as with the hip hop revolution, with its emphasis on community roots and DIY production values.

And if there was one French city that could rival Paris as an ethnic melting pot with strong community credentials and a healthy dose of urban decay, it was Marseille. Meeting point of working-class French and North African cultures, the 'capital of the South' can now boast a music scene as eclectic as the city itself. Rap and jazz are the main currents, though there are techno DJs, rockers and post-punks in there, too.

The first Marseillais band to make it big were **IAM** (pronounced 'I am'), a posse of rappers from the city's outer suburbs who joined forces in 1989; a year later, they had been snapped up by Virgin and were supporting Madonna at the huge Bercy stadium in Paris. Taking their inspiration from US acts like Public Enemy and iconic 1970s movies, IAM merged this transatlantic input with the trans-Mediterranean sounds of the Maghreb, the Middle East and West Africa. The parodic disco-rap single *La Mia* was a huge hit in 1994; later, IAM recorded a track for the soundtrack of Matthieu Kassovitz's wasted-youth movie *La*

Haine. Their 1997 album *L'Ecole du micro argent* sold half a million copies; its title – the school of the silver mike – was a reference to the group's efforts to encourage other young Marseillais rappers such as **Fonky Family**, **3 Oeil** or **Le Rat**, who were first launched via IAM's own production company.

Other influential Marseillais bands include **Massilia Sound System** (reggae) and **Quartiers Nord** (guitar-driven rock). On the jazz front, **La Squadra** is one of the most interesting of a bunch of new acts – a quintet strongly influenced by the music of West Africa, Ornette Coleman and Thelonius Monk, led by pianist JP Kwadjo, a jazz writer who has also penned a biography of Monk.

Outside of the Southern metropolis, the scene is more volatile. Nice has its share of emerging groups, too, such as the reggae-based **Radical-el-Salam**. But outside of these major centres, it's generally visiting artists that create the most excitement. Capacity concert venues in the South include the **Zénith-Omega** in Toulon – an exact copy of the Paris venue of the same name – which hosts big names such as Sting, Texas and Janet Jackson.

In the cities, club venues nurture the local hip hop scene; on the Riviera, between Cannes and Nice, live music of variable genre and quality is on offer in a number of smaller dives – many of them Anglo or Irish pubs. English-language bands make up a significant slice of the scene down on the Côte (*see box page 230*). And big-time music industry excitement comes to Cannes at the end of January, when the MIDEM trade fair rolls into town, with a retinue of live concerts and – as of the 2000 edition – the NRJ Music Awards, the European answer to the US Grammy.

Outside of one-off concerts and happenings, the colder months can be hard for music-starved Southerners. Summer, though, brings a logjam of festivals. Jazz fans are especially well served by the often overlapping **Nice Jazz Festival** and **Jazz à Juan** (*see box page 212*). The Nice festival takes place in the Roman amphitheatre of Cimiez; note that despite the label, 'straight' jazz is in the minority here: the 1999 line-up included Dee Dee Bridgewater, James Brown, Jan Gabarek, Isaac Hayes and Cesaria Evora. Jazz à Juan, staged under the pine trees of Juan-les-Pins, attracts the serious jazz buffs with a programme mixing trad greats with younger, more experimental performers.

THEATRE

The Mediterranean climate influences the theatre scene as much as anything else. Not only does the heat inspire dramatic passions and colourful spectacle, but it also fuels a blaze of summer festivals ranging from the Edinburgh-style thesp-fest of Avignon to more modest village jamborees. The quality of these events – which are often mere tourist-promotion exercises – can vary wildly. The best, though, endeavour to promote established names while showcasing new talent.

For three weeks in July, the **Festival d'Avignon** (*see box page 94*) infuses this quiet Provençal town with an infectious carnival

Tu tires, ou tu pointes?

A dusty square surrounded by lime trees, a whiff of strong tobacco, a flash of silver, and the satisfying clack as a boules player sends his opponent's ball careering into limbo. Boules is the archetypal Southern game, reflecting, warts and all, the Provençal character: stubborn but determined, passionate when crossed, as male chauvinist as they come, but oddly feminine in the balletic movements of the players. You will sometimes hear the game referred to as *la pétanque*, but this is only one form of boules, where the thrower has to stand with his feet together (from the Occitan *pé tanco* = foot fixed). The other, older version of boules – *la longue* or *le jeu provençal*, played on grounds over 12 metres long – allows players to take three hopping steps before launching the metal ball. Teams can be made up of two or three players; each team has at least one *pointeur*, who goes first, and whose job it is to throw the ball as close as possible to the wooden jack (*le cochonnet*, or 'piglet'); and at least one *tireur*, who has the enjoyable but exacting task of throwing his ball in an arc to land almost on top of an opponent's ball, sending it scudding away from the jack and – if the shot was a good one – taking its place exactly (this is to *faire le carreau*). The winning team scores one point for each ball that it has placed closer to the jack than the nearest of its opponents' balls; matches generally go up to 13 points. The end of each game is invariably marked by animated disputes over distance from the *cochonnet*, resolved with the help of the little tape-measure that every self-respecting boules player carries with him.

Hot riffs and cool licks at **Jazz à Juan**. *See page 35.*

spirit, with theatre, dance and music bursting out of every possible building and courtyard, from school playgrounds to converted warehouses, church crypts or tumbledown stone barns. Most of the productions are staged in non-theatre venues, or in temporary theatres set up for the festival; many of the main venues are open-air, the most famous being the huge courtyard of the Palais des Papes, used for the official festival's flagship productions.

> **'A rebellious theatrical spirit has always been part of Le Midi's theatre scene.'**

The fringe festival – known as **Le Off** (as in 'Off Broadway') – is the one that helps to brighten up the streets with its parading performers, frantic competition for passing trade and refreshingly anarchic spirit. Every year, its colourful presence vies with the intellectual (and financial) prestige of the official event – referred to unofficially as Le Festival In – which usually focuses on international theatre from one particular country, alongside offerings from the stalwarts of France's well-subsidised and powerful network of state theatres.

France still believes in pouring money into cultural activity, with the result that state-supported theatres have the highest profile and

attract the largest audiences, while independently run private venues have a hard time competing. In the South, the public theatres' dominance is reflected in a repertoire featuring intellectually weighty productions of classics and modern classics both home-grown and international, from Molière and Shakespeare to Genet, Tennessee Williams, Pinter and Vinaver. 'Serious' theatre in France is seen less as entertainment and more as an arena for theatrical experiment, social comment and self-consciously ground-breaking work. Occasionally, though, in deference to populism, some big theatres in the South do welcome lighter visiting productions from the boulevard or 'West End' style Parisian theatres: recent examples include Eric-Emmanuel Schmitt's *Le Libertin*, a philosophical comedy about Denis Diderot, or Jane Birkin's *Oh pardon, tu dormais!* (directed by young blood Xavier Durringer), which were recycled for audiences in Aix and Nice.

Paris does not have it all its own way, though; a rebellious theatrical spirit has always been part of Le Midi's theatre scene. Politically motivated Occitan-language companies have existed in the South since the 1960s, André Benedetto's **Le Chêne Noir** in Avignon being a prime example (Benedetto was the first to stage a fringe production alongside the official Avignon festival in 1966, and is considered to be the founding father of Le Off). Avignon had its very own summer of protest in 1968, and the anti-authoritarian streak in Southern drama has not been absent since. In 1999, a controversial street-theatre production in the working-class port town of Martigues was banned for fear that it would lead to public unrest. The South has also been the home of numerous theatre projects that attempt to kick against the comfortable drawing-room-rebellion image of the official tradition, such as the pioneering community projects of Marseillais playwright and director Armand Gatti, who has worked extensively with non-professional actors, including prison inmates. One of his most influential works, the epic play *Adam Quoi*, is based on his experiences in a concentration camp during the last war.

Large, state-funded Centres Dramatiques Nationaux like the **Théâtre de la Criée** in Marseille or the **Théâtre de Nice** are generally well behaved, but they still make important, interesting and often innovative contributions to the national theatre scene, and tend to attract large, cosmopolitan audiences. Equally active are some of the traditionally more provincial municipal theatres such as the **Théâtre du Gymnase** in Marseille or the **Jeu de Paume** in Aix.

Young writers here, as everywhere else in France, have a tough time getting their work past an army of auteur-style directors who have traditionally preferred to stamp their own professional mark on established plays rather than risk new works and names. Directors working in the region include **Gildas Bourdet** at La Criée and **Jacques Weber** at the Théâtre de Nice, both of whom enjoy international reputations. However, local talent is not lacking either, as the large number of local companies appearing at festivals such as the Avignon Off demonstrates.

DANCE

The Provençal sun, the azure sea of the Riviera and the sensual tastes and smells of the South have always had an affinity with dance. It is no accident that the legendary *train bleu* that carried well-heeled holidaymakers in comfort down to the Riviera should have inspired a ballet by Diaghilev, with a curtain by Picasso bearing an enlargement of perhaps his most exuberantly balletic painting, *Deux femmes courant sur la plage*.

It was the pioneer of modern movement, **Isadora Duncan**, who started the French Riviera dance trend in the early years of the twentieth century with her celebrated performance studio in Nice on the promenade des Anglais and her extravagent happenings at the Hôtel Negresco, where she created works with Jean Cocteau and other avant-garde artists.

After Duncan's death in 1927, **Les Ballets de Monte-Carlo** (successors to the legendary Ballets russes, founded by Diaghilev in 1909) continued the tradition. The talented **Jean-Christophe Maillot** has recently rejuvenated the company, creating new works and staging revivals of historic productions. The Ballets also organises the **Nuits de la Danse** festival on the romantically starlit casino terrace.

More than one Parisian-based choreographer has packed his or her bags since the 1980s and resettled in Provence or the Côte d'Azur, where regional culture ministries do everything they can to promote and support new companies, dance festivals and works. As a result, performance festivals abound. Even the **Festival d'Avignon** – most closely associated with theatre – regularly includes a few dance productions by such contemporary dancemakers as **Angelin Preljocaj** (head of the Centre Chorégraphique National in Aix-en-Provence) and **Mathilde Monnier** (artistic director of a similar centre in Montpellier). The **Les Hivernales** fringe festival holds a summer edition at the same time; its more internationally oriented main winter edition, running each year in February, aims to highlight small but promising regionally subsidised companies.

Though it is just outside the area covered by this guide, the **Montpellier Danse** festival (three weeks in June and July, info and bookings on 04.67.60.83.60) needs to be mentioned as one of the pillars of the dance scene in the South. The twentieth anniversary edition in 2000 featured leading choreographers such as Lucinda Childs, William Forsythe and Jan Fabre, and a selection of visiting companies from Spain, Portugal, Italy, Greece and North Africa. The other main dance event in the South, **Danse à Aix**, is usually held for three weeks from mid-July. Though more intimate than Montpellier, the programming is always equally high quality, and companies rarely overlap between the two events.

Every other December, the **Festival International de danse de Cannes**, held in the Palais des Festivals, features ballet-oriented international troupes – the 1999 edition, for example, included Mikhail Barishnikov's White Oak Dance Project, the **Ballet National de Marseille** (recently revitalised by former Paris Opera star **Marie-Claude Pietragalla**, and not to be missed if you're ever in town) and the Trisha Brown Company.

Provençal Food & Drink

A natural larder raided by natural foodies: from the local village bar to temples of gastronomy, it doesn't get much better than this.

FOOD

If the French love to eat, the people of Provence live to eat. It's their passion, and even as Provence changes, life here remains firmly anchored to the table. Wandering the narrow streets of its ancient villages at noon, you'll be rewarded with the luscious smells of lunch cooking in invisible kitchens, the result of a morning's shopping in local markets that remain authentic and full of shoppers.

The Provençal diet remains deliciously traditional, closely following the seasons, based on recipes that are passed from generation to generation. Thrift is at the heart of the cooking, as in dishes such as *daube de boeuf*, beef simmered in red wine for hours to make it tender and flavourful; vegetables are prominent

and meat is often used sparingly as a garnish or condiment. The less noble parts of the beast are used, too, as in the *pieds et paquets* of Marseille (stuffed tripe cooked in wine and traditionally served with sheep's trotters).

Above all, though, it is the natural goodness of Provençal food that has made its fame abroad. Garlic, the signature flavouring of the region, purifies the blood and is a universal panacea. Olive oil strengthens the bones, heart and liver. And, of course, fragrant herbs, growing in wild and cultivated profusion everywhere, have long been appreciated for their therapeutic qualities. The most celebrated Provençal sauces and condiments – aïoli, pistou, rouille and tapenade (*see page 50* **Provençal menu**) – work variations on these basic ingredients.

Sheep- and goat-farming produce tender free-range meat, with the delicious nuances of the herbs the flocks graze on. The region's game includes young rabbits from the *garrigue* (brush hillsides) and birds such as snipe, plover and thrush. Along the coast, Provence has developed a splendid battery of fish and seafood dishes, the most famous of which is the bouillabaisse. Less well-known but equally delicious is *bourride*, a creamy garlic-spiked fish soup made with John Dory, sea bass and monkfish. Like bouillabaisse, it's served as two courses – first the soup, garnished with croutons, aïoli and grated Gruyère, and then the fish. If you're lucky, you may find *poutargue* (also known as *boutargue*), made with grey mullet roe that has been pressed and salted the same way since Phoenician times.

The quality of the vegetables and fruit in Provence, whether they come from irrigated fields and orchards along the Durance and Var rivers, tiny coastal gardens or greenhouses, is superb, making this part of the world a rare paradise for vegetarians. In spring, the region produces some of the best asparagus in France, followed by a summer abundance of aubergines, courgettes, tomatoes and artichokes. Autumn brings wild mushrooms, pumpkins and squash, while mesclun, that distinctly Provençal salad of tender mixed leaves and herbs, is available all year round. The black truffles of the Luberon and the Var often end up in the Périgord, where they are passed off as local finds; those that remain garnish salads or end up in *pâté de foie gras truffé* (truffled goose liver paste).

Fortunately, Provence's thriving tourist scene has not corrupted its famous open-air markets. You'll find the odd stand selling scented candles and lavender sachets, but these remain squarely outnumbered by farmers touting their own tiny goat's cheeses, stout ladies selling tightly bound bunches of fresh herbs, and table after table of perfectly ripened tomatoes and glossy aubergines. You'll also find stalls specialising in olives, dried fruit and nuts, jam and honey, and cured meat and sausages. In larger towns, there are daily markets, while in smaller ones they're often held twice weekly: check with the local tourist office for market hours.

Provençal cheeses, made from goat's or ewe's milk, are often characterised by their lactic bite, which grows stronger as they age. Among the cheeses you'll encounter most often are Banon, made with ewe's or goat's milk, wrapped in chestnut leaves and aged to a pungent runniness; Brousse, a soft, mild white cheese that's frequently used to fill ravioli and is often eaten drizzled with olive oil or honey; Picodon, small discs of fresh, tangy goat's cheese from

northern Provence; and Pelardon, similar to Picodon but aged and very firm.

One of the pleasures of travelling in the South of France are the wonderfully marked differences in the cuisine from one town or region to the next. The Italian kitchen had a powerful impact in Nice and its environs, where pasta is usually on the menu. Marseillais cuisine goes well beyond its signature bouillabaisse; the city also boasts a superb selection of ethnic restaurants – especially Armenian and North African – reflecting the kaleidoscopic variety of the people who've settled there. Beyond Marseille, the Camargue has a distinct cuisine of its own – look for dishes like *boeuf à la gardiane*, an earthy stew of bull's meat. West of the Rhône, you'll start to detect a subtle Spanish nuance on menus. Many southern towns

Top ten Restaurants

Louis XV
Aristocratic surroundings, peasant food: Ducasse's first and best. See page 45.

L'Oustau de Baumanière
Luxury on a plate at this glamorous country pile. See page 47.

La Mirande
Inventive menus and heavenly desserts. See page 47.

La Fenière
Powerful, glorious cooking from the area's top woman chef. See page 47.

La Clos de Violette
Superb modern Provençal food in a garden setting. See page 48.

Bacon
Elegant fisherie, with a knockout bouillabaise. See page 50.

Chez Bruno
The wizard of the Var enchants gourmet pilgrims. See page 50.

Le Chantecler
New-generation Provençal food boldy executed. See page 52.

La Bastide St-Antoine
Home of the Riviera's hottest chef (probably). See page 54.

Restaurant Jacques Maximin
Tastemeister Maximin continues to impress. See page 54.

BANDOL

"a secret to share"
"Les Vins de Bandol"
Espace Mistral-2, Avenue Saint-Louis-83330 Le Beausset
Var-France
Tél 00 33 4 94 90 29 59
Fax 00 33 4 94 98 50 24

Shrink-wrapped just doesn't cut it in Provence: buying produce is a hands-on affair.

are renowned for a particular produce or dish; among many examples are the brandade (creamy salt cod) of Nîmes, the *calissons* (candies made from almond paste and candied melon) of Aix-en-Provence, the *socca* (chickpea-flour crêpes) of Nice and the *tellines* (tiny shellfish) of Stes-Maries-de-la-Mer.

DRINK

The glass of cloudy anise-scented pastis that leaves a wet ring on a café table is as much an emblem of southern France as the olive tree or the chant of cicadas on a hot afternoon. Ricard, the most famous brand of pastis, is made in Marseille and is served neat with a carafe of water. The two mixed together form the cloudy cocktail that is probably the region's most popular aperitif.

But Le Midi's thriving bar and café culture offers a variety of other refreshments. In the morning, many natives still like a shot of white wine with their café, which comes strong and short. If you want it weaker, ask for *allongé*; stronger is *serré*. Note that cappuccino is a treat that hasn't crossed the Italian border. The best you can hope for is a *café au lait*, or coffee with milk, but remember, this is strictly a morning brew for the French.

With a quick lunch, many natives will order *un verre de rouge/blanc* (glass of red/white wine) with *un carafe d'eau* (jug of tap water). Perrier is considered too gassy to consume with meals, so still waters such as Evian or Vitel, or the gently bubbly Badoit, are the mineral

waters of choice. If you want to try something local after dinner, order a *marc de Provence*, a sort of Provençal grappa, made by distilling pomace (grape skins and pips) left over from wine-making. Drinks consumed standing at a bar are invariably a franc or two cheaper than those you order seated at a table.

Some of the most glorious of all French wines come from the South of France, and the quality of the region's wines, from the Rhône Valley to the Italian border, have improved dramatically over the past few years.

The Rhône Valley itself produces one of the best rosés in the world – Tavel, from vineyards north of Avignon – and superb reds. Châteauneuf-du-Pape is perhaps the most famous, but other potentially excellent full-bodied reds from the region include Gigondas, Rasteau, Beaumes-de-Venise and Cairanne. Lesser known, but a real treat, is white Châteauneuf-du-Pape, which goes beautifully with fish and shellfish.

Perusing the wine list at a local bistro (or indeed buying to take home), you'll almost never go wrong with anything from the Côtes du Rhône *appellation*, which produces some of the most reliable, agreeable and affordable table wines in France. Likewise, many lists include Costières de Nîmes, Côtes du Luberon and Côtes de Ventoux, known as easy-drinking, inexpensive reds, with some up-and-coming young producers in each area who are doing much to improve quality.

In Context

Thirteen traditional grape varieties are grown in the Provence area, including Rolle, Clairette and Sémillon (white) and Syrah, Grenache, Mourvèdre, Carignan and Cabernet Sauvignon (red). *Appellations* to look for are Côteaux d'Aix, Côtes de Provence, Cassis, Bandol and Bellet.

Wine-tasting at source can be one of the delights of a Provençal holiday, though cellar-door prices are often not a great deal cheaper than their high-street equivalents. With the exception of a few big-name producers that have jumped on to the wine tourism bandwagon, and which may offer cellar tours and *son et lumière* frills in addition to the tasting, wineries are not set up for huge groups of visitors, and it is always worth ringing ahead to confirm opening days and times and – if you are interested in a particular vintage – availability, as limited-edition *crus* often sell out weeks after bottling.

The best areas for wine-touring in the South – where wineries often do observe regular opening times for the public – are the Châteauneuf-du-Pape enclave on the eastern bank of the Rhône (*see chapter* **Orange & Around**), the coastal Bandol *appellation* (*see chapter* **Cassis to Toulon**) and the heartland of the Côtes de Provence *appellation* around Les Arcs (*see chapter* **Central & Eastern Var**). A selection of vineyards are listed in these chapters; we also list one-stop wine centres, where they exist, which group together a variety of producers.

Restaurants

The South of France is heaven for the restaurant junkie. The Côte is bristling with famous chefs and their egos: in multiple-Michelin-starred establishments such as Alain Ducasse's **Louis XV** in Monte-Carlo, **La Belle Otero** or the **Villa de Lys** in Cannes, the **Chantecler** in Nice or Jacques Chibois's **La Bastide St-Antoine** outside Grasse, you'll eat sublime food and pay sublimely ridiculous prices. And tune in to the international babble on the other tables, since the locals patronise these places only on special occasions, or at lunchtime, when many renowned kitchens offer relatively affordable *prix-fixe* lunch menus.

But Provence has also become a magnet for rising young chefs, and some of the best-value, most exciting cooking is to be found one peg below the starched and liveried temples of haute cuisine, in places such as the relaxed **Relais Ste-Victoire** in Beaurecueil near Aix-en-Provence or in the dining room of the **Hôtel la Mirande** in Avignon. At a less exalted level you'll still eat very well, since outside the obvious tourist traps, the quality of the food in the region's bistros and cafés is excellent; at places such as vegetarian **La Zucca Magica**, on the port in Vieux Nice, or at **Le Safranier**, a tavern in Antibes, remarkable meals can be had for the price of a pub feed at home.

Beyond the wonderful food, one of the other pleasures of Le Midi is that its restaurants are

The most famous of the Rhône Valley's renowned reds: **Châteauneuf-du-Pape**.

Bouillabaisse

The Mother of all fish soups, bouillabaisse is the one Provençal dish that everyone has heard of. It is not always easy to disentangle fact from legend when discussing this fiercely contested kettle of fish, but its origins as a stockpot for leftovers are undisputed. It was originally cooked on the beach, over wood fires, by fishermen anxious to use fish they couldn't sell in the market. In 1895, JB Reboul listed 40 types of fish that were suitable for bouillabaisse in his book *La Cuisinière Provençal* – including mackerel and sardines, rejected today as too oily.

Everyone has a recipe, or a favourite restaurant where 'they make it specially for me'. Marseille, though, is the acknowledged home of the soup. In 1980, the city's restaurateurs got together and signed a Bouillabaisse Charter, designed to protect and defend the 'authentic' recipe, which is contested all the time by chefs from St-Tropez to Menton.

The regulation *trois poissons* that any self-respecting bouillabaisse should include are the *rascasse* (scorpion fish), *grondin* (red gurnet) and *congre* (conger eel); potatoes (cooked separately) are also de rigueur. Purists say a total of 12 different fish or shellfish should go into the pot, but a minimum of four different fish for eight people is a good rule. True aficionados

know that the addition of lobster is more for show than for substance, and can happily be done without. The final touch is to flavour the soup with a splash of white Cassis wine, olives, pepper, saffron and dried orange peel. Before tasting, three rounds of toasted baguette are vigorously rubbed with garlic, topped with a dab of *rouille* – a spicy red sauce made with garlic, olive oil and crushed red peppers – and floated on top of the soup together with a sprinkling of grated Gruyère. The soup is served first, from a steaming cauldron, followed by the fish that went to flavour it.

In restaurants, bouillabaisse is considered a complete meal (you'll understand why when you order it). Expect to pay at least 150F for a decent rendition, and quite a bit more in the acknowledged temples of the dish. The following are the best restaurants for bouillabaisse.

Bacon
See page 47.

Bijou
Golfe-Juan; see chapter **Cannes & around**.

Le Lunch
See chapter **Marseille**.

Le Miramar
See page 48.

The Ducasse empire

Known as France's only eight-star chef, Alain Ducasse was first awarded the coveted holy trinity of Michelin stars in 1990 at age 33, for his exquisite Mediterranean-inspired cuisine at the luxurious Louis XV restaurant in Monte-Carlo. After creating the quintessentially Provençal country inn, La Bastide de Moustiers, in the Riviera hinterland, he opened his wildly successful Alain Ducasse restaurant in Paris in 1997, and pocketed another three Michelin stars. A single star for La Bastide soon followed.

Ducasse's most recent Southern venture, Monte-Carlo's snazzy Bar et Boeuf – whose one Michelin star, awarded in 2000, brings Ducasse's tally to eight – is similar to Spoon, his contemporary Parisian brasserie, but with a decidedly more exotic twist. Another Spoon recently opened on the island of Mauritius, and a Tokyo branch is in the offing.

In between combing the countryside for antiques, designing cutlery, training chefs and writing books, the tall, bearded super-chef with horn-rimmed glasses can often be seen on French TV talk shows peddling his back-to-the-garden philosophy, expounded in Confucian maxims like 'even in the best of what it has to offer, nature gives nothing which is absolute; the art of cookery is the search for that absolute'.
Website: www.ducasse-online.com

Abbaye de la Celle

L'Hostellerie de l'Abbaye de la Celle, pl du Général de Gaulle, La Celle, nr Brignoles (04.98.05.14.14/fax 04.98.05.14.15). **Meals served** noon-2pm, 7-10pm daily. **Menus** 210F (weekdays), 280F. **Credit** AmEx, MC, V.

In this country inn, tucked away in a tiny village in the Var, Alain Ducasse and his 'truffle king' pal, Clement Bruno (*see page XX* Chez Bruno), have joined forces to create the ultimate *faux-paysan* Provençal menu. The exquisitely restored eighteenth-century *auberge* (rooms 1,300F-1,900F) stands between a lush vineyard and the historic twelfth-century Abbaye de la Celle, whose Benedictine cloisters give on to the vaulted dining rooms. Prepared by rising young star Benoit Witz (former chef at La Bastide de Moustiers), the delectable food – from starters like pistou soup, and a tasty combo of shrimp, rabbit and vegetables to hearty main courses like baby lamb with ricotta gnocchi and artichokes – are decidedly good value for money.

Bar et Boeuf

av Princesse Grace, Monte-Carlo (00.377.92.16.60.60). **Meals served** July-Oct 7pm-1am daily. Closed Nov-May. **Average** 600F. **Credit** AmEx DC, MC, V.

generally relaxed. Although you shouldn't come to the table in a bathing suit unless you're right on the beach, ties are rarely required and in all but the grandest establishments, T-shirts and shorts are just fine. Children, too, are almost always welcome.

THE MENU & PRICES

By law, the menu must be posted outside the restaurant. Depending on the establishment, there is usually a choice of one or more *menus prix-fixe*: basic, inexpensive, usually three-course meals at a fixed price. Such bargain meals often have hidden overheads, though: check that the menu includes wine, mineral water, cheese and/or dessert; bread is always included. There may also be a *menu gastronomique*, with a selection of regional specialities. A *menu dégustation* is a taster menu with a selection of the chef's party pieces.

If the prices at many of the top restaurants seem prohibitive, note that most offer special lunch-only menus that represent a significant

saving. In many restaurants, fish is priced by the gramme, so have it weighed before you order. By French law, service is included in the price of a meal: it's customary, however, to leave some change, up to around 5 per cent of the bill.

We list *menus prix-fixe* prices rather than average à la carte prices, as the former are a pretty accurate indication of the latter – though be warned that in the gourmet temples, a four-course meal à la carte may cost significantly more than the highest-priced menu.

OPENING TIMES

You could invade France at noon, when nothing can distract the nation's attention from lunch. Restaurants serve until 2.30pm. Dinner hours usually run from 7.30pm to 10.30pm, when the last orders are taken. If you've missed lunch, you can usually get a salad or a sandwich in a café, while brasseries in larger towns are good bets for a late meal, often serving until midnight. When you book the table it's yours

Chef Didier Elena, trained by owner Ducasse, does starters such as carpaccio, melon with *gelée de boeuf*, and fine slices of raw sea bass with a purée of caviar-garnished broccoli, and appealing main courses that run from a spit-roasted fillet of beef larded with black olives to a New Age beef stroganoff – stir-fried beef with paprika, served on sticky rice with nori seaweed and a poached egg. The setting of Ducasse's new place is refreshingly unstuffy – the po-mo designer installed black wood tables, stools, chairs and a trellis of pale wood on the terrace, where the lighting is low. High tables and bar stools inside allow you to be both visible and approachable, high priorities in Monaco.

La Bastide de Moustiers

just south of Moustiers-Ste-Marie on D952 (04.92.70.47.47). **Meals served** noon-1.30pm, 7-9.15pm daily. Closed Jan, Feb. **Menu** 225F-295F. **Credit** AmEx, DC, MC, V.
At his famed country inn, pluri-starred Alain Ducasse has eschewed luxury, setting out to cook 'just like my neighbours'. Said neighbours are mostly small farmers making wine and olive oil and raising vegetables and goats, and their cooking is hearty Provençal food. Consequently, vegetables and spit-roasted meats take pride of place on the menu. The menu might include scrambled

eggs with truffles, soupe au pistou and spit-roasted baby lamb or pigeon served with cèpes and potatoes roasted in the fire.

Louis XV

Hôtel de Paris, pl Casino, Monte-Carlo (00.377.92.16.38.40). **Meals** served noon-2pm, 8-10pm Mon, Thur-Sun. Closed last two weeks Feb, all Dec. **Menus** 500F-980F. **Credit** AmEx, DC.
This jewel-box of a dining room in the palmy Hôtel de Paris offers the ultimate Riviera gilt trip, right down to petit-point stools next to the tables for ladies' handbags and one of the most glamorous outdoor terraces in the world, overlooking the casino. Though very expensive, it's surprisingly unstuffy and the food is superb. Remember Marie Antoinette's let-them-eat-cake dictum? Ducasse turns it on its head here, feeding some of the richest and most powerful people in the world a contemporary update of the sturdy, savoury peasant food native to the coast and hinterlands from Nice to Genoa. There are superb vegetable dishes, brilliant fish cooking – check out the turbot in a crust of polenta with wild fennel and tomato condiment – and a stunning cheese tray. Add a truly remarkable wine cellar, and this becomes one of those once-in-a-lifetime meals you want to have twice.

for the evening, as there is rarely more than one sitting. For most upmarket places, reservations are recommended, and some of the top restaurants ask clients to reconfirm on the day, as they invariably have a waiting list.

A PROVENÇAL RESTAURANT TOUR

The regional chapters include extensive eating and drinking recommendations. Below we list establishments that stand out for a combination of factors: cuisine, setting, atmosphere. Some glow in the full flush of Michelin stardom, while others are decidedly more rustic. But this is the joy of eating out in Provence – mixing high and low, passing from the starched tablecloth to the raucous card game in a single afternoon.

The Rhône Delta

Le Jardin d'Hadrien

11 rue de l'Enclos, Nîmes (04.66.21.86.65). **Meals served** *Sept-June* noon-2pm Mon, Tue, Thur-Sun; 7.30-10pm Mon, Tue, Thur-Sat; *July, Aug* noon-2pm

Mon, Tue, Thur-Sat; 7.30-10pm Mon-Sat. **Menus** 95F-150F. **Credit** AmEx MC, V.
Sitting under the plane trees in the quiet garden behind this dignified nineteenth-century house is a lovely experience after battling the coach-tour throngs around the Arena in the heart of the city. And if the weather is inclement, the dining room is comfortable and attractive, too, with white stone walls, a big open hearth and beamed ceiling. Chef Alain Vinouze does appealing dishes with a local bent such as courgette flowers stuffed with the city's famed brandade, aubergine charlotte, roast lamb and *rougets* with tapenade. Wonderful list of inexpensive wines from the surrounding countryside, including a fine Costières de Nîmes.

Le Mas de Peint

Le Sambuc, 20km south of Arles on D36 (04.90.97.20.62). **Meals served** noon-1.30pm, 8-9.30pm Mon, Tue, Thur-Sun. **Closed** mid-Jan to mid-Mar. **Menus** 190F (lunch only), 245F (dinner only). **Credit** AmEx, DC, MC, V.
Le Mas de Peint is one of the most celebrated rustic-chic hotels in the South of France. Unlike other such

Château de Berne

Situated just one hour west of Nice Airport in the South of France, you will find one of the most prestigious vineyards in the Côte de Provence, Château de Berne.

A 1500 acre estate with some 250 acres of vines producing 300,000 bottles a year of some of the finest quality red, white and rosé wines you are likely to taste, with an excellent visitors' centre.

The estate also boasts a 19 room Auberge, which provides accommodation for seminars, residential wine schools and cookery schools. The Auberge, as you may expect, has an excellent restaurant.

All 19 rooms are individually decorated to an exceptionally high standard and are air conditioned. Other facilities include: tennis, swimming and a gymnasium. Beauty treatments are available.

Château de Berne is a superb combination of outstanding wine, accommodation and food. Maybe a long way for a

evening out but what an exceptional venue for a weekend!

All inclusive packages are available - for more information contact

Château de Berne or our London office (Ruxley Holdings Ltd).

Château de Berne Flayosc 83510 Lorgues France
Tel: +33 (0)4 94 60 43 60 Fax: +33 (0)4 94 60 43 58
UK Office Tel: +44 (0)1932 870915
e-mail: info@ruxley.com
www.chateau-berne.fr

exalted and expensive places, this one is actually quite charming and relaxed. Set in an old Camarguais *mas*, or farmhouse, it's a breathtakingly beautiful place, and a meal (the restaurant is open to outside guests, but book) is a convivial experience, as chef Daniel Ergeteau cooks on a stove at the back of the dining room. There's a single fixed menu, and it runs to dishes like roasted aubergine filled with aubergine caviar, fillet of beef wrapped in bacon, and chocolate tart. Most of the produce is local, and there's a fine list of local wines.

L'Oustau de Baumanière

Val d'Enfer, Les Baux-de-Provence (04.90.54.33.07). **Meals served** *Oct-May* noon-2pm, 7.30-9.30pm daily; *Nov, Dec, Apr* noon-2pm Mon, Tue, Fri-Sun; 7.30-9.30pm Mon, Tue, Thur-Sun. Closed Jan-Mar. **Menus** 490F-750F. **Credit** AmEx, DC, MC, V.

Tucked away in the fig trees at the head of a narrow ravine just off the main road leading up to Les Baux, the legendary L'Oustau de Baumanière is perhaps the most quietly glamorous country inn in France. Chef Jean-André Charial's luxurious and disciplined creations include impeccably classical leek-and-sweetbread-filled ravioli garnished with shavings of black truffle, and refined Provençal sea bass in red wine sauce with tiny black olives. This is also a great spot for vegetarians to splash out, since *la ballade dans notre jardin* is a seven-course menu (490F) of beautifully prepared vegetables from the hotel's own gardens.

Avignon & the Vaucluse

La Fenière

2km south of Lourmarin on D945 (04.90.68.11.79). **Meals served** 7.30-9.30pm Mon; noon-1.30pm, 7.30-9.30pm Wed-Sun. Closed mid-Jan to mid-Feb, last two weeks of Nov. **Menus** 230F-550F. **Credit** AmEx, DC, MC, V.

Reine Sammut, one of France's top female chefs, likes authoritative flavours but can also be subtle and inventive. To begin, try the powerfully rich shellfish soup with eel-stuffed cannelloni, or the fluffy gnocchi with summer vegetables and strips of bacon. The *petit melon* of lamb is a treat: a ball of lamb slow-roasted for seven hours and served with caponata (Sicilian-style roast aubergine and capers). There are several hotel rooms upstairs (single 550F, double 600F, suite 1,050F) if you don't want to drive after dinner.

Le Fournil

5 pl Carnot, Bonnieux (04.90.75.83.62). **Meals served** noon-1.45pm, 7.30-9.30pm Wed-Sun. Closed Dec-Jan. **Menus** 100F-190F. **Credit** MC, V.

This bistro in an old bakery in Bonnieux is the very definition of low-key Provençal style. The 170F menu is an excellent buy, with great starters of millefeuille of aubergine and tomato, or a brilliant sauté of baby squid served on salad. Depending on the season, main courses may include duckling roasted with figs in pear juice or a veal chop with whatever

fresh vegetables the market furnishes. Finish up with the delicious fig tart with a cinnamon crust or the selection of goat's cheeses.

La Mirande

Hôtel la Mirande 4 pl de la Mirande, Avignon (04.90.85.93.93). **Meals served** 12.30-2pm, 7.30-10pm Mon, Thur-Sun. Closed Jan. **Menus** 240F-480F. **Credit** AmEx, DC, MC, V.

Since the arrival of inventive Ducasse-trained chef Daniel Hebert in 1997, the restaurant of the Hôtel de la Mirande has become the place to eat in Avignon. In good weather, meals are served in the garden; the rest of the year in the sumptuous dining room. Hebert was personal chef to Peru's President Alberto Fujimori. His desserts are some of the most exciting in Provence, and include a delicious soft vanilla macaroon with *fromage blanc* ice-cream and sour cherry sauce.

Le Moulin de Lourmarin

rue du Temple, Lourmarin (04.90.68.06.69). **Meals served** noon-2pm, 7-9.30pm Mon, Thur-Sun; 7-9.30pm Wed. Closed mid-Jan to mid-Feb. **Menus** 200F-600F. **Credit** AmEx, DC, MC, V.

This handsome stone mill by the fields surrounding the chateau at the edge of Lourmarin was badly renovated in the 1970s, but that doesn't deter young cook Edouard Loubet. Loubet leans heavily on his herb and vegetable garden. His rack of Sisteron lamb is sublime, and he has some good signature dishes, such as a delicious duo of foie gras, fresh and sautéd, in a terrine with green tomato jam, served with caramelised pine cone-scented sauce. Loubet goes wrong, though, when he gets too complicated (yes, that was one of the simpler dishes). If you're staying over (rates 1,100F-2,600F), ask for a traditional room.

La Prévoté

4 rue Jean-Jacques, L'Isle-sur-la-Sorgue (04.90.38.57.29). **Meals served** noon-1.30pm, 7-9.30pm Tue-Sat; noon-1.30pm Sun. Closed last three weeks Nov & last two weeks Feb. **Menus** 145F-250F. **Credit** MC, V.

Set in an old mill, this rather formal Michelin one-star is where the antiques dealers go to splash out, but the 210F menu is an extremely good buy. The ever-changing menu has dishes such as delicate shellfish-stuffed ravioli in lobster cream, roast duckling in a sauce of lavender honey and finely diced vegetables with a side of earthy aubergine purée, and pleasant desserts such as a terrine of citrus fruits and rosemary. Service is slow, but this is the perfect place for a lazy lunch after trawling the flea market. Reservations essential.

Marseille & Aix

La Clos de la Violette

10 av de la Violette, Aix-en-Provence (04.42.23.30.71). **Meals served** 7-9.30pm Mon; noon-2pm, 7-9.30pm Tue-Sat. Closed one week mid-Feb. **Menus** 300F-600F. **Credit** AmEx, MC, V.

In a spacious garden under ancient chestnut trees, chef Jean-Marc Banzo has a knack for producing food that is at once light, healthy and unmistakeably Provençal. Banzo's carpaccio of *pintade* (poached guinea fowl on a bed of chopped black olives and fresh almonds) and grilled *rougets* (red mullet) with squid-stuffed baby cabbage spotlight the best of modern Provençal cooking, and his sublime *croustillant* of raspberries – fresh raspberries and crunchy coconut cream between layers of translucent raspberry macaroon wafers – is rapturously good. The service can be erratic, and the welcome cool.

L'Escale

2 bd Alexandre Delabre, Les Goudes (04.91.73.16. 78). **Meals served** noon-2.30pm,7.30-10pm Tue-Sun. Closed Jan. **Menu** 140F. **Credit** AmEx, DC, MC, V.

It's hard to believe that the sleepy little fishing village of Les Goudes is actually part of Marseille, but it's only 20 minutes from the centre. Come to the spacious seaside terrace for a catch of the day that doesn't get much fresher. Owner Serge Zaroukian, a former fishmonger, does a delicious sauté of baby squid and perfectly cooked monkfish served with Provençal garnishes of ratatouille and onions au gratin. Ideal for Sunday lunch, when almost everything else in town is closed – but it's very popular, so always book ahead.

Le Miramar

12 quai du Port, Marseille (04.91.91.10.40). **Meals served** 7-10pm Mon; noon-2pm, 7-10pm Tue-Sat. Closed first two weeks Jan & first three weeks Aug. **Average** 400F. **Credit** AmEx, DC.

Located on the edge of Marseille's Vieux Port, this appealing 1950s-vintage restaurant (à la carte only) is the best place to sample the city's fabled bouillabaisse. Since bouillabaisse (280F) is always a two-course meal – first, the soup, and then the fish – don't order a first course. Dessert should be a palate cleanser; we'd recommend the fantastic raspberry and basil soufflé.

Le Relais Ste-Victoire

D46 from Aix to Beaurecueil, then follow signs (04. 42.66.94.98). **Meals served** noon-1.30pm, 7.30-9.30pm Tue-Thur, Sat; 7.30-9.30pm Fri; noon-1.30pm Sun. Closed first week Jan, school holidays Feb & first week Nov. **Menus** 160F-400F. **Credit** AmEx, MC, V.

Lost amid the neatly tilled fields below the white cliffs that frame Mont Ste-Victoire near Aix, the Relais Ste-Victoire is so warm and personal that it feels like you're visiting friends. Chef René Jugy-Berges prepares a mix of French classics and Provençal recipes that changes with the season: examples are endive stuffed with lobster in celery butter with a garnish of freshly roasted hazelnuts, breaded slices of monkfish in Parmesan butter with tomato and country-ham filled ravioli and a wonderfully earthy fig tart. Don't miss the first-rate assortment of local *chèvres* on the cheese board.

Une Table au Sud

2 quai du Port, Marseille (04.91.90.63.53). **Meals served** 7-10.30pm Mon; noon-2.30pm, 7-10.30pm Tue-Sat. **Menus** 135F-185F. **Credit** MC, V.

After working for Alain Ducasse in Paris for eight years, chef Lionel Levy moved south and opened this relaxed, contemporary restaurant on the first floor of the famous Café la Samaritaine. With spectacular views of the Vieux Port, Une Table au Sud has quickly won itself a reputation for its excellent modern French cooking at reasonable prices. Levy offers dishes such as a fricassee of squid, country ham and confit tomatoes seasoned with Espelette peppers and sesame seeds, roast pigeon with hearts of fennel, and a delicious pear in a caramelised crust with rosemary-scented *crème anglaise*. Friendly, efficient service and a nice wine list.

The Western Côte

La Bouillabaisse

plage de la Bouillabaisse, St-Tropez (04.94.97. 54.00). **Meals served** mid-Feb to mid-Nov 12.30-2.30pm, 7.45-10.30pm daily. Closed dinner Tue & all Wed during May; closed mid-Nov to Jan except Christmas period. **Average** 210F. **Credit** AmEx, MC, V.

In contrast to so many other restaurants in St Tropez, both the service and food here are excellent. While away the afternoon on the terrace, enjoying simple, well-prepared dishes such as the salad of mixed leaves, tomatoes and baked, breaded mozzarella, or tagliatelle pistou with freshly made basil sauce and toasted pine nuts. Or indulge yourself with a real treat by rounding up some friends and ordering their excellent bouillabaisse a day in advance. There is a special lunchtime menu (Le Provençale, 205F) in May, otherwise it is à la carte.

Le Mas du Langoustier

3.5km west of the port, Ile de Porquerolles (04.94.58.30.09). **Meals served** 12.30-1.45pm, 7.30-9.30pm daily. Closed mid-Oct to Apr. **Menus** 330F-500F. **Credit** AmEx, DC, MC, V.

This place is head-spinningly expensive, but you can (almost) see why. Located on the Côte's most chi-chi island, L'Olivier, the gourmet restaurant of this upmarket hotel, has friendly and efficient staff and superb food, with dishes such as a wonderful fillet of John Dory on a bed of leeks in a sauce of fresh local grape juice. If you're staying at the hotel, you'll eat just as well in the guests-only set-menu restaurant, whose highlights include a sublime fish soup, grilled fillet of sea bass stuffed with black olives and tomatoes, and cheese and chocolate soufflé cake. Day-trip it across for lunch on the ferry from Hyères.

Leï Mouscardins

Tour du Portalet, St Tropez (04.94.97.29.00). **Meals served** noon-2pm, 7-10pm Tue-Sat; noon-2pm Sun.

Closed mid-Jan to mid-Feb. **Menus** 280F-340F. **Credit** AmEx, DC, MC, V.

Laurent Tarridec's quayside restaurant is easily the best and chicest table in this hotbed of hedonism, where people tend to be more concerned about their figures than their gastronomic pleasures. The menu changes seasonally: starters may include baby squid and vegetables dressed with squid's ink and a balsamic vinaigrette, or an excellent soup of tiny grey North Sea shrimp, followed by *chapon* (a white fish) stuffed with parsley, breadcrumbs and bell pepper. The wine list is pricey and not particularly original.

L'Oasis

rue Jean-Honoré-Carle, Mandelieu-La-Napoule (04.93.49.95.52). **Meals served** noon-2pm, 7-10pm daily. **Menus** 230F-680F. **Credit** AmEx, DC, MC, V.

This legendary table in La-Napoule offers a very near approximation of a classic *grande bouffe* French meal. Chef Stephane Raimbault serves solidly classic food with a few stylish touches on a terrace under the plane trees – which is about as *Toujours Provence* as you can get. The starters can be a tad tired, but main courses are more inspired: the *ballotin* of rabbit stuffed with prawn in a Thai-spiced cream sauce with pasta is delicious. The sumptuous dessert trolley has an impeccable lemon tart and old-fashioned waist-busting treats such as Dôme du Chocolat, a two-layer chocolate cake with a hazelnut-praline interior.

Les Santons

D558, 83310 Grimaud (04.94.43.21.02). **Meals served** noon-2pm, 8-11pm Mon, Tue-Sun. Closed Nov-Mar. **Menu** 265F. **Credit** AmEx, DC, MC, V.

A slightly prissy restaurant on the edge of Grimaud – but if the service is stiff, the cuisine is excellent. To get the best out of this place, order regional dishes such as the *terrine de berger*, densely packed morsels of lamb and lamb tongue in a garlicky, parslied aspic, or main courses such as the *blanquette d'agneau*, braised lamb in a herbed cream sauce, or free-range chicken breast in a sauce of ginger and preserved citrus peel.

Inland Var

Les Chênes Verts

rte de Villecroze, Tourtour (04.94.70.55.06). Call for details of service. **Credit** AmEx, DC, MC, V.

Tucked away in a tiny town in the Var, this intimate and relaxed one-star with two cosy dining rooms is worth going out of your way for, since chef Paul Balade turns out the sort of earthy, exhilirating food everyone hopes to find in Provence. His menu follows the seasons, but dishes like risotto with truffles and cèpes, *daube de sanglier* – a stew of wild boar – chicken breast stuffed with foie gras and garnished with garlicky artichoke hearts, and lavender ice-cream communicate his talent and regional allegiance, and a very good list of reasonably priced Côtes de Varois wines round out the pleasure of a meal here.

Chez Bruno

rte de Vidauban, Lorgues (04.94.85.93.93). **Meals served** *mid-June to mid-Sept* noon-1.30pm, 7.30-9.15pm daily; *mid-Sept to mid-June* noon-1.30pm, 7.30-9.15pm Tue-Sat; noon-1.30pm Sun. **Menu** 300F. **Credit** AmEx, DC, MC, V.

Heading into the magnificent back country of the Var, a trip to Bruno has a vaguely off-to-see-the-wizard feel (watch for signs outside the village). In a lovely setting, this self-taught chef has created one of the great gourmet destinations of Europe, with

Provençal menu

Sauces & pastes

aïoli a mayonnaise made with crushed garlic, egg yolks and olive oil, served as a dip or – thinned with fish stock – as an accompaniment to bourride

anchoïade anchovy mousse, eaten with raw vegetables

pistou local take on the Italian pesto, made of crushed basil, tomato, garlic and pine nuts, often dolloped into clear vegetable soupe au pistou

raito a sauce of tomatoes, red wine, garlic, black olives and capers, usually served with grilled fish

rouille a sauce made from sweet red pepper, garlic, soaked bread and olive oil – the classic companion of bouillabaisse

tapenade a variation on anchoïade with capers and olives

Fish

baudroie downmarket version of the bourride

bouillabaisse (Marseille) king of Provençal fish soups (*see box page 43*)

bourride thick fish soup, served with either aïoli or rouille

boutargue (also known as poutargue) grey mullet roe, eaten in thin slices on toast as an entrée

brandade de morue purée of salt cod with cream, potatoes, olive oil and garlic

estocaficada (Nice) salt cod stewed with garlic and tomato

fruits de mer seafood: calmar (squid), cigale de mer ('sea cricket', a rare blunt-nosed rock

an all-truffle menu for 300F. Come hungry, though – Bruno's cooking style defies modern inclinations towards light and healthy. The *carte du jour* may include pumpkin soup, summer truffle with foie gras and bacon in pastry, potatoes with cèpes in truffle sauce, or boned pigeon with foie gras in pastry in truffle sauce, then a caramel Bavarois with sliced pear and a fig and custard tart served with yoghurt ice-cream.

The Riviera: Cannes to Menton

Les Agaves

4 av Maréchal Foch, Beaulieu-sur-Mer (04.93.01.13. 12). **Meals served** 7.30-10pm Tue; 12.30-2pm, 7.30-10pm Wed-Sun. Closed Feb. **Menu** 175F. **Credit** MC, V.

Located in the Palais des Anglais building across from the train station, this stylish little bistro is popular with the locals and a reliable option if you're looking for a good meal in a relaxed setting. Chef-owner Jacky Lelu works with good-quality produce and is best when simple: his delicious home-made ravioli, for example, followed by a grill or maybe a first-rate special such as aïoli, fresh cod and steamed vegetables.

Albert's Bar

1 rue Maurice Jaubert, Nice (04.93.87.30.20). **Meals served** noon-2.30pm, 7.30-10.30pm Mon-Sat. **Average** 250F. **Credit** AmEx, DC, MC, V.

This small, shabby restaurant in the pedestrian district of downtown Nice serves absolutely fantastic (if very expensive) food to the city's ruling class. The menu changes regularly but lunch might include a superb salad of raw artichoke hearts in olive oil and lemon juice garnished with Parmesan, chives and

fava beans, a perfect sauté of sliced squid and shrimp, and one of the best desserts in town: preserved figs in a caramel sauce with vanilla ice-cream. Go with the house white, a pleasant Château Lagoulet Côtes de Provence.

Auberge du Jarrier

30 passage Bourgade, Biot (04.93.65.11.68). **Meals served** *July, Aug* noon-2pm Fri-Sun; 8-10pm daily; *Sept-Dec* noon-2pm, 8-10pm Wed-Sun; closed Jan to mid-Mar. **Menus** 180F-250F. **Credit** AmEx, MC, V.

At this relaxed old inn you might start with braised baby artichokes in a light tomato sauce (*à la barigoule*) or a warm lobster salad (50F supplement), before a flavourful main course such as baby red mullet in a sauce of olive oil and herbs with fava beans and artichokes and a garnish of courgette flower beignets, or very good risotto with morel mushrooms. The tart of pine nuts with preserved orange slices and fresh mint is a perfect and original summer dessert.

Bacon

bd de Bacon, Cap d'Antibes (04.93.61.50.02). **Meals served** noon-1.30pm, 7.30-10pm Tue-Sat. Closed Nov-Jan. **Menus** 280F-450F. **Credit** AmEx, DC, MC, V.

This Cap d'Antibes luxury fish house is all about studied casual elegance. It is also one of the best places on the Riviera to eat an authentically local catch of the day. Overlooking the Baie des Anges, the almost all-white dining room has a tented ceiling that is rolled back in good weather. The pricey menu is dead simple, starring the catch of the day – which might be anything from turbot to monkfish to John Dory. If you can afford it, try the bouillabaisse – the most luxurious version of this Med

lobster), coques (cockles), coquilles St-Jacques (scallops), crabe (crab), crevettes (prawns), écrevisse (freshwater crayfish), gambas (king prawns), homard (lobster), huître (oyster), langouste (spiny lobster), langoustines (saltwater crayfish), moules (mussels), oursin (sea urchin), palourdes (clams), poulpe (octopus), telline (small clam), violet (very strong-tasting soft-shelled crustacean) **poisson** fish: anchois (anchovies), anguille (eel), baudroie (monkfish or angler fish), barbue (brill), cabillaud (cod), carrelet (plaice), colin (hake), congre (conger eel), daurade (sea bream), grondin (red guernard), hareng (herring), lotte de mer (monkfish), loup de mer (sea bass), maquereau (mackerel), morue (salt cod), pageot (sea bream), raie (skate), rascasse (scorpion fish), rouget (red mullet), St-Pierre (John Dory), saumon (salmon), sole (sole), thon (tuna), truite (trout), turbot (turbot)

Meat

artichauts à la barigoule artichokes braised in white wine, sometimes stuffed with pork and mushroom
boeuf à la gardiane (Camargue) beef (preferably from bulls) stewed with carrots and celery
capoun fassum cabbage stuffed with sausage
cassoulet (Languedoc) bean and meat casserole
daube de boeuf beef with lard, onion, garlic and herbs, stewed in red wine
estouffade à la provençale beef stew with carrots, onions, garlic and orange zest
lapin à la provençale rabbit in white wine with tomato and mustard
pieds et paquets stuffed tripe served in a stew, sometimes with sheep's feet
viande meat: agneau (lamb), andouille (tripe sausage), boeuf (beef), biftek (steak),

▶

classic served on the coast. The lemon sorbet is a delicious palate cleanser.

La Belle Otero

Hôtel Carlton, 58 bd la Croisette, Cannes (04.92.99.51. 10). **Meals served** 7.30-10.30pm Tue; noon-2pm, 7.30-10.30pm Wed-Sat. Closed first two weeks Nov & mid-June to mid-July. **Menus** 290F-620F. **Credit** AmEx, DC, MC, V.

The Michelin guide gives this place two stars, and some of the cooking here is superb, but overall, it's just the cherry on the cake of the most important hotel in a city that runs on the dual tracks of celebrities and conventions – not the best audience for a serious chef like Francis Chauveau. There's plenty of money to take him up on extravagant dishes such as a superb starter of fresh asparagus and morel mushrooms in almost transparent pasta envelopes, but Chauveau has a hard time pleasing tycoons who are more interested in silicone-filled tarts than strawberry ones, which explains the stridency of in-your-face dishes like the lobster risotto (390F). It seems a shame that such a first-rate kitchen should be cooking for such a largely unappreciative audience.

Le Chantecler

Hôtel Negresco, 37 promenade des Anglais, Nice (04.93.16.64.00). **Meals served** noon-2pm, 8-10pm daily. Closed mid-Nov to mid-Dec. **Menus** 250F-620F. **Credit** AmEx, DC, MC, V.

Chef Alain Llorca is a key player in the new generation of Provençal cooks. He specialises in bold and authoritative combinations of texture and flavour, as seen in the canapé of lobster and mashed white beans served with a cup of gazpacho, or the pan-roasted cod served in a garlicky sauce with a garnish of grilled Jabugo ham and red peppers stuffed (yes, this is still the same dish) with cod tripe. His sandwich-style dish of potato salad layered with cuttlefish, marinated fresh anchovies, confit of tomato, fava beans and tiny squid is superb as well, and you shouldn't miss his startlingly original tomato tarte tatin served with candied black-olive ice-cream. Excellent service and a very good wine list round off the pleasure of a meal here.

La Merenda

4 rue de la Terrasse, Nice (no phone). **Menus** 150F-180F. Closed Sat, Sun & three weeks Aug. **No credit cards.**

Chef Dominique Le Stanc shed his three-star perch at the Hôtel Negresco for this rustic hole-in-the-wall bistro not far from the Cours Saleya market in 1996; he serves a full repertoire of classic Niçois dishes such as stuffed sardines, *stockfissa* (salt cod with tomatoes and olive oil) and *daube de boeuf*. Though it's crowded and hot, the food's delicious. Book (in person) if you can.

Le Moulin de Mougins

424 chemin du Moulin, Quartier Notre-Dame-de-Vie, Mougins (04.93.75.78.24). **Meals served** noon-1.30pm, 7-9pm Tue-Sun. Closed Feb. **Menus** 550F-740F. **Credit** AmEx, DC, MC, V.

In the 1970s, Roger Vergé introduced the world to the joys of Provençal cooking with his *cuisine du soleil*. Three decades on, little has changed in the kitchens of his sixteenth-century olive mill – which may explain why Vergé has recently mislaid two of his three Michelin stars. Still, the Moulin sparkles with exquisite taste and excellent Provençal fare, with signature dishes such as courgette flowers with truffles and pigeon in a walnut crust with creamed spinach. Desserts such as the vanilla crème brûlée are equally fine, and the cheeseboard features a

► ## Provençal menu (continued)

cervelle (brain), Châteaubriand (Porterhouse steak), cheval (horse), contrefilet (sirloin), entrecôte (ribsteak), faux filet (sirloin), foie (liver), jambon (ham), langue (tongue), lapin (rabbit), lard (bacon), mouton (mutton), porc (pork), rognon (kidney), rognon blanc (testicle), sanglier (wild boar), saucisson (sausage), tête de veau (calf's head jelly), tournedos (thick filet slices), tripes (tripe), veau (veal), venaison (venison)

volaille poultry: caille (quail), canard (duck), dinde or dindon (turkey), foie gras (goose liver pâté), gibier (game), oie (goose), pintade (guinea fowl), poulet (chicken)

Vegetables & side-dishes

beignets de fleur de courgette courgette flowers dipped in batter and fried

fleurs de courgettes farcis courgette flowers stuffed with mushrooms, onions and sage

légumes vegetables: (ail) garlic, artichaut (artichoke), asperges (asparagus), avocat (avocado), blette (Swiss chard), câpre (caper), cardon (cardoon – similar to an artichoke), carotte (carrot), céleri (celery), céleri rave (celery root), champignon (cultivated mushrooms – wild varieties include cèpes, chanterelles, girolles, morilles, mousserons), chou (cabbage), chou-fleur (cauliflower), endive (chicory), épinards (spinach), fève (broad bean), flageolet (white bean), haricot vert (string bean), haricot blanc (white bean), lentilles (lentils), navet (turnip), oignon (onion), panais (parsnip), petits pois (peas), pois chiches (chickpeas), poireau (leek), poivron (bell pepper), pomme de terre (potato), riz (rice), roquette (rocket), tomate (tomato), truffe (truffle)

noble selection. The wine list, with over 700 bottles, is a treasure trove. If you can't face the drive back, there are rooms (double 850F-950F, suite 1,800F).

Neat
11 square Mérimée, Cannes (04.93.99.29.19/fax 04.93.68.84.48). **Meals served** 12.15-2.30pm, 7.15-10pm Mon-Sat. **Credit** AmEx, DC, MC, V.
Slough-born Richard Neat earned his Michelin spurs at the two-star Pied à Terre in London's Charlotte Street, and after a three-year Indian trip set up his own restaurant in Cannes. Less than a year after opening the doors, Neat has earned a Michelin star, the only one currently in British hands in France. Modern French cooking is the house style, and the top dish is snails rolled in dried mushrooms and garlic.

La Petite Maison
11 rue St-François-de-Paule, Nice (04.93.85.71.53). **Meals served** noon-2pm, 7.30-10pm Mon-Sat. **Average** 300F. **Credit** AmEx, MC, V.
This venerable restaurant in an old grocery store is generally full of colourful locals. Start with the Niçois hors d'oeuvres – slices of *pissaladière* (onion, anchovy and black olive tart), veal-stuffed vegetables, courgette, aubergine and red pepper beignets with a delicious tomato sauce, grilled red peppers, artichoke salad, fresh prawns dressed in olive oil and lemon juice – and then have the sea bass cooked in a crust of salt. If there's any room left after that, the house ice-cream, with pine nuts and candied orange blossoms, is the best in town.

Le Restaurant Arménien
82 La Croisette, Cannes (04.93.94.00.58). **Meals served** noon-1.30pm, 7-10.30pm Tue-Sun. **Menu** 250F. **Credit** DC, MC, V.

At the very eastern end of the Croisette, this laid-back Armenian restaurant offers superb eating in a calm setting, with the bonus of friendly service. Sixteen different meze – including tiny sausages, pickled vegetables, three kinds of aubergine and three types of pizza-style bread – make up the first course. Main courses include rice-stuffed mussels, skewered lamb and barley pasta with pistachios. Finishing off the feast are home-made desserts, including mint-chocolate ice-cream.

La Table d'Yves
85 montée de la Bourgade, Haute-de-Cagnes (04.93. 20.33.33). **Meals served** *Mar-June, Sept* noon-2pm, Mon, Tue, Thur, Fri; 7.30-10pm Mon, Tue, Thur-Sun; *July, Aug* 7.30-10pm Mon, Tue, Thur-Sun. Closed Feb. **Menus** 128F-230F. **Credit** MC, V.
The warm, bright dining room of chef Yves Merville's relaxed and fairly priced bistro has a festive feel, enhanced by the friendly service of Isabelle, his wife. They serve some of the best fish soup in the South of France, plus delicious dishes such as mushroom ravioli in mushroom and chicken bouillon, crayfish salad with balsamic vinaigrette, and rack of lamb and potatoes roasted with onions and tomato confit.

La Taverne du Safranier
pl du Safranier, Antibes (04.93.34.80.50). **Meals served** noon-2pm, 7.30-10pm Tue-Sat. Closed mid-Dec to mid-Jan. **Menu** 62F. **No credit cards.**
The surroundings are simple and this – for once – is where the locals go. Start with the delicious *poivron du Safranier* (pepper stuffed with garlic and parsley) or mussels prepared in a variety of ways, and then try a grilled fish or a daily special such as *daube de boeuf* or braised beef served with home-made ravioli stuffed with beef and Swiss chard. Nice selection of Provençal wines.

---

mesclun salad of salad leaves and herbs
petits farcis tiny seasonal vegetables, stuffed with mushrooms, olives, herbs
ratatouille hotpot of onion, aubergine, courgette and tomato
salade niçoise (Nice) salad of tuna, eggs, beans, lettuce, eggs and anchovies
tian mixed vegetables and rice baked with cheese

Bread, pies, pasta & pizza
fougasse bread flavoured with rose, orange or almond water; there are also savoury varieties, including olive and lardons, or bacon bits
gnocchi potato dumplings, often served with truffles (truffes) or foie gras
pan-bagnat (Nice) a bread roll filled with tuna, tomatoes, onions and other ingredients, dressed with olive oil and pressed down to blend the flavours

pissaladière (Nice) pizza with anchovy and onion topping
socca (Nice) a thin pancake made using chickpea flour

Cheese
Local cheeses include Banon (nutty, wrapped in chestnut leaves), Lou Pèvre (rolled in pepper), Poivre d'Ain (pressed with wild savory) and creamy Tomme from the Alps

Dessert & sweets
calissons (Aix) diamond-shaped sweets made of almonds, sugar and preserved fruit
chichis (Nice) deep-fried dough sticks
clafoutis baked batter tart with seasonal fruit, particularly cherries
tourte de blettes swiss chard pie garnished with pine nuts and sultanas
la Tropezienne (St-Tropez) sponge cake filled with lashings of custard cream

Les Teraillers

11 rue du Chemin Neuf, Biot (04.93.65.01.59).
Meals served noon-2pm, 7-9.30pm Mon, Tue, Fri-Sun; 7-9.30pm Thur. Closed Nov. **Menus** 180F-380F. **Credit** AmEx, MC, V.
Tucked away in what was a sixteenth-century potter's workshop, this stylish place has an atmosphere almost as good as the food. The little terrace out front can be noisy. The menu offers a creative take on traditional Provençal dishes such as courgette flowers stuffed with veal in truffle butter, and sea bass cooked in a crust of salt. After perfectly aged cheeses, finish with raspberries in a lemon gratin or a millefeuille of red fruits. A good wine list and a knowledgeable sommelier complete the bliss.

La Terrasse

Hôtel Juana, La Pinède, av Gallice, Juan-les-Pins (04.93.61.08.70). **Meals served** July-Aug noon-2pm, 7-10pm daily; Apr-June, Sept, Oct 7-10pm Mon, Thur; noon-2pm, 7-10pm Tue, Fri-Sun. Closed Nov-Mar. **Menus** 230F-680F. **Credit** AmEx, MC, V.
The formal La Terrasse attracts a clientele more likely to spend the day in white linen than bathing suits. Still, it serves some really wonderful food, and is worth considering for a splurge. It was here that Alain Ducasse won the second star that propelled him to fame; chef Christian Morisset, who's been here since 1986, continues the tradition. The spiny lobster and courgette spaghetti with cherry tomatoes is luscious and refined, as is his breaded fillet of sea bream with melted baby onions and thyme. For a light dessert, try the raspberries, strawberries and wild strawberries in vanilla oil and aged balsamic vinegar.

Villa de Lys

Majestic Hôtel, 14 bd de la Croisette, Cannes (04.92.98.77.00). **Meals served** noon-2pm, 7-10pm daily. Closed mid-Nov to mid-Dec. **Menus** 260F-580F. **Credit** AmEx, DC, MC, V.
Chef Bruno Oger is one of the rising young turks on the Riviera. In the oddly decorated restaurant of this luxury hotel on the Cannes seafront, the service can be a bit bumbling, but what makes a meal here exciting is the chef's judicious, internationally inspired creativity and unexpected seasonings. He formerly worked as chef at the Oriental in Bangkok, and the Thai influence is plain in dishes like lobster in a creamy broth spiked with a bouquet garni of lemongrass, lime leaves and fresh coriander. But Oger also does more traditional offerings like anchovy tart, an excellent risotto with baby artichokes, turbot with asparagus, and Provençal style-rabbit. Don't miss the delicious pineapple confit for dessert.

La Zucca Magica

4 bis quai Papacino, Nice (04.93.56.25.27). **Meals served** noon-2.30pm, 8.30pm-midnight Tue-Sat. **Menus** 90F-130F. **No credit cards.**
In 1996, Marco Folicardi, Rome's best vegetarian chef, moved to Nice and set up shop at this grotto-like tavern next to the city's old port. Here this gruff but hospitable bear of a man serves up a remarkable lunch menu that may be the best bargain in the city. You drink the house wine – it's all there is – and you eat what Folicardi serves you: lasagne with ricotta, asparagus and lemon zest; open ravioli of leeks, tomatoes and goat's cheese; cheese-and-aubergine 'meatballs' in a superb fresh tomato sauce; a brioche filled with aubergine, onions, tomatoes, peppers and mozzarella; and fresh cherry flan. The food just keeps on coming.

Inland Alpes-Maritimes

La Bastide St-Antoine

48 av Henri Dunant, Grasse (04.93.70.94.94). **Meals served** noon-2.30pm, 8-10.30pm daily. **Menus** 250F-700F. **Credit** AmEx, DC, MC, V.
Jacques Chibois is arguably the hottest chef on the Riviera. Set in a century-old olive grove, his new *auberge* on a hillside just below Grasse looks almost Tuscan. The lunch menu is surely the best gourmet buy on the whole coast: a superb three-course shakedown starting with a sauté of lobster and shrimp on a bed of risotto cooked with cèpes and champagne, continuing with a superb roast duckling garnished with tiny olives and crushed pistachios in a sauce of liquorice juice, and ending up with cherry sorbet in a sauce of strawberry and tomato juice. Truffles and mushrooms are a seasonal speciality. It's not easy to find: ask them to fax you a map when you book.

Issautier

RN202, St-Martin-du-Var (04.93.08.10.65). **Meals served** noon-1.30pm, 7-9.15pm Wed-Sun. Closed Jan. **Menus** 270F-540F. **Credit** AmEx DC, MC, V.
Though it looks unprepossessing enough from the main Var Valley road, this is an endearing place full of old-fashioned flounces. Issautier is a lusty cook who's proud of traditional Niçois cooking and uses first-rate local ingredients. The menu changes regularly, but his home-made Nissart ravioli stuffed with tender braised beef, and his grand aïoli-boiled cod with vegetables and lashings of garlic mayonnaise are superb.

Restaurant Jacques Maximin

689 chemin de la Gaude, Vence (04.93.58.90.75). **Meals served** July, Aug noon-1.30pm, 7-9.30pm daily; Sept-June noon-1.30pm, 7-9.30pm Tue-Sat; noon-1.30pm Sun. Closed mid-Nov to mid-Dec. **Menus** 240F-350F. **Credit** AmEx, DC, MC, V.
The French food press invariably speaks of the mercurial Jacques Maximin with awed reverence, and you'll see why once you tuck into a starter like his salad of artichoke hearts, fava beans, squid, penne pasta and Parmesan, dressed in olive oil and lemon juice and served on a bed of mixed leaves. He can also do surprisingly classical dishes, such as an autumnal salad of cèpes and scallops, or a gratin of crayfish with Parmesan. It's pricey, but it's worth it, especially when they're serving outdoors in the lush subtropical garden.

The Rhône Delta

Nîmes   56
North of Nîmes   65
Around the Alpilles   68
Arles   75
The Camargue   83

Feature boxes

Féria!   63
Mistral & the Félibrige   72
Course Camarguaise   79
Van Gogh in Arles   81
Gardians   84
Gypsies of the world unite!   86

Nîmes

Roman remains and a penchant for modern design make Nîmes an invigorating Southern mélange.

In Nîmes ancient meets postmodern in a way that typifies the French Mediterranean sunbelt. It claims France's most important collection of Roman buildings, but also makes sure the Philippe Starck bus stop gets included on the tourist map of the city. Sunny, lively, friendly, with plenty of cafés and shady squares, Nîmes is too busy and self-absorbed to be a tourist trap. The Nîmois themselves take all that heritage stuff for granted, walking their dogs round the Roman amphitheatre and using the twelfth-century buildings as blank canvases for graffiti.

Nîmes competes with Arles for the title of the Rome of France, but it was a Celtic tribe that first discovered the great spring – Nemausus – that gave Nîmes its name. Such a convenient stop on the Via Domitia between Italy and Spain was bound to attract Roman attention and by 31 BC they had moved in, colonising the settlement with a legion of veterans from the Egyptian

campaign. Their emblem, a crocodile chained to a palm tree, became the symbol of the city; the Nîmes football team is known as 'Les Crocos'.

The Romans fortified the town, built roads and ramparts, a forum and a temple, the great amphitheatre, baths and fountains and, of course, the aqueduct of the **Pont du Gard**, which supplied water to a busy metropolis of 25,000 people.

After the collapse of the Roman empire, Nîmes declined in importance, wracked by war and religious squabbles. It has always been non-conformist, welcoming the twelfth-century Cathar heretics and becoming a major centre of Protestantism from the sixteenth century on. It prospered in the seventeenth and eighteenth centuries from dye-making and textiles, processing the wool and silk of the region. Many of the fine mansions in the old town date from this period. Its tough local cotton of white warp and blue weft – already known as 'denim' (de Nîmes) in London by 1695

Nîmes' croc mascot in the place du Marché, and in the Starck-designed coat of arms.

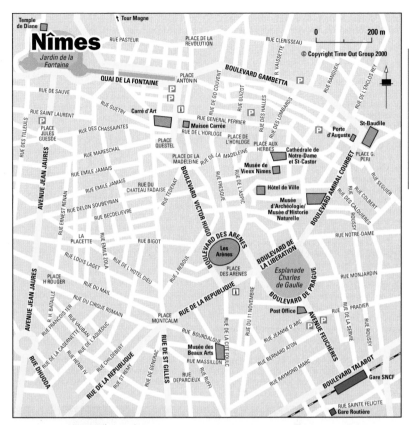

– became a contemporary icon after Levi Strauss used it to make trousers for Californian gold-diggers.

Wine is a more important product today, as the Costières de Nîmes *appellation* (known as Costières de Gard until 1989) improves in quality, thanks largely to the efforts of a number of smaller producers. Nîmes is striving to become part of the high-tech development of the Mediterranean sunbelt, and vies with Montpellier in modern architectural developments. Its dusty image took a fashionable turn in the 1980s when a flamboyant right-wing mayor, Jean Bousquet – founder of the Cacharel fashion house – commissioned several ambitious projects, including a Jean Nouvel housing estate and a new arts complex by British architect Norman Foster, as well as works of art and sculptures across the city. He was ousted from power by his political antithesis, Alain Clary, in 1995; at

the time of writing, Nîmes was the only sizeable town in France with a Communist mayor.

Sightseeing

The centre of Nîmes is small enough to visit on foot, with most of the sights inside the triangle formed by the three main nineteenth-century boulevards: Gambetta, Victor Hugo and Admiral Courbet.

North of the city centre on Mont Cavalier, the **Tour Magne** was a key component of the original pre-Roman ramparts, which were reinforced in 15 BC by the Romans to become the longest city walls in Gaul at almost seven kilometres. The viewing platform 140 steps up the tower provides a good overview of the city, its red pantile roofs spread below, the landscape of *garrigue* (the typical ground cover of aromatic plants and olives) and the hills of **Les Alpilles** (*see page 68*) beyond. The tower is accessible from the **Jardin de la Fontaine**, the beautiful formal gardens constructed in the eighteenth century around the original spring to improve the quality of the city's water supply, after the aqueduct from the Pont du Gard was abandoned.

Also to the north of the central triangle, in rue du Fort, is the **Castellum**, a recently discovered Roman water tower that was the original distribution point for the water supply from the Pont du Gard. Water reached the tower's basin and was then distributed across the city through thick lead pipes from ten holes still visible in the basin wall.

Facing each other across the north end of boulevard Victor Hugo are the **Musée d'Art Contemporain** – a modern art museum housed inside the Carré d'Art, designed by Norman Foster – and the **Maison Carrée**, a superbly preserved Roman temple surrounded by a marble-paved open space where the Roman forum stood.

To the east lies the heart of Nîmes, the pedestrianised old town, which is slowly being refurbished. Here shops and cafés are tucked within Romanesque arches, walls are half-stripped of modern accretions to reveal the ancient stonework beneath, and many seventeenth- and eighteenth-century mansions have been beautifully restored.

On rue de l'Aspic the **Hôtel Fontfroide** has a seventeenth-century double spiral staircase, while there are three early Christian sarcophagi embedded in the porch of the **Hôtel Meynier de Salinelles**. On rue de Fresque is a fifteenth-century poor man's law centre, where an early form of legal aid was once dispensed, and an

intact medieval stone shopfront. There is a well-preserved Romanesque façade with elaborate carving in rue de la Madeleine. The **place du Marché**, where Nîmes' corn market used to be held, is adorned with a fountain by Martial Raysse, a modern take on the crocodile tied to a palm tree theme.

On the central **place des Herbes** stands the much-altered eleventh-century cathedral of **Notre-Dame et St-Castor**, and the **Musée de Vieux Nîmes**, with its collection of local curiosities in the former bishop's palace.

Where boulevard Gambetta joins boulevard Amiral Courbet, the **Porte d'Auguste** remains little changed since it was one of the original Roman gates of the city; the two large arches constituted a dual carriageway for carts and chariots, while the two smaller arches were for pedestrian traffic.

Further down boulevard Courbet are the **Musée d'Histoire Naturelle** and the **Musée d'Archéologie**, both housed in the old Jesuit college.

Still further south, the **Arènes**, Nîmes' Roman amphitheatre, stands at the centre of a dizzying traffic system. For the full ancient Roman blood-lust experience, it should be visited when it echoes to the shouts of an excited crowd of bullfighting enthusiasts. For a less gory visit, come for a summer jazz concert or when the arena is not in use.

The elegantly restored **Musée des Beaux-Arts**, with its collection of French, Dutch and Italian works of the Renaissance and after, lies to the south of the city centre.

The matador statue outside **Les Arènes**.

Les Arènes

bd des Arènes (04.66.76.72.77). **Open** *May-Sept*
9am-6.30pm daily; *Oct-Apr* 9am-5.30pm daily.
Admission 28F, 20F under-16s, free under-10s. **No
credit cards.**
Encircled by two tiers of stone arcades, this is a stan-
dard-issue Roman arena of perfect classical proportions. It is smaller than the arena at Arles, but better
preserved, with two storeys of 60 stone arcades rising to a height of 21 metres, surrounding the corridors and *vomitoria* (exits) and the great oval arena
(the name comes from the *arènes*, or sands, which
were spread to soak up the blood). On the exterior
look out for the small carvings of Romulus and
Remus, the wrestling gladiators and two bulls'
heads supporting a pediment over the main entrance
on the north side. The arena is an amazing piece of
engineering, constructed out of vast blocks of stone
by teams of slaves, and could accommodate over
20,000 spectators. You can still sit on the original
stone benches and see the podium for the president
of the games and sockets for the poles that held a
huge awning to shelter the crowd. For the best view
of the structure, climb to the top tier of seats, which
were traditionally reserved for slaves and women.
The original games included gladiator fights, as well
as slaves and criminals thrown to the animals. Dogs
were set on porcupines to get the blood flowing and
the crowd excited. There were also chariot races and
even mock sea battles with the arena flooded with
water. After the departure of the Romans, the
amphitheatre was made into a fortress by Visigoths
and Frankish knights. By the Middle Ages it was a
huge tenement block; when it was finally cleared in
the early nineteenth century, centuries of garbage
had added six and a half metres to the original
ground level. The first corrida took place in 1853.
The privileged always sat at the front, nearest the
action, and still do. The *féria* (*see box p63*) today is
a key event in the chic Paris calendar; the *Figaro*
daily paper publishes a corrida special edition with
a seating plan of the rich and famous in attendance.

Cathédrale de Notre-Dame et St-Castor

pl aux Herbes. **Open** during services only.
Nîmes' cathedral is not what it was. Although it
was founded in 1096, like much of the town it was
totally wrecked during the sixteenth-century Wars
of Religion, and the current building is mainly a
nineteenth-century reconstruction. You can only
enter during services but the remains of a
Romanesque sculpted frieze, with scenes from the
Old Testament, are visible on the façade.

Jardin de la Fontaine

Open *Apr to mid-Sept* 7.30am-8pm daily; *mid-Sept
to Mar* 7.30am-6.30pm daily. **Admission** free.
The spring that bubbles up at the heart of these
lovely gardens was the reason why the Romans chose
Nîmes and named it Nemausus after the Roman river-
god. Around the neglected spring, formal gardens

were constructed in the eighteenth century, with a
complex system of reservoirs and channels for distribution of the clean water to a city where that
commodity was sadly lacking. Now a network of
canals and still green pools, with balustraded stone
terraces and marble nymphs and cupids, it provides
a perfect retreat from the summer heat.

Maison Carrée

*pl de la Maison Carrée (04.66.21.85.52/
04.66.21.91.44).* **Open** *mid-June to mid-Sept* 9am-
noon, 2.30-7pm daily; *mid-Sept to mid-June* 9am-
12.30pm, 2-6pm daily. **Admission** free.
Not *carrée* (square) at all but rectangular, this elegant, symmetrical Roman temple was built in the
first century BC and dedicated to Augustus' deified
grandsons. It is one of the best-preserved in the
world, with a great flight of stone steps leading up
to finely fluted Corinthian columns adorned with a
sculpted frieze of acanthus leaves. It has always
inspired hyperbole; Arthur Young, an eighteenth-
century British traveller, called it 'the most light, elegant and pleasing building I have ever beheld'.
Thomas Jefferson, having failed to take it home, had
it copied as the model for the Virginia state capitol.
It has remained in almost constant use, its functions
ranging from legislative seat to tomb, church to sta-
bles; briefly it was an exhibition space for US artist
Julian Schnabel. Today it contains drawings and
photos of current archaeological work, one splendid result of which is displayed here: a fresco, only
unearthed in 1992 when the Carré d'Art was being
built. Against a blood-red background sits a mythical hunter, surrounded by a border of pagan frol-
ics, most discernibly Cassandra being dragged by
her hair, and a pair of very louche-looking dwarves.
Lovely as it is, the temple could do with a clean-up,
and suffers from constant traffic pollution. Worst
of all, the huge Roman terracotta jar that always
stood outside was recently smashed by vandals.
You can still see the pieces.

Musée d'Archéologie

13 bis bd Amiral Courbet (04.66.67.25.57). **Open**
11am-6pm Tue-Sun. **Admission** *combined ticket
with Musée d'Histoire Naturelle* 28F, 20F under-16s,
free under-10s.
Housed in the old Jesuit college building, the archaeology museum has a magnificent collection of Roman
statues, sarcophagi, entablatures, coins, mosaics and
some gorgeous Roman glass, as well as a model of
Nîmes in Roman times. The pottery collection
includes a rare pre-Roman statue, the *Warrior of
Grezan.* Upstairs is a treasure trove of everyday
items from the ancient world, from oil lamps to
kitchen equipment, tools and cosmetic artefacts.

Musée d'Art Contemporain

pl de la Maison Carrée (04.66.76.35.80). **Open**
11am-6pm Tue-Sun. **Admission** 28F, 20F under-16s,
free under-10s. **No credit cards.**
Opened in 1993, the Foster-designed Carré d'Art
houses this modern art museum and the

Two square houses: the Roman **Maison Carré** viewed from the **Carré d'Art**. *See page 59.*

Bibliothèque Carré d'Art (*see below*). The gallery is constructed around a huge light-filled atrium strung with glass staircases. Its beige stone steps, glass walls and steel columns are a tribute to the ancient temple, the Maison Carrée, opposite. The restaurant terrace has a fine view over Nîmes. The collection focuses on European modern art since 1960, with particular emphasis on avant-garde movements such as Arte Povera and New Realism and work by Mediterranean artists including Martial Raysse, Christian Boltanski, Claude Viallet, Arman and Bertrand Lavier.
Website: www.mns.fr/Carréart

Musée des Beaux-Arts
rue Cité-Foulc (04.66.67.38.21). **Open** 11am-6pm Tue-Sun. **Admission** 28F, 20F under-16s, free under-10s. **No credit cards**.
The imposing façade of this early twentieth-century building leads straight into a beautiful restoration by architect Jean-Michel Wilmotte. It houses an eclectic collection of French, Italian, Flemish and Dutch works, most notably Jacopo Bassano's *Susanna and the Elders*, Rubens' *Portrait of a Monk*, and the *Mystic Matrimony of St Catherine* by Michele Giambono. The *Marriage of Admetus*, a Roman mosaic discovered in 1882, takes pride of place in the centre of the main floor.

Musée d'Histoire Naturelle
13 bd Amiral Courbet (04.66.67.39.14). **Open** 11am-6pm Tue-Sun. **Admission** *combined ticket with Musée d'Archéologie* 28F, 20F under-16s, free under-10s. **No credit cards**.
In the same building as the archaeological museum (*see above*) is the natural history collection, which

includes some important Iron Age menhirs. The college chapel, a lovely seventeenth-century structure with a spacious dome and galleries lit by skylights, now accommodates musical concerts and temporary art exhibitions.

Musée de Vieux Nîmes
pl aux Herbes (04.66.36.73.70). **Open** 11am-6pm Tue-Sun. **Admission** 28F, 20F under-16s, free under-10s. **No credit cards**.
In the tradition of Frédéric Mistral, this museum, housed in the old bishop's palace, was established in 1920 by Henri Bauquier to preserve the tools of local industries and artefacts of regional life, providing an intriguing glimpse into humdrum history. The collection includes furniture, pottery, shoes, fabrics including some early denim, shawls and silks, and lots of tools.

Tour Magne
Jardin de la Fontaine (04.66.67.65.56). **Open** *July, Aug* 9am-7pm daily; *Sept-June* 9am-5pm daily. **Admission** 15F, 12F children. **No credit cards**.
High on Mont Cavalier above the Jardin de la Fontaine is the octagonal ruin of the Tour Magne, part of Nîmes' original pre-Roman ramparts, once the longest city walls in all of Gaul. The viewing platform, 140 steps up, provides excellent views over the city.

Arts & entertainment

Ars Longa Vita Brevis
33 rue Fernand Pelloutier (04.66.67.09.98). **Open** 9am-noon, 3-5pm Mon-Wed.

A new arts centre in Nîmes that organises exhibitions and encounters with local artists in a wide range of media.

Bibliothèque Carré d'Art
pl de la Maison Carrée (04.66.76.35.50). **Open** 11am-6pm Tue-Sat.
Vast library and media centre below the contemporary art museum; particularly strong on modern art.

L'Odéon
7 rue Pierre Semard (04.66.36.65.30). **Box office** Théâtre de Nîmes, 1 pl de la Calade (04.66.36.65.10), open 10am-1pm, 2-6pm Tue-Fri. **Shows** 8.30pm Tue-Sat; 3pm Sun. **Tickets** around 100F. **Credit** AmEx, DC, MC, V.
Theatre offering a mixed, accessible programme of classic and contemporary dance, theatre and opera.

Le Sémaphore
25 rue Porte de France (04.66.67.88.04). **Tickets** 35F, 25F students, 22F under-13s. **No credit cards.**
Le Sémaf, as it is affectionately known, offers an excellent programme of original language (*version originale*) films and themed weeks showcasing a variety of foreign movies.

Théâtre de l'Armature
12 rue de l'Ancien Vélodrome (04.66.29.98.66). **Box office** 9am-noon, 2-6pm Mon-Fri. **Shows** 8.30pm Thur-Sat. **Tickets** 50F. **Credit** AmEx, DC, MC, V.
Alternative theatre that acts as a showcase for touring companies, staging works by contemporary writers such as Philippe Minyana.

Where to eat

Le Chapon-Fin
3 rue du Château Fadaise (04.66.67.34.73). **Meals served** noon-2pm, 7-11pm Mon-Fri; 7-11pm Sat. Closed Aug. **Menu** 75F (lunch only), dinner à la carte, average 150F. **Credit** AmEx, DC, MC, V.
A Nîmois institution and a true Midi brasserie with walls hung with paintings by grateful clients. Food is generous and regional, with the home-made brandade a must.

L'Enclos de la Fontaine
quai de la Fontaine (04.66.21.90.30). **Meals served** 12.15-1.30pm, 7-9.30pm daily. **Menus** 155F-360F. **Credit** AmEx, DC, MC, V.
The restaurant of the Hôtel Imperator, l'Enclos is much favoured by bullfighters at *féria* time. Try local specialities like brandade, escabèche (marinated fish) or sea bass with fennel compote.

L'Esclafidou
7 rue Xavier Sigalon (04.66.21.28.49). **Meals served** noon-2.30pm, 7-10.30pm Mon-Sat. **Menus** 56F (lunch), 92F (dinner). **Credit** MC, V.
Charming little restaurant on a tiny hidden square. Cosy in winter, and with a shady terrace for summer. Provençal cuisine with lots of olive oil, garlic and spices, generous salads, fish and omelettes – try the *omelettes aux cèpes* in season.

La Fleur de Sel
29 rue du Grand Couvent (04.66.76.04.19). **Meals served** noon-1.30pm, 7-9.30pm Mon-Sat.

Eighteenth-century elegance in the **Jardin de la Fontaine**. *See page 59.*

Menus 45F-55F (lunch), 98F (dinner). **Credit** AmEx, DC, MC, V.

Tiled walls and chairs hang Shaker-style from the ceiling here. The varied menu choices include good salads combined with smoked salmon, boudin noir, tripe or scallops, depending on the whim of the cheery chef.

La Fontaine du Temple

22 rue de la Curaterie (04.66.21.21.13). **Meals served** noon-2pm, 7.30-10.30pm Mon-Sat. **Menus** 58F-68F (lunch), 119F-139F (dinner). **Credit** AmEx, DC, MC, V.

Friendly, neighbourhood restaurant with popular bar, serving local specialities like *taureau* with anchovy sauce, lamb with thyme, brandade with lobster sauce and a good salad with tapenade. It also does takeaway, and fondues in winter.

Magister

5 rue Nationale (04.66.76.11.00). **Lunch served** noon-2pm Mon-Fri; **dinner served** 7.30-9.30pm daily. Closed 20 July-20 Aug. **Menus** 130F-220F (lunch), 185F-220F (dinner). **Credit** AmEx, CB, V.

One of Nîmes' top restaurants for smooth service and perfectly judged cooking; try its brandade, stuffed pigeon or lamb braised with red wine and mint. Cheeses are carefully selected and the wine list offers the best of local vintages.

Aux Plaisirs des Halles

4 rue Littré (04.66.36.01.02). **Meals served** noon-2.30pm, 7.30-10pm Tue-Sat; noon-2.30pm Sun. Closed third week Aug. **Menus** 88F-190F (lunch), 140F-250F (dinner). **Credit** AmEx, DC, MC, V.

Discreet, elegant little bistro near the market, serving freshly made aïoli with vegetables, home-made breads, sorbets and imaginative twists on regional classics, such as brandade with truffles and black olives.

Le P'tit Bec

87 bis rue de la République (04.66.38.05.83). **Meals served** noon-1.30pm, 8-9.30pm Tue-Sat; noon-1.30pm Sun. Closed first two weeks Aug. **Menus** 95F-225F. **No credit cards.**

Popular restaurant with a veranda and pretty enclosed garden. Seasonal specialities include baked foie gras de canard, brandade croquettes, fricassee of sole and langoustine or *pelardon* (a goat's cheese) with chestnut honey.

Vintage Café

7 rue de Bernis (04.66.21.04.45). **Meals served** noon-2pm, 8-10pm Tue-Fri; 8-10pm Sat. **Menus** 78F-142F (lunch), 142F (dinner). **Credit** V.

Sweet little café and restaurant tucked into a quiet corner of the old town, with friendly service, Provençal cooking and wine tastings on Thursday and Friday evenings.

Bars, cafés & nightlife

La Bodeguita

3 bd Alphonse Daudet (04.66.58.28.27). **Open** noon-3pm, 7.30-11pm Tue-Sat. **Credit** AmEx, DC, MC, V.

Spanish tapas bar with terrace, serving food and wine, both local and Spanish, by the glass. Themed evenings include flamenco, tango, jazz and poetry. A key hang out at *féria* time.

Villaret: if it's not crocs, then it's *croquants*.

Gilbert Courtois
8 pl du Marché (04.66.67.20.09). **Open** *July & Aug* 8am-midnight daily; *Sept-June* 8am-7.30pm daily. **Credit** AmEx, DC, MC, V.
A Nîmes institution, this Belle Epoque café with comfortable terrace serves tea, coffee, hot chocolate and a selection of cakes.

Haddock Café
13 rue de l'Agau (04.66.67.86.57). **Open** noon-2pm, 6.30pm-1am Mon-Sat. **Credit** CB, V.
Popular club and café with food served late, music and philosophy evenings.

Lulu Club
10 impasse de la Curaterie (04.66.36.28.20). **Open** 11pm-late Tue-Sun. **No credit cards**.
A late-night gay bar and disco, where heteros are also welcome.

Le Mazurier
9 bd Amiral Courbet (04.66.67.27.48). **Open** 7pm-1am daily. **Credit** AmEx, DC, MC, V.
Good old-fashioned Belle Epoque brasserie for leisurely morning coffee and *Le Figaro* on the terrace, or a pastis at the zinc bar.

Trois Maures
10 bd des Arènes (04.66.36.23.23). **Open** 6.30am-midnight daily. **No credit cards**.
Huge old-fashioned brasserie, festooned with tributes to the two main Nîmois preoccupations, bullfighting and *le foot*.

Shopping

The main produce market at Les Halles, rue des Halles, is open every morning until 1pm. There's a market selling flowers, plants and clothing on boulevard Jean Jaurès all day Monday.

F Nadal
4 rue des Marchands (04.64.67.64.06). **Open** 8am-noon, 2-6.30pm Tue-Sun. **No credit cards**.
Tiny old-fashioned shop selling olive oil from vats, hand made soaps, herbs, honey, coffee and spices.

Marie Sara Création
40 bis rue de la Madeleine (04.66.21.18.40). **Open** 9am-noon, 2-7pm Tue-Sun. **Credit** CB, V.
The place to buy your toreador outfit. Now retired, Marie Sara was famous in her day as a bullfighter.

L'Oeil du Taureau
4 rue Fresque (04.66.21.53.28). **Open** 2-7pm Mon; 10am-7pm Tue-Sat. **Credit** MC, V.
Great second-hand bookstore for art books, old cookbooks, travel books and old postcards.

Villaret
13 rue de la Madeleine (04.66.67.41.79). **Open** 7am-7.30pm Mon-Sat. **No credit cards**.
Long-established boulangerie and patisserie, with an extensive selection of bread, tarts and Nîmois speciality *croquants*.

Féria!

Nîmes' thrice-yearly *féria* draws many more visitors than the city's Roman remains, though only 25 per cent of *féria*-time visitors ever attend the bullfights that are the centrepiece of these bacchanals. For the bloodthirsty, there's the Nîmes-style *mise à mort*, in which the bulls are usually killed; for the more restrained, there's the Camarguais-style *course* (*see box page 79*). And the truly lily-livered can resort to the vicarious pleasures of discussing the aesthetics of the event over a glass of the pastis that is served in monumental quantities from bodegas all over town.

They'll be in good company: for many locals, the corrida is more an intellectual than a sporting matter. They will rate bullfighters (and bulls) for their maturity and their devotion to the traditional rules of the fight. One of the all-time heroes is a woman – tiny, blonde Marie Sara. She has retired now, having fired an entire generation of teenage girls with the desire to attend Nîmes' famous bullfighting school, but can still be seen presiding over her shop (*see opposite*), which fills with would-be toreadors during the *féria*.

The biggest *féria* takes place at Pentecost, seven weeks after Easter, when up to a million people from all over Europe descend on the city. The other two annual *férias* – coinciding with the September *vendange* and February carnival – are more domestic affairs.

Each occasion is an excuse for a week-long all-night party, with stages on every street corner. Rock and salsa compete with Gypsy guitars, African dancers and Jamaican steel bands. The narrow medieval streets are packed with exuberant conga lines. And though they mostly shun the bullfights, visitors are only too happy to adopt the *féria* look: flat black Seville hats, toreador pants with open white shirts, black leather waistcoats and Camargue leather boots are the order of the day.

Information & bookings
Bureau de Location des Arènes, 1 rue Alexandre Ducros (04.66.67.28.02). **Box office** 10am-12.30pm, 3-6pm Mon-Fri. **No credit cards**.
For corridas reservations may be made by phone and a cheque sent by post.

Where to stay

L'Hacienda

*chemin du mas de Brignon, Marguerittes
(04.66.75.02.25/fax 04.66.75.45.58).* **Rooms** 350F-
610F. **Credit** MC, V.

This country-house hotel, surrounded by olive
groves and vineyards, is six kilometres outside
Nîmes, and a convenient stop-off from the A9 motorway. Hacienda-style with a pool, large gardens, and
rooms with private terraces. Food is exceptional and
imaginative (menus 195F-310F).

Hôtel de l'Amphithéatre

*4 rue des Arènes (04.66.67.28.51/fax
04.66.67.07.79).* **Closed** Jan. **Rates** 185F-270F.
Credit AmEx, MC, V.

Surprisingly smart for the price, the hotel is housed
in a well-restored eighteenth-century building in
the old town, with antique furniture and large,
white-tiled bathrooms.

Hôtel Central

2 pl du Château (04.66.67.27.75/fax 04.66.21.77.79).
Rates 210F-320F. **Credit** AmEx, DC, MC, V.

Central (as the name suggests), cheap and convenient, tucked away in a little side street near the
Maison Carrée. Rooms near the top have views over
rooftops but some rooms, and particularly bathrooms, are rather cramped.

Lisita

*2 bis bd des Arènes (04.66.67.66.20/fax
04.66.72.22.30).* **Rates** 185F-300F. **Credit** MC, V.

Funky hotel with bullfighting as its theme, and balconied rooms with views over the arena. Although
a bit shabby with bathrooms shoe-horned into corners, it's still a very good deal.

New Hôtel la Baume

*21 rue Nationale (04.66.76.28.42/fax
04.66.76.28.45).* **Rates** 450F-510F. **Credit** AmEx,
DC, MC, V.

A seventeenth-century mansion with an elegant
classical interior around a beautiful stone staircase.
Rooms are spacious and well decorated, and bathrooms are smart. The New Hôtel also has a restaurant. One of the best deals in Nîmes.

L'Orangerie

*755 rue de la Tour Evêque (04.66.84.50.57/fax
04.66.29.44.55).* **Rates** 330F-570F. **Credit** AmEx,
DC, MC, V.

Friendly, charming hotel just outside the town
centre with pretty garden, small pool and good
restaurant (menus 110F-265F).

Le Royal Hotel

*3 bd Alphonse Daudet (04.66.58.28.27/fax 04.66.58.
28.28).* **Rates** 220F-480F. **Credit** AmEx, DC, MC, V.

Fashionable little hotel with artistically decorated
rooms and palm-filled lobby. The lively tapas and
music bar, La Bodeguita, is especially popular
during *féria* time.

Essentials

Getting there

By air

Aéroport de Nîmes-Arles-Camargue (04.66.70.06.88)
is around 10km south-east of Nîmes on the A54
autoroute. A regular shuttle bus goes from the
airport to the town centre and train station. Taxis
to the town centre cost 120F.

By car

South from Lyon/Orange or north-east from
Montpellier: A9 autoroute, exit no.50; west from
Arles: A54 autoroute, exit no.1.

By bus

All services leave from the Gare Routière in rue
Ste-Félicité, just behind the train station.
STDG (04.66.29.27.29) runs bus services between
Nîmes and Avignon direct or via Remoulins six
times a day (Mon-Sat) and twice on Sunday.
Cars de Camargue (04.90.96.36.25) runs a service
between Nîmes and Arles three times a day
Monday to Friday, twice daily Saturday; there is
no Sunday service.

By train

Nîmes station (04.66.23.50.50) is on the line between
Montpellier and Avignon.

Getting around

By bus

City buses are run by TCN (04.66.38.15.40) but all
the sights listed are within walking distance of
the Arènes.

Taxis

(04.66.29.40.11)

Tourist information

Office de Tourisme

6 rue Auguste (04.66.67.29.11/fax 04.66.51.81.04).
Open *Sept-June* 8.30am-7pm Mon-Fri; 9am-7pm Sat;
10am-6pm Sun; *July, Aug* 8am-8pm Mon-Fri; 9am-
7pm Sat; 10am-6pm Sun.

Disabled information

Accueil Information Handicap *50 bd
Gambetta (08.00.20.50.88).* **Open** 2-5.30pm Mon-
Thur; 9am-noon Fri.
Advice and education centre.

Gay & lesbian

Centre Gai et Lesbien de Nîmes *11 rue
Régale (04.66.76.26.07).* **Open** 2-6pm Mon,
Tue, Fri.
Website: www.chez.com/gayzette

Internet point

Le Pluggin *17 rue Porte d'Alès (04.66.21.49.51).*
Open 2pm-2am daily.

North of Nîmes

Historic Uzès and the magnificent Pont du Gard aqueduct are man-made monuments in Nîmes' wilderness hinterland.

Heading north from Nîmes towards Uzès, the *garrigues* – wild scrubland covering exposed limestone outcrops, tangled with aromatic herbs, *lentisque* bushes and silvery old olives – have been worn over the ages into deep river gorges. The **Gorges du Gardon** is the most spectacular of these; it is clearly visible from Pont St-Nicolas on the D979 Nîmes-Uzès road, where a fine seven-arched medieval bridge spans the chasm.

To walk along the Gorges du Gardon, detour through Poulx, taking the D135 then the D127, to pick up the GR6 footpath through the depths; at the north-east end of the gorge, the little village of Collias provides wonderful views from the paths along the riverside.

Uzès

Uzès is a charming little town, and knows it. Despite being well west of the Rhône, it seems more Provence than Languedoc, and more Italian in appearance than either. Its decorative skyline is dominated by the **Tour Fenestrelle**, a twelfth-century arcaded bell tower reminiscent of Pisa.

A major centre of Protestantism, Uzès prospered in the seventeenth and eighteenth centuries from the manufacture and merchandising of linen, serge and silk. Many fine mansions remain from the period. Uzès was also an important ducal seat, and still calls itself the first duchy of France. Republicanism notwithstanding, the Duke lives on, mainly in Paris, and his **Duché d'Uzès** – ducal palace – is open to visitors. The building spans several centuries, from a twelfth-century central tower to a Burgundian tiled chapel and ornate Renaissance façade. A guided tour includes a visit to the dungeons, complete with hologram ghost, waxwork dukes, and a fine view from the tower battlements.

By 1962, when it was designated a *ville d'art* by then-culture minister André Malraux, Uzès was sadly run down. Subsequent restoration work, in the pale, soft limestone of the district, has already taken on a time-worn look, blending in seamlessly with the historic buildings and making it a favourite location for historical films such as *Cyrano de Bergerac*.

The delightful **place aux Herbes**, with its arcaded square, sums up Uzès. Here there are shady vaulted cafés and an excellent market (all day Saturday and Wednesday morning), a great source of baskets, Provençal fabric and crockery. Come at the end of January for truffles and at Easter for pottery.

The seventeenth-century **Cathédrale St-Théodorit** contains a superb eighteenth-century organ with painted shutters, which comes into its own during the Uzès music festival, the Nuits Musicales, in July (information and booking 04.66.22.68.88). It is dominated by the twelfth-century **Tour Fenestrelle** (not open to the public), France's only round bell tower and the only part of the Romanesque cathedral to survive the Wars of Religion (it made a handy watchtower).

The **Palais Episcopal** (bishop's palace), a late seventeenth-century structure, houses a collection of local pottery and paintings, as well as a tribute to novelist André Gide, who was born here in 1869, returning as an adult to spend holidays in the town. (Uzès' other literary claim to fame is having played host to the 22-year-old Jean Racine in 1661.)

In the impasse Port Royal, in the town centre, a pretty medieval-style garden, **Jardin Medieval**, contains a remarkable collection of carefully labelled local plants and medicinal and culinary herbs used since the Middle Ages.

The recently excavated **Fontaine d'Eure**, the spring providing water for the Pont du Gard aqueduct (*see page 67*), is a short walk from the town centre (take chemin André Gide out of town to the beautiful Vallée de l'Alzon).

At Pont des Charettes, just south of Uzès, is the **Musée du Bonbon**, established by sweet manufacturer Haribo to celebrate a century of sweet-making, a nostalgia trip for adults and sheer sticky heaven for kids. North of Uzès, **St-Quentin-la-Poterie** is a mecca for pottery junkies. The area has long been famous for its fine white clay. Over the centuries, St-Quentin has churned out amphorae, roof tiles and bricks by the ton. The last large-scale factory closed down in 1974, but artisan potters have returned and revived the skill. Their work, along with that of many other potters from all over southern France, can be seen in the **Galerie Terra Viva**. For simpler lines and perfect functionality, the adjoining **Musée de la Poterie Méditerranéenne** contains examples

The twelfth-century **Tour Fenestrelle** in Uzès. *See page 65.*

from Turkey, Greece, Morocco and Egypt as well as France and Spain; there are peasant pots, jars and bowls, and even bee-smoking equipment, all in a range of particular local green or blue glazes. The village, too, is a delight, on the edge of gentrification, its crumbling ochre houses with hidden loggias and carved columns festooned with washing.

Cathédrale St-Théodorit
pl de la Cathédrale. **Open** 9am-6.30pm daily.

Duché d'Uzès
pl de Duché (04.66.22.18.96). **Open** *July to mid-Sept* 10am-1pm, 2-7pm daily; *mid-Sept to June* 10am-1pm, 2-6pm daily. **Admission** 55F, 20F-35F children. **No credit cards**.

Galerie Terra Viva
rue de la Fontaine (04.66.22.48.78). **Open** *May-Sept* 10am-1pm, 2.30-7pm daily; *Apr, Oct-Dec* 10am-1pm, 2.30-6pm Tue-Sat. **Admission** free. **Credit** DC, MC, V.

Jardin Medieval
impasse Port Royal, off rue Port Royal (04.66.22.38.21). **Open** *Apr-June, Sept* 2-6pm daily; *July, Aug* 3-7pm daily; *Oct* 2-5pm daily. Closed Nov-Mar. **Admission** 10F, free children. **No credit cards**.

Musée du Bonbon
Pont des Charettes (04.66.22.74.39). **Open** *July-Sept* 10am-7pm daily; *Oct-June* 10am-1pm, 2-6pm Tue-Sun. Closed 3 weeks Jan. **Admission** 25F, children 15F.

Musée de la Poterie Méditerranéenne
rue de la Fontaine (04.66.22.74.38). **Open** *Apr-June, Oct-Dec* 2.30-6.30pm Wed-Sun; *July-Sept* 1-7pm daily. **Admission** 18F, free under-12s.

Palais Episcopal & Musée Municipal
pl de l'Evêché (04.66.22.40.23). **Open** *Feb-Oct* 3-6pm Tue-Sun; *Nov, Dec* 2-5pm Tue-Sun. Closed Jan. **Admission** *museum* 10F; *palais* 55F, 35F children.

Where to stay & eat

In the village of Collias, the **Hostellerie le Castellas** (Grande Rue, 04.66.22.88.88, closed Jan & Feb, rates 460F-1,000F) consists of several village houses converted into a delightful hotel, with palmy garden, pool and elegant dining terrace (menus 170F-310F). The **Hôtel d'Entraigues** (pl de l'Evêché, 04.66.22.14.48, closed Nov-Mar, rates 600F-1,200F) in Uzès has antiques-furnished rooms and a pool unnervingly suspended over the dining room (menus 110F-250F).

The **Auberge de Saint-Maximin** (rue des Ecoles, 04.66.22.26.41, closed every Mon, Tue lunch in June & Sept, all Tue in Apr, May & Oct, all Nov-Mar, menus 150F-250F) in the village of St-Maximin is where locals head for a really special meal: imaginative regional fare and impeccable service. At the **Table d'Horloge** (pl de l'Horloge, 04.66.22.07.01, closed dinner Thur from May-June and Sept-Oct, Wed & Thur from Nov-Easter, menu 200F) in St-Quentin-la-Poterie, the reliable menu changes with the season.

Getting there

By car
Uzès: take the D979 from Nîmes.
St-Quentin-la-Poterie: take the D982 from Uzès and then the D5 and D23.

By bus

Services run between Nîmes and Uzès six times daily (fewer at weekends); call 04.66.29.27 29, and three times daily, except Sundays, from Avignon (04.90.82.07.35).

Tourist information

Office de Tourisme

Chapelle des Capucins, pl Albert 1er, Uzès (04.66.22.68.88/fax 04.66.22.95.19). **Open** *June-Sept* 9am-6pm Mon-Fri; 10am-1pm, 2-5pm Sat, Sun; *Oct-May* 9am-noon, 1.30-6pm Mon-Fri; 10am-1pm Sat.

Pont du Gard

'As I humbled myself, suddenly something lifted up my spirits, and I cried out "Why am I not a Roman!"'. First-time visitors to the extraordinary three-storey aqueduct of Pont du Gard – the highest the Romans ever built – are wont to come over all rhapsodic, just like Jean-Jacques Rousseau.

It is undoubtedly an astonishing sight. Frontinus, curator of Rome's aqueducts in the AD 90s, when Pont du Gard was built, labelled this piece of engineering 'the best testimony to the greatness of the Roman Empire'. What is more astonishing still is that the limestone arches, rising to a height of 49 metres, have resisted both the erosion of time and the interference of man.

The aqueduct originally carried sweet water from the springs at the Fontaine d'Eure in Uzès (*see page 65*) across the Gardon river to Nimes, along a route covering 50 kilometres, much of it through underground channels dug out of solid rock. Despite the distance travelled, the drop between Uzès and the Castellum in Nîmes (*see page 58*), the water tower where it arrived, is only 17 metres. The bridge itself is built from gigantic blocks of stone, some weighing as much as six tons, which were hauled into place by pulleys and wheels, and, of course, huge numbers of slaves. It was built with a slight bow to enable it to withstand great water pressure; in the floods that devastated Nîmes in 1988, the Pont du Gard stood firm when several other bridges collapsed.

Walking across the bridge or clambering through the water channel is now forbidden: the structure is best observed from the eighteenth-century road bridge alongside or from either river bank. There is a little beach where you can swim, and canoes can be hired for trips along the gorge.

The area around Pont du Gard is dotted with fragments of the bridges and water channels of the aqueduct, though at the time of writing, plans to protect and signpost the whole route

had not been carried through. However, you can pick up the trail at various points from Nîmes to Uzès.

South of the Pont du Gard, towards the bustling modern town of **Remoulins**, there are traces of water channels in the hills above Sernhac (the GR6 long-distance footpath passes close by), while the medieval village of St-Bonnet-du-Gard has a fortified Romanesque church, which contains stones from the aqueduct and vaulting that imitates the Pont du Gard itself. North of the Pont, just outside Vers-Pont-du-Gard, are several abandoned arches of the aqueduct. **Castillon-du-Gard** on its hilltop has good views over the Pont du Gard itself.

Where to stay & eat

Le Vieux Castillon (rue Turéon-Sabatier, 04.66.37.61.61, closed Jan to mid-Feb, rates 980F-1,920F) in Castillon-du-Gard is the area's luxury choice, with tennis courts, pool and a restaurant strong on truffle dishes. It's open every day for lunch and dinner: during the week it's the *prix fixe* menu only at 275F; at weekends it's à la carte only.

The **Hôtel Restaurant Le Vieux Moulin** (04.66.37.14.35, closed Nov-Mar, rates 310F-620F) has a pleasant restaurant (menus 80F-160F), a garden and a good view over the Pont du Gard. In nearby Vers-Pont-du-Gard is **La Beguda Saint-Pierre** (D981, 04.66.63.63.63, closed dinner Sun & all Mon from Oct-Mar, rates 350F-680F), a seventeenth-century post house in a pretty garden, with a pool and terrace restaurant (menus 170F-300F).

Getting there

By car

Pont du Gard is 14km south-east of Uzès on the D981, and around 20km north-east of Nîmes on the N86.

By bus

STDG (04.66.29.27.29) operates buses from Nîmes to the Pont du Gard seven times daily on weekdays and three times daily on Saturdays.

Tourist information

For canoe hire in the Pont du Gard area, contact Kayak Vert on 04.66.22.84.83.

Remoulins

Office de Tourisme, pl des Grands Jours (04.66.37.22.34/fax 04.66.37.22.01). **Open** *Oct-March* 9am-12.30pm, 2-5.30-6pm Mon-Fri; *April-Sept* 9am-1pm, 2-6pm Tue-Sat.
In summer, there is also an information office open on the Remoulins side of the Pont.

Around the Alpilles

The Lords of Baux, Nostradamus, Mistral and Van Gogh... south of Avignon lies a land of renegades and individualists.

The barren limestone crags of the **Alpilles**. *See page 72.*

Caught in the inverted 'V' between the Rhône and Durance rivers south of Avignon, the fertile plain of the Petite Crau is bordered to the east by La Montagnette ('the little mountain') and to the south by the craggy limestone peaks of the Chaîne des Alpilles. At the foot of the impregnable feudal stronghold of Les Baux, the Grande Crau plain and the Camargue stretch away to the south.

Châteaurenard, the Petite Crau & La Montagnette

Châteaurenard, the traffic-choked main town of the Petite Crau plain, is best known for its vast fruit and vegetable market, the outlet for the abundant produce of the plain, once a marshy swamp until the Romans came along and drained it. Two ruined towers are all that remain of the medieval castle, which came a cropper during the Revolution. More attractive by far is the hill of **La Montagnette** to the south-west, which is famous for its herbs. At the abbey of **St-Michel-de-Frigolet**,

monks make a medicinal-tasting liqueur from thyme (*férigoulo* means thyme in Provençal). The abbey church and cloisters date from the twelfth century. A new abbey, with neo-Gothic battlements and a vast and lavishly painted church was built in 1858 around the remains of the old abbey; it also contains a hotel and restaurant.

At the heart of the Petite Crau, the pleasant town of **Maillane** is the birthplace of Frédéric Mistral (*see box page 72*), revered founder of the Félibrige movement. His house and garden – now the **Museon Mistral** – have been preserved exactly as he left them. The nearby village of **Graveson** has an elegant Romanesque church and the **Musée Auguste-Chabaud**, containing the works of this local painter and sculptor who captured the landscape in a strong Expressionist style.

Abbaye de St-Michel-de-Frigolet

On the D35, between Avignon and Tarascon (04.32.74.32.74/abbey 04.90.95.70.07/restaurant 04.90.90.52.70). **Open** *abbey* group visits only 2.30pm Mon-Sat; 4pm Sun. **Meals served** *Oct-Mar*

8am-9pm Mon, Thur-Sun; *Apr-Sept* 8am-9pm
daily. **Rates** single 122F-285F, double 250F-610F.
Menus 75F-90F.

Musée Auguste-Chabaud

cours National, Graveson (04.90.90.53.02). **Open**
June-Sept 10am-noon, 1.30-6.30pm daily; *Oct-May*
1-6.30pm daily. **Admission** 20F, free under-12s.

Museon Mistral

11 av Lamartine, Maillane (04.90.95.74.06). **Open**
Apr-Sept 9.30-11.30am, 2.30-6.30pm Tue-Sun; *Oct-
Mar* 10-11.30am, 2-4.30pm Tue-Sun. **Admission**
20F, free under-10s.

Getting there

By car

Leave the A7 at exit no.24 for Châteaurenard.

By bus

Local service Rapides du Sud-Est (04.90.14.59.13) has
19 buses a day leaving every half hour or so from
Avignon to Châteaurenard.

Tourist information

Office de Tourisme

*av Roger Salengo, Châteaurenard (04.90.24.25.50/
fax 04.90.24.25.52).* **Open** *July-Sept* 8.45am-noon, 3-
7pm Mon-Sat; 10am-noon Sun; *Oct-June* 8.45am-noon,
2-6pm Mon-Sat.

Beaucaire & Tarascon

It's hard to imagine now, but **Beaucaire** was
home to one of the great fairs of Europe during
the Middle Ages. Thousands of merchants from
all over the Mediterranean would sail their
vessels up the Rhône to sell their silks, spices,
pots, skins, wines and textiles in a ten-day duty-
free spree each July on the great expanse of land
between the river and the castle. Today, shabby
streets conceal Beaucaire's former prosperity;
closer examination, however, reveals intricate
architectural details in sculpted windows,
arches and doorways.

The **Château de Beaucaire**, dismantled
in the seventeenth century on the orders of
Cardinal Richelieu after serving as a
headquarters for traitors to the crown, is now a
picturesque ruin. Dominating the town and
visible from almost everywhere, it's off-limits
to the public except during afternoon displays
of falcon-handling, which are held daily from
July to November and every day except
Wednesdays from March to June. Admission
costs 45F. The surrounding garden is a
charming retreat, and contains the **Musée
Auguste-Jacquet**. Here, odds and ends
from Roman Beaucaire (then called Ugernum),
including glass, statues, amphorae, regional

furniture, pottery and architectural fragments,
are beautifully displayed.

Four kilometres to the north-west of
Beaucaire is the **Abbaye St-Roman**, an
extraordinary fifth-century abbey with
chapels, cells, altars and 150 tombs hewn out
of sheer rock. Engulfed in a fortress during
the Renaissance, it was only rediscovered in
the nineteenth century.

Eight kilometres south of Beaucaire, **Le
Vieux Mas** is a faithful reconstruction of an
early 1900s Provençal farmhouse, with farm
animals, original equipment and regional
products. **Mas des Tourelles**, four kilometres
to the south-west on the D38, is an exact copy of
an ancient Roman winery, and produces wine
the way the Romans did.

Facing Beaucaire on the opposite bank of the
Rhône, the resolutely dilapidated town of
Tarascon is dominated by its great white-
walled **chateau**, a fifteenth-century Gothic
building that towers over the river. It was the
favourite castle of Good (as in good-living) King
René, one of the more congenial characters of
local history. To satisfy the king's love for
material comforts, the castle was lavishly
decorated with grand spiral staircases,
mullioned windows, painted ceilings and
Flemish tapestries. The roof offers extensive
views over the river, Beaucaire and hectares of
unfortunate modern industrial sprawl.

Snuggled around the castle is the old town,
where streets of pale stone contrast
picturesquely with faded pink and blue
shutters. The rue des Halles has covered
medieval arcades and, halfway along, the
fifteenth-century **Cloître des Cordeliers**,
which is used for the occasional exhibition. The
Musée Souleiado, set up by one of the main
producers of Provençal fabrics, offers a detailed
history of the local textile industry.

To the French, Tarascon is synonymous with
its fictional resident Tartarin, writer Alphonse

Tarascon's white-walled, Gothic chateau.

Daudet's character who confirmed Parisians' worst preconceptions about bumbling provincials and earned Daudet the lasting loathing of Tarascon's non-fictional citizens.

The town is also inseparable from the Tarasque, a mythical river-dwelling beast that looks like a cross between a Chinese dragon and an armadillo, which reputedly used to crawl up from the depths to devour the odd human until St Martha happened along in the ninth century or thereabouts and showed it who was who with some well-timed crucifix-wielding. St Martha's bones, unearthed in 1187, are housed in the **Collégiale Ste-Marthe**, built in the twelfth century to cope with a huge influx of pilgrims and added to, then partially destroyed on various occasions down the years. On the last weekend of June, a model of the dreaded beast is paraded through the streets amid fireworks, bullfights and other amusements.

Abbaye St-Roman

D99 (04.66.59.52.26). **Open** *Apr-Sept* 10am-6pm daily; *Oct-Mar* 2-5pm Sat, Sun & school holidays. **Admission** 20F, 10F under-12s, free under-6s.

Château de Tarascon

bd du Roi René, Tarascon (04.90.91.01.93). **Open** *Easter-Sept* 9am-7pm daily; *Oct-Easter* 9am-noon, 2-5pm Mon, Wed-Sun. **Admission** 32F, free under-18s. **No credit cards**.

Collégiale Ste-Marthe

bd du Roi Renée, Tarascon (no phone). **Open** 8am-noon, 2-6.30pm daily. **Admission** free.

Mas des Tourelles

4294 rte de Bellegarde (04.66.59.19.72). **Open** *July-Aug* 10am-noon, 2-7pm daily; *Apr-June, Sept-Nov* 2-6pm daily; *Feb-Mar* 2-6pm Sat. Closed Nov-Feb. **Admission** 28F. **Credit** MC, V.

Musée Auguste-Jacquet

In the gardens of Château de Beaucaire, Beaucaire (04.66. 59.47.61). **Open** *Apr-Sept* 10am-noon, 2-6.45pm Mon, Wed-Sun; *Oct-Mar* 10am-noon, 2-5.15pm Mon, Wed-Sun. **Admission** 13F, 3.50F children.

Musée Souleiado

39 rue Proudhon, Tarascon (04.90.91.08.80). **Open** *May-Sept* 10am-6pm daily; *Oct-Apr* 10am-noon, 2-6pm Tue-Sat. **Admission** 40F.

Le Vieux Mas

rte de Fourques (04.66.59.60.13). **Open** *Apr-Oct* 10am-7pm daily; *Nov-Mar* 10am-12.30pm, 1.30-6pm Wed, Sat, Sun & school holidays. **Admission** 30F, 20F under-16s, free under-5s.

Where to stay & eat

Tarascon is a better bet than Beaucaire for hotels and restaurants. Despite its limited menu and the fact that it's only open for lunch on

weekdays, the **Bistrot des Anges** (pl de la Mairie, 04.90.91.05.11, closed school holidays, menus 60F-95F) is popular. The small hotel **Le Provençal** (12 cours Aristide Briand, 04.90.91. 11.41, rates 140F-260F) has a restaurant (closed Mon, dinner Sun, menus 80F-140F) serving a regional menu including bourride and ratatouille. Another reasonable hotel and restaurant is **Les Echevins** (26 bd Itam, 04.90. 91.01.70, closed Nov-Easter, menus 95F-150F). Rooms cost 300F-450F.

Getting there

By car

Tarascon and Beaucaire are on the D99 between St-Rémy and Nîmes.

By train

Tarascon station (08.36.35.35.35) is on the main train line between Montpellier and Avignon.

By bus

SEYTE (04.90.93.74.90) runs one afternoon bus from Arles to Tarascon on weekdays only (except during July and August). There are also buses from Marseille. STD Gare (04.66.29.27.29) operates a regular service between Avignon, Tarascon, Beaucaire and Nîmes. From Beaucaire to Tarascon (a five-minute journey), there are around six buses daily (fewer at weekends). From Nîmes, there are about ten services a day.

Tourist information

Beaucaire

24 cours Gambetta (04.66.59.26.57/fax 04.66.59. 68.51). **Open** *July* 8.45am-noon, 2-6pm Mon-Fri; 9.30am-12.30pm, 2.15-6.15pm Sat; 9am-noon Sun; *Apr-June, Aug, Sept* 8.45am-noon, 2-6pm Mon-Fri; 9.30am-12.30pm, 2.15-6.15pm Sat; *Oct-Mar* 8.45am-noon, 2-6pm Mon-Fri.

Tarascon

59 rue des Halles (04.90.91.03.52/fax 04.90.91. 22.96). **Open** *Apr-Sept* 9am-12.30pm, 2-6pm Mon-Sat; 10am-noon Sun; *Oct-Mar* 9am-12.30pm, 2-6pm Mon-Fri.

St-Rémy-de-Provence

More second-home chic than tourist-tack, **St-Rémy** is a town of quiet pedestrianised streets, shady squares, flowery balconies, tinkling fountains and sweet-smelling herb shops. Nostradamus was born here; Van Gogh spent an anguished year in the town's asylum. And France's rich and famous flock here for urbane long weekends against the dramatic backdrop of the Alpilles hills.

The area around St-Rémy has been inhabited since neolithic times, but it was Greek-allied

Monastère St-Paul-de-Mausole.

Celts who began building the first town as long ago as the sixth century BC. Greeks had the upper hand until the first century BC, after which the Romans arrived and added their bit for four centuries or so. The result is the astonishing mismash of remains at Les Antiques and Glanum, a 15-minute stroll south of the modern town centre.

The most visible and comprehensible monuments are at **Les Antiques**, where a great Roman arch, once the entrance to the town, and the superb 'mausoleum' (in fact, a tribute to Augustus and Caesar, statues of whom can be seen inside), stand in an excellent state of preservation. The latter has amazing reliefs, with Amazons, Greeks and Trojans doing battle and wild boar being hunted.

Five hundred metres further on, the ruins of **Glanum** lay buried under river silt for centuries until 1921, when excavations began. What has come to light is certainly impressive but far from easy to make sense of, though models and plans (and a pre-emptive visit to the town's Musée Archéologique) help, as do the recently erected facsimile temple columns, which convey a powerful sense of scale. The terraces at the southern end (turn right as you enter) give a good view of the entire site.

The south end of the site is like a corner of ancient Greece, all white limestone rocks and olive trees; here you can see the sacred spring and sanctuary of the original settlers, with a deep water basin from the second century BC. The central area is the most complex, dominated by Roman temples. Signs (in English as well as French) explain the basic structure and point out evocative details such as the underfloor heating bricks of the Roman baths and the remains of mosaics and a painted bedroom.

Van Gogh sought sanctuary in St-Rémy in 1889 (*see box page 81*), checking himself into the clinic run by the nuns of the **Monastère St-Paul-de-Mausole**, opposite Les Antiques, where he churned out more than 150 paintings

of irises, starry nights, olive groves and wheatfields between bouts of abject depression. You can visit the monastery's gardens and twelfth-century cloisters.

Back in town, the **Musée Archéologique** in the Hôtel de Sade (yes, that de Sade, or his family, at least) contains a collection of architectural fragments, statues, capitals, amphorae, bas-reliefs, ceramics, jewels and coins. Most distinctive are the pre-Roman sculptures, and a stone lintel with hollows specially carved to hold the severed heads of enemies. The **Musée des Alpilles** contains a beguiling collection of humble artefacts, domestic and agricultural, along with old photos and paintings of locals at work. A display is devoted to the *chardon* thistle, which is used for brushing wool and silk threads, and to equipment for sorting seed sizes. A joint ticket (41F) gives access to Glanum, the Musée d'Archéologique and the Musée des Alpilles.

St-Rémy was long an important centre of the seed and herb trade; in the **Musée des Arômes de Provence** you can see ingredients, stills, bottles and fine glassware from Lalique and Baccarat. The elegant eighteenth-century Hôtel Estrine houses the **Centre d'Art Présence Van Gogh**, with many reproductions of the great man's work, and regular art shows.

To the east of St-Rémy is **Eygalières**, a sleepy little village with a ruined tower. Just outside the village is the pretty twelfth-century **Chapelle St-Sixte**, set deep among the olive trees that dominate the countryside and economy hereabouts.

Centre d'Art Présence Van Gogh
Hôtel Estrine, 8 rue Estrine (04.90.92.34.72). **Open** *Apr-Dec* 10.30am-noon, 2.30-6.30pm Tue-Sun. Closed Jan-Mar. **Admission** 20F. **No credit cards**.

Glanum
rte des Baux (04.90.92.23.79). **Open** *Apr-Sept* 9am-7pm daily; *Oct-Mar* 9am-noon, 2-5pm daily. **Admission** 32F. **No credit cards**.

Monastère St-Paul-de-Mausole
rte des Baux (no phone). **Open** 9am-6pm daily. **Admission** free.

Musée des Alpilles
rue du Parage, pl Favier (04.90.92.68.24). **Open** *July-Aug* 10am-noon, 2-7pm daily; *Mar-Oct* 10am-noon, 2-6pm daily; *Nov, Dec* 10am-noon, 2-5pm daily. Closed Jan, Feb. **Admission** 18F.

Musée d'Archéologique
Hôtel de Sade, rue du Parage (04.90.92.64.04). **Open** *July-Aug* 10am-noon, 2-7pm daily; *Apr-June, Sept* 10am-noon, 2-6pm daily; *Jan-Mar, Oct-Dec* 10am-noon, 2-5pm daily. **Admission** 15F.

The Rhône Delta

Musée des Arômes de Provence

34 bd Mirabeau (04.90.92.48.70). **Open** *Easter-Sept* 10am-12.30pm, 3-6.30pm daily; *Sept-Easter* 9am-noon, 2-6pm Mon-Fri; 10am-noon, 3-6pm Sat. **Admission** free.

Where to stay & eat

The **Hôtel des Antiques** (15 av Pasteur, 04.90.92.03.02, Nov-Mar, rates 370F-750F) has period furniture, frescos and overpoweringly chintzy bedrooms; the conservatory and swimming pool make up for any shortcomings, however. More than just a well-priced lodging, the **Hôtel des Arts** (30 bd Victor Hugo, 04.90.92.08.50, closed Feb, rates 290F-350F) has a café, an art gallery and a terrace bar. For a more intimate, old-fashioned experience, try the **Mas des Carassins** (1 chemin Gaulois, 04.90.92.15.48, closed Nov-Apr, rates 400F-590F), a converted farmhouse in secluded gardens. **La Maison Jaune** (15 rue Carnot, 04.90.92.56.14, closed dinner Sun from Oct-May, closed Jan-Feb, menus 120F-285F) serves Provençal classics such as roast pigeon and chicken with aïoli on its upstairs terrace. For more imaginative dishes, especially vegetable-based ones, the **Assiette de Marie** (1 rue Jaume-Roux, 04.90.92.32.14, closed Mon & Tue in Jan & Feb, menus 135F-189F) is a good bet.

Getting there

By car

St-Rémy is on the D99 between Tarascon and Cavaillon.

By bus

Cevennes Cars (04.66.84.96.86) operates buses several times a day from Tarascon to St-Rémy.

Tourist information

Office de Tourisme

pl Jean Jaurès (04.90.92.05.22/fax 04.90.92.38.52). **Open** *mid-June to mid-Sept* 9am-noon, 2-7pm Mon-Sat; 9am-noon Sun; *mid-Sept to mid-June* 9am-noon, 2-6pm Mon-Sat.

The Alpilles, Les Baux-de-Provence & the Grande Crau

The craggy outcrop of the Alpilles is one of the more recent geological formations to be thrust up from the earth's crust, and it shows: there are no smooth, time-worn edges here, just dramatically barren rock stretching for 15 kilometres between the Rhône and the Durance. Dominating the Alpilles is the bizarre eyrie of Les Baux: not, as it seems from below, a natural phenomenon but a fortified village complete with ruined chateau.

Perhaps inspired by the stark impregnability of their stronghold, the medieval Lords of Baux were an independent lot, swearing allegiance to no one and only too ready to resort to bloodshed to assert their rights and whims. Their court, however, was renowned for its chivalry: only ladies of the highest birth and learning were admitted, and quibbles over questions of gallant behaviour were often referred here from elsewhere. In 1372, the sadistic Raymond de Turenne became guardian of Alix, the last princess of Baux, and made a bid to outdo his predecessors: dubbed 'the scourge of Provence', he terrorised the countryside for miles around, taking grim pleasure in making his prisoners leap to their death from the castle walls. On Alix's death in 1426, a much more subdued Baux passed to Provence, then France, only to

Mistral & the Félibrige

Provence's secular saint, Frédéric Mistral (1830-1914), was a man with a mission: to revive Provençal, the language of the troubadours, and fight the cultural standardisation being imposed by the intellectual powers in Paris. To this end, he gathered around him a group of like-minded poets, known as the Félibrige school, and set to work creating a body of modern literature in Provençal – which is not a dialect of French, but a separate Latin-based language. His epic poem *Mireille* – a sort of Camarguais *Tess of the D'Urbervilles* – makes for stodgy reading

today; more upbeat are his *Mémoires*, flush with enjoyable details of Provençal life. His French-Provençal dictionary remains a definitive text.

Mistral's outpourings – both literary and lexicographical – gained him a Nobel prize for literature in 1904. With his prize money, he founded the **Museon Arlatan** (*see page 78*) in Arles – probably the only place in the region where you can see real people dressed in Provençal costume year round, as the writer's insistence that the museum employees should dress for the part is still strictly observed.

A light show at the **Cathédrale d'Images**, which was once an old bauxite quarry.

raise its head again as a Protestant stronghold in the seventeenth century. Cardinal Richelieu ordered the town to be dismantled and fined its inhabitants into penurious submission.

The village lay deserted for centuries, picking up again in 1822 when bauxite (named after the place) was discovered there, and subsequently when the wild and windswept became fashionable among travellers. The winding streets, cottages and noble mansions of the old town have been restored, and are visited by two million people a year. But the newer section of town has its share of interesting sights, including the **Musée Yves Brayer**, containing many of Brayer's vigorous oil paintings of the region, and the **Fondation Louis Jou**, where the presses, wood blocks and manuscripts of a typographer active until 1968 can be seen.

The fourteenth-century Tour de Brau, the entrance to the citadel, houses the **Musée d'Histoire des Baux**, which contains displays on key moments in the town's history and huge models of siege engines and battering rams outside. Inside the old town, you can clamber over masonry and walk along the battlements, discovering remnants of towers and windows, chapels scooped out of the rock, a leper's hospital with stone recesses for patients and breathtaking sheer drops to the plateau below.

From the edge of the escarpment, there are extraordinary views across the savage, unearthly rocks of the Val d'Enfer (Hell Valley), haunt of witches and spirits according to local lore. The valley is said to have inspired Dante's *Inferno* and was used by Jean Cocteau as a backdrop for *Le Testament d'Orphée*. Walkers can follow the Grande Randonnée 6 right through the valley and along the crest of the Alpilles. In the valley's **Cathédrale d'Images**,

a vast old bauxite quarry, audiovisual shows are projected on to the walls.

The lower slopes of the Alpilles are covered with vineyards producing a wine – Côteaux d'Aix-en-Provence-Les-Baux – with a growing reputation for excellence, which is much favoured (and consumed) in the area's many lavishly converted *mas* (long, low farmhouses) belonging to French film stars and wealthy Americans.

To the south-west, **Fontvieille** boasts one of France's great literary landmarks, the **Moulin de Daudet**. The stories in Alphonse Daudet's *Letters from my Windmill* (1860) capture the essence of life in the South, though he was accused of caricaturing the local bumpkins for the entertainment of a Parisian audience. He never actually lived in his windmill, preferring a friend's chateau nearby, but the view from the pine-scented hilltop is delightful and the little museum on milling is informative. Just outside town, on the road to Arles, are the remains of a Roman aqueduct and water mills.

Further along the same road stands the great abbey of **Montmajour**, one of the largest religious sanctuaries in medieval Provence. In the tenth century, a community of hermits under Benedictine rule was founded on a great rock surrounded by marshes. The monks gradually drained and cultivated the swamp. A church was built in the twelfth century, a crypt and cloisters in the fourteenth; all were massively restored in the eighteenth century, only to be broken up again by a series of careless owners, then painstakingly pieced together over the past century by the sensitive souls of Arles. The entire ensemble looks as if it has been cut from one huge limestone block: the interior is plain, serene and cold; it's at its most human in the tiny eleventh-century chapel of St Peter, with hermits' cells and an altar gouged out of a cave.

All around stretches the plain of the Crau, the 'desert' of Provence. Part of the expanse is cultivated, producing, among other things, France's only hay to be awarded an *appellation contrôlée*.

Abbaye de Montmajour

rte de Fontvieille (04.90.54.64.17). **Open** *Apr-Sept* 9am-7pm Mon, Wed-Sun; *Oct-Mar* 10am-1pm, 2-5pm Mon, Wed-Sun. **Admission** 32F.

Cathédrale d'Images

Val d'Enfer (04.90.54.38.65). **Open** 10am-6pm daily. Closed Feb. **Admission** 43F, 27F children.

Fondation Louis Jou

Hôtel Brion, Grande Rue, Les Baux-de-Provence (04.90.54.34.17). **Open** by appointment. **Admission** 20F, 10F children.

Moulin de Daudet

Allée des Pins, Fontvieille (04.90.54.60.78). **Open** *July-Sept* 9am-7pm daily; *June* 9am-6pm daily; *Oct-Dec, Feb-May* 10am-noon, 2-5pm daily. Closed Jan. **Admission** 10F, 7F 7-12s. **No credit cards.**

Musée d'Histoire des Baux & Citadel

Hôtel de la Tour de Brau, rue de Trencart, Les Baux-de-Provence (04.90.54.55.56). **Open** *July* 9am-9pm daily; *June-Aug* 9am-8pm daily; *Apr-May* 9am-7pm daily; *Sept-Mar* 9am-6pm daily. **Admission** 37F, 10F children.

Musée Yves Brayer

Hôtel des Porcelets, rue de l'Eglise, Les Baux-de-Provence (04.90.54.36.99). **Open** *Apr-Sept* 10am-noon, 2-6.30pm daily; *Oct-Mar* 10am-noon, 2-5pm daily. **Admission** 20F.

Where to stay & eat

The **Mas d'Aigret** (04.90.54.20.00, closed Jan, rates 450F-950F), situated right below the fortress on the D27A, has recently renovated rooms with balconies, wonderful views and a swimming pool. **L'Oustaloun** (pl de l'Eglise, Mausanne-les-Alpilles, 04.90.54.32.19, closed Jan to mid-Feb, rates 325F-400F) is an excellent-value accommodation option situated in a sixteenth-century abbey, with a restaurant (menus 105F-160F) serving delicious regional cuisine. Tucked away deep in the Alpilles, the **Valmouriane** (petite rte des Baux, 04.90.92.44.62, rates 590F-1,950F) is a luxurious *mas* with spacious rooms surrounded by lawn and woods, and a pool. The restaurant (menus 175F-290F) offers very stylish regional cooking, using herbs grown in the hotel garden.

The exquisitely prepared food at the **Cabro d'Or** (Mas Carita, rte d'Arles, 04.90.54.33.21, closed Mon & Tue, menus 195F-440F) is served

The **Moulin de Daudet** in Fontvieille.

on a serene garden terrace or in a stylish interior. The first hotel on the right as you enter Les Baux, the **Reine Jeanne** (04.90.54.32.06. closed mid-Oct to mid-Dec, first two weeks in Jan, menus 85F-165F) is the most reasonable option in the village, serving reliable regional dishes.

For the legendary country inn **L'Oustau de Beaumanière**, in the Val d'Enfer, *see page 47.*

Getting there

By car

Les Baux is on the D27, accessible from the D5 from St-Rémy or the D99 from Tarascon.

By bus

From Arles, there are two or three buses a day from Monday to Saturday: contact CEYTE (04.90.93.74.90). In August, regular buses run (except on Sundays) between St-Rémy and Les Baux; contact STDG (04.66.29.27.29).

Tourist information

Office du Tourisme

impasse du Château, Les Baux-de-Provence (04.90.54.34.39/fax 04.90.54.51.15). **Open** *Mar-Sept* 9am-7pm daily; *Oct-Apr* 9.30am-noon, 2-6pm daily.

Arles

Bullish, dusty and Roman – the gruff and atmospheric town of Arles is the essence of urban Provence.

Straddling the River Rhône, Arles wears its history with ease; the town's ancient monuments are not museum pieces but part of the urban fabric. The great Roman arena is encircled by the old town like a snail in its shell, while newer buildings snuggle up to the walls of the cathedral of St-Trophime. The medieval centre has an intimate feel, its tall, narrow streets providing protection from the chilly blasts of the mistral, its maze of cobbled alleys and hidden courtyards concealing centuries of history.

Arles was a Greek trading port as early as the sixth century BC, but its importance grew by leaps and bounds in 104 BC when its Roman rulers constructed a canal to facilitate river navigation between the city and the sea. In 49 BC, the city backed Julius Caesar in his victorious bid to break Marseille's stranglehold over shipping in the region, which dominated not only sea trade but the Domitian Way land route from Rome to Spain as well. Arles' moment of glory had arrived, and it began to acquire its rich heritage of no-expense-spared monuments. The city was home to a roaring trade in everything

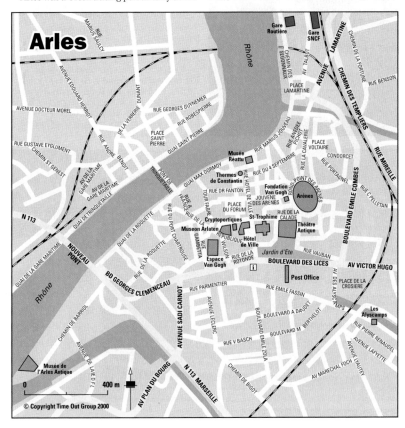

the Orient produced, as well as its own flourishing output of textiles and silverware.

Dark Ages battles involving Visigoths, Franks and Saracens took a relatively minor toll on the town, and by the Middle Ages Arles had regained its clout, becoming a major centre of religious and temporal power. At its height, the kingdom of Arles included Burgundy and part of Provence. In fact, the kingdom was so influential that, in 1178, Holy Roman Emperor Frederick Barbarossa pitched up in the town and was crowned King of Arles in the newly finished cathedral.

Gradually, however, the sea retreated, Marseille took over as the most important Rhône port and railway traffic replaced river traffic. And though Frédéric Mistral and his Félibrige freedom fighters (*see box page 72*) fought tooth and nail in the nineteenth century to restore the area's prestige, Arles never really regained its former glory.

This fact has failed, however, to dent the Arlésian attachment to local traditions. And though long-running festivals – especially bullfights in the arena – prompt the most colourful displays of local pride, just about any event will bring Arles' citizens out en masse: the **Rencontres Internationales de la Photographie** and **Sud à Arles** in July and August; the **Fêtes des Prémice du Riz** rice harvest festival in September (*see chapter* **By Season**) and the exciting climax of the bullfight *férias* in April and July (*see* **Course Camarguaise** *page 79*).

Les Alyscamps: a better class of necropolis. *See page 77.*

Though Arles is irrevocably linked with **Van Gogh**, who spent 15 months here in 1888-9, in truth the good citizens of Arles, like everybody else, rejected the unbalanced Dutchman. Somewhat embarrassed by not owning a single one of the 300 works that the artist churned out while in Arles, the city makes do with a mockup of one of Van Gogh's most famous subjects, the **Café de la Nuit**, and the **Espace Van Gogh** bookshop and arts centre. The **Fondation Van Gogh**, however, pays the right sort of homage to the misunderstood genius. Its superb collection of works by contemporary masters would have pleased Van Gogh, who so much wanted to establish a community of artists here.

Sightseeing

The best view of Arles on its hill is from the top tier of the **Arènes** (Roman amphitheatre), looking across terracotta roofs and ochre walls to the River Rhône. Adjacent to the Arènes are the crumbling remains of the **Théâtre Antique** (Roman theatre), described by Henry James as 'the most touching ruins I had ever beheld'. Today they provide a spectacular backdrop for a summer theatre season in June and July; for information contact the main tourist office

Further down the hill on place de la République stands the great Romanesque church of **St-Trophime**. The magnificent twelfth-century sculpture around the doorway on the newly scrubbed façade is equalled only by the superb cloisters next door. At the centre of the square is a fountain and an Egyptian granite obelisk, moved here from the Roman circus in the seventeenth century, and the **Hôtel de Ville** with its Versailles-like façade and celebrated vestibule vaulting. Accessible from the vestibule is the Plan de la Cour, a small square of medieval buildings, and beneath it, the **Cryptoportiques**, an underground gallery built by the Romans for purposes that have yet to be ascertained.

A block away is Frédéric Mistral's pet project, the **Museon Arlaten**, with its vast collection devoted to Provençal folklore, crafts and particularly costumes, all housed in a fifteenth-century mansion with a courtyard built round the columns of the original Roman forum.

The **place du Forum**, adjacent to the original forum site, is the centre of Arles life today, buzzing with cafés and restaurants, notably the Van Gogh-pastiche **Café de la Nuit** (*see page 81*), and the **Grand Hôtel Nord Pinus** (*see page 82*), where bullfighters and their acolytes congregate. All is watched over by a statue of Frédéric Mistral (*see box page 72*), leaning on his stick and looking, as he himself often complained, as if he's waiting for a train.

From here it is a short stroll to the banks of the Rhône, where you can walk along the *quais*, visit the partly excavated **Thermes de Constantin** Roman baths complex or browse through the collections of Picasso and other modern masters in the **Musée Réattu**, housed in an exquisite fifteenth-century priory with a façade that was once part of the city walls.

To the south of the old centre, the shady, café-lined **boulevard des Lices** is the best place to observe *le tout Arles*, especially on Wednesday and Sunday mornings, when the market held there offers Southern colours and smells. Local cheeses, olives, hams and sausages – donkey is the local speciality – are generally good buys, as are the pottery and olive wood bowls.

Further south still, the necropolis of **Les Alyscamps** lies on the ancient Aurelian Way from Rome. The avenue of marble sarcophagi is a wonderfully melancholy place to stroll, especially at dusk when the owls start to hoot. The best of the tombs and sculptures, however, have been transferred to the **Musée de l'Arles Antique**, west of the old centre. Spanking new and purpose-built for the city's collection of old marbles, the museum lies on the banks of the Rhône by the site of the Roman circus.

Before leaving Les Alyscamps, spare a thought for ancient monuments of another kind: the Jeanne Calment retirement home is named after the woman who held the title of world's oldest person before she died aged 120 in 1997.

Les Alyscamps

av des Alyscamps (04.90.49.36.87). **Open** *Apr-Sept* 9am-7pm daily; *Oct-Mar* 10am-4.30pm daily. **Admission** 12F, 7F children. **No credit cards.**
From its beginnings as a pre-Christian necropolis until well into the Middle Ages, Les Alyscamps (the name means the Elysian Fields) was one of the most fashionable places in Europe to spend eternity. Corpses from up-country were parcelled up and floated down the Rhône with the burial fee in their mouths, to be fished out by gravediggers' assistants on the Trinquetaille bridge. By the Renaissance, many of the magnificent stone sarcophagi had been stolen or presented to distinguished visitors; in the nineteenth century the railway cut through one end of the cemetery. But it remains as wonderfully atmospheric as when Van Gogh painted the avenue of remaining tombs. You can still see the tiny ruined church of St-Honorat, with its Romanesque tower, and the marks where Jesus is said to have knelt to bless the spot.

Les Arènes

rond-point des Arènes (04.90.49.36.86). **Open** *Feb* 10am-noon, 2-5pm daily; *Mar* 9am-noon, 2-5.30pm daily; *Apr to mid-June* 9am-noon, 2-7pm daily; *mid-June to mid-Sept* 9am-7pm daily; *Oct-Jan* 10am-noon, 2-4.30pm daily. Closed to the public during events. **Admission** 15F, 9F children, free under-9s. **No credit cards.**

Les Arènes: the oldest surviving Roman amphitheatre.

Les Arènes, as Arles' Roman amphitheatre is known, is one of the oldest in the Roman world, built in about 46 BC to accommodate 21,000 spectators. Like the one in Nîmes, it had three storeys of 60 arcades each, but the top floor here was plundered for building stone in the Middle Ages. Leading into the walkway around the lower arcade are tunnels through which wild beasts were released into the arena. The view across Arles from the top tiers of seats is magnificent. That so much of the amphitheatre remains today is because it was fortified for defensive purposes in the early Middle Ages. The rabble that constructed a slum town within its walls a couple of centuries later was not cleared out until 1825, when restorations began. For a true taste of Roman-style bloodlust, come for a bullfight, when the arena echoes to the sound of the spectators and the persecuted animal. Other entertainment events are also staged; *see p80*.

Cryptoportiques

rue Baize. **Open** *Apr-Sept* 9am-7pm daily; *Oct-Mar* 10am-6.30pm daily. **Admission** 12F, children 7F. **No credit cards.**
Underground Roman gallery of mysterious origins.

Fondation Van Gogh

Palais de Luppé, 24 bis, rond-point des Arènes (04.90.49.55.49). **Open** *Apr-Sept* 10am-7pm Tue-Sun; *Oct-Mar* 9am-noon, 2-5pm Tue-Sun. **Admission** 30F. **Credit** AmEx, DC, MC, V.
Work by contemporary artists in tribute to Van Gogh: a Hockney chair, a Rauschenberg sunflower in acrylic yellow and blue on steel, plus works by Bacon, Rosenquist, Lichtenstein and Viallat, and photos by Doisneau and Cartier-Bresson. The excellent catalogue explains how Vincent inspired each artist.

Musée de l'Arles Antique

av de la Première Division Française Libre (04.90.18.88.88). **Open** *Nov-Feb* 10am-5pm daily; *Mar-Oct* 9am-7pm daily. **Admission** 35F, children 25F, under-12s free. **No credit cards.**
On the fringes of the Roman circus, which is currently being excavated, this modern blue triangle (designed by Henri Ciriani) houses the many antiquities once scattered throughout Arles' museums and archeological sites. The well-displayed collection includes statues, capitals, carved friezes, pottery, jewellery, glass and villa mosaics along with maps, models and town plans. Best of all are the beautifully carved sarcophagi from the necropolis of Les Alyscamps, many of which date from the fourth century AD or earlier.

Musée Réattu

10 rue du Grand Prieuré (04.90.49.36.74). **Open** *mid-June to mid-Sept* 9am-7pm daily; *mid-Sept to 14 June* 10am-noon, 2-4.30pm daily. **Admission** 15F. **No credit cards.**
Housed in a fine fifteenth-century priory, this museum contains works by its founder, Provençal artist Jacques Réattu, along with a collection of more modern work by Léger, Dufy, Gauguin and others. Most notable are the 57 drawings made by Picasso in 1971 and donated to the museum by the artist a year later to thank Arles for amusing him with its bullfights. Also by Picasso is a delicious rendering of Lee Miller as an Arlésienne painted in Mougins in 1937.

Museon Arlaten

29 rue de la République (04.90.93.58.11). **Open** *July, Aug* 9am-1pm, 2-6.30pm daily; *Sept* 9am-noon, 2-6pm Tue-Sun; *Oct* 9am-noon, 2-5.30pm Tue-Sun; *Nov-Mar* 9am-noon, 2-5pm Tue-Sun; *Apr-May* 9am-noon,

2-6pm Tue-Sun; *June* 9am-1pm, 2-6.30pm Tue-Sun.
Admission 25F, children 20F, under-12s free.
No credit cards.
Frédéric Mistral (*see box p72*) used the money from his Nobel Prize for Literature in 1896 to set up this museum to preserve the traditions of Provence, thus establishing an enduring fashion for collections of regional memorabilia. Attendants wear Arlésien costume and captions come in French and Provençal only. Despite the stuffiness, though, this is a worthwhile and authentic collection of humble domestic and rural objects: furniture, tools, kitchen equipment, shoes and clothing. Best of all is a bizarre haul of traditional talismans: a fig branch burned to encourage maternal milk, a ring fashioned from the third nail of a horseshoe to ward off haemorrhoids and large quantities of toothache-prevention equipment. There are large tableaux, too: a home birth; a Christmas scene with the traditional 13 desserts of Provence; and a *gardian's* cabin (*see box p84*).

St-Trophime

pl de la République (04.90.96.07.38). **Open** *Apr-Sept* 9am-7pm daily; *Oct-Mar* 10am-4.30pm daily.
Admission (cloisters only) 15F.
A church has stood on this site since the fifth century. The current, stunning Romanesque cathedral was built in the twelfth century to house the relics of St Trophimus, a third-century bishop of Arles. Its austere nave is impressively tall, hung with Aubusson tapestries and dotted with Dutch paintings from the seventeenth century and Roman sarcophagi. The Romanesque bell tower is magnificent, but it is the portal that really takes your breath away. Recently restored, its vivid stone carving is clearly visible: the tympanum shows Christ in glory, with life-size apostles accommodated in the columns

below. The frieze – its style perhaps inspired by Roman sarcophagi – depicts the Last Judgement, with souls being dragged off to hell in chains or handed over to saints in heaven.

The cloister sculptures (under laser restoration at the time of writing) are Romanesque in the north and east arcades and fourteenth-century Gothic in the south and west; the two styles form a surprisingly harmonic whole. The carvings on the columns and capitals feature a rich profusion of characters and stories from the Bible. Above the cloister is a walkway that offers good views of the bell tower and the town.

Théâtre Antique

rue de la Calade (04.90.49.36.25). **Open** *Dec, Jan* 10-11am, 2-4pm daily; *Feb* 10-11am, 2-4.30pm daily; *Mar* 9am-noon, 2-4.30pm daily; *Apr to mid-June, last two weeks Sept* 9am-noon, 2-6.30pm daily; *mid-June to mid-Sept* 9am-6.30pm daily; *Oct, Nov* 10am-noon, 2-5pm daily. **Admission** 15F, children 9F.
No credit cards.
The Roman theatre, dating from the first century BC and ransacked for building stone since the fifth century, is today a mess of tumbledown columns and fragments of carved stones. Its forlorn glory makes it a particularly romantic setting for theatre and music performances during the annual Arles Festival in June and July. Vestiges of the original tiers of stone benches remain, along with two great columns of the stage wall, once used as a gallows. It was here in 1651 that the Venus of Arles, now in the Louvre, was dug up.

Thermes de Constantin

rue du Grand Prieuré. **Open** *Apr-Sept* 9am-noon, 2-7pm daily; *Oct-Mar* 10am-noon, 2-6.30pm daily.
Admission 12F, children 7F. **No credit cards**.

Course Camarguaise

The *course* Camarguaise – the Provençal style of bullfighting – is very different from the spectacular, cruel Spanish-style corrida in which the bull stands little chance of emerging from the ring alive. The *course* began as a game with animals, lions, dogs, bears and men chasing and baiting a bull. By the end of the nineteenth century, it had evolved into a battle in which human wits and dexterity were pitched against taurine speed and weight. The real competition nowadays is between the *manades* (bull breeders); bulls can become as famous as the *raseteurs* with whom they do battle.

After the initial *abrivado*, when the competitors parade around the arena, six bulls enter the arena in turn for 15 minutes each. The *raseteurs*, decked out in white,

try to snatch the *cocarde* (rosette) and *ficelles* (tassels) attached to the head of the bull, using a metal comb, called a *crochet*. The bull does not, as a rule, relish the indignity, and chases his rival round the arena, often forcing him to leap the barrier to get clear of hooves and horns. Bravery and skill earn points and prize money for the *raseteur*; the bull, on the other hand, has to make do with applause, ovations, and a burst of *Carmen* over the PA system as he is led out of the ring.

The fighting season gets under way with the April *féria* and the *gardian* festival on 1 May, when the Queen of Arles is crowned; it culminates at the beginning of July when the coveted *Cocarde d'Or* prize is awarded. *See page 80* **Les Arènes** *for further information.*

Arts & entertainment

Les Arènes d'Arles

rond-point des Arènes (04.90.96.03.70). **Box office** 9am-noon, 2.30-6pm Mon-Fri; 9am-1pm Sat. **Tickets** 180F-520F. **Credit** MC, V
The bullfighting season here runs from Easter to September and comprises principally the local *course* Camarguaise *(see box p79)*, but Spanish-style corridas also pop up on the irregular schedule. Tickets are usually available on the gate, but must be booked ahead for the *féria* and *Cocarde d'Or* events – you can make credit card bookings by phone in advance. During summer, the arena also hosts concerts and films.
Website: www.arles.org

Actes Sud

quai Marx Dormoy (04.90.93.33.56).
A lively arts centre with bookshop (Actes Sud is a respected local publishing house), original language cinema, concerts and restaurant.

Espace Van Gogh

pl du Docteur Félix Rey (04.90.49.37.53). **Open** 9am-9pm daily. **Admission** free. **No credit cards.**
A library, bookshop and space for temporary exhibits set around a garden courtyard in the hospital where Van Gogh was treated, which has been restored to look as it did when he was there.

Théâtre de la Calade

Le Grenier à Sel, 49 quai de la Roquette (04.90.93.05.23). **Tickets** approx 110F, 30F children. **No credit cards.**

Arles' main theatre company since the municipal theatre closed down. Performances, visiting companies and workshops.

Where to eat

L'Affenage

4 rue Molière (04.90.96.07.67). **Meals served** noon-2pm, 7-9.30pm Mon-Sat. Closed two weeks Aug. **Menus** 105F (lunch only), 160F (evening only). **Credit** MC, V.
An old coach house with a rustic atmosphere and a large fireplace, serving Provençal classics. There's a buffet of starters of grilled veg, tapenade, anchoïade, seafood and salads. The duck confit with cabbage is good, as is calves' liver with balsamic vinegar.

Brasserie Nord Pinus

14 pl du Forum (04.90.93.02.32). **Meals served** hours vary; call for details. Closed Feb. **Menus** 130F-180F. **Credit** AmEx, DC.
A classic grand brasserie with elegant table settings and immaculate service. The menu features stylish French regional cooking, with dishes such as cold tomato soup with croûtons and goat's cheese, red tuna with *pipérade* and *soupe de figues* with liquorice ice-cream for dessert.

L'Entrevue

23 quai Marx Dormoy (04.90.93.37.28). **Meals served** noon-2.30pm, 9-11pm daily. Closed Sun from Oct-Mar. **Menu** 130F. **Credit** MC, V.
This sociable, lively restaurant and bar offers a choice of classic or oriental menus, and is a favourite for late-night coffee and dessert.

The intricate doorway of **St-Trophime**. *See page 79.*

Van Gogh in Arles

Vincent Van Gogh (1853-90) went to Provence in February 1888 in search of light and colour, only to find a dull Arles, muddied by municipal building work and covered with thick snow. Nothing daunted, he began working furiously, painting with unprecedented passion. He encouraged his brothers-in-art to join him, declaring that 'the whole future of art is to be found in the south of France'. Van Gogh rented the Yellow House in Arles as a studio in preparation, and painted sunflowers for the benefit of his friend Gauguin. But he was almost penniless, his health was deteriorating and he was drinking heavily. When the irascible Gauguin finally arrived, he scoffed at Van Gogh's dreams of an artistic community and left, but not before Vincent, in anger and frustration, had lopped off his own earlobe and presented it to a suitably shocked prostitute.

'The Midi fires the senses, makes your hand more agile, your eye sharper, your brain clearer,' he wrote to his brother. In the space of 15 months, punctuated by the occasional stay in the town asylum, the artist produced 300 canvases of startling colours and contours. He worked in solitude, spurned by the respectable burghers of Arles, who were horrified at his wild behaviour. It must have scared him, too, because by April 1889, terrified that he was losing his artistic grip, he checked himself into the asylum at nearby St-Rémy-de-Provence, where he continued to paint haunting, anguish-tainted pictures of the faces, trees and countryside surrounding him.

Desperately homesick, Van Gogh turned his back on the South and headed for Paris in May 1890. But the north failed to calm his restless soul, and he took his own life in Auvers-sur-Oise two months later.

La Gueule de Loup

39 rue des Arènes (04.90.96.96.69). **Meals served** noon-1.30pm Mon-Thur, Sat; 7.45-9.45pm Mon-Sat. **Menus** 85F (lunch only), 120F (dinner only). **No credit cards.**
You get to this cosy first-floor restaurant through the deliciously scented kitchen; the cuisine is Mediterranean with lots of herbs. Try the *carré d'agneau* with thyme, terrine of scallops and sorrel, and gratin of pears with *marc* (an eau de vie). Booking advisable.

La Mule Blanche

9 rue du Président Wilson (04.90.93.98.54). **Meals served** noon-2.30pm, 7pm-midnight Mon-Sat. **Menu** 89F (lunch only). **Average** 110F. **Credit** MC, DC, V.
Be prepared to wait for a terrace seat in this new restaurant. Chicken with olives is a speciality.

Le Pistou

30 bis rond-point des Arènes (04.90.18.20.92). **Meals served** noon-2.30pm, 7-9.30pm Mon, Wed-Sun. Closed Feb. **Menus** 75F (lunch only), 90F-128F (dinner only). **Credit** MC, V.
A small, friendly restaurant in stone vaults opposite the amphitheatre arches. Try local favourites like tiny *tellines* (clams) with creamy garlic sauce and fresh basil or Banon cheese with peppered oil.

El Quinto Toro

12 rue de la Liberté (04.90.49.62.29). **Meals served** noon-3pm, 7pm-1am Mon, Tue, Thur-Sun. **Menus** 80F (lunch only), 120F. **Credit** AmEx, DC, MC, V.
Modest, cheerful restaurant with bullfighting theme, candles in bottles, tiled walls, red and white checked tablecloths and a fireplace for grilling brochettes, steaks or *taureau* right in front of you. Good salads, with a big bowl of fresh dressing passed around.

Bars & nightlife

Café de la Nuit

pl du Forum (04.90.96.44.56). **Open** 9.30pm-1am daily. **Credit** AmEx, DC, MC, V.
Good people-watching terrace on a sociable town square, with a bar decorated to look like Van Gogh's painting of the same name.

Cargo de Nuit

7 av Sadi Carnot (04.90.49.55.99). **Open** 8pm-5am Thur-Sat. **Admission** from 40F. **No credit cards.**
World music, rock and jazz (both live and canned) in Arles' main music venue. Open until late.

El Patio

chemin de Barriol (04.90.49.51.76). **Open** 8pm-late Sat strictly by reservation only. **Credit** AmEx, DC, V.
This Spanish restaurant on the banks of the Rhône has tapas, paella, gypsy guitar, songs and dancing from Chico et les Gypsies.

Poisson Banane

6 rue du Forum (04.90.96.02.58). **Open** evenings only Mon-Sat. **Menus** from 79F. **No credit cards.**
Late-night restaurant and jazz bar with terrace.

Shopping

Arles' market takes place on boulevard des Lices on Saturdays and on boulevard Emile Combes on Wednesdays; both have local fruit, vegetables and fish, and a vast array of nuts, spices, herbs, charcuterie and bric-a-brac. More bric-a-brac can be found on the boulevard des Lices on the first Wednesday of the month.

L'Arlésienne

12 rue de la République (04.90.93.28.05) **Open** 9am-noon, 2-7pm Tue-Sat. **Credit** AmEx, DC, MC, V.
Provençal fabrics and designs; waistcoats, frilly skirts, and *gardian* cowboy shirts.

Boitel

4 rue de la Liberté (04.90.96.03.72). **Open** 7.30am-8pm Tue-Sun. Closed three weeks Feb. **Credit** AmEx, V.
This *salon du thé* sells regional delicacies, from handmade chocolates to cakes, biscuits and nougat.

Christian Lacroix

52 rue de la République (04.90.96.11.16). **Open** 9am-noon, 2.30-7.30pm Tue-Sat; 2.30-7.30pm Mon. **Credit** AmEx, DC, MC, V.
A native son of Arles, this designer's exuberant colourful style screams Sud de France; gorgeous clothes and jewellery fill this his first shop.

Where to stay

D'Arlatan

26 rue du Sauvage (04.90.93.56.66/ fax 04.90.49.68.45). Closed two weeks Jan. **Rates** single 498F, double 798F-850F. **Credit** AmEx, DC, V.
This Provençal mansion is built over part of the Roman basilica (you can see the excavations under glass) and has many period details, carved ceilings and antiques.

Le Calendal

22 pl du Docteur Pomme (04.90.96.11.89/ fax 04.90.96.05 84). **Rates** single 250F, double 380F-450F. **Credit** AmEx, DC, MC, V.
Tucked away in a side street close to the arena, Le Calendal has a large, shady garden and a friendly, intimate atmosphere. Rooms are small but well designed, with views of the arena or the garden.

Le Cloître

16 rue du Cloître (04.90.96.29.50/ fax 04.90.96.02.88). Closed winter. **Rates** 270F-410F. **Credit** call for details.
Good-value hotel in a narrow street near the Roman theatre, with a Romanesque vaulted dining room and exposed stone walls in the bedrooms.

Grand Hôtel Nord Pinus

14 pl du Forum (04.90.93.44.44/ fax 04.90.93.34.00). **Rates** single 770F, double 840F-980F, suites 1,700F. **Credit** AmEx, DC, MC, V.
This favourite haunt of bullfighters is dramatically decorated with heavy carved furniture, giant black and white photos and mounted bulls' heads. Book well ahead in *féria* time. There's also an excellent restaurant on site.

Hôtel de Musée

11 rue du Grand Prieuré (04.90.93.88.88/ fax 04.90.49.98.15). Closed Nov, Dec. **Rates** single 230F; double 380F. **Credit** AmEx, DC.
This is a small hotel in a seventeenth-century mansion elegantly decorated with Provençal antiques. Breakfast is served in a leafy inner courtyard.

Hôtel Saint-Trophime

16 rue de la Calade (04.90.96.88.38/fax 04.90.96.92.19). Closed mid-Nov to Mar. **Rates** single 210F, double 430F. **Credit** AmEx.
Housed in an atmospheric old building in the centre of Arles with stone-arched lobby, carved ceilings and a courtyard.

Essentials

Getting there

By car

The A54 passes right through Arles; exit 5 is the closest to the centre.

By bus

Cars de Camargue (04.90.96.36.25) runs a service to Arles from Nîmes three times daily from Monday to Friday and twice on Saturdays (no Sunday service). The same company goes to Arles from Stes-Maries-de-la-Mer four times a day from Monday to Friday. There are three or four buses daily (except on Sundays) from Avignon: for details call the bus station on 04.90.49.38.01.

By train

Arles is on the main coastal rail route, and connects with Avignon for the TGV to Paris.

Getting around

Walk if possible: the centre of town is small, the streets narrow and parking a nightmare.

Taxis

Taxi-Radio (04.90.96.90.03).
Taxi-Arléan (04.90.93.31.16).

Buses

STAR (16 bd Clemenceau; 04.90.96.90.03) runs a free bus around the centre of town, starting from Musée d'Arles and stopping off at most of the town's museums and monuments.

Tourist information

Office de Tourisme

bd des Lices (04.90.18.41.20/fax 04.90.18.41.29). **Open** *Apr-Sept* 9am-7pm daily; *Oct-Mar* 9am-5.45pm Mon-Sat, 10am-noon Sun.
Websites: www.arles.org; www.cesar.fr

Arles Festival

Date June-July.
The Arles Festival starts at the beginning of June and runs throughout July. It features music, drama, dance and art from all over the French South. Main events take place in the arena, the Roman theatre and the court of the Archbishops' Palace. Tickets can be purchased in advance from branches of FNAC, Virgin, Carrefour, Auchan and the tourist office in Arles.

The Camargue

Misty mornings, startled herons, wild horses galloping across the mire: the Camargue lives up to its image.

With its marsh habitat, the Camargue is a haven for birdwatchers.

The great flat region of marsh, pasture, *étangs* (salt-water lakes) and sand dunes that nestles between the deltas of the Grand and Petit Rhônes is one of Europe's major wetlands, a vast protected area of 140,000 hectares. Eerily beautiful, with windswept, swaying grasses, pink tamarisk bushes and sun-bleached blue lagoons, it is a wonderland of flora and fauna: purple herons and pink flamingos; wild boar; the beavers that thrive again here after reaching the verge of extinction; eagles and kites; bulrushes and samphire; not to mention dense clouds of France's most bloodthirsty mosquitoes.

The marshes, with their shifting watercourses and high salinity, were eschewed by all but the occasional ancient fisherman. It was not, in fact, until the Middle Ages that they began to flourish: with the arrival of Cistercian and Templar monks, the Camargue was transformed into a valuable source of that invaluable commodity, salt, which is still harvested here in vast quantities today. With the decline of religious establishments in the region in the sixteenth century, the Camargue passed into the hands of cattle- and horse-raising *gardians* (see box page 84), descendants of whom still tend the trademark small black fighting bulls and stunning white horses. In 1970, 85,000 hectares of the Camargue, including the town of Stes-Maries-de-la-Mer,

became a regional nature reserve, protecting the area from rapacious developers with large-scale drainage plans. The reserve centres on the vast **Etang de Vaccarès**, a body of water covering 6,500 hectares that is out of bounds to the public.

The **Musée Camarguais**, about 19 kilometres out of Arles on the D570 to Stes-Maries-de-la-Mer, is a good place to begin a tour of the Camargue. Located in a converted sheep ranch, the museum explains the history of the Camargue, its produce and its people, and provides information on the trails and opening times of the nature reserve.

Further along the same road, on the banks of the small Etang de Ginès, the Centre de Ginès information centre (*see page 86* **Tourist information**) has information on horse-riding in the park, displays on the region's ecology and a good view of the avian antics from its upstairs windows. For a closer brush with the bird life, you'll need to visit the **Parc Ornithologique de Pont de Gau** nature reserve next door, which replenishes stock in its aviaries and gives access to birdwatching trails along the Ginès lagoon.

The 20-kilometre walk from Stes-Maries-de-la-Mer to the salt-processing town of **Salin-de-Giraud** along the dyke built in 1857 to protect the wetlands from the sea allows extensive views across the reserve. The dyke is off limits to cars, though mountain bikes are tolerated. If you don't wish to part with your vehicle, various points on the D37 and C134 roads allow glimpses of herring gulls and blackheaded gulls, herons, avocets and egrets as well as the slender-billed gull and the red-crested pochard, which breed nowhere else in France.

The town of **Stes-Maries-de-la-Mer** nestles cosily round its vast, fortified twelfth-century church, whose rooftop walkways offer excellent views. It is a major pilgrimage site for gypsies, who come to venerate the statue of St Sarah in the crypt (*see box page 86*). The **Musée Baroncelli** has exhibits on bullfighting and other Camargue traditions plus the odd stuffed flamingo donated by the Marquis Folco de Baroncelli-Javon, champion of the *gardians*.

Stes-Maries is primarily a seaside resort, with cafés and any number of shops for picking up that essential Provençal cowboy shirt. It's a good place to take a boat trip along the Rhône delta, hire a bike or go on a photo safari.

There is a good long sandy beach here, but for solitude strike out along the sea wall walk heading towards the Pointe de Beauduc, or the vast empty beach of Piémanson at the mouth of the Grand Rhône.

The hamlet of **Le Sambuc**, east of the Etang de Vaccarès, is home to the **Musée de Riz**, dedicated to the vital role played by rice in the agriculture of the Camargue; not only is it an important cash crop in its own right, but it also absorbs the salt in the soil, enabling other cereals to grow.

Across the salt lagoons to the north-east is **St-Gilles-du-Gard**, an important medieval port left high and dry by the receding coastline and forced to turn to agriculture for its livelihood. The tiny village is dominated by its imposing twelfth-century abbey church, originally established by Cistercian monks as a shrine to St Gilles and a resting place on the pilgrimage route to Santiago de Compostela in Spain. All that remains of the original building is the façade and the rib vaulting of the crypt; occupying Huguenot forces wreaked havoc on the structure during the Wars of Religion, and the rebuilt seventeenth-century version was half the size. The church remains, however, one of Provence's greatest artistic treasures, with carving on the three portals that rivals the stone flourishes of St-Trophime in Arles; a faithful copy can be seen at the Cloisters Museum in New York.

Opposite the church, the Maison Romane is a superb twelfth-century house with finely carved arches and elaborate

Gardians

In their black hats, high leather boots, velvet jackets and cowboy-cut shirts, Provence's *gardians* look for all the world like extras from a low-budget Western, but the Camarguais cattle herders insist airily that they predate their New World equivalents by far. But ageless mystique is all part of the *gardian* image: these men in black have always herded small black bulls destined for the bullfighting arenas of Nîmes and Arles, ridden fine white horses and lived in low white cabins with reed-thatched roofs and rounded north ends as a protection against the blasts of the Mistral wind – or so they would have us believe.

Small and sturdy with distinctive lyre-shaped horns, the black bulls of the Camargue have been raised specifically for bullfights since the nineteenth century. The region's horses are a small breed, too. They start life as brown foals, only turning white after four years.

The hardy, humble *gardians* had their finest hour when they were taken under the wing of the Marquis Folco de Baroncelli-Javon, who abandoned his aristocratic life in Avignon, where he was born in 1869, to become a Camargue cowboy. Like the vernacular poet and Provençal freedom fighter Frédéric Mistral (*see box page 72*), Baroncelli devoted his life to preserving the traditions of the Camargue, writing poetry and breeding bulls. His tomb and a museum in his honour can be seen in Stes-Maries-de-la Mer.

mouldings. Now home to the **Musée de St-Gilles**, it has a varied collection of medieval sculpture and local memorabilia.

Musée Baroncelli

rue Victor Hugo, Stes-Maries-de-la-Mer (04.90.97.87.60). **Open** 10am-noon, 2-6pm Wed-Mon. Closed mid-Nov to Apr. **Admission** 10F, free under-6s.

Musée Camarguais

Mas du Pont de Rousty, D570, Stes-Maries-de-la-Mer (04.90.97.10.82). **Open** *Oct-Mar* 10.15am-4.45pm Mon, Wed-Sun; *Apr-Sept* 9.15am-5.45pm Mon, Wed-Sun. **Admission** 30F, 15F concs, free under-10s.

Musée de Riz

rte de Salin-de-Giraud, Le Sambuc (04.90.97.20.29). **Open** 8.30am-noon, 1.30-5.30pm Mon-Fri; weekends by appointment. **Admission** 25F, 15F children.

Musée de St-Gilles

La Maison Romane, St-Gilles-du-Gard (04.66.87.40.42). **Open** *Oct-May* 9am-noon, 2-5pm daily; *June, Sept* 9am-noon, 2-6pm daily; *July, Aug* 9am-noon, 3-7pm daily. Closed Jan. **Admission** free.

Parc Ornithologique de Pont de Gau

rte d'Arles, 4km from Stes-Maries-de-la-Mer (04.90.97.82.62). **Open** *Apr-Sept* 9am-dusk daily; *Oct-Mar* 10am-5pm daily. **Admission** 35F, 18F children. **No credit cards.**

Where to eat

In Stes-Maries-de-la-Mer, if you want a sea view, try the popular **Brûleur de Loups** on the seafront (av Gilbert Leroy, 04.90.97.83.31, closed Wed in low season, menus 150F-238F), which serves specialities such as rabbit terrine, bull carpaccio and Provençal bourride. In the centre of the village, **L'Impérial** (1 pl des Impériaux, 04.90.97.81.84), closed Tue from Sept-June, closed Nov-Mar, menus 130F-180F) serves imaginative dishes such as cassoulet of snails with pine nuts, carpaccio of red mullet and curried monkfish on its shady terrace.

Further inland, the terrace restaurant at **Hostellerie du Pont de Gau** (rte d'Arles, 5km north-west of Stes-Maries-de-la-Mer on the D570, 04.90.97.81.53, closed Wed from mid-Oct to Easter, closed Jan to mid-Feb, menus 98F-270F) has stunning views over the Camargue and Provençal food.

Where to stay

In Stes-Marie-de-la-Mer, **Hôtel Camille** (13 av de la Plage, 04.90.97.80.26, rates 200F-360F) is as cheap as you'll get in the Camargue with sea views. It offers basic rooms, with or without bathrooms, and a friendly welcome. A kilometre or so outside the village on the D570 Arles road,

Mangio Fango (04.90.97.80.56, closed mid-Nov to Dec, rates 510F-600F) is a friendly ranch-style hotel with garden, swimming pool, large terraced rooms and a good restaurant (closed Tue, menus 150F-195F). Four kilometres out of town on the D38, **Le Mas de la Fouque** (rte du Bac du Sauvage, 04.90.97.81.02, closed Nov-Apr, rates 1,520F-2,050F) offers, as it should for the price, large, comfortable rooms with wooden beams and private terraces overlooking a lagoon and park. Further along the same road, **Lou Mas Dou Juge** (rte du Bac du Sauvage, Pin Fourcat, 04.66.73.51.45, rates 550F, meals extra, reservations essential) is a *chambre d'hôte* in a ranch on the Petit Rhône, with horse-riding facilities and a restaurant serving local specialities (open to the public by reservation only, menus 350F-410F).

On the east side of the Etang de Vaccarès, Le Mas de Peint (Le Sambuc, 04.90.97.20.62, closed mid-Jan to mid-Mar, rates 1,195F-2,180F) is the last word in Camargue chic: stone floors, linen sheets, wood beams and open fires, presided over by an owner happy to show you his bulls and let you to ride his horses. Delicious food is served *en famille* in the (designer) kitchen (*see page 45*).

Slightly further down the comfort scale, the **Authentiques Cabanes de Gardian de la Grand Mar** (04.90.97.00.64), 20 kilometres north of Salin-de-Giraud on the Arles road, is a collection of real (or well-faked) *gardian* cabins with horse-riding facilities. They have self-catering facilities (there's a restaurant, too) and require a minimum of two days' stay (950F per weekend, maximum six people per cabin).

Getting there

By car

Leave the A54 at exit no.4 and take the D570 to Stes-Maries-de-la-Mer.

By bus

Les Cars de Camargue (04.90.96.36.25) runs bus services from Arles train station to Stes-Maries-de-la-Mer, stopping at other destinations around the reserve. During July and August, there are about five buses a day; out of season there is only one bus in the morning and one in the afternoon.

Tourist information

You can take a boat trip on the sea and the Rhône delta on the *Tiki III* from Stes-Marie-de-la-Mer (04.90.97.81.68, Le Grau d'Orgon, closed mid-Mar to mid-Nov). Bike hire is available at **Le Vélo Saintois** (19 av de la République, 04.90.97.74.56, Stes-Maries-de-la-Mer) and four-wheel-drive trips through the reserve from **Destination Camargue** (rue de la Calade, Arles, 04.90.96.94.44).

Centre de Ginès

Information de la Réserve Naturelle, Pont de Gau, rte d'Arles, 4km from Stes-Maries-de-la-Mer (04.90.97.86.32). **Open** *Oct-Mar* 9.30am-5pm Mon-Thur, Sat, Sun; *Apr-Sept* 9am-6pm daily. This centre has displays on the region's ecology.

La Capellière

Centre d'Information, La Capellière (04.90.97.00.97). **Open** *Apr-Sept* 9am-1pm, 2-6pm daily; *Oct-Mar* 9am-1pm, 2-5pm Mon, Wed-Sun. **Admission** 20F, 10F children, free under-12s. **No credit cards**.

An information centre with exhibition halls and nature trails.

St-Gilles-du-Gard

Office de Tourisme, pl Mistral (04.66.87.33.75). **Open** *Jan-Apr* 9am-noon, 2-5pm Mon-Sat; 9am-noon Sun; *May-Dec* 9am-noon, 3-7pm Mon-Sat; 9am-noon Sun.

Stes-Maries-de-la-Mer

Office de Tourisme, 5 av Van Gogh (04.90.97.82.55). **Open** *Nov-Feb* 9am-5pm daily; *Mar, Oct* 9am-6pm daily; *Apr-Sept* 9am-7pm daily; *July, Aug* 9am-8pm daily.

Gypsies of the world unite!

Soon after the death of Christ, the legend goes, Mary Magdalene, Mary Salome (the mother of James and John), and Jesus' aunt Mary Jacob fled Palestine by sea and washed up on the shores of Provence, where they were met by Black Sarah the gypsy chief (who may, according to another version of the story, have travelled from the Holy Land with the Marys as their maid). The local populace converted en masse and Sarah was unofficially canonised by the gypsies, who adopted her as their patron saint.

Unwilling to let the gypsies and their unrecognised saint have all the glory, the Church came up with some convenient relics in 1448: three sets of bones that, recent research suggests, may be those of oriental women of the first century AD.

Gypsies from all over Europe and the Middle East converge in Stes-Marie-de-la-Mer each spring for an exuberant three-day festival, during which the streets of the tiny town throb with flamenco guitar and dancing, horse races and bullfights. On 23 May, Sarah's relics, which are kept in a little wooden boat, are lowered by ropes from the upper chapel of the great twelfth-century church that houses her statue in its crypt. On 24 May, the statue is carried in procession from its home in the crypt to the sea, surrounded by a tumultuous crowd of gypsies, Arlésiens in costume and *gardians* on horseback. The relics of Ste Marie Jacob and Ste Marie Salome follow on 25 May, the feast of Ste Marie Jacob, to be blessed by a bishop in a fishing boat. The blackened interior of Stes Maries' church is the only memory of the all-night candlelit vigil, which was banned recently to prevent further damage to the building. On 22 October, the feast of Ste Marie Salome is celebrated with a more sedate procession and blessing.

Avignon & the Vaucluse

Avignon	88
Orange & Around	102
Carpentras & Around	108
The Luberon	114

Feature boxes

The papacy in Avignon & the Great Schism	91
Festival d'Avignon	94
Les Chorégies d'Orange	104
The Jews of Carpentras	108
On the antiques trail	116

Avignon

For all its cultural and historical riches, the papal city has a shady side to its character.

For three weeks each summer, Avignon becomes France's performing arts capital, its **Festival d'Avignon** (*see box page 94*) drawing throngs of visitors from around the world. Beyond the impressive grandeur of the papal residences, the brilliant art collections of the museums, the chic antique shops and gourmet restaurants is another Avignon, best captured in Lawrence Durrell's *Avignon Quintet*: a town of gloomy, twilit streets, chill with autumn river damps or blasted by a howling mistral.

Avignon started life as a neolithic settlement on the Rocher des Doms, a cliff overlooking the Rhône. Under the Romans, the town flourished as a river port, but it was not until the twelfth century, when Avignon's clergy became a power to be reckoned with, that the village started to think big. The Romanesque cathedral was built, the bridge of St-Bénézet constructed, and towers and churches sprang up. Avignon gained a reputation for fine sculpture, superb examples of which can be seen in the Petit-Palais museum.

It was the papal presence in Avignon (*see box page 91*), however, that really transformed the town. French Pope Clement V brought his court from turmoil-wracked Rome to the safety of the Vatican-owned Comtat Venaissin (*see chapter* **Carpentras**) in 1306. Three years later, the papal court settled in Avignon, where it stayed until 1376. During the Holy See's 'Babylonian captivity', as the jealous Italians referred to it, the town became one of Europe's great artistic powerhouses and ethnic melting pots.

Even after the popes returned to Italy, Avignon remained papal territory. Without French censorship, and far enough from Rome to escape heavy-handed Vatican checks, the town flourished as an artistic, religious and publishing centre, a tradition that continued after the town was annexed to France in 1791: it was to Avignon that the Félibrige turned in the nineteenth century to get its Provençal revival works into print.

The Revolution hit Avignon hard, as anti-clerical revenge was wreaked on the town's

Avignon: home of the papal court during the fourteenth century.

'papists'; in the gruesome Glacière massacre, 60 pro-papal prisoners were flung, some still alive, into the Tour des Latrines in the Palais des Papes. Attempts by Revolutionaries to pull down the ramparts and the Palais des Papes failed, but the city was badly damaged and the

Palais was made into a barracks. It was not until 1906 that restoration got under way.

Huge parts of Avignon remain shabby and unrestored, however, and although the city is lively and cultured during the festival season, it has a tendency to rest on its laurels: theatre

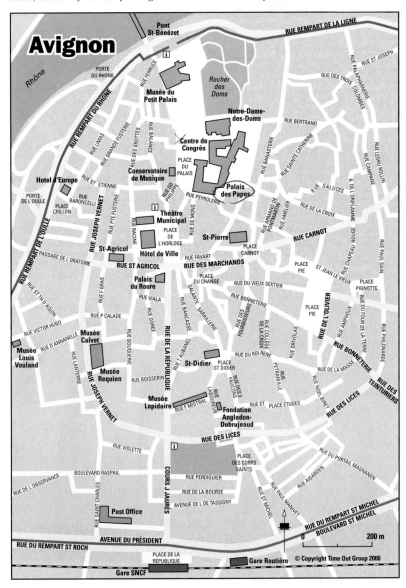

companies struggle to remain open all year, the publishing trade has moved to Arles and the legendary Roumanille bookshop, founded by the Félibrige poet Joseph Roumanille, closed its doors in 1996.

Sightseeing

The **Rocher des Doms** is where Avignon started, and it's also a good place to begin a visit. From this terraced garden perched on a cliff above the river, the view ranges over the whole city, 'its closely knitted roofs of weathered tile like a pie crust fresh from the oven', as Lawrence Durrell wrote. It also takes in a great sweep of the Rhône, as well as fertile Vaucluse countryside and Villeneuve-lès-Avignon on the opposite bank. Also clearly visible are the ramparts, now half-buried, crenellated by the ubiquitous 'improver' Viollet-le-Duc, who filled in the moat in 1860.

Just below the Rocher des Doms stands the twelfth-century **Pont St-Bénézet** (the 'Pont d'Avignon' of nursery-rhyme fame), part of which was swept away by the river in 1660. Between the Dom and the bridge, the **Musée du Petit Palais** has a superb collection of early Italian paintings, and sculptures rescued from the churches of Avignon.

The massive bulk of the **Palais des Papes**, more like an ogre's castle than a pontiff's palace, dominates the square it shares with the town's **Notre-Dame-des-Doms** cathedral.

Before entering the Palais, get a real grasp of the solidity of the place by walking along rue Peyrollerie to see its great towers, which are embedded in sheer rock. The building opposite the Palais with an elaborately swagged and furbelowed stone façade was once the Hôtel des Monnaies (the mint) and is now the **Conservatoire de Musique**.

A little further south, the **place de l'Horloge** is the centre of town life, with its people-watching cafés, opera house and grand nineteenth-century Hôtel de Ville (town hall). A Gothic clock tower, the remains of an earlier structure, gives the square its name. At festival time the place is home to a whirling carousel of musicians, minstrels and mime artists; *trompe l'oeil* paintings on the walls of the surrounding streets are a reminder of the jollity for the rest of the year.

West of here lies the smart part of town, its streets packed with fashionable restaurants and beautifully restored mansions. Lamentably unrestored, however, is the church of **St-Agricol** on rue St-Agricol (open 3-5pm Sat & one hour before services on Sun), with the celebrated carving on its fifteenth-century façade sadly obscured by pigeon droppings. An alley off rue Agricol leads to the fifteenth-century **Palais du Roure**, the family home of the Baroncellis, where the *gardian* poet Folco Baroncelli (*see box page 84*) was born, and where Frédéric Mistral (*see box page 72*) edited *Aioli*, his Provençal journal.

The **Palais des Papes**: fairy-tale castle or papal power statement? *See page 93.*

The papacy in Avignon & the Great Schism

Rome was no bed of roses for the medieval popes: the thuggish private armies of powerful barons fought pitched battles in the streets and the papal curia was not above a Machiavellian scheme or two. Little wonder, then, that the French Pope Clement V, when invited by King Philippe le Bel to leave his boltholes in Viterbo and Anagni and take refuge in France, leaped at the prospect. In 1309, Clement took up residence in Avignon, an independent enclave within the Vatican-owned Comtat Venaissin, which belonged to his allies the Counts of Provence. Clement always professed to view Avignon only as a temporary sanctuary, but on his death in 1314 six further French popes saw no reason to relocate to Rome. Their 68-year 'Babylonian captivity' – as furious Italians branded it – utterly transformed this quiet provincial backwater.

When Clement arrived, Avignon's population stood at 6,000: not many years later it had risen to 30,000. Artists, scholars, architects, weavers and jewellers flocked there for patronage and some of their handiwork remains, particularly in the wonderful collection of Italian and Avignon school paintings in the Petit Palais. The virtue industry fostered vice in equal measure: 'a sewer,' sniffed Petrarch, 'the filthiest of cities... A hell for the living, the most odoriferous on earth.' A lively demi-monde of prostitutes, heretics, refugees and criminals of all sorts flourished in Avignon's squalid streets. The town was ravaged by the plague, too; it halved the population in 1348.

Unperturbed, the papacy was digging in. It took two years to elect a replacement for Clement. In the end, the job fell to a former bishop of Avignon, who took the name John XXII and set about enlarging his palace and industriously filling the papal coffers. The austere Cistercian monk Benedict XII, who succeeded him in 1335, razed that palace to build a much bigger but much more severe fortress, the Palais Vieux.

The much more flamboyant Clement VI, elected in 1342, extended the place in the fashionable new Gothic style; he also took shrewd advantage of his landlady, Countess Jeanne of Provence. Jeanne came to beg Clement's aid when accused of murdering her first husband; when she agreed to sell the remaining portion of Avignon to the papacy in 1348, the little matter was cleared up. Gregory XI, elected in 1370, was badgered by the very persuasive St Catherine of Siena into returning to the Holy See. He took her advice, went back, and promptly died in 1378.

The Italians elected a Roman pope, but the French were loath to lose their hold on the reins of power and swiftly elected Clement VII in Avignon. The rival popes excommunicated each other, sparking the Great Schism, a 40-year period when Christendom found itself with two heirs of St Peter. Support for Rome from the French crown finally resolved the matter. The second and last Avignon anti-pope, Benedict XIII, was despatched to his native Catalonia and the Schism ended when all sides agreed on the election of Martin V in 1417.

Rue Joseph Vernet is a shopaholic's dream of designer stores and handmade chocolate emporia. Off its northern end, the grand **Hôtel d'Europe** on rue Baroncelli has long been a favourite with visiting foreign lovers, among them the eloping Brownings. John Stuart Mill and Mrs Taylor (Harriet Hardy) also checked in; when Harriet died there, Mill was so distraught that he stayed on, buying a house overlooking the cemetery where she was buried and furnishing it with the contents of their last hotel room.

Further south on rue Victor Hugo, the **Musée Vouland** is a lavishly decorated

private house museum, full of eighteenth-century French furniture and faience. Back on rue Joseph Vernet is the **Musée Calvet**, displaying an eclectic collection of sculptures and paintings in the elegant colonnaded galleries of an eighteenth-century palace around a serene courtyard. In another wing is the **Musée Requien**, an old-fashioned natural history museum crammed with stuffed animals and fossils.

Rue Joseph Vernet curves round to join rue de la République, the main thoroughfare of Avignon, a nineteenth-century 'improvement' sliced straight through the old town. To the

south it becomes cours Jean Jaurès, leading to
the main gate, train station and tourist office.

Heading north, the **Musée Lapidaire**
contains ancient sculptures displayed in a
former Jesuit chapel. In place St-Didier stands
the lovely church of **St-Didier**, in the simple,
single-aisled Provençal Gothic style. Close by
the church, the **Médiatheque Ceccano**, a
fourteenth-century cardinal's residence, is now
the town library and multimedia centre,
surrounded by a shady garden. Around the
corner in rue Laboureur is the **Fondation
Angladon-Dubrujeaud**, a worthwhile private
art museum in an eighteenth-century house.

Leading out of place St-Didier, rue du Roi
René has several fine seventeenth- and
eighteenth-century palaces; at No.22 a plaque
records that this was where the fourteenth-
century Italian poet Petrarch first set eyes on
Laura, the woman he was to idolise in verse for
the rest of his life. At the far end, rue des
Teinturiers is one of Avignon's most
atmospheric streets, winding along beside the
River Sorgue, where the water wheels of the dye
works that gave the street its name are still
visible. Production of the patterned calico
fabrics known as *indiennes* thrived here until
the end of the nineteenth century. Now the
street is home to cafés under spreading plane
trees, second-hand bookshops and art galleries.

Back at place St-Didier, the winding, partly
pedestrianised streets to the north are the heart
of the medieval town. Most of this district is
surprisingly shabby, dimly lit at night, with
empty statue niches and pigeon-daubed
churches. At the **Hôtel de Rascas** on rue des
Fourbisseurs, note the corbels of a projecting
upper storey, evidence of a cardinal's demands
for extra airspace. Place Pie to the east is home
to the fruit and flower **market** (7am-1pm Tue-
Sun). In place St-Pierre to the north stands the
Gothic church of **St-Pierre** (open for services
only), which has finely carved walnut doors
and a handsome belfry.

The winding streets behind the Palais des
Papes lead to rue Banasterie (basketmakers'
street) and the **Chapelle des Pénitents Noirs**
(open by appointment only – contact the tourist
office), with a sumptuous baroque interior.
Round the corner on rue des Escaliers Ste-Anne
is one of Avignon's liveliest cultural centres,
Utopia (*see page 96*). It's the best cinema in
Provence for foreign-language films, with a nice
little café attached; pick up a copy of its free
information sheet, *La Gazette*. Further east on
place des Carmes is the church of **St-
Symphorien** (04.90.82.10.56, open 8-9am, 6.30-
7.30pm Mon-Sat, 8.45am-noon Sun), with its
fifteenth-century Gothic façade and some lovely
polychrome wooden statues inside. Next door are

the fourteenth-century cloisters, now home to
one of Avignon's oldest theatre companies,
Théâtre des Carmes (*see page 96*), a popular
festival venue. This eastern part of town is the
university district, packed with bars, cafés and
second-hand bookstores. Past the porte St-Lazare,
avenue Stuart Mill leads to the **Cimetière St-
Véran** (04.90.82.25.02, open until sunset daily)
where Harriet Hardy and Mill are buried.

The Pass Avignon-Villeneuve gives you 20
to 50 per cent reductions (except on your first
ticket) on most major museums and sights.
Just pick up a pass at the first museum or
place you visit, or at the tourist office. It's
valid for a fortnight.

Collection Lambert

Hôtel de Caumont, 5 rue Violette (04.90.16.56.20).
Open 11am-7pm daily. **Admission** 25F,
15F children.
Housed in a renovated eighteenth-century *hôtel par-
ticulier*, this collection – due to open in July 2000 –
was donated to the city by Parisian art dealer Yvon
Lambert as part of a 20-year loan. It focuses on the
artists Lambert has long defended including Carl
André, Lawrence Weiner, Anselm Kiefer, Julian
Schnabel, Christian Boltanski, Cy Twombly, Robert
Ryman, Nan Goldin, and some younger names like
Douglas Gordon; but the museum also has a budget
for acquiring and commissioning new works.

Fondation Angladon-Dubrujeaud

5 rue Laboureur (04.90.82.29.03). **Open** *Nov-Mar* 1-
6pm Wed-Sun; *May-Oct* 1-7pm Wed-Sun.
Admission 30F, 10F children.
Housed in an eighteenth-century mansion, this new
gallery displays gems from the collection of Jacques
Doucet, hung with an eye to the right setting – thus,
Dutch oils, including a charming baby Jesus eating
cherries, are complemented by oak chests, armoires
and majolica, while eighteenth-century French por-
traits occupy a lavish salon of gilt and brocade.
Works include self-portraits by Picasso, a Derain
rose, an exquisite Foujita portrait of his wife with a
green bird, Monet's Lapin, works by Modigliani,
Degas and Sisley, a Cézanne still life and the only
Van Gogh in Provence, Les Wagons du Chemin de
Fer, with a dramatic green sky.

Musée Calvet

65 rue Joseph Vernet (04.90.86.33.84). **Open** 10am-
1pm, 2-6pm Mon, Wed-Sun. **Admission** 30F, free
under-12s.
The beautifully restored Beaux-Arts museum displays its vast collection in light, elegant, colonnaded
rooms. The ground floor has huge Gobelins tapestries and sculptures in marble, alabaster and wood;
note the exquisite fourteenth- and fifteenth-century
Flemish and Spanish painted wooden images.
Eighteenth- and nineteenth-century French paintings include works by the Avignon-based Vernet
family and David d'Angers (David's *La Mort du
jeune Bara* is the star). There is a good modern

section with works by Soutine, Sisley, Manet, Utrillo and Dufy, and Camille Claudel's head of her brother, Paul Claudel, who had his rebellious sister carted off to a mental asylum near Avignon when her relationship with Rodin became too scandalous.

Musée Lapidaire
27 rue de la République (04.90.86.33.84). **Open** 10am-1pm, 2-6pm Wed-Mon. **Admission** 10F.
Avignon's archaeological collection, part of the Esprit Calvet donation, is superbly displayed in a seventeenth-century Jesuit chapel. It includes Greek, Gallo-Roman and Etruscan finds – sculpture, pottery, bronzes, mosaics, vases and glass – and is particularly rich in Egyptian sculpture, reliefs, stele and shabti, most notably the funeral inscription of the High Priest Ptahmose. Among the Gallo-Roman selection is a depiction of the Tarasque of Noves, the man-eating monster that supposedly used to terrorise these parts. At the entrance to the museum is one of its most prized pieces, the *Scène de Halage*, a mausoleum relief in memory of a Gallic wine merchant.

Musée Louis Vouland
17 rue Victor Hugo (04.90.86.03.79). **Open** *May-Oct* 10am-noon, 2-6pm Tue-Sat; *Nov-Apr* 2-6pm Tue-Sat. **Admission** 20F, free children.
A collection of eighteenth-century French furniture and porcelain in an elegant townhouse setting.

Musée du Petit Palais
pl du Palais (04.90.86.44.58). **Open** *June-Sept* 10am-1pm, 2-6pm Mon, Wed-Sun; *Oct-May* 9am-1pm, 2-5.30pm Wed-Sun. **Admission** 30F, free children.
First constructed in 1308 for a cardinal, the Petit Palais was altered to house the local bishop in 1335, only to undergo another transformation in the late fifteenth century for Cardinal Giuliano della Rovere, the future Pope Julius II. This was when it acquired its current appearance, a symmetrical Renaissance façade with decorative tower on the north-west corner. Today, the Petit Palais houses a magnificent collection of medieval paintings and sculptures. On the ground floor are Romanesque sculptures and frescos rescued from churches destroyed during the Revolution. Note the sarcophagus of Cardinal Jean de Lagrange, with its anatomically realistic depiction of a decaying corpse, and his brutally mutilated tomb effigy.

The bulk of the Palais' painting collection was assembled by Gian Pietro Campana di Cavelli, a nineteenth-century Italian collector with such an insatiable appetite for art that he went bankrupt, allowing Napoléon III to snap up his entire estate. It provides a fine introduction to the International Gothic style, pioneered in Avignon by the mostly Sienese artists patronised by the popes, and clung to long after it had gone out of fashion elsewhere. To get an idea of the local development of the style, take a look at the *Virgin and Child with an Apple* by Enguerrand Quarton, a master of the Avignon school. Other highlights include Taddeo

Gaddi's *Virgin and Child*, Barna's exquisite *Ste Madeleine* in pure orange, gold and green garments, Allegretto Nuzi's *Virgin in Majesty*, with her delicately printed robes, and Botticelli's late fifteenth-century *Madonna and Child*.

Musée Requien d'Histoire Naturelle
67 rue Joseph Vernet (04.90.82.43.51). **Open** 9am-noon, 2-6pm Tue-Sat. **Admission** free.
An old-fashioned natural history museum, packed with rocks, minerals, stuffed animals, fossils, and, buried in the archives, a botanical section that includes John Stuart Mill's collection of dried flowers and herbs.

Notre-Dame-des-Doms
pl du Palais (04.90.82.12.24). **Open** *treasury Apr-Nov* 9am-noon, 2-7pm daily or by appointment. *Cathedral Feb-Oct* 9am-6.30pm daily; *Nov-Jan* 9am-5pm daily. **Admission** free, but donation expected.
A surprisingly unspiritual church. Any vestiges of its twelfth-century Romanesque origins have been almost obliterated by subsequent destruction or additions: a baroque gallery, a rebuilt tower and a tacky golden statue of the Virgin perched on the pinnacle of the tower. Even the Simone Martini frescos have been removed to the Palais des Papes. Still, the porch is recognisably Romanesque and there is a fine twelfth-century marble throne inside.

Palais des Papes
pl du Palais (04.90.27.50.74). **Open** *Nov-Mar* 9.30am-5.45pm daily; *Apr-Nov* 9am-7pm daily. **Admission** 45F, 36F children, free under-8s. **Credit** MC, V.
The Palais des Papes is more of a fortress than the palace of God's representative on earth; a brutal power statement, this white fortress with its towers and crenellations dominates the city. The interior is strangely empty after the devastation wreaked during the Revolution and the palace's subsequent use as a prison and barracks, when soldiers chipped off bits of fresco to sell. But many exquisite fragments remain, especially in the chapels, banqueting hall and cloister. The Palais is a complicated labyrinth with two interlocking parts: the forbidding Palais Vieux, built in the 1330s for the austere Pope Benedict XII, and the more elegant and showy Palais Neuf, tacked on a decade later by Clement VI.

You can wander at will (an audio guide in several languages is included in the entry fee), or join one of the regular guided tours (some in English). Across the main courtyard from the entrance and ticket office is the Salle de Jésus, the antechamber of the papal council room or Consistoire, where frescos by Simone Martini have been displayed since they were detached from the cathedral in 1960. In the Chapelle St-Jean next door are some delightful frescos (c1346) by Matteo Giovanetti, Clement VI's court painter. Upstairs, the vast wooden vault of the Grand Tinel banqueting hall was once coloured blue and dotted with gold stars to resemble the sky. Next door, the kitchens with their huge pyramid-shaped chimney

Festival d'Avignon

Actor Jean Vilar and his Théâtre Nationale Populaire founded the Festival d'Avignon in 1947 to bring the performing arts to the masses. If the masses that throng Avignon for most of July are now numerical rather than sociological, the spirit of Vilar's venture still permeates what has become one of the biggest events of Europe's theatrical year.

For the duration of the festival – which takes place during three or four weeks in July – the streets become a surreal carnival of medieval minstrels, Pied Pipers, fire-eaters and stilt-walkers. Churches, chapels, convents, cloisters and palaces are requisitioned for stagings – traditional and experimental – of anything from Beckett to Molière, Homer to Shakespeare. Then there's dance, ranging from Lucinda Childs to Pina Bausch, and classical music concerts, lectures and exhibitions galore. The imposing Cour d'Honneur in the Palais des Papes (*pictured right*) provides the backdrop for the official festival's main events, which include the best

of the performing arts from one selected non-European country or region each year.

Flanking the official 'In' festival is Avignon Public Off, or simply Le Off, as the fringe is known. There is no selection procedure: if you can find a space and deal with the ticketing bureaucracy, you can stage your production. And that means any space, so come early to bag your bit of street (and procure the necessary permits from local authorities). You will find yourself up against some 400 rival ventures.

Festival d'Avignon

Bureau du Festival d'Avignon, 8 bis rue de Mons (04.90.27.66.50/infodoc@festival-avignon.com). **Open** second week June-end Festival 8am-midnight daily; Aug-first week of June 9am-noon, 2-6pm Mon-Fri. **Tickets** 130F-190F. **Credit** AmEx, DC, MC, V. Bookings are accepted from the first week in June, by phone, over the Internet, at the Bureau du Festival or at any FNAC store in

could feed 3,000 guests at a time. There are more Giovanetti frescos, lavish with lapis lazuli and gold, in the Chapelle St-Martial off the side of the Grand Tinel. Beyond the Salle de Parement (robing room), Benedict XII's study and its fourteenth-century ceramic tiles were only discovered in 1963. Beyond the papal bedchamber is the Chambre du Cerf, Clement VI's study, with some delightful frescos by a follower of Giovanetti, which breathe the spirit of courtly romance. Vast as it is, the Chapelle Clementine beyond was barely large enough to hold the college of cardinals when it gathered in conclave to elect a new pope. Through the Chamberlain's Room, whose raised stone slabs mark the spot where papal treasure was discovered, stairs lead up to the battlements, with a dramatic view over the city, the Rhône and Villeneuve-lès-Avignon on the opposite bank. Back on the ground floor, the Grande Audience hall has a bevy of Biblical prophets frescoed by Giovannetti.

Palais du Roure
3 rue du Collège du Roure (04.90.80.80.88). **Open** 3pm Tue for guided tours, or by appointment. **Admission** free.
The birthplace of Marquis Folco de Baroncelli-Javon, protector of the *gardians* and romancer of the Camargue (*see box p84*), the Palais has a charming courtyard with fresco fragments on the walls, and a splendid carved doorway. It is now a literary archive and library, and the main headquarters for the Festival Provençal (*see chapter* **By Season**).

Pont St-Bénézet
rue Ferruce (04.90.27.50.83). **Open** *Apr-Oct* 9am-7pm daily; *Nov-Mar* 9.30am-5.55pm daily (ticket office closes half an hour earlier). **Admission** 19F, 15F children, free under-8s.
The original bridge was begun in 1185, by a divinely inspired shepherd boy from the Ardèche, who became St Bénézet. He lifted the first massive stone, convincing the sceptical populace that construction was possible. When completed, the bridge was 22 arches and nearly a kilometre long, and contributed greatly to the development of Avignon, although in 1660, after a huge flood, the Avignonese gave up the unequal maintenance struggle. Today, only four arches and a tiny Romanesque fisherman's chapel remain. Despite the old song *Sur le pont d'Avignon*, it seems unlikely that anyone ever danced on the narrow, traffic-packed structure. It is more likely that people danced 'sous le pont' (under the bridge): the Ile de la Barthelasse, which the bridge used to cross, was a favourite R&R spot in the Middle Ages.

St-Didier
pl St-Didier (04.90.86.20.17). **Open** 8am-6.30pm daily. **Admission** free.
This pretty example of Provençal Gothic has delicate fourteenth-century Italian frescos in the north chapel. In the Chapelle St-Bénézet are relics of the bridge-building saint himself, or his skull at least; an expert who examined it in 1984 established that he was only 25 at his death.

France, the last with a 10F booking fee. Bear in mind that 60 per cent of all available tickets are snapped up in the first week after the booking office opens. You can also buy tickets at venues, one hour before performances. Tickets are available from the Bureau until 4pm on the day of the performance.
Website: www.festival-avignon.com.festival

Avignon Public Off
Maison du Off, 18 rue Buffon, Paris 75521 (01.48.05.01.19/fax 01.48.05.40.67). **Tickets** 50F-80F.
Tickets cannot be purchased before the festival. During the festival, they can be bought from the Maison d'Off's Bureau d'Accueil in the Conservatoire de Musique on the place du Palais (open 11am-8pm daily), which also provides programme information, or from each theatre up to 20 minutes before the performance. The Carte Public-Adhérent, available in advance from the Paris office or from the Bureau d'Accueil during the event, gives a 30% reduction. It costs 75F (50F before the festival).
Website: www.avignon-off.org

Arts & entertainment

Art galleries

Galerie JE Bernard
13 rue de la Grande Fusterie (04.90.80.04.04).
Open 11am-1pm, 3-7.30pm Mon-Sat. Closed Jan.
This gallery specialises in the work of young
artists, and also runs a programme of events
including music and dance.

Galerie des Teinturiers
11 bis rue des Teinturiers (04.90.86.95.31). **Open**
11am-noon, 3-7pm Tue-Sat.
A friendly gallery for contemporary local painting
and collages.

Cinemas, cabaret & multimedia

Cyberdrome
68 rue Guillaume Puy (04.90.16.05.15). **Open** 7am-
1am Mon-Sat; 2pm-1am Sun. **No credit cards**.
Everything a cyberbuff could ask for: 15 computers
provide Internet access at 50F an hour. There's also
an alcohol-free bar with music.

L'Helicon
23 rue Bancasse (04.90.16.03.99). **Open** lunch and
dinner: days and times vary; call for details. **Musical
evenings** Thur-Sat. **Menus** 65F-115F. **Credit**
AmEx, MC, V.
Chansons are performed by guest stars or the owner
himself at the piano, with the young clientele beg-
ging for traditional favourites as they munch good
hearty fare such as seafood *pot au feu*.

Maison Jean Vilar
8 rue de Mons (04.90.86.59.64). **Open** *library* 1.30-
5.30pm Tue-Fri; 10am-5pm Sat; *videothèque* 9am-
noon, 1.30-5.30pm Tue-Fri; 10am-5pm Sat.
A library of theatre, music, dance and film.
Screenings can be arranged in advance, from the catalogue in the lobby.

Utopia
4 rue des Escaliers Ste-Anne (04.90.82.65.36). **Box
office** 11am-11pm Mon-Sat. **Shows** noon, 2pm, 4pm,
6pm, 8pm Mon-Fri; 10pm Tue, Fri, Sat. **Tickets** 32F,
250F ten-show pass. **No credit cards**.
Avignon's main *version originale* (original language) cinema has a bistro and café, too (*see below*
Where to eat).

Sport

Piscine de la Barthelasse
Ile de la Barthelasse (04.90.89.90.58). **Open** *May-
Aug* 10am-7pm daily. **Admission** 35F.
Olympic-sized open-air pool on the Ile de la
Barthelasse, for when the city gets too hot to bear.
Cross the Pont Edouard Daladier and the pool is
on your right.

Theatre

Le Chêne Noir
8 bis rue Ste-Cathrine (04.90.82.40.57). **Box office**
open just before show. **Shows** usually 8.30pm Mon-
Sat; 7pm Sun. **Tickets** 110F, 55F children. **Credit**
AmEx, DC, MC, V.
Innovative theatre specialising in performances for
and involving children, some of them matinées.

Théâtre des Carmes
6 pl des Carmes (04.90.82.20.47). **Box office** 9am-
4pm Mon-Fri. **Shows** 8.30pm Mon-Sat, 4pm Sun.
Tickets 70F, concs 40F-50F. **No credit cards**.
Avignon's oldest theatre company, based in the
restored Gothic cloister of Eglise des Carmes, is still
firmly committed to radical theatre in the original
spirit of the festival.

Théâtre du Chien qui Fume
75 rue des Teinturiers (04.90.85.95.87). **Box office**
opens one hour before show. **Shows** 8.30pm Fri, Sat.
Tickets 30F-120F. **No credit cards**.
Director Gérard Vantaggioli adamantly refuses to
allow this to become a festival-only theatre. He
stages new productions regularly, with a soirée for
fresh talent on the last Friday of the month. Booking
is recommended and tickets can be collected two
days before the show.

Théâtre Municipal
20 pl de l'Horloge (04.90.82.23.44). **Box office**
11am-6pm Mon-Sat. **Tickets** 30F-340F. **Credit**
AmEx, DC, MC, V (for tickets bought on day of show
only).
This Italianate theatre is the main permanent house
in Avignon, and stages official festival productions
in July. Tickets can be ordered by phone or bought
direct from the box office. Credit cards are accepted
but only on the same day as the show; otherwise
cheques or cash are preferred.

Where to eat

See also **Hôtel de la Mirande** (*below* **Where
to stay**).

Le Chandelier
29 rue Saraillerie (04.90.85.21.83). **Meals served** 7-
10pm Mon-Sat. **Menus** 75F-120F. **Credit** DC, MC, V.
A modest-looking place with rush-bottomed chairs,
candles and a soundtrack of quiet jazz, serving surprisingly well-cooked dishes such as fricassee of
wild mushrooms with tiny shellfish and roast black
sesame seeds. Don't miss the home-made foie gras
and bread.

Cuisine de Reine
83 rue Joseph Vernet (04.90.85.99.04). **Meals
served** noon-2.30pm, 7.30-10.30pm daily. **Menus**
110F-185F. **Credit** AmEx, DC, MC, V.
If you indulge in the sin of foie gras anywhere, do it
here, in this elegant restaurant set in a fifteenth-century cloister. The food is daringly simple, as in the

filet mignon de porc with chickpea anchoïade. For
dessert, the *assiette gourmande* has exquisite mouth-
fuls of Luberon plums in muscat, roast pear, pista-
chio ice-cream and a tiny crème brûlée. Excellent
regional wine list.

La Ferme
*chemin des Bois, Ile de la Barthelasse (04.90.82.57.
53)*. **Meals served** 7-9pm Mon; noon-1.30pm, 7-
9pm Tue, Thur-Sun. Closed Nov-Mar. **Menus** 110F-
170F. **Rates** single/double 400F-450F. **Credit**
AmEx, MC, V.
This rustic little *auberge* on an island in the Rhône,
only a five-minute journey by car or bus from the
city centre, has a piano-playing host and fresh
food that changes according to season. There's a
swimming pool, too.

Maison Nani
29 rue Théodore Aubanel (04.90.82.60.90). **Meals
served** noon-2pm Mon-Thur; noon-2pm, 7-11pm Fri,
Sat. **Average** 100F. **No credit cards.**
Charming, casual wood-panelled café with newspapers and magazines to peruse. Select from imaginative salads to accompany carpaccio of salmon, foie
gras or a variety of cheeses.

Le Mesclun
48 rue de la Balance (04.90.86.14.60). **Meals
served** *Sept-June* noon-2.15pm Mon-Sat; *July, Aug*
noon-2.15pm, 7.30-10.30pm Mon-Sat. **Plat du jour**
50F. **No credit cards.**
Great for a quick gourmet lunch, with brisk service
and good fresh dishes; try the anchoïade with raw
vegetables, the pâté and mixed green salad or the
potato tart.

Rose au Petit Bedon
70 rue Joseph Vernet (04.90.82.33.98). **Meals
served** 7-9.30pm Mon; noon-1.30pm, 7-9.30pm Tue-
Sat. Closed two weeks Aug. **Menus** 110F-165F.
Credit AmEx, DC, MC, V.
This small, cosy restaurant with velvet banquettes
serves Provençal *cuisine de ménage* (home cooking),
such as pumpkin soup or veal with sage followed by
pear cake or baked apple for dessert.

Woolloomooloo
16 rue des Teinturiers (04.90.85.28.44). **Meals
served** noon-2pm, 7-11pm daily. **Menus** 55F-85F.
Credit AmEx, DC, MC, V.
Funky candlelit restaurant in an old printing
works, complete with exotic furniture, cushions
and Indian fabrics, and serving a variety of oriental and African dishes.

Bars & nightlife

Le Bistrot d'Utopia
4 rue des Escaliers Ste-Anne (04.90.27.04.96). **Open**
11.30pm-1am daily. **No credit cards.**
This classic little bistro attached to the Utopia cinema is a good place for quiet drinks or a snack
before or after a film.

Le Bokao's
9 bis quai St-Lazare (04.90.82.47.55). **Open** 7pm-
3am Mon-Sat. **Credit** AmEx, DC, MC, V.
Admission free.
In an old wood-panelled bar, this club has a large
dancefloor and plays an eclectic selection of music.
Although admission is free, you only get in if the
staff like the look of you.

Café In et Off
5 pl du Palais (04.90.85.48.95). **Open** *May-June,
Sept* 7am-8pm daily; *July-Aug* 7am-midnight daily.
Favourite festival meeting place, with terrace tables
offering a good view of the Palais des Papes.

Le Cloître des Arts
83 rue Joseph Vernet (04.90.82.70.60). **Open** *Salon
du Thé* 9am-6.30pm Tue-Sat. **Credit** AmEx, DC,
MC, V.
Elegant café and patisserie in the serene arcades of
an ancient cloister.

L'Esclave
12 rue du Limas (04.90.85.14.51). **Open** 11.30pm-
5am daily. **Admission** free.
Gay but not exclusively so, and definitely one of the
places to be seen during the festival.

Shopping

The indoor Les Halles market in place Pie is on
from 7am to 1pm Tuesday to Sunday. There's a
flea market on the place des Carmes all day
Sunday and an antiques market in rue des
Teinturiers all day Saturday.

Annick Goutal
18 rue St-Agricol (04.90.27.95.51). **Open** 2-7pm Mon;
9am-noon, 2-7pm Tue-Sat. **Credit** AmEx, MC, V.
The only Annick Goutal shop outside Paris, for the
most exquisite perfume from all-natural products.
Try Eau de Camille or Eau du Sud.

Les Olivades
28 rue des Marchands (04.90.86.13.42). **Open**
9.30am-7pm Mon-Sat. **Credit** AmEx, DC, MC, V.
Fabric, fashions, tablecloths and napkins in a stylish range of Provençal fabrics.

Shakespeare
155 rue Carnot (04.90.27.38.50). **Open** 9.30am-
12.30pm, 2-6.30pm Tue-Sat. **Credit** MC, V.
A classically dusty second-hand bookshop with a
wide range of foreign-language titles: novels, non-
fiction, travel and so on, in English, French and
German. Tea and scones served.

La Tropézienne
22 rue St-Agricol (04.90.86.24.72). **Open** 8am-8pm
Tue-Sun. **Credit** V.
A Provençal foodie paradise: wine, preserved fruit,
marrons glacés, chocolates, jams and patisseries,
and the local speciality, *papalines* – oregano liqueur
chocolates.

Where to stay

See also page 98 **La Ferme**.

Camping Municipal

Ile de la Barthelasse (04.90.82.63.50). Closed Nov-Feb. **Rates** 64.40F-129.40F one tent with two people. **Credit** DC, MC, V.
A campsite on the Ile de la Barthelasse in the middle of the Rhône – take the Edouard Daladier bridge to reach it. The site also has bungalows (sleeping four) to rent for 2,500F per week (minimum one week).

Hôtel de Blauvac

11 rue de la Bancasse (04.90.86.34.11/fax 04.90.86. 27.41). **Rates** single 230F-340F, double 390F-545F. **Credit** AmEx, DC, MC, V.
A seventeenth-century building overlooking a quiet, winding street. The de Blauvac is very reasonably priced, with large, well-designed rooms and friendly service.

Hôtel Cloître St-Louis

20 rue Portail Boquier (04.90.27.55.55/fax 04.90.82. 24.01). **Rates** single/double 500F-850F, suite 1,400F-1,600F. **Credit** AmEx, DC, MC, V.
A clever combination of ancient and modern: a sixteenth-century cloister and chapel wing has been complemented by a modern extension designed by Jean Nouvel (architect of the Institut du Monde Arabe in Paris), with a walled garden and rooftop pool.

Hôtel d'Europe

12 pl Crillon (04.90.14.76.76/fax 04.90.85.43.66). **Rates** single/double 690F-850F, suite 2,200F-3,000F. **Credit** AmEx, DC, MC, V.
Napoléon, Victor Hugo, John Stuart Mill and Jackie Onassis are just some of the past guests to stay in this Avignon legend set in a sixteenth-century mansion complete with peaceful gardens. The elegant salons are hung with tapestries and paintings; the rooms and suites are spacious and tastefully decorated.

Hôtel de la Mirande

4 pl de la Mirande (04.90.85.93.93/fax 04.90.86. 26.85). **Rates** double 1,700F-2,600F, suite 3,700F. **Credit** AmEx, DC, MC, V.
This eighteenth-century cardinals' palace tucked away behind the Palais des Papes combines exquisitely styled period decor, tapestries, fine linen and brocade period furniture with twenty-first-century luxury and service. It also has one of Avignon's best restaurants (*see page 47*).

Hôtel Mignon

12 rue Joseph Vernet (04.90.82.17.30/fax 04.90.85. 78.46). **Rates** single 160F-220F, double 220F-260F, family room (four people) 400F. **Credit** AmEx, DC, MC, V.
A sweet little hotel with pretty Provençal furnishings. Rooms are small but prices are cheap.

Hôtel de Mons

5 rue de Mons (04.90.82.57.16/fax 04.90.85.19.15). **Rates** single 328F, double 386F. **Credit** AmEx, DC, MC, V.
A budget choice right off the place de l'Horloge, this is a quaintly converted medieval chapel, with winding stairs and rooms squeezed into nooks and crannies – some are a little too squeezed for comfort, so insist on seeing them first.

Essentials

Getting there

From the airport

Avignon's airport, Caumont-Avignon (04.90.81.51.15), is 8km south of the town. You can catch a bus to Avignon town centre; the bus stop is 500m from the airport at the Lycée Agricole, and there are about 20 buses a day (journey time 15min) – more information on 04.90.82.07.35.

By car

From the A7 autoroute, exits nos.23 (Avignon Nord) and 24 (Avignon Sud) both link with the city's outer ring road.

By bus

Daily buses connect Avignon with Carpentras, Cavaillon, St-Rémy, Orange, Nîmes, Arles, Aix, Marseille, Nice and Cannes. The bus station (04.90.82.07.35) is on av Montclar, just in front of the train station.

By train

Easily accessible by train, Avignon is at the junction of the Paris-Marseille and Paris-Montpellier lines, with frequent links to Arles, Nîmes, Orange, Toulon and Carcassonne. There are fast TGV links to Paris (3hr 20min), Lille, Nantes, Rouen, Brussels and Geneva. The train station is on bd St-Rochand, just outside Porte de la République.

Getting around

Avignon is small enough to walk around, though the car-bound locals don't think so.

Taxis

Avignonnais (04.90.82.20.20).

Buses

Espace Bus (04.90.85.44.93).
TCRA (04.90.82.68.19).

Car rental

Veo *51 av Pierre Semard (04.90.87.53.43)*. **Open** 8am-noon, 2-7pm Tue-Fri. **Credit** MC, V.
A small car costs around 260F per day if average daily mileage doesn't exceed 100km.
Loueurs de France *109 rte de Lyon (04.90.82. 49.26)*. **Open** 8am-6pm Mon-Sat. **Credit** V.
Around 200F a day.

Tourist information

Office de Tourisme

*41 cours Jean Jaurès (04.32.74.32.74/fax 04.90.82.
95.03).* **Open** *Apr-Sept* 9am-7pm Mon-Fri; 9am-1pm,
2-7pm Sat; 9am-noon Sun; *Oct-Mar* 9am-6pm Mon-
Fri; 9am-1pm, 2-5pm Sat; 10am-noon Sun; *during
festival* 9am-8pm daily.
Website: www.avignon-et-provence.com

Lost property

Police municipale, pl Pie (04.90.82.94.26). **Open** 24
hours daily.

Post office

La Poste, cours Kennedy (04.90.27.54.00). **Open**
8am-7pm Mon-Fri; 8am-noon Sat.

Villeneuve-lès-Avignon

This small settlement centred on the tenth-
century Abbaye St-André came into its own in
1307, when France's King Philippe le Bel
decided it was a prime location for keeping an
eye on the goings-on across the Rhône in

Avignon. A heavily fortified 'new town'
(*villeneuve*) sprang up, plus a watchtower – the
Tour Philippe le Bel, to the south of the
town centre – which grew higher as Avignon
became more powerful. Unjustifiably
overshadowed by its brasher neighbour,
Villeneuve is a charming little town, with some
stunning architecture, a superb view of
Avignon and the surrounding countryside, and
one matchless work of art.

For the view, head for the west tower of the
Fort St-André, the fortress built in the
fourteenth century around the abbey. Inside the
fort's massive ramparts is all that remains of
the **Abbaye St-André**: bewitching gardens,
with roses and wisteria, winding paths of
rosemary, lavender and cypress, leading to a
tiny restored Romanesque chapel, the ruins of
the thirteenth-century church and a graveyard
with sarcophagi laid out like little beds – a
place more spiritual by far than all of Avignon's
great palaces.

Below the fort, the **Chartreuse du Val de
Bénédiction** was once the largest Carthusian
monastery in France. The charterhouse has
been painstakingly restored, removing all signs
of the depredations suffered during the

Quarton's *Coronation of the Virgin* from the **Musée Pierre de Luxembourg**.

Revolution, when – to add insult to injury – the tomb of Pope Innocent VI, who founded the monastery in 1352, was converted into a white marble rabbit hutch. There are monks' cells resembling little rows of terraced cottages off the two larger, pale stone cloisters, as well as a laundry, kitchen, prisons and a herb garden funded by the beauty company Yves Rocher. A small chapel off the Cloître du Cimetière has exquisite frescos by Matteo Giovanetti, while Innocent VI's tomb, now fully restored, can be seen in the church. The Chartreuse now acts as a state-funded centre for playwrights.

The **Musée Pierre de Luxembourg** contains four floors of art, including a superb, delicately carved ivory *Virgin and Child* from the fourteenth century and sixteenth- and seventeenth-century religious paintings by Mignard and de Champaigne. The collection's masterpiece is the extraordinary *Coronation of the Virgin* (1453-54) by Enguerrand Quarton, a leading light in the Avignon school. The entire medieval world view is here: our terrestrial world is just a thin layer between the detailed torments of hell below and the vast glories of heaven above, in the centre of which is the Virgin herself, with a cloak bluer than the sky. Note the details of landscape and human activity, the devils and the damned, and the clerics, saints and martyrs among the ranks of the elect; note, too, that Jesus and God are portrayed as heavenly twins.

Just south of the museum, the fourteenth-century church of **Notre-Dame** has works by Mignard and Levieux, a lavish eighteenth-century altarpiece, a copy of Enguerrand Quarton's *Pietà* (the original is in the Louvre) and a late fourteenth-century cloister.

Chartreuse du Val de Bénédiction

allée des Muriers (04.90.15.24.24). **Open** *Apr-Sept* 9am-6.30pm daily; *Oct-Mar* 9.30am-5.30pm daily. **Admission** 32F, free children.

Fort St-André & Abbaye St-André

montée du Fort (fort 04.90.25.45.35/abbey 04.90.25. 55.95). **Open** *west tower* 10am-noon, 2-6pm daily. *Abbey* 10am-12.30pm, 2-6pm Tue-Sun. Abbey closed Jan. **Admission** *fort* 25F, free under-12s. *Abbey* 20F, 15F children.
Admission to the fort is free, but you have to pay to visit the tower and abbey.

Musée Pierre de Luxembourg

rue de la République (04.90.27.49.66). **Open** *Apr-Sept* 10am-12.30pm, 3-7pm Tue-Sun; *Oct-Jan, Mar* 10am-noon, 2-5.30pm Tue-Sun. Closed Feb. **Admission** 20F, free under-12s.

Notre-Dame

Centre Historique, pl du Chapitre. **Open** *Oct-Mar* 10am-noon, 2-5pm Tue-Sun; *Apr to mid-June, last two weeks Sept* 10am-12.30pm, 3-7pm Tue-Sun;

mid-June to mid-Sept 10am-12.30pm, 3-7pm daily. Closed Feb. **Admission** free.

Tour Philippe le Bel

rue Montée de la Tour (04.90.27.49.68). **Open** *Apr to mid-June, last two weeks Sept* 10am-12.30pm, 3-5pm Tue-Sun; *mid-June to mid-Sept* 10am-12.30pm, 3-5pm daily; *Oct-Jan, Mar* 10am-noon, 2-5.30pm Tue-Sun. Closed Feb. **Admission** 10F.

Where to stay & eat

Villeneuve's hotels absorb the overflow when Avignon's are booked out during the festival, but they're also worth considering in their own right. The luxury option is **Le Prieuré** (7 pl du Chapitre, 04.90.15.90.15, closed Nov to mid-Mar, rates 570F-1,350F), an exquisitely restored fourteenth-century palace with antiques in the bedrooms, hand-painted tiles in the bathrooms, a library, garden and pool. A cheaper option is the rustically furnished **Hôtel de l'Atelier** (5 rue de la Foire, 04.90.25.01.84, closed Nov, rates 250F-456F), with its pleasant walled patio.

Villeneuve's trendiest restaurant, **Mon Mari Etait Pâtissier** (3 bd Pasteur, 04.90.25.52.79, closed lunch daily, dinner Mon, menus 190F-250F) serves original dishes such as carpaccio of pumpkin with chanterelles and langoustine, and exquisite desserts. It functions as a *salon de thé* from 4pm. **Aubertin** (1 rue de l'Hôpital, 04.90.25.94.84, closed all day Sun and lunch Mon, menus 120F-275F) offers inventive cuisine at lower prices; try lasagne with *petits gris* (little snails) or rabbit brochette. You can consume the excellent ice-cream of the **Gelateria Notre-Dame** (8 rue Fabrigoule, 04.90.26.04.15, closed Mon) at terrace tables or take it away.

Getting there

By car

Villeneuve is just across the Pont Edouard Daladier from the centre of Avignon.

By bus

From Avignon, take bus 10 from porte l'Oulle.

By boat

From Avignon, take the Bateau-Bus (04.90.85.62.25) from allée de l'Oulle. It runs seven times a day in July and August; tickets cost 40F, 20F children.

Tourist information

Office du Tourisme

58 rue de la République (04.90.25.61.55/ fax 04.90.25.91.55). **Open** *July-Aug* 8.45am-12.30pm, 2-6pm Mon-Sat; *Sept-June* 8.45am-12.30pm, 2.30-6.30pm Mon-Sat.

Orange & Around

The Protestant stronghold of Orange has some impressive Roman monuments and a famous opera festival and is close to one of France's best-known wine regions.

Orange is where the A7 Autoroute du Soleil splits into two forks – the eastern one continuing to Marseille, Var and the Côte d'Azur, the western one heading down to Nîmes, Montpellier and the south-west. This is where the Rhône starts to get big and bloated, and its meanderings over the centuries have created a flat, agricultural landscape, rising into low hills here and there – as around the tiny wine enclave of **Châteauneuf-du-Pape**. On this eastern bank the evidence of Roman occupation is everywhere – most impressively at Orange and Vaison-la-Romaine. The western bank belonged to Languedoc and the King of France, while the east was Popish and Imperial. Today, the western side is dominated by a more modern construction – the Marcoule nuclear waste plant – but the medieval bridge of **Pont-St-Esprit** and the pretty old town of **Bagnols-sur-Cèze** are both worth a visit.

Orange

The ancient Roman city of Arausio was founded in 35 BC as a golden handshake for retiring soldiers of the Gallic second legion. During its Roman golden age, the colony was four times larger than today's town. Orange declined sharply in the Dark Ages, but picked up in the second half of the twelfth century, when it became an enclave within the Comtat Venaissin (*see chapter* **Carpentras**) governed by troubadour-prince Raimbaut d'Orange. In 1530, the town passed into the hands of a cadet branch of the German Protestant house of Nassau, and gave its name to the branch's Dutch principality 14 years later. Thereafter, Orange became a sort of Protestant buzzword and official logo – finding its way into Ulster's Orange Order and the Orange Free State – and the town itself attracted Protestant refugees from all over Provence.

The Dutch Nassaus managed to hold on to their little piece of France against the odds, and in 1622 Maurice de Nassau built an impressive chateau and fortifications around the town. Unfortunately, he used stones from the Roman monuments not previously destroyed by the Barbarians; only the Arc de Triomphe and the Théâtre Antique survived the pillaging. In

The **Théâtre Antique**.

1673, as Louis XIV was embarking on another war with Protestant Holland, he ordered the destruction of the chateau. The Treaty of Utrecht in 1713 finally gave the principality to France, but the proudly independent town has not forgotten its roots, and Queen Juliana of the Netherlands was back in 1952 to plant an oak tree on the site of the chateau above the town. The town is also home to the cavalry regiment of the French Foreign Legion and is one of only a handful of French towns with a National Front-led local council (*see box page 25*).

Geographically and emotionally, the **Théâtre Antique** dominates the town. Quite simply, this is the best-preserved Roman amphitheatre anywhere. What sets it apart from similar theatres is the unrivalled state of preservation of the stage wall, a massive, sculpted sandstone screen 36 metres high, which Louis XIV referred to as 'the finest wall in my kingdom'. The amphitheatre was a multifunctional space, like the *salles polyvalentes* that litter municipal France: it would have hosted everything from political meetings to concerts, sporting events and plays. In the fourth century, the theatre was abandoned and makeshift houses were built within the auditorium; it was not until the nineteenth century that restoration began and the famous opera festival, the **Chorégies d'Orange**, was born (*see box page 104*).

On top of the hill of St-Eutrope, into which the curve of the seats was excavated, is a pleasant park with the ruins of the **chateau** (free access) and the **Piscine des Cèdres**, an open-air swimming pool (04.90.34.09.68, open mid-June to Aug) – a temptation in a town that can get very hot and dusty in summer.

Opposite the main entrance to the theatre, the **Musée Municipal** houses an interesting collection of Roman artefacts, including a unique series of *cadastres*. These engraved marble tablets map the streets, administrative divisions and geographical features of the Orange region in Roman times over the course of three successive surveys (the earliest dates from AD 77). On the top floor is an unsuspected curiosity: a selection of post-impressionist paintings by Welsh artist Frank Brangwyn. The local tradition of the printed cotton cloth known as *indiennes* is celebrated in another series of paintings by eighteenth-century artist GM Rossetti. Modern-day *indiennes* fabric can be tracked down at **La Provençale** (5 pl Sylvain). Note that admission to the Théâtre Antique includes entrance to the museum.

The old town, in front of the theatre, is a tight knot of twisting streets that liven up in summer during the opera festival but provide little architectural competition to the towering classical monuments. The second of these monuments – at the northern edge of the old town – is the **Arc de Triomphe**, a Roman triumphal arch spanning the former Via Agrippa, which linked Lyon to Arles. Built in 20 BC in honour of the Gallic second legion that founded the city, it is the third largest arch of its kind in the world, and the north side is a riot of well-preserved carving, with military paraphernalia arranged in abstract patterns.

Musée Municipal

rue Madeleine Roch (04.90.51.18.24). **Open** *Apr-Sept* 9.30am-7pm daily; *Oct-March* 9.30am-noon, 2.30-5.30pm daily.

Théâtre Antique

junction of av Général Leclerc and rue St-Clément (04.90.51.17.60). **Open** *Apr-Sept* 9.30am-6.30pm daily; *Oct-Mar* 9.30am-noon, 1.30-5pm daily. **Admission** 30F, 25F children.

Where to eat

Aigo Bolido (20 pl Silvain, 04.90.34.18.19, closed Sun, menus 70F-150F) is a bit heavy on local colour, but handy for the Théâtre Antique, and has an interesting Provençal menu. Next door, **Le Yaca** (24 pl Silvain, 04.90.34.70.03, closed dinner Tue from Sept-July, all Wed, closed Nov, menus 65F-125F) specialises in game and traditional fare. **Le Forum** (3 rue Mazeau, 04.90.34.01.09, closed lunch Sat in July & Aug, all Mon from Sept-June, last two weeks Feb, menus 88F-230F) offers seasonal dishes such as *lièvre à la Royale* (a ritzy hare stew) and other Provençal specialities, while **La Grotte** (35 montée des Princes, 04.90.34.70.98, closed lunch Sat from Sept-June, first two weeks June, menus 60F-112F) is a fun place in a cave. The good-value menu features *Flintstones* specialities such as meat cooked on hot stones, alongside more conventional dishes.

Where to stay

Arcotel

8 pl aux Herbes (04.90.34.09.23/fax 04.90.51.61.12). **Rates** single 150F-220F, double 200F-230F. **Credit** DC, MC, V.
A charmingly positioned hotel on a small square in the old town. Basic but attractive.

St Eurotrope, patron saint of Orange.

Les Chorégies d'Orange

This spectacular festival has the muscle to attract the greatest names in opera, who come for the privilege of singing in the Roman theatre, without amplification, to upwards of 9,000 spectators. Providing the mistral doesn't get up, the acoustics are surprisingly good. There used to be no more than two performances a year, but recently these have been extended to seven or more – in July and August – amid pressure to create more of a season and make the event more relevant to the local population. Tickets should be booked well in advance, either from the main office or from FNAC stores around the country.

Bureau des Chorégies d'Orange

18 pl Sylvain, 84107 Orange (04.90.34.24.24/fax 04.90.11.04.04). **Open** *June-Sept* 9am-6pm Mon-Sat; *Oct-May* 9am-noon, 2-5pm Mon-Fri. **Tickets** 20F-990F depending on performance. *Website: www.choregies.Asso.Fr*

Arène

pl Langes (04.90.11.40.40/fax 04.90.34.85.48). **Closed** last two weeks Nov. **Rates** single 440F, double 500F, suite 700F. **Credit** AmEx, DC, MC, V. The most comfortable hotel in the town centre, on a quiet square. Not a stylish option, but the place is above average and has been recently renovated. There is no restaurant.

Château de Rochegude

Rochegude, 15km north of Orange on the D11 (04.75.97.21.10/fax 04.75.04.89.87). **Rates** single 550F-1,400F, double 700F-2,000F, suite 2,400F-3,000F. **Meals served** *July-Sept* noon-2pm, 7-9.15pm daily; *Oct-June* noon-2pm Wed-Sun; 7-9.15pm Thur-Sat. **Menus** 200F-650F. **Credit** AmEx, DC, MC, V. The ultimate luxury option. With a fine view across to the Dentelles de Montmirail and Mont Ventoux, this Relais et Châteaux hotel occupies a grand country castle, parts of which date back to the twelfth century. The atmosphere is formal but welcoming, and the hotel is set in a park, complete with pool and tennis courts. Deer gambol in the grounds, touchingly unaware of the propensity of chef Pascal Alonso to include venison on his classically assured menu. The restaurant is pricey if you go à la carte (around 500F a head), but the 200F 'menu du marché' is a good-value excuse for a treat.

Glacier

46 cours Aristide Briand (04.90.34.02.01/fax 04.90.51.13.80). **Closed** Sun from Jan-Apr, 23 Dec-23 Jan. **Rates** single 300F-340F, double 300F-360F. **Credit** AmEx, DC, MC, V. Outstandingly helpful staff and a central position on the edge of the old town make this simple hotel a useful option. No restaurant.

Getting there

By car
From the A7, take exit no.21.

By train
Although Orange's SNCF station (av Frédéric Mistral, 1.5km east of the centre) is on the main Paris-Avignon-Marseille route, the TGV doesn't stop there; from Paris, you have to change to a local train at Valence. Recorded information: 08.36.35.35.35.

By bus
Numerous buses run from Avignon to Orange and a handful of them continue on to Montélimar or Vaison-la-Romaine. The *gare routière* (04.90.81.51.15) is on cours Pourtolues, just east of the Théâtre Antique.

Tourist information
Market day is Thursday morning.

Office de Tourisme
5 cours Aristide Briand (04.90.34.70.88/fax 04.90.34.99.62). **Open** *Apr-Sept* 9am-7pm Mon-Sat; 10am-6pm Sun; *Oct-Mar* 10am-1pm, 2-5pm Mon-Sat. There is also a smaller, summer-only information bureau opposite the Théâtre Antique (open 10am-1pm, 2-7pm Mon-Sat from June-Sept).

Around Orange

Châteauneuf-du-Pape

Another of those places – like Sancerre or Roquefort – that says what it does. Just to reinforce the point, the road south from Orange has vines growing right to the edge of the tarmac, their grapes destined not only for the princely Rhône red that takes its name from the village, but also Côtes du Rhône and the Côtes du Rhône Villages, all within a few kilometres of each other. As every second farm is a wine estate, invitations to visit and taste are thick on the ground. The local tourist office offers a comprehensive list of vineyard visits in the area. A strong nerve is required to resist buying when you have sniffed, sipped and slurped every vintage from the past ten years, but the local winemakers are a philosophical crowd and will not curse or kill your first-born if you don't buy a case.

The original vineyards were planted in the fourteenth century at the instigation of the popes of Avignon – commemorated in the village's name – who summered here in the castle built by wine-lover Jean XXII in 1316. The tight rules regarding yield and grape varieties laid down by the local winemakers' association in 1923 were farsighted blueprints for France's *appellation d'origine contrôlée* regulations, and sealed the reputation of the local red, which is a blend of eight different varieties, dominated by Grenache. The alluvial soil, sprinkled with heat-absorbing pebbles, the

widely spaced vines (maximising exposure to the sun) and the cloud-dispersing mistral all contribute to the muscular alcoholic content (12.5 per cent) and complex nose of the wine. Recently, white Châteauneuf-du-Pape – a five-grape blend – has made a name for itself, too.

All that wine money has at least been put to good use. Châteauneuf-du-Pape is an outstandingly beautiful village, tastefully restored, with a characterful centre. One of the local winemakers, le Père Anselme, has had the clever marketing idea of opening a museum to celebrate the winemaking traditions of the area: the **Musée des Outils de Vignerons**. The exhibition of baskets, pruners and suchlike is

Châteauneuf-du-Pape takes its wine seriously.

Avignon & the Vaucluse

interesting enough, but the shop and tasting room at the end of the visit are what this is all about. There is also a good local chocolate factory, **Bernard Castelain** (04.90.83.54.71), on the Avignon road.

To work off that hangover, climb up to the ruins of the fourteenth-century **Château des Papes**, destroyed in the Wars of Religion in the sixteenth century. Little remains of the building, but the view over the surrounding countryside and the winding Rhône Valley below is quite exceptional.

Musée des Outils de Vignerons

pl du Portail (04.90.83.70.07). **Open** *July-Sept* 9am-7pm daily; *Oct-Mar* 9am-noon, 2-6pm daily; *Apr-June* 8am-noon, 2-5pm daily. **Admission** free.

Where to stay & eat

Châteauneuf is a good base, and a necessary one if you want to avoid drink-driving. **La Garbure** (3 rue Joseph Ducos, 04.90.83.75.08, closed Sun Oct-Jan, closed mid-Feb to mid-Mar) in the main street of the village is an attractive, simple regional choice, both for local cuisine and the comfortable rooms (345F-365F) in an old townhouse. For something more elaborate, try the **Château des Fines Roches**, two kilometres south-east off the D17 to Avignon (04.90.83.70.23, closed Sun & Mon from Oct-May, last two weeks Nov, rates 650F-1,100F), a nineteenth-century faux chateau, beautifully situated in the heart of a vineyard. It has a good but pricey restaurant (closed as hotel and every Mon, menus 175F-340F).

Seven kilometres north-east, just beyond the autoroute, is Courthezon, an unspoiled village with a well-preserved set of twelfth-century ramparts, where you can get simple *auberge* meals at **Lou Pequelet** (pl Edouard Daladier, 04.90.70.28.96, closed Sun, menus 68F-118F).

Getting there

By car

From Orange, take the D68. From Avignon, take the N7, then the D17.

By bus

The Orange-Roquemare bus service passes through Châteauneuf: contact Autocars Transports Voyages (04.66.82.64.39).

Tourist information

Office de Tourisme

pl du Portail (04.90.83.71.08/fax 04.90.34.99.62). **Open** *June-Sept* 9am-7pm Mon-Sat; 10am-5pm Sun; *Oct-May* 9am-12.30pm, 2-6pm Mon, Tue, Thur-Sat.

Pont-St-Esprit

The 'Bridge of the Holy Spirit' spans the Rhône just where it enters Provence. Built between 1265 and 1319 by a brotherhood inspired by one Jéhan de Thianges from the St-Pierre monastery, who was 'led by divine inspiration', the bridge was originally a more elaborate affair with bastions and towers, which have long since been destroyed. It remains an impressive curved structure, with 19 of the 25 arches still in their original state; a good view of it can be had from the esplanade between the churches of St-Pierre and St-Saturnin in the old town.

Pont-St-Esprit was badly bombed in World War II and was at the centre of a scandal in 1951, when the bread of the town was mysteriously poisoned. In the town itself, pretty rue St-Jacques is named after the pilgrims who stayed here on their way to Santiago in Spain. At No.2, in the twelfth-century Maison des Chevaliers, is the **Musée d'Art Sacré du Gard**. Its collection of religious paintings and artefacts might not set your pulse on fire, but the building itself is a well-preserved example of a merchant's house and was inhabited by the same family for six centuries.

More odds and ends, including a collection of 220 early eighteenth-century pharmacy jars, are on display in the **Musée Paul Raymond**, housed in the former town hall.

Musée d'Art Sacré du Gard

2 rue St-Jacques (04.66.39.17.61). **Open** *mid-June to mid-Sept* 10am-noon, 3-7pm Tue-Sun; *mid-Sept to Jan, Mar to mid-June* 10am-noon, 2-6pm Tue-Sun. Closed Feb. **Admission** 20F, 12F children.

Musée Paul Raymond

pl de l'Hôtel-de-Ville (04.66.90.75.80). **Open** call for details. Closed Feb. **Admission** 12F.

Where to stay & eat

For emergency accommodation, the **Auberge Provençale** (on the Nîmes road, 04.66.39.08.79, rates 160F-195F) is the best bet – it's simple and clean, with a popular local restaurant (menus 60F-110F). Typical Provençal fare is served up at **Lou Recati** (rue Jean-Jacques, 04.66.90.73.01, closed lunch Sat, all Mon, first two weeks Oct, menus 125F-195F), right in the centre of the old town's narrow streets.

Getting there

By car

Take the Bollène exit (no.19) on the A7, then the N86 to Pont-St-Esprit.

By bus

The Avignon-Montélimar service passes through Pont-St-Esprit: contact Cars Auran (04.66.39.10.40). Another service, Sotra (04.75.39.40.22), runs a morning bus between Avignon and Mayres via Pont-St-Esprit.

Tourist information

Market day is Saturday morning.

Office de Tourisme

1 rue Vauban (04.66.39.44.45/fax 04.66.39.51.81). **Open** 8.30am-12.30pm, 1.30-5.30pm Mon-Fri.

Bagnols-sur-Cèze

There are two reasons to come to Bagnols: it has one of the best markets in the region, and one of the most satisfying small museums. And if you are a fan of nuclear processing plants, there is a third reason: the **Centre Atomique de Marcoule**, a plutonium factory on the banks of the Rhône, which has quadrupled the town's population (by adding employees, rather than affecting the birth rate) and which has a visitor's centre. Visits can be arranged in July and August only through Bagnols' tourist office (*see below*).

The old town, though, gives no sign of the horrors beyond. Rue Crémieux, which runs up to the delightful place Mallet, is filled with fine townhouses dating from the sixteenth to the eighteenth centuries. Look up at the riotous gargoyles of No.15 and browse in the organic food shop in the courtyard. On the second floor of the town hall, a seventeenth-century mansion on place Mallet, the **Musée Albert André** is the town's big cultural draw. In 1923, a fire destroyed the museum's parochial collection of daubs. Painter Albert André, who was standing in as curator, launched an appeal – with the assistance of his friend Renoir – to the artists of France. They responded in force, and today the museum provides a snapshot of early twentieth-century figurative art, with works by Renoir, Signac, Bonnard, Matisse, Gauguin and others. Memories of the town's rich archaeological past, both Celtic-Ligurian and Gallo-Roman, are found in the **Musée d'Archéologie Léon Alègre**.

North-west of Bagnols, the valley of the Cèze provides a bucolic detour from the main Rhône flow. Perched above the river, ten kilometres from Bagnols, **La Roque-sur-Cèze** is a picture-postcard village with a fine Romanesque church, approached by an ancient single-track bridge. Just downstream from here, the Cèze cuts through the limestone to form the spectacular, swirling Cascade de Sautadet. North of La Roque, in the middle of an oak forest that would not be out of place in a medieval romance, is the **Chartreuse de Valbonne**, a thirteenth-century Carthusian monastery with glazed roof tiles and an elaborate interior, rebuilt with baroque enthusiasm and now serving as a winery. The surrounding forest is a great place for walks.

Chartreuse de Valbonne

15min after A9 turn-off (04.66.90.41.24). **Open** 9am-noon, 1.30-5.30pm daily. **Admission** 18F.

Musée Albert André

pl Mallet (04.66.50.50.56). **Open** *July, Aug* 10am-12.30pm, 2-6.30pm Tue-Sun; *Sept-Jan, Mar-June* 10am-noon, 2-6pm Tue-Sun. Closed Feb. **Admission** 20F.

Musée d'Archéologie Léon Alègre

24 av Paul Langevin (04.66.89.74.00). **Open** 10am-noon, 2-6pm Thur-Sat. **Admission** 20F.

Where to stay & eat

Five kilometres north of Bagnols on the N86, the **Hôtel Valaurie** (04.66.89.66.22, rates 270F-310F) lacks a pool, but is a comfortable enough stop. The luxury option is the **Château de Montcaud** (04.66.89.60.60, closed mid-Nov to mid-Apr, rates 944F-1,385F), a fine nineteenth-century pile with wooded grounds, a nice pool and a Turkish bath, five kilometres west of Bagnol via the D6 and D143. Its restaurant, **Les Jardins de Montcaud** (closed lunch Mon, Tue & Sat and dinner Sun except in July & Aug), is in a stone *mas,* with tables on a rose-covered patio in summer, and offers fine country cooking at a surprisingly reasonable price.

For a quick snack in Bagnols, the **Crêperie Saladerie Clementine** (12 pl Mallet, 04.66.89.42.26, average 70F) has a terrace looking over the prettiest of squares. At La Roque, the pleasant waterside inn **Le Mas du Belier** (04.66.82.78.73, call for details) is ideal for a romantic meal. **La Tonnelle** (04.66.82.79.37, closed Nov-Mar, rates 300F-340F), at the entrance to the village, has a couple of inexpensive *chambres d'hôte* rooms.

Getting there

By car

Take the Bollène exit (no.19) on the A7, then follow signs to Bagnols via Pont-St-Esprit.

By bus

The frequent Avignon-Montélimar service passes through Bagnols: contact Cars Auran (04.66.39.10.40).

Tourist information

Market day is Wednesday morning.

Office de Tourisme

Espace St-Gilles, av Léon Blum (04.66.89.54.61/fax 04.66.89.83.38). **Open** *July, Aug* 9am-7pm Mon-Sat; *Sept-June* 9am-noon, 1.30-6pm Mon-Sat.

Carpentras & Around

The historic Comtat Venaissin has a robust daily life that won't allow it to be consigned to the past.

The area around Carpentras, excluding the former principality of Orange but including Mont Ventoux and Vaison-la-Romaine, is known as the Comtat Venaissin. For over half a millennium this was a papal enclave inside French territory, a sort of huge, rural Vatican City. Ceded to the Holy See in 1274, the Comtat remained in papal hands until 1791, when it was reunited with France. Carpentras took over from Pernes in 1320 as the capital of this pretty, bucolic enclave, which has since become one of the country's main market gardens, famous for fruit, vegetables and truffles.

Carpentras

Carpentras, a bustling town of 30,000 souls, is a good, solidly provincial antidote to tourist fatigue. Though there are no must-see monuments, the place is full of character, with an independent spirit and a few surprises that make it worth a detour.

The four museums are dusty institutions, not without interest but low on presentation. The **Musée Comtadin** and the **Musée Duplessis** are in the same building; the first concentrates on the customs and history of the region, while the Duplessis floor is dedicated to local primitive painting. More charming is the **Musée Sobirats**, a well-preserved pre-Revolutionary nobleman's house. The **Musée Lapidaire** on rue des Stes-Maries, currently closed for restoration, is an eighteenth-century chapel with columns from the cloisters of the city's original Romanesque cathedral.

The **Cathédrale St Siffrein** is an extraordinary mishmash of styles and epochs, ranging from fifteenth-century Provençal Gothic to an early twentieth-century bell tower. The fifteenth-century door on the south side is

The Jews of Carpentras

When King Philippe le Bel expelled the Jews from France in the fifteenth century, many of them fled to the papal-controlled Comtat Venaissin around Carpentras, where a not entirely disinterested Pope Clement gave them shelter. In fact, conversion was very much on the agenda, and many Jews were blackmailed or bullied into a Catholic baptism. For those that declined, life was not easy: they were forced to wear a distinguishing cap, and to pay to enter and leave the ghetto. Carpentras' Synagogue (pl de la Mairie, 04.90.63.39.97, open 10am-noon, 3-5pm Mon-Fri) is the oldest in France, dating from the fourteenth century, though largely rebuilt in the eighteenth. The ancient lower floors, where there are ovens and a piscina for women's purification rites, are currently closed for restoration, but you can visit the sanctuary (men must wear a yarmulke) and

see its eighteenth-century decoration. Today, the Jewish community numbers just 122, but the culture remains strong. The Jewish cemetery just outside the town was desecrated some years ago – an event that failed to quell strong local support for the extreme-right National Front.

The **synagogue.**

known as the Porte des Juifs: here, chained Jews passed through on their way to 'conversion' (*see box*). Note the carved rats gnawing on a globe above the door, explanations of which are as numerous as they are unconvincing. The cathedral's interior is rather gloomy but the treasury (admission 2F) is worth a look for its fourteenth-century wooden statues.

Behind the cathedral, the glassed-in **Passage Boyer** – the result of a mid-eighteenth-century job creation scheme – leads to the **Hôtel Dieu**, a fine eighteenth-century building that once housed a hospital. The pharmacy contains a rich collection of decorative earthenware; there's also a baroque chapel containing the tomb of the founder.

An occasionally interesting arts festival takes place in the second fortnight of July. More lively, perhaps, is the weekly market on Fridays. If you're visiting between December and February, watch out for the area's famous black truffles (*rabasses*). Another local speciality, brightly coloured humbugs called *berlingots*, are available all year.

Devotees of the Marquis de Sade will be disappointed – or amused – to know that his château in the nearby village of Mazan is now an old people's home.

Cathédrale St Siffrein
pl St-Siffrein (04.90.63.08.33). **Open** 7am-5pm daily.

Hôtel Dieu
pl Aristide Briand (04.90.63.80.00). **Open** 9am-11am Mon, Wed, Thur. **Admission** 4F.

Musées Comtadin & Duplessis
234 bd A Durand (04.90.63.04.92). **Open** Apr-Oct 10am-noon, 2-6pm Wed-Mon; Nov-Mar 10am-noon, 2-4pm Wed-Mon. **Admission** 2F. **No credit cards**.

Musée Sobirats
rue du Collège (04.90.63.04.92). **Open** Apr-Oct 10am-noon, 2-6pm Wed-Mon; Nov-Mar 10am-noon, 2-4pm Wed-Mon. **Admission** 2F. **No credit cards**.

Where to eat

L'Atelier de Pierre (30 pl de l'Horloge, 04.90.60.75.00, closed lunch Mon, lunch Sun, menus 115F-250F), set in a delightful square near the cathedral, is the only really upmarket gastronomic choice. The central **Le Vert Galant** (12 rue de Clapiès, 04.90.67.15.50, closed lunch Sat, dinner Sun, menus 130F-390F) offers a truffle special in season. **Le Marijo** (73 rue Raspail, 04.90.60.42.65, closed Sun, menus 80F-165F) is a Provençal bistro offering local specialities such as aïoli. Tucked behind the tourist office, the **La Garrigue** pizzeria (90 rue Cottier, 04.90.63.21.24, closed Sun, average 85F-125F) offers good value for money.

Hôtel Dieu.

Where to stay

Le Fiacre (153 rue Vigne, 04.90.63.03.15, rates 190F-480F), set in a characterful old townhouse, is the best of the hotels in the centre. **La Bastide Ste-Agnès** (1043 chemin de la Fourtrounse, 04.90.60.03.01, closed mid-Nov to mid-Mar, rates 360F-750F) is a luxurious *chambre d'hôte* with pool on the outskirts of the town. **L'Hermitage** (rte Pernes-les-Fontaines, 04.90.66.51.41, closed Jan & Feb, rates 410F-500F), between Pernes and Carpentras, is a comfortable country-house style hotel with a nice garden and pool.

Getting there

By car
Autoroute A7 to Orange, then D950 to Carpentras.

By bus
Four services a day (fewer at weekends) from Marseille to Carpentras operated by Cars Arnaud (04.90.63.01.82). Also an 8am daily service (also 12.10pm Wed) from Vaison-la-Romaine, run by Cars Comtadins (04.90.67.20.25).

Tourist information

Office du Tourisme
170 av Jean Jaurès (04.90.63.00.78/ fax 04.90.60.41.02). **Open** 9am-12.30pm, 2-6.30pm Mon-Sat.

Around Carpentras

Pernes-les-Fontaines

The 37 fountains that give Pernes its name and fame date from the mid-eighteenth century. It's a good place to while away an afternoon, with fine old houses, chapels and towers. The sixteenth-century **Porte Notre-Dame** town gate – a remnant of city walls demolished in the

The **Fontaine du Cormoran**.

Where to stay & eat

The Michelin-starred **Au Fil du Temps** (pl
Louis Giraud, 04.90.66.48.61, closed dinner Tue,
all Wed, menus 105F-295F) is presided over by
young chef Frédéric Robert, whose market-fresh
dishes are still offered at affordable prices,
especially on the set menus. For simple fare and
friendly accommodation try **Hôtel-restaurant
La Margelle** (pl Aristide Briand,
04.90.61.30.36, rates 160F-240F, closed dinner
Mon, all Tue, menus 95F-145F).

Getting there

By car
D938 from Carpentras.

By bus
Cars Arnaud (04.90.63.01.82) runs seven buses daily
from Carpentras to Pernes-les-Fontaines, and its
Carpentras-Marseille service also stops off in Pernes.

Tourist information

Office du Tourisme
*pl du Comtat Venaissin (04.90.61.31.04/fax
04.92.61.33.23).* **Open** *mid-June to mid-Sept* 9am-
noon, 2-7.30pm daily; *mid-Sept to mid-June* 9am-
noon, 2-5pm Mon-Sat.

nineteenth century – incorporates the chapel of
Notre-Dame-des-Grâces. Nearby is the most
striking of Pernes' fountains, the **Fontaine du
Cormoran**, crowned by a cormorant and
featuring the town's emblem of a pearl and the
sun. Nearby, the simple church of **Notre-
Dame-de-Nazareth** has sections dating from
the eleventh century. Pernes' artistic jewels are
the thirteenth-century frescoes on the upper
floors of the **Tour Ferrande** (contact the
tourist office to arrange a visit); among the
oldest in France, they depict biblical stories and
scenes from the life of Charles d'Anjou. The
tower overlooks the **Fontaine Guillaumin** or
'du Gigot', so called because of its resemblance
to a leg of lamb. The town's other tower, the
Tour de l'Horloge (rue du Donjon), is all that
remains of the château of the Counts of
Toulouse, who ruled over Pernes from 1125 to
1320, when it was the capital of the Comtat
Venaissin. Climb to the top for views across the
Avignon plain and north to Mont Ventoux and
the Dentelles de Montmirail. Locals will tell you
that if you drink the water from the **Fontaine
de la Lune** at the base of the fourteenth-
century **Porte St Gilles**, you'll go quite, quite
mad. Should the water have no effect, console
yourself with pastries from the excellent
boulangerie in place Aristide Briand.

Mont Ventoux

When the Italian poet Petrarch reached the
summit of Mont Ventoux in 1336, he was
gobsmacked. Faced by 'the strange lightness of
the air and the immensity of the spectacle', he
wrote, 'I remained immobile, stupefied'.
Petrarch has been credited with inventing the
sport of mountain climbing with this ascent – it
had never occurred to anybody to do such a
thing just for the hell of it. Nowadays, the
summit is easily reached by a hairpin-kinked,
graffiti-daubed road built in the 1930s, though
in summer crowds of cyclists make the job as
hard as possible for themselves by panting up
to the oh-so-picturesque air force radar station
and television masts on the summit.

The spreading mass of the mountain
dominates the entire Rhône valley. As you
climb, the vegetation changes noticeably, as
does the temperature. Winds can howl across
Mont Ventoux ('windy mountain') at up to 250
kilometres an hour. At 1,909 metres, the barren
summit is snow-capped in winter and often
shrouded in mist in summer; on a clear day,
though, the view is spectacular.

An alternative approach to the summit is to
continue south towards Carpentras for three
kilometres and take the quieter and prettier D19,

which runs past the remains of a seventeenth-century aqueduct to the Belvedere du Paty viewpoint above Crillon-le-Brave. To the east, the village of **Bédoin** with its fine church is the last village of any size before the long haul to the top. It's also the starting point for a four-hour hike to the summit; information from the tourist office (*see below*), which also organises night ascents on Fridays in summer.

Mont Ventoux is famous for *épeautre*, or wild barley. Previously known (and disregarded) as the poor man's wheat, this grain has been revived as a local gastronomic treat, served in a broth and washed down with the local red wine, Côtes du Ventoux.

Where to stay & eat

The centuries-old buildings of the stunning **Hostellerie de Crillon-le-Brave** (pl de l'Eglise, 04.90.65.61.61, closed Jan to mid-Mar, rates 900F-2,600F) below the southern slopes of Ventoux have been tastefully restored, bringing a touch of Tuscany to the windy mountain. The atmosphere is welcoming, with log fires and a friendly country-house atmosphere; the cooking is sophisticated with a Provençal twist (restaurant closed dinner Mon-Fri, menus 240F-390F). East of Bédoin, six kilometres along the Mont Ventoux road, is **Le Mas des Vignes** (04.90.65.63.91; closed Dec-Easter, average

160F-220F), with fine food and spectacular views over the Dentelles. The **Hôtel Pins** (a kilometre out of Bédoin on chemin des Crans, 04.90.65.92.92, closed Dec-Mar, rates 340F-365F) is in a beautiful position and has a pool.

Getting there

By car
Take autoroute A7 to Orange, then D975 to Mont Ventoux.

By bus
Carpentras-Bédoin service operated by Cars Comtadins (04.90.67.20.25) 3 times daily.

Tourist information

For skiing information contact either the *mairie* in Beaumont-du-Ventoux (04.90.65.21.13) or the Chalet d'Accueil at Mont Serein (04.90.63.42.02).

Office de Tourisme
Espace Marie-Louis Gravier, pl du Marché, Bédoin (04.90.65.63.95/04.90.12.81.55). **Open** 9am-12.30pm, 2-6pm Mon-Sat.

Les Dentelles de Montmirail

Dentelle means lace, and the curious limestone formations of these peaks certainly decorate the skyline, though they resemble spiky teeth

Mont Ventoux rises behind the Dentelles de Montmirail.

(*dents*) more than the fringe of your grandmother's tablecloth. Formed out of Jurassic limestone pushed upwards then eroded, the Dentelles are popular with walkers, rock-climbers and artists, and are surrounded by some pretty villages that turn out a very quaffable wine.

Malaucène, on the road that separates the Dentelles from Mont Ventoux, is the jumping-off point for both. Heading south to **Le Barroux**, don't panic if you see llamas: there is an experimental farm here. In the village is a castle (admission 20F). Very little of the original twelfth-century building exists, but the views over the Dentelles are great.

On the road to **Beaumes-de-Venise** is the pretty Romanesque chapel of **Notre-Dame-d'Aubune**. A graceful terraced village, Beaumes is famous for its sweet dessert wine, made from the Muscat grape, a marketing phenomenon in Britain in the 1980s. Beaumes' olive oil is also worth a spin: see it pressed at **La Balméenne**.

Perched on the western flank of the Dentelles is the tiny village of **Gigondas**, which gives its name to the famous Grenache-based red wine: the tourist office (*see below*) will tell you where you can taste and buy it. Above Gigondas lies the **Col du Cayronis** pass, a mecca for rock-climbers. A little to the north, an excellent Côtes du Rhône Villages wine is produced around the village of **Séguret**. Car-free and oozing charm, Séguret gets more tourist attention than is good for it, with its twelfth-century church, picturesque old houses and village square with views extending to the Massif Central. On Christmas Eve, the locals turn the village into a living nativity crib.

La Balméenne

bd Jules Ferry (04.90.62.94.15). **Open** 8am-noon, 2-6pm Mon-Sat. **Admission** free.

Where to stay & eat

Near Gigondas the restaurant-hotel **Les Florets** (04.90.65.85.01, closed Jan & Feb, rates 420F) is situated in the middle of a vineyard two kilometres east of the village; it has a good restaurant with Provençal staples (menus 130F-180F). In the village of Montmirail, the **Montmirail Hôtel** (6 km south on D7 and D8, 04.90.65.84.01, closed Nov-Mar; rates 425F-475F) has a pool and garden. A sporty alternative is the fairly basic **Gîte d'Etape des Dentelles** in Gigondas (04.90.65.80.85, rates 75F), which provides courses and information on outdoor activities in the mountains.

Getting there

By car

Best access points are Malaucène, on the D938 Vaison-Carpentras road, and Beaumes-de-Venise, 18km east of the Orange Sud exit on the A7.

By bus

Sablet, 5km north of Gigondas, is served by the Orange-Vaison bus (3-4 services daily; Cars Lieutaud, 04.90.36.05.22). Malaucène is on the once-daily Vaison-Carpentras line (Cars Comtadins, 04.90.67.20.25).

Tourist information

The Club Alpin Français de Provence in Marseille (0 4.91.54.3694) organises accompanied climbing trips in the Dentelles.

Gigondas

Office de Tourisme, pl du Portail (04.90.65.85.46). **Open** *Apr-Nov* 10am-noon, 2-6pm daily; *Dec-Mar* 10am-noon, 2-6pm Mon-Fri.

Malaucène

Syndicat d'Initiative, pl de la Mairie (04.90.65.22.59). **Open** 10am-noon Mon-Sat.

Vaison-la-Romaine

Oozing history, elegant Vaison wears its origins in its name. A proudly independent, prosperous town since Roman times, when it was federated to the empire rather then colonised, its pale, red-roofed houses straddle the banks of the Ouvèze river.

This rural watercourse may not look like much, but in September 1992, swollen by heavy rains, the Ouvèze turned into a raging torrent, sweeping away houses, caravans and an entire industrial estate, and killing 37 people. Incredibly, of the town's two bridges, it was the modern road bridge that was destroyed; the 2,000-year-old **Pont Romain** lost its parapet – since rebuilt – but otherwise held up to the onslaught.

Today, Vaison has picked itself up and gone back to being chic and neat and discreet – qualities appreciated by the Parisian second-homers who converge here each summer. The old town, perched on a cliff south of the river and dominated by the twelfth-century château of the Counts de Toulouse – with a fine view of Mont Ventoux – is a web of twisting streets with picturesque medieval houses.

The modern town – built up from the eighteenth century on, when the old town was virtually abandoned – covers the original Roman nucleus of Vaison, north of the river across the Pont Romain. By the time excavations began in earnest in 1907, only the suburbs of the Roman town were left for the archaeologists to explore. Two slices were exposed – the Quartier de Puymin and the Quartier de la Villasse, which face each other on either side of avenue Général de Gaulle. The ticket gives admission to the Roman ruins, the on-site museum and the cloisters of the town's cathedral, Notre-Dame-de-Nazareth, open the same hours.

To put the site in context, start at the museum in the middle of the **Quartier de Puymin**. Admirably organised, the collection features statues, inscriptions, mosaics and domestic objects found in and around Vaison. Especially striking is a marble family group, dating from AD 121, showing a stark-naked Emperor Hadrian standing proudly next to his elaborately dressed wife, who's clearly trying to humour her husband.

Behind the museum is the Roman amphitheatre, set back into a hill as at Orange. This is the venue for the town's summer music and theatre festival, **L'Eté de Vaison**, held from mid-July to mid-August (information 04.90.28.84.49; *see also chapter* **By Season**). The rest of the ruins in this area make heavy demands on the imagination; better head out past the tourist office (which also sells regional produce) to the other chunk of excavations, the **Quartier de la Villasse**. Here the paved and colonnaded main street, with its huge paving stones and monumental scale, evokes the power and prosperity of Roman Vaison better than any other sight. On either side are the remains of shops, baths and villas, including a 5,000-square-metre property with private baths and a large hanging garden.

Notre-Dame-de-Nazareth, a ten-minute walk west on avenue Jules Ferry, is a fine and unusual example of Provençal Romanesque architecture, with particularly fine carving. Recent excavations show that the cathedral proper was built on the ruins of an important

Roman building, which you can see crushed under the foundations. Inside, the most notable feature is the eleventh-century high altar, on four delicate marble columns. Up the hill north of the cathedral is the curious **Chapelle de St Quenin**, a Romanesque building with a unique triangular apse, based on an earlier Roman temple – indeed, for centuries the locals thought it *was* Roman. You'll need to pick up the key at the tourist office (ID is required as security).

Quartiers de Puymin & de la Villasse

04.90.36.02.11 (tourist office). **Open** *June, Sept* 9.30am-12.30pm daily; *July, Aug* 9.30am-1pm daily; *Mar-May, Oct* 10am-1pm, 2-6pm Mon, Wed-Sun; *Nov-Feb* 10am-noon, 2-4.30pm Mon, Wed-Sun. **Admission** 40F.

Where to stay & eat

The best views are from the medieval town, and the **Hostellerie le Beffroi** (rue de l'Evêché, 04.90.36.04.71, closed Feb & Mar, rates 465F-650F) has one of the finest, from a charming sixteenth-century building replete with period furnishings and antiques; the attached restaurant (closed Nov-Mar, menus 145F-240F) offers good value on high-class fare. For a simpler meal in this area, **Vieux Vaison** (8 pl du Poids, 04.90.36.19.45, closed Wed & Jan, menus 55F-110F) has a pleasant terrace overlooking the lower town. Basic but neat, the **Brin d'Olivier** (4 rue du Ventoux, 04.90.28.74.79, closed lunch Sat, all Wed, rates 400F-550F, menus 80F-350F) is an attractive small hotel with a few rooms around a courtyard. **Le Bateleur** (1 pl Théodore Aubanel, 04.90.36.28.04, closed dinner Sun, all Mon and mid-Nov to mid-Dec, menus 118F-155F) is a serious family restaurant with delicious specialities such as scorpion fish soufflé).

Getting there

By car
A7 to Orange, then D975 signposted Vaison.

By bus
Orange-Vaison via Sablet: Cars Lieutaud (three to four services daily, 04.90.36.05.22); Carpentras-Vaison: Cars Comtadins (one service daily, 04.90.67.20.25).

Tourist information

Vaison's market days are Tuesday, Thursday and Saturday mornings.

Office du Tourisme
pl Chanoine Sautel (04.90.36.02.11/04.90.28.17.04). **Open** *Oct-Apr* 9am-noon, 2-5pm Mon-Sat; *May-Sept* 9am-12.30pm, 2-6.45pm Mon-Sat.

Hostellerie le Beffroi.

The Luberon

Lavender fields "Plateau de Valensole"

The Provence of popular imagination – and the reality does not disappoint.

The Luberon is classic inland Provence: perched hill villages, stone farmhouses, old fortresses and the Renaissance chateaux of a proudly unconventional land that was heavily embroiled in the sixteenth-century Wars of Religion. The area was declared a Parc Régional in 1977 and, despite the arrival of French caviar socialists and suburban Brits eager to grab a slice of the lifestyle described by former ad man Peter Mayle in *A Year in Provence*, it remains – mostly – unspoiled. Incomers can be relied on to renovate village houses and decrepit *bastides*, and there is a limit on new construction; but some villagers fear for the future, as high property prices make it hard for locals to buy in.

Montagne du Luberon

Once important for stone quarrying, the rugged northern flank of the rocky limestone massif of the Montagne de Luberon is punctuated by a string of picturesque perched hill villages. In

The Luberon lifestyle.

the west in a grandiose setting, **Oppède-le-Vieux** perfectly symbolises the rebirth of the Luberon. The old village was abandoned during the nineteenth century as residents moved down to the plain and gradually fell into ruin until resettled since the 1960s by artists, potters and writers. Just east of here you enter Peter Mayle country – literally – at **Ménerbes**, which, despite featuring heavily in *A Year in Provence*, remains a clock-stopped stone village with traces of a more prosperous past. At the top, the turreted former chateau was once a stronghold of the Waldensians (*see chapter* **History**). On the plain below the village, you can visit the cellars of the **Domaine de la Citadelle**, owned by Yves Rousset-Rouard, politician and producer of the film *Emanuelle*. The visit also takes in the corkscrew collection of the **Musée du Tire-Bouchon**.

With its medieval gateways and cobbled streets, the tiny, semi-deserted village of **Lacoste** should not be missed. The ruined castle at the top belonged to the Sade family; the scandalous Marquis lived here on and off for 30 years until his imprisonment in 1786. From here the road curves and then zigzags up the ramparts of **Bonnieux**, a typical perched village with typically perched residents; former culture minister Jack Lang has a house here. There are two churches: a twelfth-century one on the hilltop and the new parish church in the lower village, which contains four good fifteenth-century panel paintings from the old church.

In the less-known eastern half of the Luberon above Apt, the remarkably unspoiled village of **Saignon** stretches along a craggy escarpment between a square-towered Romanesque church and cemetery and a rocky belvedere, where a ruined chapel and several houses are built into the rock. Its remote location and strategic mountain site made the nearby hamlet of **Buoux** an important refuge during the Wars of Religion: on the hillside are traces of the fortress demolished by Louis XIV to deter Huguenots from taking refuge here.

The southern edge of the range, sloping towards the Durance river, is known for its trio of Renaissance chateaux. One of the largest and liveliest of the Luberon villages, **Lourmarin**, with its cluster of grey-shuttered stone houses and medieval church, is de facto gastronomic capital of the area. Despite all the antiques

Camus' grave in **Lourmarin**.

the midst of a swamp between 1175 and
Perhaps the plainest of the three – partly
centuries of abandonment reversed only in 1949,
but also to the extreme austerity of the Cistercian
rule and the style it generated – the abbey has a
sober church and impressive vaulted chapter
house. Just to the west, the village of **La Roque-
d'Anthéron** is known for its international
summer piano festival (*see page 290*).

Back on the Luberon side of the Durance, east
of Lourmarin on the D27, the ancient winding
streets of **Cucuron** are less touristed than those
of many other Luberon villages, although its
moulin à l'huile (olive press) is a favourite with
some of the super-chefs, who claim it produces
the best olive oil in France.

On **place de l'Horloge**, a fortified bell-
tower gateway leads to a ruined keep. At the
other end of the village is the surprisingly large
Eglise Notre-Dame-de-Beaulieu, with a
baroque altarpiece by Puget and Gothic side
chapels. On the northern side of the village,
surrounded by plane trees, the stone-walled
reservoir once fed three flour mills. Beyond here
various footpaths lead from Cucuron and
nearby Cabrières d'Aigues up the **Mourre
Nègre**, the highest point of the Luberon
(1,125 metres), with fine views.

Ansouis is dominated by its Renaissance
chateau, still fully furnished and inhabited by
the Sabran-Pontevès family – who sometimes
give the tours themselves. The visit takes in
plenty of baronial halls and massive kitchens,
but the highlight is the terraced gardens.
Further east at **La Tour-d'Aigues**, amid
rolling vineyards, are the remains of what was
once the finest of the Renaissance chateaux,
destroyed by fire in 1792. The pedimented
entrance and part of the wings survive; the
département is slowly rebuilding the rest. Two
small museums, **Musée des Faïences** and
Musée de l'Histoire du Pays d'Aigues,
are housed in the cellars; the first is the most
interesting, with a collection of ceramics from a
local eighteenth-century factory.

Abbaye de Silvacane
*6km south-west of Cadenet on D943 and D561
(04.42.50.41.69).* **Open** *Apr-Sept* 9am-7pm daily;
Oct-Mar 10am-1pm, 2-7pm Mon, Wed-Sun.

Château d'Ansouis
rue Cartel, Ansouis (04.90.09.82.70). **Open**
2.30-6pm daily. **Admission** 30F, children 15F.
No credit cards.

Château de Lourmarin
Lourmarin (04.90.68.15.23). **Guided tours** *May-
Sept* 10am, 11am, 2.30pm, 3.30pm, 4.30pm, 5.30pm;
Oct-Dec & Feb-Apr 11am, 2.30pm, 3.30pm, 4.30pm
daily. Closed Tue Nov-Mar. **Admission** 30F,
children 15F. **No credit cards**.

shops, art galleries, gift shops and estate
agents, tourism here remains restrained and
civilised, with action centred on the main street,
where **Café Gaby** and **Café de l'Ormeau**
enjoy a friendly rivalry. From here rue du
Temple leads to the mainly sixteenth-century
chateau, with its square tower and large
Renaissance windows. It was restored and
furnished with period furniture by Laurent
Vibert in the early 1900s and since 1925 has
received artists and writers in residence. It is
also used for chamber music in summer. Albert
Camus lived on the edge of the village and is
buried in the cemetery alongside his wife.
Visits are by guided tour only.

More workaday than chic neighbour
Lourmarin, **Cadenet** nonetheless has some
charming stepped streets and ancient houses, as
well as the small **Musée de la Vannerie**,
devoted to basketmaking, once one of the
principal activities in the area. The main square
has statue of the drummer boy of Arcole, born
in the village, who saved French troops in the
war against Austria in 1796. On the hill above
the village are the foundations of a chateau.

The best thing to do in Cadenet, though, is to
continue south across the Durance and head for
the **Abbaye de Silvacane**, the third of
Provence's great Romanesque abbeys, built in

All set: **Le Moulin de Lourmarin**.

Musée des Faïences
Château de la Tour-d'Aigues (04.90.07.50.33).
Open year round; call for times. **Admission** 5F,
10F children.

Musée du Tire-Bouchon
*Domaine de la Citadelle, Le Chataignier, chemin de
Cavaillon, Ménerbes (04.90.72.41.58).* **Open** *Apr-
Sept* 9am-noon, 2-7pm daily; *Oct-Mar* 9am-noon,
2-6pm Mon-Fri. **Admission** 24F, free under-15s.

Musée de la Vannerie
*La Glaneuse, av Philippe de Girard, Cadenet
(04.90.68.24.44).* Closed Nov-Mar.

Where to stay & eat

In the pretty village of Goult, just north of the
main N100 Avignon-Apt road, three kilometres
after the Ménerbes turn-off, the **Café de la
Poste** (pl de la Libération, 04.90.72.23.23,
closed lunch Wed, dinner daily, Nov to mid-
Mar, plat du jour 70F) gained fame in Mayle's
A Year in Provence and Jean Becker's film
L'Eté meurtrier. Join the locals and show up
early to watch the panting folks on guided
cycling trips being informed that the plat du
jour is sold out.

Bonnieux is home to a marvellous bistro,
Le Fournil (*see page 47*), and two fine hotels:
the **Hostellerie de la Prieuré** (rue Jean-
Baptiste Auvard, 04.90.75.80.78, closed Nov-
Mar, restaurant also closed lunch Tue-Fri,
rates 350F-640F, menus 125F-220F), in an
eighteenth-century stone building on the
descent to Lacoste, and the more upmarket
La Bastide de Capelongue (1.5km east on
the D232, 04.90.75.89.78, closed mid-Nov to

mid-Dec, mid-Jan to mid-Mar, rates 1,100F-
2,600F), in a tastefully decorated modern
bastide with a swimming pool.

In Saignon, the **Auberge du Presbytère**
(pl de la Fontaine, 04.90.74.11.50, closed Wed
Oct to mid-May, closed 15 Nov-5 Dec & 5-31
Jan, rates 260F-570F) has individually
decorated rooms in an ancient presbytery

On the antiques trail

Antiques dealers began settling in L'Isle-
sur-la-Sorgue after the first *foire à la
brocante* was held in 1962 and there are
now an estimated 300, concentrated along
avenue de la Libération, avenue des Quatre
Otages and around the station, some of
them in picturesque canalside locations. On
Sunday, the antiques shops and arcades
(open from 10am to 7pm on Saturdays,
Sundays and Mondays) are joined by stalls
of junkier *brocanteurs* along avenue des
Quatre Otages, with major antiques fairs at
Easter and on 15 August. Merchandise
ranges from high-quality antiques to quirky
collectibles, including many specifically
Provençal items, such as pretty gilt mirrors,
often carved with vines or laurel leaves,

carved *buffets*, printed fabrics and
Moustiers faience. There are also
architectural salvage specialists offering
old zinc bars, bistro fittings and entire hotel
reception booths. Le Rendezvous des
Marchands (91 av de la Libération,
04.90.20.84.60) is a bar-cum-
antiques shop where you can stop off for a
drink among a clutter of items for sale.

Even if there are few true bargains (some
shops seem to pack up entire crates of
furniture for shipping direct to stores in the
US, and it's not uncommon to hear prices
being discussed in dollars), prices are
noticeably lower than in Paris, where a fair
number of the goods end up. Needless to
say, the usual bargaining rules apply.

overlooking the village square. The restaurant (menu 175F) is closed for lunch on Wednesdays and Thursdays. **Chambre de Séjour avec Vue** (04.90.04.85.01, rates 380F) is an old village house that has been transformed with a remarkable eye for colour and design by Kamila Regent; she invites artists in residence to work and exhibit in the house, while also letting out three bedrooms and an apartment.

Down south in Lourmarin, **La Fenière** (*see page 47*) is the gourmet stop of choice, though **Le Moulin de Lourmarin** (*see page 47*) runs it a close second; both also offer comfortable, stylish accommodation. For a less demanding meal, **Maison Ollier** (pl de la Fontaine, 04.90.68.02.03, closed Tue dinner & all Wed except in July & Aug, closed mid-Nov to mid-Dec, menus 115F-300F), in a restored village house with garden, has a Mediterranean-inspired menu ranging from tagliatelle to tagines. The affordable **Hostellerie du Paradou** (route d'Apt, 04.90.68.04.05, closed mid-Nov to Jan, rates 330F-610F), a short walk from the village, is a stone *mas* with spacious lawns beside the Aiguebrun river; the restaurant serves regional fare accompanied by well-chosen local wines (closed all day Thur, lunch Fri, menus 120F, 145F).

In the panoramic village of Cucuron, **L'Horloge** (55 rue Léonce Brieugne, 04.90.77.12.74, closed Wed and during Feb school holidays, menus 95F-140F) is housed in two vaulted cellars that provide a cool summer retreat for some prettily presented, quietly creative Provençal cooking, including a superb-value 110F menu. **L'Arbre de Mai** (rue de l'Eglise, 04.90.77.25.10, closed dinner Mon, all Tue and from mid-Jan to Feb, menus 85F-140F) is a basic, comfortable hotel and restaurant serving traditional food.

Getting there

By car

A7 autoroute exit no.25 (Cavaillon) for northern Luberon, no.26 (Sénas) for southern Luberon. From the N100 Avignon-Apt road, side roads branch off south for Oppède-le-Vieux and the other northern Luberon villages. To the south, the D973 runs from Cavaillon via Mérindol to Cadenet, where the D943 heads north to Apt via Lourmarin, crossing the range. For La Tour d'Aigues, continue along the D973 to Pertuis, then take the D956.

By bus

Cars Sumian (04.91.49.44.25) runs two buses a day from Marseille to Apt stopping at Cadenet, Lourmarin and Bonnieux; twice daily buses from Aix to Apt also stop at Cadenet and Lourmarin.

Tourist information

Bonnieux
Office de Tourisme, 7 pl Carnot (04.90.75.91.90/fax 04.90.74.92.94). **Open** 2-6pm Mon; 9.30am-noon, 2-6pm Tue-Sat.

Cucuron
Office de Tourisme, rue Léonce Brieugne (04.90.77.28.37/fax 04.90.77.17.00). **Open** *May-Sept* 9am-noon, 3-7pm daily. *Oct-April* 9am-noon Mon-Sat.

Lourmarin
Office de Tourisme, 17 av Philippe de Girard (tel/fax 04.90.68.10.77). **Open** 9.30-1pm, 3-7pm Mon-Sat; 9.30am-noon Sun.

La Tour d'Aigues
Office de Tourisme, Château (04.90.07.50.29). **Open** 9.30am-noon Mon-Sat; 2-5pm Mon, Wed-Sun.

L'Isle-sur-la-Sorgue & Fontaine-de-Vaucluse

L'Isle-sur-la-Sorgue, literally, and descriptively, 'island on the Sorgue', is known as the 'Venise Comtadin' (the Venice of the Comtat Venaissin) for its ring of canals. Countless dripping wheels recall a past when water powered first a silk industry and later paper mills. Upstream, the

Collégiale Notre-Dame-des-Anges. *See p118.*

Partage des Eaux, a large pool at the point where the river divides into two, is a popular stroll for the locals. But what makes the town tick today is its concentration of antiques dealers, the largest in France outside Paris (*see box page 116*).

Star sight is the **Collégiale Notre-Dame-des-Anges** on place de la Liberté, an extraordinary baroque church with heavens full of cherubim over the west door. Sculpted pairs of gilded virtues and graces fly over the arches along the nave, while the sanctuary boasts a gleaming carved altarpiece and choir stalls and barley-sugar twists. The side chapels – all worth exploring – reveal frescos, faux marble, delicate wood carving and painted altarpieces by the Mignard family and Lebrun, among others. Outside is a square containing the pretty **Café de France**, galleried houses and the tourist office, located inside a former granary. Nearby, the **Musée Donadeï de Campredon**, a restored *hôtel particulier* built in 1773 for the Marquis de Campredon, puts on high-quality temporary exhibitions of modern and contemporary art. The eighteenth-century former **Hôtel Dieu** hospital is also worth a look, with its chapel and pharmacy lined with glazed apothecary jars in Moustiers earthenware.

Upstream, pretty **Fontaine-de-Vaucluse** clusters around the source of the Sorgue river: water mysteriously gushes out of a sheer cliff face into a jade-green coloured pool, giving the name Vallis Clausa (closed valley) or Vaucluse to the whole *département*. Numerous divers, including the late Jacques Cousteau, have attempted without success to find the source; their exploits, and the geological wonders of the area, are explained in the underground museum **Le Monde Souterrain de Norbert Casteret**. Fontaine's most famous resident was the Italian Renaissance poet and scholar Petrarch (1304-74). The **Musée Pétrarque** stands on the site of the house where he lived and wrote most of his poetry, having fallen in eternal, helpless love with Laure de Noves (the 'Laura' of his verses), whom he first spied at church in Avignon on 6 February 1327. Already married, to Hugues de Sade, she died in the Black Death in 1348, and Petrarch's *Canzoniere* is a reflection on his great platonic love and his grief after her death. Recent scholars have pooped the party by suggesting that Laura never actually existed.

East of Fontaine-de-Vaucluse is a section of the **Mur de la Peste**, built in 1720 to keep the Marseille plague from spreading north into the papal Comtat Venaissin; it spread anyway. Between April and December, the Sorgue can be navigated by canoe between Fontaine-de-Vaucluse and Partage des Eaux. Canoes can be hired at **Canoë Evasion** (on D24 at Pont de Galas, 04.90.38.26.22).

Collégiale Notre-Dame-des-Anges
pl de la Liberté. **Open** 10am-noon, 3-5pm Tue-Sat.

Hôtel Dieu
quai des Lices, L'Isle-sur-la-Sorgue (04.90.21.34.00). **Open** 10.30-11.30am, 2.30-4pm daily. **Admission** free. Closed for work until 2001.

Monde souterrain de Norbert Casteret
chemin de la Fontaine, Fontaine-de-Vaucluse (04.90.20.34.13).

Musée Donadeï de Campredon
20 rue du Docteur Taillet, L'Isle-sur-la-Sorgue (04.90.38.17.41). **Open** (during exhibitions) 9.30am-noon, 2-6pm Tue-Sun. **Admission** 35F, 30F children.

Musée Pétrarque
quai du Château Vieux, Fontaine-de-Vaucluse (04.90.20.37.20). **Open** *Apr, May* 10am-noon, 2-6pm Wed-Mon; *June-Sept* 10am-12.30pm, 1.30-6pm Mon, Wed-Sun; *Oct* 10am-noon, 2-5pm daily. Closed Nov-Mar. **Admission** 20F, children 10F, free under-12s.

Where to stay & eat

Hungry antiques merchants and browsers are served by a rash of restaurants and cafés along the canals and within the markets of L'Isle-sur-la-Sorgue. Two of the best are the stylish bistro **Le Carré des Herbes** (13 av des Quatres Otages, 04.90.38.62.95, closed Tue & Jan or Feb, meuns 80F-160F), now under the wing of fêted Paris chef Bernaud Pacaud, and the formal but delicious **La Prévoté** (*see page 47*). By the riverside at Partage des Eaux, **Le Pescador** (04.90.38.09.69, closed Wed & Jan to mid-Feb, rates 290F-350F) is an affordable place to kip, with a reliable restaurant (menus 105F-145F). On the N100 Apt road, six kilometres south-east, Le Mas des Grès (04.90.20.32.85, closed mid-Nov to mid-Mar, rates 430F-1,300F) offers rustic hospitality in a restored *mas*, with pool.

In Fontaine-de-Vaucluse, the **Hostellerie Le Château** (quai du Château Vieux, 04.90.20.31.54, closed Dec-Mar, rates 230F) is a good budget hotel in an attractive waterside setting, whose veranda restaurant is open year round (menus 119F-189F).

Getting there

By car
A7, exit no.24 (Avignon sud), then D25 to L'Isle-sur-la-Sorgue, or no.25 (Cavaillon), then D938 to L'Isle-sur-la-Sorgue. From central Avignon take the N100. Fontaine-de-Vaucluse is 7km east of L'Isle-sur-la-Sorgue on D938/D25.

By train/bus

TGV to Avignon, then the local train to L'Isle-sur-la-Sorgue; some of these trains are replaced by SNCF TER buses. Fontaine-de-Vaucluse is served by six or so shuttle buses daily from L'Isle-sur-la-Sorgue, run by Cars Arnaud (04.90.38.15.98).

Tourist information

L'Isle-sur-la-Sorgue

Office de Tourisme, pl de l'Eglise (04.90.38.04.78/fax 04.90.38.35.43). **Open** 9.30am-12.30pm, 2.30-6pm Mon-Sat.

Fontaine-de-Vaucluse

Office de Tourisme, chemin de la Fontaine (04.90.20.32.22/fax 04.90.20.21.37). **Open** 10am-6pm Mon-Fri.

Main arcades

Hôtel Dongier

9 pl Gambetta (04.90.38.63.63).

L'Isle aux Brocantes

7 av des Quatre Otages (04.90.20.69.93).

Village des Antiquaires de la Gare

2 bis av de l'Egalité (04.90.38.04.57).

Le Quai de la Gare

4 av Julien Guigue (04.90.20.73.42).

Cavaillon

Sprawling over the flat Durance plain with the St-Jacques hill as backdrop, Cavaillon is renowned as the melon capital of France. The juicy globes are celebrated in a festival in July, and crop up in everything from jam to chocolates. In recent years the town has been more associated with militant farmers dumping spectacular mounds of produce in protest at European agricultural policy than with sightseeing, but past the anonymous periphery of roundabouts and fruit warehouses is an old town with relics from what was once an important medieval diocese.

The earliest visible reminder of Cavaillon's past is the spindly first-century **Arc Romain** (pl du Clos), bearing traces of sculpted flowers and winged victories, rebuilt in its present location in the 1870s. Left of the Arc, a footpath zigzags up the cliff to the medieval **Chapelle St-Jacques**, which has a good view over the town and the surrounding countryside. At the foot of the Arc, on place du Clos, scene of a lively Monday morning market, be sure to peer into the time-capsule **Fin de Siècle** café.

Wedged inside the Cours – tree-lined avenues that replaced the ramparts in the nineteenth century – the raggedy old town is presided over

Prévot: famed for its use of melons.

by the Romanesque **Cathédrale Notre-Dame et St-Véran** (closed Mon), with its cloister, octagonal tower and a sundial on the side with a winged angel. Nearby, tree-shaded **place Philippe de Cabassole** has a couple of fine eighteenth-century houses. On the other side of the church, the Grand-Rue leads to the **Musée de l'Hôtel Dieu**, where archaeological finds from a neolithic settlement on St-Jacques hill are displayed in part of the former hospital and its eighteenth-century chapel.

Like nearby **Carpentras** (*see box page 108*), Cavaillon had a sizeable Jewish community, and its light-filled **synagogue** (built 1772-4) is one of the finest in France. The upper level, with bronze chandeliers, baroque tabernacle and delicate wrought ironwork, was reserved for the men. Below, connected by an external staircase, the lower level, dominated by a large bread oven, doubled as a bakery. It now contains the **Musée Juif Comtadin**, housing the tabernacle doors from the earlier synagogue on the site, prayer books and other possessions that had belonged to the community.

Musée de l'Hôtel Dieu

Grand-Rue (04.90.76.00.34). **Open** *Oct to mid-Apr* 10am-noon, 2-4.30pm Mon, Wed-Fri; *mid-Apr to Sept* 10am-12.30pm, 3-6.30pm Mon, Wed-Sun. **Admission** 20F, free children.

Synagogue/Musée Juif Comtadin

rue Hébraïque (04.90.76.00.34). **Open** *Oct to mid-Apr* 10am-noon, 2-4.30pm Mon, Wed-Fri; *mid-Apr to Sept* 10am-12.30pm, 3-6.30pm Mon, Wed-Sun. **Admission** 20F, free children.

Where to eat & drink

Cavaillon's hotels leave quite a lot to be desired, but culinary prospects are more promising. Upmarket, old-fashioned **Prévot** (353 av de Verdun, 04.90.71.32.43, closed dinner Sun, all Mon, menus 135F-320F) is famed for its inventive summer melon menu. **Le Pantagruel** (5 pl Philippe de Cabassole, 04.90.76.11.30, closed lunch Mon & Tue, all Sun, menus 135F-195F) has a striking high-ceilinged dining room with a huge open fire on which meat is grilled in winter. In summer, start with the gigantic anchoïade before roast lamb with herbs and honey. **Côté Jardin** (49 rue Lamartine, 04.90.71.33.58, closed dinner Sun, all Mon, three weeks Jan, menus 86F-150F) has tables around a courtyard fountain and good-value Provençal cooking, especially fish. The belle Époque **Le Fin de Siècle** (46 pl du Clos, 04.90.71.12.27, closed dinner Tue, all Wed and Aug to mid-Sept, menus 65F-220F) has kept its mosaic frontage, mouldings and large mirrors inside; downstairs is a café, upstairs a more formal restaurant.

Getting there

By car

From autoroute A7, exit Cavaillon (no.25). From Apt and northern Luberon, by N100 and then D2 at Coustellet; from southern Luberon by D973, which follows the Durance.

By train/bus

The station is at the end of av du Maréchal Joffre. There are regular trains from Avignon via Isle-sur-la-Sorgue, some of which are replaced by SNCF TER buses. Société Villardo-Bernard (04.90.74.36.10) runs buses to Avignon, Apt and Forcalquier (around two a day).

Tourist information

Office de Tourisme

pl François Tourel (04.90.71.32.01/fax 04.90.71.42.99). **Open** *summer* 9am-12.30pm, 2-7pm Mon-Sat; 9.30am-12.30pm Sun; *winter* 9am-12.30pm, 1.30-6.30pm Mon-Sat.

Apt

At first sight there is not much going on in Apt, with its industrial outskirts – Apt is the centre of the *fruits confits* (candied fruit) industry – plane trees and sleepy squares along the murky River Calavon. But it comes alive on Saturday morning with the largest market for miles around, with dozens of food stalls and others selling Aptware marbled faience, which can also be picked up at **Faïence d'Apt**.

Arriving from Avignon, **place de la Bouquerie** is the main access point for the old town, via the narrow main street, rue des Marchands. The bell tower of the **Ancienne Cathédrale Ste-Anne** throws an arch across the street; the cathedral itself, now demoted to the status of parish church, is a curious mix of Gothic and baroque. The treasury contains an Arabic standard filched in the First Crusade and later revered as the shroud of St Anne, Jesus' grandma.

The church's two crypts reveal the ancient origins of the building: the upper one dates from the eleventh century, the lower from the fourth.

Nearby, the **Maison du Parc** has information about the flora, fauna and geology of the Parc Régional du Luberon, plus the small, child-oriented **Musée de la Paléontologie**. The **Musée d'Histoire et d'Archéologie** has displays of faience and archaeological finds. If all this mind-candy whets your appetite for the real thing, head for **Aptunion**, the town's biggest manufacturer of candied fruits.

Ancienne Cathédrale Ste-Anne

rue de la Cathédrale (04.90.74.36.60). **Open** *Oct-June* 10am-noon, 2-4pm Tue-Fri; 10am-noon Sat, Sun; *July-Sept* 10am-noon, 3-6pm Tue-Fri; 10am-noon Sat, Sun. **Treasury open** *July-Sept* guided tours only 11am, 5pm Mon-Sat, 11am Sun. **Admission** free.

Aptunion

Salignan, 2km along Avignon road (04.90.76.31.43). **Factory open** call for details. **Shop open** 8.30am-noon, 2-6pm Mon-Sat.

Faïence d'Apt

12 av de la Libération (04.90.74.15.31).

Maison du Parc & Musée de la Paléontologie

60 pl Jean Jaurès (04.90.04.42.00). **Open** *Apr-Sept* 8.30am-noon, 1.30-7pm Mon-Sat; *Oct-Mar* 8.30am-noon Mon-Sat; 1.30-6pm Mon-Fri. **Admission** *Maison du Parc* free; *museum* 10F, free under-18s.

Musée d'Histoire et d'Archéologie

rue de l'Amphithéâtre (04.90.74.00.34). **Open** *Oct-May* 2-4.30pm Mon; 2-5pm Tue, Thur, Fri; 10am-noon, 2-5pm Sat; *June-Sept* 10am-noon, 2.30-4.30pm Mon; 10am-noon, 2-5pm Wed, Thur, Fri; 10am-noon, 2-5.30pm Sat; 2-5.30pm Sun. **Admission** 12F, free under-16s.

Where to stay & eat

At the **Auberge du Luberon** (8 pl du Fbg Ballet, 04.90.74.12.50, closed dinner Sun, all Mon and Christmas & New Year, menus 240F-420F), chef Serge Peuzin offers a special menu *aux fruits confits* in which candied fruit features in every course; there are also 14 bedrooms (295F-495F). Otherwise, give Apt a miss and stay in a nearby village such as Saignon (*see below* **Montagne de Luberon**). The **Queen Victoria** pub (94 quai de la Liberté, 04.90.04.76.30) offers Internet facilities and live music.

Getting there

By car

N100 from Avignon, D943 from Cadenet and the south.

By bus

Frequent daily buses from Avignon set down at pl de la Bouquerie, near the tourist office, or at the *gare routière* in av de la Libération. There are two buses a day to and from Cavaillon, Forcalquier, Aix-en-Provence and Marseille. For times, ring the *gare routière* (04.90.74.20.21).

Tourist information

Office de Tourisme
20 av Philippe de Girard (04.90.74.03.18/fax 04.90.74.03.18). **Open** *Sept-June* 9am-noon, 2-6pm Mon-Sat; *July, Aug* 9am-1.30pm, 3-7pm Mon-Sat; 9am-1.30pm Sun.

Plateau de Vaucluse

Fiefdom of the *gauche caviar*, France's champagne socialists – or the *gauche tapenade* as some dub them here – **Gordes** is too pretty for its own good, with a spectacular hilltop setting, dominated by the machicolated turrets of its chateau, and steep, stepped alleys weaving down the hill. Today renovation and wealth have given Gordes a rather chi-chi sheen, but it is precisely this combination of historic stones and worldly buzz that draws most of the well-dressed people-watchers who loll at its café tables. Tasteful shops sell all the usual Provençal crafts and produce, while the chateau, which long displayed kinetic art by Vasarely, now has a semi-permanent exhibition by the Pop Art-influenced Belgian painter Pol Mara.

Just west of Gordes, the **Village des Bories** is a group of restored drystone, beehive-shaped structures, inhabited between the sixteenth and early nineteenth centuries; they may have been built over – or on the model of – much earlier dwellings. An attempt has been made to reconstruct the simple rural lifestyle of the Borie dwellers, and a photo exhibition shows similar drystone structures in other countries.

North of Gordes, at the base of a wooded valley, the **Abbaye Notre-Dame-de-Sénanque**, founded in 1148, is one of the great triumvirate of Provençal Cistercian monasteries (with Silvacane and Thoronet). Set amid lavender fields, the beautifully preserved Romanesque ensemble – church, cloister, dormitory, chapter house – still houses a monastic community.

Surrounded by strangely eroded outcrops of ochre-red rocks, **Roussillon** is among the most picturesque of all the Luberon villages. Despite the crowds of tourists, it remains unbelievably appealing. The houses are painted in an orange wash, which makes the entire village glow. Walk past the belfry-sundial of the **Eglise St-Michel** to an orientation table, and note also

Unbelievably appealing **Roussillon**.

the eighteenth-century façades on place de la Mairie. To the left of the village cemetery, above car park 2, the **Sentier des Ocres** (10F, free under-10s), a footpath with information panels, offers spectacular views amid peculiar rock formations, the result of centuries of ochre quarrying. On the D104 towards Apt, the former ochre works have reopened as the **Conservatoire des Ocres et Pigments Appliqués**, with displays showing how the rock was purified and made into pigment (entry on tours only).

Abbaye Notre-Dame-de-Sénanque
4km north of Gordes on D177 (04.90.72.05.72). **Open** *Mar-Oct* 10am-noon, 2-6pm Mon-Sat; 2-6pm Sun; *Nov-Feb* 2-5pm Mon-Fri; 2-6pm Sat, Sun. **Admission** 30F, 12F children.

Château de Gordes
Gordes (04.90.72.02.89). **Open** 10am-noon, 2-6pm daily.

Conservatoire des Ocres et Pigments appliqués
Usine Mathieu, D104, Roussillon (04.90.05.66.69). **Tours** 11am, 2pm, 3pm, 4pm, 5pm; plus 10am, 6pm in July, Aug. **Admission** 25F, free under-11s.

Village des Bories
Les Savournins, 2km west of Gordes (04.90.72.03.48). **Open** 9am-sunset daily. **Admission** 32F, 20F children.

Where to stay & eat

In Gordes, **La Bastide de Gordes** (rte de Combe, 04.90.72.12.12, closed Nov to mid-Dec, Jan to mid-Feb, rates 520F-1,350F) is an upmarket hotel on the ramparts, with spectacular views. The **Domaine de l'Enclose** (rte de Sénanque, 04.90.72.71.00, closed mid-Nov to mid-Dec, rates 580F-980F) offers all mod cons in a garden setting; ground-floor rooms have private gardens, the restaurant (menus 238F; closed lunch to non-residents) serves creative seasonal cooking, **Café-Restaurant La Renaissance** (pl du Château, 04.09.72.02.02, menus 75F-200F), adjoining the chateau, has tables on the square and five affordable bedrooms (rates 300F-470F). In Roussillon, **David** (pl de la Poste, 04.90.05.60.13, closed Mon, 20 Nov-20 Mar, menus 128F-300F) is the most reliable of several bistros and snack bars.

Getting there

By car
From Avignon, N100/D2 to Gordes, continuing on D2/D102 to Roussillon. From Apt, N100/D4/D104 to Roussillon. There are no bus or train services.

Tourist information

Gordes
Office de Tourisme, Le Château (04.90.72.02.75/fax 04.90.72.02.26). **Open** *July, Aug* 9am-12.30pm, 2-6.30pm Mon-Sat; *Sept-June* 9am-noon, 2-6pm Mon-Sat.

Roussillon
Office de Tourisme, pl de la Poste (04.90.05.60.25/fax 04.90.05.63.31). **Open** 2-6pm Mon-Sat.

Manosque

Though it nestles at the eastern edge of the Luberon range, Manosque is very much a Durance Valley town – the largest in the sparsely populated *département* of Alpes de Haute Provence. Housing and industrial parks now sprawl over the hillside, but for a long time the town remained within the city walls, where the not-yet-tarted-up network of narrow streets, squares and covered passageways gives an interesting perspective on what the rest of the Luberon must have been like before it became so hip. Manosque is positively moribund on a Sunday out of season and liveliest on a Saturday, when a market takes over the whole centre.

Porte Saunerie leads into **rue Grande**, Manosque's main shopping street. At No.14, a plaque marks the house where novelist Jean Giono (1895-1970), son of a shoemaker, was born. At No.21 is a branch of **Occitane**, the phenomenally successful Manosque-based cosmetics company that is now one of the town's main employers. Note also the fine eighteenth-century balcony at No.23. There are two historic churches, **St-Sauveur**, which features in Giono's swashbuckler *Le Hussar sur le Toit*, and **Notre-Dame-de-Romigier** on place de l'Hôtel de Ville, which has a fine Renaissance doorway and a black Virgin inside. From here rue des Marchands leads into rue Soubeyron and out to a gateway-belfry, the Porte Soubeyron.

The Giono link is exploited to the full with literary competitions and walks on the theme of 'Jean Giono, poet of the olive tree' (Haute-Provence olive oil gained an *appellation contrôlée* in 1999). The **Centre Jean Giono** has temporary exhibitions and a permanent display about the writer's life and work. His own house, **Lou Paraïs** (montée des Vraies Richesses, 04.92.87.73.03), north of the old town, is open for guided visits on Friday afternoons (ring ahead).

Centre Jean Giono
1 bd Elémir Bourges (04.92.70.54.54). **Open** 9am-noon, 2-6pm Tue-Sat. **Admission** 21F, 11F students, free under-12s. **No credit cards**.

Where to eat

Manosque's top chef is **Dominique Bucaille**, whose same-name restaurant (43 bd des Tilleuls, 04.92.72.32.28, closed dinner Wed, all Sun and mid-July to mid-Aug, menu 150F) offers refined classical cooking and seasonal Provençal dishes at surprisingly reasonable prices; a great place to try the local Sisteron lamb.

Getting there

By car
From Aix, A51 autoroute, exit no.18.

By bus
The *gare routière* on bd Charles de Gaulle has services to Marseille, Aix, Gap and Sisteron, plus two buses daily to Apt: ring 04.92.87.55.99 for timetable information.

By train
Regular trains from Marseille via Aix and Gap via Sisteron arrive at Manosque-Gréoux-les-Bains station, south of the centre on av Jean Giono.

Tourist information

Office du Tourisme
pl du Docteur Joubert (04.92.72.16.00). **Open** *Sept-June* 9am-noon, 1.30-6pm Mon-Sat; *July, Aug* 9am-noon, 1.30-6.30pm Mon-Sat; 10am-noon Sun.

Marseille & Aix-en-Provence

Marseille & Around   124
Aix-en-Provence   139

Feature boxes

The Olympique spirit   133
Château d'If   134
Cézanne & Montagne
   Ste-Victoire   142
Cours Mirabeau   144
Festival International
   d'Art Lyrique   146

Marseille & Around

A Parisian would scoff at the very suggestion, but Marseille is rapidly becoming one of France's most dynamic cities.

After an auspicious nineteenth century, when Marseille grew wealthy and cultivated as the busiest port on the Mediterranean, it struggled through most of the twentieth century with an unsavoury reputation as corrupt, strike-prone, dangerous and definitely best avoided. In fact, until very recently, if tourists paused here, it was only to flit in and out of town for a bowl of bouillabaisse before the plane or ferry departed.

Within the past ten years, though, Marseille has been undergoing a slow but steady revival. A new generation of local politicians and a variety of intelligent urban renewal projects – most notably Euroméditerranée, a vast redevelopment of the old docklands – have boosted the city's economy. Word has spread that it has a magnificent setting, striking architecture and a world-class constellation of museums and cultural institutions. Statistics have shown that it's no more dangerous than any other large French city. And as the rest of the country grapples uncomfortably with its new multi-ethnic identity, Marseille can boast that it got to grips with that problem years ago.

Slowly but surely, the city is emerging as an important new tourist destination and cultural pace-setter for twenty-first-century France.

HISTORY

Around 600 BC, a band of Phocaean Greeks sailed into Marseille harbour on the very day that a local chieftain's daughter, Gyptis, was to choose a husband. The Greek's good-looking commander Protis mingled with the crowd and was immediately picked out by Gyptis as the man for her. The bride came with a donation of land, a hill near the mouth of the

The **Vieux Port**: spiritual heart of Marseille.

River Rhône, where the Greeks founded a trading post named Massalia.

Or so the story goes – and there's nothing legendary about the fact that the history of Marseille is irrevocably linked to its development as a port. By 500 BC, Massalia's Greeks were trading throughout Mediterranean Europe and from Cornwall to the Baltic. Had they not made the mistake in the first century BC of backing Pompey against the ultimately victorious Caesar, the Massalians might have gone on to even greater things. As it was, Caesar besieged the city in 49 BC, seized almost all its colonies, and Massalia's Greeks were left with little more than their famous university and their much-vaunted independence, which was to be lost and regained several times over the years.

After a harsh buffeting from Saracens and marauding latter-day Greeks, Marseille reactivated its port swiftly in the twelfth century and made a killing from embarking, and maintaining, supply lines to Crusaders. The city was seized by Charles d'Anjou in 1214 and was then annexed to France by Henri IV in 1481, but kept up its time-honoured tradition of fighting every battle available… often on the losing side.

It was Louis XIV who ushered in the first great transformation of Marseille since the arrival of the Greeks; he pulled down the city walls in 1666 and expanded the port to the Rive Neuve, or eastern banks of the original U-shaped harbour. The city was devastated by plague in 1720, losing more than half its population of 90,000. By the time of the Revolution, however, it was flourishing once more, its traditional industries – soap manufacture, oil processing and faience – supplying the whole of France and much of the Mediterranean. The demand for labour sparked a wave of immigration to the city from Provence and Italy.

Marseille supported the Revolution enthusiastically, only to turn monarchist under the First Empire and republican under the Second. By the time of Napoléon III, Algeria had become a French *département*, leading to a huge increase in trans-Mediterranean shipping. Realising that the city would play a pivotal role in achieving his colonial aims, the emperor

occupiers gave the 40,000 residents of the Vieux Port area 24 hours to leave their houses, which were then razed. More damage was done by Allied bombardments in 1944.

Following the French defeat in Indochina in 1954, and the independence of Tunisia in 1956 and Algeria in 1962, Marseille received a mass exodus of French colonists, North African Jews and North Africans who had been involved in colonial administration. At the same time, the loss of these colonies hit Marseille's shipping trade, and the city's traditional industries went into decline. From 1954 to 1964, the population grew by 50 per cent, creating a severe housing shortage. New neighbourhoods were rapidly constructed to cope with the influx. Areas of high unemployment throughout the 1970s and '80s, these neighbourhoods were infamously home to drug dealing and crime.

This explosive ethnic mixture was fertile ground for Jean-Marie Le Pen and his henchman Bruno Megret, mayor of neighbouring Martigues, whose 'France for the French' brand of extreme-right politics received enthusiastic support in Marseille in the 1980s and '90s (*see chapter* **Le Midi Today**).

After centuries in which local brawn was what counted, Marseille is now seeking its white-collar place in the sun: the city is repositioning itself as a service and research centre, and is learning to capitalise on its spectacular setting and cultural facilities. The city centre is being slowly renovated and repopulated. And although it has yet to shake off its reputation as a mob fiefdom, Marseille's image is improving rapidly.

Notre-Dame-de-la-Garde. *See page 130.*

initiated the construction of an entirely new port, La Joliette, on the coast running west from the original harbour, to accommodate the steamships that were replacing old schooners. One of the largest public works projects ever undertaken in Europe, the port opened in 1853. Three years later, the Paris-Lyon-Méditerranée (PLM) railway line acquired the right to construct warehouses to service the new port; Les Docks, modelled on London's St Katharine's Dock, opened in 1866. In 1869, the Suez Canal opened and Marseille became the greatest boom town in nineteenth-century Europe. Between 1851 and 1911, the population rose by 360,000. As immigrants arrived from all over southern Europe, it acquired the astonishingly cosmopolitan population that it maintains to this day. In 1915, the city received some 20,000 Armenians fleeing Turkish genocide.

But Marseille's heyday was soon to come to an abrupt halt. In 1934, King Alexander of Yugoslavia and Louis Barthou, the French foreign minister, were assassinated on La Canebière, the city's main artery. In 1939, the city was placed under national guardianship when widespread corruption in local government was revealed. This, combined with frequent violent strikes in the port, tarnished the city's image nationally and, eventually, internationally. In 1943, Marseille's German

Sightseeing

Marseille's neighbourhoods are as heterogeneous as its population, while its honeycomb-like layout contains fascinating architectural diversity. The city was born on the edges of the **Vieux Port**: this harbour, now filled with pleasure craft and the odd fishing trawler, remains the centrepiece of the city.

La Canebière (from *canèbe*, hemp in Provençal, after a rope factory once located here) is the city's main drag. It runs from the **Palais Longchamp** – a grandiose nineteenth-century monument celebrating the arrival of an aqueduct carrying the diverted waters of the Durance river to the previously drought-prone city – to the Vieux Port. Though this boulevard lost much of its glory with the decline of Marseille as the bridge between France and its North African colonies, it still makes for an interesting walk, lined as it is with nineteenth-century wedding-cake façades, including the now-defunct Grand Hôtel

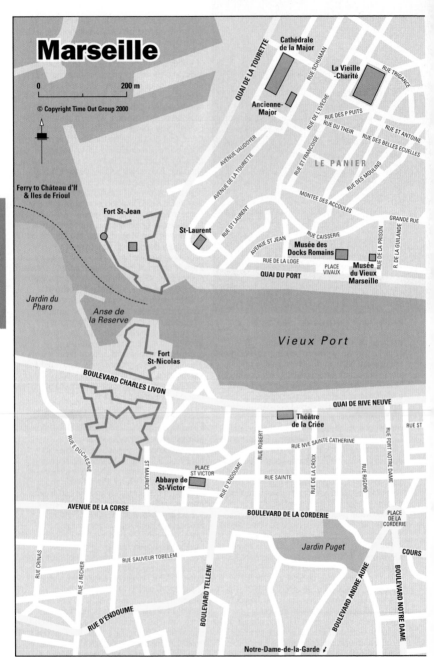

Marseille

0   200 m

© Copyright Time Out Group 2000

Ferry to Château d'If
& Iles de Frioul

QUAI DE LA TOURETTE

Cathédrale
de la Major

RUE SCHUMAN

La Vieille
-Charité

RUE TRIGANCE

Ancienne-
Major

RUE DE L'EVECHE

RUE DES P PUITS

RUE DU THEIR

RUE ST ANTOINE

RUE DES BELLES ECUELLES

AVENUE VAUDOYER

RUE ST FRANCOISE

LE PANIER

RUE DES MOULINS

AVENUE DE LA TOURETTE

MONTEE DES ACCOULES

GRANDE RUE

Fort St-Jean

St-Laurent

RUE ST LAURENT

RUE CAISSERIE

Musée des
Docks Romains

RUE DE LA PRISON

R. DE LA GUILANDE

AVENUE ST JEAN

RUE DE LA LOGE

PLACE
VIVAUX

Musée
du Vieux
Marseille

QUAI DU PORT

Jardin du
Pharo

Anse de
la Reserve

Fort
St-Nicolas

BOULEVARD CHARLES LIVON

Vieux Port

QUAI DE RIVE NEUVE

Théâtre
de la Criée

RUE ST

RUE E'DUCHESNE

RUE ROBERT

RUE NVE SAINTE CATHERINE

RUE FORT NOTRE DAME

ST MAURICE

PLACE
ST VICTOR

RUE D'ENDOUME

RUE DE LA CROIX

RUE RIGORD

Abbaye de
St-Victor

RUE SAINTE

AVENUE DE LA CORSE

BOULEVARD DE LA CORDERIE

PLACE
DE LA
CORDERIE

RUE CRINAS

RUE J RECHER

RUE SAUVEUR TOBELEM

BOULEVARD TELLENE

Jardin Puget

BOULEVARD ANDRE AUNE

COURS

BOULEVARD NOTRE DAME

RUE D'ENDOUME

Notre-Dame-de-la-Garde ↙

Marseille & Aix

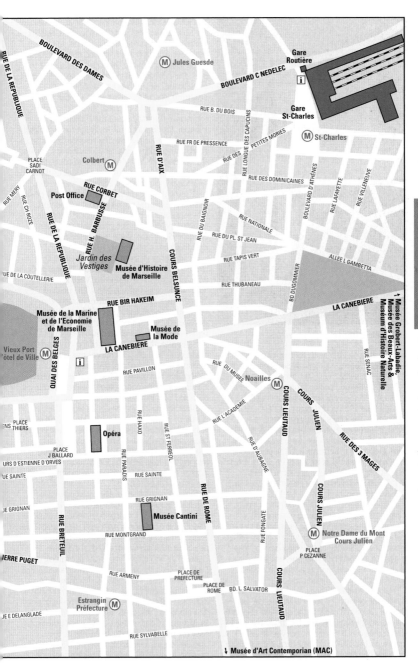

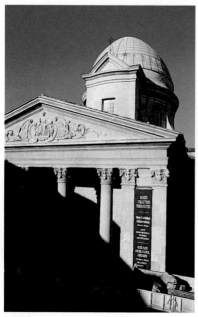

La Vieille-Charité. *See page 131.*

Louvre et de la Paix with its four caryatids at the door representing Europe, Asia, Africa and the Americas.

Marseille is laid out in 16 *arrondissements*, the first of which encompasses the north bank of the Vieux Port and runs up to the Gare St-Charles, the city's main train station.

Sitting in a café on the Quai des Belges, the eastern edge of the Vieux Port, the two huge forts guarding the entrance to the port come into view: **Fort St-Jean** (only open for special exhibitions) on the north bank and **Fort St-Nicolas** (closed to the public) on the south. The former was built in the twelfth century and the latter under Louis XIV; both testify to the former strategic importance of the port. Tellingly, the guns in these forts faced towards, rather than away from, the city: the Marseillais, whose local identity has always been at least as strong as their national one, are still proud of this display of the king's (quite justified) doubts about their allegiance.

The city's most famous landmark, the neo-Byzantine basilica of **Notre-Dame-de-la-Garde** rises on a peak to the south of the port. Below, on the Quai Neuve, the **Théâtre de la Criée** was created from the city's old fish market in the 1970s, while a thriving restaurant and café district has sprung up around the former arsenal buildings constructed by Colbert for Louis XIV. Nearby is the **Musée Cantini**, the modern art museum, which has just reopened after a lengthy period of restoration.

Continuing around the southern flank of the port, the **Abbaye St-Victor** is a forbidding, crenellated, eleventh-century abbey with a stunning Romanesque interior. On the point beyond the Fort St-Nicolas, there's a superb view from the gardens of the **Palais du Pharo**, which was built for Emperor Napoléon III. Further south, along the seaside Corniche road, is the fishing hamlet of Vallon des Auffes, the spectacular **Musée de la Faïence**, the delightful fishing port of Les Goudes and the *calanques* (*see box page 153*).

A ferry service from the Quai Neuve deposits passengers on the northern edge of the port, where a mass of post-war housing blocks is punctuated only by the gorgeous seventeenth-century **Hôtel de Ville**, one of the few buildings left standing in 1943.

Heading away from the port towards the district of Le Panier, the **Maison Diamantée**, which houses the **Musée du Vieux Marseille**, was built in 1570. The nearby **Musée des Docks Romains** houses the vestiges of the Roman port of Marseille, uncovered during a construction project to replace the area devastated in World War II.

Le Panier, the oldest part of the city and the traditional first stop for successive waves of immigrants, is a warren of narrow streets and old houses surrounding **La Vieille-Charité**, a stunning stone poorhouse, now a museum, built in 1745. From La Vieille-Charité, there's a splendid view over the docks along the northern shoreline: the **Docks de la Joliette**, handsome stone warehouses that have recently been converted into smart offices; the *port moderne*; and beyond, **L'Estaque**, a small, formerly industrial village that attracted many artists, including Cézanne, at the beginning of the twentieth century.

Depending on the weather, you may also catch a glimpse of the **Château d'If** (*see page 134*) on the Ile d'If, where Alexandre Dumas set *The Count of Monte Cristo*, and the larger Ile de Frioul. Nestling behind the Joliette docks is the neo-Byzantine **Cathédrale de la Major**.

East of the Vieux Port, at the beginning of La Canebière, the remains of Massalia's original Greek walls are visible in the **Jardins des Vestiges**, a garden behind the grandiose but dignified 1860-vintage Chambre d'Industrie et de Commerce, which is home to the **Musée de la Marine**. Continuing along La Canebière, past the new **Musée de la Mode**, is the up-and-coming neighbourhood of Belsunce, known for its handsome eighteenth-century *hôtels particuliers* (and, to wary locals, as the best place to be mugged). The souk-like rue d'Aubagne and surrounding streets offer a vibrant experience of Marseille today: busy market streets selling everything from Algerian dates to Armenian sausage. The Cours Julien on the site of the former vegetable market is now the heart of a district of restaurants, alternative bars, art galleries and funky boutiques, as well as live music and performances at the **Espace Julien** (No.39; 04.91.24.34.10).

Further east, where La Canebière merges with boulevard de Longchamp, is a bourgeois nineteenth-century neighbourhood: the **Musée Grobert-Labadie** contains the diverse collections of a rich merchant, housed in a private mansion that offers an atmospheric peek at life in the city during its heyday. Just beyond, the **Palais Longchamp**, winsomely grandiose, contains the city's excellent **Musée des Beaux Arts** and the **Muséum d'Histoire Naturelle**.

Along boulevard Michelet to the south of the centre is Le Corbusier's **Cité Radieuse**, the prototype for innumerable modern housing developments. Cutting across towards the coast, the **Musée d'Art Contemporain** contains one of southern France's most important public collections of contemporary art.

Le Corbusier's innovative **Cité Radieuse**.

La Cité Radieuse

280 bd Michelet (04.91.77.81.74). **Open** guided tours only; contact the tourist office (04.91.13.89.00).
La Maison de Fada, or the House of the Madman, as the Marseillais once scornfully but now affectionately call Le Corbusier's 1952 reinforced-concrete apartment block, is one of the architect's most successful and original projects. Perched on piles with an open ground floor to create an impression of lightness, the building was meant to reinvent the village idiom for the twentieth century. In addition to balconied flats that house 1,600 people, it contains a floor that functions as a 'village street', with a hotel (*see p136* **Hôtel Le Corbusier**), post office, café, restaurant and shops. On the roof are an open-air theatre, a gym and a nursery school. The flats themselves are mostly duplexes in which the architect designed everything down to the knobs on the kitchen cupboards.

Docks de la Joliette

10 pl de la Joliette (04.91.91.17.70). **Open** 9am-7pm Mon-Sat.
Les Docks, as the Marseillais call the handsome stone warehouses that run along the waterfront for almost a mile, were modelled on St Katharine's Dock in London and were state of the art when they opened in 1866. As port traffic declined and cargo shifted to containers, the buildings fell into disuse and there were plans to raze them. However, they have been brilliantly renovated into office space by architect Eric Castaldi and are the centrepiece of the Euroméditerranée redevelopment project.

Churches

Abbaye de St-Victor

3 rue de l'Abbaye (04.96.11.22.60). **Open** 8am-7pm daily. **Admission** 10F.
Dominating the south bank of the Vieux Port, this spectacular, crenellated medieval citadel was built on the remains of an antique necropolis. The earlier church, founded in the fifth century by St Jean Cassian, was the city's first basilica. Saracens destroyed the original basilica in the eleventh century; it was rebuilt and fortified in the fourteenth. In the thirteenth-century crypt are remains of the fifth-century Chapelle Notre-Dame-de-Confession, which contains the tomb of St Victor, ground to death between two millstones by the Romans.

Cathédrale de la Major

pl de Major (04.91.90.53.57). **Open** 9am-noon, 2-5.30pm Tue-Thur; 2.30pm-6pm Fri-Sun.
The largest cathedral built in France since the Middle Ages, the neo-Byzantine Nouvelle-Major, tucked between the port and the Panier neighbourhood, was started in 1852 and completed in 1893. More rewarding, however, is the Ancienne-Major, the eleventh-century church, which was severely hacked about to make room for its larger neighbour. The chancel and part of the transept and nave

remain. The older church contains a Renaissance altarpiece by Francesco Laurana and Thomas de Como, as well as a ceramic Deposition attributed to the Della Robbia workshop.

Notre-Dame-de-la-Garde
rue Fort du Sanctuaire (04.91.13.40.80). **Open** *July, Aug* 7am-8pm daily; *Sept-June* 7am-7pm daily.
Perched on top of a 162m-high peak, the church that is the emblem of Marseille, with its monumental gilded statue of the Virgin holding the Christ child, was begun in 1853 and completed in 1870, while the interior decoration continued until 1899. Deeply loved by the Marseillais, its Byzantine-like interior is filled with remarkable ex votos, including one for Olympique de Marseille, the local football team (*see box p133*), and others for car accidents, military and boating accidents, diseases and so on. The mosaic floors were made in Venice, and alternating red and white marble pillars add to the richness of the surprisingly intimate chapel. Outside, the esplanade running around the basilica offers spectacular views of the city and its complicated geography. Come here early in your visit to get your bearings.

Museums & galleries

Jardins des Vestiges
Centre Bourse, 1 square Belsunce (04.91.90.42.22). **Open** noon-7pm Mon-Sat. **Admission** 12F, 6F children.
While the foundations for the Centre Bourse shopping centre were being dug in the 1970s, remains of Marseille's original Greek walls and a corner of the Roman port were unearthed. They're conserved here in a roofed shelter. The star feature of the adjoining Musée d'Histoire de Marseille is a remarkably well-preserved ship dating from the third century and hauled from the seabed in 1974.

Musée d'Art Contemporain (MAC)
69 av d'Haifa (04.91.72.17.27). **Open** *June-Sept* 11am-6pm Tue-Sun; *Oct-May* 10am-5pm Tue-Sun. **Admission** 18F, free under-10s.
Marseille's specialist contemporary art museum, the MAC, is located in a hangar-like space that opened in 1994 to house post-1960s works that no longer fitted in the Musée Cantini. It's a wide-ranging international collection that includes Rauschenberg, César, Roth, Balkenhol, Absalon and Laffont, as well as varied temporary exhibitions.

Musée des Beaux-Arts & Muséum d'Histoire Naturelle
Palais Longchamp, bd de Longchamp. **Open** *Musée des Beaux-Arts (04.91.14.59.30): June-Sept* 11am-6pm Tue-Sun; *Oct-May* 10am-5pm Tue-Sun; *Muséum d'Historie Naturelle (04.91.14.59.50):* 10am-5pm Tue-Sun. **Admission** *Musée des Beaux-Arts* 12F, 6F children; *Muséum d'Histoire Naturelle* 12F, 6F children.
No other monument expresses the ebullience of nineteenth-century Marseille – with Chicago, the fastest-growing city in the world at the time – better than the Palais Longchamp. This grandiose complex, inaugurated in 1869, was built to celebrate the completion of an 84km aqueduct bringing the diverted waters of the Durance river to the drought-prone port. A massive neo-classical, horseshoe-shaped colonnade, with a triumphal arch at its centre and museums at the head of each wing, crowns a hill landscaped into a massive series of fountains. On the ground floor of the Musée des Beaux-Arts are works by Marseillais painter and sculptor Pierre Puget (1620-94). On the first floor is a fine collection of sixteenth- and seventeenth-century French, Provençal, Italian and Flemish paintings, while on the second are French eighteenth- and nineteenth-century works, and old master drawings. The Muséum d'Histoire Naturelle has zoological and prehistoric artefacts, plus a tankful of exotic fish.

Musée Cantini
9 rue Grignan (04.91.54.77.75). **Open** *June-Sept* 11am-6pm Tue-Sun; *Oct-May* 10am-5pm Tue-Sun. **Admission** 12F, 6F children.
The city's modern art museum, which contains works from around 1945 to 1960, including many Surrealist paintings, was closed for restoration for years. It reopened in May 2000.

Musée des Docks Romains
pl du Vivaux (04.91.91.24.62). **Open** *June-Sept* 11am-6pm Tue-Sun; *Oct-May* 10am-5pm Tue-Sun. **Admission** 12F, 6F children.
During post-war reconstruction in 1947, the remains of a first-century Roman shipping warehouse on the edge of the Vieux Port were uncovered. This museum preserves the site intact, and documents the equipment and techniques used in maritime trade with exhibits of terracotta jars, amphorae and coins.

Musée de la Faïence
157 av de Montredon (04.91.72.43.47). **Open** *June-Sept* 11am-6pm Tue-Sun; *Oct-May* 10am-5pm Tue-Sun. **Admission** 12F, free under-10s.
Surrounded by a magnificent park that evokes the days when this rural part of Marseille was a popular place for the city's bourgeoisie to build summer and weekend homes, the elegant Château Pastre was built during the eighteenth century by a family that had grown rich trading with Egypt. Its beautiful interiors have been restored and today it houses the Musée de la Faïence, where more than 1,200 pieces of ceramic and porcelain are displayed. However low pottery comes on your list of sightseeing priorities, the beauty of these pieces may grip you, and the chateau itself is well worth a visit.

Musée Grobert-Labadie
140 bd de Longchamp (04.91.62.21.82). **Open** *June-Sept* 11am-6pm Tue-Sun; *Oct-May* 10am-5pm Tue-Sun. **Admission** 15F, free under-10s.
An intimate and atmospheric place, the Musée Grobert-Labadie houses the private art collection of a wealthy nineteenth-century couple. Their 1873 mansion, scrupulously renovated, offers an intriguing

glimpse of the cultivated tastes of the time in a domestic setting. Its diverse collection ranges from fifteenth- and sixteenth-century Italian and Flemish paintings to Fragonard and Millet, medieval tapestries and sculpture, and seventeenth- and eighteenth-century Provençal furniture and faience.

Musée de la Marine et de l'Economie de Marseille
Palais de la Bourse, 9 La Canebière (04.91.39.33.33). **Open** 10am-6pm daily. **Admission** 12F, 6F children.
This grandiose building housing the city's Chamber of Commerce was designed by architect Pascal Coste and inaugurated by Emperor Napoléon III in 1860. Medallions in the main hall celebrate the ports of the world, from Liverpool to Montevideo, with which the city was trading at the time. The museum charts the maritime history of Marseille from the seventeenth century with paintings, models and engravings.

Musée de la Mode
11 La Canebière (04.91.56.59.57). **Open** noon-7pm Tue-Sun. **Admission** 18F, free children.
Marseille's costume history and fashion museum has a rich permanent collection comprising more than 2,000 pieces, with a special emphasis on the last 70 years of fashion.

Musée du Vieux Marseille (Maison Diamantée)
rue de la Prison (04.91.55.10.19). **Open** *Maison Diamantée* (guided tours only) 3pm Sat, 11am Wed; call 04.91.55.28.68 for details.
The Maison Diamantée, so named because of its diamond-faceted Renaissance façade, was built in 1570 by Pierre Gardiolle, a rich merchant. It's the only surviving example of what the neighbourhood surrounding the Vieux Port looked like in the sixteenth century. Inside, the Musée du Vieux Marseille has Marseillais costumes, furniture, household utensils and other local artefacts, mainly from the eighteenth and nineteenth centuries. One room focuses on the plague of 1720 and another has a scale model of the city in 1848. Closed at the time of writing, the museum is due to reopen sometime in 2001. However, the *maison* itself, with its fine staircase, can be visited twice a week on free guided tours.

La Vieille-Charité
2 rue de la Charité (04.91.14.58.80). **Open** *June-Sept* 11am-6pm Tue-Sun; *Oct-May* 10am-5pm Tue-Sun. **Admission** 15F.
This seventeenth- to eighteenth-century ensemble designed by Pierre and Jean Puget has beautiful open loggias on three storeys around a courtyard, which is dominated by a magnificent chapel with an oval-shaped dome. Originally built as a shelter for the poor and homeless, it was renovated and reopened in 1986 as a cultural complex. The former chapel houses temporary exhibitions. Permanent collections include the Musée d'Archéologie Méditerranéenne and the Musée d'Arts Africains,

Océaniens et Amerindiens (MAAOA). The former has a superb collection of archaeological finds from around Provence and the Mediterranean, including the most important Egyptian collection in France outside Paris. Aside from mummified people, cats and ibises, there are statues and ceramics from ancient Greece, Etruscan burial urns and Roman glassware, bronzes and portrait busts. The MAAOA has artefacts from Africa, the South Pacific and North and South America, including masks, ceremonial paddles and a variety of human skulls, some of them tastefully engraved. A section of the Vieille-Charité complex is set aside for finds from the neolithic site at Roquepertuse.

Arts & entertainment

Cité de la Musique
4 rue Bernard Dubois (04.91.39.28.28). **Box office** 8.30am-7pm Mon-Fri. **Shows** 8.30pm Mon-Fri. **Tickets** 70F. **No credit cards.**
This well-equipped, city-sponsored conservatory offers modestly priced music lessons and diverse concerts that reflect the city's ethnic diversity.

La Friche la Belle de Mai
41 rue Jobin (04.91.85.42.78). **Open** 2-6pm Mon-Sat. **Admission** free.
A disused industrial complex in the scruffy Belle de Mai quarter north of the centre, La Friche started life as an artists' squat, but is now home to numerous artistic, musical and theatrical groups. Its gallery is used for exhibitions put on by its resident artists and associations, and for outside shows. For general information, contact the Astérides association at the number above. Among the other resident groups, Triangle (04.91.11.45.61) organises exchanges with foreign artists, and Vidéochroniques (04.91.11.48.70/www.lafriche.org/ videochroniques) produces and promotes video and multimedia works.

Galérie Roger Pailhas
19 quai Rive Neuve (04.91.54.02.22/04.91.55.66.88). **Open** 11am-1pm, 2-6pm Tue-Sat.
Among Marseille's commercial galleries, this is the one that has long set the agenda. Over the years it has collaborated with major international artists including Dan Graham and Daniel Buren.

Opéra Municipal
2 rue Molière (04.91.55.11.10). **Box office** 7am-7pm daily. **Shows** *Oct-June* 8.30pm Mon-Sat; 2.30pm, 8.30pm Sun. **Tickets** 55F-340F. **Credit** AmEx, DC, V.
The original Marseille opera was one of the city's great eighteenth-century buildings. Partially destroyed by fire in 1919, it was rebuilt in art deco style, conserving only the original façade and reopening in 1925. Today, it also houses the Ballet National, founded by Roland Petit – who retired last year, banning the use of any of his choreography when the city fathers disregarded his advice and took on Marie-Claude Pietragalla as the corps

Marseille & Aix

director. Pietragalla has come up trumps, however, producing an entire new repertoire in the space of a year. The ballet headquarters, which also houses a Centre Chorégraphique National, is located at 20 bd Gabès (info and bookings 04.91.71.03.03).

Théâtre de la Criée
30 quai Rive Neuve (04.91.54.70.54). **Box office** 11am-6pm Tue-Sat. **Shows** 8.30pm Tue, Fri, Sat; 7pm Wed, Thur; 3pm or 5pm Sun. **Tickets** 35F-160F. **Credit** MC, V.
Created from the former fish market in 1981, this theatre under the direction of Gildas Bourdet has two stages, one for mainstream shows and a smaller one for contemporary pieces by young authors.

Théâtre du Gymnase
4 rue du Théâtre-Français (04.91.24.35.35). **Box office** noon-6pm Mon-Sat. **Shows** 8.30pm Mon, Tue, Fri; 7pm (premières 8.30pm) Wed, Thur. **Tickets** 100F-170F. **Credit** MC, V.
This beloved candy-box of a theatre dates from 1834 and was completely restored in 1986 with a grant from the late oil tycoon Armand Hammer, whose parents landed in Marseille after fleeing a pogrom in Russia. Directed today by Dominique Bluzet, it's one of the best-attended and most innovative theatres in France, staging its own take on everything from French and international classics to contemporary French drama.

Théâtre de la Minoterie
9-11 rue d'Hozier (04.91.90.07.94). **Box office** 45 min before shows. **Shows** 9.02pm Tue, Fri, Sat; 7.23pm Wed, Thur. **Tickets** 70F. **No credit cards.**
One of the most famous experimental theatre venues in France, right down to its unusual location in the middle of the industrial zone flanking the port, and its unconventional show times. This stage is used by regional theatre companies and is also known for its dance festival.

Where to eat

Marseille restaurants reviewed in our **Provençal Food & Drink** chapter are **L'Escale** (*page 47*), **Le Miramar** (*page 48*) and **Une Table au Sud** (*page 48*).

Les Arcenaulx
25 cours d'Estienne d'Orves (04.91.59.80.30). **Meals served** noon-2.30pm, 7-11.30pm Mon-Sat. **Menus** 155F-285F. **Credit** AmEx, DC, MC, V.
In a restored eighteenth-century arsenal building, this charming restaurant serves delicious home-style, old-fashioned Provençal dishes: stuffed veal cutlets in tomato sauce or tagliatelle pistou.

Café Parisien
1 pl Sadi Carnot (04.91.90.05.77). **Open** 4am-10pm daily. **Meals served** noon-3pm, 7-10pm daily. **Menus** 52F-65F. **Credit** MC, V.
A beautifully renovated 1901 café with handsome stucco mouldings. This is where the night people

come when the clubs close, for quiet breakfasts, light lunches or dinners. There are also first-rate tapas (20F a portion) on Thursdays and Fridays from 6.30pm to 9pm.

Caffè Milano
43 rue Sainte (04.91.33.14.33). **Meals served** noon-2pm, 8-10pm Mon-Fri; 8-10pm Sat. **Average** 130F. **Credit** MC, V.
This popular spot serves Italian and Provençal dishes in a buzzy atmosphere. Try dishes such as the ribbon pasta with locally made fresh goat's cheese, batter-dipped and fried squid, beef braised in wine, and pork in ginger sauce. The house wines are good and inexpensive.
Branch: Le Milano des Docks Les Docks Atrium 10.4, 10 pl de la Joliette (04.91.91.27.10).

César's Place
21 pl aux Huiles (04.91.33.25.22). **Meals served** 7-11pm Mon, Sat; noon-2.15pm, 7-11pm Tue-Fri. **Menus** 60F-150F. **Credit** AmEx, MC, V.
An excellent bistro with very good service, this is an oasis of good Provençal food, though the menu, which changes seasonally, actually puts an appealing contemporary spin on the classics. Try dishes such as salad garnished with duck breast and cêpe mushrooms, gnocchi with *brousse* (soft white cheese), and spicy Corsican sausage. The house red, a Costières de Nîmes, is very good, too.

Chez Vincent
25 rue Glandeves (04.91.33.96.78). **Meals served** noon-11pm Wed-Sun. **Average** 100F. **No credit cards.**
In the mini red-light district near the Vieux Port, this old-fashioned Italian place has a clubby crowd of regulars and is popular with night owls, including singers from the nearby Opéra. It offers southern Italian cooking (with a Provençal twist) at low prices: try the spaghetti with *clovises* (baby clams) or the lasagne. It also does decent pizzas.

La Grotte
1 av des Pebrons, Calanque de Callelongue (04.91.73.17.79). **Meals served** noon-2.30pm, 7.30-10pm daily. **Average** 150F. **No credit cards.**
Extremely popular with a lively young crowd, including hikers and walkers from the nearby trails, this simple little restaurant bar does great pizzas and grilled fish at the water's edge. Book ahead if you want a table outside.

Des Mets de Provence Chez Maurice Brun
18 quai Rive Neuve (04.91.33.35.38). **Meals served** 8-10.30pm Mon; noon-2pm, 8-10.30pm Tue-Sat. Closed first two weeks Aug. **Menus** 220F-300F. **Credit** MC, V.
Founded in 1936, this place proudly perpetuates the traditional kitchen of Provence. There's a big rotisserie in the fireplace, and pretty mix-and-match table settings. There's no printed menu: the proprietor recites the daily offerings, part of a substantial,

The Olympique spirit

Say 'Marseille' to a Parisian, and the associations are likely to be crime, corruption, pastis and bouillabaise – in that order. Marseille is seen as a 'problem city', with high rates of unemployment, and social unrest. Recently, the rap music of bands such as IAM (*see chapter* **Arts & Entertainment**) has provided some outlet for Marseille's wounded pride. But it is still Olympique de Marseille (OM), the city's soccer team – what one national magazine called the city's 'armed wing' – that does most of the fighting back. For most supporters, few moments can compare with the joy of beating Paris-St-Germain.

Marseille lives, breathes and breeds *le foot*. Legends like Eric Cantona grew up on the city's backstreets, and the team commands the sort of fervour that separatist movements might elsewhere. The night before a match you'll see a slow procession of supporters traipsing up to the cathedral of Notre-Dame-de-la-Garde to light candles. Next day, in the stadium, some less pious supporters may still be sporting the T-shirts that were all the rage in 1999, adorned with the legend 'J'enc… Paris' (Up yours, Paris).

OM needed plenty of fighting spirit in 1993, when the bottom fell out of the team's world. Shiny saviour-president Bernard Tapie (*see chapter* **Le Midi Today**), a former socialist minister, who had hoisted them to four league titles and a European Cup title, was shown to have feet of clay. Or soil rather – the money he set up to buy OM's victory over fellow leaguer Valenciennes had been buried in a player's garden. The result was scandal, the second division and insolvency.

The club has clawed its way back with determination, finally taking second place in the UEFA club and the French league in 1999. Part of the reason is the crop of fresh talent brought in by its new president, Adidas boss Robert-Louis Dreyfus: stars such as Fabrizio Ravenelli and Laurent Blanc, plus French internationals Christophe Dugarry and Robert Pires. But the club's recovery is also due to the tenacity of its fans. They take their role to heart; 60,000 of them pay to get the team's cable TV channel OMTV.

Olympique de Marseille

Club office *441 av du Prado (04.91.76.56.09).* **Stade Vélodrome** *3 bd Michelet. Métro line 2 Rond-point du Prado (exit on bd Michelet).* The largest stadium in France after the Grand Stade, with 60,000 seats. The best ones – costing 200F – are in the Jean-Bouin stand. For a cheaper (100F-150F) but still relatively peaceful viewpoint, head for the Ganay stand. Tickets can be bought from the stadium on match day or in advance from L'OM Café, 3 quai des Belges, Vieux Port, or the Virgin Megastore, 75 rue St-Ferreol. *Website: www.olympiquedemarseille.com/*

delicious *prix-fixe* meal that might include *galinette* (a local white fish) boned and stuffed with vegetables, or a *daube* of wild boar.

Orient Extreme

9 rue Dejean (04.91.33.54.15). **Meals served** 7-11pm Mon; 11am-2pm, 7-11pm Tue-Sat. **Menu** 84F. **No credit cards.**

The neo-Egyptian wall paintings aren't terribly alluring, but the cooking – a variety of Egyptian and Middle Eastern dishes – is authentic and copiously served. Lounge on big leather pillows around the brass tray tables upstairs and try the couscous or *kefta* (minced lamb and bulghur). Wash it all down with Moroccan or Algerian wine.

Le Panier des Arts

rue du Petit Puits (04.91.56.02.32). **Meals served** 7.30-11.30pm Mon-Sat. Closed last two weeks Aug. **Menus** 98F-150F. **No credit cards**.

Château d'If

This tiny islet of sun-bleached white stone is today inhabited by salamanders and seagulls. Its two most famous residents – Edmond Dantès and l'Abbé Faria, the main characters of Alexandre Dumas' *The Count of Monte Cristo* – never existed.

Aware that control over the island meant control over Marseille's harbour, François I had a fortress built here in 1524. With its massive stone wall, and three stout towers – added at the end of the sixteenth century – the effect of this chateau was sufficiently formidable that it never saw combat and was eventually converted into a prison. Mirabeau ran up enough debts in Aix to be imprisoned here. Thousands of Protestants met grisly ends here after the Edict of Nantes was revoked in 1685.

But it was Dumas who put the island on the map of the world's imagination by making it the prison from which Dantès escaped: wily administrators soon caught on and kept tourists happy by hacking out the very hole through which Edmond slid to freedom in the story.

The chateau is easily visited in half an hour: there's little there aside from a few placards about the history of the building and the life of Alexandre Dumas, including a family tree that shows he was one-quarter black, his grandfather having married a slave on his sugar plantation in the Dominican Republic. So bring a picnic and enjoy the clean sea water. Off-season, the one café on the island is likely to be closed, making for a long, cold wait between ferries.

Château d'If

04.91.59.02.30. **Open** 9.30am-6.30pm daily. **Admission** 25F. GAMC (7 quai des Belges, 04.91.55.50.09) runs six to eight crossings daily; times vary depending on the weather and season. A round-trip ticket is 50F.

This small, easygoing bistro just steps from La Vieille-Charité is a fine spot for a meal in the old Panier neighbourhood. The kitchen does a diverse Mediterranean menu, including dishes such as tuna steak dressed with olive oil, and a *pastilla* (flaky pastry parcel) of rabbit with cinnamon.

Bars & nightlife

Le Bar de la Marine
15 quai Rive Neuve (04.91.73.46.90). **Open** 8am-11pm daily. **No credit cards.**
Formerly frequented by sailors and fishermen, this tiny waterfront bar has a fading but slightly raffish air. It attracts a diverse crowd depending on the time of day. It functions as a café in the daytime and as a bar at night, when it's a popular place for a drink before heading to the nearby clubs.

L'Intermédiaire
63 pl Jean Jaurès (04.91.47.01.25). **Open** 7pm-2am Tue-Sat. **Admission** free.
The hippest venue for jazz, blues and rock in town (concerts 10.30pm Wed-Sat; jam session Tue) is an easygoing place: small and crowded but friendly. It also has a pool table. If you're interested in the local music scene, watch out for Gachempega, a group that has a contemporary take on traditional southern French music.

Le Moulin
47 bd Perrin (04.91.06.33.94). **No credit cards.**
This former cinema has become one of Marseille's main venues for visiting French and international rock and world music bands.

The New Cancan
3 rue Senac-de-Meilhan (04.91.48.59.76). **Open** 11pm-5am Thur-Sun. **Admission** 70F Thur, 80F Fri, 90F Sat, Sun. **Credit** MC, V.
The New Cancan is Marseille's largest gay club. It sweeps up the city's arty odd bods and local glamour pusses, as well as muscle boys, the hardcore dance crowd from the suburban council flats and a smattering of lesbians. The music ranges from techno and house to 1970s disco. Smallish and rundown, its low-attitude factor make it a lot of fun. There's a drag show on Thursdays.

La Part des Anges
33 rue Sainte (04.91.33.55.70). **Open** 9am-2am daily. **Credit** MC, V.
Georges, the friendly proprietor of this trendy wine bar, hunts good wines from all over France and sells his hundred or so vintages by the glass (14F-52F) or the bottle. Food includes tasty cheese and charcuterie plates, and a few hot dishes (25F-50F). Open until 2am every day, La Part des Anges attracts a wonderfully eclectic crowd, from young local trendies to arty types and ladies with steel-spiked high heels taking a break from plying their trade on the nearby pavement.

Le Trolleybus
24 quai Rive Neuve (04.91.54.30.45). **Open** 11pm-5am Thur-Sun. **Admission** free Thur, Fri, Sun; 60F Sat. **Credit** AmEx, DC, MC, V.
This sprawling club is the ground zero of Marseille nightlife, with something to please all the punters. Different zones offer techno, salsa and funk-acid-jazz... and *pétanque*. You'll find a heterogeneous crowd, from young bankers to rappers wearing tracksuits and trainers.

Shopping

Arax
24 rue d'Aubagne (04.91.54.11.50). **Open** 8am-12.30pm, 3-7pm Mon-Sat. **No credit cards.**
This fragrant little cavern of a shop is an edible reflection of the city's astonishing ethnic diversity, selling everything from Black Sea anchovies and Armenian dried beef to stuffed grape leaves, dried apricots, couscous ingredients and a huge variety of herbs and spices.

Arterra
1A rue du Petit Puits (04.91.91.03.31). **Open** 9am-1pm, 2-6pm Mon-Fri. **No credit cards.**
Santons (Christmas crib figures) can be cloying, but a visit to this workshop in the Le Panier district shows how charming they are when dosed with a bit of artful talent. In addition to the Holy Family, there are lots of secular Provençal figurines.

Bataille
25 pl Notre-Dame-du-Mont (04.91.47.06.23). **Open** 8am-8pm Mon-Sat. **Credit** AmEx, MC, V.
The most venerable *traiteur* (caterer) in Marseille is the perfect place to shop for a picnic: there's an excellent cheese counter and delectable prepared salads and cold cuts. The olive oils are wonderful, too.

Compagnie de Provence
1 rue Caisserie (04.91.56.20.94). **Open** 10am-5pm Mon-Sat. **Credit** MC, V.
This simple shop is the place to come for Savon de Marseille, the celebrated blocks of soap that are one of the city's most famous products. The classic soap is a non-perfumed olive-oil green, but lavender, lemon, rose and other scents are also available.

Faïence Figuères
10/12 av Lauzier (04.91.73.06.79). **Open** 8.30am-noon, 1-6pm Mon-Fri. **Credit** AmEx, MC, V.
This charming, family-owned and operated atelier has almost single-handedly revived a tradition of faience and delightful ceramic *tromp l'oeil* centrepieces and decorative objects in Marseille, a craft that dates from the early seventeenth century.

Four des Navettes
136 rue St-Marseille (04.91.33.32.12). **Open** 7am-8pm Mon-Sat; 9am-7.30pm Sun. **Credit** MC, V.
Founded in 1781, this bakery is famous for its boat-shaped *navettes*, orange-scented biscuits that are a local delicacy and are modelled on the tiny boat in

which Mary Magdalene and Lazarus supposedly arrived on continental shores.

La Thuberie
14-16 rue Thubaneau (04.91.90.84.55). **Open** 10.30am-7pm Tue-Sat. **No credit cards.**
This hip new boutique is a sign of the reviving (though not wholly revived – watch out for bag-snatchers or worse) fortunes of the Belsunce neighbourhood, where the narrow streets are lined with gorgeous eighteenth-century mansions built by the city's bourgeoisie. Run by designer Linda Cohen, it's a showcase for local talent with some wonderful clothing – look for Tectus and Benoît Missolin designs – plus housewares and furniture.

Torrefaction Noailles
56 La Canebière (04.91.55.60.66). **Open** 7am-7pm Mon-Sat. **Credit** AmEx, MC, V.
Marseille's most famous coffee-roaster sells a variety of different roasts, ground or as beans, in this attractive café-shop on the city's main avenue.

Where to stay

Bonneveine Youth Hostel
47 av Joseph Vidal (04.91.17.63.30). Closed mid-Dec to mid-Jan. **Rates** 65F-175F per person. **Credit** MC, V.
Just 200m from the sea and very near the *calanques*, this comfortable youth hostel is a good bet if you're looking for a holiday in nature.

Château de la Panouse
198 av de la Panouse (tel/fax 04.91.41.01.74). Closed Feb. **Rates** double 230F-640F. **No credit cards.**
Just three double bedrooms (with breakfast) are available in this elegant nineteenth-century chateau on a hill near a nature reserve with walking trails. The peaceful but very remote location makes private transport a must. There's a pool and a superb view of the city. Book by letter or fax only.

Hôtel Hermès
2 rue Bonnetière (04.96.11.63.63/fax 04.96.11.63. 64). **Rates** single 300F-350F, double 395F-470F. **Credit** MC, V.
Though its rooms are small, this simple hotel just steps from the Vieux Port is good value. Several rooms on the top floor have small terraces with superb views of the harbour and Notre-Dame-de-la-Garde. There's a top-floor sundeck, too.

Hôtel Le Corbusier
280 bd Michelet (04.91.16.78.00/fax 04.91.16.78. 28). **Rates** single 265F, double 295F, triple 395F. **Credit** MC, V.
Though rooms veer more towards the cheap than the cheerful, Le Corbusier fans won't want to pass up the opportunity to spend a night at this hotel on the seventh floor of the Modernist architect's famous Cité Radieuse.

Mercure Beauvau
4 rue Beauvau (04.91.54.91.00). **Rates** single 570F-660F, double 690F-780F, suite 1,600F. **Credit** AmEx, DC, MC, V.
This old-fashioned hotel, where Chopin and George Sand once stayed, overlooks the Vieux Port. Public rooms have Louis Philippe- and Napoléon III-style furniture; bedrooms are done up in Provençal prints.

Le Petit Nice
anse de Maldormé, corniche JF Kennedy (04.91.59. 25.92/fax 04.91.59.28.08). **Rates** single 1,000F-1,200F, double 2,200-2,600F, suite 3,100F-4,300F. **Credit** AmEx, DC, MC, V.
A luxurious villa with 13 rooms and a swimming pool, the Petit Nice overlooks the Mediterranean and is the address of choice for visiting stars. Though the setting is splendid, the hotel's Michelin two-star restaurant has its ups and downs.

Sofitel Vieux Port
36 bd Charles Livon (04.91.15.59.00/fax 04.91.15. 59.50). **Rates** single 1,240F-1,680F, double 1,340F-1,780F, suite 3,300F-5,000F. **Credit** AmEx, DC, MC, V.
This low-rise modern hotel has comfortable and attractive rooms, plus spectacular views over the Vieux Port, and an excellent restaurant.

Essentials

Getting there

From the airport
The Aéroport CCI Marseille-Provence (flight information 04.42.14.14.14) is located 25km northwest of the city in Martignane. From the airport, Cartreize (04.91.50.59.34) runs bus services every 20 minutes from 6.30am to 9.50pm from Terminals 1 and 2 to the St-Charles railway station in the city centre, and from the station to the airport from 6.30am to 8.50pm. The trip takes 25 minutes, and costs 45F one-way. A taxi to the Vieux Port should cost around 230F.

By car
Marseille is served by three major autoroutes: A51-A7 (north) heads to the airport, Aix and Lyon. The A55 runs west along the coast to the airport. The A50 (east) runs east to Toulon, Nice and Genoa. The Prado-Carenage tunnel (13.50F toll) links the A55 to the A50 without travelling through city streets. For directions or other driving information (in French only), call CRICR (Centre Régional d'Information et de Coordination Routières) on 04.91.78.78.78, which is open 24 hours daily. There are public car parks at the Bourse (04.91.91.19.26), Hôtel de Ville (04.90.91.62.83) and Vieux Port (04.91.54.34.38).

By bus
The *gare routière* (3 pl Victor Hugo, information 04.91.08.16.40) is the hub for coach services to the Camargue and most other destinations in the Bouches du Rhone. Phocéens Cars (04.93.85.66.61) operates long-distance bus services between

Marseille and Avignon, Nice via Aix-en-Provence
(four buses a day), Venice, Milan and Rome (one a
day), and Barcelona and Valencia (one a day).

By train
The main station is the Gare St-Charles (sq Narvik,
information and reservations 08.36.35.35.35). In the
station, SOS Voyageurs (04.93.82.62.13, open 9am-
noon, 3-6pm Mon-Fri) helps with stolen or lost
luggage, missed trains, parents with children and
elderly passengers. The TGV service due to begin in
2001 will cut the travel time between Paris and
Marseille from five and a half hours to three hours.

By boat
There are regular ferry services to Algeria, Tunisia,
Morocco, Corsica and Sardinia. The main passenger
terminal is the Gare Maritime de la Joliette
(information 04.91.39.42.42). SNCM (61 bd des
Dames, open 8.30am-7.45pm Mon-Fri) is the primary
passenger line serving the port. For ferries to
Sardinia, Corsica or Italy, call 08.36.67.95.00; for
Algeria, Tunisia or Morocco, call 08.36.67.21.00.

Getting around

By bus & metro
RTM (04.91.91.92.10) runs a comprehensive system
of 81 bus lines, as well as the city's two metro
(underground) lines and a tram. For metro
information, call Espace Information, 6 rue des
Fabres (04.91.19.55.55, open 8.30am-6pm Mon-Fri,
9am-5.30pm Sat). The same tickets are used on
buses, metros and the tram, and can be purchased in
metro stations, on the bus (exact change only) or at
tabacs and Maisons de Presse. An individual ticket
costs 9F and entitles the user to one hour's travel on
any bus, metro or tram. A one-day ticket is 25F, a
weekly pass 58F, monthly pass 280F.

By taxi
Marseille's taxis are expensive, and it's a good idea
to look at a map to have some idea as to where
you're going before setting out. There are cab ranks
located on most main squares in the city, or you can
call a cab: try Marseille Taxi (04.91.02.20.20),
Eurotaxi (04.91.97.12.12), Radio Taxi (04.91.85.80.00),
Taxi Plus (04.91.03.60.03) or Taxi Radio Tupp
(04.91.05.80.80). The pick-up fare is 11F, then 7.24F
per km during the day, 9F per km at night.

Tourist information

Office du Tourisme
*4 La Canebière (04.91.13.89.00/fax 04.91.13.89.20/
destination-marseille@wanadoo.fr).* **Open** *July-Sept*
9am-8pm Mon-Sat; 10am-7pm Sun; *Oct-June* 9am-
7pm Mon-Sat; 10am-5pm Sun.
There are branch offices at the St-Charles station
and place des Pistoles.
Website: www.destination.marseille.com

Lost property
18 rue de la Cathédrale (04.91.90.99.37). **Open**
8.30am-11.30am, 2.30-5.30pm Mon-Fri.

Post office
Central Post Office *Poste Colbert, rue Henri
Barbusse (04.91.15.47.00).* **Open** 8am-7pm Mon-Fri,
8am-noon Sat.

Around Marseille

Heading west from Marseille, the faded
industrial town of **L'Estaque** looks like an
unlikely place to have swayed the history of
modern art, but it did. When Paul Cézanne first
visited it in 1870, the little fishing village was
already evolving into a working-class suburb
living off its tile factories and cement works.
The transition clearly intrigued him, because
his most famous painting of the town, *Le Golfe
de Marseilles vu de L'Estaque* (1885) – now in
the Art Institute of Chicago – has a factory
chimney smoking in the lower right-hand
corner of the canvas.

The main attraction for Cézanne (and Derain,
Braque, Dufy and the others who came in their
wake) – the remarkable light and profusion of
different forms on the landscape – survives
today. Amid the urban sprawl it's not easy to
pick out the locations the painters immortalised,
but the main Marseille tourist office (*see page
137*) will help if you take its guided Circuit des
Peintres walking tour.

Beyond L'Estaque is a charming and
surprisingly unspoiled stretch of coastline
known as La Côte Bleu, much frequented by the
Marseillais at weekends. **Carry-le-Rouet**, with
its crowded beach, is the largest town on the
coast. **La Redonne** and **Carro** have
picturesque yacht and fishing ports.

Inland, **Martigues** is a pretty little town of
pastel houses built along canals, on the edge of
the heavily industrialised Etang de Berre, a
lagoon that is surrounded by one of the largest
petrochemical and oil refining complexes in
Europe. Martigues (where the recent political
scene has been far from attractive) is the result
of a fusion of three villages: Jonquières,
Ferrières and the Ile Brescon. In **Jonquières**,
the church of **St-Genies**, built between 1625
and 1669, has elaborate baroque twirls in its
chapelle de l'Annonciade. Next door is the
baroque **Eglise de la Madeleine**. Over in
Ferrières, the **Musée Ziem** contains works
by local landscape artists and some
archeological bits and pieces.

Heading east from Marseille, the scenic
Route de Gineste (D559) runs through such
beautiful rural landscapes of vineyards and
forests that it's hard to believe that the centre
of France's third-largest city is just minutes
away. From this road, walking tracks lead to
the coast where there are magnificent views
of the dramatic *calanques*.

Heading north, the rural outskirts of Marseille are Pagnol country.

Born in Aubagne in 1895, Marcel Pagnol is the modern writer most closely associated with twentieth-century Provence. Among his best known works, many of which have been made into films, are *Fanny*, *Manon des Sources*, *La Femme du Boulanger* and *Souvenirs d'Enfance*. The Aubagne tourist office will provide instructions for the Circuit Pagnol, for which you'll need your own wheels to reach many sites mentioned in his works. Included on the circuit is the quiet village of **La Treille**, inside Marseille's city limits, which appears in *Jean de Florette* and *Manon des Sources*, and is where the writer is buried.

Aubagne itself is a busy commercial centre and seems unappealing from the outside, but its *vieille ville* is pleasant and dotted with tree-lined squares. The town is renowned for its ceramics industry, especially for its *santons* (Christmas crib figures – *see box page 291*). There are a dozen *santon* workshops in town: the tourist office will provide a complete list with opening hours.

Aubagne's other claim to fame is as the headquarters of the French Foreign Legion. The **Musée du Kepi Blanc** – named after the legionnaires' signature white caps (*képi*) – pays homage to this legendary military fraternity with displays of medals, weaponry, uniforms and some wonderful photographs.

Musée du Képi Blanc

Caserme Vienot, west of Aubagne on the D44 (04.42.03.03.20). **Open** *June-Sept* 10am-noon, 3-7pm Tue-Sun; *Oct-May* 10am-noon, 2-6pm Wed, Sat, Sun. **Admission** free.

Musée Ziem

bd du 14 Juillet (04.42.80.66.06). **Open** *July, Aug* 10am-12.30pm, 2.30-6.30pm Wed-Mon; *Sept-June* 2.30-6.30pm Wed-Sun. **Admission** free.

Where to eat

On the coast west of Marseille in Sausset-les-Pins, locals delight in the imaginative cooking – red mullet salad with mint, monkfish with mangoes – of Joelle Boudara at **Les Girelles** (rue Fréderic Mistral, 04.42.45.26.16, closed Tue, lunch Mon-Wed in July & Aug, dinner Sun, two weeks Jan, two weeks Nov). Menus 138F-290F.

In Martigues, try the *poutargue*, a delicacy of dried, pressed and salted fish eggs, at **Le Miroir** (4 rue M Galdy, 04.42.80.50.45, closed Mon, lunch Sat, dinner Sun, two weeks Apr, two weeks Aug, menus 118F-175F). In Aubergne, **La Farandole** (6 rue Martino, 04.42.03.26.36, closed Sun, dinner Mon, menus 68F-145F) serves delicious, home-style Provençal cooking.

Getting there

By car

From central Marseille, the N568 passes through L'Estaque and then heads inland for Martigues and the Etang de Berre; 6km out of L'Estaque, the D5 branches off left to Carry-le-Rouet and the Côte Bleu. South of the city, the D559 skirts behind the *calanques* to Cassis. For Aubagne, take the A50/A501 autoroute (exit no.6 on the A501) or the N8.

By bus

There are regular services to Aubagne, Martigues, and L'Estaque from the *gare routière* (04.91.08.16.40).

By train

The main coast line stops in Aubagne and L'Estaque, while a branch line from Marseille stops in localities along the Côte Bleu, and Martigues.

Tourist information

Aubagne

Office du Tourisme, av A Boyer (04.42.03.49.98). **Open** 9am-12.30pm, 2.30-6pm daily.

Martigues

Office du Tourisme, 2 quai Pierre Doumer (04.42.42.31.10/fax 04.42.4.31.10). **Open** *Easter to mid-Sept* 9am-7pm Mon-Sat; 10am-noon Sun; *mid-Sept to Easter* 8.45am-6.30pm Mon-Sat.

Aubagne is famous for its *santons*.

Aix-en-Provence

Famed for its arts festivals and its elegant architecture, sophisticated Aix is the golden city of the South.

Aix, the intellectual and elegant, is the eternal rival of rough diamond Marseille. It's not that it doesn't have its share of housing estates around the edges, but the overall impression is one of golden stone buildings, sophisticated cafés and tinkling fountains: for Aix's origins as a restful place to take the waters go back to Roman times. Aquae Sextiae was founded in 122 BC by Roman consul Sextius after he had defeated the Celto-Ligurian *oppidium* at Entremont, the remains of which lie just outside the city.

In the twelfth and thirteenth centuries, the independent Counts of Provence held court in Aix, but it was in the fifteenth century that the city saw a true resurgence. In 1409, the university was founded by Louis II of Anjou, and under Good King René (1409-80), a patron of the arts, the city flourished. After its absorption into France in 1486, Aix became the capital of the *parlement* of Provence – the southern arm of the country's strongly centralised administration. In decline for a couple of centuries, Aix picked up again in the 1600s, when the newly prosperous political and merchant class began building elegant townhouses to the south of the *vielle ville*, virtually doubling the city's size. Aix has expanded even more rapidly in the past 20 years, as new housing, business and university districts have swallowed up rural villages and the grandiose agricultural *bastides* built by the nobility outside the city.

Despite a reputation as the haughty bastion of the bourgeoisie, and the highbrow image of its summer arts festivals, Aix is a surprisingly young city, with some 40,000 students and a thriving café society.

Sightseeing

Vieil Aix

At the heart of the city – and its most quintessential location – is the **cours Mirabeau** (*see box page 144*), a broad avenue lined with plane trees and elegant stone houses. At one end is place Charles de Gaulle, better known as **La Rotonde**, marked by a grandiose

Place d'Albertas, with its cobblestones and classical façades, in Vieil Aix.

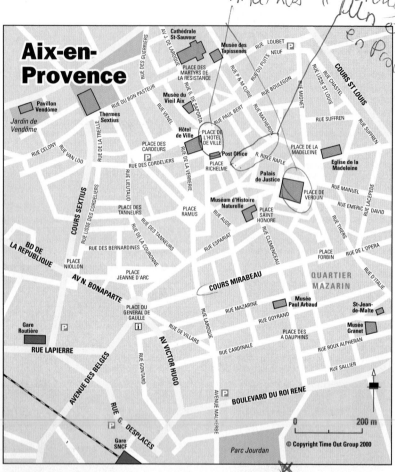

Aix-en-Provence

markets il poterie en Provence

Marseille & Aix

fountain in black and white marble, with lions
at the base and figures of Justice, Agriculture
and Fine Art on the top.

North of cours Mirabeau lies Vieil Aix, the
oldest part of the city, where squares and smart
mansions alternate with winding _ruelles_.
Fountains splash in almost every square,
statues peer out of niches on street corners
and the whole place is buzzing with small
bistros, cafés and shops.

Parallel to the cours runs rue Espariat, where
the baroque church of **St-Esprit** and the bell
tower of a former Augustinian monastery nestle
amid cafés and shops. At its north-east end, rue
Fabrot is home to the smartest designer
boutiques in Aix. To get there you cross the
glorious, cobbled **place d'Albertas**, a
U-shape of uniform classical façades with

Corinthian pilasters, which was built in 1745
as a speculative venture by the powerful
Albertas family. Almost opposite is the elegant
1672 **Hôtel Boyer d'Eguilles**, now part
pharmacy, part school and part **Muséum
d'Histoire Naturelle**.

Busy shopping streets rue Aude and rue
Maréchal Foch lead to **place Richelme**, which
comes alive on Tuesday, Thursday and
Saturday mornings, with a fruit and vegetable
market under the plane trees. The door of the
late seventeenth-century **Hôtel Arbaud**
(7 rue Maréchal Foch) is framed by two
muscular male slaves. In beautiful **place de
l'Hôtel de Ville**, the Gothic belfry with
astrological clock and rotating figures of the
seasons was a former town gateway. The **post
office** next door to the Hôtel de Ville occupies a

magnificent eighteenth-century former grain market, whose pediment, an allegory of the Durance and Rhône rivers by Chastel, is given a wonderful spark of life by a leg dangling lasciviously out of the frame.

Running north from Hôtel de Ville, rue Gaston de Saporta contains some of Aix's finest *hôtels particuliers*: **Hôtel Etienne de St-Jean** (No.17) contains the **Musée du Vieil Aix**; **Hôtel de Châteaurenard** (No.19), where Louis XIV stayed in 1660, has a staircase painted with *trompe l'oeil* by Daret (it now houses the city's social services, but you can visit the entrance hall); **Hôtel Maynier d'Oppedé** (No.23) belongs to the university, which stretches away to the left.

Opposite is the composite structure of the **Cathédrale St-Sauveur**, with its sculpted portals and fortified towers. Next door, the baroque **Palais de l'Archevêché** contains a **Musée des Tapisseries** (tapestries) and hosts productions in the courtyard during the **Festival International d'Art Lyrique** (*see box page 146*).

West of the town hall, long **place des Cardeurs** is lined with ethnic restaurants. Underground car park aside, it looks as ancient as any of the other squares in Aix but in fact was created only in the 1960s, when an area of slums, historically the Jewish quarter, was demolished. From here, narrow streets lead to the **Thermes Sextius** (the thermal baths), a last surviving fortified tower and, on rue des Etuves, some fragments of medieval city wall.

South-east of the town hall, the colonnaded mass of the **Palais de Justice** was built in the 1820s. In front, place des Prêcheurs is used for a big food and junk market on Tuesday, Thursday and Saturday mornings and a flower market on other days, in the shadow of the neo-classical **Eglise de la Madeleine**. Further east from the Palais de Justice lies the Villeneuve quartier, which replaced the royal gardens in the late sixteenth century. Several ornate *hôtels particuliers* remain on **rue de l'Opéra**. Cézanne was born at No.25; at No.17 is the Jeu du Paume, a real tennis court built in 1660 and transformed into the **Théâtre du Jeu de Paume** a century later.

Cathédrale St-Sauveur

pl de l'Université (04.42.21.10.51). **Open** *church* 7.30am-noon, 2-6pm daily (closed to tourists during services); *cloister* 9.30-11am, 2.30-4.30pm Mon-Sat (hours may vary).

Aix cathedral is a hotchpotch of Romanesque, Gothic, Renaissance and baroque, reflecting its long on-off construction from the fifth to the eighteenth centuries. At first sight the interior looks unremarkable, with three curiously linked naves, Gothic vaults and classical domes. But it has two jewels.

The first is off the right-hand nave: a polygonal, fifth-century Merovingian baptistry, with crisply carved capitals and traces of frescos (the hole in the ground is a throwback to the days of total immersion baptism). Further along to the right is a cloister, with paired capitals carved with mysterious beasts and foliage.

In the central nave is the second treasure: Nicolas Froment's symbolically loaded fifteenth-century triptych of Mary in the Burning Bush, with King René and Queen Jeanne praying in the wings. At the end of the left nave, the seventeenth-century Corpus Domini chapel has a fine wrought iron grille and a painting by Jean Daret.

Eglise de la Madeleine

pl des Prêcheurs (04.42.38.02.81). **Open** 8-11.30am, 3-5pm daily.

This former Dominican convent was rebuilt in the 1690s in the baroque style. A neo-classical façade, busy with swags and garlands, was added in the nineteenth century. Inside there is a good Annunciation (1444), attributed to Flemish painter Barthélemy Van Eyck.

Hôtel de Ville

pl de l'Hôtel de Ville (04.42.25.95.95) **Open** *Salle des Etats de Provences* 10am-noon, 3-5pm Mon-Fri. **Admission** free.

The town hall was built between 1655 and 1678 by Pierre Pavillon. A wrought-iron gateway leads into an elegant cobbled courtyard. At the back, a double stairway leads up to the Salle des Etats de Provences, hung with portraits and mythological subjects.

Muséum d'Histoire Naturelle

6 rue Espariat (04.42.26.23.67). **Open** 10am-noon, 1-5pm daily. **Admission** 10F, free children.

Mineralogy and palaeontology collections, including a huge collection of dinosaur eggs, in a fine seventeenth-century hôtel.

Musée des Tapisseries

pl des Martyrs de la Résistance (04.42.23.09.91). **Open** 10-11.45am, 2-5.45pm Mon, Wed-Sun. **Admission** 10F, free children.

In the former bishop's palace, whose courtyard hosts the annual opera festival (*see box p146*), the Musée des Tapisseries houses a collection of seventeenth- and eighteenth-century tapestries discovered in the palace in the nineteenth century.

Musée du Vieil Aix

17 rue Gaston-de-Saporta (04.42.21.43.55). **Open** *Apr-Sept* 10am-noon, 2.30-6pm Tue-Sun; *Oct-Mar* 10am-noon, 2.30-5pm Tue-Sun. **Admission** 10F, free under-14s.

This small but worthwhile collection housed in a seventeenth-century nobleman's residence focuses on folk art, with *santons* (Christmas crib figures – *see box p291*) and puppets from a mechanical crèche, plus some fine lacquered furniture and faience. Two folding wooden screens and a fragile line of mechanical puppets depict the *Fête-Dieu* (Corpus Christi) procession that was a feature of Aix life every June until the beginning of the last century.

Thermes Sextius

55 cours Sextius (08.00.63.96.99). **Open** 8.30am-7.30pm Mon-Fri; 8.30am-1.30pm, 2.30-6.30pm Sat.
Behind a wrought iron grille and classical façade, the Thermes now house the glass and marble pyramids of an ultra-modern health spa. You can wander in and look at the small fountain, which still marks the original warm spring of the fashionable eighteenth-century establishment and, to the right of the entrance, the remains of first-century BC Roman baths fed by the *Source Imperiatrice*.

Quartier Mazarin

Laid out on a strict grid plan in 1646, the Quartier Mazarin gradually became the aristocratic quarter; it still feels very refined today. There are few shops or restaurants, but plenty of balustrades and fine balconies. The fitfully interesting **Musée Paul Arbaud** lies on rue du 4 Septembre, the quarter's main thoroughfare, which leads into **place des Quatre Dauphins**, with a baroque fountain.

On the square, at the rear of an arcaded courtyard, is the beautiful 1650 **Hôtel de Boisgelin**, while nearby, on rue Cardinale, is the **Collège Mignet** (formerly Bourbon), where Cézanne and Zola went to school. At the far end of rue Cardinale stands the Gothic **Eglise St-Jean-de-Malte**, built by the Knights of Malta (note the Maltese cross on the fountain in front) at the end of the thirteenth century. It was one of the first edifices constructed outside the city walls, and has a wide nave and side chapels but no transept; it was once the burial place of the Counts of Provence. Beside the church, the **Musée Granet** in the Commanderie of the Knights of Malta houses the city's fine art and archaeology collections.

Musée Granet

pl St-Jean-de-Malte (04.42.38.14.70). **Open** 10am-noon, 2-6pm Mon, Wed-Sun. **Admission** 15F, 10F children.
Aix's fine art museum is at the centre of an ambitious expansion project that should eventually quadruple the exhibition area. At the time of writing, though, there is disappointingly little to see; an important collection of seventeenth-century Provençal painters

Cézanne & Montagne Ste-Victoire

Montagne Ste-Victoire is inextricably linked with Cézanne: although he spent periods in Paris and Auvers-sur-Oise, it was the Southern landscapes and, above all, the looming bulk of Montagne Ste-Victoire, which he had known since childhood, that provided the greatest inspiration for his work. The artist painted some 60 canvases and watercolours of the mountain in the 1880s and '90s, as he gradually moved away from the Impressionists' idea of painting with light, towards his own interest in underlying structure, searching out the geometrical forms in the landscape, for which the triangular massif provided the perfect motif.

The best way to approach the Montagne Ste-Victoire is in a loop, leaving Aix on the D17, which climbs up through woods towards Le Tholonet (marked as **route de Cézanne**). Just before Le Tholonet is the **Château Noir**, where Cézanne rented a room in 1887. Here he painted canvases such as *Le Rocher Rouge* and *Dans le Parc du Château Noir*, which replace the calm order of earlier works with wilderness and ravines.

The D17 continues along the wild, rocky southern edge of the mountain, from where

several footpaths climb up to the **Croix de Provence** (the metal cross on the 945-metre lower summit, erected after the 1870 Franco-Prussian war). After the rugged perched village of **Puyloubier**, head south-east to Pourrières, then take the D23 along the eastern flank of the massif. Return to Aix, on the gentler, lusher northern slopes, along the D223 and the D10, which offers the easiest access for walkers. Picasso is buried due north of the main peak, in the grounds of the **Château de Vauvenarges** (private), which he bought in 1958. Just after Les Bonfillons, a track leads to the **Carrière de Bibemus** quarry, where Cézanne rented a hut in 1895, before building his own last studio on the Lauves hill, the **Atelier Cézanne** (*see opposite*).

The Montagne Ste-Victoire is included in a bus tour of sites associated with the artist, (**Les Sites Cézanniens du Pays d'Aix**). The tour departs at 2pm on Thursdays from April to November, returning to Aix at 7pm. For information and reservations, call 04.42.16.11.61. The tourist office in Aix issues a guide for those wishing to do the tour in their own cars. There are also organised walking visits on Saturdays.

and Flemish masters is not on show. Upstairs, there is a room with several small Cézannes, including an early landscape, a self-portrait and the *Apotheosis of Delacroix*, and several works by the museum's founder, the now obscure François Granet, an early nineteenth-century Aixois painter and pupil of David. Granet's donations also include Ingres' huge *Jupiter et Thétis*, in which a monumental Jupiter looms over Thétis and an eagle. In the basement, the archaeological collection includes statues and other finds from Entremont and Roman Aix.

Musée Paul Arbaud

2 rue du 4 Septembre (04.42.38.38.95). **Open** 2-5pm Mon-Sat. **Admission** 15F, 10F children.
A rag-tag collection of drawings, old masters and Provençal faience in an eighteenth-century hotel.

Further out

Circling the old town, the busy peripheral boulevards follow the former ramparts. Beyond here lies 'new Aix', a post-war sprawl, which includes an entire new district, the Quartier Sextius Mirabeau, home to the dynamic **Cité du Livre**. It is still dotted with former country

Atelier Cézanne, the artist's last studio.

villas and *bastides*. One such is the **Pavillon Vendôme**, west of the Thermes Sextius, another the **Jas de Bouffon**, a country residence bought by Cézanne's father in 1859, and now at the centre of a redevelopment zone near the Fondation Vasarely. Further out at **Les Milles** is a former tile factory turned prison camp where numerous Jews of foreign origin, among them Surrealist Max Ernst, were interned during World War II. North of Vieil Aix, past the pyramidal **Mausoleum of Joseph Sec** – a rare example of Revolutionary architecture dating from 1792 – a steep hill climbs to the Lauves where Cézanne built his last studio, the **Atelier Cézanne**. The remains of the Celto-Ligurian **Oppidium d'Entremont**, site of Sextius' victory in the second century AD, lie just outside the city to the north-west.

Atelier Cézanne

9 av Paul Cézanne (04.42.21.06.53). **Open** *Apr-Sept* 10am-noon, 2.30-6pm daily; *Oct-Mar* 10am-noon, 2.30-5pm daily. **Admission** 25F, free under-16s. **Credit** V.
Cézanne built this studio in 1902, and worked here until his death in 1906. Then outside the town with views of the rocky ravines of the Montagne Ste-Victoire, it now overlooks post-war housing developments. The first-floor studio is a masterpiece of artistic clutter, with Cézanne's easels and palettes and many of the props – fruit, vases, a broken cherub statue – that are familiar from his still lifes. To reach the Atelier, take bus no.1 from La Rotonde.

Fondation Vasarely

1 av Marcel Pagnol, Jas de Bouffan (04.42.20.01.09). **Open** 10am-1pm, 2-7pm Mon-Fri; 10am-7pm Sat, Sun. **Admission** 35F, 20F students, 10F under-7s. **Credit** AmEx, MC, V.
This *centre architectonique*, two kilometres west of the centre by the A8/A51 autoroute junction, is the former studio of Hungarian-born abstract artist Victor Vasarely, who made geometric and kinetic art on a truly architectural scale. The building itself is composed of hexagonal structures of black and white squares and circles that reflect off water and act as a foil for the typically Cézanne-esque landscape. Within the building are large-scale paintings and tapestries and thousands of drawings explaining his theories. To reach the Fondation, take bus no.8 from La Rotonde.

Oppidium d'Entremont

2km north-west of centre via av Solari (D14), just before junction with N296 (04.42.21.97.33). **Open** 9am-noon, 2-6pm Mon, Wed-Sun. Closed 1 May, 1 & 11 Nov. **Admission** free.
This Celto-Ligurian hilltop settlement developed sometime around the second century BC and was destroyed by Romans in the second century AD at the request of the land-hungry Marseillais. Excavated sections of wall laid out on a grid reveal a residential zone, plus traces of shops, warehouses

Jewellery, carved tablets and statues · can be seen in the **Musée Granet** each the *oppidium*, take bus no.20 ...La Rotonde; a path off the D14 to the right leads to the hilltop.

Pavillon Vendôme

32 rue Célony (04.42.21.05.78). **Open** 10am-noon, 2-5.30pm Mon, Wed-Sun. **Admission** 10F, free under-25s. **No credit cards**.

This perfect pleasure dome was built by the aptly named Pierre Pavillon for the Duc de Vendôme in 1665. Set in landscaped gardens, the original one-storey pavilion was later extended to three storeys following the classical hierarchy of Doric, Ionic and Corinthian orders. Giant Atlantes hold up the balcony and the interior is adorned with seventeenth- and eighteenth-century furniture.

Arts & entertainment

Pick up *Le Mois à Aix*, a monthly listings magazine published by the tourist office (also on **www.aix-en-provence.com**), and the freebie weekly *César*, distributed in hotels and some restaurants in the Gard, Vaucluse and Bouches du Rhône *départements*.

Cité du Livre

8-10 rue des Allumettes (04.42.25.98.65/04.42.25.98.88). **Open** noon-6pm Tue, Thur, Fri; 10am-6pm Wed, Sat. **Admission** free.

Cours Mirabeau

The heart and soul of Aix was laid out in 1649 as a broad carriageway following the course of the ramparts that once marked the frontier between the old town and the brand-new Quartier Mazarin. Soon the southern side became the favoured spot for local nobility to construct their mansions: there was space for a show-off façade (see Nos.20 and 38) and extensive gardens. Nowadays, cafés hog the sunny side, banks and businesses the shade. At No.53, the legendary **Café des Deux Garçons** is still the city's artistic and intellectual hub (*see page 145*). **Espace 13** at No.21 bis puts on exhibitions of contemporary art and photography (*see above*). There are three fountains on the cours itself: the **Fontaine des neufs canons**, the **Fontaine d'eau chaude**, a mossy lump out of which warm (34°C) water gurgles, and the **Fontaine du Roi René**, with a statue of the wine-loving king holding a bunch of grapes.

Despite the name, this converted match factory is a multi-disciplinary arts centre. As well as hosting an annual literary festival in October and housing the historic Bibliothèque Méjanes public library, it is also the home of the Institut de l'Image (repertory cinema, video screenings and December short film festival) and the Fondation St-John Perse, plus a library of opera on video.

Espace 13

21 bis cours Mirabeau (04.42.93.03.67). **Open** 10.30am-6pm daily. **Admission** free.

Run by the Conseil Général des Bouches du Rhône, Espace 13 puts on exhibitions of modern and contemporary art and photography.

Théâtre du Jeu de Paume

17 rue de l'Opéra (04.42.29.71.51/box office 04.42.99.12.12). **Box office** 10am-5pm Mon-Sat. **Shows** 8.30pm. **Tickets** average 150F. **Credit** MC, V.

This beautiful vintage theatre was founded in 1756 on the site of the city's old real tennis court and is due to reopen, following major renovation work, in June 2000. In the past the municipal theatre has had a rather low brow reputation, but new boss Dominique Bluzet is making changes by bringing in successful Paris plays and visiting companies from Marseille and elsewhere.

Théâtre des Ateliers

29 pl Miollis (04.42.38.10.45). **Box office** 10am-noon, 2-8pm Mon-Sat. **Shows** times vary. **Tickets** 35F-75F. **No credit cards**.

A smallish theatre that works on co-productions of new work with other subsidised theatre venues.

Where to eat

For excellent Provençal cuisine in or near Aix, *see also page 48* **La Clos de la Violette** and **Le Relais Ste-Victoire**.

A la Cour de Rohan

10 rue Vauvenargues (04.42.96.18.15). **Meals served** noon-3pm, 7-10pm daily. **Menus** 85F, 120F, 220F. **Credit** MC, V.

This tea room-cum-restaurant overlooking the Hôtel de Ville is furnished with old dressers and tables in a pretty plant-filled courtyard. The hot dishes are rather expensive, but it's an elegant spot to enjoy afternoon tea.

Antoine Côté Court

19 cours Mirabeau (04.42.93.12.51). **Meals served** noon-2.30pm, 7-11pm Tue-Sat. Closed Sun. **Average** 200F. **Credit** MC, V.

The fashionable folk of Aix comes to this stylish, lively Italianate restaurant, which serves veal dishes, gnocchi and pasta.

Au Pain Quotidien

5 pl Richelme (04.42.23.48.57). **Meals served** noon-11pm daily. **Average** 90F. **Credit** MC, V.

Visit the classical interiors and landscaped gardens of the **Pavillon Vendôme**.

After success in Paris, this Belgian franchise has opened its first bakery-cum-café in the south. The focus is, as the name suggests, on bread – great crusty varieties to accompany home-made soups and salad plates; you can choose to sit at a small table or join in at the large communal one.

Café des Deux Garçons

53 cours Mirabeau (04.42.26.00.51). **Meals served** noon-3pm, 7-11.30pm daily. **Menus** 74F, 129F. **Credit** AmEx, DC, MC, V.

Alias 'les 2 G', the historic Deux Garçons café, founded in 1792 and named after the two waiters who bought it in 1840, still has its original canopied entrance and *consulaire* interior with tall mirrors, chandeliers, an old-fashioned cashier's desk and a salon off the side where you can read the papers or write your novel. A hangout of Cézanne, Zola and a long list of famous names from Piaf, Picasso and Cocteau to Churchill. The food is proficient brasserie fare, but it's the elegant café buzz that counts.

Chez Féraud

8 rue du Puits Juif (04.42.63.07.27). **Meals served** 7-10pm Mon; noon-1.30pm, 7-10pm Tue-Sat. Closed Sun & Aug. **Menus** 115F, 145F. **Credit** AmEx, MC, V.

Provençal cooking is served up amid summery southern decor. Specialities include *soupe au pistou*, peppers stuffed with salt cod, and rabbit with basil; good desserts, too.

Chez Maxime

12 pl Ramus (04.42.26.28.51). **Meals served** 7-10pm Mon; noon-2pm, 7-10pm Tue-Sat. Closed Sun & 15-20 Jan. **Menus** 98F, 135F, 150F, 270F. **Credit** MC, V.

The *raison d'être* of Chez Maxime is meat, which Maxime himself saws up in full view of guests. Big hunks of good-quality beef and lamb grilled on charcoal are a treat, especially if you opt for the *côte de boeuf* for two, rather than one of the *menus*. Starters and vegetables can be rather lacklustre. There are good, but very pricey, Southern wines to enjoy and a big outdoor terrace.

Le Grillon

49 cours Mirabeau (04.42.27.58.81). **Meals served** 8am-2am daily. **Menus** 69F, 100F, 150F. **Credit** MC, V.

Sit on the terrace or in the deliciously pretty, pastiche eighteenth-century upstairs dining room. Plenty of Aixois eat here as well as tourists. Roast lamb with herbs and daily fish dishes are simple but proficient (the pasta is best forgotten), service affable and wines by the carafe affordable.

L'Hacienda

7 rue Mérindol (04.42.27.00.35). **Meals served** noon-2pm, 7-10pm Mon-Sat. Closed Sun, three weeks Aug & 25 Dec-1 Jan. **Menus** 62F, 90F, 120F. **Credit** MC, V.

This homely, low-ceilinged budget eaterie offers Provençal food with salads, Mexican grills and paella, all served under the eye of a motherly *patronne*. It's not great cooking, but the 62F menu is a bargain. There are tables on the square in summer.

Bars & nightlife

For a drink, the cafés of cours Mirabeau and rue Espariat are the obvious choices, beginning with the **Deux Garçons** (*see above*). **Le Verdun** (20 pl de Verdun, 04.42.27.03.24) is a lively café near the Palais de Justice, known for its wide range of beers; salads, steaks and snacks are served until 12.15am.

Aix's best jazz venue is the **Hot Brass** (rte d'Eguilles, 04.42.21.05.57), which offers live funk, soul, rock and blues as well as jazz at 10.30pm on Fridays and Saturdays. Other live bands play at **La Fonderie** (14 cours St-Louis, 04.42.63.10.11); the roster ranges from jazz to local hard rock and garage outfits.

There's also sometimes live music (along with beer and sangria) at the **Unplugged Pub** (25 rue du Bon Pasteur, 04.42.23.40.84, closed Sun), a studenty corner bar. **Le Richelm** (24 rue de la Verrerie, 04.42.23.49.29) is a

Festival International d'Art Lyrique

Aix's cultural reputation today rests squarely on its opera festival, which fills out the month of July. Founded in 1948, the event soon began to attract chic audiences, with its inventive outdoor productions featuring innovative directors, international divas such as Berganza and Caballe, and sets designed by leading artists such as Balthus, Masson and Derain.

The tradition continues today with directors like Stéphane Braunschweig, Klaus Michael Grüber and Adrian Noble, and the faithful participation of conductors Pierre Boulez, William Christie and Simon Rattle. Mozart has been a feature since the start, but more recently the festival has widened its scope to take in the early repertoire and, at the other end of the spectrum, the twentieth century.

The **Cour de l'Archevêché** in the **Musée des Tapisseries** (*see page 141*) remains the main venue, but lyric productions and related concerts also use the **Cité du Livre**, the **Théâtre du Jeu de Paume**, and the **Domaine du Grand St-Jean**, a park ten kilometres north-west of Aix.

If opera isn't your thing, there are further cultural blow-outs on offer at the **Aix Jazz Festival** (04.42.63.06.75) in early July and the **Festival Danse à Aix** from mid-July to early August (*see page 290*).

Festival International d'Art Lyrique

Box office: 11 rue Gaston de Saporta (04.42.17.34.34). **Open** *postal bookings* Nov-May; *telephone bookings* 1 Mar-July. **Tickets** 150F-1,200F. **Credit** AmEx, MC, V.
Website: www.aix-en-provence.com/festartlyrique.

---

bar/club with a small dancefloor. Across the street is the **Bugsy Club** (25 rue de la Verrerie, 04.42.38.25.22), which offers beer, music videos and billiards.

Shopping

Undoubted leader of the fashion brigade is **Gago** (21 rue Fabrot, 04.42.27.60.19, closed am Mon & all Sun) with up-to-the-minute men's and women's designer wear and accessories. For simpler, casual wear **Sugar** (4 rue Maréchal Foch, 04.42.27.48.33, closed am Mon & all Sun) is worth a look. A clutch of good children's wear shops include **Catimini** (9 pl des Chapeliers, 04.42.27.51.14, closed am Mon & all Sun), colourful **Marese** (4 rue Aude, 04.42.26.67.00, closed lunch Fri & all Sun), and the excellent-value **Du Pareil au Même** (14 rue Maréchal Foch, 04.42.26.48.49).

Aix's culinary speciality is the *calisson d'Aix*, diamond-shaped sweets made out of almonds, sugar and preserved melon; the **Calissons du Roi René** (7 rue Papassaudi, 04.42.26.67.86, closed Sun) are the most reputed. Aix's most celebrated *santon* (Christmas figurine) maker is **Santons Fouque** (65 cours Gambetta, 04.42.26.33.38, closed Sun).

There are numerous antique and interior design shops on place des Trois Ormeaux and neighbouring rue Jaubert. **Scènes de Vie** (9 rue Jaubert, 04.42.21.13.90, closed am Mon) stocks sophisticated Provençal pottery. Upmarket antique and fabric shops congregate in the Quartier Mazarin, especially along rues Cardinale and Granet.

Of Aix's bookshops, the **Librairie de Provence** (31 cours Mirabeau, 04.42.26.07.23, closed fine art section) has a good fine art section, while **Librairie Paradox** (15 rue du 4 Septembre, 04.42.26.47.99, closed Sun) stocks books, videos and CD-Roms in English.

Where to stay

Grand Hôtel Nègre Coste

33 cours Mirabeau (04.42.27.74.22/fax 04.42.26.80.93). **Rates** double 420F-750F, breakfast 50F. **Credit** AmEx, MC, V.
The hospitable, old-fashioned Hôtel Nègre Coste has a prime location on the cours Mirabeau, and is a temple of eighteenth-century splendour. Upstairs, the corridors are a little dark, but bedrooms are colourful, with Provençal print fabrics and antique wardrobes. Those at the front look over cours Mirabeau, quieter ones at the back have a view over rooftops to the cathedral.

Hôtel Aquabella

2 rue des Etuves (04.42.99.15.00/fax 04.42.99.15.01). **Rates** single 590F-720F, double 670F-850F, suite 950F, breakfast 60F. **Credit** AmEx, DC, MC, V.
This modern, 110-room hotel adjoining the revamped Thermes Sextius may lack the character of Aix's older hotels but compensates with spacious, comfortable rooms, helpful staff and a good location for exploring Vieil Aix. There's an airy reception area and a glass-walled restaurant, L'Orangerie. Special spa treatment packages are available.

Hôtel des Augustins

3 rue de la Masse (04.42.27.28.59/fax
04.42.26.74.87). **Rates** single/double 600F-1,500F,
breakfast 50F. **Credit** AmEx, DC, MC, V.
On a sidestreet off the cours Mirabeau, this very
appealing hotel was part of an Augustine convent
until the Revolution, becoming a hotel in the 1890s.
The reception has been inserted into a spectacular
vaulted space. Rooms are comfortable even if they
don't quite live up to the expectations of the lobby.

Hôtel la Caravelle

29-31 bd du Roi René (04.42.21.53.05/fax
04.42.96.55.46). **Rates** single 380F, double 350F.
Credit AmEx, MC, V.
Despite a rather unprepossessing 1950s concrete
exterior, the Caravelle is a popular option with
budget travellers. Pricier rooms overlook gardens.

Hôtel Cardinale

24 rue Cardinale (04.42.38.32.30/fax
04.42.26.39.05). **Rates** single 300F, double 350F,
suite 400F-450F. **Credit** AmEx, DC, MC, V.
The decor in this eighteenth-century building may
be somewhat lacking, but the rooms are clean, inexpensive and large, and dotted with eclectic furniture
and artworks. Suites in the annexe have a small
kitchenette – useful if you're travelling with kids.

Hôtel de France

63 rue Espariat (04.42.27.90.15/fax 04.42.26.11.47).
Rates single 260F, double 210F-360F. **Credit**
AmEx, MC, V.
The interior looks fusty (flock wallpaper lift) and in
need of renovation, but this is an inexpensive option
in a town that has fewer central hotels than you
might expect. Most rooms are a good size; those at
the front overlook the cafés of a busy shopping
street in Vieil Aix.

Hôtel des Quatre Dauphins

54 rue Roux Alphéran (04.42.38.16.39/fax
04.42.38.60.19). Closed one week Feb. **Rates** single
295F-335F, double 335F-420F, triple 520F, breakfast
42F. **Credit** MC, V.
A simple but tastefully decorated building on a
corner of one of the most pleasant streets of the
Quartier Mazarin. The 12 rooms are hardly enormous,
and there's no air-conditioning, but most guests are
returnees, so book well ahead.

Villa Galici

av de la Violette (04.42.23.29.23/fax 04.42.96.30.45).
Rates double 950F-3,050F, suite 2,100F-3,300F.
Credit AmEx, DC, MC, V.
Slightly out of the centre in an elegantly renovated
bastide, Villa Galici offers plush comfort, with
Italianate trimmings. Some rooms have private
gardens, and there's a swimming pool.

Resources

Getting there

By car

Leave the autoroute A8 at exit nos.29-31. Take the
N7 from Avignon or St-Maximin-la-Ste-Baume. From
Marseille, take the A51.

By train

Aix is on the slow Marseille Sisteron line; trains run
roughly every hour from Marseille St-Charles. The
new high-speed TGV Méditerranée line (due to open
in June 2001) will put Aix back on the national grid,
with a station 10km west of the city.

By bus

For information on services to Avignon (six to ten
daily) and the hourly shuttle to Marseille airport, ring

The glorious Gothic **Basilique de Ste-Marie-Madeleine**. *See page 148.*

the *gare routière* on 04.42.91.26.80. Aix is also one of the stops on the Marseille to Nice airport service (three to four daily in each direction) operated by Phocéen Cars (04.93.85.66.61).

Getting around

The centre of Aix, including Vieil Aix and the Quartier Mazarin, is relatively compact and is best explored by foot. Visitors without cars can use the local buses to reach attractions further afield. Alternatively, **Cycles Zammit** (27 rue Mignet, 04.42.23.19.53) offers bikes for hire.

Tourist information

Office de Tourisme
2 pl du Général de Gaulle (04.42.16.11.61/hotel reservations 04.42.16.11.84). **Open** *June, Sept* 8.30am-8pm Mon-Sat; 10am-1pm, 2-6pm Sun; *July, Aug* 8.30am-10pm Mon-Sat; 10am-1pm, 2-6pm Sun; *Oct-Mar* 8.30am-7pm Mon-Sat; 10am-1pm, 2-6pm Sun.

Around Aix

St-Maximin-la-Ste-Baume

In the farming country west of Aix lurks the ugly grid-pattern town of St-Maximin-la-Ste-Baume. Hidden like a Sleeping Beauty behind the residential and industrial sprawl, though, is the finest Gothic edifice in Provence – and one of the very few outposts of this style in the largely Romanesque South. The **Basilique Ste-Marie-Madeleine** (pl de Prêcheurs, 04.42.38.01.78) was founded in 1295 by Charles II, King of Sicily and Count of Provence, who was keen to improve his standing in the region by building a resplendent shrine for the relics of Mary Magdalene (*see box page 86*), which had been discovered in a cave (*baume* in Provençal) in the **Massif de la Ste-Baume**. Its interior contains a wealth of fascinating decoration carried out by the Dominican monks, such as the 94 seventeenth-century choirstalls carved in walnut by Brother Vincent Funel. The altarpiece of the Passion by Antoine Ronzen was painted in 1520. Over the altar is a gilded plaster sunburst of cherubs and saints (1678-82) by Lieautaud. The monumental eighteenth-century organ (free recitals in summer on the first Sunday of the month) was saved from destruction during the Revolution by Lucien Bonaparte, Napoléon's youngest brother, who used it for spirited performances of the *Marseillaise*. The fourth-century crypt contains the finely carved sarcophagi of saints Mary Magdalene, Maximin, Marcelle and Suzanne.

Adjoining the basilica is the **Couvent Royal**, a royal foundation begun at the same

time as the basilica, now converted into a hotel and restaurant. You can visit a chapel, the refectory and the Gothic cloister; the capitular room, originally the monks' assembly room, is now part of the restaurant.

The town is a good starting point for exploring the limestone hills of the **Massif de la Ste-Baume**, which stretches south-west of the town, and the villages of **Rougiers** (with ruined castle), **Mazaugues** and **St-Zacharie**. The cave hidden in the cliff above **Aups-Ste-Baume** has been a centre of pilgrimage since the fifth century; legend claims it was the one-time residence of Mary Magdalene. It was closed at the time of writing.

Where to stay & eat

Hôtellerie du Couvent Royal
pl Jean Salusse (04.94.86.55.66). **Rates** double 220F-350F, breakfast 50F. **Credit** AmEx, MC, V.
Forget the hotels on the edge of town, there's only one place worth staying here: the royal convent, adjoining the basilica, is worth the trip in itself. Bedrooms in former monks' cells have been converted with simplicity and good taste to keep a sense of monastic calm; those in the 'modernised' wing overlooking the cloister offer more mod cons. There's a walled garden, and a restaurant and wine bar.

Getting there

By car
The town is 35km west of Aix on the A8 autoroute, exit no.34. It is also accessible via the N7.

By bus
Autocars Blanc operates around six buses a day from Aix (info from Aix *gare routière*, 04.42.91.26.80).

Tourist information

Office de Tourisme
Hôtel de Ville, St-Maximin-la-Ste-Baume (04.94.59.84.59/fax 04.94.49.82.92). **Open** *Oct-Mar* 9am-12.30pm, 2-6pm daily; *June-Sept* 9am-12.30pm, 2-6.30pm daily.

Salon-de-Provence

It might sound like the drawing room of Provence to you and me, but the French associate Salon above all with the Air Force flying school, whose presence is announced by the periodic scream of jet engines overhead. The chief tourist draw of this rather characterless town on the edge of the Crau plain between Aix and Arles is the **Maison de Nostradamus**, the house where the astrologer and doctor wrote his *Centuries* and lived from 1547, after his

The market at **St-Maximin-la-Ste-Baume**.

second marriage to a Salonaise, Anne Ponsard, until his death in 1566. A CD-guided visit talks you through some kitsch waxwork tableaux: podgy little Michel being schooled in cabalism by his uncle, his medical studies at Montpellier, the Plague (when Nostradamus became famous for his miraculous remedies, despite the fact that his first wife and two children died), and the final, consecratory visit in 1564 from a busty, satin-clad Catherine de Médicis. Nostradamus's tomb consists of a simple tablet set into the wall of the chapel of the Virgin in the fourteenth-century Gothic **Collégiale de St-Laurent** (Paroisse St-Laurent, 04.90.56.06.40) beyond the medieval city wall.

Salon's skyline is dominated by the **Château de l'Emperi**, built between the tenth and thirteenth centuries as a residence for the bishops of Arles. A fortified medieval outer courtyard ringed by square turrets leads through to an impressive arcaded Renaissance inner courtyard. Within is a military museum and some Napoleonic memorabilia. The Romanesque/early Gothic church of **St-Michel** in the old town is also worth a look, as are two surviving town gateways: the **Tour de Bourg Neuf**, guarded by a black Virgin, and the **Porte de l'Horloge**, topped by a wrought iron belfry. Modern town life centres on the tree-lined avenues surrounding the over-restored *vieille ville*, around the baroque **Hôtel de Ville** and the shops of cours Gimon, and on pl Croustillat, where cafés overlook a lumpy, mossy fountain.

Around 1900, the arrival of the railway and the town's strategic position at the crossroads between Marseille, Aix, Arles and Avignon made Salon (southern capital of oil, soap and coffee) a boomtown. Prosperous soap barons (much of what is called *Savon de Marseille* is actually made here) built themselves fanciful *faux-châteaux*. Several remain, especially around the station. Installed in a nineteenth-century *bastide*, the **Musée de Salon et de la Crau** focuses on the soap industry and Salon's *belle époque* heyday.

Outside Salon, the **Château de la Barben** was originally a fortress belonging to the Abbaye de St-Victor in Marseille, before becoming a residence of King René. Later it was home to the powerful Forbin family, who remodelled it rather more comfortably during their five-century residence, bringing in André Le Nôtre of Versailles fame to redesign the gardens. The adjoining **Zoo de la Barben** is a popular family attraction. Overlooking the lush plain further east, sleepy **Lambesc** boasts a neo-classical church, an old *lavoir* and some fine houses, which hint at the village's 14 decades of fame (1646-1786), when it was the seat of the regional assembly.

Château & Zoo de la Barben

11km east of Salon on D572/D22 (chateau 04.90.55.25.41/zoo 04.90.55.19.12). **Open** *chateau* 10am-noon, 2-5.30pm daily; *zoo* 10am-6pm daily. **Admission** *chateau* 40F, 20F children; *zoo* 55F, 25F children. **Credit** V (chateau only).

Château de l'Emperi

pl des Centuries (04.90.56.22.36). **Open** 10am-noon, 2.30-6.30pm Mon, Wed-Sun. Closed Tue. **Admission** 20F, 15F children. **No credit cards.**

Maison de Nostradamus

13 rue Nostradamus (04.90.56.64.31). **Open** *Sept-June* 9am-noon, 2-6pm Mon-Fri; 2-6pm Sat, Sun; *July, Aug* 9.30am-noon, 2-6.30pm Mon-Fri; 2-6.30pm Sat, Sun. **Admission** 20F, 15F children. **No credit cards.**

Musée de Salon et de la Crau

av Roger Donnadieu (04.90.56.28.37). **Open** 10am-noon, 2-6pm Mon, Wed-Fri; 2-6pm Sat, Sun. **Admission** 20F, free under-17s. **No credit cards.**

Where to stay & eat

The grandest place to stay is the **Relais & Châteaux Abbaye de Ste-Croix** (rte du Val de Cuech (D16), 04.90.56.24.55, closed 5 Nov-end Mar, rates 800F-2,500F) five kilometres out of town in a twelfth-century monastery. Most rooms have private gardens, there's a pool, and a Michelin one-star restaurant (closed lunch Mon & Thur, menus 345F-595F). In Salon, try the **Hôtel Vendôme** (34 rue Maréchal Joffre, 04.90.56.01.96, rates 240F-300F). The best restaurant in town is **La Salle à Manger** (6 rue Maréchal Joffre, 04.90.56.28.01, average 125F), which has tables outside.

Getting there

By car

Salon is at the junction of the A7 (exit no.27) and A54 (exit nos.14/15) autoroutes.

By train/bus

The Gare SNCF is on av Emile Zola, 500m west of the centre. There are several trains daily (irregular intervals) from Avignon; to reach Salon from Marseille or Arles, change at Miramas. There are over 20 buses a day (various companies) from Aix-en-Provence, and seven buses Monday to Saturday (two only on Sun) from Arles with CTM; for information ring the *gare routière* on 04.90.49.38.01.

Tourist information

Office de Tourisme

56 cours Gimon (04.90.56.27.60). **Open** *Sept-June* 9am-noon, 2-6.30pm Mon-Sat; *July, Aug* 9am-1pm, 2-7pm Mon-Sat; 10am-noon Sun.

The Western Côte

Cassis to Toulon   152
Hyères to the Maures   161
St-Tropez & Around   168
St-Raphaël & Around   175

Feature boxes

Les calanques   153
Pink drink   155
Diving into history   158
The Massif des Maures   166
Beach babes   170

ssis to Toulon

Tuned-in French holidaymakers choose this laid-back stretch of coast over the crowds and hustle of the Riviera.

Cassis

A quiet fishing village out of season, and a mecca for *flâneurs* and sun-worshippers in summer, Cassis is best known for its delicate white wines and its dazzling fjord-like *calanques* (*see box*). Though the Académie Française considers the final 's' to be silent, locals consider that to be for Parisians and snobs, and pronounce it anyway.

The quarries in the white marble cliffs above the town yielded stone for the Suez Canal among other things. The pretty smattering of colourful houses attracted early twentieth-century artists including Dufy, Matisse and Vlaminck, all of whom holidayed here.

Besides having two pleasant beaches within easy reach – **Plage de la Grande Mer** on the sea side of the breakwater, and the sheltered **Plage du Bestouan** at the western end of the port – Cassis offers a variety of watersports and some of southern France's best rock-climbing: any of the town's numerous sports shops will provide equipment and guides.

Cassis' wines can be tasted and purchased at **La Ferme Blanche** (rte de Marseille, 04.42.01.00.74, open 7am-7pm daily) and at **Clos Ste-Magdeleine** (chemin du Revestel, 04.42.01.70.28, open 9am-noon, 3-7pm Mon-Fri).

Heading east out of Cassis, the vertiginous **route des Crêtes** (D141) climbs to Cap Canaille and the highest cliffs (416 metres) in France, offering spectacular views.

Where to stay & eat

On Plage du Bestouan, the **Hôtel-Restaurant Le Jardin d'Emile** (23 av Amiral Ganteaume, 04.42.01.80.55, rates 400F-650F) stands in a tropical garden against the old city walls. The restaurant (menus 165F-295F) serves the best Provençal cuisine in town. On the port, **Restaurant Panisse** (4 pl Mirabeau, 04.42.01.93.93, closed dinner Sun, all Mon and mid-Nov to mid-Dec, menus 98F-159F) has tables out on the cobbled street and a delightful view over the harbour. An hour's hike west of Cassis, **La Fontasse** hostel (04.42.01.02.72, closed Jan & Feb, rates 50F) requires reservations for its ten beds; bring your own food and water. The only three restaurants in

Fishing boats in the harbour at **Cassis**.

the *calanques* are **Le Nautic-Bar** in Morgiou (04.91.40.06.37, reservations essential, average 150F), **Le Lunch** in Sormiou (04.91.25.05.37, closed mid-Nov to mid-Mar), a low-key but actually rather chic beach shack, and **La Grotte** in Callelongue (04.91.73.17.79, average 130F-150F), a simple restaurant/bar popular with a lively young crowd.

Getting there

By car

Leave the A50 autoroute at exit no.8 and take the D559 (5km).

By bus/train

More or less hourly local trains on the Marseille-Toulon line stop at Cassis station, 3km back from the coast; frequent buses connect the station with the town centre.

Tourist information

Office du Tourisme

pl Baragnon (04.42.01.71.17/fax 04.42.01.28.31). **Open** *July, Aug* 9am-8pm daily; *June, Sept* 9am-6pm daily; *Oct-May* 9am-12.30pm, 1.30-5.30pm Mon-Fri; 10am-12.30pm, 1.30-5.30pm Sat; 10am-12.30pm Sun.

La Ciotat & St-Cyr

When the Krupp dockyard in La Ciotat closed down in 1989, 10,000 people in a town with a population of 30,000 lost their jobs. Yet the tiny medieval port still manages to put on a lively face, with café tables spilling on to the streets and fishermen selling their catch on the dock.

Les calanques

Les calanques – spectacular sea-eroded gashes in the limestone cliffs – are the reason why most people visit Cassis. Of the eight *calanques* only the first, **Port-Miou**, is fully accessible by car. If you choose only one to visit, make it **En-Vau**, the most beautiful and unspoiled.

Getting there

By boat
Small craft begin ferrying visitors from the quay in Cassis towards the *calanques* at around 10am each morning for sightseeing boat trips (50F-90F). If you'd rather walk back, you can ask to be set down in one of the calanques.

On foot
The clearly marked GR98 footpath runs along the clifftop for 28 kilometres from Cassis to Marseille. However, the section between the Calanque d'En-Vau and Marseille is often closed between mid-June and mid-September, depending on the level of fire risk. From Cassis, it's 30 minutes' walk to Port-Miou, another half hour to Port-Pin, and two hours to En-Vau. The western *calanques* of Sormiou and Morgiou can be reached on direct footpaths from Marseille, open year round. Tents and campfires are banned throughout.

Information

Visite des Calanques
13 rue Lamartine, Cassis
(04.42.01.03.31). **Open** *Feb-May, Sept-Nov* 10am-4pm daily; *June-Aug* 9.30am-6pm daily. Closed Dec, Jan.
Though this is a privately run boat company, the friendly staff are also a good source of information on hiking in the Calanques.

Sormiou.

Since the mid-nineteenth century, La Ciotat has served as a genteel summer residence. Among illustrious guests were Auguste and Louis Lumière, the pioneering brothers of cinema. Their short film of a train pulling into La Ciotat station was the first ever made; viewers are supposed to have leaped from their seats in terror when it was first projected in September 1895 at the **Eden**. This venerable cinema still stands on the seafront on boulevard Anatole France, next to the fire station; it is open to the public on one weekend in mid-September for a short Lumière film season (information 04.42.08.88.68). The **Espace Lumière** continues the theme with a display of photos and posters and a film archive. The station is still there, too, adorned with movie posters to celebrate its place in cinema history. Overlooking the old port, the **Musée Ciotaden** presents the maritime history of La Ciotat from the time of its foundation by Greek colonists from Marseille.

On the eastern side of the Baie de la Ciotat, **St-Cyr-sur-Mer** has a market, cafés and a small golden replica of the Statue of Liberty. St-Cyr's seaward extension, **Les Lecques**, is a clutter of fashion shops and holiday eateries. The long beach is family-friendly, with sand brought in by barge each June. Les Lecques claims to have been the Greek trading post of Taureontum, and to prove it, the **Musée de Taureontum** contains a display of Greek and Roman artefacts in two first-century AD Roman villas. Past the museum, the coast gets rocky. A stunning nine-kilometre hiking trail (waymarked in yellow) sets off from just beyond the hamlet of La Mandrague, clinging to the coastline through pine and oak forests. It takes three and a half hours to reach Bandol; four daily buses (Cariane Buses; 04.42.08.41.05) ease the return to Les Lecques.

Espace Lumière
20 rue Foch (04.42.71.61.70). **Open** *Sept-June* 10am-noon, 3-6pm Wed-Sat; *July, Aug* 10am-noon, 3-6pm Wed-Sat; 10am-noon Sun.

Musée Ciotaden
Ancien Hôtel de Ville, Quai Ganteaume (04.42.71.40.99). **Open** *Sept-June* 3-7pm Mon, Wed-Sat; *Oct-Apr* 3-6pm Mon, Wed-Sat. **Admission** 20F, 10F children.

Musée de Taureontum
rte de la Madrague (04.94.26.30.46). **Open** *June-Sept* 3-7pm Mon, Wed-Sun; *Oct-May* 2-5pm Sat, Sun. **Admission** 15F, 5F children.

Where to stay, eat & drink

The **Grand Hôtel des Lecques** (24 av du Port, St-Cyr-sur-Mer, 04.94.26.23.01, closed Nov-Mar, rates 455F-695F) has old-world charm and an exotic garden, plus a pool and a restaurant, **Le Parc** (menus 180F-450F). Surrounded by greenery but handy for the centre, **Le Petit Nice** (11 allée du Docteur Seillon, St-Cyr-sur-Mer, 04.94.32.00.64, closed Nov to mid-Mar, rates 280F-360F) has a pool shaded by swaying trees.

In La Ciotat, hungry local fishermen head for **La Mamma** (Vieux Port, 04.42.08.30.08, closed lunch Mon-Wed, closed Nov, two weeks Feb, menus 98F-125F), where La Mamma herself, Madame Dessolis, cooks up lasagne and ravioli to serve with the freshest possible seafood on her port-side terrace. The **Riviera del Fiori** (Nouveau Port des Lecques, 04.94.32.18.20, closed Wed and two weeks Feb, menus 70F-210F) uses the local catch in its bouillabaisse.

Tourist information

La Ciotat
Office de Tourisme, bd Anatole France (04.42.08.61.32/fax 04.42.08.17.88). **Open** *May-Sept* 9am-8pm Mon-Sat, 10am-1pm Sun; *Oct-May* 9am-noon, 2.30-6pm Mon-Sat.

St-Cyr-sur-Mer
Office de Tourisme, pl de l'Appel du 18 Juin (04.94.26.73.73/fax 04.94.26.73.74). **Open** *June & Sept* 9am-6pm Mon-Fri; *July, Aug* 9am-7pm Mon-Sat; 10am-1pm, 4-7pm Sun; *Oct-May* 9am-6pm Mon-Fri; 9am-noon, 2-6pm Sat.

Getting there

By car
The A50 autoroute skirts both La Ciotat (exit no.9) and St-Cyr (exit no.10).

By bus/train
Trains leave Marseille station for La Ciotat and St-Cyr hourly between 6am and 1am. La Ciotat station is 3km from the centre; bus no.4 provides a regular service to the port until 7pm. One morning bus (Mon-Sat) connects St-Cyr station with Les Lecques and Taureontum; there are two (morning and afternoon) in the other direction (info from tourist office).

Bandol

Bandol is a curate's egg of a town. Its port, built in 1715 to ship the wine and olive oil of the hinterland, is grey and unappealing. Head for the *ruelles* around the eighteenth-century church of St-François-de-Sales, however, and you'll find an area buzzing with shops and restaurants. Westwards towards the Baie de Renécros are some of the *belle époque* houses that once made Bandol famous. It is still a popular family resort, its population swelling in summer from 7,000 to 45,000. Palm trees line the quays, where tanned tourists chat in cafés and boats set out to nearby islands.

The **Ile de Bendor**, two kilometres out to sea, was just a rock in the Mediterranean until the 1950s, when Paul Ricard (of pastis fame) bought it. Today, the island has mostly been cemented over; what nature remains can be seen on the half-hour walking trail. As befits an island created by an alcohol magnate, the main attraction is the **Exposition Universelle des Vins et Spiritueux**, with 8,000 bottles of booze on show. At the western tip, the **Daddy & Milou** restaurant provides sunbeds and umbrellas: plunge off the rocks or slink down a ladder for a swim. The **Fun Plage** behind the port has a sandy beach and pedalos for hire.

There are 20 vineyards on and around the D559 road between Bandol and the medieval hilltop village of **La-Cadière-d'Azur** (*see box page 155*). A representative, reasonably priced range of local wines is on sale at the **Cave Cooperative La Cadièrenne** next to exit no.11 of the A50 autoroute. Ten more wineries line the D626, which meanders via Brulat to **Le Castellet**, a fortified village once owned by King René of Provence, with ramparts, an eleventh-century castle and a sprinkling of artsy shops. From Le Castellet, the D226 takes you past seven vineyards to **Le Beausset**, where an olive-press millstone serves as an altar in the twelfth-century church, and where more wines can be sampled at the **Cave Cooperative Les Maîtres Vignerons du Beausset**. From here, the N8 continues north to **Ste-Anne-d'Evenos**, above which perches Evenos, a little-visited ruined village built on ancient lava rock with sweeping coastal views.

Exposition Universelle des Vins et Spiritueux
Ile de Bendor, signposted from ferry quay (04.94.24.44.34). **Open** *Apr-Sept* 10am-noon, 2-6pm Thur-Tue. Closed Oct-Mar. **Admission** free.

Where to stay, eat & drink
Escape holiday crowds on the private beach of the **Golf Hôtel** (plage Renécros, end of bd Lumière, 04.94.29.45.83, closed Nov-Mar, rates 290F-550F). **Hôtel L'Oasis** (15 rue des Ecoles, 04.94.29.41.69, closed Dec, rates 295F-340F) is convenient for the old town and port. Near the church in the old town, **L'Oulivo** (19 rue des Tonneliers, 04.94.29.81.79, closed dinner Mon, Tue, all Wed, also closed dinner Sun from May-Sept, closed two weeks Feb, menus 75F-120F) offers fine Provençal dishes.

In Bandol vineyard country, **Le Bérard** in La Cadière (av Gabriel Péri, 04.94.90.11.43, closed Jan, rates 405F-870F) has rooms in an old convent and a gourmet restaurant (closed lunch Mon, lunch Sat, menus 450F-1,370F) where snazzy Provençal fare is served by sometimes sullen staff. In the grey-stone village of Ste-Anne-d'Evenos, the **Marquise Dutheil de La Rochère** (04.94.90.35.40, rates 450F) offers chambres d'hôte at the Château-Ste-Anne vineyard (the track to the Château is signposted opposite the butcher's). There's a pool under the olive trees and tastings (8am-noon, 2-7pm daily) of the Château's exquisite reds.

Getting there

By car
From Marseille leave A50 at exit no.12; from Nice take A8 to Le Luc, A57 to Toulon, and then A50.

By bus/train
A 15-minute walk from the beach, Bandol station is on the Marseille-Toulon line, with regular trains.

Getting around

By boat
To the Ile de Bendor: Paul Ricard Boats (06.11.05.91.52). Services run hourly between 7am and 7pm from October to May. Fishing trips are

organised by Hooker (Key Largo Hôtel, 19 corniche Bonaparte, 04.94.29.46.93, open June-Oct, rates 5,000F per day for six people).

By bike
François at Holiday Bikes *127 rte de Marseille, Bandol (06.84.81.36.58).* **Open** *Apr-Sept* 9am-12.30pm, 3-7pm daily. *Oct-Mar* on request. **Rates** bikes 80F per day; scooters 170F-240F per day.

Tourist information

Office de Tourisme
allées Alfred-Vivien (04.94.29.41.35/fax 04.94. 32.50.39). **Open** *July, Aug* 9am-1pm, 2-7pm daily; *Sept-June* 9am-noon, 2-6pm Mon-Fri; 9am-noon Sat.

Ollioules & Sanary

The N8 winds gently south by the River Reppe through the Gorges d'Ollioules below steep rocky cliffs riddled with caves that once hid Gespard, the bandit-hero of local folk stories.

Ollioules is set amid terraced hills where locals tend olives, wines, vegetables and – most importantly – flowers, which end up in the town's wholesale cut-flower market, the largest in France. Medieval streets climb beneath

Pink drink

The grapes that go into Bandol's wines grow on terraced vineyards in hills that slope down to the Mediterranean, protecting the vines from winds and ensuring a long growing season. The variety that has made Bandol famous is Mourvèdre, a rare black grape. It gives Bandol wines their character, making for spicy, rich reds and full, fresh rosés.

In the sea off Bandol, terracotta wine casks dating back to 2,500 BC have been found. The Greeks were the first to produce wine here; the Romans took over, exporting them as far  as Egypt. In 1941, Bandol was one of the first appellations issued in France.

Every year on the first Sunday in December, the Fête du Millésime is held on the port of Bandol. The 52 vintners of the region bring keg-loads of their three-month-old wines for a public

tasting, before putting them to bed in wooden casks for 18 months.

The following wine centres offer year-round tasting and sales at vineyard prices:

Maison des Vins de Bandol
29 allée Vivien (04.94.29.45.03). **Open** 10am-noon, 3-6pm Mon, Tue, Thur-Sat. **Credit** AmEx, DC, MC, V.

Caveau des Vins de Bandol
allée Vivien, across from Embarcadère (04.94.29.60.45). **Open** *Sept-June* 9am-12.30pm Mon-Wed, Fri, Sat; 3.30-6.30pm Mon-Wed, Fri-Sun. **Credit** MC, V.

Cave Cooperative La Cadièrenne
by La Cadière exit (no.50) of A8 autoroute (04.94.90.11.06). **Open** 8am-noon, 2-5.30pm Mon-Sat. **Credit** MC, V.

Cave Cooperative Les Maîtres Vignerons du Beausset
southern edge of Le Beausset on N8 to Ollioules (04.94.98.70.17). **Open** 9am-noon, 2-6pm Mon-Sat. **Credit** MC, V.

The Western Côte

Between Provence and French Riviera...

Toulon

The heart of your holidays

Palms and fishing nets at **Sanary-sur-Mer**.

arched walkways, and the ruins of a thirteenth-century chateau rise above the town. The spectacular GR51 footpath climbs west to the peak of Gros Cerveau (430 metres) and east to Le Croupatier (580 metres); allow two hours return for either hike.

On the coast to the south-west, **Sanary-sur-Mer** is an old fishing port lined with palms and pastel-coloured Provençal houses. In the 1930s, the village became the refuge of anti-Nazi German writers, including Thomas Mann; Aldous Huxley was another visitor. The square tower at the western edge of the port houses the **Musée Frédéric-Dumas** diving museum. A 90-minute seaside trail runs from Sanary port past Pointe de la Cride to Baie de Bandol and the sandy Plage Dorée, mostly carved up by private beach concessions.

Further south on the wind-battered Sicié peninsula, **Six-Fours-les-Plages** is a string of modern beach bars and restaurants. When the mistral is blowing, angry waves pound the sand at Plage Brutal, making it a surfer's paradise. On a hill just to the north, the eleventh-century **Collégiale St-Pierre-aux-Lions** is all that remains of the old village of Six-Fours. Three kilometres further north, the fifth-century chapel **Notre-Dame-de-Pépiole**

(open for guided tours in the afternoon), one of France's oldest Christian buildings, has three unusual vaulted naves.

The little port of **Le Brusc** is the starting point of a fine trail over the cliffs to the pilgrimage chapel of **Notre-Dame-du-Mai** and the rocky headland of Cap Sicié. Most visitors to Le Brusc stay only long enough to get on a ferry for the **Iles des Embiez** (*see below* **Getting around**). Once a salt-panning centre, the four islands were bought up by pastis king Paul Ricard in 1958. The main island, Les Embiez, is now home to the **Fondation Océanographique Paul Ricard** with its fine examples of Mediterranean marine life, the **Domaine Iles des Embiez** vineyard, and miles of trails for walking or cycling.

Collégiale St-Pierre-aux-Lions

montée du Fort Militaire, Six-Fours (04.94.34.24.75). **Open** *Oct-May* 2-6pm Mon-Sat; 10am-noon Sun; *June-Sept* 3-7pm Mon-Sat; 9am-noon Sun. Guided visits (available in English) by arrangement. **Admission** small donation.

Fondation Océanographique Paul Ricard

Les Isles des Embiez; follow signs from quay (04.94.34.02.49). **Open** *Apr-Oct* 10am-12.30pm, 1.30-5pm daily; *Nov-Mar* 10am-12.30pm Wed, Sat, Sun. **Admission** 25F; children (4-11) 12F.

Musée Frédéric-Dumas

pl de la Tour, Sanary-sur-Mer (04.94.34.76.76). **Open** *July, Aug* 10am-noon, 3-7pm daily; *Sept-June* 10am-noon, 2-6pm Sat, Sun, school holidays. **Admission** free.

Where to stay, eat & drink

Two kilometres outside Ollioules, the Domaine de Terrebrune not only offers tastings of its Bandol wines but serves good Provençal lunches at its terrace restaurant, the **Table du Vigneron** (chemin de la Tourelles, 04.94.88.36.19, closed Jan, menus 230F-350F), where reservations are essential.

On the port in Sanary, the **Restaurant de la Tour** (24 quai Général de Gaulle, 04.94.74.10.10, rates 300F-500F) serves some of the freshest seafood on the coast (closed dinner Tue, all Wed, closed Dec, menus 125F-250F).

In Le Brusc, the **Restaurant Le St-Pierre** (47 rue de la Citadelle, 04.94.34.02.52, closed dinner Tue, all Wed, closed Jan, menus 98F-198F) serves grilled fish and good bouillabaisse in a garden above the port. For campers, the **Jardin de la Ferme** (688 chemin des Faisses, 04.94.34.01.07) has cabins (2,000F-3,500F/week) and rooms (350F) or you can pitch your tent (74F/two people) on the farm.

Diving into history

In 1991, Henri Cosquer, a professional diver from Cassis, swam into a long, narrow tunnel 37 metres below sea level between the *calanques* of Sormiou and Morgiou. The tunnel climbed upwards, eventually emerging into a huge grotto. On the walls, he found the world's oldest cave paintings, dating back 27,000 years: bison, horses and hand-prints, the outlines drawn in charcoal and filled in with red and ochre dyes. They include the first recorded use of the three-quarter portrait technique, showing both eyes. And the unknown artists gave experts plenty to puzzle over: are the fingers missing from the hand-prints symbolic, or the result of amputations? And what are those three

playful creatures floating on the ceiling: figments of the artist's imagination, or did penguins really live in the colder Mediterranean of 27 millennia ago? The cave has been sealed since its discovery, but Cosquier still accompanies divers into less artistic grottos.

Henri Cosquer of Cassis Service Plongée can be found on his boat *Cro-Magnon* on the port of Cassis (across from the pizzeria 82) or at his shop (3 rue Michel Arnaud, 04.42.01.89.16/fax 04.42.01.23.76, open 8:30am-12.30pm and 2.30-7pm daily from Mar-Nov). He organises two dives daily at 9am and 3pm from 18 March to 12 November. Reservations are advised.

The Western Côte

On the main Les Embiez island, the **Hôtel Le Canoubié** (above quay on left, 04.94.74. 94.94, closed Nov-Mar, rates 350F-700F) is a fine romantic hideaway. Also on the island, you can eat glorious seafood on salt-encrusted tables at the **Bar-Restaurant Acceuil** right in front of the ferry quay (04.94.74.93.90, closed lunch except in July & Aug, menus 80F).

Getting there

By car
Heading east on the A50 autoroute, take the Bandol exit (no.12), then the D559 to Sanary; heading west, exit no.12 for Six-Fours and Sanary.

By bus/train
On the Marseille-Toulon line (regular trains), Sanary-Ollioules station is 2km from Sanary and 3km from Ollioules. Littoral Cars (04.94.74.01.35) runs eight daily services from the station into Sanary and Ollioules and five buses (three on Sun) from Toulon to Sanary via La Seyne, Six-Fours and Le Brusc. Orlandi (04.94.63.42.73) runs a regular urban bus service (no.12) between Toulon and Ollioules.

Getting around

Iles des Embiez
Ferries (information: 04.94.10.65.20) depart regularly from Le Brusc quay (7am-12.45am June-Sept; 7am-8pm Oct-May). Tickets are 35F. On the island, bikes can be hired from Cycles Merviel by the ferry quay (04.94.88.15.51, open daily Apr-Oct).

Six-Fours
Bikes can be hired from Cap 83 Cycles, 34 rue de la République (04.94.07.48.29, closed Sun, also closed Mon from Oct-Mar). Rates go from 50F.

Tourist information

Ollioules
Office de Tourisme, 16 rue Nationale (tel/fax 04.94.63.11.74). **Open** *Oct-Apr* 8am-noon, 3-6pm Mon-Fri; *May-Sept* also open 8am-noon Sat.

Sanary-sur-Mer
Maison du Tourisme, jardins de la Ville, opposite av Jean-Jaurès (04.94.74.01.04/fax 04.94.74.58.04). **Open** *mid-Sept to Apr* 9am-noon, 2-5.30pm Mon-Sat; *May, June* 9am-noon, 2-6pm Mon-Sat; *July to mid-Sept* 9am-noon, 2-7pm Mon-Sat.

Six-Fours-les-Plages
Pavillon du Tourisme, plage de Bonnegrâce (04.94.07.02.21/fax 04.94.25.13.36). **Open** *Sept-June* 8.30am-noon, 2-6pm daily; *July, Aug* 9am-7pm Mon-Sat; 9am-noon Sun.

Toulon

Toulon's raison d'être is its port. The streets of the old town run down to the port. From the hills, the view ranges over the port and out to sea. Even Toulon's tough reputation has blown into the port like flotsam: from prisoners working their terms as galley slaves to sex-hungry sailors. Toulon is a city of contrasts: ugly with post-war high-rises and beautiful in its medieval streets; a place with some frankly dodgy nightlife and yet by day a charming and colourful café scene. At the time of writing, the extreme-right Front National was installed in the city hall, presiding over a huge North African community.

The Greeks and Romans knew about the impressive natural harbour, and exploited the local deposits of murex shells to make purple dye. During a recent submarine search for the aeroplane of writer Antoine de Saint-Exupéry, thought to have crashed just offshore in July 1944, hundreds of amphorae were found. But only since 1481, when the city became part of France, has the port become strategically important. A major shipyard was constructed in the sixteenth century, and the town fortified with star-shaped bastions in the seventeenth.

In 1793, royalist Toulon fell to an unknown young Revolutionary officer called Napoléon Bonaparte and narrowly escaped being razed to the ground. The royalists scuppered their ships and blew up the shipyards to stop the Revolutionaries getting their hands on them. In a remarkable rerun, the French scuttled their Mediterranean fleet in the harbour in 1942 as German forces advanced; much of what still stood of the old town was destroyed by air-raiding Allies and retreating Germans in 1944.

Nowadays, the **vieille ville** has pavement cafés lining the sunny quays where grey warships anchor at the docks. Several companies run boat tours around the harbour (average 45F per hour from quai Cronstadt). At the old Mairie (town hall) on the quai Cronstadt are two caryatid Atlantes carved in 1657 by soon-to-be-famous local sculptor Pierre Puget.

The **Musée de la Marine** juts out into the westerly Darse Neuve, the 'new dock' built in 1680, and houses figureheads, model ships and maritime paintings. The eighteenth-century façade was once the entrance to the dockyards. Nearby are the heavily guarded gates of the military port (closed to the public); inside, an ancient wall is all that remains of the gruesome La Bagne penal colony (1748-1854), described vividly by Victor Hugo in *Les Misérables*.

Back from the port lies the gritty **red-light district**, known locally as Petit Chicago. Sex shops and 'American bars' (read fleshpots) line avenue Micholet. The neighbourhood is currently undergoing the biggest civic restoration in France; however, the few remaining slums in rue Auban exude infinitely more character than the Disney-heritage image that is being projected elsewhere. Where the sex industry doesn't have a stranglehold, the *vieille ville*'s maze of streets is packed with designer shops and crafts workshops. On place Vezzani, a six-metre head of Neptune by Pierre Puget sticks out of a tenement wall, while in place Raimu there's a life-size sculpture of the card game from Marcel Pagnol's film *César*.

In the heart of the *vieille ville*, **place Puget** was the site of a grain market in the seventeenth century; Victor Hugo lived at No.5 while researching *Les Misérables*. The pretty, mossy Fontaine des Trois Dauphins (1780) can be admired from surrounding cafés. To the south-east, the atrociously lit **cathedral of Ste-Marie** (closed noon-3pm) was built and rebuilt between the eleventh and seventeenth centuries, escaping destruction during the Revolution only because it was used as an arms depot. One block east, cours Lafayette becomes a colourful morning market (Tuesday to Sunday). Halfway along the street, the **Musée du Vieux Toulon** documents Toulon's history.

Rising above the town, Mont Faron can be reached by funicular (closed Dec, Jan). As well as offering spectacular views, it is the site of the Musée-mémorial du Débarquement, commemorating the 1944 liberation of Provence.

Toulon's **Opera House** is one of the city's more impressive buildings.

Along the western shore in depressing, industrial **La Seyne**, Fort Balaguier is where Napoléon staged his capture of Toulon in 1793, commemorated in the Fort's **Musée Naval**. Past the beach villages of **Tamaris** and **Les Sablettes** to the south, the wooded peninsula of **St-Mandrier-sur-Mer** has walking trails.

East of the city, the wealthy suburb of **Le Mourillon** has parks, nightlife, a good beach and a fort dating back to 1514; beyond, garden-filled **Le Pradet** abounds in trails and beaches. The rue du Pin de Galle leads to the sea, from where a five-kilometre path (yellow markers) winds along the wild coastline into a succession of beaches and coves: sandy Plage du Monaco, accessible only to hikers and boaters; Plage des Bonnettes, where the east wind blows up a serious surf; Plage de la Garonne; and Plage des Oursinières, with a small port. The trail continues into the woods of Le Bau Rouge and the **Musée de la Mine du Cap Garonne**, where you can descend a shaft to experience conditions in the mine where copper was extracted between 1862 and 1917.

Musée de la Marine
pl Monsenergue (04.94.02.02.01). **Open** *May-Sept* 10am-6pm Mon, Wed-Sun; *Oct-Apr* 10am-noon, 2-6pm Mon, Wed-Sun. **Admission** 29F, 19F children.

Musée-mémorial du Débarquement
Tour Beaumont, rte du Faron (04.94.88.08.09). **Open** 9.45-11.45am, 2-4.30pm Tue-Sun. **Admission** 25F, 10F children, free under-5s.

Musée de la Mine de Cap Garonne
chemin du Bau Rouge, Le Pradet (04.94.08.32.46). **Open** *Sept-June* 2-5pm Wed, Sat, Sun; *July, Aug* 2-5pm daily. **Admission** 40F, 20F children.

Musée Naval du Fort Balaguier
924 corniche Bonaparte (04.94.94.84.72). **Open** *Sept-June* 10am-noon, 2-6pm Tue-Sun; *July, Aug* 10am-noon, 3-7pm Tue-Sun; closed Jan. **Admission** 10F, 5F children, free under-5s.

Musée du Vieux Toulon
cours Lafayette (04.94.62.11.07). **Open** 2-6pm Mon-Sat. **Admission** free.

Where to stay, eat & drink

In the heart of the *vieille ville*, **Le Grand Hôtel Dauphiné** (10 rue Berthelot, 04.94.92.20.28, 270F-310F) is a little frayed at the edges but clean and friendly. The Michelin-starred **La Chamade** (25 rue Denfert-Rochereau, 04.94.92.28.58, closed lunch Sat, Sun, closed Aug, menu 195F) has good if sometimes over-exotic cuisine. Sip an evening aperitif at **Le Nautique** brasserie (carré du Port, quai Cronstadt, 04.94.93.49.88, average 75F) by the

breakwater, and watch boats sail into the sunset. Despite its sombre interior, **Chez Odette Le Cellier** (52 rue Jean-Jaures, 04.94.92.64.35, closed Sat, Sun and two weeks Aug, menus 83F-160F) serves good local specialities. For couscous, join the North African community at **Le Régal** (25 rue Chevalier Paul, no phone, menu 35F), where they show Algerian TV and seat single women well away from the men in the front room.

In a pretty bay south of Le Pradet, the **Hôtel L'Escapade** (75 rue de la Tartane, port des Oursinières, 04.94.08.39.39, rates 695F-980F) has a lovely garden and pool. Across the street, gourmet Provençal cuisine is served on the patio of **La Chanterelle** (50 rue de la Tartane, port des Oursinières, 04.94.08.52.60, closed Wed, closed Jan & Feb, menus 160F-240F). On the Pointe de Carqueiranne headland south of here, the terrace of the split-level, log-cabin-effect **L'Oursinado** (chemin du Pas des Gardéens, 04.94.21.77.06, closed dinner Tue, all Wed and Jan & Feb, menus 180F-250F) offers a romantic setting and Mediterranean seafood.

Getting there

By air
The cunningly named Toulon/Hyères airport (04.94.00.83.83) is in fact in Hyères, 35km east of Toulon. A taxi will cost around 260F (Taxi-Hyères, 04.94.38.55.55). Sodetrav (04.94.12.55.12) buses coincide with most flights (56F one-way).

By car
Exit nos.15 or 16 from the A50 autoroute.

By train
Trains for Toulon leave hourly from Marseille (5am-1am) and Nice (5am-9pm).

Getting around

By ferry
Allo Bus, quai Cronstadt (04.94.03.87.03). **Tickets** 10F one-way. **To La Seyne** line 8M; hourly 6am-7pm Mon-Sat; 9am-6pm Sun. **To St-Mandrier-sur-Mer** line 28M; hourly 6am-8pm daily. **To Sablettes/Tamaris** line 18M: hourly 7am-7pm daily.

Tourist information

Toulon
Office du Tourisme, pl Raimu (04.94.18.53.00). **Open** *May-Sept* 9am-6pm Mon-Sat; 10am-noon Sun; *Oct-Apr* 9.30am-5.30pm Mon-Sat; 10am-noon Sun. Occasional guided tours of the *vieille ville* go from here, costing 20F.

Le Pradet
Office de Tourisme, pl Général de Gaulle (04.94.21.71.69). **Open** 10am-noon, 3-6pm Mon-Fri.

Hyères to the Maures

Unspoiled beaches, dizzying views and the wild Massif des Maures – some unfortunate developments aside, this is the Côte at its most pristine.

Hyères & Around

At the western extremity of the Côte d'Azur, Hyères isn't typical Riviera: the attitude's missing, as are the filthy-rich yachts. The regional airport gives the area clout, however, and Bregançon, the president's summer residence across the bay, lends it a certain institutional dignity.

In the nineteenth century, Hyères was much frequented by the wintering British. Queen Victoria paid a one-off visit, introducing the locals to Irish stew. According to local legend, Robert Louis Stephenson found inspiration for *Treasure Island* on the Ile de Porquerolles.

Hyères & Giens

Once on the coast, Hyères is now five kilometres inland, looking down from its height over the flat coastal strip with its airport, salt pans and beaches. Cut flowers and date-palm rearing play a large part in the town's economy: the latter grace all the wide boulevards of modern Hyères, as well as being exported as far afield as the Middle East.

Hyères' medieval *vieille ville* clusters around the ruins of the old thirteenth-century chateau (a half-hour hike uphill from the Parc St-Bernard, *see below*), from where the view over town and coast is stunning. The *vieille ville* is approached through the medieval Porte Massillon and rue Massillon, which leads to the beautiful café-filled **place Massillon**. In the square, where a daily produce market is held, the twelfth-century Tour St-Blaise is all that remains of a Templar monastery. Up the steps, the **Collégiale St-Paul** has a large collection of ex-votos from the seventeenth century on.

To the west, **Parc Ste-Claire** (open 8am-6pm daily), which surrounds the nineteenth-century castle – once the home of novelist Edith Wharton, who restored it extensively – of the same name, is packed with exotic plants. Up rue du Paradis, **Parc St-Bernard** (open 8am-6pm daily) is equally lush. The park contains the **Villa Noailles** (1924), a cubist design by Robert Mallet-Stevens that has a restored cubist garden and was the scene, in its day, of trysts and parties frequented by A-list bohemians

including Man Ray (who shot part of his film *Mystère du Château de Dé* here), Picasso and filmmaker Luis Buñuel.

In **place de la République**, the thirteenth-century church of St-Louis (open 7am-8pm daily) is where King Louis IX prayed in 1254 when he got back from crusading.

Nineteenth-century Hyères is a palm-lined sprawl, containing, in place Lefebvre, the **Musée Municipale**, with its collection of artefacts from local ancient settlements.

Heading south out of town on avenue Thomas, the pseudo-Moorish **Villa Olbius Riquier** is surrounded by lush subtropical gardens, complete with hothouse and mini-zoo.

The beach, nowadays, is to be found below the town, a long stretch of sand reaching around the Rade d'Hyères bay from beyond the airport and south to the Giens peninsula. The esplanade by the marina is a fiesta of activity morning to night during the long high season. A market sprawls along the palm-lined quayside, where portraits are painted and ethnic jewellery sold.

Joining what used to be the Ile de Giens to the mainland is the narrow strip of land called La Capte, to the west of which are the Etang des Pesquiers salt pans. On the western shore of the isthmus, the beach of **Almanarre** is home each year to heats for the world windsurfing championships.

The bulge at the end of the isthmus is the **Giens** peninsula, with its stunningly situated namesake hilltop village. The main square, place Belvédère, affords fantastic views and hosts a market on Tuesday mornings. Tour Fondue on the southern tip of the peninsula is where boats leave for the islands.

Collégiale St-Paul
Hyères (no phone). **Open** *Apr-Oct* 3-6pm Mon; 10am-noon, 4-6.30pm Wed-Sat; 10am-12.30pm Sun; *Nov-Mar* 3-6pm Mon, Wed-Sun.

Jardins Olbius Riquier
av Amboise Thomas, Hyères (04.94.00.78.65). **Open** *May-Sept* 7.30am-8pm daily; *Oct-Apr* 7.30am-6pm daily. **Admission** free.

Musée Municipale
Cité Administratif, pl Théodore Lefebvre, Hyères (04.94.00.78.42). **Open** 10am-noon, 2.30-5.30pm Mon, Wed-Fri. **Admission** free.

ATLANTIDE

**Discover the
Mediterranean Coast
from Marseille to Porquerolles
in luxury**

**Departures from
the Port of Bandol Quai d Honneur
opposite La Mairie**

BOAT EXCURSIONS

**Reservations & Information
Gare Maritime
04 94 32 51 41
and at local tourist offices**

Villa Noailles

montée de Noailles (04.94.12.70.63). **Open** *June-Oct* 10am-noon, 4-7pm Mon, Wed-Sun; *Nov-May* 10am-noon, 2-5.30pm Wed-Sun; guided tours by appointment (04.94.01.84.40). **Admission** free.

Where to stay, eat & drink

Situated above the roulette wheels, the **Casino des Palmiers** (1 rue Amboise Thomas, 04.94.12.80.80, rates 590F-800F) is Hyères' only seriously grand hotel. The vine-covered **Hôtel du Soleil** (rue de Rempart, 04.94.65.16.26, rates 180F-390F) offers a warm welcome and has a small terrace where breakfast is served. Overlooking the La Gavine pleasure port, the **Potinière** (27 av de la Méditerranée, 04.94.00.51.60, closed Jan & Feb, rates 330F-490F) not only has large rooms and a private beach, but also serves great food – try the sumptuous seafood platter at its excellent-value restaurant **Giorgo** (menu 95F).

In Giens, the **Provençal** (pl St-Pierre, 04.98.04.54.54, closed Nov-Mar, rates 280F-600F) has a shady garden and a pool.

Deep in the *vieille ville*, **Bistrot de Marius** (1 pl Massillon, 04.94.35.88.38, closed Tue, menus 92F-195F) serves authentic Provençal cuisine, including bouillabaisse and other seafood dishes. In the modern town, the **Jardins des Bacchus** (32 av Gambetta, 04.94.65.77.63, closed lunch Sat and all Mon in July & Aug, dinner Sun and all Mon from Sept-June, menus 151F-300F) does good prawns with salad and Parmesan and a great rack of lamb. Three kilometres west of town in La Bayorre, **La Colombe** (663 rte de Toulon, 04.94.65.02.15, closed Mon in July & Aug, lunch Sat and dinner Sun from Sept-June, menus 145F-195F) serves carefully prepared specialities. It's a bright and highly popular space, so book ahead.

In Giens, the **Tire Bouchon** (1 pl St-Pierre, 04.94.58.24.61, closed dinner Tue, all Wed, menus 140F-180F) does an excellent *fricassée de poulpe et poulon*, a variation on bouillabaisse. In the tiny cove of Port du Niel, **L'Eau Salée** (Presqu'île de Giens, 04.94.58.92.33, closed dinner Sun & all Mon from Oct-Mar, closed Jan, menus 150F-195F) serves fish (and clients) straight off the boat(s); don't miss the delicious and very original mango tarte tatin.

Getting there

By air

Only internal flights serve Toulon/Hyères airport (04.94.00.83.83). The centre of town is ten minutes away by taxi.

By car

Leave the A57 at the Hyères interchange between exit nos.5 and 6; Hyères is on the RN98 coast road.

By bus

Phocéens Cars (04.93.85.66.61) runs two services a day (Mon to Sat) between Nice airport and Hyères. Sodétrav (04.94.12.55.12) operates several bus lines between Toulon and Hyères (one bus about every 30min); Sunday services are less frequent.

By train

Hyères station is on a branch line that separates from the main coast line just east of Toulon, with several trains a day between Toulon and Hyères.

Tourist information

Office de Tourisme

3 av Amboise Thomas (04.94.01.84.50/fax 04.94.01.84.51). **Open** *July, Aug* 8am-8pm daily; *Sept-June* 9am-6pm Mon-Fri; 10am-4pm Sat.

Iles d'Hyères

Strung across the entrance to Hyères bay are the Iles d'Hyères, of which Levant, Port-Cros and Porquerolles are the largest.

In the possession of the monks of Lérins until 1160, when they were seized by Saracens, the islands were home to these pirates until the sixteenth century. After turfing them out, King François I offered the islands as an asylum for ne'er-do-wells – who turned to piracy in their turn. A century later they were evicted, and the islands were used for various nefarious official purposes, including an army shooting range on Levant that all but decimated the island.

The village on **Ile de Porquerolles** was built as a retirement colony for Napoleonic officers, and it still bears a striking resemblance to a North African colonial post, despite the fact that for 60 years from 1911 it was the private property of Belgian engineer Joseph Fournier, who introduced the exotic flora still to be seen there. If your wallet doesn't stretch to dining in the Mas de Porquerolles (*see below*), pack a picnic, rent a bike from one of the outlets in the port and cycle through the pine and gum tree woods. The beaches on the northern side of the island are best for swimming.

The hilly, lush **Ile de Port-Cros** is a nature reserve with no cars, no smoking (!) and nature paths that extend under the sea for swimmers and divers to look at marine flora. Eighty per cent of the **Ile du Levant** is still military property, though no longer a shooting range. The remaining area, Héliopolis, is a nudist colony where participating visitors, as opposed to voyeurs, are welcome.

Where to stay & eat

On Porquerolles, the **Mas du Langoustier** (04.94.58.30.09, closed Nov-Apr, rates 1,200F-1,500F), three kilometres west of the port, has simple but luxurious accommodation and a restaurant that has foodies swooning (*see page 48*). If simpler (and cheaper) is more your style, **Les Glycines** (pl d'Armes, 04.94.58.30.36, rates 390F-890F) is a charming spot with lovely rooms in Provençal hues, and a restaurant (menus 99F-169F) where the simpler dishes usually prove the best. **L'Oustaou** (pl d'Armes, 04.94.58.30.13, closed mid-Nov to Feb, rates 500F-900F) is a good bet, too. **Le Manoir** (04.94.05.90.52, closed Oct to mid-Apr, rates 700F-1,060F incl dinner) is the only hotel on Port-Cros, so book well in advance in high season; it also has a restaurant (menus 250F-320F) serving Provençal classics. Levant is better served for hotels and campsites, though be warned that the majority are clothes-free zones. The upmarket, mimosa-swathed **La Villa Delphes** (chemin du Couvent, 04.94.05.90.63, closed Oct-Mar, 350F-450F) has a pool and a private beach. The pleasant rooms of **Brise Marine** (pl du Village, 04.94.05.91.15, rates 260F-520F) open on to a pretty courtyard.

Getting there

There are frequent ferry services to and between all three islands during the summer, and less frequent ones during the winter, from Hyères port (04.94.57.44.07), La Tour Fondue on the Giens peninsula (04.94.58.21.81), Cavalaire (04.94.64.08.04), Le Lavandou (04.94.71.01.02) and Toulon's quai Stalingrad (04.94.62.41.41).

Le Lavandou & the Massif des Maures

The rugged Corniche des Maures, which extends from Hyères to St-Tropez, offers the nearest thing to unspoiled beauty along the Côte d'Azur. The beaches shine silver, due to the mica in the sand. Hills and *calanque*-studded cliffs rise up from the coast, topped with thick pine, cork and eucalyptus forests. And although property developers have tried hard to wreak their usual havoc, the real horrors are outnumbered by the secluded villas and low-rise resorts beloved of family holiday-makers and the more retiring type of star.

From Hyères to Le Lavandou

La Londe-les-Maures, the first town after Hyères along the traffic-choked coast road, offers sandy beaches and some fairly ghastly seaside sprawl at the end of the mile-long tree-lined boulevard leading down to the sea.

Set back in the hills, the much-restored medieval village of **Bormes-les-Mimosas** affords wonderful sea views without the hustle and bustle of the coast. The floral handle was added to the name in 1968, when Bormes sought to drive home the point that it had the highest density of these yellow-puffball bearing trees on the Riviera. (The mimosa, a Mexican native, was only introduced to France in the 1860s). The **Musée d'Art et d'Histoire** has nineteenth-century landscapes by local artists that are of decidedly limited interest, though its

Villa Noailles: a cubist design by Robert Mallet-Stevens. *See page 161.*

historical section dedicated to illustrious eighteenth-century natives Ippolite Bouchard (who set up the Argentinian navy) and Ippolite Mourdeille (who was killed while chasing the Spaniards from Montevideo) is gripping. There's also a section on the history of the Chartreuse de La Verne (*see box page 166*).

South of Bormes, the Cap Bénat peninsula is a forest of no-entry signs, and getting down to the coast can be difficult. On the pleasant beaches around the old fishing hamlet of **Cabasson**, at the south-west point of the peninsula, you'll find yourself swimming under the watchful eye of secret-service men. For here, at the **Fort de Bregançon**, is the French president's official summer retreat, a sixteenth-century edifice whose restoration was initiated by a youthful Bonaparte. Reached by a causeway, the fortress stands on the heavily guarded high ground of the peninsula, but the lowlands remain open to the public. Further east, Borme-les-Mimosas' beach suburb of **La Favière** is a resort of the sardine-tin variety in the high season, with a seriously ugly port. From here, however, a delightful coastal path winds back around the Cap Bénat, allowing access to lovely, unspoiled beaches.

On the eastern coast of the peninsula, **Le Lavandou** has a pleasantly low-rise seafront looking on to the Ile du Levant. Watersports are big here, and equipment of all ilks is easily hired in town. Locals after a bit of calm make for the quieter St-Clair beach to the east.

Musée d'Art et d'Histoire de Bormes

103 rue Carnot (04.94.71.56.60). **Open** 9-10am, 2.30-5.30pm Mon, Wed-Fri; 9-10am, 2.30-5pm Sat; 10am-noon Sun. **Admission** free.

Where to stay & eat

In Cabasson, the **Palmiers** (240 chemin du Petit Fort, 04.94.64.81.94, closed mid-Nov to mid-Feb, rates 400F-675F) is one of the nicest hotels around, with steps down to the beach and a reliable restaurant (menus 160F-250F).

In Bormes, the **Mirage** (38 rue de la Vue des Iles, 04.94.05.32.60, closed Jan-Mar, Nov & Dec, rates 650F-900F) has a stunning view out across to the Iles d'Hyères, as well as pretty rooms, a pool and tennis courts. **La Terrasse** (19 pl Gambetta, 04.94.71.15.22, closed Nov &, Dec, rates 120F-190F) and **Bellevue** (14 pl Gambetta, 04.94.71.15.15, rates 180F-245F), both in the old town, are more downmarket but clean. **L'Escoundudo** (2 ruelle du Moulin, 04.94.71.15.53, closed Oct-Mar, menu 170F) serves simple but good food alfresco. The tiny **Lou Portaou** (1, rue Cubert des Poètes,

Set back in the hills, **Bormes-les-Mimosas**.

04.94.64.86.37, closed Tue, menus 68F-140F) has a short but excellent choice of Provençal dishes.

Le Lavandou's most luxurious option is **Les Roches** (1 av des Trois Dauphins, 04.94.71.05.07, closed Nov-Mar, rates 2,100F-3,000F), located four kilometres west of town at the head of a *calanque*, which has its own beach, antiques-furnished rooms and a fittingly upmarket restaurant (average 400F). In town, the **Auberge de la Calanque** (62 av Général de Gaulle, 04.94.71.05.96, closed mid-Oct to mid-Apr, rates 1,050F-1,630F) has a pool and a garden; some rooms have balconies with sea views; its Algue Bleue restaurant serves good Provençal fare with an Italian twist. To the east of the centre, in St-Clair, the **Belle-Vue** (chemin du Four des Maures, 04.94.00.45.00, closed Nov-Mar, rates 300F-800F) does, indeed, have a *belle* view, as well as a lovely garden and friendly hosts. Also in St-Clair, **Les Tamaris** (chez Raymond, Plage de St-Clair, 04.94.71.07.22, closed mid-Jan to mid-Feb, no menus) is an excellent fresh fish restaurant.

The Western Côte

The Massif des Maures

Stretching north-east of Bormes is the Massif des Maures. Though it rises only to 800 metres, the Massif's dramatic pine-clad crags give it a far loftier feel, while its wild inaccessibility – even to walkers in some areas – makes it seem very removed from the milling throngs a stone's throw away on the coast.

Beyond the Col de Gratteloup pass, a hair-raisingly winding road forks off the RN98 to Collobrières, the main town of the Massif, where cork has long been the economic mainstay and which is surrounded by the massive, gnarled trees from which cork is hewn. *Marrons* – chestnuts – are important, too, and a chestnut fair is held each year in early October. Ten kilometres north of town, off the road to Gonfaron, is the Village des Tortues (*see page 294*), not the tacky theme park the name implies but a centre for tortoise research. Twelve kilometres east of Collobrières, off the D14 to Cogolin, stands the recently restored Chartreuse de La Verne, the moody, brooding ruins of a twelfth-century Carthusian monastery.

Still further east, La Garde-Freinet was the last bastion of the Moors before they retreated from France in the tenth century.

The ruins of the Moorish fort can still be seen beside the remains of the fifteenth-century castle.

To get to the heart of the Massif, experience it from the GR9 walking route, which crosses it east-west, or the GR90, which cuts north-south.

Chartreuse de La Verne

(04.94.43.45.41). **Open** 11am-5pm Mon, Wed-Sun. Closed Jan. **Admission** 30F, children 15F. **No credit cards**.

Where to eat

In Collobrières, good, simple, local food is served at **La Petite Fontaine** (1 pl de la République, 04.94.48.00.12, closed dinner Sun, all Mon, two weeks in Sept & Feb, menus 130F-160F). For a truly rustic experience, sample the home-made delights at the **Chèvrerie du Peigros** (8km off RN8 on rte de la Môle, 04.94.48.03.83, closed dinner from Sept-June, menu 130F) near the Col du Babaou. In La Garde-Freinet, **La Faucado** (31 bd de L'Esplanade, 04.94.43.60.41, closed Tue and mid-Jan to mid-Mar, menu 150F) serves classic dishes in an old-world ambience.

Tourist information

Bormes-les-Mimosas

Office de Tourisme, 1 pl Gambetta (04.94.01.38.38/fax 04.94.01.38.39). **Open** *Apr-Sept* 9am-12.30pm, 2.30-6.30pm daily; *Oct-Mar* 9am-12.30pm, 2-6pm Mon-Sat.

Le Lavandou

Office de Tourisme, quai Gabriel Péri (04.94.00.40.50/fax 04.94.00.40.59). **Open** 9am-noon, 2.30-6pm Mon-Sat.

Getting there

By car

RN98 goes from Hyères to Bormes then cuts along the south of the Massif des Maures. Take the D559 turn-off at Bormes for the slow-moving coast road to Le Lavandou.

By bus

Sodétrav (04.94.12.55.00) runs frequent daily services along the coast from Hyères to St-Tropez.

Cavalaire & around

Between Le Lavandou and Cavalaire-sur-Mer is some of the Côte's most unspoiled scenery. Villas there are, but they're tree-swamped on the whole, and the view uphill from the silver-sand beaches scattered along the coast is, in many places, unimpeded by development. Pramousquier and Cavalaire both have lovely beaches.

The pretty village of Le Rayol-Canadel is home to the **Domaine du Rayol**, undoubtedly one of the most beautiful spots on the Corniche des Maures. Set amid ancient cork tree forests on a headland running down to sea cliffs, the Domaine was created in 1910 by Parisian banker Alfred Courmes, who packed the grounds with exotic plants from Chile, South Africa, Australia and New Zealand before losing all his money in the crash of 1929. Gullies, bowers and secret paths are dotted about this jungle of green and dramatic vistas. Outdoor concerts (information 04.94.05.32.50) are held in July and August.

Above Le Rayol-Canadel, spectacular sea views can be had from the Col du Canadel pass.

The idyll comes to an abrupt halt at **Cavalaire-sur-Mer**, a built-up sprawl with a long beach much frequented by unglamorous families, and one of the best charcuteries in the region, Au Bec Fin.

Slightly back from the coast, **La Croix-Valmer** is a residential town with fine views across cliffs dotted with the holiday villas of discreetly well-heeled French families. Though the *croix* (cross) in its name refers to an airborne one allegedly seen around here by the co-Emperor Constantine – a forerunner of the burning one he was to see as he crossed Rome's Milvian bridge on the way to a successful battle for total control of the Roman empire – the town was only built in 1934. From here, there is easy access to the stunning coastal conservation area on the **Cap Lardier**.

Au Bec Fin

275 av des Alliés (04.94.64.00.20). **Open** 7am-1pm, 3-7pm Tue-Sun. **Credit** AmEx, DC, MC, V.

Domaine du Rayol

ave des Belges, Le Rayol-Canadel (04.94.05.32.50). **Open** *Feb to mid-Nov* 9.30-12.30pm, 2.30-6.30pm daily; *July, Aug* 9.30am-12.30pm, 4.30-8pm daily. **Admission** 40F, 20F children.

Where to stay & eat

Between Le Lavandou and Le Rayol, **Le Club de Cavalière** (04.94.05.80.14, call for current details) on the beach of the same name is a dream of a place, with Caribbean-style thatched beach huts. In the restaurant, chef Marc Dach produces interesting takes on local specialities. In Pramousquier, **Le Mas** (9 av du Capitaine Ducourneau, 04.94.05.80.43, closed mid-Nov to Feb, rates 250F-410F) has lovely views and a pool, and the Beau Site (plage de Pramousquier, 04.94.05 80.08, closed Oct-Apr, rates 250F-390F) has rooms with balconies and sea views, as well as a restaurant (menus 95F-135F).

In Le Rayol-Canadel, the **Maurin des Maures** (04.94.05.60.11, closed dinner from mid-Nov to mid-Dec, menus 68F-144F) serves excellent, simple seafood. One kilometre east of La Croix-Valmer on the D93, the **Parc Hôtel** (av Georges Selliez, 04.94.79.64.04, closed Nov-Apr, rates 430F-560F) is full of old-world charm and stands in pleasant grounds. The elegant **Château de Valmer** (rte de Gigaro, 04.94.79.60.10, closed Nov-Apr, rates 900F-1,700F) is eight kilometres south-east of town, and close to less crowded beaches. Nearby, in La Croix's beach suburb of Gigaro, the soberly elegant **Souleias** (plage de Gigaro, 04.94.55.10.55, closed mid-Oct to mid-Apr, rates

550F-1,530F), is situated on the clifftop; its restaurant (menus 190F-370F) serves classic Provençal food. Between La Croix and Cavalaire, in the suburb of Barbigoua, the **Petite Auberge** (av des Gabiers, 04.94.54.21.82, closed lunch Mon-Sat in July & Aug, lunch Tue, all Mon at other times, closed Nov-Mar, menus 150F-170F) serves Niçois favourites with a smile.

Getting there

By car

D559 runs all along the coast and up to La Croix-Valmer.

By bus

Sodétrav (04.94.12.55.00) runs frequent daily services (fewer on Sun) from Toulon and Hyères to Le Rayol-Canadel, Cavalaire-sur-Mer and La Croix Valmer.

Tourist information

Cavalaire-sur-Mer

Office de Tourisme, Maison de la Mer, Cavalaire-sur-Mer (04.94.01.92.10/fax 04.94.05.49.89). **Open** *mid-June to mid-Sept* 8.30am-7.30pm daily; *mid-Sept to mid-June* 9am-12.30pm, 2-6pm Mon-Sat.

La Croix-Valmer

Office de Tourisme, Les Jardins de la Gare (04.94.55.12.12/fax 04.94.55.12.10). **Open** *June-Sept* 9am-8pm Mon-Sat; 9am-1pm Sun; *Oct-May* 9.15am-noon, 2-6pm Mon-Fri; 9.15am-noon Sat.

Chartreuse de La Verne: *see box opposite.*

St-Tropez & Around

Been there, got the T-shirt? Despite – or maybe because of its – overblown reputation – navel (and naval) gazing 'San Trop' remains absorbing.

So inconspicuous and unimportant was the rocky headland on which St-Tropez stands that no one thought to supply it with roads until early last century, while the railway bypassed it completely. Today, the approaches to St-Tropez are a purgatory of slow-moving traffic during the summer season. Up on the vine-covered headland, however, things are calmer: apart from Chapelle Ste-Anne, all you'll find are luxury homes and badly lost beach babes.

St-Tropez

Given the hedonistic reputation of St-Tropez, it's fitting that the arch-hedonist Nero should have put the place on the map. In the first century AD, the emperor had a Christian centurion by the name of Torpes beheaded in Pisa. Torpes' headless trunk was loaded aboard a boat and set adrift with a rooster and a dog. When the boat washed up on the beach now named after the hapless centurion, the starving dog hadn't taken so much as a nibble of the corpse, a sure sign of sainthood.

In the Middle Ages, the small fishing community at St-Tropez was harried by Saracens, until the fifteenth century when tough Genoese settlers were imported to show the pirates who was who. But the place was still a tiny backwater in 1880 when Guy de Maupassant sailed his boat in briefly to give the locals their first taste of bohemian eccentricity. A decade later, post-Impressionist Paul Signac, driven into port by a storm, liked the place so much that he stayed, inviting his whacky friends – including Matisse, Derain, Vlaminck and Dufy – down, and converting their palettes from dark northern tones to brilliant St-Tropez hues. Colette lived here, too: her only complaint about the place was that in order to concentrate on writing, she had to turn her back on the attention-monopolising view.

Another wave of personalities washed up in St-Tropez in 1956 after Roger Vadim, his young protégée Brigitte Bardot and a film crew descended on the town to make *Et Dieu créa la femme* (*And God Created Woman*). Like Signac, Bardot stayed, giving the village a glamorous sheen. It was no time before St-Tropez became the world's most famous playboy playground.

The millionaires and superstars are still there (including Bardot, who alternates between her house up in the hills and her near-legendary seafront home at La Madrague, now officially the headquarters for her animal rights group). Nowadays, however, they're locked in a bitter love-hate relationship with the Instamatic hordes who come to gawp. When a French magazine

The legendary **Vieux Port** at St-Tropez, where luxury yachts back up to the quayside.

contacted various St-Tropez faces to sign a spoof 'anti-pleb' charter, many said yes. (To his credit, veteran rocker Johnny Hallyday honourably refused. 'Plebs! Those are my fans,' he stormed.)

Though the yacht-and-champagne scenario around the Vieux Port is oddly compelling, St-Tropez has other attractions, beginning with the **Musée de l'Annonciade**, situated between the old and new port areas. Signac had long wanted to set up a permanent exhibit of his friends' works here, but it was not until 1937 that it came to pass. In the best collection of early twentieth-century art outside Paris, the brilliant effects of St-Tropez light upon Signac's mates can be seen. Pointillists like Signac, Fauves, Nabis, Expressionists and Cubists are all represented in this extraordinary – and extraordinarily under-visited – gallery.

East of the Vieux Port, the huge **Château de Suffren**, where the occasional art show is staged, dates back to 980. Back from the quai Jean Jaurès, heading towards the Port de Pêche (yes, even in glitzy St-Tropez there are real, working fishermen), the place aux Herbes and rue de Ponce are quieter, less sanitised, distinctly more lived-in areas of town. The former is home to a lively daily fish market.

Still further around the seafront, the sixteenth-century citadel contains the fairly bland **Musée Naval**, and allows access on to ramparts with a fantastic view over the town and coast. South-east of the port, the plane-tree lined **place des Lices** is where St-Tropez's *pétanque*-playing fraternity hangs out. It's also home to a market on Tuesdays and Saturdays, when the Provençal characters come to town. Fruit, vegetables, charcuterie, honey and wine fill the stalls but traders are really there to catch up on the local gossip and see friends. Bardot is a regular customer.

On the hill a kilometre out of town, the pretty **Chapelle Ste-Anne** (closed to the public) commands spectacular views over the bay, and hosts flash weddings.

But like it or not, you'll find yourself being drawn to the **Vieux Port**, where multi-million-pound yachts back up to the quayside to give the quay-strolling crowds a ringside view of their owners' champagne-swilling antics.

Musée de l'Annonciade

pl Gramont (04.94.97.04.01). **Open** *June-Sept* 10am-noon, 3pm-7pm Mon, Wed-Sun; *Oct-May* 10am-noon, 4-6pm Mon, Wed-Sun. **Admission** 30F-35F, 15F-20F children.

Musée Naval

Mont de la Citadelle (04.94.97.59.43). **Open** *Apr-Oct* 11am-6pm Mon, Wed-Sun; *Nov-Mar* 10am-noon, 1-5pm Mon, Wed-Sun. **Admission** 25F, 15F children.

Where to eat & drink

St-Tropez restaurants reviewed in the **Provençal Food & Drink** chapter are La Bouillabaisse and Leï Mouscardins, *see page 48*.

Le Café

pl des Lices (04.94.97.44.69). **Open** daily; hours vary with season. **Menus** 138F-178F. **Credit** AmEx, MC, V.
In the hinterland, away from the flashbulbs, this place is on the site of the Café des Arts, the legendary watering hole for the place des Lices boules players. Take a drink at the bar with the locals and cast an eye over the wooden boules lockers by the front door; on the wall above is the boules league table. The restaurant at the rear is used as a hideout by summertime celebrities hoping to avoid the hordes. In winter a fire blazes in the grate. The grilled sea bass is a treat, as is the home-made apple tart.

Café de Paris

15 quai Suffren (04.94.97.00.56). **Open** *summer* 7am-4am daily; *winter* 7am-1am daily. **Menus** 80F-120F. **Credit** MC, V.
Philippe Starck gave this old bar a makeover and it now has a long counter, red velvet banquettes, chandeliers and a sushi menu. In summer it's packed, and the terrace is a prime position for people-spotting.

Café Le Senequier

quai Jean Jaurès (04.94.97.00.90). **Open** *mid-Dec to June, mid-Sept to Nov* 8am-6.30pm daily; *July, Aug* 8am-3am daily. **No credit cards**.
This vast terrace filled with scarlet chairs may no longer attract the glamorous, but it remains a thoroughly entertaining place for aperitifs, people-watching and yacht-gazing at sunset.

Chez Fuchs

7 rue des Commerçants (04.94.97.01.25). **Open** 7am-11pm Mon, Wed-Sun. Closed Tue. *Meals served* noon-2.30pm, 8-11.30pm daily. **Menus** 180F-280F. **Credit** MC, V.
A tiny, moderately priced bistro that doubles as a *bar-tabac* cigar shop, with tasty regional beef stew, stuffed vegetables and a friendly atmosphere. It's a legendary hangout for the local thirty something crowd.

Le Frégate

52 rue Allard (04.94.97.07.08). **Open** noon-2pm, 7-11pm daily. **Menus** 145F. **Credit** MC, V.
This unassuming restaurant, which seats just 25, serves unpretentious Provençal cuisine.

Le Gorille

1 quai Suffren (04.94.97.03.93). **Open** *summer* 24 hours daily; *winter* 6am-8pm daily.
No credit cards.
A corner caff, Le Gorille is open 24 hours a day in summer, when its menu is honed down to burgers or steak served with the house *frites*.

The Western Côte

Beach babes

After parading on the poop deck, even the super-rich must make for the beach and the St-Tropez headland is one long string of them, fringed with non-stop beach restaurants.

The most easily accessible beaches from town are the built-up **La Bouillabaisse** to the west, **Les Graniers** in the Baie des Cannebiers just past the Citadel and the horribly crowded **Les Salins** (a five-kilometre drive, or a 12-kilometre hike round the headland path, if you feel so inclined). Les Salins has a 5,000-capacity free car park, watched by an attendant whom you are advised to tip handsomely. If you find the occupants of those 5,000 cars (or the seaweed that frequently washes on to the beach) off-putting, turn left (north) on the shore and follow the winding coast path for less peopled stretches of sandy beach, including the isolated **Plage de la Moutte**.

But these are not where you'll find the yachties. For decades, the two big names in bathing St-Tropez-style have been the **Tahiti** (04.94.97.18.02; at the north end of the beach) and **Club 55** (04.94.79.80.14) beach clubs, both of which are along the five kilometres of white sand in the **Baie de Pampelonne**. It was here that topless bathers first shocked the world; on some stretches even that is *de trop* these days.

When Club 55 opened in the 1950s, it was a lone shack on a very deserted beach. The location appealed to Roger Vadim and Brigitte Bardot, who made it their unofficial headquarters between takes of *Et Dieu créa la femme* (*And God Created Woman*). To reach it, turn off the D93 coast road by the municipal parking lot on boulevard Patch before the road curves towards Ramatuelle. At the far (southern) end of this car park is **NiouLargo** (04.94.79.82.14), a private beach with good restaurants and a thriving afternoon backgammon scene. At the southern end of Pampelonne beach, the walking track resumes, continuing past **Cap Camarat** and various lesser-known coves, skirting verdant luxurious residential developments, towards **La Croix-Valmer**.

La Madrague

résidences du Nouveau Port (04.94.97.14.70). **Meals served** *summer* 8pm-2am daily; *winter* noon-2am daily. **Menus** 120F-400F. **Credit** AmEx, MC, V.
Designer gilt and high-back second-empire chairs are the order of the day in this most overtly trendy of eating houses. Models and glitterati consider it a home from home, not least because the owner, Jean Roch, has another branch in Paris on the Champs Elysées.

Popoff

quai Frédéric Mistral (04.94.97.13.54). **Open** hours vary according to season. **No credit cards**.
This classic St-Trop ice-cream parlour on the port is still family-run. Held in particularly high esteem are the chocolate and banana flavours, but the pièce de résistance is the creamy coconut.

La Table du Marché

38 rue Georges Clemenceau (04.94.97.85.20). **Open** 7.30am-10.30pm Tue-Sun. Annual holidays vary. **Meals served** noon-2.30pm, 7-10.30pm Tue-Sat; noon-2.30pm Sun. **Menu** 330F. **Credit** AmEx, MC, V.
A mouthwatering spread of regional specialities and superb wines in a cosy bistro/deli with an afternoon tea room and a new sushi bar, masterminded by celebrity chef Christophe Leroy. Try for the upstairs dining room, set up like a theatre stage with antique bookshelves and overstuffed armchairs.

Nightlife

Caves du Roy

Hôtel Byblos, av Paul-Signac (04.94.97.16.02). **Open** *June-Sept* 11pm-dawn daily; *Oct-May* 11pm-dawn Fri, Sat. **Admission** first drink 140F. **Credit** AmEx, DC, MC. V.
Though VIP (*see below*) has made a splash, this old institution in the cavernous basement of the Hôtel Byblos (*see below*), with an open-air terrace, has not faltered. Swingers d'un certain age like rocker Johnny Hallyday and France's club king Eddie Barclay party until dawn. It may be big, but getting in ain't always easy.

L'Esquinade

2 rue du Four (04.94.97.87.45). **Open** *Oct-Easter* 11pm-6am Fri, Sat; *Easter-Sept* 11pm-6am daily. **Admission** free. **Credit** V.
This old favourite is packed with locals year-round.

Octave Café

pl de la Garonne (04.94.97.22.56). **Open** 11pm-5am daily. **Admission** first drink 90F. **Credit** AmEx, MC, V.
A stylish piano bar with soft music, squishy cushioned chairs, low black marble tables and a chic clientèle. Liza Minelli and the inimitable Johnny Hallyday have been known to pop in and croon a few tunes just for fun.

Though some smaller coves and short stretches of Pampelonne beach are free, much of the sand around the St-Tropez peninsula is sewn up by beach establishments. Expect to spend 500F a day for your sun lounger, parasol, towel and aperitif on a private beach, whether it be chic or family-oriented.

Where to eat & drink

Eateries are shoulder to shoulder along the peninsula, where ever-changing fashion dictates the place to be seen.

A few places seem immune to the whims of fashion, including **Club 55** (*see above*) where owner Patrice de Colmont oversees the serving of great fresh grilled fish and salads under a white-canvas-shaded deck, surrounded by tamarisk trees; a meal costs around 300F and booking is essential. Also evergreen are **La Voile Rouge** (rte de Tamaris, Ramatuelle, 04.94.97.22.56, closed Nov-early June, menu 400F), the

extreme Tropezien party scene, where siliconed string-bikini starlets dance on tables, the rock booms out at mega-decibels and champagne flows at exorbitant prices; and the more laid-back **L'Esquinade** (rte des Plages, 04.94.79.83.42, closed Nov-Mar, menu 120F), a glitz-less, affordable beach with authentic funky beach-shack charm; Bardot's favourite night-time haunt, this is a friendly family spot that evokes the St-Trop of the '50s.

Of the newer arrivals, the **Cachelot Plage** (rte de l'Epi, 04.94.79.82.04, closed Nov, menus 105F-250F) boasts the most delicious and affordable Provençal menu of fresh salads and grilled fish of all the Pampelonne beaches, with a lovely shaded deck and pool. The style is casual chic but extremely convivial, and best of all, it stays open during the off-season. On Les Salins beach, **Les Salins** (rte des Salins, 04.94.97.04.40, closed Oct-Mar), run by Portuguese chef Manu, is a good bet for a drink and a meal of fresh fish.

Le Papagayo

résidences du Nouveau Port (04.94.97.07.56). **Open** *late Apr-Nov* 11.30pm-5am daily. **Admission** 100F. Ever since the '60s, this legendary club has attracted the showbiz crowd; it's still one of the nocturnal hotspots, particularly if the VIP (*see below*) is full.

Le VIP Room

résidences du Nouveau Port (04.94.97.14.70). **Open** *Apr-Oct* midnight-dawn. **Admission** first drink 120F. **Credit** AmEx, V.
Downstairs at the Madrague (*see above*), this is St-Trop's hippest new joint. It's no easy job getting in: you'll need to work on your St-Trop look. Naomi Campbell celebrated a birthday here and photos from this dancefloor end up on glossy pages worldwide. The music is modern and edgy, with the accent on hip hop and techno.

Shopping

Rue Sibille and rue Clemenceau are home to every designer name imaginable.

Claire l'Insolite

1 rue Sibille (04.94.97.10.74). **Open** *mid-June to mid-Sept* 10am-1pm, 3-10pm daily; *mid-Sept to mid-June* 9am-1pm, 3-8pm daily. **Credit** AmEx, DC, MC, V.
Since the time before the onslaught of designer boutiques, this established prêt-à-porter shop has

offered a little bit of everything from the world of trendy haute couture and glamour bikinis, along with friendly service.

La Maison des Lices

2 bd Louis Blanc (04.94.97.64.64). **Open** *Sept-May* 10am-1pm, 3-7pm Tue-Sat; *June-Aug* 10am-1pm, 3-8.30pm Tue-Sat. Closed Mon, Sun. **Credit** AmEx, MC, V.
Old-fashioned home linens, sweet-smelling soaps, Provençal pottery and unusual objets d'art.

Where to stay

If you're planning to stay in St-Tropez in high season, book months ahead.

Château de la Messardière

rte de Tahiti (04.94.56.76.00/fax 04.94.56.76.01). Closed Dec-Apr. **Rates** single 1,000F-2,000F, double 1,200F-3,500F, suite 2,500F-7,000F. **Credit** AmEx, DC, MC, V.
Perched on a hilltop of parasol pines, this restored nineteenth-century castle, complete with turrets and canopy beds, once belonged to an aristocratic family whose spirit lives on in the tarot card-inspired art adorning the arches of the elegant lobby, designed by the current Countess de la Messardière. From the olive branch-patterned carpets and Provençal fabrics down to the terracotta tiles and marble bathrooms, all is luxurious Mediterranean splendour.

The Western Côte

Hôtel Les Bouis

rte des Plages-Pampelonne (04.94.79.87.61/ fax 04.94.79.85.20). Closed 2 Nov-Easter. **Rates** single/double 750F-1,220F. **Credit** AmEx, DC, MC, V.

Slightly out of town, opposite **Tahiti Beach** (*see box* **Beach babes**), Les Bouis offers all the creature comforts in the wilds of St-Tropez beachland.

Hôtel Byblos

av Paul Signac (04.94.56.68.00/fax 04.94.56.68.01). Closed mid-Oct to Easter. **Rates** single 1,200F-1,950F, double 1,550F-2,500F, suites 6,500F-9,000F. **Credit** AmEx, DC, V.

An eclectic mix of Byzantine kitsch and Provençal neo-rustic, the Byblos has twee chalets along pathways through lush palm- and fountain-filled gardens, right in the centre of town. Perennially trendy, it is a must for the jet set: the hotel lobby in August is starpacked. Food is taken very seriously since the arrival in 1998 of chef Georges Pelissier. Specials include a light bouillabaisse with garlic chips.

Les Palmiers

pl des Lices (04.94.97.01.61/fax 04.94.97.10.02). **Rates** single 430F-670F, double 670F-1,050F. **Credit** AmEx, DC, MC, V

A verdant path leads to reception and in season the branches are loaded with limes, mandarins and grapefruits. Rooms giving on to the courtyard each have a mini-patio. Service is friendly and the bar spacious enough for guests to welcome friends for a pre-clubbing apéritif.

Le Pré de la Mer

rte des Salins (04.94.97.12.23/fax 04.94.97.43.91). Closed Oct-Easter. **Rates** 520F-1,420F. **Credit** AmEx, V.

Three conventional bedrooms and eight self-contained studio apartments in a pretty Provençal setting slightly outside town.

Résidence de la Pinede

plage de la Bouillabaisse (04.94.55.91.00/fax 04.94.97.73.64). Closed mid-Oct to Easter. **Rates** double 1,925F-4,125F, suite 4,455F-8,690F. **Credit** AmEx, DC, MC, V.

Only a stone's throw from the mad summer hordes of downtown St-Trop, this tranquil oasis of luxury has its own private beach, a spillover pool, an unbeatable view of the bay and one of the best restaurants around (meals served noon-2.30pm, 7.30-10pm daily, menus 280F-560F). Try Belgian chef Alois Vanlangeenaeker's delectable *menu Provence*.

Le Sube

15 quai Suffren (04.94.97.30.04/fax 04.94.54.89.08). Closed three weeks Jan. **Rates** single 390F-590F, double 590F-1,500F. **Credit** AmEx, DC, MC, V.

Plum in the centre of the port, the Sube is woody and cosy, and a favourite with yachting enthusiasts. The unusually large bar has a view on to the port, with a balcony so popular it can be difficult to squeeze on

to in high season. Don't worry, just ease back into a leather armchair and admire the nautical artefacts that deck the mantlepiece and tables. Breakfast is served to hotel guests on the balcony.

Getting there

The right sort arrive by large boat or helicopter. There is no train station.

By car

Sweat it out on the notoriously busy RN98 coast road. There are plans for an expressway in 2005.

By bus

SODETRAV (04.94.49.97.88.51) runs frequent bus services daily between St-Tropez, Toulon and Nice, around the St-Tropez peninsula, and to Ramatuelle, Gassin, Grimaud and St-Raphaël.

By boat

MMG (04.94.96.51.00) runs regular daily boat services (every hour) from Ste-Maxime to St-Tropez from April to October .

Tourist information

Office de Tourisme

quai Jean-Jaurès (04.94.97.45.21/fax 04.94.97.82 66). **Open** 9am-noon, 2pm-6pm daily.

Around St-Tropez

The St-Tropez peninsula

Ramatuelle and the smaller **Gassin** are perfect hilltop villages, packed with artsy-craftsy shops and surrounded by Côtes de Provence vineyards. Ramatuelle was a Saracen stronghold; it was razed in 1592 during the Religious Wars, then rebuilt in 1620, as many inscriptions above doors testify. Gassin sits at the end of some frightening hairpin bends, and is a delightful place to stroll around picturesque alleyways when it's too hot to breathe down on the coast. Gassin was where Mick and Bianca Jagger honeymooned after an action-packed wedding in St-Tropez' Chapelle Ste-Anne in the early 1970s.

When the sun-worshipping gets too much, the peninsula's vineyards offer a welcome alternative. On route Ramatuelle (D61 towards Gassin), **Château Minuty** produces a highly rated rosé and fine reds. The cellars, grounds and eighteenth-century chapel can be visited. Further along the D61 is the equally charming **Château de Barbeyrolles**. Local co-operative **Les Maîtres Vignerons de St-Tropez**, by the La Foux junction on the RN98, is the place to sample a quality rosé. On Sunday mornings in summer, there's a farmers' market here.

Ramatuelle, once a Saracen stronghold.

Château de Barbeyrolles
04.94.56.33.58. **Open** *summer* 9am-8pm daily;
winter 9am-5pm Mon-Sat. **Credit** AmEx, MC, V.

Château Minuty
04.94.56.12.09. **Open** 9am-noon, 2-6pm daily.
Admission free. **Credit** AmEx, MC, V.

Les Maîtres Vignerons de St-Tropez
04.94.56.32.04. **Open** *Oct-May* 8.30am-noon, 2-
6.30pm Mon-Fri; 10am-noon, 2-6.30pm Sat; *June-Sept*
9am-12.30pm, 3-6.30pm Mon-Fri; 10am-12.30pm, 3-
6.30pm Sat; 9am-1pm Sun. **Credit** MC, V.

Where to stay, eat & drink

Below Ramatuelle, heading for the Pampelonne
beach, **Les Moulins** (rte des Plages,
04.94.97.17.22, closed mid-Nov to Mar, rates
950F-1,450F) has six pretty rooms and an
excellent restaurant (closed lunch Thur, all
Wed, menus 300F-580F) in a glorious, quiet
country-meets-beach setting.

In Ramatuelle, the **Terrasse-Hostelleries
le Baou** (av Gustave Etienne, 04.94.79.20.48,
closed mid-Oct to Easter, rates 950F-3,500F),
has spectacular views across the vine-clad
peninsula, pleasant rooms, a pool and a
restaurant (menus 190F-360F) serving good,
reliable Provençal favourites. In a converted
blacksmith's shop, **La Forge** (rue Victor Léon,
04.94.79.25.56, closed winter, call for details)
chef Pierre Fazio, too, serves up good Provençal
cuisine. The **Café de l'Ormeau** (pl de
l'Ormeau, 04.94.79.20.20) is pure central casting:
the terrace is covered by a canopy of creepers,
inside is a long wooden bar and to the rear are
painted evergreen tables where you can order
your *chocolat chaud* or local charcuterie.

In Gassin, the **Bello Visto** (pl des Barrys,
04.94.56.17.30, closed winter) is the perfect place
to down a pastis while admiring the view, but it
also has a few simple rooms and a restaurant.
Le Micocoulier (pl des Barrys, 04.94.56.14.01,
closed lunch Mon and mid-Oct to Apr, menus
160F-260F) serves some of the best food for
miles around: Provençal, with an Italian twist.

Getting there

By car
Ramatuelle is on the D61 south of St-Tropez; for
Gassin take one of the signposted roads off the
D61 or D559.

By bus
Sodetrav (04.94.12.55.12) runs one morning service a
day between St-Tropez, Ramatuelle and Gassin
during summer and on Tuesday, Wednesday Friday
and Saturday in winter.

Tourist information

Office de Tourisme,
pl de l'Ormeau, Ramatuelle (04.94.79.26.04). **Open**
mid-Oct to Mar 8.30am-12.30pm, 2-8pm Mon-Fri;
Apr-June, Sept-mid Oct 8.30am-12.30pm, 2-8pm Mon-
Sat; *July, Aug* 8.30am-12.30pm, 2-8pm daily.

Cogolin, Grimaud & Ste-Maxime

West of St-Tropez, **Cogolin** wins no prizes for
beauty, but it does qualify as a real town, with
real – rather than tourist-oriented – crafts being
carried out. Local specialities include corks,
pipes carved from briar roots, reeds for wind
instruments, bamboo furniture and Armenian
carpets, a trade imported by Armenian
immigrés in the 1920s. In the few medieval
streets at the top of the village, the eleventh-
century church of **St-Sauveur** (open 8am-7pm
daily) has a lovely sixteenth-century alterpiece
by Hurlupin. The **Espace Raimu** museum has
a collection of memorabilia of the actor Jules
Muraire, alias Raimu.

Further north, picture-perfect *village perché*
Grimaud was a Saracen stronghold before
falling to the Templars. Nowadays, the quaint
shops brigade is firmly in command. Up top are
the ruins of an eleventh-century castle. Rue des
Templiers has basalt arcades and imposing
doorways, and there's a pretty Romanesque
church, St-Michel (open 9am-6pm daily).

Back down on the coast, **Port Grimaud** was
built in the late 1960s on reclaimed land,
designed by architect François Spoerry to look

The Western Côte

like a perfect miniature Murano, complete with canals instead of streets. Kitschily pretty, this is real estate for the seriously rich, but the owners magnanimously let visitors wander along the brasserie-lined canals to admire the yachts parked at the bottoms of gardens.

Ste-Maxime is in sharp contrast to the rarified glamour of St-Tropez across the gulf, and the residents are proud of the small-town welcome they offer. They're also happy to take up the slack of big-spending holiday-makers who found no room at the inn in St-Tropez, and ferry them across by regular boat services to soak up the flasher atmosphere. The esplanade is crowded with family restaurants facing on to the pines and the port.

Espace Raimu

18 av Clemenceau (04.94.54.18.00). **Open** 10am-noon, 3-6pm Mon-Sat, 3-6pm Sun; later in summer. **Admission** 20F, 10F children, free under-11s.

Where to stay, eat & drink

In Cogolin, the centrally located **Hôtel Coq** (pl de la Mairie, 04.94.54.13.71, rates 200F-320F) has a wide selection of rooms. The simple **Hôtel Clemenceau** (pl de la République, 04.94.54.15.17, rates 170F-650F) has an English-speaking host. Outside Cogolin, heading towards

Port Grimaud: real estate for the very rich.

St-Tropez, **Relais de Font-Mourier** (domaine Bellevue, 04.94.56.60.61, closed Oct-Mar, rates 350F-600F) has a pool and tennis courts.

Grimaud's only hotel is the **Côteau Flori** (pl des Pénitentas, 04.94.43.20.17, closed mid-Nov to mid-Dec, rates 275F-550F), a gem with views over the Massif des Maures. It also has the excellent **Santons** restaurant (*see page 50*). In Port Grimaud, the luxurious **Giraglia** (pl du 14 Juin, 04.94.56.31.33, closed Oct-May, rates 890F-2,200F) is perfect for watching the water traffic.

In Ste-Maxime, the elegant **Belle Aurore** (4 bd Jean Moulin, 04.94.96.02.45, closed mid-Oct to mid-Mar, rates 800F-3,950F) has white-jacketed staff, a view of the sea across the golf course, a swimming pool and a good restaurant (closed Wed from Sept-June, menus 210F-450F). The **Mas des Oliviers** (Quartier de la Croisette, 04.94.96.13.31, rates 250F-750F), a kilometre west of the centre in Quartier de la Croisette, has 20 rooms, some with balconies and sea views, plus a pool and tennis courts.

Of the town's restaurants, **La Marine** (6 rue Fernard Bessy, 04.94.96.53.93, closed Nov-Feb, menus 150F-200F) serves reliable seafood and **La Maison Bleue** (48 rue Bert, 04.94.96.71.69, closed Tue, menus 55F-138F) serves fresh pasta and equally fresh fish alfresco.

Of Ste-Maxime's bars, the **Café de France** (pl Victor Hugo, 04.94.96.18.16, open 7am-8pm daily) and **Le Wafu** (pl Victor Hugo, 04.94.96.15.74, open 7am-8pm), both with sun-kissed terraces, are institutions.

Getting there

By car

Ste-Maxime is on the D98 coast road; alternatively, leave the A8 at exit no.36 and take the D25 to the coast.

By bus

Sodatrav (04.94.54.62.36) runs services to Cogolin, Grimaud and Ste-Maxime ten times a day during the summer season, five in winter.

Tourist information

Cogolin

Office de Tourisme, pl de la République (04.94.55.01.10). **Open** *summer* 9am-12.30pm, 2.30-7pm daily; *winter* 9am-noon, 2-6.30pm Mon-Fri; 9am-noon Sat.

Grimaud

Office de Tourisme, 1 bd des Aliziers (04.94.43.26.98). **Open** *summer* 9am-12.30pm, 3pm-7pm daily; *winter* 9am-12.30pm, 2.30-6.30pm daily.

Ste-Maxime

Office de Tourisme, promenade St-Lorière (04.94.55.75.55). **Open** 9am-noon, 2pm-6pm daily.

St Raphaël & Around

Vertiginous cliff views, seaside towns, a scattering of history and the dramatic heights of the Massif d'Estérel.

The conurbation-resort of St-Raphaël and Fréjus stands at the western end of the Corniche de l'Estérel, where the high red volcanic rocks of the Massif de l'Estérel loom over the deep blue sea, providing the most striking colour contrasts on the Côte d'Azur. There are pines and cork oaks on this lush rock face, but their numbers are sadly reduced: since 1943, fires – accidental and set deliberately by property developers – have ravaged the eco-system and reduced much of the area to brushland. Wildlife abounds nonetheless: wild boar, deer, hares, pheasant and partridge are common sights. In spring, the lavender is spectacular and fragrant.

St-Raphaël

St-Raphaël's beach strip, which stretches eastwards from the *vieux port* around the headland past the casino to the big seafront hotels, is peopled by Rollerbladers and mountain bikers. All the multicoloured paraphernalia of sea sports, from windsurfing boards to the latest fluorescent garb, spill out of shops. This is the nearest the Côte d'Azur gets to Bondi or Miami Beach. Gounod composed *Roméo et Juliette* here; F Scott Fitzgerald worked on *Tender is the Night*. But St-Raphaël is also home to timeshares, making it an un-flashy, family- and pensioner-oriented destination.

Just as it was for the staid Romans who came down from Fréjus to take the sea air here. The Saracens who ravaged the place in the Middle Ages had other ideas, however. So, presumably, did Napoléon when he made the village famous by landing here in 1799 after taking a beating at the hands of the British in Egypt.

St-Raphaël's medieval and Belle Epoque centre was largely destroyed by wartime bombing. From the west, the skyline is dominated by the neo-Byzantine **Notre-Dame-de-la-Victoire-de-Lépante**, built in 1883 and surrounded by apartments with all the allure of office blocks. Beneath the railway arches on rue Victor Hugo, the daily market is a rare patch of local character: all manner of produce, including cut flowers, is noisily sold. Beyond the railway line, the twelfth-century church of **St-Pierre-des-Templiers** stands beside the remains of the Roman aqueduct. Next door, and overseeing

visits to the church, the **Musée Archéologique** contains ancient artefacts from the harbour, plus a display on underwater archaeology.

Musée Archéologique
pl de la Vieille Eglise (04.94.19.25.75). **Open** 10am-12pm, 2-5.30pm Tue-Sat. **Admission** 20F, 10F children, including entry to St-Pierre-des-Templiers.

Where to stay & eat

Slap bang on the seafront, the gleaming new **Continental** (100 promenade René Coty, 04.94.83.87.87, menus 410F-1,190F) is cruise-liner shaped and very smart. Equally well-placed but somewhat cheaper, the **Excelsior** (193 bd F Martin, 04.94.95.02.42, rates 630F-900F) is family-run and friendly. Five kilometres east of town, by the Boulouris railway station, **La Potinière** (169 av de la Gare de Boulouris, 04.94.19.81.71, rates 390F-790F) is a villa by the sea surrounded by eucalyptuses. Just down the road, the youth hostel (chemin de l'Escale, 04.94.95.20.58, closed Sept-June, rates 115F-150F) is chic-er and costlier than most but does have double rooms.

In the city centre, **L'Arbousier** (6 av de Valescure, 04.94.95.25.00, closed dinner Wed & Sun, all Mon, menus 145F-320F) continues to merit its reputation as St-Raphaël's finest; moreover, its 145F weekday lunch menu is the best value you'll find for miles. Behind the *vieux port*, **La Gargoulette** (29 rue Pierre Aublé, 04.94.95.48.18, closed dinner Sun, all Mon, menus 120F-320F) offers a mix of Med classics and innovative dishes such as coquilles St-Jacques with truffle, and millefeuille of roast veal. **Pastorel** (54 rue de la Liberté, 04.94.95.02.36, closed dinner Sun, all Mon, menus 170F-210F), which has been serving tasty local specialities for 70 years, is a St-Raphaël institution. **Le Nautic** (52 cours Jean Bart, 04.94.95.03.80, lunch menus 69F-78F), where St-Raphaël's young crowd eats Tex-Mex, is a relative newcomer. **La Bouillabaisse** (50 pl Victor Hugo, 04.94.95.03.57, closed 1-26 Dec, menus 230F-280F) by the market serves no-frills seafood. The **San Pedro** (890 av du Colonel Brooke, 04.94.19.90.20, menus 80F-280F) has a dining room overlooking its swimming pool, and offers accommodation, too (rates 390F-850F).

The cloisters of
**Cathédrale St-
Léonce** in Fréjus.

Getting there

By car

Leave the A8 autoroute at exit nos.37 or 38. St-Raphaël is on the RN98 coast road.

By bus

Cars Phocéens (04.93.85.61.81) runs regular services from Nice's *gare routière* to St-Raphaël.

By train

St-Raphaël is on the main coastal line; frequent services from Nice and Marseille.

Tourist information

Office de Tourisme

210 rue Waldeck-Rousseau (04.94.19.52.52/fax 04.94.83.85.40). **Open** *Sept-June* 9am-12.30pm, 2-6.30pm Mon-Sat; *July, Aug* 9am-7pm daily. *Website: www.st-raphael.com*

Fréjus

Two kilometres inland from St-Raphaël but linked by the sprawl of modern beach suburbs, Fréjus was founded – as Forum Julii – by Julius Caesar in 49 BC and became a base for Augustus' swift-sailing galleys, which beat Antony and Cleopatra at the Battle of Actium in 31 BC. The silting up of the harbour, combined with a Saracen attack or two, turned the once-crucial staging post into a tiny backwater. It wasn't until the Middle Ages that Fréjus began to grow again. Even today Fréjus is smaller than Forum Julii was in its heyday. It's a town of Provençal pastels, each house sticking rigidly to the municipal colour chart.

Facing on to the place Formigé, the twelfth-century **Cathédrale St-Léonce** is at the heart of the unusual fortified **Cité Episcopale** (cathedral close). The carved sixteenth-century cathedral doors show Mary and Saints Peter and Paul amid scenes of Saracen butchery. Opposite, the octagonal baptistry, with its black granite columns, may date back to the fourth century and is certainly one of France's oldest ecclesiastical structures. The beautiful thirteenth-century cloisters have double columns topped by pointed arches, and delicate fifteenth-century paintings of fanciful animals on the ceiling. Upstairs is the **Musée Archéologique**, with artefacts dug up around the city.

It takes the best part of a day to see Fréjus' scattered Roman remains. To the west of the modern town, the second-century AD **Arènes** (amphitheatre) can still seat 10,000 and is used for bullfights and summer theatre productions. Towards the railway station, the **Porte des Gaules** was part of the Roman ramparts.

Further south-east, the **Butte St-Antoine** once stood on the since-receded shore; one of the remaining towers – only the base of which is Roman – was probably a lighthouse. Following the signposted path to the end of the Roman quay, the medieval tower called the **Lanterne d'Auguste** also stands on the site of a lighthouse. At the eastern extreme of the ancient walls (not visible) along rue Sieyès is a platform used as a military headquarters. From avenue du XV Corps d'Armée, stretches of the Roman aqueduct are visible. Further north, the Roman theatre lacks its original seats, but modern ones are installed for summer concerts.

North-west of Fréjus, **Roquebrune-sur-Argens** has traces of medieval fortifications surrounding arcaded streets of houses dating back to the sixteenth century. The first left fork on the D7 into town leads to the red sandstone outcrop of the Rocher de Roquebrune.

North of Fréjus, a Vietnamese pagoda (on the RN7) and a Sudanese mosque (on the D4) rise above the graves of colonial troops slaughtered in World War I. The D4 also leads to the **Parc Zoologique**. Another prime attraction for kids, the **Aquatica** water park is situated off the RN98, south of Fréjus, heading west.

Aquatica

RN98, Quartier Le Capou (04.94.51.82.51). **Open** *June, Sept* (weather allowing) 10am-6pm daily; *July, Aug* 10am-7pm daily. **Admission** 125F; 100F children. **Credit** AmEx, MC, V

Les Arènes

rue Henri Vadon (04.94.51.34.31). **Open** *Apr-Oct* 10am-1pm, 2.30-6.30pm Mon, Wed-Sun; *Nov-Mar* 10am-noon Mon, Wed-Sun. **Admission** free.

Cité Episcopale

48 rue de Fleury (04.94.51.26.30). **Open** *Apr-Sept* 9am-7pm daily; *Oct-Apr* 9.30am-noon, 2-5pm Tue-Sun. **Admission** 25F.

Musée Archéologique

pl Calvini (04.94.52.15.78). *Nov-Mar* 10am-noon, 1.30-5.30pm Mon, Wed-Sat; *Apr-Oct* 10am-1pm, 2.30-6.30pm. **Admission** free.

Parc Zoologique de Fréjus

04.94.40.70.65. **Open** *Oct-Apr* 10am-5pm daily; *May-Sept* 9.30am-6pm daily. **Admission** 62F, 38F children. **Credit** MC, V.

Where to stay & eat

The **Aréna** (145 bd Général de Gaulle, 04.94.17.09.40, closed Nov, rates 480F-650F) in the old town offers a warm welcome, pleasant rooms, a garden and a pool; and as if that weren't enough, its restaurant (menu 140F-250F, closed lunch Mon, lunch Sat) is easily the

The Western Côte

best in town. Also central, the **Bellevue** (pl
Paul Vernet, 04.94.17.27.05, rates 180F-250F) is
a cheaper option, while down on the beach, the
modern **Sable et Soleil** (158 rue Paul Arène,
04.94.51.08.70, closed mid-Nov to mid-Dec, rates
220F-350F) is a pleasant option.

Café-Galerie du Monde (49 pl Formigé,
04.94.17.01.07, plat du jour from 40F) has a café
serving light meals downstairs, a basement art
gallery, and three self-contained holiday flats
(rates 2,300F-4,000F per week) upstairs. Hidden
away in a tiny backstreet, **Les Potiers** (135
rue des Potiers, 04.94.51.33.74, closed lunch
Wed, all Tue, menus 125F-175F) serves reliable
classics in a pleasant ambience. The **Bar du
Marché** (5 pl de la Liberté, 04.94.51.29.09), with
tables outside under spreading boughs, offers a
filling *plat du jour* at 45F. In Fréjus port, the
Port Royal (pl du Tambournaire,
04.94.53.09.11, closed dinner Tue, all Wed,
menus 145F-290F) is difficult to find and
surprisingly unfishy, but consistently tasty.

Getting there

By car
Leave the A8 at exit nos.37 or 38.

By train
Fréjus station is on the main coast line; regular
services from Nice and Marseille.

By bus
Estérel Bus (04.94.52.00.50) runs a regular daily
service between Fréjus and St-Raphaël until
around 8pm.

Tourist information

Office du Tourisme de la Culture et de l'Animation de Fréjus
*325 rue Jean Jaurès (04.94.51.83.83/fax
04.94.51.00.26).* **Open** *Sept-Mar* 9am-noon,
2-6pm Mon-Sat; *Oct-Apr* call for times.

The Corniche de l'Estérel

Pull the top down and enjoy the curves,
hairpins and red rock on the last long
stretch of the dramatic clifftop road
before the high rises and beach commerce
of the urban coastline between Cannes
and Nice. Even in an area of such
dramatic coastal views, the **Pointe de
Dramont**, ten kilometres east of St-
Raphaël, stands out. Certainly Auguste
Lutaud thought so when he bought tiny Ile
d'Or just off the point in 1897. On it, he built a
four-storey mock-medieval tower constructed
from the local red porphyry. He then
proclaimed himself King Auguste I of the Ile

d'Or and threw some of the wildest society
parties on the Côte. Hergé's Black Island, of the
eponymous Tintin adventure, was inspired by
Lutard's bit of rock.

For a spectacular view over the island, and
for miles along the coast, take the paved and
signposted one-hour walk up to the Sémaphore
de Dramont from the RN98. Alternatively, just
enjoy the Plage du Dramont.

A strategic inlet discovered by the ancient
Greeks, in a ravine beneath towering red cliffs,
Agay is one of the Côte's more relaxed resorts.
The Romans prized the local blue porphyry,
from which they cut columns. Daredevil author
of *Le Petit Prince* Antoine de St-Exupéry
crashed his plane just around the bay in
World War II.

Similarly laid-back, the beach of **Anthéor** is
dominated by the **Plateau d'Anthéor**, from
where a marked half-hour path leads up to the
Rocher de St-Barthélemy and a beautiful view
over the sea and the Pic du Cap Roux. At the
Pointe de l'Observatoire on the coast road,
ruins of a blockhouse give on to a fine view
over some very rocky crags.

At **Le Trayas**, small creeks running down
to the sea offer pleasant but modest beach
possibilities. The bay of **La Figueirette**, with
its little beach, was a tuna-fishing centre from
the seventeenth century. **Miramar** is another
small resort giving access to La Figueirette,
and to the **Pointe de l'Esquillon** and yet
another dramatic view.

The coast road then leads into **La Galère**, a
small family resort with shady trees and a

A figure from the
roadside **pagoda**
north of Fréjus.
See page 177.

An eccentric's folly built from the ruins of a Saracen Castle: the **Fondation Henry Clews**.

The Western Côte

questionable housing development designed in the 1970s by architect Jacques Couelle. Small beaches are also to be found at Théoule-sur-Mer, almost a suburb of Mandelieu-la-Napoule.

On a hill overlooking the Napoule Gulf, Mandelieu has little to recommend it but its golf links. Its seaside extension **La Napoule** would be much like any Riviera resort were it not for the **Fondation Henry**, an outsize pseudo-medieval folly conjured out of the ruins of a Saracen castle in 1917 by the extremely wealthy, extremely eccentric Henry himself. Mr and Mrs Clews and their servants dressed in costume (the valet wore Algerian Zouave gear), gave medieval banquets and crusaded against galloping modernity. Henry's sculptures, still visible in the garden, tend towards the gargoyle.

When you tire of the coast, the **Massif de l'Estérel** can be traversed by car along the RN7, which cuts around the north of the Massif following the ancient Via Aurelia, or along the many tortuous tracks that wend between the RN7 and the RN98 coast road. **Mont Vinaigre**, the cork-tree clad highest point of the range, offers stunning views from the belvedere near the summit. For hardy trekkers, the GR49 traverses the Massif north-south, and the GR51 east-west.

Fondation Henry Clews

Château de la Napoule, av Henry Clews (04.93.49.95.05). **Open** *Mar-Oct* 2.30-5.30pm Mon, Wed-Sun. Closed Nov-Feb. **Admission** 25F, 20F children.

Where to stay & eat

The Corniche is dotted with perilously perched hotels and restaurants. Overlooking the Ile D'Or, the isolated **Sol et Mar** (rte Corniche D'Or, 04.94.95.25.60, closed mid-Nov to Mar, rates 400F-770F) has saltwater pools and a restaurant (menus 150F-210F). In Agay, the **Hôtel L'Estérella** (bd de la Plage, 04.94.82.00.58, closed mid-Nov to Apr, rates 250F-420F) is an inexpensive option right on the beach.

The **Relais des Calanques** (04.94.44.14.06, rates 300F-580F) near Le Trayas is a green world leading down to the water's edge, a jet-set idyll without the price tag; it has a good fish restaurant (closed Oct-Mar, plat du jour 80F), too. Cheaper still is the **Auberge Blanche** (1061 rte des Calanques, 04.94.44.14.04, closed Oct-Mar, rates 350F-495F) at the Le Trayas bus stop. Two hard kilometres uphill from here, the youth hostel

Red cliffs and a rugged landscape: heading to Cap Roux on the **Corniche de L'Esterel**.

(9 av de la Véronèse, 04.93.75.40.23, closed Oct-Feb, rates 49F) is beautifully situated: but book ahead to avoid a long, pointless walk if you don't have a car.

Théoule-sur-Mer is home to one of the area's best restaurants, the **Etoile des Mers** (47 av de Miramar, 04.93.75.05.05, closed Nov to mid-Dec, menus 180F-395F), where chef Serge Gouloumès does wonderful mod-Med things; it's also a hotel, the Miramar Beach hotel (rates 500F-1,800F), with massage and mud treatments and a private beach.

In Mandelieu-la-Napoule, the **Ermitage du Riou** (av Henry Clews, 04.93.49.95.56, rates 735F-3,130F) has delightful rooms, some with private balconies looking out towards the Iles de Lérins, a private beach and a pool; the restaurant (menus 240F-450F) offers deceptively simple, exquisite dishes and has an equally impressive wine list. There's also some fine cooking at **L'Oasis** (*see page 50*), a restaurant serving classical French food. **La Calanque** (bd Henry Clews, 04.93.49.95.11, closed Nov-Jan, rates 195F-360F) has views over the Clews' folly; the **Acadia** (681 av de la Mer, 04.93.49.28.23, closed Nov & Dec, rates 295F-840F) has a pool and tennis courts. The restaurant **Le Coelacanthe** (pl du Château, 04.93.49.95.15, closed lunch Mon, lunch Tue, menu 110F-195F) not only serves excellent modern Provençal fare, but has a *fumoir* (smoking room), too.

Getting there

By car
The D2098 coast road joins the coastal towns above. For Mandelieu-la-Napoule, leave the A8 at exit no.40.

By bus
To get from Nice to Mandelieu-la-Napoule, you have to go via Cannes. Buses between Mandelieu and Cannes (04.92.99.20.05) run roughly once an hour from 6am to 8pm. Buses between Cannes and Nice (04.93.39.11.39) run every 20min (every half-hour on Sun).

By train
Frequent services from Nice and Marseille to Mandelieu-la-Napoule.

Tourist information

Agay
Office de Tourisme d'Agay, pl Giannetti (04.94.82.01.85/fax 04.94.82.74.00). **Open** *mid-June to Sept* 9am-7pm daily; *Oct-Mar* 9am-noon, 2-6pm Mon-Fri; *Apr to mid-June* 9am-noon, 2-6pm Mon-Sat.

Théoule-sur-Mer
Office de Tourisme, 1 Corniche D'Or (04.93.49.28.28/fax 04.93.49.00.04). **Open** 9am-6.30pm Mon-Sat; 10am-1pm Sun.

Mandelieu-la-Napoule
Office de Tourisme et de l'Animation, av Henry Clews (04.93.49.95.31/fax 04.92.97.99.57). **Open** 9am-12.30pm, 2.30-6pm Mon-Sat.

Inland Var

Western Var   182
Central & Eastern Var   187
Les Gorges du Verdon   193

Feature boxes

Days of wine & roses   189
Walking & rafting
  the Grand Canyon   195

Western Var

The Western Var is a land of truffles, medieval stonework and tuned-in expatriates.

The western villages of the Var lie in the softly sloping highlands above Toulon, where the sun shines dazzling green through the giant leaves of plane trees. This is the land the tourist brochures promote as the Green Var, where visitors come as much for the kayaking, rock-climbing and camping as for the craft shops, hidden country inns and medieval villages.

Brignoles & around

Brignoles is the busy commercial centre of the western villages, with a steady stream of traffic. Once famous for its plums, it later turned to bauxite quarrying. In the old town, stroll up the covered stairway of rue du Grand-Escalier past the church of St-Sauveur to the thirteenth-century Palais des Comtes de Provence, which now houses the **Musée du Pays Brignolais**, with an eclectic collection of Provençal curiosities including santons, a concrete canoe and a play-it-safe half-pagan, half-Christian tombstone from around AD 200. There's a packed flea market on the riverside promenade du Carami every second Sunday of the month. Brignoles is also a springboard for the **Vallon Sourn** 'sombre valley' 14 kilometres further north on the D554 to Barjols; rock-climbing and kayaking are among the activities on offer in this steep upper valley of the Argens river.

On the southern outskirts of Brignoles, the tiny village of **La Celle** (D405) once attracted those seeking religious solace at the twelfth-century royal abbey; today's visitors have more venal aims, as the abbey is now a luxury hotel/restaurant under the sway of Provençal super-chef Alain Ducasse (*see box page 44*). South from here stretch wooded hills pitted with red bauxite quarries. **La Roquebrussanne** (15 kilometres south via the D405 and D5) is reached through woods that cross the mountains just under the peak of La Loube (830 metres), which boasts some odd-shaped rock formations. The village sits squat on a plain of Coteaux Varois vineyards that stretches for miles in all directions. A country lane – marked as the D64 – leads east of here past two small lakes to a turn-off on the left for the British-owned **Domaine des Chaberts** vineyard, a reliable producer of rosés and reds that offers tastings (04.94.04.92.05).

The D5 winds south from La Roquebrussanne through seven kilometres of vineyards (other good producers are the Domaine des Laou and Domaine la Rose des Vents) to the sleepy village of Méounes-les-Montrieux. Nine kilometres east of here is **Signes**, another small and attractive farming community at the foot of the **Ste-Baume massif**. This is good hiking country; from the village, the GR9 long-distance footpath heads north-west to the holy site of St-Pilon at the panoramic summit, while the GR99 strikes north-east across thickly forested hills to Mazaugues, with its turn-of-the-last-century ice factory.

Musée du Pays Brignolais

pl des Comtes de Provence, Brignoles (04.94.69.45.18). **Open** 9am-noon, 2.30-6pm Wed-Sun. **Admission** 20F, children 10F, free under-8s.

Where to stay & eat

There are two ways to play it in Brignoles. The first is to stock up with supplies in the town and head for the **Camping Municipal le Grand Jardin** in Correns, downstream from the Vallon Sourn (enquiries to the Mairie, 04.94.37.21.95, closed Nov-Mar, tent 20F, adult 15F, child 10F, car 10F). The second is to throw caution – and canvas – to the wind, and check into the **Hostellerie de l'Abbaye de la Celle** (*see page 44*), whose elegant rooms (rates 1,150F-1,900F) are the only appropriate follow-up to dinner at the gourmet restaurant. In sleepy La Roquebrussanne, Annie and Jean-Pierre Pouillard's **Hôtel-Restaurant de la Loube** on place de l'Eglise is a stylish and cheerful country inn (04.94.86.81.36, closed dinner Mon, all Tue, rates 380F, menus 99F-149F). At **L'Olivier** in Méounes (11 rue Neuve, 04.94.33.96.01, closed Sat lunch & July, menus 75F-130F), Gilbert Giraud serves one of the oldest recorded delicacies in Provence: tiny snails called *sucarelles* that you suck out of their shells. Archeologists have found shells from the creatures dating back 2,000 years in local caves. In Signes, Françoise Penvern opens her home, **La Vieille Bastide**, as a charming *chambres d'hôte* (plan de Hedron, 04.94.90.81.45, rates 310F).

Getting there

By car

A8 autoroute Brignoles exit (no.35); then follow directions in text

By bus

Les Autocars Blanc (04.94.69.08.28) runs the following services: Brignoles-Marseille (six to seven daily); Brignoles-Toulon via La Roquebrussane and Méounes (three to four daily); Brignoles-Cotignac (several times a day Monday to Saturday); Brignoles-Barjols via Correns and the Vallon Sourn (once daily Monday to Saturday); Brignoles-Carcès-Sillans-Aups (twice daily); Brignoles-Carcès-Entrecasteaux-Salernes-Villecroze (once daily Monday to Saturday). Autocars Phocéens (04.93.85.66.61) operates a twice-daily service between Brignoles and Nice Airport.

Note that the train line that passes through Brignoles is goods-only.

Tourist information

Brignoles & surrounding region

Maison du Tourisme, La Provence Verte, carrefour de l'Europe, just north of river, Brignoles (04.94.72.04.21/fax 94.72.04.22). **Open** *June-Sept* 9am-12.30pm, 2-7.30pm daily; *Oct-May* 9am-12.30pm, 2-6.30pm Mon-Sat.

Brignoles

Office du Tourisme, Hôtel de Clavier, rue des Palais (04.94.69.2751/fax 04.94.69.44.08). **Open** 10am-noon, 2-4pm Mon-Fri.

Signes

Maison du Tourisme, 29 rue Pasteur (04.94.90.83.53/fax 94.90.68.30). **Open** *July-Sept* 10am-noon, 3-6pm Mon-Sat; *Oct-June* 2-6pm Sat.

Cotignac & around

English expatriates home in on **Cotignac**, a lively, authentically Provençal village with a high estate-agent count. Locals and would-be-locals hang out at the pavement cafés under the huge old plane trees that line the cours Gambetta; the chatter from the tables is amplified on Tuesday mornings by a bustling weekly market. The town is dominated by a pink cliff honeycombed with caves, some of which can be reached along promenade du Rocher.

The D13/D560 road to Barjols (16 kilometres) affords good views back over the ruins of two towers, vestiges of a feudal castle. Beyond here is a countryside of truffle-rich woods, green fields, grazing horses and rolling vineyards.

Just before Barjols, the village of **Pontevès** sweeps into view atop the hills to the left. From the D560, a stone bridge and tiny rural road wind up through grassy meadows to the village, whose ruined chateau makes a good picnic spot. The road continues down to **Barjols**, which lies in a valley fed by springs. Twelve wash basins and 30 fountains – the most original being a giant mossy mushroom next to the town hall – have earned this town the hopeful nickname of 'the Tivoli of Provence'. In **Réal**, the old part of

Cotignac is the perfect Provençal village and a favourite with English expatriates.

A design masterpiece: **Abbaye du Thoronet**'s beauty lies in its geometric lines.

town north of the Romanesque church, warehouses that now house galleries and artists' studios were once tanning factories. Sombre Barjols comes alive every year on 16 January16 for the decidedly pagan Fête de St Marcel, when the saint's bust is paraded through town with a garlanded ox that is later sacrificed, roasted and eaten by the townspeople.

Continuing straight on along the D13 from Cotignac past the Barjols turn-off, you end up in **Fox-Amphoux**, which locals still pronounce 'foks-amfooks' in true Provençal style. There are precious few locals in the village itself, though, which has been turned into a Northern European vision of what a Provençal village should look like. In ruins only 20 years ago, it is now a soulless place full of over-restored second homes and slow-moving hire-cars (handily distinguished by their '51' licence plates).

East of Fox-Amphoux – or six kilometres north-east of Cotignac on the D22 – is **Sillans-la-Cascade**, a pretty village with a sunny square and two restaurants facing the River Bresque. Just in front of the old chapel, a hand-painted wooden sign marks the start of the 30-minute hike to la cascade itself, a waterfall that crashes down 45 metres into a refreshingly cool pool. For the road east to Salernes, *see below.*

Due east of Cotignac, nine kilometres along the remote D50, lies the village of **Entrecasteaux**, dominated by a magnificent seventeenth-century **chateau** (04.94.04.43.95). Saved from destruction during the Revolution, the chateau was in ruins when Scottish painter Ian McGarvie-Munn – whose chequered life included a stint as commander of the Guatemalan navy – purchased

the property and began repairs in the 1970s. The castle is open for guided tours, which – if a sufficiently motivated group rings ahead – may even be conducted personally by the current owner, historian Hervé Girard. It is surrounded by a formal garden designed by Le Nôtre, the landscaper of Versailles, which is open to the public. A few kilometres east of here on a road with beautiful views back over Entrecasteaux is the hamlet of **St-Antonin-du-Var**, a farming community that is about as far as you can get from the glitz of the coast.

The **Abbaye du Thoronet**, a twelfth-century Cistercian abbey nestling in the middle of the Darboussière forest, is a silent and imposing place. The beauty of the building lies in its sparse, geometric lines: pure and stripped of ornaments, they reflect the austere lifestyle of this back-to-basics order. Even cement is shunned: the blocks of warm pinkish stone are glued together by the force of gravity alone. The first of the three great Cistercian foundations of Provence (*see also page 115* Silvacane and *page 121* Sénanque), Thoronet stays faithful to the Romanesque, though by 1160, when work on the abbey started, northern France was already under the sway of the Gothic. Stairs lead up to the monks' dormitories, which look very much as they must have done in the Middle Ages, apart from the glass in the windows. The arcaded cloister, built on different levels to accommodate the slope of the ground, has a charming fountain house.

Abbaye du Thoronet

15km south-east of Cotignac via Carcès on the D13/D279 (04.94.60.43.90). **Open** *Apr-Sept* 9am-

7pm daily; *Oct-Mar* 10am-1pm, 2-5pm daily. Closed for tourist visits during Sun mass (noon-2pm). **Guided tours** eight per day, in French and German with printed notes in English. **Admission** 35F, free children. **No credit cards.**

Where to stay, eat & drink

Cotignac is renowned for honey, wine and olives; the latter grow in abundance around the friendly *chambres d'hôte* **La Radassière** (rte d'Entrecasteaux, 1km east of centre, 04.94.04.63.33, rates 400F), run by Richard and Maryse Artaud. The nature's bounty theme continues at breakfast, when Maryse serves jam made of *coing* (quince), the fruit that gave its name to Cotignac. The **Modern Bar** (12 cours Gambetta, 04.94.04.65.92, closed Mon & Jan) is the best place for a drink on the town's main drag. The locals play cards inside, while tourists take the edge off their northern pallor at the pavement tables. **La Fontaine** (27 cours Gambetta, 04.94.04.79.13, closed Mon) is good for lively terrace lunches, especially on market Tuesdays, or for a late dinner (it stays open till 2am, and dinner is served until 11.30pm in July and Auguest, 10pm the rest of the year). Near Pontevès, the **Domaine-de-St Ferréol** offers upmarket *chambres d'hôte* in an eighteenth-century farm set in vineyards with a superb pool (1km north of Pontevès on other side of D560, 04.94.77.10.42, closed mid Nov to mid Mar, rates 300F-480F). For an antidote to the sterile prettiness of Fox-Amphoux, phone ahead (particularly on Thursdays, for some reason) to book a table for lunch at **Chez Jean**, at the roundabout of La Bréguière north of the village (04.94.80.70.76, closed dinner, average 130F). Under the vigilant gaze of a stuffed owl and boar, Jean and Chantal Serre serve abundant, wholesome fare, with wine charged according to how much of the bottle you drink.

Getting there

By car
For Cotignac, A8 autoroute, Brignoles exit (no.35), then D554/D562 to Carcès, D13 to Cotignac. For other destinations see text.

By bus
See above **Brignoles & around**.

Tourist information

Barjols
Office de Tourisme, bd Grisolle (tel/fax 04.94.77.20.01). **Open** mid-April to mid June 10am-noon, 3-6pm Mon-Fri; 10am-noon Sat; *mid June to mid Sept* 10am-noon, 3-7pm Mon-Fri; 10am-noon, 4-6pm Sat. Closed Sept-Apr.

Cotignac
Office de Tourisme, rue Bonaventure (04.94.04.61.87/fax 04.94.04.78.98). **Open** times vary; usually 10am-noon, 2-4.30pm daily.

Entrecasteaux
Office de Tourisme, cours Gabriel Péri (tel/fax 04.94.04.40.50). **Open** year-round: times vary; call for details.

Sillans-la-Cascade
Office de Tourisme, 12 pl Verger (04.94.04.78.05). **Open** call for details. Closed winter.

Salernes, Aups & around

Salernes, 12 kilometres north-east of Cotignac, makes floor tiles – the small, hexagonal, russet tiles that are a Provençal trademark. It is believed to be Europe's oldest terracotta site: production has been traced back to 5000 BC. Of the town's 15 ceramic workshops, the most interesting is that of **Alain Vagh**, whose creative mosaic work includes a pink-tiled Harley-Davidson and a grand piano with green-tiled keys – a symbolic protest against the ivory trade.

Aups – as its name suggests – is almost up in the Alps, at least in Provençal terms. Just south of the spectacular Gorges du Verdon, this is a lofty village that can get seriously cold in winter. It's also the Var truffle capital: every Thursday morning at 10am between the end of November and the end of February there is a high-stakes truffle auction in the main square, where the precious commodity – all the more valuable as it is exempt from taxes – is sold right out of the trunks of Citroën station wagons. At the **Grand Café du Cour** on the corner of the square, wizened men in berets play cards, and the shop next door sells essential shooting supplies – Kodak film and hunting rifles. Every morning at the **Boulangerie Canut** on rue du Marché you can watch the bakers cutting pastry dough for their *pains au chocolat*.

The picturesque village of **Villecroze** (seven kilometres southeast of Aups on the D557), with its medieval, arcaded streets, grew up around a series of caves, later turned into dwellings by a sixteenth-century feudal baron. Between May and September, the caves can be visited on guided tours organised by the tourist office (2.30-7pm daily, admission 10F, children 5F). Up above Villecroze, **Tourtour** has a breathtaking view over the plains and hills of the Var. Unlike Fox-Amphoux, Tourtour has been sensitively restored, and the main square is a good place to imbibe Provençal vibes over a glass of wine. The village also has a still-operative seventeenth-century olive press and the medieval **Tour Grimaldi** watchtower.

Inland Var

Troglodyte dwellings in the village of **Villecroze**. *See page 185.*

Alain Vagh
rte d'Entrecasteaux, Salernes (04.94.70.61.85). **Open** 9am-noon, 2-6pm Mon-Sat. **Credit** AmEx, MC, DC, V.

Where to stay, eat & drink

Aups comes alive in January for the Fête des Truffes, when the town's restaurants vie to find new ways of serving truffles. The rest of the year, Catherine at **Le Yucca** (3 rue Foch, 04.94.70.12.11, closed dinner Mon & all Tuesday from Sept to June, menus 65F-140F) prepares divine ravioli with truffles and New Mexican salsa barbeques on her garden terrace. In Tourtour, **La Petite Auberge** (relais du Silence, 04.94.70.57.16, closed Nov-Feb, restaurant closed lunch Thur, rates 450F-900F, menu 180F) has a great view; specialities include *daube provençal* stew and aubergine terrine. Just outside the village, on the route d'Aups, **Le Mas l'Acacia** (04.94.70.53.84, rates 290F-650F) offers *chambres d'hôte* with spectacular views and a pool. Two kilometres out of town on the Villecroze road, **Les Chênes Verts** (04.94.70.55.06) is a gourmet restaurant with a great line in truffles (*see page 50*); it also has three charming rooms (closed June, rates 600F). For lap-of-luxury experience, **La Bastide de Tourtour** (on D77 rte de Flayosc just behind the church of St-Denis, 04.98.10.54.20, rates 520F-1400F) has the lot: a 35 hectare park, swimming pool, tennis courts and a restaurant with herb-laden Provençal dishes (closed lunch Mon, lunch Tue, menus 160F-280F). In Villecroze, the **Auberge des Lavandes** (pl de Gaulle, 04.94.70.76.00, closed dinner Tue, all Wed from Sept-June, menus 55F-150F) is a cheerful restaurant with pasta and regional dishes such as *tian d'agneau* (lamb and rice casserole); there are also a few rustic rooms at 280F-310F (hotel closed Jan & Feb).

Getting there

By car
From Cotignac (*see above*), D22 to Sillans-la-Cascade, then D560 to Salernes.

By bus
See above **Brignoles & around**. There is also a Salernes-Draguignan bus (one daily Monday to Thursday) run by Les Cars Brémond (04.94.68.15.34).

Tourist information

Aups
Office de Tourisme, pl Mistral (04.94.70.00.80/fax 94.84.00.69). **Open** *Sept-June* 2-4pm Mon; 10am-noon, 2-4pm Tue-Sat; *July-Aug* 9am-noon, 3-7pm daily.

Salernes
Office de Tourisme, rue V Hugo (04.94.70.69.02/fax 04.94.70.69.02). **Open** *Sept-June* 9.30am-12.15pm, 3-6.15pm Mon-Sat; July, Aug 9.30am-7pm Mon-Sat, 9.30am-noon Sun.

Villecroze
Office de Tourisme, rue Ambroise Croizat (tel/fax 04.94.67.50.00). **Open** *Oct-May* 8.30am-12.30pm, 1.30-5.30pm Tue, Thur, Fri; *June-Sept* 8.30am-12.30pm, 1.30-6.30pm daily.

Central & Eastern Var

Wine, roses and golden stone: the villages of this fertile area exude bucolic charm.

The centre of the Var *département*, traversed by the fertile valleys of the Argens and the Nartuby, is one of the great market gardens of France. Though towns like **Draguignan** or **Le Muy** make a good attempt at urban sprawl, there are still plenty of secret Provençal villages to explore. Above all, though, this is Côtes de Provence wine country, and the most popular activity sport is the estate crawl – something best done by bicycle, with a solemn promise that you'll come back later with the car to pick up the 15 cases of rosé.

To the east, the hill villages strung out across the foothills of the Alps seem light years – rather than the 30 minutes they are – away from the glitz of Cannes. Built as fortified Roman strongholds, they were plagued down the centuries by the usual Germanic hordes, Saracens and medieval mercenaries. Once isolated, and still picturesque, these stone-built villages have lately undergone yet another invasion of northern tribes; but despite the second homes and the estate agents, their charm shines through.

Draguignan & around

The *Year in Provence* brigade has a real downer on Draguignan, mainly because, with its military barracks (the town hosts the French army artillery school) and Parisian-style boulevards, it doesn't conform to all those boules, lavender and village fountain clichés. And as far as the outskirts go, they have a point: the approach roads are lined with tacky shopping malls, discount stores and fast food joints. But the town centre is a surprisingly pleasant place to while away a couple of hours. Baron Haussmann used Draguignan as a mini-pilot for his geometrical reorganisation of Paris, and during the day at least, the town tries to live up to the comparison: **boulevard Clemenceau** buzzes with shoppers and big-name boutiques, and the old town behind has its share of elegant townhouses, adorned with blue shutters and hanging plants.

The town's name derives from the legend of a fifth-century bishop of Antibes, St Hermentaire, who killed a troublesome local dragon. There are two worthwhile rainy-day museums in the old town: the **Musée Municipal**, housed in the summer palace of

Chez Bruno, foodie heaven. *See page 188.*

the Bishop of Fréjus, with a patchy collection of paintings plus antique furniture, porcelains and archeology from local Gallo-Roman sites; and the nearby **Musée des Traditions Provençales**, which recreates traditional life in Provence through displays of agricultural tools, home furnishings, glassworks and tiles, plus a collection of *santons*.

The vile beastie hung out, it seems, in the **Gorges de Châteaudouble** north of town, reached via the scenic D955. First stop on this road (signposted) is the **Pierre de la Fée** (fairy stone), a giant dolmen dating from 2400 BC. Further along the D955, a dirt road on the right edging a beautiful vineyard leads to the **Domaine du Dragon**, once the twelfth-century fortified Castrum de Dragone of the Draguignan family, where archeologists have recently discovered the **Chapel St-Michel-du-Dragon**, a medieval chapel on first-century foundations. The D955 winds along the gorge floor past jags of rock, descending on the left to

Inland Var

Rebouillon, a hamlet built like a horseshoe around a large central meadow on the banks of the Nartuby. From the gorge road, **Châteaudouble** appears high on the spectacular red cliffs to the west. In 1027, the name of this mountaintop fortress was wisely changed from Château du Diable; the village's medieval houses are highly picturesque, with stunning panoramas of the Gorges below.

West of Draguignan is a flatter landscape, ripe with vineyards and fruit trees. The D557 heads into **Flayosc**, a village with a timeworn feel and an excellent country restaurant (*see below* **Where to stay & eat**). In a bucolic hamlet one kilometre north of Flayosc, the thirteenth-century **Moulin du Flayosquet** is the oldest continually operating olive mill in the Var. Fifth-generation owner Max Doleatto offers guided visits and tastings of olive oil and other local products. Oil – from olives and grapeseed – is also big news at **Lorgues**, which lies 13 kilometres south-west of Draguignan on the D562. Park at the massive eighteenth-century **Collégiale St-Martin** and look in at the multi-coloured marble altar. Lorgues is a pleasant town, its main street lined with peeling old plane trees, fountains and cafés; it also has one of the Var's top foodie meccas, **Chez Bruno** (*see below* **Where to stay & eat**). The little *ruelles* of the old town, full of mainly unrestored medieval houses, run up behind the main square. This is prime Côtes de Provence wine country; good producers include the **Château de Berne**, with its impressive modern caves.

Château de Berne

rte de Salernes, 3km north of Lorgues (04.94.60.43.60). **Open** 10am-6pm daily. **Admission** free. **Credit** AmEx, DC, MC, V.

Domaine du Dragon

off D955 (04.94.68.14.46). **Open** *wine-tasting* 10am-noon, 4-6pm Mon-Fri; 10am-12.30pm Sat, Sun. **Admission** free. **Credit** AmEx, MC, V.

Moulin du Flayosquet

1km north of Flayosc (04.94.70.41.45). **Open** *Jan, Dec* 9am-12.30pm, 2.30-7.30pm daily; *Feb-June, Sept-Nov* 9am-noon, 2-6.30pm Tue-Sat; *July, Aug* 9am-12.30pm, 2.30-7.30pm Mon-Sat. **Admission** free. **No credit cards.**

Musée Municipal

rue Edmond Poupé, Draguignan (04.94.47.28.80). **Open** *all year* 9am-noon, 2-6pm Mon-Sat. **Admission** free.

Musée des Traditions Provençales

15 rue Roumanille, Draguignan (04.94.47.05.72). **Open** *all year* 9am-noon, 2-6pm Tue-Sat; 2-6pm Sun. **Admission** 20F; 8F children.

Where to stay & eat

In Draguignan, **Les Milles Colonnes** (2 pl aux Herbes, 04.94.68.52.58, closed dinner late Aug to mid-June, plat du jour 90F) is a lively brasserie and Internet café (sarlmilco@ wanadoo.fr) in the heart of the old town serving up fresh market dishes. The view's the thing at the panoramic **Restaurant de la Tour** in Châteaudouble (pl Beausoleil, 04.94.70.93.08, menus 95F-160F), but the food comes a close second – try the excellent brouillade truffle omelette, if you're around here between the end of November and the end of February. In Flayosc, **L'Oustaou** (5 pl Brémond, 04.94.70.42.69, closed Mon & dinner Thur & Sun, menus 125F-280F) is a well-regarded regional restaurant with terrace tables on the village square, where you can sample Provençal specialities such as *pieds e paquets* (tripe stuffed with onion and salt pork). Annie and Henri Duhaut offer upmarket *chambres d'hôte* hospitality at their pink, palmy turn-of-the-century **Mas du Flayosquet** (on the D57 1km north of Flayosc, 04.94.84.66.27, rates 320F), which has a swimming pool and can arrange meals on request. **Chez Bruno** in Lorgues is the Var temple of truffles (*see page 50*) – but be warned, guests have been known to heli in from Monaco, so don't expect rock-bottom prices.

Getting there

By car

For Draguignan, leave the A8 autoroute at exit no.36 and take the N555; the town is 12km from this junction.

By train/bus

The closest station is Les Arcs, 9km south of Draguignan, with regular local trains from Marseille/Nice. From the station, Les Rapides Varois (04.94.47.05.05) runs hourly buses into Draguignan. There are other regular bus services between Draguignan and St-Raphaël (Estérel Cars, 04.94.52.00.50) and Toulon (Transvar, 04.94.28.93.28). For connections between Draguignan and nearby villages, ring the *gare routière* (04.94.68.15.34), which is south of the centre on the bd des Fleurs.

Tourist information

Châteaudouble

Secretariat, Hôtel de Ville, pl de la Fontaine (04.98.10.51.35). **Open** 9-11am Mon, Tue, Thur, Fri.

Draguignan

Office de Tourisme, 2 bd Carnot (04.98.10.51.05). **Open** 9am-6pm Mon-Sat; 10am-noon Sun.

Days of wine & roses

Roseline de Villeneuve was one of those archetypal medieval saints, born in 1263 into a rich family with a tyrannical father, who opposed his daughter's charitable impulses. During Saracen invasions, she used to sneak out of the family castle to distribute food to the starving peasants. One night, she was stopped by a suspicious guard, and lo! the bread she was carrying in her pinafore miraculously became a bouquet of roses. She later became the prioress of the local abbey, now occupied by the prestigious Côtes de Provence wine estate of **Château Ste-Roseline**.

After Roseline's death in 1329 her body refused to decompose, and since then (apart from a few years when the holy corpse was mislaid), she has reclined in a glass casket in the Chapelle de Ste-Roseline. But she still makes herself useful by watching over the grapes: when other vineyards in the area experience hail or frost, the Château Ste-Roseline is always spared.

The mainly baroque chapel has a couple of unexpected works by modern masters: Diego Giacometti, brother of the more celebrated Alberto, sculpted the music stands and the doors of the rather ghoulish reliquary that holds the saint's eyes; while a mosaic by Marc Chagall depicts the miracle of angels preparing food for pilgrims. In the past few years, the Château Ste-Roseline has become a bit of a wine factory, with new buildings that jar in this idyllic setting.

Château Ste-Roseline

D91 4km E of Les Arcs, also accessible from N555 (04.94.99.50.30/tours Service Municipal Tourisme Culture Patrimoine 04.94.47.56.10). **Open** *chapel 2-7pm Tue-Sun. Guided tours by appointment only. Wine tasting 9am-noon, 2-7pm Mon-Fri; 10am-noon, 2-7pm Sat, Sun.* **Admission** *chapel free; guided tours 50F (incl wine).* **Credit** *AmEx, DC, MC, V.*
Website: www.chateau-ste-roseline.

Flayosc
Office de Tourisme, pl Pied-Barri (04.94.70.41.31). **Open** *Sept-June 9am-noon, 3-6pm Mon-Fri; 9am-noon Sat; July, Aug 9am-noon, 3-6pm Mon-Fri; 9am-noon Sat, Sun.*

Lorgues
Office de Tourisme, pl d'Entrechaus (04.94.73.92.37). **Open** *mid-Sept to June 9am-12.30pm, 3-6pm Mon-Fri; 9am-12.30pm Sat; July to mid-Sept 9am-1pm, 3-7pm Mon-Sat; 9am-noon Sun.*

The Argens Valley

South of Draguignan, the Côtes-de-Provence *appellation* moves into top gear, with vineyards lining the gentle slopes on either side of the Argens river. Most French visitors think of **Le Muy** as the A8 motorway exit for St-Tropez. But this small, flat, militantly working-class town (one of the few in the Côte d'Azur region to have had a Communist mayor) has been caught in the crossfire of history a couple of times: once when the locals tried to assassinate the Holy Roman Emperor Charles V (they failed, nailing a stand-in instead, and were promptly nailed themselves); and again when Le Muy was chosen as the parachute bridgehead for Operation Dragon, the August 1944 Allied liberation of Provence. The **Musée de la Libération** is the only one of its kind in the

Var, and its authentic memorabilia (including cockpits, jeeps, parachutes, documents) complement a visit to the **American War Cemetery** in Draguignan.

Betwen Le Muy and Les Arcs is one of the area's biggest tourist pulls: the vineyards and medieval chapel of the **Château Ste-Roseline** (*see box* **Days of wine & roses**). **Les Arcs** is a pretty town with cream-coloured buildings and a medieval centre that twists up steeply to the dungeon tower of the eleventh-century Villeneuve castle, once a fortified look-out that now offers dining and accommodation (*see below* **Where to stay & eat**), with good views over red-tiled rooftops to the vineyards that give the town its *raison* (or *raisin*) *d'être*. Their produce – squeezed, fermented and bottled – is on sale at the **Maison des Vins** on the main N7 road south of town, an excellent one-stop shop for those who don't have the time, or the patience, to tour the vineyards; though it also has route maps and brochures for those who do. In the Maison's yellow *bastide* houses, over 650 different Côtes de Provence wines are available to taste and purchase.

Vidauban, five kilometres further west along the N7, is another quiet village amid the vineyards, and a great base for estate hopping. The D48 north to Lorgues (pick it up behind the Office du Tourisme) crosses the Argens river on a stone bridge and winds between giant plane trees to the forests of **Château d'Astros**, the magnificent residence featured by Marcel Pagnol (*see box page 14*) in his film *Le Château de ma mère*. North of Vidauban, just outside the pretty village of Taradeau with its Saracen tower, is the **Château St-Martin**, where a son et lumière show in the fifteenth-century wine cellar portrays the history of Provençal wines in French or English, depending on the audience.

Château d'Astros
off D48 (04.94.73.00.25). **Open** *wine-tasting* 8.30am-noon, 1.30-6pm daily. **Admission** free. **Credit** MC, V.

Château St-Martin
off D10, 1.5km south of junction with D73 (04.94.73.02.01). **Open** *mid-Oct to Mar* 9am-6pm Mon-Sat; *Apr to mid-Oct* 9am-6pm daily. **Admission** free; *son et lumière* 30F; *tastings* 15F-70F. **Credit** MC, V.

Maison des Vins Côtes de Provence
D555, 200m west of Les Arcs exit (04.94.99.50.20). **Open** *Apr-June, Sept* 10am-1pm, 3.30-7pm daily; *July & Aug* 10am-1pm, 1.30-8pm daily. **Credit** MC,V.

Musée de la Libération
Tour Charles-Quint, Le Muy (info & tours Office du Tourisme 04.94.45.12.79). **Open** *Apr-Sept* 10am-noon Thur, Sun; *Oct-Mar* (by reservation only) 10am-noon Tue, Thur.

Where to stay & eat
The jovial Boeuf brothers have the gourmet eating scene in Vidauban sewn up. Alain runs the hearty **La Concorde** on the pleasant central square (pl de la Mairie, 04.94.73.01.19, closed dinner Tue & all Wed, menus 148F-260F), while brother Christian recently opened the more designer-elegant **Bastide des Magnans** (D48, rte de La Garde-Freinet, 04.94.99.43.91, closed all Mon & dinner Sun, menus 140F-180F); both offer solid but elegant *cuisine de terroir*. In Les Arcs, the hotel-restaurant **Le Logis du Guetteur** (04.94.99.51.10, hotel closed Feb, rates 650F, menus 155F-350F) occupies the remains of the eleventh-century chateau that tops the medieval village; it has charming rooms and dining in vaulted stone chambers.

Getting there

By car
The A8 autoroute runs through the Argens valley; for all villages mentioned take the Le Muy exit (no.36) and continue on the N7.

By train/bus
From Marseille and Nice regular local trains serve Le Muy, Les Arcs and Vidauban. From St-Raphaël, Estérel Cars (04.94.52.00.50) runs frequent daily buses to Le Muy; Transvar (04.94.28.93.28) runs around five daily buses to Les Arcs and Vidauban.

Tourist information

Les Arcs
Office de Tourisme, pl Général de Gaulle (tel/fax 04.94.73.37.30). **Open** *Sept-June* 9am-noon, 2-5pm Mon-Fri; 9am-noon Sat; *July, Aug* 9am-noon, 2-6pm Mon-Fri; 9am-noon Sat.

Le Muy
Office du Tourisme, rte de la Bourgade (04.94.45.12.79/fax 04.94.45.06.67). **Open** *Sept-June* 9.30am-noon, 3-5pm Mon-Fri; 9.30am-noon Sat. *July, Aug* 9.30am-noon, 4-7pm Mon-Fri; 10am-noon Sat, Sun.

Vidauban
Office de Tourisme, pl Fernand Maurel (04.94.73.10.28/fax 04.94.73.07.82). **Open** *mid-Sept to May* 9am-noon, 3-6pm Mon-Fri; *June to mid Sept* 9am-noon, 3-7pm Mon-Fri; 9am-noon Sat, Sun.

Bargemon & around

The stone houses of **Callas** cluster around a Romanesque church and a ruined castle with spectacular views southwards towards the Maures and Estérel massifs. North of town, the D25 crosses the Boussague Pass towards Bargemon. It's worth detouring through the ravine that flanks the D425 to **Claviers**, a quaint village with a fiercely patriotic church clock on the main square; admire it from the shady tables outside the **Auberge Le Provençal** (*see below* **Where to stay & eat**).

   Bargemon was the last link in a chain of six Roman fortifications stretching from here to **Montauroux** (*see page 192*) via Fayence. The chapel of **Notre-Dame-de-Montaigu** houses a hidden, miracle-working statue of the Virgin, which is brought out once a year on Easter Monday. In the fourteenth-century church of St-Etienne – built into the town wall next to a so-called 'Roman', but in fact twelfth-century gate – are a fascinating collection of votive offerings.

   To the north, the D25 loops ever upwards in steep hairpin curves, with dizzying views of the Mediterranean, to the **Col de Bel Homme** look-out. The road flattens out across the mountain plateau and military training grounds of Camp Canjuers. At the fork of La Colle, head left on the D37 for **Bargème**, a windswept village, which blends into the rocky limestone terrain. At 1,097 metres it is the highest in the Var, with a population of just 115. The tourist information office in the

town hall runs guided tours to the fortified
gateways, the twelfth-century church of St-
Nicholas and the Pontevès family chateau,
which was destroyed during the Wars of
Religion in the fifteenth century. For hikers,
the GR49 passes just to the north of the town
on its way to the **Gorges du Verdon**.

Where to stay & eat

At the southern entrance to Callas on the D225,
the **Camping Les Blimouses**
(04.94.47.83.41, rates 70F for two adults & tent)
offers the usual two-star campsite facilities.
Far more imposing – and expensive – is the
hospitality on offer at the **Hostellerie Les
Gorges de Pennafort** (04.94.76.66.51, closed
15 Jan-15 Mar, rates 620F-1,100F, menus 190F-
550F), an elegant *bastide* in a dramatic rocky
gorge seven kilometres south of Callas on the
D25. Host Phillipe da Silva does excellent
regional dishes in the classic cordon bleu
tradition and succulent desserts. Twelve
rooms and four suites are on hand for those
who want to get far, far away from it all. In
Claviers, the **Auberge le Provençal** (2 pl du
8 Mai 1945, 04.94.47.80.62, closed Jan, menus
68F & 98F) is good for a cheap meal, with lots
of salads and fish, and tables in the main
square in summer. The **Hôtel-Restaurant
Auberge des Arcades** (2 av Pasteur,

04.94.76.60.36, rates 250F-300F, menus 98F &
185F) in Bargemon is an old Provençal inn
with a huge shady terrace. In tiny Bargème,
Annie Noel provides *chambres d'hôte* rooms
and good home cooking at **Les Roses
Trémières** (Le Village, 83840 Bargème,
04.94.84.20.86, closed Nov-end Mar, rates
320F), in the ruins of the chateau.

Getting there

By car
Callas is 15km north-east of Draguignan on the D562
and D225; for the other villages, folllow the
indications in the text.

By bus
From Draguignan, Gagnard (04.94.76.02.29) buses
run three times a day, Mon-Sat, to Callas, Bargemon
and Claviers, continuing to Seillans, Fayence, Callian,
Montauroux and Grasse. There are only two daily
buses in the other direction.

Tourist information

Bargème
Mairie, Bargème (04.94.76.81.25). **Open** *Sept-June*
2-5pm Mon, Tue, Thur, Fri; *July-Aug* 2-6pm daily.

Bargemon
Syndicat d'Initiative, av Pasteur (04.94.47.81.73).
Open 9am-noon daily.

Inland Var

Steep cobbled streets, and plenty of pottery and antiques, in **Fayence**. *See page 192.*

Callas
Syndicat d'Initiative, pl du 18 Juin (04.94.39.06.77).
Open *Sept-June* 10am-12.30pm Tue, Thur; *July, Aug*
9am-12.30pm, 4-7pm Mon-Sat.

Claviers
Mairie, ensemble Victor Audibert (04.94.76.62.07).
Open 10am-noon, 2.30-5.30pm Mon-Fri;
10am-noon Sat.

Around Fayence

Leaving Bargemon, the D19 swings around
testing mountain curves to **Seillans**, its cream-
coloured houses seemingly cut out of the forest
like a cubist sculpture. Seillans is the oldest of
six fortified Roman villages in the Eastern Var.
Three Roman gates lead into town where steep
cobbled streets ascend to a chateau and tower. A
reminder of troubled times, the name Seillans is
derived from the Provençal word *seilhanso* – the
pot of boiling oil that villagers dumped over the
ramparts onto the heads of Saracen attackers.
Less bellicose now, the village concentrates its
energies on honey, perfume and flower
cultivation. It was home to German surrealist
Max Ernst during the last years of his life.

From Seillans, the D19 passes the Romanesque
chapel of **Notre-Dame-de-l'Ormeau**, with a
fine sixteenth-century altarpiece, en route to
Fayence, a hotbed of British subversives
plotting to make Provence drive on the left.
Pottery and antiques are big around here. On
place St-Jean-Baptiste, with its glorious view
over the mountains to the south, stands the
eighteenth-century church of **Notre-Dame**, with
a marble altarpiece by Provençal mason
Dominique Fossatti. Cobbled streets lead into the
village and the **Four du Mitan**, an old bakery
with a *tableau vivant* breadmaking display.

A stone's throw from Fayence, **Tourrettes**
is named after the two square towers of its
feudal chateau, home of the powerful
Villeneuve family. In the history of south-
eastern France, only the Grimaldis of Monaco
held equal sway. **Callian**, a few kilometres
east of Tourrettes, is tiny and pedestrian, its
lanes spiralling up to the impressive feudal
chateau that tops the village. In summer, chill
your feet in the ancient fountain on **place
Bourguignon**, courtesy of the same Roman
aqueduct that once supplied water to Fréjus.
From Callian, it's two kilometres along the D37
through olive terraces to **Montauroux**. The
main square opens on to a fine view and boules
players congregate for pastis at the corner bar.
Ignoring its Roman and medieval influences,
Montauroux has lately taken to selling itself as
'the village of Christian Dior'. The Dior family
once owned the exquisite twelfth-century
Chapelle St-Barthélemy above the village,

bequeathing it to the community when
Christian died. Montauroux is handy for
watersports on the **Lac St-Cassien**, six
kilometres south-east along the D37.

Where to stay, eat & drink

The old-fashioned charm and reliable Provençal
cooking of the **Hôtel des Deux Rocs** (pl Font
d'Amont, 04.94.76.87.32, restaurant closed Dec-
Mar, rates 300F-600F, menus 90F-210F) in
Seillans makes it a favourite with the back-
country brigade. In Fayence, **Hôtel La Sousto**
(4 pl du Paty, 04.94.76.02.16, rates 240F-360F)
offers a taste of village life with its cheerful
rooms. Just around the corner, the tiny
Restaurant Patin Couffin (pl de l'Olivier,
04.94.76.29.96, closed Mon & Nov, menus 90F-
125F) is a *très* rustic experience with dishes such
as lamb or rabbit in sage, garlic and olives. Four
kilometres back along the Seillans road, **Le
Castellaras** (04.94.76.13.80, closed dinner Mon
& all Tue, menus 185F-295F) is the area's
gourmet pull, offering excellent Provençal food
(including a vegetarian menu) and wines in a
lovely garden setting, with the bonus of a
swimming pool. Note that it's closed during
March and from mid-November to mid-
December. In the heart of Montauroux, the
Hôtel-Restaurant Le Marina (2 rue Droite,
04.94.76.43.33, hotel closed Jan, restaurant closed
all Fri & lunch Sat except during July & Aug,
rates 130F-180F, menus 70F-140F) moves outside
in summer to occupy place de la Rougière.

Getting there

By car
Fayence lies halfway between Draguignan and Grasse;
from either, take the D562 (signed as the D2562 from
Grasse), then the D563 3km north to Fayence.

By bus
See p191 **Bargemon & around**.

Tourist information

Fayence
*Office de Tourisme, pl Léon Roux
(04.94.76.20.08/fax 04.94.84.71.86).* **Open** 8.30am-
noon, 2-6pm Mon-Sat.

Montauroux
*Office de Tourisme, pl du Clos (04.94.47.75.90/
fax 04.94.47.61.97).* **Open** 9am-12.30pm, 2.30-6pm
Mon-Sat.

Seillans
*Office de Tourisme, pl du Valat (04.94.76.85.91/fax
04.94.76.84.45).* **Open** *Oct-May* 9.30am-12.30pm,
2.30-6pm Mon-Sat; *June-Sept* 9.30am-12.30pm, 3-7pm
Mon-Sat; 10am-1pm, 3-6pm Sun.

Les Gorges du Verdon

The precipitous limestone gorges of the Verdon river form a natural spectacle of Gothic scale.

The beetling crags of **Moustiers-Ste-Marie**. *See page 194.*

Europe's largest canyon slices through the high limestone plateau that runs between Avignon and Nice at the southern edge of Haute Provence. Towards the east, the upper gorge is between 215 and 1,650 metres wide. The lower section narrows claustrophobically to between six and 108 metres. All along the route, dizzying cliffs range from 270 to 770 metres in height.

The Grand Canyon proper runs for 21 kilometres from just south of Rougon to the reservoir at the Lac de Ste-Croix. The high fluorine content of the River Verdon's water in the upper sector makes it an unnaturally vibrant green; it also makes it undrinkable. West of the lake, the cliffs of the lower gorge climb no higher than 500 metres. It is, however, a pleasant enough place to splash about on a pedalo.

Few people, save the locals, even knew about the existence of this natural wonder until its depths were fully explored in 1905. Even then, some avid Parisian nature-lover suggested that the best thing to do with such a large, unproductive hole would be to wall it up and flood it to make a dam. In the event, the dams were built further downstream, at the Lac de Ste-Croix and below the Basses (lower) Gorges (*see page 196*). The whole spectacular, sparsely populated but much-visited area was made into a Parc Naturel Régional in 1977.

The Grand Canyon: the road circuit

Though fraught with hairpin bends and heavy traffic in high season, the 130-kilometre circuit on the perilous road perched above the canyon is an experience not to be missed. From the the route is best tackled from **Castellane**, a small town packed with accommodation and eateries for canyon-visitors situated on the Route Napoléon. The great man himself stopped off here for a bite in March 1815, at what is now the **Conservatoire des Arts et Traditions Populaires** museum.

The town nestles beneath a massive rocky outcrop topped by the **Notre-Dame-du-Roc** chapel, a 20-minute ascent from the centre. If you want to look inside the chapel, a mainly eighteenth-century affair packed with *ex votos* left by pilgrims, collect the key in town at 35 rue de la Merci. But it's the view that makes the climb worthwhile: though the canyon is not

Bungee heaven: **Pont d'Artuby**.

does not set your pulse racing sufficiently, tourist offices in towns around the Gorges will direct you to sports clubs that organise bungee-jumping over the edge. Further along at the Etroit des Cavaliers, the Corniche Sublime road begins, winding above stretches of the gorge that plunge to depths of 440 metres as it approaches the town of Aiguines.

Perched splendidly between water and sky, wild and windy **Aiguines** has the western entrance to the canyon to one side and the sapphire waters of Lac Ste-Croix to the other. The fairy-tale castle – a faux-Renaissance pile from the seventeenth century, with multicoloured towers – is not open to the public. Once famous for its wood-turning, and its boules-making in particular (using box wood gathered by intrepid climbers from trees at the base of the gorge), Aiguines' crafts are commemorated in the **Musée des Tourneurs sur Bois**. But it is tourism that keeps the pretty, airy town alive today. In **Les Salles-sur-Verdon**, directly below Aiguines on the shores of the lake, all kinds of watersports equipment can be hired. The lake is great for swimming unless the water level is low, when it becomes muddy.

The northern and southern routes meet in **Moustiers-Ste-Marie** to the north of the Lac de Ste-Croix. Built in the shape of an amphitheatre on the edge of a precipice, Moustiers enjoys a Mediterranean climate despite its altitude. On a rock above town is the medieval **Notre-Dame-de-Beauvoir** chapel, with a stunning view over the canyon. Suspended from a chain between two rocks above the chapel is a star said to have been hung there by a grateful local knight, relieved at having returned from the Crusades unscathed.

Moustiers achieved fame in the seventeenth and eighteenth centuries for its faience pottery. After 200 years of production it was dethroned by the fashion for porcelain and English bone china, and the last oven went cold in 1874. Recently, attempts have been made to resuscitate the dead craft, and there are now 19 workshops in operation, the output of which is given a very hard sell in the town's all too numerous crafts and souvenir shops.

visible, the majestic entrance to the Gorges is, along with the town and its ramparts.

Twelve kilometres out of Castellane, the D952 Gorges road forks. Turn left along the D955 to Trigance and then the narrow, winding D90 for access to the Corniche Sublime, which runs along the canyon's southern flank. For a more immediate scenic fix, continue straight on to the aptly named Point Sublime viewpoint at the head of the canyon (for walks from here, *see box*). A sequence of death-defying bends follows, above cliffs that plunge a sheer 800 metres to the ribbon of river below. Further on, the small town of **La Palud-sur-Verdon**, the nearest place of habitation to the brink, has plenty of accommodation, including a youth hostel.

Just before La Palud, the D23 Route des Crêtes branches off to the left, offering an airy circular route that is not for the faint-hearted. The road climbs more than 500 metres before plunging halfway down the side of the canyon to the Chalet de la Maline, point of departure for a spectacular walk along the valley floor (*see box*). From here it's another eight kilometres back to La Palud via a series of scenic viewpoints.

On the D71 southern route, the canyon is first glimpsed from the Balcon de la Mescla lookout. Shortly beyond, the **Pont d'Artuby** is Europe's highest bridge, suspended 650 metres above the Artuby torrent. If a simple crossing

Conservatoire des Arts et Traditions Populaires
34 rue Nationale, Castellane (04.92.83.71.80). **Open** *mid-June to mid-Sept* 9am-noon, 2-6pm Tue-Sun; *mid-Sept to mid-June* 9am-noon Wed and by appointment. **Admission** 10F, 5F children.

Musée des Tourneurs sur Bois
Village centre, Aiguines (04.94.70.20.89). **Open** *July & Aug* 10am-noon, 2-6pm Mon, Wed-Sun; *Sept-June* by appointment. **Admission** 10F.

Inland Var

Where to stay & eat

Aiguines

The **Auberge Altitude 823** (04.94.70.21.09, closed Oct-Mar, rates 230F-320F) is a good budget option. The **Hôtel du Grand Canyon** (71 Falaise des Cavaliers, 04.94.76.91.31, closed mid-Oct to mid-Apr, rates 300F-460F), east of town on the Falaise des Cavaliers, is a little more upmarket, and has a restaurant; prices reflect the spectacular view more than the service offered.

Castellane

Castellane abounds with mid-range hotels, gîtes, campsites and bed and breakfast accommodation. The **Hôtel de Commerce** (pl Marcel Sauvaire, 04.92.83.61.00, closed Nov-Feb, rates 250F-365F) has an excellent restaurant (closed lunch Wed and all Tue between Mar and mid-June and again between mid-Sept and Oct, menus 95F-115F), run by a pupil of Alain Ducasse (*see box page 44*), while the **Canyons du Verdon** (bd St-Michel/rte de Digne, 04.92.83.76.47, closed winter) has a pool and rents out mountain bikes. The accommodation in the **Auberge du Teillon** in the nearby hamlet of Garde (Route Napoléon, 04.92.83.60.88, closed mid-Dec to mid-Mar, rates 110F-240F) is nothing special but the restaurant is (closed dinner Sun and all Mon from mid-June to Sept, menus 110F-230F; book well ahead).

Some way south of Castellane, the **Grand-Hôtel-Bain** in Comps-sur-Artuby (2 av de Fayet, 04.94.76.90.06, closed mid-Nov to 25 Dec, rates 265F-340F) has been run by the same family for eight generations, while the 11th-century **Château de Trigance**, in the delightful hilltop village of the same name (rte Château de Trigance, 04.94.76.91.18, closed Nov-Mar, rates 650F-950F) also has a pleasant restaurant (closed Nov to late-Mar, booking advisable) with menus at 210F, 270F and 320F.

Moustiers-Ste-Marie

There are several acceptable mid-range hotels here: **La Bonne Auberge** (04.92.74.66.18, closed mid-Nov to Mar, rates 320F-520F), **Le Belvédère** (rue d'Orville, 04.92.74.66.04, closed Dec to mid-Feb, rates 280F-380F) and **Le Relais** (village centre, 04.92.74.66.10, closed Jan, rates 320F-500F). **Les Santons** restaurant (pl de l'Eglise, 04.92.74.66.48, open Wed-Sun and sometimes Mon & Tue, call for details, closed Dec & Jan, menus 220F-300F) is pricey but well worth a visit (you may need to book). For a true gourmet experience, head for super-chef Alain Ducasse's **La Bastide de Moustiers** (04.92.70.47.47; *see box page 45*), in the nearby village of La Grisolière, which also has 11 delightful rooms (rates 1,000F-1,520F).

La Palud-sur-Verdon

The dramatically situated youth hostel here (04.92.77.38.72, closed Nov-Mar, rates from 48F) has an adjacent campsite. The **Le Provence** hotel (rte de la Maline, 04.92.77.38.88, closed winter) also has stunning views, a terrace, and a restaurant (menus 65F-100F).

Walking & rafting the Grand Canyon

You can hike along most of the Grand Canyon, though it's no easy task, and all but the most experienced walkers should consider hiring a guide on more demanding routes. If you're determined to go it alone, the full two-day Sentier Martel canyon trail from Rougon to Maireste is explained in a walker's guide that can be picked up from tourist offices in Castellane and Moustiers-Ste-Marie. Remember to check the latest weather forecast in any tourist office before setting out, and ask about the water level, too: the EDF electricity generating company controls the flow artificially, and opens the floodgates at intervals (recorded information 04.92.83.62.68).

For the less adventurous, there are a host of much less demanding hikes. The walk through the 670-metre Couloir Samson (Samson corridor) is a two-hour round trip from the **Point Sublime** lookout (*see opposite*). The trail, which is clearly signposted from the car park, takes you down to a footbridge spanning the River Baou and through a series of tunnels through the rock (take a torch and a sweater), from which you emerge to a fantastic panorama of the Chaos de Tréscaïre rock formations. From Point Sublime you can also take the much more strenuous waymarked six- to eight-hour hike to Chalet de la Maline on the Route des Crêtes. There's also an easier path to the Chalet de la Maline from the **Etroit des Cavaliers**, a two-hour descent.

Kayaking and rafting in the canyon is definitely for experts, though placid Lac de Ste-Croix offers an easier option. The tourist office in Aiguines has leaflets and information. If it's whitewater rafting you're after, head for the tourist information office in La Palud.

...ke the Grasse exit
...low the N85 to
... the A8 take the N555
... through the military
...ern rim of the canyon.

By bus

Public transport is very limited. Sumian (04.42.67.60.34) runs services from Marseille to Castellane via Aix-en-Provence, La Palud-sur-Verdon and Moustiers-Ste-Marie three times a week in summer (Mon, Wed and Sat) and on Saturday only the rest of the year. VFD (04.93.85.24.56) runs a daily service from Grenoble to Nice via Digne-les-Bains and Grasse, which stops in Castellane en route. Shuttle buses run around the canyon in July and August only (Mon-Sat), linking Castellane with Point Sublime, La Palud and La Maline (information 04.92.83.40.27).

Tourist information

Aiguines

Office de Tourisme, Les Buis (04.94.70.21.64). **Open** *July & Aug* 9am-12.30pm, 3-7pm Mon-Sat; *Sept-June* 9-noon, 2-5pm Mon-Fri.

Castellane

Office de Tourisme, rue National (04.92.83.61.14/fax 04.92.83.76.89). **Open** *July & Aug* 8.30am-12.30pm, 1.30-7pm daily; *Sept-June* 9am-noon, 2-6pm Mon-Fri.
Staff can provide driving and walking itineraries for the area, including the nearby lakes of Chaudanne and Castillon, and point you in the direction of the Moulin des Soleils (04.94.76.92.62) at Trigance, one of Provence's few remaining working flour mills.

La Palud-sur-Verdon

Syndicat d'Initiative, Le Château (04.92.77.32.02). **Open** summer only; call for details.

Moustiers-Ste-Marie

Office de Tourisme, Hôtel Dieu (04.92.74.67.84/fax 04.92.74.60.65). **Open** *July & Aug* 9am-8pm daily; *Sept-June* 2-5pm daily.

Riez & the Basses Gorges du Verdon

Only half as sheer as the Grand Canyon, the Basses Gorges are still pretty dramatic. Though part of the Parc Naturel, this area is more given over to agriculture. Lavender is the main crop on the Plateau de Valensole, which separates the Basses Gorges from the town of Riez; it colours and perfumes the whole area in summer.

West of the Lac de Ste-Croix, **Riez** is a pretty, unspoiled little place whose impressive main street suggests it has seen better days. Four seven-metre columns in a field on the western outskirts bear witness to the town's Roman past. On the opposite bank of the river stands a rare early Christian monument: a sixth-century Merovingian baptistry with more plundered Roman columns inside. Ramparts surround the old town, which is dominated by a sixteenth-century clocktower. The western gate into the old town, the **Porte Saint-Sols** or Sanson, opens onto la Grande Rue with its flamboyant Renaissance constructions: note the Hôtel de Mazan at No.12, which has a beautiful sixteenth-century staircase with Gothic flourishes. Important to the lavender industry, Riez is also a hive of honey-making activity. The market, on Wednesdays and Saturdays, is a good place to pick up local produce, including truffles, honey, lavender and faïence pottery.

The **Basses Gorges** themselves are not easily accessible; the best approach is from **Quinson** at the eastern end, 21 kilometres south-west of Riez. This tiny village is the site of an ambitious, partially underground **Musée de la Préhistoire**, designed by Norman Foster and Partners, due to open in July 2000 (information from Office de Tourisme, pl de la Maire; 04.92.74.01.12); Quinson is already proclaiming itself 'the European capital of prehistory'. South of the village, a path descends to a broad, partially dammed stretch of the river; there's a swimming area, and pedalos for hire. On the southern flank, paths lead from the road to the end of the abyss but no further.

Where to stay & eat

In Riez, the ugly **Carina** hotel (Quartier St-Jean, 04.92.77.85.43, closed mid-Nov to Mar, rates 250F-320F) is more acceptable when looking out, with lovely views from the rooms. The **Château de Pontfrac** (rte de Varenson, 04.92.77.78.77, rates 300F) is between Riez and Valensole. For creative but modestly priced Provençal cooking (aïoli a speciality), try **Les Abeilles** (10 allée Louis-Gardiol, closed Sun, menu 72F).

Getting there

By car

Leave the A8 motorway at St-Maximin and take the D560 and D13 to Quinson.

Tourist information

Office de Tourisme

4 allée Louis Gardiol, Riez (04.92.77.99.09/ fax 04.92.77.99.08). **Open** *June-Sept* 8am-12.30pm, 1.30-6.30pm daily; *Oct-May* 8am-noon, 1.30-5.30pm Tue-Sat.

The Riviera

Cannes & Around	198
Antibes to Cagnes	210
Nice	218
The Corniches	235
Monaco & Monte-Carlo	242
Menton & Around	250

Feature boxes

Iles de Lérins	199
Top ten beaches in the South	203
Hôtel du Cap Eden-Roc	210
Jazz à Juan	212
Le Nissart	225
Rosbif rock	230
Faites vos jeux	247

Cannes & Around

Cruise La Croisette or go rustic in Mougins – just make sure it's on the expense account.

Classic **Cannes**, iconic heart of the French Riviera, in a rare quiet moment.

Cannes

When Napoléon landed in the nearby dunes after escaping from Elba in 1815, Cannes was just a sleepy fishing village. So it had been for centuries: a few Celto-Ligurians dwelt about the place until the Romans turfed them out in 42 BC. A handful of Genoese made a living fishing among the reeds (*les cannes*); in the twelfth century, the abbots of Lérins (*see box opposite*), under whose care they were placed by the Counts of Provence, provided them with fortifications against Saracen attacks.

It was not until 1834 that Cannes was 'discovered'. An outbreak of cholera in fashionable Nice forced former British Chancellor Lord Brougham to winter in the town, on what was then the French side of the border. He liked the place, had a villa built, and for the next 34 years came back for the winter season, joined by a growing number of emulators. At Brougham's insistence, King Louis-Philippe spent two million francs on a harbour wall, the essential prerequisite of a decent, strollable seaside promenade.

So the little resort grew, quietly and classily, until 1946, when Cannes hosted its first ever

Festival International de Cinéma. It had been selected for this purpose in 1939, in order to wrest the monopoly on cinematic prize-giving from the Italian Fascists who did it annually in Venice, but a world war disrupted the preparations. The beginning of the first edition was inauspicious: when the first **Palais des Festivals** was built (where the Noga Hilton now stands) the architects forgot that the projection booth needed windows to project the film through. After several embarrassed minutes of hammering and chiselling, a glamorous audience was able to enjoy their first festival movie. The rest is history (*see box page 30*).

Capitalising on its film festival kudos, Cannes has launched itself as the European media festival hub. The Palais des Festivals swarms at various times of the year with advertisers (MIPCOM), music-makers (MIDEM), TV producers (MIP-TV) and a vast range of other conference-goers who keep the town buzzing and the hotels full.

Lounging with a cocktail, dressed in clothes that dare not speak their price, is an important pastime in Cannes, and **La Croisette** – the sea-front drag – is the place to be seen doing it. There are flash bars and luxury hotels with sugar-icing façades, the Palais des Festivals with its array of star hand-prints outside, and, from **Pointe de la Croisette**, glorious views across the bay of La Napoule. Modern art exhibitions are held at **La Malmaison**, part of the old Grand Hotel.

To the west is the port and, perched on a hill above, the old town of **Le Suquet** where Cannes' only museum of note, the **Musée de la Castre**, occupies what's left of the town's twelfth-century fortifications; it displays archaeological and ethnographical finds from around the world and offers spectacular views.

East of the centre, the **Quartier de la Californie** is packed with exotic *belle époque* villas in lush gardens. Further north, the hilltop suburb of **Le Cannet** has eighteenth-century houses standing in pretty, leafy squares.

La Malmaison

47 La Croisette (04.93.99.04.04). **Open** 10am-noon, 2-5.30pm Mon, Wed-Sun. **Admission** 10F.
This nineteenth-century mansion now houses regular art exhibitions.

Musée de la Castre

Château de la Castre, pl de la Castre (04.93.38.55.26). **Open** *Oct-Mar* 10am-noon, 2-5pm Wed-Mon; *Apr-June* 10am-noon, 2-6pm Wed-Mon; *July-Sept* 10am-noon, 3-7pm Wed-Mon. **Admission** 10F, free children.

Palais des Festivals

1 La Croisette (04.93.39.01.01). **Tours** (in French) occasional Wed 2.30pm, 3.30pm; admission free; ring Office de Tourisme (04.93.39.24.53) to check.

Iles de Lérins

A 15-minute boat ride from the Gare Maritime on the old port of Cannes, the Iles de Lérins are a dramatic contrast to the glitz of La Croisette. Known to the ancients as Lero and Lerina, these two oases, where secluded paths criss-cross thick forests of aleppo pine and eucalyptus, now go by the names of St-Honorat and Ste-Marguerite, after the religious siblings who formed monastic communities here in the fourth century. By the seventh century, Lérins was one of Europe's key monastic institutions. Today it's a religious backwater where a handful of Cistercian monks make a liqueur called Lerina.

Honoratus, credited with being one of the founders of monasticism, had the usual early Christian attributes of extreme asceticism and a way with snakes: it was he who did away with the smaller island's venomous inhabitants, and it was here that St Patrick trained in the same art before setting out for Ireland – or so the story goes. The little that remains on **St-Honorat** of the earlier monastery buildings was incorporated into the current **Abbaye de Lérins** in the nineteenth century. The nearby keep – the **Monastère Fortifié** – built by the monks in 1073 to protect themselves when Saracens attacked, still has a decidedly impregnable air.

Ste-Marguerite is more touristy, but quiet corners can still be found. The **Musée de la Mer** in the **Fort Ste-Marguerite** is visited not so much for its collection of artefacts gleaned from underwater archaeological expeditions as for its reputation as the prison of the mysterious Man in the Iron Mask.

Made lastingly famous by novelist Alexandre Dumas and by countless cinematic tall tales, the Man may have been Louis XIV's twin brother – or so that story goes. It is a fact, however, that many hapless Huguenots were confined here during Louis XIV's religious crackdown, and that the place was re-fortified in 1712 by royal architect Vauban, though why – seeing as it faces landwards and is fairly useless for defensive purposes – is difficult to imagine. The port is awash with rather overpriced fish restaurants, but at least the sea around the islands is cleaner than over on the mainland.

Musée de la Mer

Fort Ste-Marguerite (04.93.43.18.17). **Open** *Oct-Mar* 10.30am-12.15pm, 2.30-4.30pm Wed-Mon; *Apr-June* 10.30am- 12.15pm, 2.30-5.30pm Wed-Mon; *July-Sept* 10.30am-12.15pm, 2.30-6.30pm Wed-Mon. **Admission** 10F, free children.

Monastère Fortifié

St-Honorat (04.92.99.54.00). **Open** *mid-Sept to mid-June* 9am-5pm daily; *mid-June to mid-Sept* 10.30am-12.30pm, 2.15-5pm daily. Closed during Sunday mass. **Admission** 10F.

Getting there

By boat

Compagnie Esterel Chantelclair (04.93.39.11.82) runs boats to the islands from the Gare Maritime in Cannes, every hour from 10am to 5pm daily; the crossing takes 15 minutes.

The Riviera

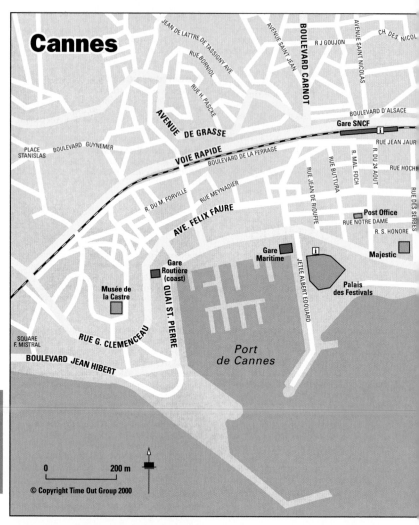

Cannes

JEAN DE LATTRE DE TASSIGNY AVE
RUE BORNIOL
RUE H. PASCKE
AVENUE SAINT-JEAN
BOULEVARD CARNOT
AVENUE SAINT NICOLAS
R J GOUJON
CH DES NICOL
AVENUE DE GRASSE
BOULEVARD D'ALSACE
Gare SNCF
PLACE STANISLAS
BOULEVARD GUYNEMER
RUE JEAN JAUR
VOIE RAPIDE
BOULEVARD DE LA FERRAGE
R. DU M. FORVILLE
RUE MEYNADIER
RUE BUTTURA
R. MAL. FOCH
R. DU 24 AOUT
RUE HOCH
AVE. FELIX FAURE
RUE JEAN DE RIOUFFE
RUE DES SERBES
Post Office
RUE NOTRE DAME
R. S. HONORE
Gare Maritime
Gare Routière (coast)
Majestic
Musée de la Castre
QUAI ST. PIERRE
JETÉE ALBERT EDOUARD
Palais des Festivals
SQUARE F. MISTRAL
RUE G. CLEMENCEAU
BOULEVARD JEAN HIBERT
Port de Cannes

0   200 m

© Copyright Time Out Group 2000

The Riviera

Restaurants

See also **La Belle Otero** (*page 52*), **Neat**, **Le Restaurant Arménien** (*both page 53*) and **Villa de Lys** (*page 54*), in our food and drink chapter.

Astoux et Brun
27 rue Félix Faure (04.93.39.21.87). **Meals served** noon-3pm, 7-11.30pm daily. Closed July. **Average** 135F. **Credit** AmEx, MC, V.
Crewed by men in gumboots who swab the decks with brush and hose, Astoux et Brun serves abundant *fruits de mer* of impeccable freshness. Specials include fish casserole and the ultimate seafood platter, *l'assortiment royale*.

Au Bec Fin
12 rue du 24 Août (04.93.38.35.86). **Meals served** 9am-2.30pm, 4-10.30pm Mon-Sat. **Menu** 105F. **Credit** MC, V.
A film festival favourite that serves unpretentious family cooking of quality. Seafood is the speciality here, though the restaurant even stretches to curry, and portions are generous.

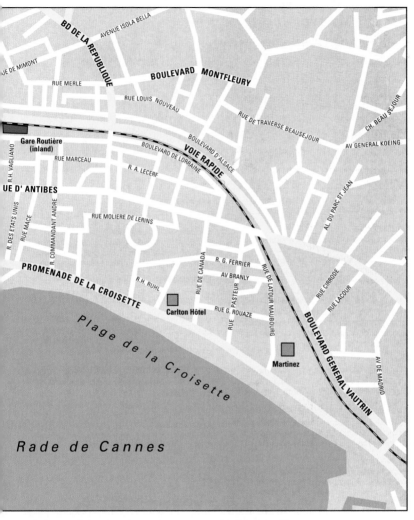

The Riviera

L'Auberge Provençal

10 rue St-Antoine, Le Suquet (04.92.99.27.17). **Meals served** noon-3pm, 6pm-midnight daily. **Menu** 148F. **Credit** AmEx,V.

Dating back to 1860, L'Auberge Provençal claims to be the oldest restaurant in Cannes, and the old-fashioned open fireplace and aged wooden beams certainly lend credence to the claim. The menu remains classic: Bouillabaisse is served at 220F for a two-person portion, while those with a more delicate palate can opt for the likes of omelette with violet artichokes.

Le Caveau 30

45 rue Félix Faure (04.93.39.06.33). **Meals served** noon-2.15pm, 7pm-midnight daily. **Menus** 120F, 172F. **Credit** AmEx, DC, MC, V.

Don't be put off by the faux art deco look: this place is good value, and full of locals. Though seafood is the speciality, lamb and other classic dishes are available.

Chez Astoux

43 rue Félix Faure (04.93.39.06.22). **Meals served** 8am-1am daily. Closed July. **Average** 220F. **Credit** AmEx, MC, V.

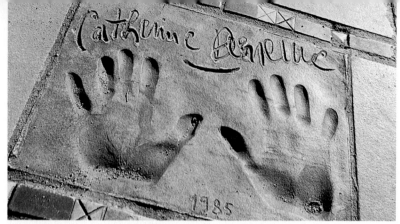
Star handprints outside the **Palais des Festivals**. *See page 198.*

Splendid seafood in refined surroundings: overflowing platters cost anything up to 460F.

Le Farfalla

1 La Croisette (04.93.68.93.00). **Meals served** 10am-1am daily. **Menus** 75F, 98F (both lunch only). **Average** 150F. **Credit** AmEx, MC, V.
Since opening in 1995, this steak house with milk bar decor has established itself as the rendezvous for the bright young things of Cannes. There's a full menu to choose from, or a lighter selection of salads or snacky items. The terrace is for grade-A people-watching; alternatively, seek refuge in an intimate booth on the mezzanine or look down on your fellow festival-goers from a first-floor table.

Félix

63 La Croisette (04.93.94.00.61). **Meals served** noon-2.45pm, 7.30pm-midnight daily. Closed mid-Nov to mid-Dec. **Menu** 220F. **Credit** AmEx, MC, V.
Crispy white-linen preserve of the showy and deep-pocketed. This pristine Croisette restaurant with its immaculately tended little garden likes to be seen to charge for the privilege of eating there.

Jade

24 rue Pasteur (04.93.94.33.49). **Meals served** noon-2.30pm, 7-10.30pm Mon-Sat. Closed mid-Nov to mid-Dec. **Menu** 75F (lunch only). **Average** 150F. **Credit** AmEx, DC, V.
Beautifully presented Vietnamese food. It's considered a local gem, and charges accordingly, but the restaurant does offer a lunchtime budget menu. The crispy chicken cooked with lemon and ginger is a house speciality.

Le Mandarin

rond-point Doboys d'Angers (04.93.38.37.60). **Meals served** noon-2.30pm, 7-10.30pm daily. **Menus** 89F, 140F. **Credit** AmEx, V.
Swathed in greenery, this is the nearest thing to an oriental garden to be found in Cannes. Dragon motifs and red and gold decor make this the grandest Chinese restaurant in town.

Le Marais

9 rue du Suquet, Le Suquet (04.93.38.39.19). **Meals served** 7.30-11pm Tue-Sun. Closed mid-Nov to mid-Dec. **Menu** 135F. **Credit** MC, V.
Friendly, informal place with a menu that makes the most of local ingredients. House specials include home-made ravioli and foie gras. Always busy.

Stromboli

3 sq Mérimée (04.93.39.20.10). **Meals served** 6.30am-2am daily. **Menu** 110F. **Credit** AmEx, MC, V.
With the biggest of the terraces facing the Palais des Festivals, this is a no-nonsense establishment offering an extensive bistro menu with predictable fare, plus some Provençal goodies.

Bars, cafés & snacks

Le Crillon

4 rue Jean Riouffre (04.93.39.34.78). **Open** *Apr-Oct* 6.30am-2am daily; *Nov-Mar* 6.30am-2am Mon-Sat. **Credit** AmEx, V.
Head here for that neighbourhood bar experience. Star snaps along the wall behind the bar are a reminder that this is where the paparazzi gather at festival time. Reliable *plats du jour* (50F-55F) are a good alternative for those suffering from cordon bleu fatigue.

North Beach Café

10 rue 24 Août (04.93.38.40.51). **Open** 7am-7.30pm Mon-Sat. **Average** 80F. **Credit** MC, V.
This airy corner restaurant in the town centre serves appetising Italian food. During the summer the terrace gets packed out. When the festival's on, it stays open till after midnight.

Le 72 Croisette

71 La Croisette (04.93.94.18.30). **Open** 24 hours daily. **Credit** AmEx, MC, V.
Of all the Croisette bars this remains the most feistily French. You'll have to battle hordes of locals to get a ringside seat from which to watch the rich and famous enter the Martinez hotel next door.

Beaches in the South

Don't believe anyone who tells you that Le Midi is beached out. There are still plenty of secluded coves, many of them reachable only by boat or cliff-top footpath, and even in the crowded resorts, there are still a few civilised places to bask. From west to east, here is our choice.

Calanque d'En-Vau, near Cassis

A two-hour stroll or short boat-ride from Cassis, En-Vau is one of the most beautiful and secluded of the *calanques*. Nudism is de rigueur on the sandy beach, whose high cliffs make for plenty of shade. See page 153.

Clos des Plages, La Ciotat

This tranquil strip to the north of the centre of La Ciotat, and overlooked by a newly landscaped promenade, is great for families. See page 153.

Bain de Diane & La Grotte, Ile de Levant

Nudism is compulsory on these two rocky beaches with clear, blue-green water, on the easternmost of the Iles d'Hyères. See page 163.

La Londe to Cap de Bregançon

A succession of quiet beaches stretching to the north of the fishing village of Cabasson provide some of the seclusion of the French president's nearby Cap de Bregançon residence, without the armed guards. See page 165.

L'Esquinade, Plage de Pampelonne, St-Tropez

The north end of Pampelonne is deckchair to deckchair, but towards Cap Camarat the scene gets more relaxed and bohemian –

nowhere more so than at the ramshackle L'Esquinade, a resto-shack run by Edna, former Norwegian motorcycle queen and one of Brigitte Bardot's best friends. See page 170.

La Batterie, Cannes

Straight and gay nude beach. Take the main N7 road out of Cannes for Antibes and park in the lot next to the Shell station. A pedestrian tunnel exits on to La Batterie beach. The woods behind are a favourite gay cruising area.

Juan-les-Pins

Sunbathing was invented here, and this sandy sweep of white sand beneath the pines still works the old magic for diehard sun worshippers. See page 212.

Castel Plage, Nice

Nice isn't about seclusion, but for an urban beach experience, the private Castel Plage, right in front of the *vieille ville*, is stylish enough, with bronzed locals playing chess over coffee in a friendly, relaxed atmosphere. See page 220.

Plage Paloma, St-Jean-Cap-Ferrat

At the luxury-villa end of the headland, just before the chapel of St-Hospice, is this small, pebbly, family-friendly beach, with great views across the gulf to Beaulieu. See page 237.

Plage Mala, Cap d'Ail

A ten-minute walk down from the Basse Corniche at Cap d'Ail. Sandy, with a good snack bar, Mala features a democratic mix of Riviera socialites, Italian daytrippers and kids building sandcastles. See page 239.

Nightlife

Le Cat Corner

22 rue Macé (04.93.39.31.31). **Open** times vary; call to check. **Admission** 100F. **Credit** AmEx, MC, V.
Formerly the slinky Le Velvet, this club has undergone a name change and facelift designed to increase its 'cosy' factor. Attracts the smart hairdresser set.

Les Coulisses

29 rue de Commandant André (04.92.99.17.17). **Open** 5.30pm-2.30am daily. **Credit** AmEx, V.
Beautiful people flock to this club, and during the warm summer months, the action spills out on to

the streets as well. This is the place to go to pick up flyers for late-night events. During the film festival it takes on a more Parisian air as the trendy media folk move in.

Le Jimmy'Z

Casino Croisette, 1 La Croisette (04.93.68.00.07). **Open** *Sept-June* 11pm-6am Thur-Sun; *July, Aug* 11pm-6am daily. **Admission** 50F Mon-Thur, 70F Fri, 100F Sat, Sun. **Credit** AmEx, DC, MC, V.
This uptown establishment caters for high rollers and local wannabes. It also has a rich film festival history: Stevie Wonder tinkled the ivories here at Spike Lee's *Jungle Fever* party, and Madonna had a reunion dance with Sean Penn.

Le Queens

48 bd de la République (04.93.90.25.58). **Open**
11pm-dawn daily. **Admission** varies, depending
on event.

Don't be fooled by the name. This is where the local
mecs (lads) go to meet the *meufs* (chicks). An
imposing structure that fills nightly with local
colour. At festival time, the large capacity makes
it an indispensible venue for grand soirées with
guest lists running the full gamut, from Prince
Albert of Monaco to Naomi Campbell.

Le Sept

7 rue Rouguière (04.93.39.10.36). **Open** 11.30pm-
6am daily. **Admission** varies, depending on event.
Credit MC, V.

If Genet's Querelle was in town he'd sink a drink
here. This long-running back-alley hole-in-the-wall
hosts a nightly drag act. Recently the venue has used
its sleaze chic to attract top club DJs for one-nighters.

Zanzibar

85 rue Félix Faure (04.93.39.30.75). **Open** 6pm-
dawn daily. **Credit** AmEx, V.

One of France's oldest gay haunts. On the cellar
ceiling is a frisky fresco of sailors with bulging
biceps in striped T-shirts. *Bonjour, matelot.* These
days the scene is less nautical and more disco dolly,
with old hands watching the new recruits with a
weather eye from the bar.

Shopping

Most shops in Cannes are open from 9am-noon
and 4-7pm from Monday to Saturday. **La
Croisette, rue d'Antibes** and the streets that
link the two are the places for luxury purchases.
For typical Provençal articles make for **rue
Meynadier** or the winding streets of **Le
Suquet**. In **allée de la Liberté**, a Saturday
morning market offers regional crafts. The
magnificent covered **Forville** produce market
behind the old port is open on Tuesday to
Sunday mornings.

   Cannes English Bookshop (11 rue
Bivouac Napoléon, 04.93.99.40.08, closed Sun) is
a well-stocked emporium providing English-
language material for festival bluffing or beach
reading. British and US dailies can be found at
Espace Loisirs (4 rue d'Antibes,
04.92.98.32.32, open daily) and **Le Temps de
Vivre** (7 La Croisette, 04.93.39.14.51, open
daily) among other places, but they tend to run
out early. **Ceneri** (22 rue Meynadier,
04.93.39.63.68, closed Sun, Mon) is the place for
cheese and gourmet goodies, while **Le Cave
du Vieux Port** (6 rue Emile Négrin,
04.93.39.30.12, open daily) has a good wine
selection. **Jacques Loup** (21 rue d'Antibes,
04.93.39.28.35, closed Sun) stocks major fashion
labels. The essential accessory for any Croisette
stroll is best picked up at **Sunglass Hut**

The **Carlton**: epitome of Riviera glamour.

(37 rue d'Antibes, 04.93.39.78.88, closed Sun), a
veritable supermarket of sunglasses offering an
agony of choice.

Sport & leisure

To keep that body beautiful, join joggers on
La Croisette or make for the **Fitness Centre**
(10 bd de Moulin, 04.93.99.66.16, 60F per day),
which has all the latest equipment but no
sauna. For horse riding try **La Ferme
d'Anais** (1 av Borde, 04.92.92.29.65, closed
Thur), which organises hour-long (90F) or day-
long (300F) rides through nearby forests.

   Behind the Martinez hotel, a knockabout at
Tennis Cannes Martinez (11 rue Lacour,
04.93.43.58.85) costs 90F per hour, while the
Tennis Municipal de la Bastide (230 av
Francis Tonner, 04.93.47.29.33) near the airport
has hard courts at 60F an hour.

   For sailing (160F), water-skiing (210F),
surfing (190F) or diving (195F), the **Centre
Nautique Municipal** (9 rue Esprit Violet,
04.93.47.40.55) organises activities on beaches
along the coast around Cannes.

Where to stay

Hotels

Beverly

14 rue Hoche (04.93.39.10.66/fax 04.92.98.65.63).
Closed Dec. **Rates** single 130F-230F, double 240F-
300F. **Credit** AmEx, DC, MC, V.

Situated on a shopping street parallel to La Croisette. Book ahead if you want to secure one of the rooms with a balcony at the back.

Carlton Hôtel

58 La Croisette (04.93.06.40.06/fax 04.93.39.67.82). **Rates** single 2,040F-2,520F, double 3,435F, suite 6,490F-8,960F. **Credit** AmEx, DC, MC, V.

Built in 1911, the Carlton Hôtel is a trademark of Riviera glamour and an enduring symbol of the film festival. Though some top stars have deserted the hotel in recent years for the super-swank Hôtel du Cap Eden-Roc in Cap d'Antibes (*see box p210*), the Carlton remains the first choice for festival purists, and its terrace is a prime location for people-spotting. The wedding-cake façade so impressed one wartime *New York Times* correspondent that he persuaded the American commander to spare it from bombardment. On each end of the façade of the two-star restaurant, La Belle Otero (*see p52*), is a black coupole, inspired, it's said, by the breasts of the gypsy courtesan after whom the restaurant is named.

Hôtel des Allées

6 rue Emile Négrin (04.93.39.53.90/fax 04.93.68.63.63). Closed mid-Nov to mid-Dec. **Rates** single 260F-390F, double 360F-540F. **Credit** MC, V.

A happy family atmosphere compensates for the lack of a lift and the cramped rooms.

Hôtel du Bourgogne

11 rue du 24 Août (04.93.38.36.73/fax 04.92.99.28.41). **Rates** single 150F, double 450F. **Credit** MC, V.

Opposite the station, this clean if spartan hotel is run by the formidable Madame Nicole. Breakfast is served outside the kitchen on the first floor in front of the television. You'll certainly feel at home.

Majestic

14 La Croisette (04.92.98.77.00/fax 04.93.38.97.90). Closed mid-Nov to Dec. **Rates** single/double 1,290F-10,260F, suite 3,300F-10,900F. **Credit** AmEx, DC, MC, V.

During the film, music or advertising festivals the Majestic throbs as industry folk loudly renew acquaintances, slapping backs and hustling for the Big Deal. The hotel's Villa des Lys restaurant (*see p54*) offers one of Cannes' best hotel dining experiences. Beside the restaurant is the only *fumoir* – cigar room – on the Côte, with all the havanas and coronas any self-respecting mogul could want. The Majestic bar is mythical, the Cecil B DeMille decor paying homage to the Pharaonic ambitions of the film types who frequent the place.

Martinez

73 La Croisette (04.92.98.73.00/fax 04.92.18.85.25). **Rates** single/double 1,300F-2,800F, suite 4,000F-15,000F. **Credit** AmEx, DC, MC, V.

Constructed at the end of the Roaring Twenties, the Martinez prides itself on its art deco appeal,

which is lovingly preserved by its owners, the bubbly Taittinger family. This is the most relaxed of Cannes' big three; the discreet rich can be found of an evening snacking at the hotel's Palm d'Or restaurant, the only Michelin two-star on the Croisette. The other notable feature of the Martinez is Jimmy at the piano in the bar. Jimmy hires (and fills) Carnegie Hall in New York for an annual one-nighter: you can hear him play here for the price of a dry martini.

Le Mondial

1 rue Teisseire (04.93.68.70.00/fax 04.93.99.39.45). **Rates** single 480F, double 600F, suite 800F. **Credit** AmEx, DC, MC, V.

This 1930s edifice dominates the rue – only a short walk from La Croisette – and looks down to the sea, facing *plein sud*. It's newly renovated, with smart, soundproofed, modern rooms, many with tiny balconies, and friendly staff.

Savoy

5 rue François Einsey (04.92.99.72.00/fax 04.93.68.25.59). **Rates** single/double 1,050F-1,530F, suite 3,100F-5,900F. **Credit** AmEx, DC, MC, V.

The rooftop terrace-with-pool of this designer hotel is considered Cannes' best: a restful crow's nest with a magnificent view over the city, it's a mecca for high-density sunbathers.

Splendid

4 rue Félix Faure (04.97.06.22.22/fax 04.93.99.55.02). **Rates** single 560F-860F, double 580F-960F, suite 1,280F-1,380F. **Credit** AmEx, DC, MC, V.

Across from the festival HQ, the Splendid stands wedding-cake proud with flags fluttering, making it clear to all and sundry that this was the original Cannes palace hotel. It's picture-postcard charms lure a loyal, mostly American clientele. Despite the installation of a Planet Hollywood restaurant downstairs, some of the mystique remains.

Self-catering

Résideal

11 rue Bertrand Lepine (tel/fax 04.93.05.50.00). **Rates** from 3,400F per week for a five-person apartment. **Credit** AmEx, DC, MC, V.

Tall trees shade this secluded block, providing privacy poolside where top talent greets the world's media during the festival. The modern apartments each have a balcony. Breakfast in the grounds is a real treat.

Pierre et Vacances Résidences

6 rue de la Verrerie, La Bocca (04.93.90.72.00/fax 04.93.99.56.50). **Rates** 4,420F per week for four to five people. **Credit** AmEx, DC, MC, V.

This modern complex offers high-quality holiday flats a few minutes' drive west of Cannes. Stunning views from the large balconies. It's a good base from which to explore the Riviera and the hinterland.

The Riviera

Art deco style and a relaxed atmosphere ensure the **Martinez** stays popular. *See p205.*

Essentials

Getting there

By car
Leave the A8 at exit no.41 or no.42.

By train
Cannes is on the main coastal route, with frequent services from Nice and Marseille. There is also a service from inland towns, such as Grasse.

By bus
There are two *gares routières* in Cannes: the main one by the port (pl Cornut Gentille) serves coastal destinations, including Nice; the one by the train station serves Mougins, Grasse and various other inland destinations. RCA (04.93.18.16.03) runs hourly services between Cannes and Nice airport from 9am to 9pm and has no fewer than 43 daily services between Cannes and Nice's central *gare routière*. It also runs 20 services per day to Marseille airport (via Aix) between 7.30am and 9.15pm.

Tourist information

Office de Tourisme
Palais des Festivals, 1 bd de la Croisette (04.93.39.24.53/fax 04.92.99.84.23). **Open** 9am-7pm Mon-Fri, 10am-6pm Sat, Sun. *Website: www.cannes-on-line.com*

Around Cannes

Mougins

Almost a satellite of Cannes and yet still charmingly rural, Mougins is the place where film people come to get away from the crush on the Croisette. Though its star eaterie, the Moulin de Mougins, was recently downgraded to just one Michelin star, the various tasteful, upmarket restaurants sprinkled around the village still make Mougins one of the gastronomic capitals of Le Midi.

A Ligurian hill fort and a Roman staging post with walls dating from the Middle Ages, when Mougins was bigger than Cannes, the village grew rich from the eighteenth century onwards on its luxury crops: olives, wine, jasmine and roses. In the 1920s and '30s, as the Côte became fashionable, Mougins was discovered by artists such as Picabia, Cocteau and Man Ray. Picasso spent the last 12 years of his life here, between 1961 and 1973. Today Mougins bristles with second homes for the better sort of resident, often given away by all the closed-circuit cameras peeping out from behind the bougainvillea. The worst sort of residents are welcome, too, as long as they are discreet: Haitian dictator Baby Doc used to have a bolt-hole here.

Views from the medieval centre are spectacular, ranging over Cannes and out to the Iles de Lérins; for the best panorama, climb the bell tower of **St-Jacques-le-Majeur** in rue des Orfèvres. The old village is full of private art galleries, and there are a couple of worthwhile public spaces, too. **Le Lavoir**, once the village laundry, is now an exhibition centre that showcases local artists. The **Musée de la Photographie** stands next to the twelfth-century Porte Sarassin (Saracen gate). On three floors, the permanent collection includes old cameras and endless photos of Picasso by André Villers, as well as works by photographic masters such as Doisneau and Lartigue. Outside the village, five kilometres south-east on the A8 autoroute (access from the Aire de Bréguières service station) is the **Musée de l'Automobiliste**. Adrien Maeght, son of Aimé and Marguerite Maeght (*see page 263*), set up this state-of-the-art glass and concrete tribute to cars and motorbikes and things that go. Around a hundred sleek racing cars are on rotating display here; there are also temporary exhibitions, auctions and fairs for people who find carburettors sexy.

Le Lavoir

av Charles Mallet (04.92.92.50.42). **Open** *Mar-Oct* 11am-7pm daily. **Admission** free.

Musée de l'Automobiliste

chemin de Font-de-Currault (04.93.69.27.80). **Open** *Apr-Sept* 10am-7pm daily; *Oct to mid-Nov, mid-Dec to Mar* 10am-6pm daily. Closed mid-Nov to mid-Dec. **Admission** 40F, 25F children.
Website: www.weblane.fr/musee-auto-mougins

Musée de la Photographie

67 rue de l'Eglise (04.93.75.85.67). **Open** *Sept-Oct, Dec-June* 2-6pm Wed-Sun; *July, Aug* 2-11pm daily. Closed Nov. **Admission** 5F.

St-Jacques-le-Majeur

rue des Orfèvres. **Open** *Mar-Oct* 2-6pm Mon, Wed-Sun. **Admission** free. Key from Musée de la Photographie.

Where to stay & eat

Mougins may be small, but it packs a gastronomic punch. Star player is Roger Vergé's **Le Moulin de Mougins** (*see page 53*), a temple of modern Provençal cuisine that also hosts works and installations by artists such as César, Arman and Folon. If you can't face the drive back, there are three rooms (from 850F) and four suites (1,800F). Chefs from the restaurant also run cookery courses at the **Ecole de Cuisine de Soleil** in Mougins village (04.93.75.35.70, 300F for a two-hour lesson); each multilingual session is organised around a menu or seasonal theme. At **Le Feu**

Moulin de Mougins, down to one Michelin star but still a gastronomic landmark.

Follet (pl de la Mairie, 04.93.90.15.78, closed Sun eve, all Mon, menus 135F-175F), English-speaking chef and owner Jean-Paul Battaglia heads a battalion of young chefs in an open-plan kitchen. Battaglia likes to take orders and discuss his local market discoveries in person. Sit on the terrace and enjoy dishes like *salade-Feu Follet* with smoked salmon and foie gras. There is an excellent wine list, with the accent on Provence (Domaine Tempier, Château Real Martin, and it's great value for money.

Les Muscadins (18 bd Courteline, 04.92.28.28.28, open daily, closed Nov, menus 185F-250F) is where Picasso fell in love with Mougins in 1936. A bit cash-strapped at the time, he covered his room and the outside walls with art, to pay for his board and lodging; the enraged owner made the still obscure artist erase them with whitewash the next day. In the kitchen, chef Noël Mantel, a Ducasse graduate, creates Italo-Provençal dishes like hare stuffed with polenta. Excellent service, by English-speaking staff, on the shady terrace underneath the spreading chestnut tree. The restaurant also has seven rooms (850F) and a luxurious 'Picasso' suite (1,800F). **La Terrasse à Mougins** (31 bd Courteline, 04.92.28.36.20, open daily, closed Nov, menus 130F-230F) is a new, happening restaurant at the entrance to the village with super-chic decor and panoramic views over the Alps, Cannes and the islands. Inside is a state-of-the-art rotisserie on which the freshest meat, fish and offal are grilled to order. Vegetarians will love the vegetable, pasta and rice dishes. Desserts such as the mousse zabaglione with lime are worth every calorie.

For some country calm, head for **Le Manoir de l'Etang** (bois de Fontmerle, allée du Manoir, 04.93.90.01.07, rates 680F-1,380F), a bastide hotel/restaurant with swimming pool in a peaceful bucolic setting.

Getting there

By car

3.5km north of Cannes on N85.

By bus

RCA (04.93.39.11.39) runs a half-hourly service from Cannes railway station's *gare routière* to Grasse. For Mougins, get off at the Val de Mougins stop and walk up the hill to the village.

Tourist information

Office du Tourisme

15 av Jean-Charles Mallet (04.93.75.87.67/fax 04.92.92.04.03). **Open** *mid-June to mid-Sept* 10am-1pm, 3-8.30pm daily; *mid-Sept to mid-June* 10am-5.30pm Tue-Sat.
Website: www.mougins-coteazur.org

A sprawling village perched on a hillside dotted with greenhouses, pink villas, orange trees and fragrant mimosa bushes, Vallauris overlooks the sandy beaches, ports and harbours of Golfe-Juan. It would have little but scenery to offer the visitor were it not for the artistic and marketing genius of Pablo Picasso. Holed up in Antibes castle in 1946, Picasso was introduced to the joys of clay by Georges and Suzanne Ramié, who owned the Madoura pottery workshop in Vallauris. Not only did the wily Spaniard discover a new passion, but he single-handedly rekindled the town's moribund ceramics industry. A mixed blessing, in view of some of the crimes committed in the name of *céramique artistique* in Vallauris' main drag, **avenue Georges Clemenceau**, which is a riot of kitsch water fountains and ceramic budgies. But there are a few serious workshops lurking behind the souvenir tat.

One of the best is the **Galerie Madoura** itself, now run by the son of the original owners. It still has the rights to reproducing the master's designs, over 630 of which are available in signed and numbered limited editions. Prices start at around 3,000F for the smallest model – but they have postcards, too. The other tutelary god of Vallauris is Jean Marais, the iconic film and stage actor whose boyish good looks were first launched by Jean Cocteau in his film *Orphée*. A writer and sculptor of some talent as well as an actor, Marais came to Vallauris in 1973, attracted by the quality of the local clay, and fell in love with the village.

But the biggest draw in Vallauris is hidden inside a tiny, medieval chapel in the courtyard of the village castle (once a priory, and one of the few Renaissance buildings to have survived on the Côte). By 1949 Picasso's passion for clay was waning; worried perhaps, that such a prestigious resident was about to desert them, the good burghers of Valauris gave him carte blanche to decorate the bare, deconsecrated chapel, which is now the **Musée National Picasso**. In such a confined space, this slapdash, speed-painted essay on the theme of war and peace can appear either trite or moving, depending on one's mood. The ticket also gives admission to the **Musée Magnelli/Musée de la Ceramique** on the second floor of the castle, with more Picasso ceramics. The final P-connection is the bronze statue of a man and sheep that stands beside the castle in the main **place de la Libération**. The artist presented the work to his adopted town in 1949, on the condition that children be allowed to climb all over it.

Vallauris: a sprawling hillside village made legendary by Picasso.

Vallauris' seaward extension, **Golfe-Juan**, has a fine kilometre-long sandy beach, sheltered from the worst of the mistral. This is where Napoléon landed on 1 March 1815, on his way back from Elba, at the beginning of the Hundred Days that would see his triumphant return to Paris, rapid popular disaffection, Waterloo and a second, permanent exile on St Helena. An almost certainly apocryphal story relates that one of the first people he met after setting foot on dry land was the Prince of Monaco, who told Napoléon that he was on his way back to reclaim his realm, now that the Revolution had blown over. 'Then, sir, we are in the same business', replied the short Corsican. Those who wish to retrace his route as far as Grenoble can do so on the **Route Napoléon** (*see page 258*), which begins in Golfe-Juan.

Musée National Picasso, Musée Magnelli, Musée de la Céramique

Château de Vallauris (04.93.64.16.05). **Open** *June-Sept* 10am-6.30pm Mon, Wed-Sun; *Oct-Mar* 10am-noon, 2-6pm Mon, Wed-Sun. **Admission** 15F.

Where to stay, eat & drink

In Vallauris, old-fashioned style (shorts are frowned on) is the hallmark of **La Gousse d'Ail** (11 av de Grasse, 04.93.64.10.71, closed Mon and mid-Nov to mid-Dec, average 120F), just behind the church, a classic but good-value restaurant with a 95F lunch menu. It's the bouillabaisse that's the draw at the excellent, upmarket **Bijou** (bd Guillaumont, 04.93.61.39.07, menus 110F-280F).

Good hotels are thin on the ground in Vallauris; it's better to stay down at Golfe-

Juan, for example at the **Auberge du Relais Impérial** (21 rue Louis Chabrier, 04.93.63.70.36, closed mid-Oct to mid-Nov, rates 250F-400F). Tucked away in a courtyard opposite the *vieux port*, this family-run hotel has seven rooms, all with air-conditioning, and an above-average restaurant (closed lunch Mon in July, Aug). For a pleasant drink in convivial surroundings, head for **Le Café Bleu** (port Camille Rayon, 04.93.63.48.02, closed Mon and Nov to mid-Dec), a lively meeting place with live jazz on Fridays between February and October.

Getting there

By car

A8 motorway, exit Antibes and follow signs to Vallauris on the D435. The N7/N98 runs through Golfe-Juan along the coast.

By bus/train

Trains stop off roughly every 30 minutes at the Golfe-Juan SNCF station, which is connected to Vallauris by regular STGA shuttle buses. Direct buses (about every 20 minutes) link Golfe-Juan with Cannes and Nice (RCA, info/sales 08.36.35.35.35, recorded timetable 08.36.67.68.69).

Tourist information

Vallauris

Office de Tourisme, sq du 8 Mai 1945 (04.93.63.82.58). **Open** *July-Aug* 9am-7pm daily; *Sept-June* 9am-noon, 2-6pm Mon-Sat.

Golfe-Juan

Office de Tourisme, 84 av de la Liberté (04.93.63.73.12). **Open** *July-Aug* 9am-7pm daily; *Sept-June* 9am-noon, 2-6pm Mon-Fri; 9am-noon Sat.

Antibes to Cagnes

The Riviera was invented in Antibes and Juan-les-Pins. Today ritzy hotels vie with soulless high-rises – but there are some charming medieval surprises inland.

Where Cannes is brash and glitzy, Antibes is elegant and discreet. St-Tropez may become Paris-by-the-sea in summer, but Antibes – with its beachside satellite of Juan-les-Pins, site of a high-profile summer jazz festival (*see box page 212*) – attracts the rich and famous all year round. The most exclusive of the private mansions nestle on the wooded promontory of Cap d'Antibes, which also boasts the Riviera's most expensive hotel, the Hôtel du Cap (*see box*).

The seaward extensions of the next towns east along the coast, Villeneuve-Loubet and Cagnes-sur-Mer, are more downmarket, and harbour some of the worst architectural crimes on the Riviera. But both have attractive medieval citadels, set well back from the coastal horrors.

Antibes Juan-les-Pins

The Greeks set up their trading post of Antipolis in the fifth century BC. Ligurian tribes fought hard to get their hands on the town over the following centuries, forcing Antibes' residents to turn to Rome for protection in 154 BC. Under Roman rule, their town became the region's

largest. But the fall of Rome left Antibes prey to attacks from every passing marauder, from Barbarians to Vandals, Visigoths, Burgundians, Ostrogoths and Franks. In the tenth century, Antibes fell into the hands of the Lords of Grasse before passing to the bishops of Antibes and, at the end of the fourteenth century, to the Grimaldi family of Monaco. It remained that way until 1608, when Henri IV of France purchased Antibes for his kingdom, turning it into the front line of defence against the Savoy kingdom across the bay in Nice.

The tourist invasion of Antibes and the rocky, pine-forest clad headland of Cap d'Antibes got under way in the early years of the twentieth century, when artists, writers and alcohol-fuelled socialites such as F Scott and Zelda Fitzgerald hightailed it down to what was the Riviera's first chic society resort. Antibes had been 'discovered' some years before by – among others – Queen Victoria's son the Duke of Albany. To host the initial trickle of Europe's titled and wealthy who came seeking winter sunshine, a local entrepreneur had opened the Grand Hôtel du

Hôtel du Cap Eden-Roc

Of all the hotels on the French Riviera, the Hôtel du Cap Eden-Roc is probably the most exclusive, certainly the most expensive. Originally built in 1863, the main building – gleaming white in the bourgeois style – nestles a little way back from the coast in 25 acres of woodland.

Until the 1920s, many Riviera hotels shut down in July and August. But a bad winter season persuaded Antoine Sella, Italian owner of the Hôtel du Cap, to keep his doors open through the summer of 1923. American society hosts Gerald and Sara Murphy came down from Paris, were charmed, and told all their friends. The summer season was born, together with the cult of the suntan. The Murphys were immortalised as Dick and Nicole Diver in F Scott Fitzgerald's *Tender is the Night*, in which the Hôtel du Cap was recast as the Hôtel des Etrangers.

A super-luxurious annexe, the Eden Roc pavilion, perched on the rocks at the water's edge, was added in 1914. Staying at the Hôtel du Cap Eden Roc involves a certain effort, even if you do have the money – it's pretentious enough not to accept credit cards, and can be annoyingly overrun by celebrities and their bodyguards. On the other hand, the hotel does its best to live up to the Eden tag, with impeccable service, classically refined decor and those fabulous views – across to the Iles des Lérins from the private park.

Hôtel du Cap Eden-Roc
bd Kennedy, Cap d'Antibes
(04.93.61.39.01/fax 04.93.67.76.04).
Closed Nov-Mar. **Rates** single 1,600F-2,500F, double 2,500F-3,000F, suite 4,850F-6,550F. **No credit cards**.

Antibes' rocky seafront.

Cap in 1870. But it was Coco Chanel and US tycoon Frank Jay Gould who turned Antibes and its glitzy satellite beach resort, Juan-les-Pins, into a year-round playground.

The conurbation of **Antibes Juan-les-Pins** is a mainly unappealing, sprawling mass wedged between the sea and the A8 autoroute. The old quarters are best approached from the **Fort Carré**, which stands on the point separating the St-Roch inlet from Baie des Anges. The original fort was constructed in the sixteenth century to counter the Savoy threat to the east; in the seventeenth century, the architect Vauban gave it its eight-pointed star shape. Just to the south of the fort, the marina of **Port Vauban** is Europe's largest yacht harbour, harbouring some of Europe's largest pleasure craft and plenty of glitzy boutiques. South of the marina, along the city's ramparts, is the **Musée d'Histoire et d'Archéologie**, containing reminders of the town's multi-faceted past, including Greek and Etruscan amphorae. Also squeezed within the ramparts is the **Eglise de l'Immaculée-Conception**, Antibes' former cathedral, built on the site of a Roman temple to Diana. Only a fraction of the original Romanesque church remains, hidden behind a resolutely seventeenth-century exterior; in the south transept is an altarpiece (1515) by Louis Bréa.

The **Château Grimaldi** next door was built on the site of a Roman fort, and its layout remains basically Roman, despite rebuilding in the sixteenth century, when it was home to the Grimaldi family. In 1946, when Picasso rented a cold, damp room on the second floor, it belonged to a certain Romuald Dor, and already contained a small archaeological collection. Dor had ulterior motives in his offer of such prime Riviera studio space; the works Picasso left behind in lieu of rent enabled him to upgrade his lacklustre collection and re-baptise it the **Musée Picasso**. This was a fertile period for the bald Spaniard with the stripy vest; his Mediterranean exuberance is enhanced here by the eclectic range of media. As proper artists' materials were almost impossible to get hold of in 1946, Picasso used ships' paint slapped on to some odd-looking bits of wood, and discovered the joys of pottery (*see page 208* **Vallauris**). Just inland from the castle, the **Cours Masséna**, the Greek town's main drag, plays host to one of the region's liveliest and best-supplied produce markets, open every morning (except Monday in winter).

Four kilometres east of Antibes on the RN7 is **Marineland**, an outdoor marine park and entertainment complex staging shows with performing whales, dolphins and sealions. Other attractions include Aquasplash (with giant waterslides), a Provençal-style farm, a butterfly farm and the ubiquitous crazy golf.

Heading south out of Antibes, the scenery changes dramatically from built-up citadel to leafy lap of luxury. The peninsula of **Cap d'Antibes** is a playground for the very, very wealthy, and it makes no bones about it. To appreciate the prosperity to the full, rent a bike from one of the many outlets along boulevard Wilson and take in the views as you wend your way up to **Parc Thuret**, a botanical testing site established in 1856 with the aim of introducing more varied flora to the Riviera. If that sounds like too much exertion, take advantage of the Cap's surprisingly long stretches of public beach, Plage de la Salis and Plage de la Garoupe. Between the two, and a fair hike uphill, the **Sanctuaire de la Garoupe** has a great collection of unlikely ex-votos, and a superb view from outside. At the southern tip of the peninsula, the **Musée Naval et Napoléonien** has model ships and charts and mementoes of the great man, who parked his mother in Antibes on one occasion. Next to the museum is another historical landmark where most people would opt to park themselves, rather than their mothers: the **Hôtel du Cap** (*see box page 211*).

To the west of the peninsula, **Juan-les-Pins** has no pretensions to history: a sandy, forested,

For ten days towards the end of July each year, Juan-les-Pins becomes the centre of world jazz – a tradition that now dates back 40 years. Although the first official Jazz à Juan festival wasn't held until 1960, Juan has had jazz in its bloodstream since the 1920s, when the Fitzgeralds and other well-heeled, well-oiled Americans blew into town. All the jazz greats have passed through Juan-les-Pins at one time or another: Sidney Bechet, Ray Charles, Miles Davis, Ella Fitzgerald, Louis Armstrong, Count Basie, Dizzy Gillespie... The festival, which takes place under the pine trees of the Pinède Gould in the centre of town, still attracts the big names, but gives space to up-and-coming musicians, too, and has resisted the neighbouring Nice Jazz Festival's tendency to define jazz as any kind of music that isn't classical.

For further information, call 04.92.90.53.00 or check the tourist office's website: www.antibes-juanlespins.com.

The Riviera

Yacht rivalry at Antibes.

deserted headland until the 1920s, it was
conceived as, and still is, a mecca for the
Riviera's hedonists. The town centre is a
seething mass of boutiques and restaurants –
but if it seems frantic during the day, you
should see it at night: Juan-les-Pins isn't in the
habit of wasting good partying time on sleep.
The beach – one of the most beautiful in the
South – has public and private sections; on the
latter, a patch of sand with sunbed will set you
back around 60F a day (or 300F on the Hôtel du
Cap's private strip). If playing at sardines on the
strand is not your thing, there are watersports
galore; it was in Juan-les-Pins, they say, that
water-skiing was invented, in the 1930s. And if
sweating in nightclubs doesn't grab you, come
for the summer jazz festival (*see box*).

Eglise de l'Immaculée-Conception
rue de la Paroisse, Antibes (04.93.34.06.29). **Open**
8am-noon, 3-6.30pm daily.

Fort Carré
rte du Bord de Mer, RN 98 (06.14.89.17.45). **Open**
mid-June to Sept 10am-7pm Tue-Sun; *mid-Sept to*
Nov 10am-4.30pm Tue-Sun; *Nov-June* 10am-4pm
Wed, Sat, Sun and public holidays. **Guided tours**
every half hour 10.15am-3.15pm. **Admission** 30F,
free under-17s.

Marineland
4km east of Antibes on RN7 (04.93.33.49.49). **Open**
July, Aug 10am-midnight daily; *Sept-June* 10am-4pm
daily. **Admission** (combined ticket) 124F, 82F
children; tickets to individual elements also available.
Credit MC, V.
Crazy Golf is open on Wednesdays, Saturdays,
Sundays and school and bank holidays only.

Musée d'Histoire et d'Archéologie
Bastion St-André, Antibes (04.92.90.54.35). **Open**
Dec-Oct 10am-noon, 2-6pm Tue-Sun. Closed Nov.
Admission 20F, free under-16s.

Musée Picasso
Château Grimaldi, pl Mariejol, Antibes
(04.92.90.54.20). **Open** *June-Sept* 10am-6pm Tue-
Sun; *Oct-May* 10am-noon, 2-6pm Tue-Sun.
Admission 30F, free under-16s.

Musée Naval et Napoléonien
av Kennedy (04.93.61.45.32). **Open** *Nov-Sept*
9.30am-noon, 2.15-6pm Mon-Fri; 9.30am-noon Sat.
Closed Oct. **Admission** 20F, free under-16s.

Parc Thuret
62 bd du Cap, Cap d'Antibes (04.93.67.88.00).
Open *May-Sept* 8am-6pm Mon-Fri; *Oct-Apr* 8.30am-
5.30pm Mon-Fri. **Admission** free.

Where to eat

In Antibes, up on the ramparts, **Les Vieux
Murs** (promenade Amiral de Grasse,
04.93.34.06.73, closed dinner Sun, all Mon in
winter, menus 200F-300F) serves mod-
Provençal cooking. **L'Eléphant Bleu** (28 bd
d'Aguillon, 04.93.34.28.80, menus 75F-215F)
serves up good Thai and Vietnamese in one of
Antibes' busier quarters, while **Le Brulot** (3
rue Frédéric Isnard, 04.93.34.17.76, closed lunch
Mon-Wed & Sun from end-Aug to May, closed
three weeks Aug, menus 60F-200F) specialises
in dramatic grills. For fish to die for, including a
knockout bouillabaisse, check out **Bacon** (*see
page 51*), and for the full-on local experience,
try **La Taverne du Safranier** (*page 53*).
In Juan-les-Pins, the lively **La Bodega** (av
Docteur Dautheville, 04.93.61.07.52, closed Wed,
menu 85F) stays open until all hours in summer
to feed revellers from local nightlife haunts, while
the **Bijou Plage** (bd Guillaumont, 04.93.61.39.07,
menus 110F-280F) serves reliable seafood on the
seafront. **La Terrasse** (*see page 54*) is a far
more formal, gourmet option.

Bars & nightlife

If Juan-les-Pins' annual jazz festival (*see box*)
earns the town most international attention,
most local punters will settle for music of any
kind, as long as it's loud and danceable. **Le J's**
(av Georges Gallice, 04.93.67.22.74, open daily
mid-June to Aug, open Fri & Sat Sept-mid June,
admission 100F incl one drink) and **Le Duc** (2
av Guy de Maupassant, 04.93.67.78.87, open Fri
& Sat Sept-June, daily July & Aug, admission
100F) are favourites.
Though most of the action is in Juan-les-Pins,
La Siesta (rte du Bord de Mer, 04.93.33.31.31,
admission free), just east of Antibes, is a
restaurant, bar, casino and nightclub (note the
free admission is balanced out by costly drinks).

Outdoor pursuits

Parascending
Plage du Garden Beach, Juan-les-Pins (04.90.20.56.93).
Open June-Sept. **Credit** AmEx, DC, MC, V.
A 15-minute session costs 350F, parachute included.

The Riviera

Tennis

*Tennis Municipal, av Jules Grec, Antibes
(04.93.33.24.49).* **Courts** 70F for two people
per hour.

Waterskiing

*Cap d'Antibes Ski Nautique, Plage de la Baie Dorée,
Cap d'Antibes (04.93.67.30.67).* **Open** June-Aug.
The cost is 140F per person per ten minutes, all
equipment included.

Where to stay

If the Hôtel du Cap Eden-Roc is too much of a
challenge to your credit limit, don't despair:
there are alternatives.

Though expensive, the **Hôtel Le Passy**
(15 av Louis Gallet, Juan-les-Pins,
04.93.61.11.09, closed Jan-Mar, rates 300F-
600F approx) is in a great location, while the
less expensive **Hôtel Juan Beach** (5 rue de
l'Oratoire, Juan-les-Pins, 04.93.61.02.89, closed
Nov-Mar, rates 190F-430F approx) is in a
beautiful position 15 minutes' walk out of
town. The **Hôtel Castel Mistral** (43 rue
Bricka, Juan-les-Pins, 04.93.61.21.04, closed
mid-Oct to mid-Mar approx, rates 220F-295F)
is a charmingly dilapidated place, and handy
for the beaches. The staff of the **Auberge
Provençale** (61 pl Nationale, Antibes,
04.93.34.13.24, rates 250F-550F) are friendly
enough to make up for the hotel's lack of
finesse. And budget travellers can find a bed
just a stone's throw from the beach at the
Relais International de la Jeunesse (60
bd de la Garoupe, Cap d'Antibes,
04.93.61.34.40, closed Oct-Easter, rate 170F).

Getting there & around

By car

Leave the A8 at the Antibes exit (no.44).

By bus

The local operator is STGA (04.93.34.37.60). Bus
no.200 to Nice and Cannes every 20min.

By train

Antibes' Gare SNCF is on the main south coast route,
served both by high-speed TGV trains from Paris
and Lyon and more frequent local trains, which also
stop at Juan-les-Pins.

Bike hire

Access FRL *43 bd Wilson, Antibes
(04.93.67.62.75).* **Open** 9am-noon, 2.30-6pm
Mon-Sat. **Rates** one day 70F, three days 210F,
one week 320F.

Holiday Bikes *122 bd Wilson, Antibes
(04.93.61.51.51).* **Open** *mid-Mar to mid-Nov* 9am-
6pm Mon-Sat. Closed mid-Nov to mid-Mar. **Rates**
one day 80F.

Tourist information

Antibes

11 pl de Gaulle (04.92.90.53.00/fax 04.92.90.53.01).
Open 9am-12.30pm, 2-6.30pm daily. Closed Sun from
Oct-Mar.

Juan-les-Pins

51 bd Guillaumont (04.92.90.53.05). **Open** 9am-
noon, 2-6pm daily. Closed Sun from Oct-Mar.

Villeneuve-Loubet & Cagnes

The coast road between Antibes and Nice
passes through a sprawl of increasingly
downmarket resorts. The interest lies inland, in
the medieval centres of Villeneuve-Loubet and
Cagnes – towns that also give their names to
their beachside offshoots.

Villeneuve-Loubet Plage stretches for three
kilometres around the Marina Baie des Anges, a
huge pyramid-shaped apartment complex,
arguably the low-water mark of 1970s Riviera
architecture. Ignore it if you can, and head
instead across the A8 to the delightful town of
Villeneuve-Loubet proper, where the twelfth-
century castle in which François I signed a
decidedly shaky peace treaty with Charles V in
1538 is intact, though not open to the public.

The **Musée de l'Art Culinaire** celebrates
one of Villeneuve's most famous sons, Auguste
Escoffier, who was taken under the wing of
Britain's King Edward VII after transforming
cooking from a trade to an art. Escoffier later
became head chef of the Savoy in London. A
photograph of opera star Nellie Melba – after
whom the peachy sundae was named – just
about sums up the modest charms of this
collection, whose highlights are its artistic
sculptures in sugar and chocolate.

Obscured by the traffic system that thunders
through the sprawl of suburbs south-west of
Nice, **Cagnes** is in fact three separate entities:
unalluring Cros-de-Cagnes on the seafront,
misleadingly named Cagnes-sur-Mer, which is
in fact inland, and medieval Haut-de-Cagnes,
perched on high and home to the Unesco-
sponsored Festival International de la Peinture
(International Painting Festival) each summer.

Cros-de-Cagnes was once a fishing village
but today offers little more than crowded
beaches, oversubscribed watersports facilities,
and a string of restaurants and hotels of
varying qualities along the beachfront.

On the other side of the busy A8 lies
Cagnes-sur-Mer, best known for Auguste
Renoir's estate, **Les Collettes**. The artist had
the house built in 1908 after his doctor
prescribed a drier, warmer seaside climate for
his rheumatoid arthritis. Renoir spent the last

years of his life here, working right up until his death in 1919, and battling against the growing paralysis in his hands. The house is preserved pretty much as the artist left it, and his olive tree-filled garden still remains. There's also a collection of paintings of the artist by his friends, as well as a few of the works he made here.

Rising above its noisy, polluted neighbours is **Haut-de-Cagnes**, a favourite spot for contemporary artists of all persuasions, drawn not only by the annual arts festival but by the **Musée Mediterranéen d'Art Moderne** and the **Donation Suzy Solidor**, both of which are housed (along with the Musée de l'Olivier, a tribute to that local mainstay, the olive tree) in the dramatic fourteenth-century Château Grimaldi. The 40 portraits from the collection of popular chanteuse Suzy Solidor include works by Cocteau, Dufy, Friesz and many others, many of whom also feature in the modern art museum. The Renaissance interior of the chateau is worth a look in itself.

Château-Musée Grimaldi
4 pl Grimaldi, Cagnes-sur-Mer (04.93.20.85.57).
Open *May-Sept* 10am-noon, 2-6pm Mon, Wed-Sun; *Oct-Apr* 10am-noon, 2-5pm Mon, Wed-Sun. **Admission** 20F, children 10F.

Les Collettes
av des Collettes (04.93.20.61.07). **Open** *May-Sept* 10am-noon, 2-6pm Wed-Mon; *Oct-Apr* 10am-noon, 2-5pm Wed-Mon. Closed Nov **Admission** 20F, children 10F, free under-5s.

Musée de l'Art Culinaire
3 rue Escoffier, Villeneuve-Loubet (04.93.20.80.51).
Open *Apr-Sept* 2-7pm Tue-Sun; *Oct-Mar* 2-6pm Tue-Sun. **Admission** 25F, 15F children.

Where to stay, eat & drink

The area's most luxurious accommodation option is **Le Cagnard** (rue Sous-Barri, 04.93.20.73.21, rates 900F-2,600F) in Haut-de-Cagnes. Its many modern comforts have failed to disturb the twelfth-century magic of the building, and the hotel has spectacular views, and an excellent restaurant (closed Nov to mid-Dec), with menus starting at 330F. **Le Grimaldi** (6 pl du Château Haut-de-Cagnes, 04.93.20.60.24, rates 200F-300F) is a cheaper option, in Haut-de-Cagnes. Down the hill in Cros-de-Cagnes, the recently refitted **Hôtel Beaurivage** (39 bd de la Plage, 04.93.20.16.09,

Go all glassy-eyed at the **Verrerie de Biot**. *See page 217.*

The **Musée National Fernand Léger** at Biot.

closed Nov, rates 300F-450F) has rooms with balcony and sea view.

Haut-de-Cagnes' leading eating place, after Le Cagnard, is the **Restaurant des Peintres** (71 montée de la Bourgade, 04.93.20.83.08, closed dinner Sun and all Mon from Nov-June, menus 148F-340F), offering simple Provençal elegance with views over Cap d'Antibes. But **Entre Cour et Jardin**, with its cosy vaulted cellar (102 montée de la Bourgade, 04.93.20.72.27, closed Mon, menus 140F-250F) is a reliable alternative, and the bistro fare of **La Table d'Yves** (*see page 53*) has many admirers. Good seafood can be found at the port in Cros-de-Cagnes at **La Bourride** (04.93.31.07.75, closed dinner Sun, all Wed, menus 198F-380F).

Getting there

By car
Cagnes: leave the A8 at exit no.48.
Villeneuve: leave the A8 at exit no.47.

By bus
Buses run between Cagnes and Nice (RCA; 04.93.85.61.81), Grasse (SOMA; 04.93.62.12.22) and Vence (SAP; 04.93.58.37.60). The Cagnes-Grasse bus runs once an hour, the others run every 40-45min.
Villeneuve-Loubet is served by the RCA no.200 Nice-Cannes bus (*see above*). It also stops at Villeneuve-Loubet-Plage.

By train
Cagnes: Cagnes-sur-Mer station is on the local south coast line; shuttle buses for Haut-de-Cagnes meet every train. Cros-de-Cagnes has its own station.
Villeneuve: local trains stop at Villeneuve-Loubet-Plage, from where a shuttle bus leaves regularly for the old town.

Tourist information

Cagnes-sur-Mer
6 bd Maréchal Juin (04.93.20.61.64/fax 04.93.20.52.63). **Open** *July, Aug* 9am-1pm, 3-7.30pm Mon-Sat; *Sept-June* 8.30am-12.15pm, 2-6pm Mon-Sat; 9am-1pm, 3-7pm Sun.

Villeneuve-Loubet
pl de l'Hôtel de Ville (04.93.20.20.09/fax 04.93.20.16.49). **Open** *July-Aug* 9am-noon, 2-7pm daily; *Sept-June* 9am-noon, 2-6pm Mon-Sat.

Villeneuve-Loubet-Plage
15 av de la Mer (04.93.20.49.14/fax 04.93.20 40.23). **Open** *July-Aug* 9am-7pm daily; *Sept-June* 9am-noon, 1.30-5.30pm Mon-Sat.

Biot

Once, long ago, a clever PR company was sent into the hinterland of the Côte d'Azur to give its villages instant brand recognition. That, at least, is how it sometimes appears. Grasse is perfume, St-Paul-de-Vence is art, Vallauris is pottery (and Picasso), and Biot (pronounced

Bee-ot) is glass (and Léger). But it was not always so. In fact, until as late as the 1950s, the name of this picturesque old village, perched on a volcanic outcrop above the River Brague, was linked to pottery. One of Fernand Léger's protégés set up a ceramic workshop in Biot dedicated to reproducing the master's designs, and Léger himself spent his last few years here.

Fifteen days before he died, in 1956, the artist acquired a piece of land in Biot, intending to build a house. His widow, Nadia, used the site to build a fitting tribute to her husband's long and varied career, the **Musée National Fernand Léger**. The low-slung building – its façade dominated by a huge ceramic mosaic commissioned for Hanover Stadium – is set back from the road in undulating sculpture gardens. It traces the work of this restless, politically committed artist from his first Impressionist stirrings in 1905, through the boldly coloured, strongly outlined 'machine art' canvases of the 1920s and 1930s to his later work in other media, including murals, stained glass, ceramic and tapestries. An annual exhibition links Léger to an artist or designer with whom he worked.

Glass came to Biot only at the end of the 1950s, when the **Verrerie de Biot** fired up its furnaces. Half a working glass factory and half a gallery-cum-showroom, the Verrerie lies just off the main D4 road, below the town walls. One can watch the unique Biot 'bubble glassware' (*verre bullé*) being blown, and there are plenty of chances to buy the end result both here and in the village itself, where **rue St-Sébastien**, the main street, is lined with glass workshops. Also here – at No.9 – is the **Musée d'Histoire et de Céramique Biotoises**, with a patchy but charming collection of local costumes and artefacts, including the domestic ceramics (jars, cisterns) that the town was once renowned for. Past the boutiques and bars is the pretty **place des Arcades**, surrounded by Italianate loggias – a home-from-home touch brought by Genoese settlers who moved in to repopulate Biot after the Black Death. The village church, which overlooks the square, has two good altarpieces by those stalwarts of fifteenth-century Niçois religious art, Ludovico Bréa and Giovanni Canavesio. Classical concerts and recitals are held in the square on summer evenings.

Musée d'Histoire et de Céramique Biotoises

9 rue St-Sébastien (04.93.65.54.54). **Open** *July-Sept* 10am-6pm Wed-Sun; *Oct-June* 2-6pm Wed-Sun. Closed three weeks Nov. **Admission** 15F.

Musée National Fernand Léger

chemin de Val de Pome (04.92.91.50.30). **Open** *Sept-June* 10am-12.30pm, 2-5.30pm Mon, Wed-Sun; *July, Aug* 11am-6pm Mon, Wed-Sun. **Admission** 30F.

Verrerie de Biot

chemin des Combes (04.93.65.03.00). **Open** *July, Aug* 9am-8pm Mon-Fri; 10am-1pm, 3-6.30pm Sat, Sun; *Sept-June* 9am-6pm Mon-Fri, 10am-1pm, 3-6pm Sat, Sun. **Admission** free. **Guided tours** 20F. **No credit cards.**

Where to stay & eat

The hotel of choice is the delightful **Hôtel des Arcades** (16 pl des Arcades, 04.93.65.01.04, closed mid-Nov to mid-Dec, rates 280F-450F). The decor of this fifteenth-century mansion mixes ancient (huge fireplaces, four-poster beds) and modern: the owner is a collector, and the gallery/restaurant (a good, reasonably priced alternative to the two more serious eating options given below) displays works by artists such as Vasarely, Léger and Folon, among others. At the other end of the price scale is the campsite **Des Oliviers** (chemin des Hautes Vignasses, 04.93.65.02.79).

Brigitte Guignery is chef and owner of the Michelin-starred **Auberge du Jarrier** (*see page 51*), a relaxed restaurant serving Mediterranean dishes, located at the end of a nondescript, laundry-festooned passageway in a converted jar factory. Also in a converted factory – a sixteenth-century pottery factory, natch – is **Les Terraillers** (*see page 54*). With a vine-draped terrace and flower-adorned dining room, it wins on aesthetics, and competes strongly on food too, with showpiece dishes including a whole sea bass presented at the table in a baked salt crust, then returned to the kitchen to be boned, and cold lobster soup, and a strong wine list.

Getting there

By car

Take the A8 motorway to Antibes (exit no.44), then follow the signs to Biot; heading east on N7 coast road, turn left on to D4 Biot-Valbonne road 3km after Antibes.

By train/bus

Biot has a little railway station near the seafront, on the Nice-Cannes line, or there is a shuttle bus running every hour from Antibes railway station (STGA no.10A).

Tourist information

Office du Tourisme

pl de la Chapelle (04.93.65.78.00/fax 04.93.65.78.04). **Open** *July, Aug* 10am-noon, 2.30-7pm Mon-Fri, 2.30-7pm Sat, Sun; *Sept-June* 9am-noon, 2-6pm Mon-Fri; 2-6pm Sat, Sun. *Website: www.biot.ed.fr/biot*

The Riviera

Nice

Resilient, beautiful Nice still does things its own way despite the glamorous image forced upon it.

Nice: less glamorous, but the beauty remains.

Some 400,000 years ago, prehistoric man set up elaborate camp at the site known as Terra Amata at the foot of Mont Boron, not far from where Sir Elton John's hilltop mansion now sprawls. In the fourth century BC, Phocaean Greeks from Marseille sailed into the harbour and founded a trading post around another prominent hill – now the Colline du Château – and named their city Nikea (derived from Nike, goddess of victory).

The Romans arrived in 100 BC and built an entire, no-expense-spared city (replete with thermal spa, shops and sports facilities, including a huge stone arena) on a third hill that they called Cemenelum (today's Cimiez). Cimiez's prime location made it an obvious target in the Dark Ages for invading Saracens and Barbarians, who left it in ruins; it was to take many centuries – and a bunch of wintering Brits – before it regained its exclusive status.

By the fourteenth century, the once-Greek part of the city – including the port – was thriving again, and the population was determined to stay that way. After sizing up the local balance of power, they opted to shun Louis d'Anjou and ally themselves with the Counts of Savoy, thus opening up huge new Italian markets for their commerce. The Savoys fortified this key outpost against France. An artistic school flourished around Louis Bréa in the late fifteenth and early sixteenth centuries. By the seventeenth century, the city was beginning to spread beyond its walls.

But so rich a prize was Nice that France laid hands on it several times during the seventeenth and eighteenth centuries; on one occasion Louis XIV took advantage of temporary control to have the medieval fortifications blown up. The city finally passed to France under the Treaty of Turin in 1860, which was ratified later in a plebiscite. (The final result of some 25,000 pro-French to 160 anti-French votes had a strong smell of election-rigging about it.)

Over a century before that, however, this sunny and conveniently non-French spot had been discovered by British travellers seeking winter warmth. So fond were they of the place that they raised a subscription in 1822 for the building of a seafront esplanade, still called the promenade des Anglais in their honour. By the time Queen Victoria visited later that century, the Cimiez district, filled with stately villas, was the place to stay. The queen pitched camp in the Régina palace-hotel, as did Henri Matisse in the 1940s. The Musée Matisse now stands just across the road.

Now the fifth-largest city in France, twentieth-century Nice was beset by high crime levels and tainted (not to mention financially damaged) by the shenanigans of its long-time mayor, Jacques Médecin (*see page 16*).

Nice's golden era of seaside palaces, casinos, red Bugattis and unmitigated glamour has receded. Some essential things, however, really haven't changed: city residents, never tired of the beauty of the place, get up early to buy baskets of vine tomatoes, perfect peaches and wild mushrooms at the daily market. On Sundays, families roam the promenade des Anglais en masse on bicycles or Rollerblades or

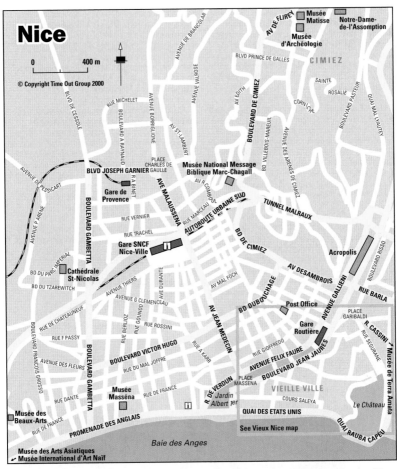

Nice

0   400 m

© Copyright Time Out Group 2000

Musée Matisse   Notre-Dame-de-l'Assomption

Musée d'Archéologie

AV DE FLIREY

BLVD PRINCE DE GALLES   CIMIEZ

SAINTE ROSALIE

AVENUE DE BRANCOLAR

AVENUE VALROSE

RUE MICHELET

AVENUE BORRIGLIONE

BOULEVARD A RAYNAUD

BLVD DE CESSOLE

BOULEVARD DE CIMIEZ

AV EDITH

CORNICHE

BOULEVARD PASTEUR

QUAI MAL LAUTEY

AV ST LAMBERT

AVENUE DES ARÈNES DE CIMIEZ

BD VILLEBOIS-MAREUIL

PLACE CHARLES DE GAULLE

BLVD JOSEPH GARNIER

R A BINET

Musée National Message Biblique Marc-Chagall

AV R COMBOUL

Gare de Provence

AVE MALAUSSENA

AV MARCEAU

AUTOROUTE URBAINE SUD

TUNNEL MALRAUX

RUE VERNIER

RUE TRACHEL

RUE MARCEAU

BD DE CIMIEZ

Acropolis

BOULEVARD RISSO

AVENUE DU PESSICART

AVENUE P ARÈNE

BOULEVARD GAMBETTA

Gare SNCF Nice-Ville

Cathédrale St-Nicolas

BD DU PARC IMPERIAL

BD DU TZAREWITCH

AVENUE THIERS

AVENUE G CLEMENCEAU

AV DURANTE

AV MAL FOCH

AV DESAMBROIS

AVENUE GALLIENI

RUE BARLA

RUE DE CHATEAUNEUF

RUE F PASSY

RUE BERLIOZ

RUE GOUNOD

RUE ROSSINI

BD DUBOUCHAGE

Post Office

PLACE GARIBALDI

R CASSINI

RUE SEGURANE

BOULEVARD FRANÇOIS GROSSO

AVENUE DES FLEURS

BOULEVARD GAMBETTA

BOULEVARD VICTOR HUGO

RUE DU MAL JOFFRE

AV JEAN MEDECIN

RUE A KARR

RUE GIOFFREDO

Gare Routière

AVENUE FELIX FAURE

BOULEVARD JEAN JAURÈS

Musée de Terra Amata

RUE DANTE

Musée Masséna

RUE DE FRANCE

R. DE VERDUN

PLACE MASSENA

Jardin Albert 1er

COURS SALEYA

VIEILLE VILLE

Le Château

Musée des Beaux-Arts

RUE DE FRANCE

PROMENADE DES ANGLAIS

QUAI DES ETATS UNIS

See Vieux Nice map

QUAI RAUBA CAPEU

Baie des Anges

Musée des Arts Asiatiques
Musée International d'Art Naïf

pushing strollers. Unlike 20 years ago, there's a surge of cultural attractions and a youthful nightlife: if you're up until dawn, check out the early-opening bars by the market, where you'll find sun-wizened farmers about to set up their wares quietly sipping espresso beside bleary-eyed twentysomething clubbers.

Sightseeing

Nice breaks down neatly into old and new parts of town, making it easy to get your bearings. Vieux Nice lies at the foot of the **Colline du Château**, a grassy park with an impressive waterfall but no chateau: this was destroyed in the eighteenth century. If you don't fancy the long slog up to the magnificent view from the

top, interpreted by a radial map, there's a lift (open 8am-6pm daily) by the Tour Bellanda, home of the **Musée Naval**, on the quai des Etats-Unis. East of the Colline du Château, the **Parc Forestier le Mont Boron** is an idyllic spot for a picnic or a stroll, with winding paths through acres of Aleppo pines and breathtaking views of the coast. Between the two hills, the **Musée Terra Amata** documents the area's earliest settlement.

At the western foot of the Château, the *vieille ville* is Nice's most colourful neighbourhood – tiny serpentine alleys with countless shops, galleries and restaurants nestling among the stacked medieval buildings with laundry hanging outside the windows like pastel banners. Once shunned as crime-plagued and poverty-stricken, it is fast becoming the city's trendiest district. The main square, **place Rosetti**, is home to two places of pilgrimage: the **Cathédrale de Ste-Réparate**, Nice's patron saint, and the **Fennocchio** ice-cream parlour (*see page 229*). Another favourite with the locals is the nearby baroque **Chapelle de l'Annonciation**. A few blocks north-east, through bustling streets of little shops, the **Palais Lascaris** is a fascinating museum in a lavishly decorated seventeenth-century home.

But the heart of the *vieille ville* lies to the south, along the **cours Saleya**, where stalls piled high with lush fruit and vegetables, olives and candied fruit operate from dawn to lunch, Tuesday to Sunday, and cut flowers perfume the air all day. On Monday, there are antiques, the lacy-lineny contents of grandma's trunk, junk and second-hand clothes. All around, shoppers and onlookers crowd bars and eateries. On the neighbouring **place du Palais de Justice**, there's a book and print market on Saturdays. Towards the seafront, the **Opéra** is grandly *belle époque*. Just east of the *vieille ville* is the attractive old port, lined with tall, colour-washed houses and plenty of simple cafés where you can snack on a *pan-bagnat* and watch the comings and goings of ferries to Corsica.

Dividing the old town from the nineteenth-century new town is the River Paillon, though you'd never know it, as it is covered over for most of its length. **Place Masséna** and the **Jardins Albert I**, which run down the river's course to the promenade des Anglais, form the centrepiece of the area. Among the twentieth-century buildings in variable taste to the north of place Masséna is the striking **Musée d'Art Moderne et d'Art Contemporain** (MAMAC).

On the seafront west of the rivermouth, the **promenade des Anglais** is nineteenth-century Nice's most famous landmark; getting safely across to it through manic traffic can be a challenge, and the palm trees ain't what they used to be, but the grandiose *belle époque* and art deco palaces that line it – such as the Hôtel Negresco (*see page 232*) and the Musée Masséna – are a joy. A couple of blocks back from the western end, the **Musée des Beaux-Arts**, in a villa built in the 1880s, has a delightful collection. A kilometre further on is the **Musée International d'Art Naïf Anatole Jakovsky**, while right before the airport, the **Parc Floral Phoenix** has the **Musée des Arts Asiatiques** nestling among its thousands of botanical species and giant hothouse.

The beach itself, though long, is not particularly spectacular: pebbly, and not sparklingly clean (though it's OK to swim).

The nineteenth-century **promenade des Anglais**, now popular with Rollerbladers and cyclists.

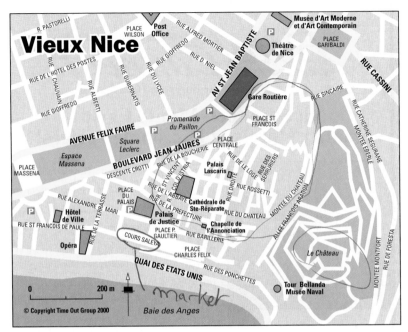

Parts of it are carved up by private beach concessions, some run by hotels for their guests and some open to paying customers. One of the nicest of the latter is **Castel Plage** (admission 60F), across the street from the *vieille ville*. It's got comfy mattresses, bronzed pretty people and some artsy local celebs playing chess over coffee in a friendly, relaxed ambience.

Slicing north-west through the new town from place Masséna, avenue Jean Médicin is Nice's prime shopping street, and home to every chain store imaginable. At its northern end is the main train station, to the west of which, across boulevard Gambetta, stands the **Cathédrale St-Nicolas**, the Russian church that, thanks to its flow of visiting Russians, is the Riviera's second most-visited attraction after Monaco's Musée Océanographique.

To the north of the centre, Cimiez is Nice's best-heeled suburb, an affluent hillside swathed in large villas. Just off the lower reaches of the boulevard de Cimiez is the **Musée National Message Biblique Marc-Chagall**. At the top of the hill, the **Musée Matisse** stands behind the ruins of the Roman amphitheatre and the **Musée d'Archéologie**, which charts Nice's history from prehistoric times. The nearby church of **Notre-Dame-de-l'Assomption** and its sixteenth-century

Franciscan monastery are flanked by a glorious rose-perfumed garden, with a great view over the city.

Churches

Cathédrale St-Nicolas (Eglise Russe)

bd du Tzarewich (04.93.96.88.02). **Open** *June-Sept* 9.30am-noon, 2.30-6pm daily; *Oct-May* 9.30am-noon, 2.30-5pm daily. **Admission** 15F, free under-12s.

The six brilliantly coloured onion-domed cupolas of Nice's turn-of-the-century Russian Orthodox cathedral are a startlingly surreal sight against the flat red-tile rooftops of the central western suburbs. If you visit only one church, go and see this beautiful pink and grey marble oddity, filled with intricate wood carving, icons and frescos, and a marvellous iconostasis.

Cathédrale de Ste-Réparate

pl Rossetti (04.93.62.34.40). **Open** 7.30am-noon, 2-6pm daily.

Located on Vieux Nice's most charming square, this seventeenth-century church, replete with stucco, marble and a colourfully tiled dome, is named after a 15-year-old virgin martyred in the Holy Land, who was towed here in a flowery boat by angels (landing, naturally, in what is now the Baie des Anges) in the fourth century. An important venue for baroque concerts and other musical events.

The Riviera

Pebbly, and not sparklingly clean, the beach is still a good place to relax. *See page 220.*

Notre-Dame-de-l'Assomption (Musée Franciscain)

pl du Monastère (04.93.81.00.04). **Open** *church* 8.30am-12.30pm, 2.30-6.30pm daily; *museum* 10am-noon, 3-6pm Mon-Sat. **Admission** free.

At the edge of the gardens of Cimiez, this church is a heavy-handed nineteenth-century reworking of a sixteenth-century building. Inside, two Louis Bréa altarpieces survive. The adjoining sixteenth-century monastery is intact, and includes a couple of pretty cloisters – one with some strange, perhaps alchemical murals – as well as the Musée Franciscain, where the uncomfortable ends of Franciscan martyrs are documented. Outside, the fragrant rose garden (7.30am-6.30pm daily) offers fine views over the city. Matisse and Dufy are buried in the nearby cemetery.

Chapelle de l'Annonciation

1 rue de la Poissonnerie (04.93.62.13.62). **Open** 7.30-noon, 2.30-6.30pm daily.

Join a steady trickle of locals in this lovely little gilded baroque gem and light a candle for Ste Rita – the patron saint of miserable middle-aged women – to whom the chapel is dedicated.

Museums & galleries

All museums are free on the first Sunday of the month. Various discount passes are available from any branch of the Office de Tourisme; the Passe-musées (40F), for example, gives free entrance to all Nice museums for a week.

Castel Plage: a relaxed private beach, open to paying customers. *See page 221.*

Musée d'Archéologie

160 av des Arènes (04.93.81.59.57). **Open** *museum & ruins Apr-Sept* 10am-1pm, 2-6pm Tue-Sun; *Oct-Mar* 10am-noon, 2-5pm Tue-Sun. **Admission** 25F, 15F children.

The smart archeological museum charts Nice's history from 1100 BC through Roman times and up to the Middle Ages through its impressive display of ceramics, sculpture, coins, jewellery and tools. Outside are the first- to fourth-century ruins on the ancient site of Cemenelum, with vestiges of the Roman public baths, paved streets and a 4,000-seat stone amphitheatre that once served as the playground for javelin-throwing gladiators and now is a concert venue during the Nice Jazz Festival.

Musée des Arts Asiatiques

405 promenade des Anglais (04.92.29.37.00). **Open** *May to mid-Oct* 10am-6pm Mon, Wed-Sun; *mid-Oct to Apr* 10am-5pm Mon, Wed-Sun. **Admission** 35F, 15F children, free under-6s.

This impressive minimalist glass and metal structure at the duck pond in the Parc Floral Phoenix boasts a small but stunning collection of rare pieces that range from 2000 BC Chinese jade knick-knacks to the latest in oriental high-tech design. Don't miss the tea pavilion under the ginko trees, with a display of ceremonial clay bowls.

Musée d'Art Moderne et d'Art Contemporain (MAMAC)

promenade des Arts (04.93.62.61.62). **Open** 10am-6pm Mon, Wed-Sun. **Admission** 25F, free children.

The city's sprawling, multi-level marble home of contemporary European and American works

stages first-rate seasonal shows. There's also a permanent collection from the Nice school, with works by Arman, César and Sosno and a stunning room filled with electric-blue works by the late Yves Klein.

Musée des Beaux-Arts

33 av des Baumettes (04.92.15.28.28). **Open** 10am-noon, 2-6pm Tue-Sun. **Admission** 25F, free children.

Built for a Russian prince, this splendid Genoese-inspired villa houses an unmissable collection of seventeenth- to early twentieth-century works of art. Highlights include works by Niçois pastel artist and pioneering lithographer Jules Cheret, canvases by Van Dongen, Sisley and Dufy, and newly acquired paintings by Signac and Kisling.

Musée International d'Art Naïf Anatole Jakovsky

Château Ste-Hélène, av de Fabron (04.93.71.78.33). **Open** 10am-noon, 2-6pm Mon, Wed-Sun. **Admission** 25F, free children.

Once the home of perfume creator René Coty, this lovely pink villa now houses a private collection that traces the history of naive art from the eighteenth century to the present. Great for kids, who will enjoy spotting the canvases that could have been done by a child of three; there's even a grassy park nearby.

Musée Masséna

65 rue de France (04.93.88.11.34). **Open** *Dec-Apr, Oct* 10am-noon, 2-5pm Tue-Sun; *May-Sept* 3-6pm Tue-Sun. Closed Nov. **Admission** free. Closed until 2002.

Heavy, Empire-style salons with a heavy if eclectic mix of Nice primitive painters and water-colourists, medieval armour, costumes and Napoléon's coronation robe and death mask. Note that the museum is closed until 2002.

Musée Matisse

164 av des Arènes (04.93.81.08.08). **Open** *Apr-Sept* 10am-6pm Mon, Wed-Sun; *Oct-Mar* 10am-5pm Mon, Wed-Sun. **Admission** 25F, free children.

This renovated seventeenth-century villa, with a modern extension, houses a fascinating collection, tracing Matisse's development from his early works – dark, brooding, almost Rembrandt-like – through his archaic-style sculptures, Pointillisme and Lautrec-like graphic simplicity on to his stark line-drawings and colourful paper cut-outs. One room is devoted to his massive sketches for the Chapelle du Rosaire in Vence (*see page 265*). There are excellent temporary shows, too.

Musée National Message Biblique Marc-Chagall

av du Docteur Menard (04.93.53.87.20). **Open** *July-Sept* 10am-6pm Mon, Wed-Sun; *Oct-June* 10am-5pm Wed-Mon. **Admission** 30F, free children.

This is long-time Riviera resident Chagall at his best, a purpose-built space with a stunning selection of large paintings on Old Testament themes, notably the Song of Songs. Chagall provided stained glass, mosaics and sketches for the gallery, which holds frequent temporary shows on Jewish art.

Musée Naval (Tour Bellanda)

Parc du Château (04.93.80.47.61). **Open** *June-Sept* 10am-noon, 2-7pm Wed-Sun; *Oct-June* 10am-noon, 2-5pm Wed-Sun. **Admission** 15F, free children.

On the western flank of Nice's grassy Colline du Château park, this circular nineteenth-century tower, once the home of Hector Berlioz, offers an exhibition of model boats, arms and navigation instruments. The park above is accessible by the elevator at the foot of the hill from 8am to 6pm daily, or take the countless stairs for a good workout.

Musée de Terra Amata

25 bd Carnot (04.93.55.59.93). **Open** 9am-noon, 2-6pm Tue-Sun. **Admission** 25F, free children.

Find out what life was like on the Riviera 400,000 years ago. The highlights of this museum, built on an excavation site, include a reconstituted prehistoric cave, a human footprint in limestone, traces of fire and records of ancient elephant hunters.

Palais Lascaris

15 rue Droite (04.93.62.05.54). **Open** 10am-noon, 2-6pm Tue-Sun. **Admission** free.

A treasure trove of ornate furnishings, seventeenth-century paintings, Flemish tapestries, Provençal costumes and agricultural tools, in a miniature palace with vaulted frescoed ceilings and a dramatic balustraded staircase.

Villa Arson

20 av Stephen Liegeard (04.92.07.73.73). **Open** 2-7pm Tue-Sun. **Admission** free.

Le Nissart

Vourehe saupre parla lou nissart? It may not be the world's most useful language – spoken for the most part by Niçois old-timers up narrow alleyways or in market places – but if you'd like to impress your friends at cocktail parties or simply love the way it sounds, Nice's quintessential local lingo is on the up.

Derived from Provençal (and not from Italian, despite similar intonation), Nissart, its champions will tell you, is a language in its own right and not a mere dialect. To prove the point, those champions are fighting, with some success, to have it recognised as such. Many of Nice's street signs are now bi-lingual, in French and Nissart; there's a bi-monthly magazine, *Lou Sourgentin*; there are Nissart columns in the *Nice-Matin* daily; and hip local bands such as Nux Vomica have taken up the cause with Nissart lyrics.

Linguistic militants also lurk within the regional education system. And though parents grumble that Nissart won't help their kids to trade stocks on the Internet, the language has entered the primary school curriculum and become a whopping success. Five-year-old *pichoun* (little ones) gleefully sing the praises of *Nissa la Bella, Regina de li flour* (queen of flowers) and its grand *souleu d'or* (golden sun).

If you're interested in taking classes, contact Jan Blaquiera, editor of *Lou Sourgentin* magazine (information 04.93.55.19.79).

The cutting edge of the adventurous, young and contemporary avant-garde, with plenty of performance art and seasonal shows.

Arts, entertainment & sport

Acropolis

1 esplanade Kennedy (04.93.92.83.00).
A modern mega-structure that hosts special events, conventions, concerts, ballet and opera.

Casino Ruhl

Hôtel Le Méridien, 1 promenade des Anglais (04.97.03.12.33). **Open** 10am-5am daily. **Admission** 65F. **Credit** AmEx, DC, MC, V.

A gamblers' paradise: a modern expanse of gaming rooms with French and English roulette, blackjack, punto banco, craps and clanging slot machines galore. If you just want to go and play the slots, there's no need to dress up.

The Riviera

Cinémathèque de Nice

3 esplanade Kennedy (04.92.04.06.66). **Shows** 2.30pm, 8pm Tue-Thur; 2.30pm, 10pm Fri, Sat; 3pm Sun. **Tickets** 20F; 40F for a three-film pass. **No credit cards.**

Offers an international selection of classics and quality recent films in their original version.

Galerie Soardi/Espace d'Art Contemporain

8 rue Desiré Niel (04.93.13.98.97). **Open** 9am-7pm Mon-Sat. **Credit** AmEx, DC, MC, V.

This was once the atelier of Henri Matisse, and it was here that he sketched *La Danse* with a long pole and charcoals. Today, it's a private gallery presenting innovative seasonal shows featuring the Ecole de Nice. It also sells lithographs, frames and artsy gift items.

Opéra de Nice

4 rue St-François-de-Paule (04.92.17.40.40). **Box office** 10am-5pm Mon-Sat. **Shows** 8pm. **Tickets** opera 40F-400F, concerts 40F-130F. **Credit** AmEx, MC, V.

A small nineteenth-century gem of an opera house, done out in sumptuous red velvet with crystal chandeliers and lashings of rococo gold. The Opéra attracts top-notch visiting artists for symphonies, ballet and opera.

Musée d'Art Moderne. *See page 224.*

Palais des Sports Jean Bouin

esplanade de Lattre de Tassigny (04.93.80.80.80). **Open** *pool* 4-9pm Tue, Thur; noon-6pm Wed; 9pm-11pm Fri; 9-6pm Sat, Sun; ice rink 9-11.30pm Tue, Thur; 2-6pm Wed; 9pm-1am Fri; 10pm-1am, 2-6pm Sat; 9-noon, 2-6pm Sun. **Admission** 28F; skate rental 17F. **No credit cards.**

A vast municipal sports complex with a well-kept indoor Olympic-sized pool and covered ice rink.

Théâtre de Nice

promenade des Arts (04.93.13.90.90). **Box office** 9am-7pm Tue-Sat. **Shows** *La Petite Salle* 7pm; *La Grande Salle* 8.30pm; matinées 3pm Sun. **Tickets** 60F-170F. **Credit** AmEx, DC, MC, V.

One of the most important theatres in the South of France – alongside Marseille's La Criée – this impressive venue stages high-profile productions of French and foreign classics and contemporary work, covering everything from the well-known to the ground-breaking with an intellectual twist.

Théâtre de la Photographie et de l'Image

27 bd de Dubouchage (04.92.04.99.70). **Open** 10am-noon, 2-6pm Mon-Wed, Sun. **Admission** free.

A recently restored pink *belle époque* theatre, now a vast space for big-name photography shows, lectures, an Internet archive and a convivial coffee bar.

Where to eat

Nice restaurants reviewed in our **Provençal Food & Drink** chapter are **Le Chantecler** (*page 52*), **Albert's Bar** (*page 51*), **La Merenda** (*page 52*), **La Petite Maison** (*page 52*) and **La Zucca Magica** (*page 54*).

Acchiardo

38 rue Droite (04.93.85.51.16). **Meals served** noon-1.30pm, 7-9.30pm Mon-Fri; noon-1.30pm Sat. **Menus** 70F-130F. **No credit cards.**

This family-run, check-tableclothed Niçois dining spot is a long-standing *vieille ville* favourite for the budget-minded. Daily specials include home-made *ravioli au pistou*, *merda de can* (dog-turd shaped pasta swirls – delicious once you get over the resemblance), *daube de boeuf* and ratatouille.

L'Auberge de Théo

52 av Cap de Croix (04.93.81.26.19). **Meals served** noon-2pm, 7pm-1am Tue-Sun. Closed 25 Aug-25 Sept. **Menus** 95F-150F. **Credit** V.

This is a perfect place for lunch on your way to or from the Chagall and Matisse museums. In a residential Cimiez neighbourhood, this charming Italian trattoria, with an open-air patio and Tuscan farm atmosphere, is known for its varied pasta dishes, pizza and grilled fish.

Le Barachois

12 rue Amiral de Grasse (04.93.88.92.50). **Meals served** noon-1.30pm, 7-9.30pm Tue-Sat. Closed Aug. **Menus** 65F-150F. **Credit** V.

Located on a backstreet near the train station, this modest 12-table restaurant specialises in exotic, spicy dishes from the Indian Ocean island of Réunion. Try the fried *samoussas* (meat or vegetable fritters) for starters, followed by a pork or shrimp curry or coconut chicken, served with huge portions of rice and red beans; end in totally tropical style with a salad of passion fruit, sugar bananas and papaya.

Bistro les Viviers

22 rue Alphonse Karr (04.93.16.00.48). **Meals served** noon-2.30pm, 7.30-10pm Mon-Fri; 7.30-11pm Sat. Closed mid-July to Aug. **Menus** 180F-230F. **Credit** AmEx, MC, V.

This recently opened brasserie, replete with mirrors, comfy booths and chalkboard menus, is one of the best seafood addresses in town. It's popular both at lunch and dinner, so reservations are a must. Highlights include a lobster and avocado salad, duck foie gras with pears, and sea bass with fennel and saffron sauce. Alternatively, splash out on the all-lobster menu (390F).

Chez Simon

275 rte de St-Antoine-de-Ginestière (04.93.86.51.62). **Meals served** noon-2.30pm, 7.30-11.30pm Tue-Sun. **Menu** 170F. **Credit** MC, V.

A 15-minute drive inland, this rustic-style *auberge* in the hills is a family-run local landmark for tasty Niçois specialities. The lemon- and plane-tree shaded terrace makes you feel miles away from the city, and everything from the olive and aniseed bread to the luscious home-made ravioli and crêpes topped with honey, pine nuts and pastis bring out the Riviera flavours. You'll need to take a taxi or drive to get here: it's two kilometres west along the promenade des Anglais from avenue de Verdun, then turn right into bd Carlone and follow the signs to St-Antoine.

Chez Thérèse

Marché de cours Saleya (no phone). **Open** 6am-2pm daily. **No credit cards.**

You can't miss Thérèse, with her gypsy earrings and black hair, as she cheerfully touts her delicious socca – the cheap but filling snack that is to Nice what the hotdog is to New York City – from a stand in the cours Saleya market. Made from chickpea flour and olive oil and cooked in huge open pans, socca has the consistency of a crêpe and is eaten hot with a sprinkling of black pepper.

Indyana

11 rue Deloye (04.93.80.67.69). **Meals served** noon-2.30pm, 7.30pm-midnight Mon-Sat. **Menus** 60F-140F. **Credit** AmEx, MC, V.

Thirty- and fortysomething hipsters finally have their own stylish but affordable dining spot, run by enterprising brothers Christophe and Pascal Ciamos, whose 'fusion cuisine' menu matches the eclectic decor mix of New York loft, art deco, Asian and Moroccan. Global dishes range from sushi, vegetable chop suey and Japanese duck to classic but copious beef and fish platters served with mouthwatering potato or courgette gratin. Don't miss out on Christophe's scrumptious home-made fruit tarts and cakes.

La Part des Anges

17 rue Gubernatis (04.93.62.69.80). **Open** 10.30am-8pm Mon-Thur; 10.30am-10.30pm Fri, Sat. **Meals served** noon-2pm daily; 7-8pm Mon-Thur; 7-9.30pm Fri, Sat. **Menus** 110F-130F. **Credit** MC, V.

The captivating aroma as you walk past this intimate wine cellar and bistro draw you inside, where owner and sommelier Olivier Labarde offers expert advice on his superb selection of local and rare vintages. The delicious home-cooked southwestern specialities served at five tables at the back are one of the best gastronomic bargains in town. Booking advised.

Pelican's Station

3 rue de la Préfecture (04.93.85.58.48). **Meals served** noon-2pm, 8-11pm Mon-Fri; 8-11pm Sat. Closed June. **Menus** 80F-150F. **Credit** AmEx, MC, V.

The world cuisine trend really works in this superbly decorated Louisiana-style bistro, serving copious portions of traditional French meat and seafood dishes, Tex-Mex specialities and home-made pasta in cast iron pots. Convivial and always packed.

Cours Saleya flower market. *See page 220.*

Palais Lascaris: a treasure trove in a miniature palace. *See page 225.*

Le Safari

1 cours Saleya (04.93.80.18.44). **Meals served** noon-2.30pm, 7-11pm daily. **Menu** 200F. **Credit** DC, MC, V.
Overlooking Nice's most colourful market, the Safari's terrace fills quickly on market days, but it's pleasant inside, too. Ideal for a light lunch or supper: food on offer includes delicious pizzas cooked in a wood oven, Niçois specialities such as ravioli stuffed with braised beef in beef stock, courgette flower beignets, a salade Niçoise that defines the term and the Cascade Safari starter, an assortment of Niçois specialities including grilled red peppers, *accra* (salt cod fritters), artichoke salad and squid beignets.

La Table Alziari

4 rue François Zanin (04.93.80.34.03). **Meals served** noon-2pm, 7-10.30pm Tue-Sat. **Menus** 90F-140F. **Credit** MC, V.
From the family that sells the best local olive oil in town (*see below* **Shopping**), this low-key but authentic Nissart bistro hidden on a sidestreet off rue Pairolière offers home-style cooking with the freshest ingredients. Don't miss the stuffed sardines, delicate courgette flower beignets or the regional pride and joy, morue (cod) Niçoise.

L'Univers de Christian Plumail

54 bd Jean Jaurès (04.93.62.32.22). **Open** noon-2pm, 7.30-10pm Mon-Fri; 7.30-10pm Sat. **Menus** 100F-290F. **Credit** AmEx, MC, V.
Renowned Niçois chef Christian Plumail took charge of this former brasserie and turned it into an unpretentious haven for simple but refined Mediterranean cuisine at surprisingly affordable prices. Regulars

rave about the ever-changing but reliably delicious menus, which include dishes such as purple artichoke salad with Parmesan, grilled fish with coriander sauce, rabbit stew and macaroons with pine nuts and mascarpone sauce.

Cakes & ice-cream

Fennocchio

2 pl Rossetti (04.93.80.72.52). **Open** 9am-midnight Mon, Wed-Sun. Closed Jan, Feb. **Credit** MC, V.
The terrace of this ice-cream maker in Vieux Nice is a fine destination on a warm afternoon. Settle in at a table overlooking the fountain and choose from a superb range of home-made ice-cream and sorbets, including what's surely the world's best peach ice-cream and a killer blackcurrant sorbet.

Pâtisserie Cappa

7-9 pl Garibaldi (04.93.62.30.83). **Open** 7.30am-7.30pm Tue-Sun. **Credit** V.
Venture under the Italianate arches for the most heavenly chocolate pastries (try the *petit marquis*), fruit mousse cakes and *tourte de blettes* – a sweet Niçois tart of swiss chard, pine nuts and raisins, jazzed up with apples and rum – to take away or consume in the miniature tea room.

Bars & nightlife

Le Bar des Oiseaux

5 rue St-Vincent (04.93.80.27.33). **Open** 11am-3pm, 7pm-1am daily. **Admission** concerts 80F-120F. **Credit** MC, V.

The Riviera

Lots of local atmosphere at this popular restaurant, bar and theatre. Live bands and live birds, too – in cages, most of the time – and uproarious comic sketches, written by proprietor Noëlle Perna, whose plays target the Niçois and city politics.

Blue Boy Enterprise
9 rue Spinetta (04.93.44.68.24). **Open** 11pm-late; days vary. **Credit** MC, V.
An all-night gay club with a split-level dancefloor and stage for live drag shows. Music of every genre, clientele of every gender.

La Bodeguita del Havana
14 rue Chauvain (04.93.92.67.24). **Open** *Oct-May* 5pm-2.30am Tue-Sun; *June-Sept* 5pm-2.30am daily. **Credit** MC, V.
The current Cuban Latino trend has turned this club into a mecca for Buena Vista Social Club groupies and hot-to-trot dancers. Free salsa lessons on Tuesdays and Wednesdays.

La Casa del Sol
69 quai des Etats-Unis (04.93.62.87.28). **Open** *Oct to mid-May* 7pm-2.30am Tue-Sat; *mid-May to Sept* 7pm-2.30am Mon-Sat. **Credit** MC, V.
A before- and after-hours tapas bar with a lively atmosphere and a Spanish-Latin background beat (DJs Wednesdays and Thursdays). Dress cool, clean and casual or you might not get past the door.

Cherry's Café
36 rue des Ponchettes (04.93.13.85.45). **Open** *Oct-Mar* noon-midnight Tue-Sun; *Apr-Sept* noon-midnight daily. **Menus** 110F, 160F. **Credit** AmEx, MC, V.
This popular gay bar/restaurant has an inviting miniature terrace overlooking the promenade des Anglais; it offers a variety of salads and an affordable *plat du jour*.

Chez Pipo
13 rue Bavastro (04.93.55.88.82). **Open** 5.30-10pm Tue-Sun. **Menus** 50F. **No credit cards**.
A lively port-side spot, with a huge wood-burning oven and long tables where old-timers gossip in Niçois dialect. The perfect place for an early evening snack (the socca costs 13F) and a glass of local rosé.

Dizzy Club
26 quai Lunel (04.93.26.54.79). **Open** 11pm-5am Wed-Sun. **Credit** MC, V.
One of the few clubs where you can actually have a conversation at the bar. Sleek decor, piano-bar music, a dancefloor with live bands and DJs, for pretty people from 25 to 50.

Shopping

Agnès B
17 rue des Ponchettes (04.93.62.32.39). **Open** 10am-7pm Mon-Sat. **Credit** AmEx, MC, V.
An oasis of beautifully cut stylish but sober classics for men and women, on the edge of the *vieille ville*.

Alziari
14 rue St-François-de-Paule (04.93.85.76.92). **Open** 8.15am-12.30pm, 2.15-7pm Tue-Sat. **Credit** MC, V.

Rosbif rock

For some reason, Bono, Mick Jagger, Dave Stewart and Tina Turner rarely emerge from their Riviera hideaways to give impromptu concerts down the local Irish pub. But who cares when the likes of Fat Cat Hackett are more than happy to oblige?

A small army of expatriate rockers work the English-language pubs and clubs of the Côte d'Azur. A few of these fly in for the summer season and aim to meet their living – and drinking – expenses by playing covers in well-known watering holes. Others have chosen to base themselves here all year round, preferring small-pond notoriety – and a great climate – to the cold shoulder of the music business back home.

Many acts operate as buskers, even if they are playing inside the pub. They bring in business for the landlord, and in return get to pass the hat around after the concert. As a general rule, if entrance is free and you like the band, you should give at least ten francs.

ARTISTS
In a rootless community, band members come and go at quite a rate. Among the acts to have survived long enough to build up a certain following are:
Fat Cat Hackett and his Band – a singing soul drummer, the Fat Cat works the coast all year round.
Running Birds – ever yearned to hear an Italian band in Nice singing *Stairway to Heaven* in English? Now's your chance.
Calligagan – Anglo-French rockers who mix covers with their own songs; the singer sounds like Lenny Kravitz – sort of.
Donal – Irish one-man-band who sings inside and outside pubs with his Ovation pick-up and portable speaker.

VENUES
Nice is where most of the action is, and it's also where most of the authentic pubs – as opposed to their synthetic clones – are

Since 1879, the Alziari family has been producing a superb nutty-flavoured olive oil, sold in distinctive yellow and blue tin drums. There is also a selection of other natural products. Don't miss their green tapenade or the gorgeous lavender, honey and olive oil soap.

Le Centre du Monde

6 rue du Lycée (04.93.80.23.63). **Open** 10.30am-noon, 2.30-7pm Tue-Sat. **Credit** AmEx, MC, V.
Fluxus artist Ben, enfant terrible of the Nice school, now has his own gallery and shop, selling everything from his provocative proverb-scrawled T-shirts to whimsical objets d'art. The store also hosts monthly philosophical debates on art-world trends and ideas.

Le Chandelier

7 rue de la Boucherie (04.93.85.85.19). **Open** 9.30am-7pm daily. **Credit** AmEx, MC, V.
For attractive and authentic Provençal fabrics, make a beeline for this tiny boutique, where you'll find a dizzying choice of high-quality tablecloths, place mats and napkins in sunny colours and original patterns.

Façonnable

7 & 10 rue Paradis (04.93.87.88.80). **Open** 10am-7pm Mon-Sat. **Credit** AmEx, DC, MC, V.
What began as a small Nice-based menswear label in this small shop is now a huge company – with stores in every major international city – selling elegantly preppy sportswear, suits and ties in all stripes and colours.

Fayences de Moustiers

48 rue du Marché (04.93.13.06.03). **Open** 9.45am-1pm, 2-7pm Mon-Sat. **Credit** AmEx, MC, V.
The only shop in Nice with delicately hand-painted porcelain from Moustiers; everything from cream jugs to fruit bowls. Pricey, but the real thing.

Fleur de Cactus

12 rue du Marché (04.93.80.66.51). **Open** 10am-7pm Mon-Sat. **Credit** AmEx, MC, V.
A tiny boutique in the *vieille ville* with the latest in women's clothing, jewellery and shoes. Trendy labels (Cop Copine, Lola, Scooter) and personalised attention.

Marché de la Brocante

cours Saleya. **Open** 8am-5pm Mon. **Credit** varies.
Antiques galore at this inviting outdoor market, where you'll find vintage phonographs, blue seltzer bottles, old linen tablecloths, art deco jewellery, assorted attic junk and dazzling silver cutlery.

Movida

2 rue Longchamp (04.93.88.90.80). **Open** 10am-1pm, 2-7.15pm Mon-Sat. **Credit** AmEx, MC, V.
Chic labels for men and women, with a mix of cool French (Comme les Garçons, Mugler) and Italian (Ferretti, Moschino) sportswear, for that climb-into-my-Ferrari look.

Nocy-Be

4-6 rue Jules Gilly (04.93.85.52.25). **Open** 10.30am-1pm, 2.30-8.30pm Mon, Wed-Sun. **Credit** MC, V.
If you're looking for ethnic bric-a-brac or unusual handcrafted lamps, this cosy boutique, which

clustered. For live music listings, pick up a copy of the weekly French-language *Semaine des Spectacles* (5F from newsagents). The following dives all attract a mixed crowd of expats and locals, and offer live music:

Le Bull Dog Pub

16 rue de l'Abbaye (04.93.85.04.06). **Open** 8pm-2.30am daily. **Credit** MC, V.
Plenty of decibels, free munchies with cocktails and 25 brands of beer. Live pop and rock bands and a 25- to 35-year-old crowd of listeners.

Chez Wayne

15 rue de la Préfecture (04.93.13.46.99). **Open** 5pm-midnight daily. **Credit** AmEx, DC, MC, V.
Buzzing live-music pub with a decent-sized stage, run by East End lad Wayne. A magnet for English students and Sophia Antipolis

high-tech workers. Drinks can be pricey, especially during the summer.

Jonathan's

1 rue de la Loge (04.93.62.57.62). **Open** 7pm-midnight Mon-Sat. **No credit cards.**
Cosy cellar bar with live one- or two-piece bands of varying quality.

The Klomp

6 rue Mascionat (04.93.92.42.85). **Open** 5.30pm-2.30am Mon-Sat. **Credit** AmEx, DC, MC, V.
Jazz-oriented dive with draught Guinness, presided over by English barman Howard.

Thor Pub

32 cours Saleya (04.93.62.49.90). **Open** noon-3am daily. **Credit** AmEx, DC, MC, V.
Large venue in the heart of Nice's old town, with a huge terrace in summer, attracting a better-than-average selection of acts.

The Riviera

Look again: marzipan fruit and veg at the **cours Saleya** market. *See page 220.*

doubles as a Moroccan tea room, is a place where
you can literally shop till you drop... on to a comfortable floor cushion, for some invigorating mint
tea and pastries.

Village Ségurane

main entrance on rue Ségurane (no phone).
Open 10am-noon, 3-6.30pm Mon-Sat. **Credit**
AmEx, MC, V.
When Elton John went on a decorating spree for his
villa in Mont Boron, this is where he shopped: a two-
storey miniature village of antiques shops, stacked
together on one square block.

Where to stay

Luxury

Hôtel Negresco

36 promenade des Anglais (04.93.16.64.00/
fax 04.93.88.35.68). **Rates** single 1,350F, double
2,750F, suite 3,400F-8,200F. **Credit** AmEx, MC, V.
You can't miss this enormous pink and white
wedding cake of a palace across from the Baie des
Anges, built by Eduoard Niermans, known as the
Offenbach of architecture. At the entrance, the
parking valet, with his blue tailcoat, breeches and
red feather in his hat, sets the mood. In the lobby,
the modern world pales beside the glitter of a huge
Baccarat crystal chandelier, expansive Aubusson
carpet and a dazzling glass and metal dome
designed by Gustave Eiffel. Considered a folly at
the time when Cimiez was the chic place to be, the
Negresco eventually drew everyone, from the

crowned heads of Europe to the stars of stage
and screen. There's no pool or jacuzzi, but sumptuous bedrooms range in style from oriental splendour to Louis XIV and Napoléon III pomp and
circumstance. Oddly, many of the bathrooms have
kitsch Las Vegas-style sparkly baths rather than
the expected claw-foot tub... it's all part of this
hotel's eclectic charm.

Hôtel Palais Maeterlinck

30 bd Maurice Maeterlinck (04.92.00.72.00/fax
04.92.04.18.10). Closed mid-Jan to mid-Mar. **Rates**
single & double 1,450F-2,900F, suites 1,950F-7,000F.
Credit AmEx, DC, MC, V.
Once a villa belonging to Belgian writer Count
Maurice Maeterlinck, this entirely renovated
modern structure – a sprawling 'neo-classic style'
palace – on the edge of the sea on the Basse
Corniche between Nice and Villefranche-sur-Mer,
is now a hotel boasting luxurious rooms, an excellent restaurant and a lovely outdoor pool. The
atmosphere is somewhat stiff and formal, but
the views are superb.

Upmarket

Hôtel Atlantic

12 bd Victor Hugo (04.93.88.40.15/fax
04.93.88.68.60). **Rates** single 750F-950F, double
850F-1,050F. **Credit** AmEx, MC, V.
Beyond the sumptuous *belle époque* stained-glass
lobby – used by François Truffaut as a location in
Day for Night – the modern, renovated rooms are
spacious and comfortable.

Hôtel Beau Rivage
24 rue St François-de-Paule (04.92.47.82.82/fax 04.92.47.82.83). **Rates** single 650F-950F, double 1,100F, suites 1,950F. **Credit** AmEx, DC, MC, V.
Thoroughly modernised since the days when Matisse had a seafront apartment here, this comfortable 1930s hotel has its own private beach and excellent restaurant across the street.

Hôtel Château des Ollières
39 av des Baumettes (04.92.15.77.99/fax 04.92.15.77.98). **Rates** single & double 950F, suite 2,800F-3,300F. **Credit** AmEx, MC, V.
Only steps away from the Musée des Beaux-Arts, this turretted *belle époque* palace, formerly owned by a Russian prince, is an ornate mini-museum of marble statues, stained glass, crystal chandeliers and embroidered tapestries, with excellent cuisine and friendly staff.

Hôtel La Perouse
11 quai Rauba-Capeu (04.93.62.34.63/ fax 04.93.62.59.41). **Rates** single 745F-950F, double 1,490F-2,000F, suite 3,500F. **Credit** AmEx, MC, V.
This bright, airy hotel, ideally situated between the port and *vieille ville*, has an unbeatable sea view and a rooftop garden and spill-over pool.

Moderate

Hôtel Les Camélias
3 rue Spitalieri (04.93.62.15.54/fax 04.93.80.42.96). **Rates** single 300F, double 380F. Closed Nov. **Credit** MC, V.
A haven of faded kitschy splendour in the heart of the city, next to the Nice Etoile mall, with a lobby filled with artificial flowers, set back in a palm-shaded patio. Low-budget charm at its best.

Hôtel Excelsior
19 av Durante (04.93.88.18.05/fax 04.93.88.38.69). **Rates** double 330F-497F. **Credit** AmEx, MC, V.
An impressive turn-of-the-century building on a quiet street, with clean, old-fashioned rooms and a small garden where breakfast is served.

Hôtel Gounod
3 rue Gounod (04.93.16.42.00/fax 04.93.88.23.84). **Rates** single 400F-600F, double 650F-750F, suite 890F-990F. Closed mid-Nov to mid-Dec. **Credit** AmEx, DC, MC, V.
A lovely dusty rose *belle époque* exterior and chic but standard modern rooms with balconies. Guests can use the rooftop pool next door at the four-star Hôtel Splendid.

Hôtel Le Grimaldi
15 rue Grimaldi (04.93.16.00.24/fax 04.93.87.00.24). **Rates** single 490F, double 630F-790F, suite 1,200F-1,400F. **Credit** AmEx, MC, V.
An elegant, upmarket bed and breakfast, offering guests the kind of personalised hospitality often lacking in the glitzy Riviera palaces. All the rooms are different, tastefully decorated with countrified furnishings and Provençal fabrics.

Hôtel Oasis
23 rue Gounod (04.93.88.12.29/fax 04.93.16.14.40). **Rates** single 300F-350F, double 390F-440F. **Credit** AmEx, MC, V.
Centrally located, and slightly set back from the street, this tranquil hotel once lodged illustrious Russians such as Chekhov and Lenin. The biggest rooms – numbers 110, 124 and 210 – have a view of the splendid shady garden.

Hôtel Windsor
11, rue Dalpozzo (04.93.88.59.35/fax 04.93.88.94.57). **Rates** single 525F, double 700F. **Credit** AmEx, MC, V.
An artsy oasis with its own exotic garden, aviary and pool. The spacious rooms are all individually decorated by renowned contemporary painters; there's also a wonderful Moroccan-style hammam (bath-house) and small gym.

Essentials

Getting there

From the airport
Bus no.23 runs every 25 minutes between the airport and the main SNCF station: the fare is 8.50F. ANT (04.92.29.88.88) also runs a coach service (every 20 minutes) to the *gare routière* for 21F. From the airport to the promenade des Anglais, a taxi costs about 160F from Terminal 1 or 180F from Terminal 2.

By train
Timetable information for all stations is available on 08.36.35.35.35. The main SNCF station is at 3 av Thiers. In the station, SOS Voyageurs (04.93.82.62.13, open 9am-noon, 3-6pm Mon-Fri) helps with stolen or lost luggage, missed trains, children and elderly passengers. Local services to Menton also stop at the smaller Gare SNCF Riquier, which is handy for the port and the old town. The closest station to the airport is the Gare SNCF St Augustin. The private Gare de Provence, just north of the main station, is the departure point for the narrow-gauge Var Valley Train des Pignes (*see box p270*).

By bus
The *gare routière* (04.93.85.61.81) on Nice's main traffic artery, the promenade du Paillon, is the hub for most Côte d'Azur coach services. Others leave direct from the aiport. For coach services from Nice to other towns inland and along the Riviera, see the Getting There listings in the relevant chapter. Phocéens Cars (04.93.85.66.61) operates long-distance services to Avignon via St-Raphaël and Aix-en-Provence (two daily); to Marseille via Aix-en-Provence (four daily); and two international routes: Rome-Nice-Barcelona (three weekly) and Venice-Milan-Nice-Valencia (three weekly).

By car
Leave the A8 at exit no.54 or no.55. The coastal RN7 and RN98 roads go through Nice.

Hôtel Negresco, byword for glitter and glamour, and choice of the stars. *See page 232.*

Getting around

By bus

Local services are run by Sunbus, 10 av Felix Fauré
(04.93.16.52.10; open 7.15am-7pm Mon-Fri; 7.15am-
6pm Sat). Single tickets cost 8.50F. Bus-hop passes
cost 25F (one-day), 85F (five-day) and 110F (seven-
day) and are available from the Sunbus office and at
tabacs and newsagents. Useful routes include the
no.23, from the SNCF station via rue de France (a
block back from promenade des Anglais) to the
airport; and the no.15 from place Masséna to Cimiez.

By taxi

Nice taxis are notoriously expensive, and you should
keep your wits about you: drivers have been known
to place a jacket strategically over the meter, or
switch it off seconds before arrival. To order a taxi,
call Central Taxi Riviera (04.93.13.78.78).

Tourist information

Office du Tourisme et des Congrès

*5 promenade des Anglais (04.92.14.48.00/fax
04.93.92.48.03/otc@nice-coteazur.org).* **Open** *Oct-*
May 9am-6pm Mon-Sat; *May, June, Sept* 8am-8pm
daily; *July, Aug* 9am-6pm daily.
Website: www.coteazur.org
Branches: Aéroport Nice Côte d'Azur, Terminal 1
(04.93.21.44.11/fax 04.93.21.44.50); Gare SNCF, av
Thiers (tel & fax 04.93.87.07.07).

Internet point

Webstore *12 rue de Russie (04.93.87.87.99).* **Open**
10am-12.30pm, 2-7pm Mon-Sat. **Credit** AmEx, DC,
MC, V.
Thirteen consoles available for Net junkies at 30F
per half hour, 50F per hour. A one-month subscription costs 199F.
Website: www.webstore.fr

Lost property

Police Municipal *10 cours Saleya
(04.93.80.65.50).* **Open** 8.30am-5pm Mon-Thur;
8.30am-3.45pm Fri.

Post offices

Bureau de Poste *35 av Thiers (04.93.82.65.00).*
Open 8am-7pm Mon-Fri; 8am-noon Sat.
Bureau de Poste *pl Wilson (04.93.13.64.26).*
Open 8am-7pm Mon-Fri; 8am-noon Sat.

The Riviera

The Corniches

Roll the roof off the Rolls and join the traffic on the triple-decker Nice to Menton run.

The Corniches are the quintessence of the Riviera. The name refers to three roads – high, middle and low – between Nice and Menton, and, by extension, to the strip of coastline in between. But it also conjures up visions of sun-bronzed boys and babes speeding along in convertible sports cars. Unfortunately, the reality is more prosaic. In summer the traffic often slows to a crawl – which at least gives you plenty of time to admire some of southern France's most glorious panoramas.

The Basse Corniche (N98 – also known as the Corniche Inférieure) hugs the coast, passing through all the towns and resorts; most of the year it is a vehicle-packed nightmare. To take some of the strain, the wider Moyenne Corniche (N7) was hacked through the mountains in the 1920s. The highest route – the Grande Corniche (D2564) – is also the oldest: it follows the route of the ancient Roman Aurelian Way, and is easily the most spectacular of the three drives.

The glamour of the Corniches has its tragic side, too. On 13 September 1982 at about 10am, a car carrying Princess Grace of Monaco and her daughter Stéphanie swerved off the RN53, a treacherous descent full of hairpin bends that leads from the Grande Corniche down to the Moyenne Corniche. Stéphanie survived; her mother didn't. There's no memorial, but a bunch or two of fresh flowers can generally be seen by the roadside.

The Basse Corniche

Villefranche-sur-Mer

Founded in the fourteenth century by Charles d'Anjou II as a duty-free port, Villefranche's slanted narrow streets and stacked cluster of dusty rose, ochre and apricot houses with *trompe l'oeil* frescos redefine the term 'picturesque'. On the tiny cobblestoned port, you might still see old women mending hand-woven fishing nets. In the old town, **rue Obscure**, a dark and eerie vaulted passageway, has changed little since the Middle Ages. And the **Combat Naval Fleuri**, held each year on the Monday before Ash Wednesday, is a surreal sight: dozens of fishing boats bedecked with flowers invade the harbour.

The deep **harbour** between the headlands of Mont Boron to the west and Cap-Ferrat to the east was used as a US naval base until France withdrew from the military wing of NATO in 1966. The quayside has settled down since the days when it used to service sailors; lined with restaurants and brasseries, it overlooks a strip of beach. At the western end of the old port is the postage stamp-sized **Chapelle de St-Pierre-des-Pêcheurs** – once a storehouse for fishing nets. In 1957, Jean Cocteau covered the walls with lively and lyrical frescos recounting the life of St Peter. Perched at the summit of the old town, the **Eglise St-Michel** (04.93.01.73.13, open 9am-7pm daily) is a handsome eighteenth-century Italianate church that boasts an impressive organ built in 1790 by the Niçois Grinda brothers, still played during Sunday mass.

To the west, the imposing **Citadelle** dominates the harbour. A sixteenth-century stone fort replete with drawbridge built by the

fumes in the 1920s, the artist's spirit lives on in the decor. Many of the small but airy rooms have sunny balconies that give on to the port. **La Mère Germaine** (7 quai Corbet, 04.93.01.71.39, closed Nov-25 Dec, menus 210F), just a few metres from the cobblestoned quay, is the best bet for traditional fish soup and seafood. But for ambience and good value head for **Michel's** (pl Pollonais, 04.93.76.73.42, closed Tue, menus 150F-200F), which serves simple seafood, meat and pasta dishes, as well as copious ice-cream sundaes, on a sunny terrace overlooking the Cocteau chapel or inside the cheerful bistro. **L'Echalote** (7 rue de l'Eglise, 04.93.01.71.11, open dinner only, closed Sun, menus 125F-185F) is an intimate bistro perched up a steep alley that serves tasty dishes at very affordable prices: heavenly vegetable and Parmesan tarts, sirloin of pork with dried figs, and polenta with almonds.

Getting there

See page 237 **Beaulieu**.

Tourist information

Office de Tourisme

Jardin Binon (04.93.01.73.68/fax 04.93.76.63.65). **Open** 9am-noon, 2-6pm Mon-Sat. *Website: www.villefranche-sur-mer.com*

Cap-Ferrat

This lush, secluded peninsula jutting out between Villefranche and Beaulieu is a millionaires' paradise of luxurious, high-hedged, security-gated mansions (part-time residents include Hubert de Givenchy and Andrew Lloyd Webber), but it is also a walker's dream. A rocky ten-kilometres path shaded by umbrella pines winds around the Cap, affording glimpses of the most expensive real estate on the Côte en route to the Plage des Fosses, a pebbly horseshoe beach that is ideal for small children.

The narrow approach to the Cap is dominated by the **Villa Ephrussi-de-Rothschild**, an Italianate extravaganza built for the extravagant Béatrice de Rothschild in the early 1900s. Inside, Béatrice had appropriate settings recreated for her immense art and *objet* collection, which focuses on her favourite century, the eighteenth. There are also impressionist paintings and fascinating oriental knick-knacks. Surrounding the villa are seven hectares of exotic Mediterranean plants, Spanish and Japanese gardens, Renaissance fountains, gargoyles and an incomparable view.

Chapelle de St-Pierre-des-Pêcheurs.

Dukes of Savoy, it houses the **Musée Volti**, an exhibit of voluptuous female figurines by contemporary local sculptor Antoniucci Volti, and the **Musée Goetz-Boumeester**, containing 100 minor works by modern artists such as Picasso, Hartung, Picabia and Miró.

Chapelle de St-Pierre-des-Pêcheurs

pl Pollonais (04.93.76.90.70). **Open** *July-Sept* 10am-noon, 4-8.30pm Tue-Sun; *Oct to mid-Nov* 9.30am-noon, 2-6pm Tue-Sun; *mid-Dec to Feb* 9.30am-noon, 2-5pm Tue-Sun; *Mar-June* 9.30am-noon, 2-7pm Tue-Sun. Closed mid-Nov to mid-Dec. **Admission** 12F.

Musée Volti & Musée Goetz-Boumeester

Citadelle, av Sadi Carnot (04.93.76.33.33). **Open** *July, Aug* 10am-noon, 3-7pm Mon, Wed-Sat; 3-7pm Sun; *June, Sept* 10am-noon, 3-6pm Mon, Wed-Sat; 3-6pm Sun; *Oct, Dec-May* 10am-noon, 3-5pm Mon, Wed-Sat; 3-5pm Sun. **Admission** free.

Where to stay & eat

The **Hôtel le Welcome** (1 quai Amiral Courbet, 04.93.76.27.62, closed mid-Nov to Dec 23, rates 500F-950F) is a splendid pink- and green-trimmed port-side hotel, and though it unfortunately bears little resemblance to the hotel of the same name where Jean Cocteau fraternised with young sailors amid opium

On the eastern side of the peninsula, luxury yachts have replaced fishing boats in the harbour of **St-Jean-Cap-Ferrat**, which remains a pleasant enough town, good for an evening drink followed by a stroll along the marina. Further west, the **Zoo du Cap-Ferrat** is a miniature tropical park with 300 species, from flamingos and talking cockatoos to Himalayan bears and Siberian tigers – all more likely to impress tots, however, than adult animal-lovers.

Villa Ephrussi-de-Rothschild

1 av Ephrussi-de-Rothschild (04.93.01.45.90). **Open** *mid-Feb to June, Sept, Oct* 10am-6pm daily; *Nov to mid-Feb* 2-6pm Mon-Fri; 10am-6pm Sat, Sun; *July, Aug* 10am-7pm daily. **Admission** 49F, children 37F.

Zoo du Cap-Ferrat

117 bd du Général de Gaulle (04.93.76.07.60). **Open** *Apr-Oct* 9.30am-7.30pm daily; *Nov-Mar* 9.30am-5.30pm daily. **Admission** 58F, children 42F.

Where to stay & eat

You almost expect to see gentlemen in top hats strolling through the manicured gardens of the stately **Grand Hôtel du Cap-Ferrat** (71 bd Général de Gaulle, 04.93.76.50.50, closed Jan & Feb, rates 1,200F-7,100F), hidden away near the tip of the peninsula. Non-guests can stop for a drink at its Somerset Maugham Bar, where the writer occasionally wandered from his nearby home to meet friends for *gin tonics* at sunset, or eat at the classically elegant Le Cap restaurant (menu 520F); for a 300F entrance fee, they can also take the funicular to Le Club Dauphin, a spectacular spill-over pool at the water's edge with a restaurant. Set on a hill inland, the more affordable **Hôtel le Panoramic** (3 av Albert 1er, 04.93.76.00.37, closed mid-Nov to mid-Dec, rates 600F-780F) has airy, comfortable rooms with terraces and a dazzling view of the harbour. **La Voile d'Or** (av Jean Mermoz, 04.93.01.13.13, closed Nov-Mar, rates 1,100F-3,500F) might be mistaken for an impressive family villa at the edge of the Port St-Jean. The excellent but traditional cuisine (menus 270F-360F) and 1950s decor may not be trendy, but starlit nights at its breezy terrace restaurant make up for the stuffiness of the place. **Hôtel Brise Marine** (58 av Jean Mermoz, 04.93.76.04.36, closed Nov-Jan, rates 730F-790F), a splendid ochre- and turquoise-trimmed villa with a tangled garden, is the quintessential Riviera experience, a stone's throw from the lovely La Paloma beach. **Hôtel Résidence Bagatelle** (av Honoré Sauvan, 04.93.01.32.86, closed Nov-Feb, rates 380F-480F), tucked away on a quiet residential

backstreet linking St-Jean and Beaulieu, has modestly priced rooms and an overgrown citrus garden where breakfast is served.

Getting there

See page 237 **Beaulieu.**

Tourist information

Office de Tourisme

59 av Semeria (04.93.76.08.90/fax 04.93.76.16.76). **Open** *June-Aug* 8.30am-6pm daily; *Sept-Apr* 8.30am-noon, 1-5pm Mon-Fri.

Beaulieu-sur-Mer

A charming Belle Epoque resort that was long a mecca for holidaying Russian and British aristocrats, Beaulieu still has an old-world feel, with its neat rows of genteel but non-designer boutiques on peaceful village streets lined with orange trees and the ubiquitous palms. Well-heeled Sunday strollers and their yapping dogs jostle each other for space on **promenade Maurice Rouvier**, a paved seaside path linking the port of Beaulieu to St-Jean-Cap-Ferrat via the late David Niven's pink castle; go early in the morning or at sunset to get the best of the view.

Gustave Eiffel (he of the tower) and Gordon Bennet, legendary director of the *New York Herald Tribune*, lived here. So did archeologist Theodore Reinach, who was so enamoured of his specialist subject – ancient Greece – that he built a fastidious and not-to-be-missed reconstruction of a fifth-century BC Athenian house. Now a museum, the **Villa Kerylos** boasts a sunken marble bath, reclining sofas and antique-looking frescos galore (plus some hidden modern amenities such as showers, loos and pianos). The villa's outdoor café, smack in front of the glittering **Baie des Fourmis** – so called because of the ant-like black rocks dotted about – is one of the coast's best-kept secrets for breakfast, snacks or a glass of wine.

The **casino**, a small turn-of-the-century jewel across from the palm-lined seafront offering roulette, blackjack and baccarat for the staid, wealthy Cap-Ferrat crowd, is deliciously retro. So, too, is the **Tennis Club de Beaulieu-sur-Mer** (4 rue A de Yougoslavie, 04.93.01.05.19), a quaint Riviera-style club with eight clay courts and a mini-clubhouse; non-members are welcome (from 100F per day).

East of Beaulieu, the Basse Corniche continues towards Monaco through the nondescript ribbon development of Eze-Bord-de-Mer and on to Cap-d'Ail, which would have little to recommend it were it not for a splendid

Ancient Greek mod cons at the **Villa Kerylos**.

(and well-signposted) pebbly beach, **Plage la Mala**, a democratic favourite equally prized by the Monaco jetset and Italian day-trippers. It's only a ten-minute walk from the Basse Corniche, but be prepared for a considerable trek down (and up!) the stone steps. Top up your energy reserves with the surprisingly good food at the beach shack.

Casino
4, rue Fernand Dunan (04.93.76.48.00). **Open** 11am-5am Fri, Sat; 11am-4am Mon-Thur, Sun.

Villa Kerylos
impasse Gustave Eïffel (04.93.01.01.44). **Open** *mid-Dec to mid-Feb* 2-6pm daily; *mid-Feb to June, Sept to mid-Nov* 10.30am-6pm daily; *July, Aug* 10.30am-7pm daily. **Admission** 43F, under-8s free.

Where to stay & eat

Stylish bistro **Les Agaves** (*see page 51*) in the Palais des Anglais building opposite the station is reviewed in the Provençal Food & Drink chapter. The Italianate **Le Métropole** (15 bd Leclerc, 04.93.01.00.08, closed mid-Oct to mid-Dec, rates 1,800F-4,100F) has its own flower-lined walkway by the sea and excellent restaurant (menus 330F-530F) serving an inspired mix of classic and Provençal dishes by chef Christian Metral; it makes a refreshing change from the formality of most Riviera luxury hotels. The *fin de siècle* Florentine **Hôtel La Réserve** (5 bd Leclerc, 04.93.01.00.01, closed mid-Jan to Feb, rates 980F-5,690F), where celebrities and royalty once flocked, is still a discreetly elegant landmark, recently refurbished in sumptuous marble to match the refined but pricey Mediterranean cuisine (menus 480F-850F) orchestrated by chef Christophe Cussac. **Hôtel Le Havre Bleu** (29 bd du Maréchal Joffre, 04.93.01.01.40, closed two weeks Jan, rates 280F-300F) is a Victorian-style villa with simple, clean rooms, some with terraces.

The **Pâtisserie Lac** (35 bd Marioni, 04.93.01.35.85, closed Wed) is a must for sweet fiends: try its famous featherlight *fraisier*, a divine strawberry mousse cake. The retro-colonial **L'African Queen** (port de Plaisance, 04.93.01.10.85, à la carte only) is always lively, especially in the summer; it offers standard brasserie fare – pizza, salads, pasta and grilled fish – plus a chance to rub elbows with stars like Jack Nicholson or Bono, who occasionally turn up for dinner.

Getting there

By car
From the Vieux Port in Nice, take bd Carnot, which becomes the Basse Corniche (N98).

By bus
Broch and RCA run services along the Basse Corniche from bus stations in Nice and Menton every 20min: information from Nice's *gare routière* (04.93.85.61.81).

By train
Stations at Villefranche, Beaulieu, Eze-Bord-de-Mer and Cap-d'Ail are served by regular stopping trains from Nice, some of which continue on to Ventimiglia in Italy. Beaulieu is also served by faster Italian trains on the Nice-Genova run, but not by French TGVs, which go direct from Nice to Monaco.

Tourist information

Office de Tourisme
pl Clemenceau (04.93.01.02.21/fax 04.93.76.16.67). **Open** *Sept-May* 9am-12.15pm, 2-5.30pm Mon-Sat; *June-Aug* also open 9am-12.30pm Sun. *Website: http://www.rivierafr/bsmhome.htm*

The Moyenne Corniche

Eze

Perched photogenically on a pinnacle of rock 430 metres above sea level, Eze started life as a Celto-Ligurian settlement, passing over the ages from Phoenicians to Romans and from Lombards to Saracens. A centre of local power in the sixteenth century, its twisting stone alleys and vaulted passageways had become virtually deserted by the 1920s.

The village's glorious vistas inspired Friedrich Nietzsche, who would stride up here from his Eze-Bord-de-Mer home in the 1880s, composing the third part of *Thus Spake Zarathustra* in his head. The steep mule path he followed – now called **sentier Frédéric-Nietzsche** – snakes through olive and pine groves. Allow an hour and a half for the upward slog.

Eze hosts the **Eze d'Antan Festival** in the third week of July, when the village is swamped by sword-toting knights and colourful pageantry. Cutesy Provençal boutiques go some way to marring Éze's charm the rest of the year, but a place where donkeys still haul groceries up the steep lanes can't be entirely ruined (unless, of course, they're financed by the tourist board).

In what remains of Eze's castle, at the summit of the village, the **Jardin Exotique** is a spiral of paths inside the ruins, lined with a prickly blaze of flowering cacti and succulents, offering a sweeping panorama over the village's red-tiled roofs to the coast.

The Riviera

Don't be put off by the tourist hype outside: the family-run **Parfumerie Fragonard** is an outlet for one of Grasse's oldest perfume factories (*see box page 258*). The gift shop has everything from mint-lavender massage oil to wild thyme-scented candles.

Jardin Exotique
rue du Château (04.93.41.10.30). **Open** *Sept-Feb* 9am-5pm daily; *Mar, Apr* 9am-6.30pm daily; *May, June* 9am-7pm daily; *July, Aug* 9am-8pm daily. Closed Sept-Feb. **Admission** 15F, free under-12s. **No credit cards.**

Parfumerie Fragonard
quartiers des Condamines (04.93.41.05.05). **Open** 8.30-noon, 2-6pm Mon-Sat. **Credit** MC, V.

Where to stay & eat

Nestling beneath the castle ruins, the **Nid d'Aigle** (rue du Château, 04.93.41.19.08, closed Wed & Jan, menus 130F-180F) is an informal, family-run restaurant specialising in Provençal dishes, including a tasty *daube niçoise*. The sumptuous rooms at the **Château de la Chèvre d'Or** (rue du Barri, 04.92.10.66.66, closed end-Nov to Mar, rates 1,900F-3,200F) have sweeping views along the coast, and there's a pool, too. At the Château's gourmet restaurant (menus 320F-680F), chef Jean-Marc Delacourt specialises in classic Med-inspired dishes; if you're not up to the splurge, put on your finery and sip cocktails at sunset in the bar, a romantic hideaway with the best view onto the Riviera. The **Château Eza** (rue de la Pise, 04.93.41.12.24, closed mid-Oct to Mar, rates 2,000F-4,000F), a mini-castle at the top of endless steep, crooked steps, has pricey rooms bordering on the kitsch, with a choice of medieval armour or chintzy frills; the highlight is the outdoor terrace restaurant (closed Tue and Wed from Jan-Apr, closed Nov-25 Dec, menus 250F-530F) with romantic balconies for two, a sublime panorama and equally exquisite food. The **Auberge du Troubadour** (rue du Brec, 04.93.41.19.03, closed Mon lunch, all Sun & Feb to late-Dec, menus 170F-245F) may be one of the few dining spots here without a view, but it offers reliably good regional specialities and an extensive choice of wines at affordable prices.

Getting there

By car
Take Corniche André de Joly from the pl Max Barel roundabout in Nice; this soon becomes the N7 Moyenne Corniche, which climbs to Eze via the Col de Villefranche. From the A8 autoroute take exit no.57.

Eze, the ultimate *village perché*.

By bus/train
RCA's (04.93.85.61.81) fairly frequent Nice-Beausoleil service (no.112) stops in Eze (and terminates there on Sun). There are also regular shuttle buses (more frequent in summer) from Eze-Bord-de-Mer railway station (*see above* **Beaulieu**).

Tourist information

Office de Tourisme
pl Général de Gaulle (04.93.41.26.00). **Open** *Apr-Oct* 10am-1pm, 2-7pm Mon-Sat; 9am-7pm Sun; *Nov-Mar* 9am-6.30pm Mon-Sat; 9.30am-1pm, 2-6.30pm Sun. Guided tours of the town start from here at 10.15am and 3pm daily and cost 30F. *Website: http://www.eze-riviera.com*

The Grande Corniche

The Grande Corniche winds for 32 kilometres along the breathtaking precipices of the Alpes-Maritimes, climbing to 62 metres above sea level. Built under Napoléon along the route of the Aurelian Way (known in this stretch as the Via Julia Augusta), it's a favourite recreational route for wannabe Formula One drivers, masochistic cyclists, scenery-lovers who don't suffer from vertigo and *To Catch a Thief* fans.

Dominating the road is **La Turbie** (from *tropea*, Latin for trophy), a spectacularly located village that is often shrouded in mountain mist. Basking in sleepy charm, it is little more than a row of ochre eleventh- to thirteenth-century houses, two ancient town gates and an eighteenth-century church, **St-Michel-Archange**, with a host of 'attributed to' and 'school of' works that are clearly not by Bréa, Rembrandt, Raphael or Murillo themselves. What puts the village on the map, however, is the Roman **Trophée des Alpes**, a partly restored curve of huge white Doric columns set in a beautiful hilltop park. The Trophée was erected in 6 BC to commemorate the victories of Augustus' troops over rowdy local tribes who had taken advantage of the momentary confusion after the death of Julius Caesar to overrun the place; a copy of an inscription praising Augustus can be seen on the trophy, though the huge statue of the victor that once adorned it has long since gone. Inside the adjoining museum is a scale model of the original, and diverse artefacts unearthed from the site.

If it's sport, not history, you're after, the **Monte-Carlo Golf Club** is an 18-hole course with a vertiginous view from impeccably kept grounds. Star-gazers, on the other hand, should head for the **Eze Astrorama**, a wildly popular astronomical show (planetarium, telescopes, videos) a couple of kilometres up the hill north of La Turbie.

Eze Astrorama

Rte de la Revere (04.93.41.23.04). **Open** 6-10pm Fri, Sat. **Admission** 40F, children 30F. **No credit cards**.

Monte-Carlo Golf Club

rte du Mont Agel (04.92.41.50.70). **Open** *June-Sept* 8am-8pm daily; *Oct-May* 8am-6pm daily. **Price** 400F Mon-Sat, 500F Sun. **Credit** AmEx, MC, V.

Trophée des Alpes

18 av Albert 1er (04.93.41.20.84). **Open** *mid-Sept to Mar* 10am-5pm Tue-Sun; *Apr to mid-June* 9.30am-6pm daily; *mid-June to mid-Sept* 9.30am-7pm daily. **Admission** 25F, children 15F.

Where to stay & eat

Besides offering pleasant rooms, La Turbie's **Hôtellerie Jérome** (20 rue de Compte de Cessole, 04.92.41.51.51, rate 420F) boasts a restaurant (closed Mon, Tue & mid-Oct to mid-Dec, menu 240F) in which chef Bruno Cirino concocts great country recipes with a Ligurian twist, such as roast chicken with chestnut stuffing and candied fennel, and caramelised apples with ricotta. Hanging off a cliff off the

Corniche by exit no.58 off the A8, the **Roquebrune Vista Palace** (La Grande Corniche, 04.92.10.40.00, closed Feb to mid-Mar, rates 1,600F-4,000F) is an architectural eyesore of monstrous proportions; inside, however, the vast, sharp-edged triangular rooms have a luxury-liner feel, with countless spellbinding vantage points. Its restaurant, **Le Vistaero** (menus 250F-580F), has become a temple of classic French cuisine with a hint of Provençal whimsy: try the grilled fish with citrus fruit and saffron, served with pumpkin and carrot gratin with Parmesan and pine nuts.

Getting there

By car

From Nice, take the bd Riquier north and turn right at the sign marked Grande Corniche. From Roquebrune, follow signs to the Grande Corniche from the Basse or Moyenne Corniches

By bus

RCA (04.93.85.61.81) runs three services daily, except on Sundays and public holidays, between Nice and Peille (no.115), via La Turbie.

Tourist information

La Mairie (town hall)

La Turbie (04.92.41.51.61). **Open** 9am-noon, 2-5pm Mon-Fri; 9am-noon Sat.

The **Trophée des Alpes** in La Turbie.

The Riviera

Monaco & Monte-Carlo

Small, smart and discreetly loaded, Monaco has made plenty of mileage out of its historical isolation.

Controlled by the Grimaldi family since 1297, the principality of Monaco is the last European state – apart from the Vatican – with an autocratic ruler. It's a perfect set-up: the prince holds benevolent but absolute sway over 32,000 residents – of whom only 6,000 are Monégasque citizens – and they, in return, are happy to barter democracy for tax breaks.

One look at the square in front of the casino – lined with Lamborghinis and Rolls-Royces, with white-gloved *gendarmes* directing traffic past carefully manicured lawns – and you know this is a world apart. Here you can indulge your dress-code daydreams: from sables to labels, you can never be too ostentatiously rich. As for jewels, the bigger the better, and if they're real, never fear: there's a policeman for every 60 residents (not to mention as many gardeners); and around 150 sophisticated surveillance cameras – in trees, at traffic lights, even in lifts – watch every movement in this two-kilometre-square principality.

It wasn't always like this. When Menton and Roquebrune were whisked away from Grimaldi control in 1848, Europe's poorest state lost its main source of revenue: a tax on lemons. Then-ruler Charles III had the idea of replacing lemons with gambling. He called in financier François Blanc, who set up the Société des Bains de Mer (SBM) to operate a casino on a hill named after the prince: Monte-Carlo. The crown took 10 per cent of SBM profits.

Blanc gave the French government a low-interest 4.8-million franc loan so it could finish building the Paris Opéra; in return, he got the Opéra's architect, Charles Garnier, to design the casino, plus a French-built railway to ship in gamblers by the wagon-load. So fruitful was the venture that in 1870 the flourishing principality abolished taxes for nationals and anyone meeting certain residence requirements, and for companies based and trading here. That rule still stands, much to the delight of the world's top earners and tax-dodgers.

Nowadays, Monaco has a government of sorts, the 18-member National Council elected by Monégasque citizens (not residents) for a five-year term, with a chairman who must be a French citizen. The Council's main job is to pass French legislation on to the reigning prince: if he approves, it becomes law in Monaco, too; if

he doesn't, it doesn't. Apart from a tiff with France in 1962, when Paris tired of its richer citizens taking tax-refuge in Monaco and stationed troops along the border in protest, relations between the principality and its bigger neighbour run pretty smoothly.

Much more smoothly, indeed, than the tragic and/or torrid affairs of the Grimaldi family. Dapper Rainier III's marriage to ravishing Hollywood star Grace Kelly in 1956 was the stuff of fairy tales. But it was one with a sad ending, when Princess Grace was killed in a car accident on the Corniche in 1982. Her daughter, Princess Caroline, has had her share of troubles, too: her first marriage ended disastrously, and her second husband, Stefano Casiraghi, was killed in 1990 in a speedboat race. Her sister Stéphanie – once considered the wild child of the family – was stung by scandal when former bodyguard husband Daniel Ducruet was photographed in a compromising position with a Belgian stripper. The real pressure, though, seems to be on Prince Albert, who has been properly groomed to inherit his father's tiny kingdom and 200-million-franc fortune, but has so far produced no heir.

Sightseeing

Glitzy Monte-Carlo is just one of Monaco's five districts. It packs in the **casino**, which houses the **Salle Garnier** opera house, most of the principality's shops and hotels, and the slightly creepy **Musée National Automates et Poupées** doll museum.

To the west, Fontvieille is a concrete sprawl of high-rise, high-price apartments, many of them built on land reclaimed over recent decades from the sea. The area has some rather antiseptic museums (one for Prince Rainier's car collection, another for his model ships, a coin collection and a zoo) plus a lovely rose garden dedicated to Princess Grace and – up the hill – the cactus-filled **Jardin Exotique**.

Le Rocher – or Monaco-Ville – is the medieval town, dominated by the fairy-tale Palais Princier. A labyrinth of winding streets, the Rocher abounds in shops purveying touristic paraphernalia. The neo-Byzantine **Cathédrale de Monaco** is the final resting place of numerous Grimaldi princes and of Princess

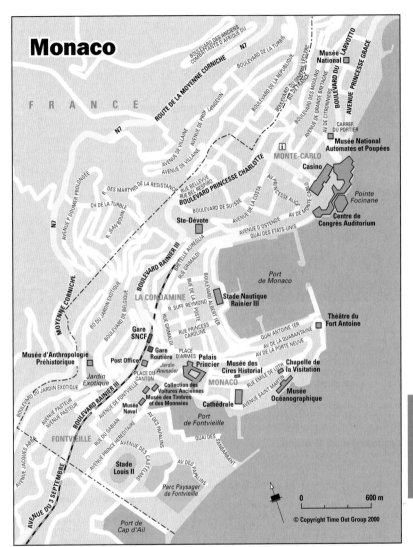

Monaco

F R A N C E

BOULEVARD DES ANCIENS
COMBATTANTS D'AFRIQUE DU

ROUTE DE LA MOYENNE CORNICHE

BOULEVARD DE LA TURBIE

N7

BOULEVARD DE LA REPUBLIQUE

BOULEVARD DU GÉNÉRAL LECLERC
BD DE FRANCE

BOULEVARD DES MOULINS

AVENUE DE GRANDE BRETAGNE

AVENUE DE CITRONNIERS

BOULEVARD DU LARVOTTO

AVENUE PRINCESSE GRACE

Musée
National

CARREF.
DU PORTIER

N7

AVENUE DE VILLAINE

AVENUE DE VILLAINE

AVENUE DE PROF. LANGEVIN

AVENUE DE VILLAINE

Musée National
Automates et Poupées

MONTE-CARLO

Casino

AVENUE P. DOUMER PROLONGÉE

DES MARTYRS DE LA RESISTANCE

RUE BELLEVUE
RUE BEL RESPIRO

BOULEVARD PRINCESSE CHARLOTTE

AV. PRINCESSE ALICE

AV. PRINCESSE ALICE

Pointe
Focinane

CH DE LA TURBIE

BOULEVARD DE SUISSE

AVENUE DE LA COSTA

AV DE MONTE-CARLO

Centre de
Congrès Auditorium

N7

R. DES MARTYRS DE LA RESISTANCE

R. JEAN BOUIN

Ste-Dévote

AVENUE D'OSTENDE
QUAI DES ETATS-UNIS

Port
de Monaco

BOULEVARD RAINIER III

BRETELLE AUREGLIA
RUE GRIMALDI

BOULEVARD ALBERT 1ER

Stade Nautique
Rainier III

MOYENNE CORNICHE

BD DU JARDIN EXOTIQUE

BOULEVARD DE BELGIQUE

RUE DE LA

R. SUFF. REYMOND

R. SUFF. REYMOND

RUE DE LA POSTE

RUE PRINCESSE
CAROLINE

QUAI ANTOINE 1ER

QUAI DE LA QUARANTAINE
AV DE LA PORTE NEUVE

Théâtre du
Fort Antoine

Musée d'Anthropologie
Préhistorique

Gare
SNCF

Gare
Routière

Post Office

RUE GRIMALDI

PLACE
D'ARMES

Palais
Princier

PLACE DU
CANTON

Jardin
Animalier

Musée des
Cires Historial

RUE EMILE DE LOTH

Chapelle de
la Visitation

BOULEVARD DU JARDIN EXOTIQUE

Jardin
Exotique

BOULEVARD RAINIER III

AVENUE PASTEUR

AVENUE PASTEUR

AVENUE DE FONTVIEILLE

Collection des
Voitures Anciennes

Musée des Timbres
et des Monnaies

Musée
Naval

AVENUE DES PAPALINS

MONACO

Cathédrale

AVENUE SAINT MARTIN

Musée
Océanographique

Port
de Fontvieille

QUAI DES SANBARBANT

FONTVIEILLE

RUE DU GABIAN

RUE PRINCE HEREDITAIRE

AVENUE DES CASTELANS

AVENUE DES

AVENUE PRINCE HEREDITAIRE

Stade
Louis II

AV DES PAPALINS

AV DES PAPALINS

AVENUE JACQUES ABBÉ

AVENUE DU 3 SEPTEMBRE

Parc Paysager
de Fontvieille

Port de
Cap d'Ail

0   600 m

© Copyright Time Out Group 2000

Grace. More Grimaldis can be seen in the **Historial des Princes de Monaco** waxworks museum. Alternatively, head for the infinitely more fascinating aquarium in the **Musée Océanographique** or the impressive array of old masters housed in the **Musée de la Visitation**.

La Condamine, the harbour area, has a good daily food market, and a number of industrial lofts on the port quay that have been turned into ateliers for a select group of international artists – Arman, Botero, Sosno, Adami and Matta. This Cité des Artistes boasts an art gallery and a brasserie where creative ideas can be swapped over an aperitif. The area is also home to the nineteenth-century **Eglise Ste-Dévote**. If you're on the celebrity watch, **Larvotto**, the easternmost strip where Monaco's beaches are located, is your best bet: you may glimpse residents Boris Becker, Ringo

Le Rocher, Monaco's powerhouse.

Starr or Claudia Schiffer at events at **Le Sporting Club**.

● The international phone code for Monaco is 00 377. If you're calling from France, dial 00 377 then the number. When phoning a Monégasque number from inside the principality, omit the code. To call abroad – including France – from Monaco, use the international prefix 00 then the country code (33 for France).

Cathédrale de Monaco

4 rue du Colonel Bellando de Castro (00.377.93.30.87.70). **Open** 7am-7pm daily. **Admission** free.

Built in 1875 on the ruins of a thirteenth-century chapel, this Romanesque-y, Byzantine-y cathedral has an altarpiece by fifteenth-century local artist Louis Bréa, a grandiose altar in Carrara marble, tombs of the former princes of Monaco, and a simple pavement slab for Princess Grace, inscribed 'Gratia Patricia Principis Rainierii III Uxor'.

Collection des Voitures Anciennes

terrasse de Fontvieille. (00.377.92.05.28.56). **Open** 10am-6pm daily. **Admission** 30F, 15F children.

Prince Rainier's snazzy vintage car collection, with everything from a 1903 De Dion Bouton to a 1986 Lamborghini Countach.

Eglise Ste-Dévote

pl Ste-Dévote (00.377.93.50.52.60). **Open** 9am-6.30pm daily. **Admission** free.

This portside church was built in 1870 on the ruins of the site where, according to legend, the third-century martyr Ste Dévote – Monaco's patron saint – was miraculously guided ashore by a dove after surviving a shipwreck off Africa. The saint's relics were stolen by pirates in the Middle Ages; they were caught, and their ship burnt. A replica goes up in flames in the square in front of the church every 26 January.

Jardin Animalier

esplanade Rainier III (00.377.93.25.18.31). **Open** Oct-Feb 10am-noon, 2-5pm daily; Mar-May 10am-6pm daily; June-Sept 9am-noon, 2-7pm daily. **Admission** 20F, 10F children. **No credit cards.**

After a visit to Africa in 1954, Prince Rainier procured countless varieties of monkeys and sundry other wild beasts and exotic birds for this mini-zoo.

Jardin Exotique et Grotte de l'Observatoire

bd du Jardin Exotique (00.377.93.15.29.80). **Open** mid-May to mid-Sept 9am-7pm daily; mid-Sept to mid-Nov, Jan to mid-May 9am-6pm daily. Closed mid-Nov to Dec. **Admission** 40F, 19F children (includes entry to garden, grotto and Musée d'Anthropologie Préhistorique). **No credit cards.**

Inaugurated in 1933, this succulent wonderland of nearly 7,000 bizarrely shaped tropical specimens has everything from giant agaves from the Aztec plateau to prickly ball-shaped cacti known as 'mother-in-law's cushions'. The grotto inside the garden contains a stalactite- and stalagmite-lined Neolithic dwelling 60 metres underground.

Musée d'Anthropologie Préhistorique

bd du Jardin Exotique (00.377.93.15.80.06). **Open** mid-May to mid-Sept 9am-7pm daily; mid-Sept to mid-Nov, Jan to mid-May 9am-6pm daily. Closed mid-Nov to Dec. **Admission** 40F, 19F children (includes entry to museum, Jardin Exotique and Grotte de l'Observatoire).

Relics of Stone Age life on the Riviera when mammoths, elephants and hippos ruled. Bones galore of extinct animal species and impressive Cro-Magnon skeletons, all found in the Grimaldi caves (which can be visited in Balzi Rossi, just over the border in Italy).

Musée de la Chapelle de la Visitation

pl de la Visitation (00.377.93.50.07.00). **Open** 10am-4pm Tue-Sun. **Admission** 20F, 10F children.

This seventeenth-century chapel houses a private collection of sacred works by Rubens, Zurbaran and Italian baroque masters.

Musée des Cires Historial des Princes de Monaco

27 rue Basse (00.377.93.30.39.05). **Open** Oct-Feb 10am-4pm daily; Mar-June 10am-6pm daily; July, Aug 10am-7pm daily. **Admission** 12F, 6F children.

Everything you've ever wanted to know (and probably rather more) about the Grimaldi dynasty in wax, with life-sized figures in full regalia.

Musée National Automates et Poupées

17 av Princesse Grace (00.377.93.30.91.26). **Open**
Oct-Apr 10am-12.30pm, 2.30-6.30pm daily; *Apr-Oct*
10am-6.30pm daily. **Admission** 30F, 20F children.
One of the world's biggest collections of eighteenth-
and nineteenth-century dolls and mechanical toys,
set into motion several times daily.

Musée Naval

esplanade Rainier III (00.377.92.05.28.48). **Open**
10am-6pm daily. **Admission** 25F, 15F children.
Prince Rainier's private collection of 180 scale repli-
cas of famous sea vessels.

Musée Océanographique

av St-Martin (00.377.93.15.36.00). **Open** *Apr-Sept*
7am-7pm daily; *Oct-Mar* 10am-6pm daily.
Admission 60F, 30F children.
Founded in 1910 by Albert I, who sank much of his
fortune into underwater research, the aquarium contains some of nature's most bizarre creatures, such
as the diaphanous leafy sea dragon, plus glinting
bream circling endlessly in their cylindrical tank
like bored Monégasque millionaires. Upstairs are
awesome displays of whale skeletons and stuffed
marine fauna. At the time of writing, a live coral
reef containing the world's rarest species was
due to go on show.

Musée des Souvenirs Napoléoniens et Collection des Archives Historiques du Palais

Pl du Palais (00.377.93.25.18.31). **Open** *June-Sept*
9.30am-6.30pm daily; *Oct, Nov* 10am-5pm daily; *Dec-
May* 10.30am-12.30pm, 2-5pm Tue-Sun. **Admission**
20F, 10F children.
Bonaparte buffs will enjoy the vast display of
objects and documents from the First Empire, while
the more Monaco-smitten can peruse an exhibit of
historic charters and Grimaldi medals.

Musée des Timbres et des Monnaies

esplanade Rainier III (00.377.93.15.41.50). **Open**
Sept-June 10am-5pm daily; *July, Aug* 10am- 6pm
daily. **Admission** 20F, 10F children.
More conspicuous money in this coin and stamp display covering four centuries of Monégasque minting.

Palais Princier

pl du Palais (00.377.93.25.18.31). **Open** *June-Sept*
9.30am-6.30pm daily; *Oct* 10am-5pm daily. Closed
Nov-May. **Admission** 30F, 15F children.
The salmon-pink palace, built over a thirteenth-
century Genoese fortress, is closed to the public
when the prince is in residence – signalled by the
red and white banner. During the 30-minute tours,
you'll be able to catch a glimpse of the frescoed
gallery, the sumptuous chambers with canopied
beds and Venetian furnishings in the state apartments, the throne room where official ceremonies
are held, and the mosaic courtyard. The changing
of the guard takes place at 11.55am daily in the
huge palace square.

Arts & entertainment

Le Cabaret du Casino

pl du Casino (00.377.92.16.36.36). **Shows** 10.30pm
Tue-Fri, Sun; 8.30pm, 10.30pm Sat. **Admission**
350F. **Credit** AmEx, MC, V.
Slick French cabaret shows *pour les touristes*, such
as Parisian import Le Crazy Horse, featuring tastefully lit barebreasted dancers, set in a red-velvety
nightclub atmosphere.

Casino

*pl du Casino (00.377.92.16.23.00/opera box office
00.377.92.16.23.67).* **Casino open** noon-late daily.
Opera *box office* 10am-5.30pm Tue-Sun;
performances 8.30pm; *tickets* 170F-720F.
Belle Epoque gilded splendour, designed by Charles
Garnier in 1863, where elegant cigar-puffing gamblers plunk down serious money in a muted old-
glamour atmosphere (*see box page 247*). Inside the
Ionic-columned atrium is the **Salle Garnier**, a
splendid chocolate-box concert hall, replete with
frescoed ceilings, dusty pink and green walls, and
wreath-toting sculpted cherubs. It's an ideal setting
for Monaco's top-notch opera series and innovative
performances by the Ballet de Monte-Carlo's ultra-
modern choreographer Jean-Christophe Maillot.

The **Grand Prix**. See page 289.

Monte-Carlo Beach Club

av Princesse Grace (04.93.28.66.66). **Open** *Apr-Oct* 9am-7pm daily. **Admission** 200F Mon-Fri, 300F Sat, Sun. **Credit** AmEx, DC, MC, V.

The favoured summer playground for Hermès-towel-toting socialites. Most of the action is by the huge heated seawater pool where Princess Stéphanie does her laps. Extras include jet-skiing, parasailing, water-skiing and windsurfing.

Monte-Carlo Country Club

155 av Princesse Grace (04.93.41.30.15). **Open** *July, Aug* 8am-9pm daily; *Sept-June* 8am-8.15pm daily. **Admission** 220F daily, 35,000F for a year's membership. **Credit** AmEx, DC, MC, V.

The swankiest club on the Riviera, with clay tennis courts, squash, and a heated open-air pool (open May-Oct) with airjets, waterfalls and a counter-current basin for aquatic workout enthusiasts.

Stade Louis II

7 av des Castelans (00.377.92.05.40.11). **Open** guided tours by appointment at 2.30pm & 4pm Mon, Tue, Thur, Fri. **Admission** 25F, 2.50F children. **No credit cards**.

This unsightly circular concrete block houses a gigantic sports complex – gyms, an athletics track, a pool – and the soccer pitch where AS Monaco play their home games. They may have almost no supporters (when they won the French league in 1997, Prince Albert, ringleader of the hardline fans, had to bus in 2,000 schoolchildren for the victory party), but an annual subsidy of 50 million francs keeps the team in winning form.

Stade Nautique Rainier III

quai Albert I (00.377.93.30.64.83). **Open** *May-June, Sept-Oct* 9am-6pm daily; *July, Aug* 9am-8pm.daily. **Admission** 24F. **No credit cards**.

This beautiful Olympic-sized seawater outdoor pool is a great place for serious swimming. Leave your designer swimsuits behind: no one's watching.

Théatre du Fort St-Antoine

av de la Quarantaine (00.377.93.25.66.12). **Box office** one hour before shows. **Shows** July, Aug. **Tickets** 60F, 80F, 30F concs. **No credit cards**.

A lovely stone theatre-in-the-round built on the ruins of an eighteenth-century fortress, perched on a rock overlooking the sea and magical for open-air concerts on starry summer nights. The venue also hosts theatre productions.

Les Thermes Marins de Monte-Carlo

2 av de Monte-Carlo (00.377.92.16.40.40). **Open** 8am-8.30pm daily. **Credit** AmEx, DC, MC, V.

A luxurious temple of thalassotherapy with state-of-the-art fitness centre and heated seawater pool. Special packages include quit-smoking cures and a back-in-shape programme for new mothers. A one-day package with four treatments and use of facilities costs 730F.

Monégasque haute cuisine is dominated by super-chef Alain Ducasse (*see box page 44*). But there are alternatives…

Le Café de Paris

pl du Casino (00.377.92.16.21.24). **Open** 8am-1.30am daily. **Menus** 180F-260F. **Credit** AmEx, DC, MC, V.

The principality's renowned turn-of-the-century brasserie next to the casino has a sprawling outdoor terrace so perfect for people-watching that it compensates somewhat for the pricey espresso. The reliably good bistro fare ranges from fresh oysters and grilled fish to hamburgers-frites and salads. Try the crêpe suzette, which was inadvertently invented here in the 1900s when a dessert-creation by Escoffier caught fire.

Castelroc

pl du Palais (00.377.93.30.36.68). **Meals served** mid Sept-Nov, Feb to mid-June noon-2.30pm Mon-Fri, Sun; *mid-June to mid-Sept* noon-2.30pm, 7.30-11pm Mon-Fri, Sun. Closed Dec, Jan. **Menus** 125F, 245F. **Credit** AmEx, MC, V.

Don't be put off by the touristy allure of the ultra-scenic outdoor terrace smack in front of the palace: this affordable family-run bistro is an established local haunt for seafood such as stockfish and steamed scampi.

La Coupole

Hôtel Mirabeau, 1 av Princesse Grace (00.377.92.16.65.65). **Meals served** noon-2pm, 8-10pm daily. **Menus** 270F-470F. **Credit** AmEx, DC, MC, V.

Ever since the recent takeover by talented chef Michel de Matteis, this restaurant has become a mecca for enlightened gastronomes. Specialities include ravioli stuffed with lobster, swiss chard and ricotta, coquilles St-Jacques in truffle sauce, and a divine caramelised apple soufflé.

Quai des Artistes

4 quai Antoine I (00.377.97.97.97.77). **Open** noon-11.15pm daily. **Menus** 135F-250F. **Credit** AmEx, DC, MC, V.

Brasserie with oysters, mussels and seafood galore, its decor an artsy mix of original frescos and a monstrous crystal chandelier. You can also dine at the marble counters near the zinc-topped bar and watch the beau monde, or drop in between meal-times for tea and pastry.

Stars & Bars

6 quai Antoine I (00.377.97.97.95.95). **Open** *Sept-June* 11am-4am Tue-Sun; *July, Aug* 10am-5am daily. **Menus** 175F-260F. **Admission** *club* 60F. **Credit** AmEx, MC, V.

This lively portside American-style sports bar is always packed with a mix of locals, racing drivers and the occasional rock or film star. Tex-Mex dishes are served by rollerskating waitresses with

The Riviera

Faites vos jeux

The majestic hush of Old World splendour hits you as soon as you step into the Belle Epoque atrium of the casino, with its towering marble Ionic columns and colossal bronze candelabras. One of the oldest casinos in the world, this ornate gambling house was dreamed up by Monaco's reigning Prince Charles III in 1863, to generate new revenue. When his early attempts failed, he turned it over to shrewd businessman François Blanc, who quickly found the necessary capital, sought out Paris' star architect Charles Garnier to build the new casino, and founded the now all-powerful Société des Bains de Mer (SBM) to run it. In 1951, just after Prince Rainier III came to the throne, Aristotle Onassis took over ownership, but his power was short-lived: Rainier made the state the principal shareholder in 1962. Today, old-fashioned precepts still apply: no clergymen or Monégasque citizens are allowed into the gaming rooms; if the Grimaldis want to attend an opera or ballet in the Salle Garnier, they have to slip in through the side door.

First stop is the casino entrance desk, where all those who want to gamble (who must be over 21) are required to present a passport or identity card. For men, a sports jacket and a tie are de rigueur in the evening; women glide from table to table in anything from a little black cocktail dress to elegant trousers.

Most of the novices begin with roulette, which has a 20 franc minimum bet, or play the endless rows of slot machines. The stakes are much higher in the Salons privés and the Club Anglais, which offer chemin de fer, *trente-et-quarante*, blackjack, American roulette and craps. Four predictably expensive restaurants are also housed within the casino's gilded walls. Note that all sections of the casino stay open until the last gambler slouches off home – which can be as late as 6am.

Casino de Monte-Carlo

pl du Casino (00.377.92.16.23.00). **Open** *Salons européens* noon-late daily, *slot machines* 2pm-late daily; *Salons privés* 3pm-late; *Club anglais* 10pm-late. **Admission** *Salons européens & slot machines* 50F; *Salons privés & Club anglais* 100F.

high-tech headphones in a forced-fun atmosphere. There is a playroom for kids, a backroom with video games, and a small after-hours club with live groups upstairs.

Il Triangolo
1 av de la Madone (00.377.93.30.67.30). **Lunch served** noon-2pm Mon-Fri; **dinner served** 8-11pm daily. **Menus** 100F (lunch only), dinner à la carte only, average 150F. **Credit** MC, V.
A centrally located Italian bistro with the best thin-crust pizza in the principality.

Le Vista Mar
Hôtel Hermitage, square Beaumarchais (00.377.92.16.40.00). **Meals served** noon-2.30pm, 7.30-10pm daily. **Menus** 280F-380F. **Credit** AmEx, DC, MC, V.
On the hotel's rooftop terrace, this elegant seafood restaurant, designed like a cruise liner, offers a refined extravaganza of Mediterranean-inspired fish dishes, exquisitely prepared by chef Joel Garault, whose daily catch of the day is delivered to the kitchen door straight from the boat. The copious three-course business lunch during the week is well worth the price.

Zia Teresa
Galerie du Metropole, pl du Casino (00.377.93.30.12.29). **Meals served** noon-10pm daily. **Menu** 100F. **No credit cards**.
The perfect lunch spot in this upmarket shopping centre, serving generous portions of homemade pasta dishes at modest prices – a rarity at this glitzy end of town.

Nightlife

Bombay Frigo
3 av Princesse Grace (00.377.93.25.57.00). **Open** 11am-3.30pm, 6pm-1am Tue-Sun. **Credit** AmEx, DC, MC, V.
Colonial decor and DJs – the new place to be seen for the chic beau monde.

Cherie's Café
9 av des Spelugues (00.377.93.30.30.99). **Open** *bar* 10pm-5am daily. **Meals served** noon-2pm, 7pm-midnight Mon-Sat. **Credit** AmEx, DC, MC, V.
A small restaurant and piano bar on the main drag with live soul, rock and blues groups.

La Rascasse
quai Antoine I (00.377.93.25.56.90). **Open** 1pm-5am Tue-Sun. **Admission** free. **Credit** AmEx, DC, MC, V.
This informal all-night pub has an outdoor terrace, a superb view of the harbour, and features live jazz and rock music plus DJs. Upstairs, the more upscale candlelit seafood restaurant (open 7pm-midnight, closed Mon, menu 200F) is known for its *rascasse* soup.

Sass Café
11 av Princesse Grace (00.377.93.25.52.00). **Open** 10pm-late daily. **Admission** free. **Credit** AmEx, DC, MC, V.
A hotspot offering live music and a pricey menu of international dishes, with the quintessential Monte-Carlo mix of Eurotrash, club-hoppers, and a bevvy of dressed-to-kill gold-laden women who'll be dancing on the tables by 2am.

A lion fish meditating in the **Musée Océanographique**. See page 245.

The Riviera

Le Sporting Club

av Princesse Grace (00.377.92.16.22.77). **Open**
10.30pm-late daily. **Admission** 200F. **Credit** AmEx,
DC, MC, V.

This six-hectare complex is a glittery seaside landmark, frequented by European royalty, models, pop
stars, Middle Eastern princes and mini-skirted demoiselles in Cartier. Jimmy'z (open Apr-Nov 11.30pm-
dawn Wed-Sun, reservations 00.377.92.16. 36.36), the
disco for beautiful people, requires chic dress and an
amply stuffed wallet. Le Sporting d'Eté, a multi-level
entertainment complex, hosts the principality's charity balls, plus big-name crooners and bands.

Shopping

Luxury knows no bounds in Monte-Carlo's
couturier-glutted streets, from the rash of
jewellery shops near the casino, to the endless
rows of designer boutiques that stretch along the
boulevard des Moulins and avenue Princesse
Grace. In the place du Casino, the Galerie du
Metropole is an upscale three-storey mall. Rue
Grimaldi offers the flip, hip side of fashion. True
Monégasques shop in the Centre Commerciale in
Fontvieille, a large mall with mega-supermarket.

Where to stay

Hôtel Helvetia

*1 bis rue Grimaldi (00.377.93.30.21.71/
fax 00.377.92.16.70.51)*. Closed two weeks Dec.
Rates single 390F-430F, double 420F. **Credit** AmEx,
MC, V.

A stone's throw from the port, this clean, affordable
hotel has unremarkable decor but friendly staff.

Hôtel Hermitage

*square Beaumarchais (00.377.92.16.40.00/
fax 00.377.92.16.69.10)*. **Rates** single 1,700F-
2,722F, double 1,902F-3,017F, suites 4,010F-4,920F.
Credit AmEx, DC, MV, V.

A lovely Belle Epoque landmark of understated
elegance, with a floral stained-glass-domed *jardin
d'hiver* designed by Gustave Eiffel. Comfortable modern rooms; the more expensive ones have balconies
with harbour views.

Hôtel de Paris

*pl du Casino (00.377.92.16.30.00/fax
00.377.92.16.69.10)*. **Rates** single 2,000F-3,706F,
double 2,200F-3,706F, suites 1,700F-10,000F. **Credit**
AmEx, DC, MC, V.

The most luxurious of the three hotels owned by
the Grimaldi-run Société Bains de Mer, this rococo-
style palace built in 1865 was once frequented
by grand dukes, royals, and everyone from
Sarah Bernhardt to Winston Churchill. Majestic
grandeur still prevails, bath soaps are Hermès, and
breakfast is served on gold-trimmed Limoges
porcelain. If funds are short, soak up the atmosphere in its Old World bar.

Monte-Carlo Grand Hôtel (formerly Loews)

*12 av des Spelugues (00.377.93.50.65.00/fax
00.377.93.93.30.01)*. **Rates** single 1,700F, double
2,050F, suites 5,500F. **Credit** AmEx, DC, MC, V.

This high-rise hotel built over the sea may be glitz-
less and efficiently modern, but it's also family-friendly, with a choice of restaurants and bars, a fitness
centre, rooftop swimming pool, and the Sun Casino.

Essentials

French banknotes are legal tender in Monaco;
French coins are not. Monégasque coins can be
used in the principality and Alpes-Maritimes, but
no further afield in France. Letters sent from
Monaco must bear Monégasque stamps.

Getting there

By car

Leave the A8 autoroute at exit no.57 or no.58.

By bus

From Nice, Gare Routière RCA and Broch
(information 04.93.21.30.83) run services every 15min
Mon-Sat, and every 20min Sun.

By helicopter

Heli-Air Monaco, Fontvieille (00.377.92.05.00.50). A
seven-minute flight from Nice airport costs 435F,
40% discount for under-12s; free under-2s.

By train

Monaco-Monte-Carlo station is served by regular
trains on the Cannes-Nice-Menton-Ventimiglia line.

Getting around

By bus

Four local bus lines cover the whole principality:
two leave from the railway station and two from
Monaco-Ville.

Lifts & escalators

Seven public lifts and a number of escalators ferry
people from car prksea-level areas up to Monaco-
Ville and Monte-Carlo.

Tourist information

Direction des Tourismes et des Congés de la Principauté de Monaco

*2A bd des Moulins (00.377.92.16.61.16/fax
00.377.92.16.60.00)*. **Open** 9am-7pm Mon-Sat,
10am-noon Sun.
Website: www.monaco-congres.com

Postes et Télégraphes

*Palais de la Scala, 1 av Henri Dunant
(00.377.97.97.25.25)*. **Open** 8am-7pm Mon-Fri;
8am-noon Sat.

The Riviera

Menton & Around

Lemons, invalids and tropical gardens have long been Menton's speciality. For something more bracing, head for Roquebrune and the hill villages.

Menton

Sheltered by a circle of mountains, Menton, last stop on the Côte before the Italian border, has preserved a certain geriatric charm. It claims to have the mildest climate on the Riviera, with 316 cloudless days a year. Lemon trees thrive here – and the humble lemon – juiced, iced, or printed on plates and floor tiles – is slowly replacing the zimmer frame as Menton's official symbol.

After more than six centuries of Monégasque domination, Menton voted to become French in 1860. With invasion or takeover no longer a threat, the town expanded beyond its fortified walls and over the terraced green hillsides.

In 1860, British physician Henry Bennet recommended Menton, with its bright sunny winters, as the ideal site for a seaside health resort. Before long, wealthy Britons and Russians – including royal celebrities such as Empress Eugénie, Queen Victoria and Edward VII – began gracing Menton's shores. With them, they brought an affinity for fashionable tea rooms and elaborate botanical gardens. Writers, artists and musicians – among them Guy de Maupassant, Gustave Flaubert and Franz Liszt – also came to sojourn in the lemon-scented city.

But the sea air wasn't always as restorative as doctors imagined. Tuberculosis sufferers like Robert Louis Stevenson (who discovered the virtues of opium in Menton) and Katherine Mansfield, holed up in her tiny villa Isola Bella, found that the seaside dampness only worsened their condition.

The tone of present-day Menton is still set by its charmingly dilapidated Belle Epoque villas, by the public **Jardin Biovès**, with its palms and bitter orange trees, and by numerous statue-filled historic tropical gardens. But there's modernity here, too, if you know where to look: Jean Cocteau left his mark, as did architect Eileen Gray, whose miniature 1930s cube-house, later owned by painter Graham Sutherland, is clearly visible on route de Castellar.

Out of season, Menton has few nocturnal hotspots, and the gambling at the casino is low-key. Year-round, however, youthful crowds and smartly dressed Italians can be seen strolling along the seafront **promenade du Soleil**, scooping up fruit in the municipal covered market in the *vieille ville*. In the

The Menton trademark.

summer, they sunbathe topless on the city's uninspiring pebbly beaches.

The **Musée des Beaux-Arts** stands a little to the west of the city centre. A sumptuous seventeenth-century villa and former summer retreat for the Princes of Monaco, the museum has an extensive collection of European paintings, ranging from Italian primitives to a beautiful *Virgin and Child* by Louis Bréa, and works by major contemporary artists, including Graham Sutherland, an honorary Mentonnais. The palace is surrounded by a vast garden, the **Jardin des Agrumes**, an extravaganza of 400 fragrant citrus trees.

The *salle des mariages* (registry office) of the **Hôtel de Ville** was decorated by Jean Cocteau in the 1950s. A whimsical set of variations on Riviera symbols, it features splendid murals of swirling seas, a fish-eyed fisherman and his straw-hatted bride, as well as kitsch palm tree candelabras and a mock panther-skin carpet.

It's not perhaps the most auspicious background for a wedding: the bride's mother looks royally pissed off, as does the groom's angry ex-wife and her well-armed brother. There's more Cocteau in a miniature seventeenth-century stone bastion on the waterfront, where the **Musée Cocteau** contains works donated by the artist. It's an eclectic collection, ranging from beach-pebble mosaics and Aubusson-inspired tapestries to ceramic vases and pastels.

Two blocks north of the Hôtel de Ville, the **Musée de Préhistoire Régionale** shows what life was like on the Riviera a million years ago, with remains from sites such as the Vallonet, Lazaret and the Grimaldi caves. East of here, the pink and ochre Italianate *vieille ville*, a pedestrian zone, runs uphill to the mosaic-paved parvis St-Michel overlooking the sea; this pretty square hosts Menton's **Chamber Music Festival** each August (*see chapter* **By Season**). On one side of the square, the magnificent baroque church of **St-Michel** (open 10am-noon, 3-5pm Mon-Fri, Sun; 3-5pm Sat) has an ochre and green two-tier façade, double towers and a gilded marble Genoese-style interior. There's a fine sixteenth-century altarpiece of a dragon-slaying St Michael, and a *trompe l'oeil* dome.

Higher still in the *vieille ville* is the **Cimetière du Vieux-Château**, a terraced cemetery with a breathtaking view, perched on the site of a medieval castle, where artist Aubrey Beardsley and the Reverend William Webb Ellis – credited with being the first person to pick up a soccer ball and run with it, thus inventing rugby – rest in peace.

Heading east from the *vieille ville*, promenade de la Mer leads into **Garavan**, a leafy and luxurious quarter of private villas. Just off the promenade on chemin de St-Jacques is the **Jardin Val Rahmeh**, a glorious botanical garden founded in 1905 by an English resident, Lord Radcliffe, and now a branch of Paris' Musée d'Histoire Naturelle. Among the 700 tropical and subtropical species is the rare Easter Island pagoda tree, *Sophora toromiro*, plus *passiflora*, guava, kiwi and avocado plants galore.

Cimetière du Vieux-Château
pl du Cimitière, Vielle Ville. **Open** *May-Sept* 7am-8pm daily; *Oct-Apr* 7am-6pm daily. **Admission** free.

Hôtel de Ville
17 rue de la République (04.92.10.50.00). **Salle des mariages open** 8.30am-noon, 1.30-5pm Mon-Fri. **Admission** 10F, children free. **No credit cards**.

Jardin Val Rahmeh
chemin de St-Jacques, Garavan (04.93.35.86.72). **Open** *May-Sept* 10am-12.30pm, 3-6pm daily; *Oct-Apr* 10am-12.30pm, 2-5pm daily. **Admission** 20F, children 10F. **No credit cards**.

Musée des Beaux-Arts & Jardin des Agrumes
Palais Carnolès, 3 av de la Madone (04.93.35.49.71). **Open** 10am-noon, 2-6pm Mon, Wed-Sun. **Admission** free.

Musée Cocteau
Le Bastion, quai Napoléon III (04.93.57.72.30). **Open** 10am-noon, 2-5pm Mon, Wed-Sun. **Admission** 20F, free children.

Musée de Préhistoire Régionale
rue Loredan-Larchey (04.93.35.84.64). **Open** 10am-noon, 2-6pm Mon, Wed-Sun. **Admission** free.

Where to eat & drink

Bar Le Cap
1 pl du Cap (04.93.35.91.06). **Open** *Sept-June* 5.45am-8pm daily; *July, Aug* 5.45am-2am daily. **Credit** V.
A quick, inexpensive meal is sometimes hard to find in Menton, but this ordinary-looking bar in a lovely square is an ideal stop for delicious *bruschetta* toast.

Braijade Meridiounale
66 rue Longue (04.93.35.65.65). **Meals served** *Sept-June* noon-1.30pm, 7-10.30pm Thur-Tue; *July, Aug* 7pm-midnight. Closed mid-Nov to mid-Dec. **Menus** 75F-245F. **Credit** MC, V.
This rustic stone-vaulted dining spot in the heart of the *vieille ville* is a favourite for local specialities, such

Here lies the inventor of rugby.

as marinated brochettes grilled over an open fire, and tripe and aïoli. As charming as they come.

Le Darkoum

23 rue St-Michel (04.93.35.44.88). **Meals served** noon-2pm, 7.30-11pm Wed-Sun. **Menus** 90F-128F. **Credit** AmEx, DC, MC, V.

At the end of a pedestrian street lined with touristy shops in the *vieille ville*, this small family-run Moroccan restaurant serves up authentic dishes at reasonable prices. Try the *briouates de keftas* (crisp fried pastry filled with beef and coriander) or the assorted plates that include stuffed sardines, *zaalouk* (cumin, tomato and aubergine caviar) and grilled peppers, or choose from eight variations of couscous.

Le Lion d'Or

7 rue des Marins (04.93.35.74.67). **Meals served** *June-Aug* 7.30-11pm Mon-Sat; *Sept-May* noon-2pm, 7.30-11pm Tue-Sat; noon-2pm Sun. **Average** 200F-350F. **Credit** MC, V.

Known for its classic regional cuisine and seafood, the Lion d'Or has its fish of the day delivered straight from the town's fishing boats. Traditional but reliable, and much frequented by the locals.

Le Midi

103 av de Sospel (04.93.57.55.96). **Meals served** noon-2pm Mon-Sat, 7.30-9.30pm Mon, Tue, Thur-Sat. Closed July. **Menus** 72F-170F. **Credit** MC, V.

It may be out on the road leading towards the motorway and Sospel, but the regional cooking at Le Midi – with dishes such as salade niçoise, squid in tomato sauce, home-made gnocchi and aubergine fritters – is better and cheaper than at most of the restaurants in the scenic heart of town.

Where to stay

Hôtel Aiglon

7 av de la Madone (04.93.57.55.55/fax 04.93.35.92.39). Closed Nov-20 Dec. **Rates** single 295F-430F, double 360F-760F, suite 690F-960F. **Credit** AmEx, DC, MC, V.

Set back from the main road, this Belle Epoque villa is the epitome of old Riviera charm. It has everything from a peaceful garden lined with century-old palms and towering banana trees to ceiling frescos, mouldings and marble columns in the comfortable rooms. It also boasts a good pool-side restaurant, the Riaumont (open lunch and dinner daily, menus 100F-300F), offering classic French cuisine such as beef fillet with wild mushrooms and a home-made verbena sorbet splashed with gin.

Hôtel des Ambassadeurs

3 rue des Partouneaux (04.93.28.75.75/fax 04.93.35.62.32). **Rates** double 600F-1,350F, suite 1,350F-1,650F. **Credit** AmEx, DC, MC, V.

This turn-of-the-(last)-century pink and bronze green mini-palace, bordered by magnolias and towering palms, has a faded splendour and unbeatable central location.

Getting there

By car

Leave the A8 at exit no.59 (if you don't, you'll end up in Italy).

By bus

RCA Menton (04.93.21.30.83) runs a regular daily service along the Basse Corniche to Nice and Nice airport.

By train

There are regular stopping services to Menton and Menton-Garavan stations (information: 08.36.35.35.35) from Nice, some of which continue across the Italian border to Ventimiglia; also daily TGV connections between Paris and Menton.

Tourist information

The Office du Patrimoine (Hôtel d'Adhemar de Lartagnac, 24 rue St-Michel, 04.92.10.33.66, open 9am-noon, 2-5pm Mon-Fri) arranges visits or guided group tours of historical sights and private gardens.

Office de Tourisme

Palais de l'Europe, 8 av Boyer (04.92.41.76.76/fax 04.92.41.76.78). **Open** *Oct-May* 8.30am-12.30pm, 2-6pm Mon-Sat; *June-Sept* 8.30am-6pm Mon-Sat; 10am-noon Sun.

Roquebrune-Cap-Martin

Wedged between Monaco and Menton, Cap-Martin is one of the Riviera's loveliest stretches of wild coast, cloaked in pines, firs, olive and mimosa trees and studded with luxury hideaways. Celebrities ranging from Churchill and Coco Chanel to Le Corbusier and WB Yeats have lived (and, in the case of the latter two, died) here. A white rocky seaside footpath, the Sentier Douanier, winds around the peninsula, passing by **Le Cabanon**, Le Corbusier's tiny modular beach cottage, situated just before the Pointe de Cabbé. West of here, the vast curved beach of the **Plage du Golfe Bleu** is a favourite landing spot for hang-gliders.

The architect, who drowned while swimming in the sea here in 1965, had the foresight to design himself an impressive memorial in the cemetery (open 10am-noon, 2-5pm daily) in the old village of **Roquebrune**, which dominates the Cap-Martin peninsula. Carved into the rock above the Grande Corniche, this handsome *village perché* started life in the tenth century as a fortified Carolingian fiefdom. For five centuries, from 1355, it belonged to the Grimaldis. Up the steep stairways at the top of the village is the **chateau**, which was almost fairy tale-ified by a tasteless English owner in the 1920s, until the locals kicked up a stink. It

Roquebrune's ancient olive tree.

now has four floors of historical displays, lordly armour galore and a tenth-century dungeon. On the chemin du St-Roch, not far from the cemetery, stands one of the oldest trees in the world: a 1,000-year-old olive.

For intrepid hikers, the Sentier Massolin is little more than a giant staircase leading from Roquebrune village to the Cap-Martin coast walk, which leads into Menton. Allow 20 minutes for the descent and a lot more for the climb back up.

Le Cabanon

promenade Le Corbusier, Cap-Martin (04.93.35.62.87). **Open** by appointment only 10am Tue; 2.30pm Fri. **Admission** 30F. **No credit cards.**

Château de Roquebrune

pl du Château (04.93.35.07.22). **Open** *June-Sept* 10am-12.30pm, 3-7.30pm daily; *Oct-Jan* 10am-12.30pm, 2-5pm daily; *Feb-May* 10am-12.30pm, 2-6pm daily. **Admission** 20F, children 10F, free under-7s.

Where to stay & eat

Tucked away off the Basse Corniche in Cap-Martin is a small, reasonably priced gem on the water's edge, the **Hôtel Westminster** (14 av Louis Laurens, 04.93.35.00.68, closed Dec-Feb, rates 220F-475F), with a glorious view and a peaceful secluded cove just down the street. In

old Roquebrune, the excellent **Au Grand Inquisiteur** (18 rue du Château, 04.93.35.05.37, closed lunch Tue, all Mon and Nov, Dec, menus 148F-245F) was once the castle's sheep pen. It serves classic Southern French dishes and a whopping assortment of cheeses. For a breathtaking view, you can also dine on the terrace of the **Hôtel-Restaurant des Deux-Frères** (pl des Deux Frères, 04.93.28.99.00, closed 15 Nov-Dec 15, rates 425F-595F), an impeccably run inn on the esplanade at the foot of the village, with marvellous views from the rooms (go for number one or two) and traditional French cuisine (restaurant closed dinner Sun, all Mon, menus 120F-245F). Back in the main square – on to which its tables spill in summer – the atmospheric brasserie **La Grotte** (3 pl des Deux Frères, 04.93.35.00.04, closed Wed and Nov, average 150F) is carved out of the rock face. The food is simple: salads, hot *plats du jour* and pretty good pizzas.

Getting there

By car

Leave the A8 at exit no.58 and follow the Grande Corniche down to Roquebrune.

By bus

RCA Menton (04.93.21.30.83) runs a reasonably frequent shuttle bus service from Carnolès station to Roquebrune village daily.

By train

Local trains on the Nice-Ventimiglia line stop at Roquebrune-Cap-Martin (just before the headland) and Carnolès (just beyond), which is the last station before Menton proper.

Tourist information

Office de Tourisme

218 av Aristide Briand, Carnolès (04.93.35.62.87/fax 04.93.28.57.00). **Open** *May-June, Sept* 9am-12.30pm, 2-6.30pm Mon-Sat; *July, Aug* 9am-1pm, 3-7pm daily; *Oct-Apr* 9am-12.30pm, 2-6pm Mon-Sat.

North of Menton

From Menton, a series of narrow roads fans out northwards through dramatic mountain scenery to a cluster of *villages perchés*.

Gorbio sits high on a hilltop surrounded by olive groves, which used to provide the town's only livelihood. It now makes money from tourists, too, who are attracted to its narrow arched streets all year round, but especially during the famed Procession des Limaces (snails) on the feast of Corpus Christi in June. Don't expect a live snail race, however: it's a

Gorbio (*see p253*) moves at a snail's pace.

procession of villagers carrying snail shells that have been turned into tiny oil lamps. The seventeenth-century baroque church of **St-Barthélemy** has a striking black marble holy water stoop.

Up the tortuous D22 road from Menton, scenic **Ste-Agnès** hangs from the rock at 780 metres above sea level. The tangle of narrow cobblestoned streets have gradually succumbed to the inevitable quaint shops selling tourist-oriented clutter. But the spectacular panorama of the Italian and French coastline is reason enough for a visit. The **Fort Maginot**, built in the 1930s when the village was a strategic point in Riviera defences, has some impressive cannons.

Castillon, known as the 'artists' village', is a regrettably prettified town whose modern Arcades du Serre along the main square and the rue Haute contain Disneylandish crafts boutiques. Its main redeeming feature, in fact, is an exit: the ancient mule trail through the lemon and olive groves to Ste-Agnès, which makes for a lovely two-hour hike.

After skirting the *vieille ville* of Menton, the route de Castellar (D24) winds uphill through lemon groves to the tiny medieval fortressed village of **Castellar**, a *village perché* without a trace of cute gentrification. Once the home of the illustrious seigneurs of Lascaris-Vintimille, it's now a mecca for Sunday lunchers from Menton. The pretty baroque church of **St-Pierre** (pl de l'Eglise, open Nov-Mar 10am-noon, 3-5pm daily, 10am-noon, Apr-Oct 3-6pm daily) has a pink façade and onion-domed bell tower.

Fort Maginot

Ste-Agnès (04.93.35.84.58). **Open** *July-Sept* 2.30-5.30pm daily; *Oct-June* 2.30-5.30pm Sat, Sun. **Admission** 20F, children 10F. **No credit cards**.

Where to stay & eat

In Gorbio, the **Restaurant Beau-Séjour** (pl de la République, 04.93.41.46.15, closed Wed, menus 188F-175F) dishes up tasty specialities such as courgette flower fritters, marjoram-sautéed rabbit and large fried ravioli stuffed with swiss chard, cheese and rice. The **Hôtel St-Yves** (rue des Sarrasins, 04.93.35.91.45,

closed 20 Nov-10 Dec, rates 190F-260F) in Ste-Agnès offers small but comfortable rooms. For typical regional fare, such as home-made vegetable *tourtes* and ravioli, try the country inn **La Vieille Auberge** (Ste-Agnès, 04.93.35.92.02, closed Wed and Jan, menus 70F-150F), on the pine-shaded road just before the village, or the bar/restaurant **Le Logis Sarrasin** (rue des Sarrasins, 04.93.35.86.89, closed Mon and mid-Oct to mid-Nov, menus 85F-125F). In Castillon, the **Hôtel La Bergerie** (chemin Strauss, 04.93.04.00.39, closed Nov, rates 490F-750F) has rustic rooms, and a moderately priced restaurant (closed Mon, menu 150F) that serves standard pasta, fish and salads. In Castellar, the **Hôtel des Alpes** (1 pl Clemenceau, 04.93.35.82.83, closed Nov & Dec, rates 240F-280F with half-board) offers a variety of family-style Provençal dishes (restaurant closed Fri, menus 85F-100F) and a few cheerful rooms with a sweeping view of the coast. More rustic is the **Palais Lascaris** (58 rue de la République, 04.93.57.13.63, closed Mon and Oct, menus 90F-120F), which specialises in Ligurian and Provençal peasant dishes like courgette pie and polenta with grilled aubergines.

Getting there

By car

Note that it is almost impossible to drive directly between these villages without going almost all the way back to the coast. Gorbio is 9km north-west of Roquebrune-Cap-Martin on the narrow D23 road. For Ste-Agnès, take the route des Castagnins from Menton, which becomes the D22 (13km). Castillon is 10km up the wider and much more trafficked D2566 Sospel road from Menton. For Castellar (6km), take the D24.

By bus

Breuleux Cars in Menton (04.93.35.73.51) runs services to all villages.

Tourist information

Castellar

Refer to the tourist office at Menton (*see above*) for information on the area.

Castillon

Syndicat d'Initiative (04.93.04.32.03). **Open** 10am-noon, 2.30-5.30pm daily.

Gorbio

Hôtel de Ville (04.92.10.66.50/fax 04.93.41.49.60). **Open** 8.30am-12.30pm, 1.30-4pm Mon-Fri.

Ste-Agnès

Espace Culturel des Traditions, 51 rue des Sarrasins (04.93.35.87.35). **Open** 10am-1pm, 2-5.30pm daily.

Inland Alpes-Maritimes

Grasse & Around   256
Vence & Around   263
The Arrière-pays
 & the Var Valley   268
Into the Alps   271

Feature boxes

The smell of Grasse   258
Sophia-Antipolis   262
The Train des Pignes   270
La Vallée des Merveilles   272
The Parc National du
 Mercantour   280

Grasse & Around

Surrounded by natural spectacle, gentle Grasse is as redolent of Provençal life and tradition as it is of the perfumes that made its name.

Grasse

Perfume may be what Grasse is all about today, but in the Middle Ages this self-contained hill town with sweeping views down to the Mediterranean below was best known for its tanneries. An independent republic, Grasse (from *grâce*, as in grace, rather than *gras*, fat) cured skins supplied by its allies Genoa and Tuscany. It was a Tuscan, King Henri II's wife Catherine de' Medici, who first suggested that these hills, whose balmy microclimate ensures that flowers flourish year-round, would be a good place to turn out the perfumed gloves she loved. Grasse's inhabitants became *parfum-gantiers*, then, as gloves went out of fashion, just *parfumiers*. And so they have remained: 30 factories now extract precious essence of jasmine, rose, orange, tuberose, jonquil, violet, mimosa and lavender to be transformed into fragrances by Dior, Chanel, Yves Saint Laurent and other leading fashion houses.

Grasse's medieval *vieille ville* retains its villagey, workaday atmosphere, despite the droves of souvenir shops and tourist-trap restaurants. The produce and flower market, every morning except Mondays, in the **place aux Aires** is good for stocking up on picnic fare. Surrounded by a jumble of arcades, the cobbled square was once a meeting point for tanners as they hauled their pelts to and from a nearby canal for washing. Now it has elbow-to-elbow pavement cafés from which to admire the intricate wrought iron balconies of the Hôtel Isnard (1781) at No.33. East of the square is the rue de l'Oratoire, where the portal and Gothic window of a former Franciscan church can be seen incorporated into a later façade. Still further east, in rue Droite (crooked, despite its name), the Hôtel Doria Roberti at No.24 has a remarkable Renaissance stairwell and terraces. The street ends in the place des Herbes, once Grasse's herb and vegetable market. Nearby, nineteenth-century Grasse has been reconstructed in the **Musée Grasse d'Antan**, where 150 miniature figures set in a miniature land- and townscape recreate the history of Grasse's perfume industry.

Rue de la Poissonnière leads from here to **place du Petit Puy**, dominated by the Romanesque cathedral of **Notre-Dame-du-Puy**. Built in the twelfth century, the church underwent radical overhauls in the seventeenth and eighteenth centuries, but the interior remains a perfect example of simple, sparse Provençal Romanesque, its high narrow nave topped by heavy ogive arches. The columns are unusually thick and the stonework around the altar pitted by a fire that swept through the church in the late eighteenth century. In the right aisle are several paintings by the very young Rubens, *The Washing of the Disciples' Feet* by local boy Fragonard and a beautiful sixteenth-century triptych by Ludovico Bré. Across the square, the *hôtel de ville* (town hall) occupies the old bishop's palace, and incorporates a tenth-century watchtower, the Tour de Guet.

South-west of the cathedral lies the **Musée d'Art et d'Histoire de Provence**. Housed in the magnificent eighteenth-century home of the Marquise de Clapiers-Cabris, sister of the flamboyant Revolutionary politician Mirabeau, the museum's eclectic collection charts high-class Provençal daily life in the 1800s, with a fully equipped kitchen, faience ceramics, *santons*, plus a luxurious Turkish bed and Mirabeau's death mask. The **Musée Provençal du Costume et du Bijou** around the corner in rue d'Ossola houses a quaint collection of eighteenth- and nineteenth-century costumes and jewellery. D'Artagnan, musketeer to King Louis XIV, stayed down the road at No.14. Nearby, the **Musée International de la Parfumerie** (*see box page 259*) is an indispensable introduction to the area's chief industry.

At the far end of the Jardin Public stands the **Villa-Musée Fragonard**, the elegant seventeenth-century country house where artist Jean-Honoré Fragonard (1732-1806) sought refuge when he fell from favour with the Revolutionary powers-that-were. The son of a not particularly successful glove-maker, Fragonard took himself to Paris at a young age to study painting. In the capital, his chocolate-box works soon became all the rage, but they were little liked by the children of the Revolution who, in any case, had decapitated most of his clients. The villa has *trompe l'oeil* wall and ceiling paintings by Fragonard *fils*, and, upstairs, a collection of original sketches and etchings by

Post-prandial fun at the **Bastide St-Antoine**.

Fragonard. Downstairs are copies of four panels commissioned but then rejected by one of Fragonard's greatest patrons, Louis XV's mistress Madame du Barry; the originals are in the Frick Collection in New York.

On the busy boulevard du Jeu de Ballon, the eighteenth-century Hôtel Pontevès-Morel houses the **Musée de la Marine**, dedicated to the life and career of Admiral François-Joseph-Paul (1722-88), Count of Grasse, whose naval defence of Chesapeake Bay during the siege of Yorktown was decisive in bringing the American War of Independence to an end.

Musée d'Art et d'Histoire de Provence

2 rue Mirabeau (04.93.36.01.61). **Open** *June-Sept* 10am-7pm daily; *Oct-May* 10am-12.30pm, 2-5.30pm Wed-Sun. **Admission** 20F.

Musée Grasse d'Antan

3 rue Moulinets (04.93.36.01.09). **Open** *May-Sept* 10.30am-7pm daily; *Oct-Apr* usually 10am-noon, 2-5pm daily but call first. **Admission** 25F.

Musée de la Marine

2 bd du Jeu de Ballon (04.93.40.11.11). **Open** *June-Sept* 10am-7pm daily; *Oct-May* 10am-noon, 2-6pm Mon-Sat. Closed Nov. **Admission** 20F, 10F children.

Musée Provençal du Costume et du Bijou

2 rue Jean Ossola (04.93.36.44.65). **Open** *Sept-June* 10am-1pm, 2-6pm daily; *July, Aug* 10am-7.30pm daily. **Admission** free.

Villa-Musée Fragonard

23 bd Fragonard (04.93.40.32.64). **Open** *June-Sept* 10am-7pm daily; *Oct-May* 10am-noon, 2-5pm Wed-Sun. **Admission** 20F; includes free entry to the botanical gardens.

Eating, drinking & nightlife

The Michelin-starred **Bastide St-Antoine** offers one of the best-priced gourmet lunches in the region; for details *see page 54*. For something a little less demanding, there is

La Toque Blanche (83 av Auguste Renoir, 04.93.36.20.64, menus 130F-230F) in Magagnosc, four kilometres east of Grasse on the D2085 Nice road, which serves fragrant local dishes and excellent desserts. Back in town, close by the cathedral, **Le Gazan** (3 rue Gazan, 04.93.36.22.88, closed dinner, menus 84F-200F) is a simple, lively restaurant with an outside terrace that fills up fast in summer. The kitsch décor will raise a smile, but the 110F *menu au parfum*, which includes roast quail with *confit de roses* is spot-on. **La Flute Enchantée** (5 rue Thouron, 04.93.36.14.18, closed Mon and Sept-June) has a selection of hearty snacks, including *pan-bagnat*: a huge bap filled with lettuce, tuna, anchovies, egg, tomato and olives, seasoned with a garlicky Provençal dressing.

The **Little Pub** (6 rue Maximin Isnard, 04.93.36.34.93, closed Sun) is about as good as nightlife gets in Grasse. Locals meet to devour bruschetta on the terrace and peruse the pub's collection of books to read there or borrow. The cybercafé **Le Petit Caboulet** (escalier Maximin Isnard, 04.93.40.16.01, closed Sun) is Grasse's only Internet café but there's little competition for the one computer: Grassois prefer the Caboulet's crêpes (10F-12F) and steak and chips (45F) to its technological offerings. The useful bar tabac **Le Celtic** (4 cours Honoré Cresp, 04.93.36.06 78) has a shady terrace. The house speciality is *panscotta*, a doorstep of toasted bread moistened with olive oil and topped with tomato, ham and grilled red peppers.

Where to stay

The friendly **Hôtel des Parfums** (rue Eugene Charabot, 04.92.42.35.35, rates 330F-780F) has a jacuzzi and gymnasium as well as fabulous views from rooms geared more to travelling salesmen than tourists. The **Hôtel Panorama** (2 pl du Cours Honoré Cresp, 04.93.36.80.80, rooms 300F-485F) is within walking distance of the town centre, and front rooms have nice views, but the style is 1950s M&S. For a touch of Provençal chic, try the **Bastide Saint-Antoine** (48 av Henri Dunant, 04.93.70.94.94, rooms 1,020F-2,160F). Set amid perfumed gardens and manicured lawns, the Bastide has a pool and views down to the sea and the Esterel mountains – along with its Michelin-starred restaurant. If you prefer to pitch a tent, try the **Camping Municipal** (27 av de Rothschild, 04.93.36.28.69, 23F per person) or the **Camping de la Paoute** (160 rte de Cannes, 04.93.09.11.42, closed mid-Sept to mid-June, 110F two people, 30F extra adults, 20F under-10s).

Getting there

By car
N85 from Cannes, or A8 from Nice, exit no.42 Cannes-Grasse, then N85.

By bus
Bus services are operated by Rapides du Côte d'Azur (RCA; 04.93.36.37.37). From Cannes bus station take bus 600-605, RCA's Cannes-Grasse service. From Nice Airport take RCA bus 500. The *gare routière* (04.93.36.37.37) is on place de la Buanderie.

Tourist information
Grasse plays to its floral heritage with some fragrant annual events. In May, rose-growers from all over the world display their blooms at Expo-Rose, and during the annual Jasmine Festival over the first weekend of August there are processions, swathes of flowers and elections for Miss Jasmine.

Office de Tourisme
22 cours Honoré Cresp (04.93.36.66.66/fax 04.93.36.03.56). **Open** 9am-12.30pm, 1.30-6pm daily. *Website: wwwtourism@ville-grasse.fr*

Around Grasse

West of Grasse
The Route Napoléon heads north-west out of Grasse, and winding for 12 pastoral kilometres before reaching the medieval village

The smell of Grasse

Grasse's perfume industry blossomed during the eighteenth and nineteenth centuries, when the distilleries stopped perfuming gloves made by local leatherworkers and started putting their distillates, still used as bases for the costly concoctions of Paris' fashion houses, straight into bottles. There are now around 30 major perfume houses in the town, many of which welcome visitors, explain the essence-extracting process and sell their scents at factory-door prices.

The *parfumeries* manufacture their essences by straightforward distilling, by *enfleurage* (in which the raw materials are placed between layers of animal fat that absorb the perfume and then are broken down by alcohol to leave the essence) or by extraction (in which solvents are used to get the perfume out). The end result is a highly concentrated substance: perfumes contain

Inland Alpes-Maritimes

of **St-Vallier-de-Thiey**, a good vantage point for spotting *bories*, stone igloos once occupied by shepherds. Nearby is the grandly named **Souterroscope de Baume Obscure**, a cave system where underground waterfalls crash past helictites, stalactites, stalagmites and other natural phenomena. Bring a sweater even in summer, as it's a constant 12°C. Heading south towards the *village perché* of Cabris are the **Grottes des Audides**. This atmospheric limestone cave system, inhabited in prehistoric times, was discovered by a shepherd in 1988. Dioramas in the park outside (admission 20F, 15F children) illustrate the lives of the original inhabitants, using implements found there.

Cabris, a sleepy, sunny little village with a mountainous backdrop, was a favourite haunt of Sartre and Camus, and still has its share of creative souls, mostly of the arts-and-crafts type. It's also popular with perfume magnates, and has a pleasant green where expatriates play cricket.

A little further west lies the unspoiled medieval village of **St-Cézaire-sur-Siagne**, where the twelfth-century chapel in the cemetery is Provençal Romanesque at its untrammelled best. Neolithic man roamed here; the Romans marched in much more purposefully. According to local legend, Julius Caesar set up an observation post at the top of the village, and the view over the Siagne valley is certainly worth conquering for. On the road outside town, the **Puits de la Vierge** are nine wells, probably Roman. But most visitors pass this way to see yet more caves, the **Grottes de St-Cézaire**. Plunging to depths of over 60 metres, they contain stalagmites and stalactites

only 10-25 per cent of essence and eau de cologne between two and six per cent, while aftershave can have as little as 0.2 per cent.

The finished product is an alcohol-based blend of over 100 different ingredients. These include the flowery essences produced in Grasse, but also a host of decidedly less savoury items, such as ambergris (a waxy substance found in sperm whales' intestines), civet (a secretion from the anal glands of the civet cat) and musk (from the glands of the musk deer).

The grisly details are dwelt on at length in Patrick Suskind's novel *Perfume*. For a quicker technical and historical overview of the perfume-making process, start at the **Musée International de la Parfumerie**. Small but well thought out, this museum has a display of perfume bottles dating from classical Greece to the present day. It offers a chance to test your sense of smell in the lush greenhouses, and provides children's entertainment, too.

Down the road towards Cannes, the modern **Parfumerie Fragonard** (*pictured*), set in a delightful garden, offers guided tours in English. When Peter Mayle decided to cap his literary genius with a sortie into smelliness, he used the Fragonard plant to create the fragrance Une Année en Provence. For sale in the factory shop at a mere 190F a bottle, this lavender-based scent is far better than *A Year in Provence*, and easier to wash off.

Three generations of the Biancalana family still cultivate roses and jasmine at the **Domaine de Manon**. Flowers from the Domaine find their way into Chanel N°5, Guerlain's Jardin de Bagatelle and Patou's Joy.

If watching is not your scene, mix your own personal *parfum* at the **Parfumerie Galimard**. Your exclusive creation will be funnelled into a charming glass bottle and the formula registered on Galimard's computer; you can have further supplies whipped up on demand and sent to you anywhere in the world. A bottle of your own perfume with a factory tour thrown in costs 200F.

Domaine de Manon
36 chemin de Servan, Plascassier (04.93.60.12.76). **Open** *May-June 10am-5pm daily; July to mid-Nov around 8-10am* daily. Closed mid-Nov to April. **Admission** 25F. **No credit cards**.

Musée International de la Parfumerie
8 pl du Cours Honoré Cresp (04.93.36.80.20). **Open** *June-Sept 10am-7pm daily; Oct-May 10am-noon, 2-5pm Wed-Sun.* **Admission** 25F. **No credit cards**.

Parfumerie Fragonard
Les Quatre Chemins, rte de Cannes (04.93.77.94.30). **Open** *Feb-Oct 9am-6.30pm daily; Nov-Jan 9am-12.30pm, 2-6pm daily.* **Admission** free.

Parfumerie Galimard
rte de Pegomas (04.93.09.20.00). **Open** *shop 9am-12.30pm, 2-6pm daily; factory 10am-noon, 2-5pm daily.* **Admission** free. *Website: www.galimard.com*

Inland Alpes-Maritimes

Waterfalls dot the **Gorges du Loup**.

of a uniform rusty red that, when struck, turn into an eerie natural organ.

Grottes des Audides

rte de Cabris (04.93.42.64.15). **Open** *July, Aug* 10am-6pm daily; *Sept-Oct* 10am-6.30pm Wed-Sun; *Nov-Feb* by appointment; *Feb-June* 2-5pm Wed-Sun. **Admission** 30F, 20F children. **No credit cards**.

Grottes de St-Cézaire

9 bd du Puit d'Amon (04.93.60.22.35). **Open** 15 *Feb-May* 2.30-5pm daily; *June* 10.30am-noon, 2-6pm daily; *July, Aug* 10.30am-6.30pm daily; *Sept* 10.30am-noon, 2-6pm daily; *Oct-14 Feb* 2.30-4.30pm Sun. **Admission** 30F, 13F children. **No credit cards**.

Souterroscope de Baume Obscure

Rte de St-Vallier-de-Thier (04.93.42.61.63). **Open** 10am-6pm daily. Closed Oct to mid-Feb. **Admission** 50F, 25F children). **No credit cards**.

Where to stay & eat

Le Préjoly in St-Vallier-de-Thiey (pl Rougière, 04.93.42.60.86, closed mid-Dec to mid-Jan, rates 280F-320F) is a welcoming country inn with 17 rooms and a bustling restaurant. **L'Hostellerie des Chênes Blancs** (2020 rte de St-Vallier, 04.93.60.20.09, rooms 335F-565F, bungalows 555F-755F) has a pool and tennis courts, and a restaurant with menus from 128F to 220F.

In Cabris, **L'Horizon** (100 promenade St-Jean, 04.93.60.51.69, closed mid-Oct to Easter, rates 350F-620F) has a scenic suntrap terrace and prettily renovated bedrooms but no restaurant. **Le Vieux Château** (pl du

Panorama, 04.93.60.50.12, closed dinner Tue, all Wed) is a charming hotel/restaurant carved out of the old castle, with Provençal menus from 130F to 320F and just four double rooms (360F-570F) that need to be booked far in advance.

Handy for a meal near the caves in St-Cézaire is the **Auberge du Puits d'Amon** (2 rue Arnaud, 04.93.60.28.50, closed dinner Sun, all Wed, dinner mid-Oct to mid-Mar, menus 105F-210F), a real village inn offering superb bouillabaisse and bourride. Booking is advisable.

Getting there

Check tourist offices in Grasse, Nice, Cannes and St-Raphaël for bus tours to the caves.

By car

Cabris, St-Cézaire: D4 from Grasse to Cabris, then D13 to St-Cézaire.
St-Vallier-de-Thiey: N85 from Grasse.

By bus

Cabris, St-Cézaire: RCA (04.93.36.37.37) runs one bus daily from Grasse to St-Cézaire via Cabris and a more frequent direct service.
St-Vallier-de-Thiey: Two RCA buses run from Grasse in the morning (Mon-Sat) and return in the afternoon.

Tourist information

Cabris

Office de Tourisme, 9 rue Frédéric Mistral (04.93.60.55.63/fax 04.93.60.55.94). **Open** *Sept-*

June 9.30am-12.30pm, 2-5.30pm Mon-Sat; *July, Aug* 9.30am-12.30pm, 2.30-6.30pm Mon-Sat.

St-Cézaire
Office de Tourisme, 1 bd Courmes (04.93.60.84.30/fax 93.60.84.40). **Open** *Sept-June* 10am-noon Sat, Sun; *July, Aug* 10am-noon, 5-7pm Mon-Sat.

St-Vallier-de-Thiey
Office de Tourisme, 10 pl du Tour (tel/fax 04.93.42.78.00). **Open** *Sept-June* 9am-noon, 3-5pm Mon-Sat; *July, Aug* 9am-noon, 3-6pm Mon-Sat.
A free guided tour of the village departs from here every Thursday morning at 10am.

Gorges du Loup

Le Bar-sur-Loup is the best setting-out point for a visit to the spectacular Gorges du Loup. Le Bar's old stone houses cling to hillsides covered with orange orchards and olive groves, grouped around the church and the castle where American War of Independence hero Admiral de Grasse (*see above* **Grasse**) was born and raised. The Gothic church of St-Jacques contains a fifteenth-century altarpiece, possibly by Louis Bréa, of tiny, intricate courtly dancers being shot by Death, their souls being judged unworthy by St Michael and hurled into the gaping maw of hell. When he's in the area, a less saintly Michael – Schumacher – takes his go-kart to **Fun Kart**, where a 160CC Honda Kart costs 50F for five minutes.

Beyond Le Bar, the road plunges down into the Gorges du Loup, sawing back and forth around tortuous bends, beneath overhanging cliffs, to the sound of crashing waterfalls. Swinging back and up along the western cliff, it leads to **Gourdon**, an eagle's nest of a village perched between Grasse and the Loup Valley. Gourdon was first a fortress and later a medieval citadel, keeping watch for marauding Saracens. Today's invading hordes are met by ranks of souvenir shops. The thirteenth-century **Chateau de Gourdon**, which dominates the village and the Loup valley, comes as a blessed relief from the hard sell. Blending French and Italian Romanesque influences, the castle has gardens designed by Le Nôtre and now houses two museums: the Musée Historique has the usual weaponry and torture implements plus a Rembrandt, a Rubens and Marie Antoinette's writing desk, while the Musée de la Peinture Naïve has a collection of Douanier-Rousseau-type daubs, along with an example of the real thing.

Chateau de Gourdon
04.93.09.68.02. **Open** *June-Sept* 11am-1pm, 2-7pm daily; *Oct-May* 2-6pm Mon, Wed-Sun. **Admission** 25F, 15F children. **No credit cards.**

Fun Kart
Plateau de la Sarée, rte de Gourdon (04.93.42.48.08). **Open** *June-Sept* 10am-8pm daily; *Oct-May* 10.30am-5pm Mon, Wed, Fri-Sun. **No credit cards.**

Where to stay & eat
Gastronomic pickings in Le Bar are slim: try **La Jarrerie** (av Admiral de Grasse, 04.93.42.92.92, closed dinner Mon, all Tue), which serves hearty Provençal fare with menus from 145F to 250F. L'Ecole des Filles (av Admiral de Grasse, 04.93.09.40.20, closed dinner Mon, all Sun, menus 148F-195F) is a good bet for snacks, while the **Confiserie Florian** in Le Pont du Loup (04.93.59.32.91, closed Nov-Mar) is a must if you're after jams or confectionery. In Gourdon, the **Auberge de Gourdon** (04.93.09.69.69) is a bar-tabac-restaurant with local charm, heavy Provençal accents and simple honest dishes at 88F to 120F.

There are few accommodation options at the Grasse end of the gorge. If you have a tent, the **Camping des Gorges du Loup** (965 chemin des Vergers, 04.93.42.45.06) is a well-organised site in a lovely setting, with caravans and mobile homes to rent, but call first as its future is uncertain.

Getting there

By car
A8 autoroute from Nice or Marseille, exit no.42 at Cannes, follow signs to Valbonne, Opio and Le Bar-sur-Loup.

By bus
PACAVL (04.93.36.06.79) operates several services a day (Mon-Sat) between Grasse and Le Bar-sur-Loup.

Tourist information

Le Bar-sur-Loup
Office du Tourisme, pl Francis Paulet (04.93.42.72.21/fax 04.93.42.92.60). **Open** 9am-noon, 2-5pm daily.

Gourdon
Syndicat d'Initiative, pl de l'Eglise (tel/fax 04.93.09.68.25). **Open** *Oct-June* noon-5pm daily; *July-Sept* 10am-7pm daily.
Website: www.gourdon-france.com

Valbonne

East of Grasse, Valbonne was rebuilt on a grid plan in the sixteenth century as part of a bid to repopulate a region that had been devastated by plague. At the heart of the

Inland Alpes-Maritimes

village is the seventeenth-century place des Arcades; further uphill, in place de l'Eglise, the parish church is in reality an abbey founded in the twelfth century. Below the village a pastoral footpath, the Sentier de la Couverte de la Brague, follows the course of the River Brague.

South-west of Valbonne, just off the main N85 Grasse-Cannes road, **Mouans-Sartoux** is a mecca for contemporary art lovers. The town's sixteenth-century chateau was converted into the **Espace de l'Art Concret** in 1990; it houses a permanent collection with works by Josef Albers, Carl André and other concrete artists, and rotating three- or four-month themed exhibitions dedicated to abstract and minimalist art.

Espace de l'Art Concret

Château de Mouans-Sartoux (04.93.75.71.50). **Open** *Oct-May* 11am-6pm Mon, Wed-Sun; *Jun-Sept* 11am-7pm Mon, Wed-Sun. **Admission** 15F, children free.

Where to stay & eat

The **Hôtel Les Armoiries** (pl des Arcades, 04.93.12.90.90, rates 550F-900F) has 16 tastefully decorated rooms. Valbonne's best

food is to be found at **Lou Cigalon** (4-6 bd Carnot, 04.93.12.27.07, closed Mon, Sun, two weeks Jan, menus 180F-410F). Alain Parodi, the owner and chef, specialises in simple Provençal cuisine with a light, modern spin. The restaurant can get crowded, so booking is advised.

Getting there

By car
A8 autoroute, exit at Antibes or Cannes, follow signs to Valbonne.

By bus
STGA bus 3VB runs from Cannes direct to Valbonne about every hour (with fewer buses on Sunday). The 5VB (four services daily Monday-Friday) goes via Sophia-Antipolis. More detailed information is available from Cannes train station.

Tourist information

Office de Tourisme
11 av St-Roch (04.93.12.34.50/fax 04.93.12.34.57). **Open** 9am-5pm daily. *Website: www.alpes-azur.com/vsa*

Sophia-Antipolis

In the shadow of ancient Valbonne lies the Riviera's 15,000-hectare bid for high-tech power and prestige on a truly Californian scale: Sophia-Antipolis. Work on this perfectly landscaped, perfectly soulless science park began in 1969, with the first company moving in to a shady spot beneath the umbrella pines in 1974. Since then, it has grown exponentially, with around 1,200 high-tech companies currently sharing the site, which is set to double in size over the next decade. Information technology and telecommunications are the main sectors, with electronics and biotechnology not far behind; the University of Nice also has a research faculty on the site. Over 20,000 people currently work in what has been described as 'Milton Keynes on the Riviera' – not least because of the park's lack of a centre and endless roundabouts.

One in four of those who work here are foreigners, most high-earners in their 20s and 30s – something that keeps the already high rents and property prices in the surrounding area bubbling over, and explains the density of upmarket restaurants in the Mougins-Valbonne-Biot triangle. The park is run by the semi-private SAEM consortium, which maintains a Sophia-Antipolis website at http://www.saem-sophia-antipolis.fr.

Vence & Around

A source of inspiration for saints, conquerors and some of the twentieth century's greatest artists, Vence and its satellites retain a magnetic appeal.

St-Paul-de-Vence

Four kilometres due north from Cagnes and the coast is St-Paul-de-Vence, a picturesque village that might have been just another charming *village perché*, with its fortified walls looming majestically over the surrounding countryside. Instead, St-Paul-de-Vence has become a regional *quartier général* of modern art, helped along by a heritage of illustrious artistic visitors and by the presence of one of the most important modern art museums in France, the Fondation Maeght.

A strategic defence point, St-Paul flourished in the Middle Ages thanks to its vines, figs, olives and orange trees, as well as hemp and linens. Of the twelfth-century castle, only the dungeon remains. The almost-intact ramparts were put up in 1540 as a thank-you present by François Ier, in recognition of the town's role in beating off his arch-enemy, the Holy Roman Emperor Charles V. After this moment of glory, the town went into a decline until the twentieth century, when an influx of artists gave it a much-needed makeover. Picasso, Matisse, Braque and Dufy were just some of the impoverished daubers who pitched up here after World War I, paying for their board and lodging at the town's only inn, La Colombe d'Or, with paintings that still adorn the hostelry's walls. In the 1960s, art dealer-collectors Aimé and Marguerite Maeght created the Fondation Maeght, a remarkable container for their remarkable private collection.

Inside the ramparts, St-Paul's narrow, crowded medieval lanes are lined with bougainvillea, jasmine and geraniums along with hard-sell artists' studios and shops selling antiques, crafts and souvenirs for all tastes and purses. The pedestrianised main street, rue Grande, runs between the north and south gates; peek through the gaps in the houses on either side for picture-postcard views. In the **Eglise Collégiale**, the town's main church, only the choir remains from the original twelfth-century building; later adornments include the baroque stucco masterpiece of St Clément's chapel in the south transept and a painting of St Catherine of Alexandria, attributed to Tintoretto, which hangs in the north aisle.

From a café in the place de Gaulle, observe France's most famous *terrain de boules*, shaded by plane trees. This was the late Yves Montand's favourite pitch. Celebrities line up to challenge local champions and Japanese players travel huge distances for regional tournaments, but rookies are always welcome (boules can be rented from the tourist office at 20F a set). At the urn-shaped fountain and *lavoir* in place de la Grande Fontaine, the locals queue to fill bottles, cans and buckets with pure spring water.

The walk around the town's ramparts affords spectacular views from the Alps to the sea. The gate on the south side, the Porte de Nice, leads to the cemetery where Chagall lies beneath cypress trees.

In a pinewood just north-west of St-Paul, the **Fondation Maeght** is unquestionably one of the Côte's star attractions. Opened in 1964, this extraordinary low-slung construction set in grounds bristling with artworks was designed by Catalan architect José Luis Sert specifically to house Aimé and Marguerite Maeght's collection of contemporary classics. As you prepare to join the 200,000 people who cross the threshold each year, it helps to throw away any preconceptions of what a gallery should look like. The Fondation is a maze, with no fixed route and nothing resembling a hanging plan. Some works do have places of their own, by virtue of being part of the fabric of the place: Giacometti figures in the courtyard; a Miró labyrinth peopled with sculptures and ceramics, including the half-submerged *Egg*; mural mosaics by Chagall and Tal-Coat; the pool and stained glass window by Braque; Pol Bury's fountain; Calder's bobbing mobiles. But the Fondation's more moveable collection of Braques and Légers, Kandinskys and Mirós, Bonnards and Chagalls comes and goes inside, shifting places or disappearing altogether into storage to make way for temporary exhibitions, including the annual summer show.

Eglise Collégiale
pl de la Mairie. **Open** 8am-8pm daily.

Fondation Marguerite et Aimé Maeght
Montée des Trious (04.93.32.81.63). **Open** *Oct-June* 10am-12.30pm, 2.30-6pm daily; *July-Sept* 10am-7pm daily. **Admission** 50F, children 35F; photography fee 15F.

Art break hotel: penniless artists left paintings at **La Colombe d'Or** in lieu of payment.

Where to stay & eat

Accommodation is scarce and generally expensive in St-Paul: head for Vence for more choice. Book well ahead for a meal or a bed if you're hoping to get even a glance inside **La Colombe d'Or** (pl des Ormeaux, 04.93.32.80.02, closed 3 Nov-20 Dec, rates 1,350F-1,600F). The artworks left here in lieu of payment by penniless clients of the hostelry's rustic founder Paul Roux – including works by then-unknowns like Picasso, Modigliani, Miró, Matisse and Chagall – are only on view to guests of the hotel and restaurant. A meal on the celebrated, fig-shaded terrace (average 300F) is pleasant enough but it's art and atmosphere that count here, not the adequate but unexciting Provençal cuisine.

Le Saint-Paul (86 rue Grande, 04.93.32.65.25, rates 1,300F-1,600F) offers four-poster beds in a sixteenth-century mansion in the heart of town. The restaurant (menu 290F) is, gastronomically speaking, a couple of notches up from the Colombe d'Or; chef Frédéric Buzet offers a modern Provençal menu, backed by a fine list of local wines. It's closed all January, on Wednesdays between October and December and for Wednesday and Thursday lunches between February and April.

Set in an eight-hectare park with views across the Mediterranean on the road to La Colle-sur-Loup, **Le Mas d'Artigny** (20 rte de la Colle, 04.93.32.84.54, rates 1,000F-3,000F) has rooms, suites and self-catering apartments, plus a venerable restaurant that has recently been given a new direction by young chef Francis Scordel (menu 290F-395F). The **Auberge le Hameau** (528 rte de la Colle, 04.93.32.80.24, closed mid-Nov to mid-Feb, rates 580F-790F), with pretty rooms in a terraced garden, is a somewhat cheaper hotel option, but it doesn't have a restaurant.

Back in the old town, the tiny **Couleur Pourpre** restaurant (7 rempart Ouest, 04.93.32.60.14, closed lunch Wed, all Tue and mid-Nov to Dec, average 200F) offers excellent, refined local fare including wonderful desserts. The **Café de la Place** (pl de Gaulle, 04.93.32.80.03, closed 11 Nov-25 Dec) is the best café for watching the action on the boules pitch.

Getting there

By car

D7 from Cagnes-sur-Mer via La Colle-sur-Loup. Note that the D36 to Vence bypasses St-Paul.

By bus

The 400 bus from Nice to Vence via Cagnes makes a stop at St-Paul-de-Vence. It runs every half hour daily (services are slightly less frequent on Sundays).

Tourist information

Office de Tourisme

2 rue Grande (04.93.32.86.95). **Open** *June-Sept* 10am-7pm daily; *Oct-May* 10am-noon, 2-6pm daily. Closed first 2 weeks Dec. *Websites: www.stpaulweb.com www.saint-paul-de-vence.com*

Inland Alpes-Maritimes

Vence

When the Emperor Caesar Augustus led his jack-sandalled hordes into what they were to call Vintium, it had long been inhabited by a Ligurian tribe. Set five kilometres north of St-Paul-de-Vence in a strategic position ten kilometres back from the sea, Vence has always been important. A bishopric from the fourth to the nineteenth centuries, it boasts not one but two patron saints. The first was fifth-century bishop Véran, who successfully organised the town's defences against Visigoth invaders (though Saracens would later succeed where the Barbarians had failed, razing the cathedral and much of the rest of Vence to the ground). The second cleric to earn the gratitude of the Vençois was Lambert, a twelfth-century bishop who is best remembered for defending the town's rights against its rapacious new baron, Romée de Villeneuve, thus setting a trend of bitter rivalry between nobility and clergy that was to last until the bishopric was dissolved after the Revolution.

Perhaps Vence's most popular prelate – though this one was never canonised – was seventeenth-century bishop Antoine Godeau, a gallant dwarf, poet and renowned wit who was the first ever member of the newly formed Académie Française.

In the 1920s, Vence became a popular creative pitstop for artists and writers, including Paul Valéry, André Gide and DH Lawrence, who died here in 1930. In 1941, Matisse took refuge in Vence from the Allied bombs that were raining down on Nice; he fell ill, and was nursed back to health by the town's Dominican sisters. To repay the favour, he designed what is perhaps Vence's best-known sight, the Chapelle du Rosaire (*see below*).

Walls still encircle some of the *vieille ville*, Vence's medieval heart, which manages to retain its old-world feel despite the modern sprawl outside. Right outside the western Porte Peyra, one of five original gates into the town, the **place du Frêne** is named after its giant ash tree planted, according to legend, to commemorate Pope Paul III's visit to Vence in 1538. The porte leads into place Peyra in what was once the Roman forum. Between the two squares, the seventeenth-century **Château de Villeneuve** was home to the barons of the same name, and now hosts modern and contemporary art exhibitions.

At the centre of the *vieille ville*, the **ancienne cathédrale** was built over a Roman temple of Mars, a column from which can still be seen in place Godeau to the east of the church. A fifth-century church was replaced by a Romanesque one, which has itself been reworked more than

once over the centuries. The Roman legacy can be seen in inscriptions incorporated into the baroque façade, and in the pre-Christian sarcophagus (third chapel on the right) in which St Véran is said to have been buried. There's a mosaic of Moses in the bulrushes by Chagall in the baptistry, and some stunning – and charmingly irreverent – fifteenth-century carvings by Jacques Bellot on the choir stalls. Three steep stairways lead up from the centre towards boulevard Paul André, which follows the old ramparts and offers sweeping views across to the Alps.

Vence's biggest tourist attraction, the **Chapelle du Rosaire**, lies slightly north of the *vieille ville*. Matisse himself always maintained that this chapel, entirely conceived and created between 1947 and 1951, was his masterpiece, 'the result of a lifetime devoted to the search for truth'. Though not a believer, the elderly artist threw himself wholeheartedly into this project for the nuns who had nursed him through illness. Bedridden, he splashed out the designs for his towering figures using a paintbrush tied to a bamboo pole. From the outside, the chapel looks fairly traditional, but inside, it is an icebox of stark white tiles disturbed only by the scrawled, black, faceless figures of St Dominic, the Virgin and Child, and the Stations of the Cross. Stained glass windows in the south and west walls cast an eerie light.

Also slightly north of the old centre is the **Centre d'Art VAAS**, a sculpture garden and exhibition space for contemporary art that Jean Dubuffet used as a studio from 1955 to 1970. Another private gallery, the **Galerie Beaubourg**, housed in a château, lies west of the centre on the Grasse road. Terraced sculpture gardens are dotted with pieces by Niki de St Phalle, Arman and Julian Schnabel, part of a permanent collection assembled by Parisian gallery owners Marianne and Pierre Nahon, which also continues inside.

The pièce de résistance is the Jean Tinguely chapel, featuring his weird and wonderful *Grande odalisque*.

Ancienne cathédrale
pl de la Cathédrale (04.93.58.42.00). **Open** 9am-6pm daily.

Centre d'Art VAAS
14 traverse des Moulins (04.93.58.29.42). **Open** *Apr-Sept* 9.30am-noon, 2.30-6pm Tue-Sat; *Oct-Mar* by appointment only. **Admission** free.

Chapelle du Rosaire
468 ave Henri Matisse (04.93.58.03.26). **Open** *Sept-June* 10-11.30am, 2.30-5.30pm Tue, Thur; *July-Aug* 2.30-5.30pm daily; mass 10am daily. **Admission** 13F.

Inland Alpes-Maritimes

Matisse-designed vestments in the **Chapelle du Rosaire**. *See page 265.*

Galerie Beaubourg

Château Notre Dame des Fleurs, 2618 rte de Grasse (04.93.24.52.00). **Open** *Apr-Sept* 11am-7pm Mon-Sat; *Oct-Mar* 11am-5.30pm Tue-Sat. **Admission** 30F.

Where to stay & eat

The recently renovated **La Closerie des Genêts** (4 impasse M Maurel, 04.93.58.78.50, rates 180F-450F) has 12 chintzy rooms and a good restaurant. The **Hôtel Diana** (79 av des Poilus, 04.93.58.28.56, rates 440F), in a modern building, serves breakfast in a tiny courtyard garden. Slightly out of the centre, **La Roseraie** (14 av H-Giraud, 04.93.58.02.20, rates 385F-730F) has a magnificent garden with pool. The **Château du Domaine Saint-Martin** (rte de Coursegoules et du col de Vence, 04.93.58.02.02, rates 3,000F-4,500F), now under the same ownership as the **Cap Eden Roc** (*see box page 210*), offers not only elegant accommodation and stunning views but an excellent restaurant with lunch menus starting at 300F. Best of all, you can cut out all those winding roads by availing yourself of the hotel's private helipad. The **Auberge des Templiers** (39 av Joffre, 04.93.58.06.05, closed Mon, menus 205F-325F) has great mod-Med cuisine cooked up by young internationally trained (but Vence-born) chef Stéphane Demichelis in a pretty setting with tables in the garden in summer. For the innovative Provençal cooking of super-chef Jacques Maximin at **Restaurant Jacques Maximin**, *see page 54*.

Getting there

By car

A8 autoroute, Cagnes-sur-Mer exit (no.48), then D36 to Vence.

By train/bus

The 400 bus runs from Nice to Vence via Cagnes-sur-Mer and St-Paul-de-Vence. Services are every half hour (slightly less frequent on Sundays).

Tourist information

Office du Tourisme

8 pl du Grand Jardin (04.93.58.06.38). **Open** 9am-noon, 2-5.30pm Mon, Sat.

Around Vence

The houses of tiny medieval **Tourrettes-sur-Loup**, west of Vence, are circled around like wagons to form their own defensive wall. Tourrettes is famous for its violets, which grow in abundance under the olive trees in spring and star in the Fête des Violettes in early March. The village's main drag, the Grand'Rue, is lined with craft shops, most of them more earnest than their souvenir-oriented cousins in St-Paul and correspondingly more expensive. To the north-east, **St-Jeannet** is a wine-making village dominated by the dramatic rock outcrop known as le Baou, which can be ascended by a waymarked path. East of Vence, **La Gaude** is a very friendly little village

Inland Alpes-Maritimes

dating from 189 BC. It's a good place to start a pedestrian exploration of the surrounding countryside: there are six marked walks, the one to Vence taking an hour and ten minutes, and the one to le Baou an hour and a half. The tourist office (*see below*) has maps.

Where to stay, eat & drink

In Tourrettes, you can rent a luxury, furnished, hand-painted American-Indian teepee from 195F per day (plus 20F membership fee) at **L'Espace de la Vie** campsite at nearby Les Rives-du-Loup (7 pl Anthony Dors, 04.93.58.30.85).

In St-Jeannet, dawdle for dinner or just an ice-cream on the terrace at **La Tourelle** (6 rue Euzigre, 04.93.24.91.27, closed Mon) or join hepcats from all over the Côte at **La Seguinière** (rte de St-Laurent, 04.93.24.42.92, closed Mon-Wed & Sun), one of the best jazz bars in the region, which also serves simple à la carte food (Fri, Sat dinner only; average 150F), including ice-creams and sorbets imported from Fenocchio in Nice.

Rest up before or after the hike up le Baou at the **Hôtel du Baou** (le plan du Bois, 04.93.59.44.44, rates 400F-520F) in La Gaude, which has a swimming pool and tennis courts. Alternatively, replace those burned-up calories with the sweet and savoury pastries on sale **Chez Amandine** (rue les Nertiers 04.93.24.75.25, closed Wed).

Getting there & around

By car
From Vence, D2210 west to Tourrettes-sur-Loup, D2210 east to St-Jeannet, then D18 to La Gaude.

By bus
The area is not well-served by local bus services, though the 400 service from Nice covers some of this area, and there's a bus from Vence to St-Jeannet. For details, contact Vence's tourist office (*see above*).

Tourist information

La Gaude
Syndicat d'Initiative, 20 rue Centrale (04.93.24.47.26/fax 04.93.24.70.06). **Open** *Apr-Aug* 9am-noon, 2-4pm Tue-Sat
Website: www.mairie-lagaude.fr

St-Jeannet
Syndicat d'Initiative, 35 rue de la Soucare (04.93.24.73.83). **Open** 10am-noon, 2-5pm Mon-Fri.

Tourrettes-sur-Loup
Office de Tourisme, 2 rte de Vence (04.93.24.18.93). **Open** 10am-noon, 2-6pm Tue-Sat.

Crafty **Tourrettes-sur-Loup**.

Inland Alpes-Maritimes

The Arrière-pays & the Var Valley

When Nice gets too hot, the rural villages of the *arrière-pays* and the Var Valley soothe the soul.

Ask any full-time Riviera residents where they spend their weekends, and they're likely to tell you that they head for the hills. Known as the *arrière-pays*, these backlands are a world apart from the coast – a mini-wilderness of pine forests, wild flowers and medieval *villages perchés* built into the steep rocky slopes, offering spectacular panoramas, clear night skies, pristine cool breezes in the summer months and traditional rustic cuisine based around local produce such as olive oil and goat's cheese. Art enthusiasts can explore pastel Italianate architecture and a trove of painted chapels, from the frescos of fourteenth-century primitives to the gilded ornamental follies of the baroque era.

The Arrière-pays

Once a Roman settlement, the village of **Contes**, 18 kilometres north of Nice on the D2204/D15, juts out from a steep slope overlooking the Paillon de Contes torrent. The town only found itself in the historical limelight in 1508 when the bishop of Nice was called in to rid the place of a nasty plague of caterpillars. The **Musée de Contes** includes the **Site des Moulins** where olives are still pressed (Dec-Mar) in a seventeenth-century water-generated mill, and the **Musée de la Vigne et du Vin**, a wine-making museum. Olive oil, salted olives and olive paste are on sale at the museum and at the **Gamm-Vert agricultural cooperative** (rte de Châteauneuf, 04.93.79.01.51, open 8am-noon, 2-6pm Tue-Sat). From **Châteauneuf-de-Contes**, a tiny village four-and-a-half kilometres west of Contes on the side of the mountain, there is a good 30-minute walk to the old, abandoned village of **Vieille Châteauneuf**, an atmospheric, overgrown cluster of ruins amid the crags, with splendid views.

Continuing upvalley from Contes, the D15 leads in ten kilometres to **Coaraze**, the self-styled *village du soleil* (village of the sun). On the main square, the outer walls of the *mairie* (town hall) are decorated with dazzling modern sundials by Jean Cocteau and other artists. The village is a maze of vaulted passageways and

cypress-lined gardens and fountains. At the top of the village is the old cemetery, with cement boxes for burials because the rocks are too hard even for pickaxes. The name Coaraze, locals will tell you, derives from *caude rase* (cut tail): wily medieval inhabitants caught Old Nick napping and grabbed hold of him, obliging him to shed his lizard-like tail to escape; a modern pavement mosaic commemorates the event.

Only 16 kilometres from Nice on the D2204/D21, isolated on a rocky spur above olive groves, **Peillon** has not a single quaint boutique, the wise residents having banned all touristic upscaling. To compensate, there are narrow cobblestoned streets and an unbeatable panorama of the valley. Not to be missed is the miniscule **Chapelle des Pénitents Blancs** at the entrance of the village. The chapel is kept closed to protect the fifteenth-century frescos of the Passion attributed to artist Giovanni Canavesio, but the works can be viewed through a grating with coin-operated lights. Further upstream – or a lovely one-and-a-half-hour ridge walk from Peillon – **Peille** is a quiet village with some handsome Romanesque and Gothic doors, windows and fountains and a ruined feudal castle. Peille's feisty inhabitants, who accepted numerous excommunications in the Middle Ages rather than paying taxes to the bishop, speak a dialect all their own known as *pelhasc*.

At the bottom of the main Paillon Valley, the agricultural township of **L'Escarène** was once an important staging post on the old *Route du Sel* (salt road) from Nice to Turin; for once, a piece of modern engineering – the arched viaduct of the Nice-Sospel railway – complements the view of the old town. The ornate baroque church of **St-Pierre** (04.93.79.50.73), renowned for its eighteenth-century organ, is generally closed, but the mayor's office (04.93.91.64.00) can sometimes be prevailed on to produce a key. The **Association ADO** (Les Amis de l'Olivier) located across from the post office (19 bd du Docteur Roux, 04.93.91.44.29, closed Sat, Sun) takes great pride in its superb extra-virgin olive oil, and offers a tasting initiation, a tour of the town's oil mill, a hike through the groves and a

Inland Alpes-Maritimes

Head for the hills: the *arrière-pays*.

The Arrière-pays & the Var Valley

and endless fruit orchards is a treat for city-sore eyes. Try the *giboulette de lapin* (rabbit stew) and heavenly home-made nougat ice-cream. Rooms (rates 360F-510F) are simple but comfortable, and overlook the valley. In Peillon, the **Auberge de la Madone** (04.93.79.91.17, closed three weeks Jan, mid-Oct to mid-Dec, rates 470F-960F, menus 150F-350F) is a long-standing romantic hideaway with small but lovely antiques-filled rooms and refined authentic Nissart specialities in the restaurant. It's closed on Wednesdays throughout the year. The stunning view from the flower-lined terrace makes up for the slightly overpriced fare. In peaceful Peille, stop for a pastis and some *pissaladière* (onion pie) at the café **Chez Cauvin** (pl Carnot, 04.93.79.90.41, closed Tue, Wed, and mid-June to mid-July, menus 100F, 150F).

Getting there

By car
The starting point for all these villages is the D2204 Paillon Valley road, which begins at the Acropolis roundabout in Nice as bd J-B Verany.

By train/bus
the Nice-Sospel line (four-six trains daily; *see also p275*) winds up the Paillon valley, stopping off at Peillon, Peille and L'Escarène, but only L'Escarène has a station within easy reach of the town; Peillon and Peille are a 5km walk from their respective stations. There are buses from Nice to Peillon and Peille (three daily Mon-Sat), L'Escarène and Lucéram (four daily Monday-Saturday), and Contes and Coaraze (two daily Monday-Saturday); for details ring Nice *gare routière* (04.93.85.61.81).

Tourist information

Coaraze
Office de Tourisme, montée du Portal (04.93.79.37.47/fax 04.93.79.31.73). **Open** *Oct-Mar* 10am-noon, 2-5pm Mon-Fri; *Apr-Sept* 10am-noon, 2-5pm daily.

Contes
Office de Tourisme, pl Albert-Olivier (04.93.79.13.99/fax 04.93.79.26.30). **Open** 2-6pm Mon-Fri.

Lucéram
Office de Tourisme, Maison du Pays, pl Adrien Barralis (04.93.79.46.50). **Open** 9am-noon, 2-6pm Tue-Sat.

Peille
Syndicat d'Initiative, Mairie, pl Carnot (04.93.91.71.71/fax 04.93.91.71.78). **Open** 9am-noon Mon-Fri.

Peillon
Syndicat d'Initiative, Mairie, 672 av de l'Hôtel de Ville (04.93.79.91.04/fax 04.93.79.87.65). **Open** 8.30am-noon, 2-5pm Mon-Fri.

traditional Niçois olive-centric feast at a nearby restaurant. Further up the Route du Sel, the fortified medieval crossroads of **Lucéram** is worth a detour for the fifteenth-century church of **Stes-Marguerite-et-Rosalie** (rue de l'Eglise, closed Mon & Tue), with a striking Italianate onion-domed yellow and pink bell tower rising above the grey stones. Don't miss the silver reliquary and outstanding *rétables* by the Bréa school that recount the story of Ste Marguerite, a popular third-century shepherdess-martyr burned at the stake, who was one of Joan of Arc's favourite voices-in-her-head.

Musée de la Vigne et du Vin
rue Scuderie (04.93.79.19.17). **Open** 10.30am-12.30pm, 2-5pm second and fourth Sun of month. **Admission** 5F, free children.

Le Site des Moulins
Quartier Le Martinet. **Open** 9am-12.30pm, 2-5.30pm Sat; by appointment Mon-Fri. **Admission** 5F, free children.

Where to stay & eat

In Contes, **Le Cellier** (3 bd Charles Alunni, 04.93.79.00.64, restaurant closed two weeks Aug & Sun, menus 68F-138F), in the modern lower section of town, dishes up tasty family-style cuisine at reasonable prices; there are also a few double rooms (rates 180F-195F). One of the most quietly celebrated *arrière-pays* destinations is the **Auberge du Soleil** (04.93.79.08.11, closed Nov to mid-Feb, menus 118F-142F) in Coaraze, where the bucolic vista from the sun-warmed bay window dining room over distant blue mountains

Inland Alpes-Maritimes

The Train des Pignes

Trains are a good way of resort-hopping on the Riviera, and the SNCF line up the valleys of the Bévéra and Roya (*see page 271*) offers spectacular views. But on the independently run Train des Pignes, which chugs up the lower Var Valley on its way to Digne-les-Bains, north of the Gorges du Verdon in the remote rural *département* of Alpes-de-Haute-Provence, the journey itself becomes part of the fun.

The Chemins de Fer de Provence line was part of an ambitious plan to provide a direct rail link between the Alps and the Côte d'Azur. Built between 1891 and 1909, the narrow one-metre gauge railway runs over 31 bridges and viaducts and through 25 tunnels, climbing to an altitude of 1,000 metres. Trains leave from the **Gare de Provence** in Nice, five minutes' walk north of the main Nice-Ville SNCF station, but those with cars should head for the second station, **Lingostière** (from exit no.52 on the A8 autoroute, take the N202 north-signposted Digne – for one kilometre, then turn left on to chemin de la Glacière, which has a free car park).

The first part of the line out of Nice follows the lower Var Valley through an uninspiring landscape of *centres commercials* and industrial estates, though there is one jewel lurking amid the drabness: the marvellous **Issautier** restaurant in St-Martin-du-Var (*see page 54*). Beyond Plan du Var the mountains close in on either side at the forbidding Défilé de Chaudan, beyond which the Var abruptly changes direction, heading west. **Villars-sur-Var**, the first stop of interest, is a *village perché* with some good Renaissance art in the church of **St-Jean-Baptiste**; but its main claim to fame is as the centre of the tiny Bellet wine *appellation*, which occupies a mere 31 hectares; the white is definitely worth trying. **Touët-sur-Var**, ten minutes further up the line, clings precariously to the side of the cliff. Space is so tight up here that the village church straddles a mountain stream. The valley opens out a little at **Puget-Théniers**, an old Templar stronghold and the birthplace of Auguste Blanchi, one of the leaders of the Paris Commune of 1870, who is commemorated by a stirring Aristide Maillol monument on the main road.

If you stop anywhere, make it **Entrevaux**, a handsome fortified village an hour and a half along the line from Nice. It's cradled in a curve of the river and dominated by a fort that has seen a lot of action since it was built by Louis XIV's military architect Vauban in the 1690s. Until 1860, this was a frontier town, just upstream from the border between France and Italian Savoy. The twin towers that guard the entrance to the village across a single-arched bridge are almost Disney-picturesque, but once inside this is a sturdily practical place, with tall houses, narrow lanes and a seventeenth-century cathedral built into the defensive walls, complete with turreted bell tower. The chateau itself is a steep, appetite-building climb from the town up a zigzag ramp; it's an atmospheric old pile, with dungeons and galleries to explore.

Beyond Entrevaux, the line plunges further into underpopulated, sheep-ridden Alpes-de-Haute-Provence, via the old town of **Annot** with its houses built right up against huge sandstone boulders, towards Digne. **St-André-les-Alpes**, almost two and a half hours along the line, is the jumping-off point for Castellane at the head of the **Gorges du Verdon** (*see page 193*), via a bus that meets the 9am train from Nice daily except Sundays.

The Train des Pignes is operated by Chemins de Fer de Provence (info/bookings 04.97.03.80.80). Trains depart from the **Gare de Provence** in Nice (4 bis rue Alfred Binet, 04.93.82.10.17) and terminate at the **Gare Digne-les-Bains** (av Pierre Sémard, 04.92.31.01.58). There are four daily departures in each direction; Nice to Digne takes just over three hours and costs 111F one-way; Nice to Entrevaux takes an hour and a half and costs 56F. Trains are modern, with two carriages, but steam trains still ply the route on Sundays from May to October; ring for details.

Into the Alps

The dramatic landscapes and subtler pleasures of the Alpes-Maritimes and the Parc du Mercantour.

It's not the first thing that springs to mind when sipping a dry martini on the terrace of the Carlton Hôtel in Cannes, but the *département* of Alpes-Maritimes – which hosts the glitziest stretch of the Riviera – also contains some of the most spectacular mountain scenery in France. Less than an hour's drive north of Nice, the olive groves and *villages perchés* of the immediate hinterland make way for some serious Alpine crags, dominating the deeply scored valleys of the Roya, the Vésubie, the Tinée and the Haut Var. Outdoor activities such as walking, skiing, canyoning and mountain biking bring visitors in droves, but there are more sedate reasons to come up here: the views, the cool summer evenings, the Renaissance frescos hidden in out of the way chapels. The flora- and fauna-rich **Parc National du Mercantour** (*see box page 280*) covers a huge swathe of territory near the border with Italy, and offers walkers plenty of waymarked paths and mountain refuges; it also has one of the area's more unusual sights – the rock-hewn Bronze Age engravings of the **Vallée des Merveilles** (*see box page 272*). And, though the region is one of the biggest blanks on the *Guide Michelin*'s restaurant and hotel map of France, it does at least offer rustic hospitality of a kind (and at a price) that's sadly lacking on the coast.

One really needs a car – or even better, a motorbike or mountain bike – to make the most of this area. Trains serve only the Bévéra and Roya Valleys to the east – and a charming route it is, too, climbing doggedly from Nice to Sospel and then on via Tende into Italy, even looping back on itself at one point to gain altitude. In the other valleys, the only alternative to the infrequent buses is to walk – not a bad option, if you have the time.

Saorge.

The Vallées de la Roya & de la Bévéra

When the rest of the county of Nice devolved to France in 1860, the valleys of the Roya and its tributary the Bévéra stayed Italian – the reason being that King Vittorio Emanuele II liked to go hunting there. It was not until 1947 that the French-speaking inhabitants of these most

Mediterranean of Alpine valleys were allowed to decide which side of the border they wanted to be on – and after 20 years of Mussolini and five of total chaos, it was hardly surprising that they plumped en masse for France. The Italian influence makes itself felt in the colourful houses and churches of towns such as Sospel and Saorge, and in the valleys' artistic legacy – notably the remarkable set of fifteenth-century frescos in the chapel of Notre-Dame-des-Fontaines near the village of La Brigue.

Sospel, a sleepy, sprawling town that hangs over the olive groves beside the River Bévéra, is the mountain gateway to the Roya Valley, and a mecca for soft-core ramblers who prefer classic hilly countryside to jagged peaks. The streets abound with charming squares and sculpted fountains, but the main highlight is the **Eglise St-Michel** (open 3-6pm daily) on place St-Michel, with its peach and frothy stucco façade,

La Vallée des Merveilles

Is it a long-horned cow? Is it a beetle? Is it a woman giving birth? The great thing about the prehistoric rock engravings of the Vallée des Merveilles, a remote, rock-strewn valley dominated by the 2,872-metre peak of Mont Bego, is that they allow us all to become amateur archaeologists, as very few have been deciphered with any degree of certainty.

Over 50,000 engravings have been catalogued, most dating from between 2,500 BC and 500 BC, although there are a few more recent interlopers – Christian crosses, Napoleonic slogans and even a Mickey Mouse. The Bronze and Iron Age shepherds who grazed their flocks here chipped away at the red rocks (the colour is caused by the lichen that once grew on them, and is only skin deep) to create line drawings of apparently familiar objects – cattle, ploughs, field systems. A few, though, seem clearly ritual in intent. One of the most famous – and a symbol of the Vallée des Merveilles, which is part of the Mercantour National Park – is the so-called Sorcerer, a bearded giant who appears to be shooting lightning bolts from his hands.

As with Stonehenge, the scholarly debate on the meaning and purpose of these prehistoric leavings is as wide-ranging as it is inconclusive. For some, they are markers on

a processional way that led in the direction of Mount Bego, considered a sacred mountain that symbolised the union of sky and earth; for others, they are simply doodles.

The fascination of the Merveilles engravings is enhanced by their setting – a magnificent rockscape studded with lakes, where chamoix, marmosets and eagles are common sights. Access is from the town of St-Dalmas-de-Tende, an unremarkable market village five kilometres south of Tende. A paved mountain road branches west from St-Dalmas to the hamlet of Casterino, jumping-off point for two waymarked walking tracks into the valley – the direct route via the Refuge de Fontalbe, or the longer northern route via the Refuge de Valmasque. Both routes converge on the main Merveilles trail, which heads south down the valley to the lakeside Refuge des Merveilles. The Association des Taxi Accompagnateurs (04.93.04.60.31) can provide transport to the start of walking trails from Tende or St-Dalmas.

It is possible to visit the engravings in a day from Nice, but it's more rewarding to spread the visit over two days, spending the night in one of the refuges. Better still, hire a guide from the official Bureau des Guides in Tende, and get to see some of the less well-known engravings. Next door to the guides' HQ is the small but well-organised **Musée des Merveilles** (*see opposite*), which provides a good introduction to the history and interpretation of the site.

Bureau des Guides du Val des Merveilles
11 av du 16 Septembre 1947, Tende (04.93.04.77.73). **Open** 9am-noon, 3-6pm Wed-Sun.
Accompanied walking tours from 35F per person.

Refuge de Valmasque
04.93.21.91.20/Club Alpin Nice 04.93.62.59.99.
Open between June and September.

Refuge de Fontanalbe
04.93.04.89.19/warden 04.93.04.69.22.
Open between June and September.

Refuge des Merveilles
04.93.04.64.64/Club Alpin Nice 04.93.62.59.99.
The refuge is open daily between mid-June and September and during school holidays, and on Saturdays and Sundays only the rest of the year.

The Sorcerer.

trompe l'oeil murals and François Bréa's splendid early sixteenth-century *Immaculate Virgin* surrounded by angels. The tourist office, on the half-demolished eleventh-century bridge, provides useful hiking maps.

North of Sospel, the D2204 climbs over the 879-metre Col de Brouis before dropping down into the Roya Valley proper at **Breil-sur-Roya**. A tranquil village of red-tiled pastel houses surrounded by olive trees, Breil has also become an internationally known centre for canyoning, rafting and kayaking. Visit the flamboyantly ornate eighteenth-century church of Sancta-Maria-in-Albis (open 9am-noon, 2-5pm daily), which has a fine gilded organ from the seventeenth century. Organs are big news in the churches of the Roya-Bévéra area: there are no fewer than seven historic, finely decorated instruments made by Tuscan or Lombard craftsmen, all in perfect working order.

Saorge is the most spectacular Roya village: a cluster of ochre, rose and burnt sienna Italianate houses and bell towers with shimmering fish-scale tile roofs, clinging to the side of a mountain at the entrance to the breathtaking Roya Gorge. A narrow cobbled street winds up to the fifteenth-century church of St-Sauveur, with another of those magnificent carved organs, this one from the nineteenth century. South of the village is the not-to-be-missed **Couvent des Franciscains** (Franciscan Monastery), whose lovely rectangular cloister is filled with painted sundials and eighteenth-century frescos depicting the life of St Francis of Assisi. Beyond the monastery's cypress-lined terrace with its meditation-provoking view, a former mule track leads to the Madone del Poggio, an isolated Romanesque church with a crumbling octagonal tower, the remains of a former abbey, which is privately owned (and therefore not open to visitors).

As one approaches **Tende**, 20 kilometres further on, the surrounding peaks become seriously Alpine. The dark, narrow streets and grey slate houses of this frontier town offer little distraction for the wandering tourist. At the end of a passageway on rue de France, however, is a surprising splash of colour – the fifteenth-century church of **Notre-Dame-de-l'Assomption** on place de l'Eglise (open 9am-6pm daily), with an elaborately sculpted russet and ice-blue façade and pink Lombard bell tower. Anyone intending to visit the rock engravings of the Vallée des Merveilles should not miss the **Musée des Merveilles**, which has a diorama and interactive exhibits explaining the history and significance of these prehistoric scratchings, as well as an array of hunting tools and fossils from the Bronze Age.

Inland Alpes-Maritimes

Downstream from Tende, a pretty side road leads east to **La Brigue**. Postcard picturesque, the village boasts no fewer than three baroque churches, of which **La Collégiale St Martin** (La Place, open 9am-6pm daily), with some fine primitive paintings of the Nice school, is the only one open to the public. The real cultural treat, though, lies a few kilometres further east, where the plain mountain chapel of **Notre-Dame-des-Fontaines** conceals a series of frescos that has earned it the moniker the 'Sistine of the Alps'. Those in the chancel are by Jean Baleison; but it is the nave frescos of the Passion and Last Judgment by Giovanni Canavesio (born 1420) that stand out, pushing beyond the Gothic into a touching, though still primitive, foretaste of the Renaissance. Don't just turn up at the chapel: visits are arranged through the tourist office in La Brigue (*see below*).

Saorge

Couvent des Franciscains
04.93.04.55.55. **Open** *April-Oct* 2-6pm Mon, Wed-Sun; *Nov-March* 2pm-5pm Sat, Sun. **Admission** 25F, children 15F

Tende

Musée des Merveilles
av du 16 Septembre 1947 (04.93.04.32.50). **Open** *May-Oct* 10.30am-6.30pm Mon, Wed-Fri, Sun; 10.30am-9pm Sat; *Nov-Apr* 10.30am-5pm Mon, Wed-Sun. **Admission** 30F, 15F children.

Where to stay & eat

Breil-sur-Roya
The reasonably priced bistro **L'Etoile 'Chez Camolio'** (19 bd Rouvier, 04.93.04.41.61, closed Wed from Oct-May, menus 70F-150F) offers simple home cooking. Set back from the road right alongside the Roya river is the **Hôtel Restaurant Castel du Roy** (1km out of town on RN204, 04.93.04.43.66, doubles 320F-440F), whose comfortable rooms and country-style restaurant (menus 125F-225F) look out on to grassy parklands. Best of all is the exquisitely served regional cuisine, well worth a day trip from the coast. Highlights include a pan-fried *loup* (sea perch) served with Provençal tian and fruit sauce; local river trout with mustard sauce and vegetables; and a rosemary crème brûlée.

La Brigue
La Cassoulette (20 rue du Général de Gaulle, 04.93.04.63.82, closed Mon, dinner Sun, menus 75F-175F) is a tiny convivial bistro, chock-a-block with kitsch statuettes of barnyard birds;

it's also one of the best-kept gastronomic secrets in the *arrière-pays*, offering divine home-made foie gras, duck confit, olive-tree smoked salmon, mouthwatering desserts and an excellent selection of wines, all reasonably priced. Not surprisingly, reservations are recommended. **Hôtel Restaurant Le Mirval** (3 rue Vincent Ferrier, 04.93.04.63.71, closed Nov-Mar, rates 260F-350F, menus 90F-150F) has comfortable modern accommodation and also organises four-wheel-drive excursions into the surrounding valleys.

Saorge
The only two restaurants in this tiny ancient town are **Le Bellevue** (5 rue Louis Périssol, 04.93.04.51.37, closed Thur from Sept-June, menus 98F-138F), a cheerful brasserie/tea salon with a huge panoramic bay window facing south, and **Lou Pontin** (rue Revelli, 04.93.04.54.90, closed Wed from Sept-May, menus 70F-100F), with good home-made pastas and savoury flans. There are no hotels in Saorge but trekkers flock to the rustic **Gîte Bergiron** (04.93.04.55.49, rate 160F), on the hill behind the Franciscan monastery.

Sospel
For a leisurely gastronomic meal, try the **Bel Acqua** restaurant at the **Hôtel des Etrangers** (9 bd de Verdun, 04.93.04.00.09, closed Tue from Sept-June, menus 105F-185F) for typical Ligurian-style pastas and stews. Rooms cost 105F to 185F and the whole place closes down for January.

Tende
L'Auberge Tendasque (65 av du 16 Septembre 1947, 04.93.04.62.26, closed lunch Mon & Tue, dinner Sat, menus 60F-125F) serves tasty trout soufflé and is always full of locals. In nearby St-Dalmas-de-Tende – jumping-off point for the Vallée des Merveilles – the **Hôtel Restaurant Le Prieuré** (av Jean Médecin, 04.93.04.75.70, rates 260F-310F, menus 90F-135F) offers a comfortable stop for trekkers who are allergic to mountain refuges.

Getting around

By car
A8 from Nice, Menton exit (no.59), then the D2566 to Sospel; from Sospel, follow the D2204 north for Breil-sur-Roya and beyond. Alternatively, the Roya Valley can be ascended in its entirety from Ventimiglia in Italy on the S20, which crosses into France at Olivetta San Michele, 10km before Breil.

By bus
All the main villages are served by coaches from Nice run by private operators under the TAM (Transports des Alpes Maritimes) banner: call

Inland Alpes-Maritimes

04.93.89.47.14 for information. Transports Rey
(04.93.04.01.24) runs services from Sospel to most
destinations in the Roya valley.

By train
Around five trains a day travel the winding,
picturesque Nice-Sospel-Tende route; for timetable
information, ring the general SNCF number
(08.36.35.35.35).

Tourist information

Sospel
Office de Tourisme, Le Pont-Vieux (04.93.04.15.80).
Open *Sept-June* 9.30am-noon, 2.30-5pm daily; *July,
Aug* 9am-12.30pm, 2-6pm daily.

Breil-sur-Roya
*Office de Tourisme, pl Bianchéri (tel/fax
04.93.04.99.76).* **Open** *Oct-Mar* 9am-noon, 1.30-
5pm Mon-Fri; *Apr-Sept* 9am-noon, 1.30-5pm;
9am-noon Sun.

Tende
Office de Tourisme, pl de Gaulle (04.93.04.73.71).
Open *Oct-May* 9am-noon, 1-5pm Mon-Sat; *June-Sept*
9am-noon, 2-6pm daily.

La Brigue
*Office de Tourisme, ground floor, La Mairie, pl St-
Martin (04.93.04.36.07/fax 04 93 04 36 09).*
Open *Sept-May* 8.30am-noon, 1.30-5pm Tue-Sat;
8.30am-noon Sun; *June-Aug* 8.30am-noon, 1.30-6pm
Mon-Sat; 8.30am-noon Sun.

The Vallée de la Vésubie

The best way into the high mountains of the
Vésubie is the D19 out of Nice, which rises
almost imperceptibly past villas and pastures to
the village of Levens, an atmospheric cluster of
stone houses with an excess of burbling
fountains. Beyond Levens the mountains begin
with a vengeance as the road clings to the sheer
side of the **Gorges de la Vésubie** – which can
also be negotiated on the lower D2565 route.
Soon after the two roads meet is the turn-off for
Utelle, another *village perché*, whose church
has a pretty Gothic porch and wooden doors
carved with scenes from the life of local boy St
Verain. The shrine of **Madone d'Utelle** stands
on a barren peak six kilometres further on; try
to visit in the morning, as the clouds often roll
up here later in the day. A plain terracotta-red
barn of a church, rebuilt several times, it owes
its existence to a ninth-century shipwreck on
the patch of sea that – on a clear day – can be
seen far down below. Saved from drowning by
the Virgin, who appeared on the mountainside
bathed in light, the grateful mariners climbed
up here to set up a rudimentary shrine, which in
time became the chapel of **Notre-Dame-des-
Miracles**. The road up to St-Martin continues

past Lantosque to Roquebillière, a crumbling
old village on the east side of the valley with a
modern offshoot opposite, built after a landslide
in 1926 that claimed 17 lives. Right down by the
river – on the same, western side as the modern
village – is one of the valley's more unusual
churches: **St-Michel-de-Gast-des
Templiers**, of eighth-century origin. Built by
the Knights Templars, who were active in this
valley, and later taken over by the Knights of
Malta, it is full of abstruse Templar symbolism;
on one ancient capital there is even a carving of
the Egyptian baboon god Thot. The key is kept
by the voluble Madame Périchon, who can be
found in the house opposite the church.

It may look sleepy enough if you've just
come up from the coast, but the ancient market
town of St-Martin-Vésubie is where the local
action is. Though most walkers head higher
up, the town is a good place to refuel and pick
up supplies and information (*see below*). The
town's entrance hall is the pocket-sized **place
Félix Faure**, which links the main valley
road with Rue Cagnoli, St-Martin's steeply
inclined pedestrian backbone. A little paved
channel of water runs the whole way down
the steeply inclined street. Known as a
gargouille, this is a rare feature today; the
only other example is in Briançon.

Easy riders at **La Colmiane**. *See page 276.*

Stare it out with a mountain goat at **Madone de Fenestre.**

The road west to the church of **Madone de Fenestre** criss-crosses a mountain stream that offers plenty of excuses for a paddle, a picnic or some serious raspberry-picking. But it's worth pushing on to the end, where a large mountain refuge and a tin-roofed church stand in a spectacular position, surrounded by a cirque of high peaks. The church is only two centuries old, but its miraculous icon of the Madone de Fenestre (which lives down in St-Martin in winter) dates from the twelfth century. Allow at least an hour and a half for the rewarding walk up past a lake to the Col de Fenestre on the Italian border. Madone de Fenestre is also the classic western access point for the **Vallée des Merveilles** (*see page 272*), via the high-altitude Refuge de Nice (information from the Club Alpin, 04.93.62.59.99). Another way into the Mercantour National Park (*see page 280*) is to head north from St-Martin to the Swiss-chalet style hamlet of **Le Boréon**, which is the departure point for a number of good walks. The village of **Venanson** – perched on a rocky spur overlooking St-Martin – is home to the tiny chapel of Ste-Claire. Inside is a lively fifteenth-century cycle of frescos with scenes from the life of St Sebastian. If it's closed, ask Roger the butcher (opposite) for the key.

West of St-Martin, the D2565 continues up to the Col St-Martin (1,500 metres), which links the Vésubie and Tinée valleys. Just below the pass is the aspiring resort of **La Colmiane**, where, in summer (June and July), you can career down

the mountain on a *trottinerbe* – a sort of kid's scooter with huge soft tyres – from the top of the Pic de Colmiane lift (23F return, 28F with *trottinerbe*). The charms of **St-Dalmas-de-Valdeblore**, the first village over the pass, are more sedate. The Eglise de l'Invention de la Ste-Croix, a fine Romanesque church with original twelfth-century masonry and its very own piece of the Holy Cross, once belonged to a powerful Benedictine priory. St-Dalmas, now a pretty backwater, was a local grain basket and market centre in the Middle Ages, when many traders chose the high Alpine routes over the pirate- and brigand-infested coast road.

Where to stay & eat

Utelle
Le Bellevue (tel/fax 04.93.03.17.19, closed Nov & Jan, rates 200F-290F), just above the village on the Madone d'Utelle road, has views over the village rooftops and down the valley that live up to its name. It has a restuarant (open all year, closed Wed from Oct-May, menus 70F-150F) and a good-sized outdoor swimming pool with bar.

Lantosque
L'Ancienne Gendarmerie (Le Rivet, 04.93.03. 00.65, closed Oct-Mar, rates 350F-710F), on the valley road below the village, really was a police station – hence the sentry box outside. With its eight rooms and small

swimming pool perched above the river, this place is worth bookmarking, not least for its restaurant (closed Mon and Oct-Mar, menus 145F-285F), which offers one of the few serious gourmet experiences in the area. The cuisine rises well above the sedate décor in dishes like *mousse de St-Jacques et sa noix grillée* (scallop mousse) and *ris de veau aux chanterelles* (veal sweetbreads with chanterelle mushrooms), and the desserts are equally fine. Up in the village, the **Bar des Tilleuls**, with a view over the valley, is a good place to sip a pernod under the eponymous lime trees; it also does lunchtime salads and a hot plat du jour at 60F.

St-Martin-Vésubie

La Treille (68 rue Cagnoli, 04.93.03.30.85, open daily school holidays, Fri-Tue rest of year, closed Dec & Jan, menus 100F-125F), towards the top end of the winding main street, is a friendly restaurant with good pizzas made in a wood oven, classic meat and fish dishes, excellent *foie gras maison*, and tables on a panoramic terrace at the back. Further down the same street, on place Marché, **La Trappa** (04.93.03.21.50, open daily school holidays, Tue-Sun rest of year, menus 85F-140F) specialises in pasta and fondues, and has tables outside in the pretty square. Of the five hotels in the centre of town, the two that face each other across the allée de Verdun are the best bets. **La Bonne Auberge** (La Place, 04.93.03.20.49, closed mid-Nov to Jan) lives up to its name, offering solid mountain hospitality in a cheerful building overlooking the valley. The slightly more luxurious **Edward's Parc Hôtel La Chataigneraie** (04.93.03.21.22, closed Oct-May, rates incl breakfast 390F-480F), set in a park of chestnut trees, is a little frayed at the edges but still a good place to relax, with the aid of a heated outdoor swimming pool and a mini-golf course. One hotel we suggest you avoid is the **Des Alpes** in place Félix Faure, where cleanliness and service are not strong points. There are two much better reasons to be in this main square: the **Pâtisserie A Barraja**, a must for sweet addicts, and the **Café-Boulangerie La Maverine** (closed Wed from Sept-June), which offers outsized breakfasts with coffee, bread and home-made jam at 30F and, later in the day, *bruschettas* – not the small Italian version, but a meal-sized 'bread' pizza with various toppings. Note that there is a bank but no cash dispenser in St-Martin; the nearest is in Roquebillière, nine kilometres south.

Madone de Fenestre

The imposing **Refuge de la Madone de Fenestre** (04.93.02.83.19/04.93.03.20.73, closed Mon-Fri from Oct to mid-June) has 62 dormitory beds. It's also a good place to stop for lunch (average 80F); don't miss the home-baked tarts.

Getting there

By car

Take the N202 Var Valley road from Nice airport (exit 50 on A8 autoroute), turn right on to the D2565 after 24km, then follow the route described above.

By bus

All destinations in the Vésubie Valley are served by thrice-daily TRAM buses from Nice (Nice 04.93.89.47.14/St-Martin-Vésubie 04.93.03.20.23). One a day continues to La Colmiane; services to Le Boréon and Madone de Fenestre are much less frequent.

Tourist information

St-Martin-Vésubie's helpful tourist office is well stocked with leaflets, while the Bureau des Guides du Mercantour can arrange guided walks in the mountains, as well as canyoning, climbing and parascending courses.

Office de Tourisme

pl Félix Faure, St-Martin-Vésubie (tel/fax 04.93.03.21.28). Open Oct-May 10am-noon, 2.30-5.30pm Mon-Sat; June-Sept 9am-noon, 3-7pm daily.

Bureau des Guides du Mercantour

rue Cagnoli, St-Martin-Vésubie (04.93.03.26.60).

The Vallée de la Tinée

Most Niçois see this road as a bit of scenery on the way to the ski resorts of Isola 2000 or Auron, but the upper reaches of the Tinée Valley are worth a visit in their own right. Walking up to views (or skiing down from them) is the main attraction, but there is no lack of charmingly frescoed chapels or unspoiled mountain villages.

The Tinée flows into the Var just where the latter changes direction to head south to Nice. But the gorge traversed by the D2205 road up the valley is never quite so precipitous as in the lower reaches of the Vésubie. A few side roads even manage to wind their way up to *villages perchés* such as **La Tour** – which has some vivacious fifteenth-century scenes of vices and virtues in the Chapelle des Pénitents-Blancs and an ancient but still-working oil mill – and **Clans**, one of the best-preserved medieval villages in the whole *département*, where the Chapelle de St-Antoine has frescos of the life of the saint. The last of this trio of villages on the east side of the valley, **Marie**, is a pretty hamlet of only 60 inhabitants with an excellent hotel/restaurant (*see below*). Back on the valley

Inland Alpes-Maritimes

road, just past the turn-off for Marie, the D2565 heads across to St-Dalmas-de-Valdeblore and St-Martin-Vésubie (*see above*).

Approaching St-Sauveur-sur-Tinée, the iron-rich cliffs turn a garish shade of puce – quite a sight at sunset. St-Sauveur itself is a one-horse town, strung out along the road, with little to detain the visitor (the highlight, perhaps, is the lintel of a house that once belonged to the village barber opposite the church, with the tools of his trade proudly carved into the stone). But it is also the jumping-off point for a spectacular route west via the ski resort of Valberg into the valley of the Haut Var, which can be followed to its source just below the Col de Cayolle, one of the most rewarding of all the gateways into the Mercantour.

Above St-Sauveur the Tinée valley heads north through the Gorges de Valabre before broadening out below **Isola**, a siesta of a village amid chestnut groves, with a solitary fifteenth-century bell tower and – rather incongruously, given the pace of life around these parts – a brand new covered fun pool, **Aquavallée**. Further incongruities lie in wait up the side road that ascends the Chastillon torrent to the purpose-built ski resort of **Isola 2000**. The 1970s British design of this blight on the landscape has not aged well, and the only reasons to come up here in the summer are to walk up into the high peaks that surround the resort or to continue by car over the Col de la Lombarde pass into Italy. The tourist office chalet down in Isola village (*see below*) can advise on walks in the area.

St-Etienne-de-Tinée, near the head of the valley, is a surprisingly lively market town of tall, pastel houses and Gothic portals, which celebrates its shepherding traditions in the *Fête de la Transhumance* on the last Sunday in June. But the town also has a cluster of interesting churches. There's a catch, however – artistic jewels like the **Chapelle de St-Sébastien**, with frescos (1492) by Jean Canavesio and Jean Baleison, or the **Chapelle des Trinitaires**, which has, of all things, a marvellously graphic seventeenth-century depiction of the Venetian naval Battle of Lepanto, or the **Chapelle de St-Maur**, with sixteenth-century frescos so rustic you can almost smell the hay – are closed to individual visitors. The only way to get to see them is to go on the tour organised by the Maison du Tourisme (*see below*).

Prize for the most unexpected sight in the Maritime Alps goes to the **Chapelle de St-Érige** in the ski resort of **Auron**. This little wooden chapel – commissioned by wealthy parishioners in the fifteenth century, when this upland plain was covered in summer cornfields – is almost overwhelmed by the faux-Swiss chalet hotels, ski-lifts and roller discos that surround it. Inside, though, it's another story – a series of stories, in fact, told in vivid frescos dating back to 1451. The central scenes of the life of Mary Magdalene alternate religious mysticism with the secular spirit of the troubadour poets, at its most touching in the scene above the central niche in which Mary counts off on her fingers a series of arguments designed to convert the good citizens of Marseille to the true faith (for more on Mary Magdalene's Provençal jaunt, *see page 86*). The key to the chapel can be picked up from the tourist office at the other end of town. Back in the modern world, with 130 kilometres of pistes and 25 ways of getting up there (between téléphériques, télésièges and téléskis), Auron fulfils its purpose depressingly well, and even out of season remains the liveliest of the three big Alpes-Maritimes ski resorts, thronged with families escaping the heat.

North of St-Etienne the D2205 soon becomes the D64 to Barcelonnette, the highest paved road in Europe. When the pass is open (between June and September) bikers, motorists and even cyclists slog up through rugged mountain scenery to the **Col de la Bonette**, where the road loops to encircle the bare peak of Cime de la Bonette. From the highest snack bar in Europe (2,802 metres), a short path takes you up to the viewing table at 2,860 metres for a spectacular 360° panorama. Alternatively, for more rustic pleasures, leave the D2205 five kilometres north of St-Etienne and head left to **St-Dalmas-le-Selvage**, one of the prettiest mountain villages in the whole *département*. Most of the houses still have their original *bardeaux de mélèze* larchwood roofs, open under the eaves where the corn was laid out to dry. The pretty parish church has two good early sixteenth-century altarpieces, and inside the tiny Chapelle de Ste-Marguerite in the centre of the village are frescos by Jean Baleison, discovered behind the altar in 1996. A homely *gîte d'étape* and a better-than-average restaurant make St-Dalmas a good base for walks in the surrounding mountains.

Aquavallée

Isola (04.93.02.16.49). **Open** 11am-8pm Mon-Fri; 10am-8pm Sat, Sun. Admission 25F, 20F children. **No credit cards.**

Where to stay & eat

It's worth planning a lunch or dinner stop in Marie, where the family-run hotel/restaurant **Le Panoramique** (rte de Station de Sports d'Hiver, 04.93.02.03.01, closed Thur, menus 90F-148F) provides fine views and fine meals; the *menu du pêcheur* (135F) is particularly

Unmistakably Alpine: three views of the **Vallée de la Tinée.**

recommended. There are also five equally scenic rooms (160F-200F), for those seeking total rest and relaxation. In Isola (the village, not the ski resort), the hotel/restaurant **Au Café d'Isola** at the entrance to the old village (pl Jean Gaïssa, 04.93.02.17.03, menus 69F-159F) does decent pizzas, salads and full meals; it also 'welcomes bikers' – attracted, no doubt, by the flowers and the baby-blue décor. Sheep-crazed St-Étienne-de-Tinée is hardly crawling with three-star chefs, but the restaurant at the comfortable **Le Régalivou** hotel (8 bd d'Auron, tel/fax 04.93.02.49.00, closed May & mid-Oct to mid-Dec, rates 290F-350F) serves up solid regional dishes (menus 90F-120F) at very reasonable prices. The town also has a well-run municipal campsite on a small watersports lake only three minutes' walk from the centre (Plan d'Eau, 04.93.02.41.57, 55F tent and two people). **L'Auberge de l'Etoile** (04.93.02.44.97, closed Oct to mid-June, lunch menus 55F & 95F, average 120F) in St-Dalmas-le-Selvage hides not a little sophistication beneath its rustic décor, which is enlivened by fake Van Goghs courtesy of Paul – half of the laid-back young couple that run the place. Of an evening, regional specialities are served by candlelight. Booking is essential. There is also a basic *gîte d'étape* in the village, designed for walkers doing the GR5 long-distance path, but open to all-comers (04.93.02.44.61).

Getting there

By car
N202 Var valley road from Nice airport (exit no.50 on the A8), turn right on to the D2205 after 31km, then follow the route described above.

By bus
Santa-Azur (04.93.85.92.60) runs daily services between Nice, St-Etienne-de-Tinée and Auron, and between Nice, Isola and Isola 2000.

Tourist information

Isola
Chalet d'Accueil, at entrance to village (04.93.02.18.97). **Open** *school holidays* 10am-noon, 4-6pm Mon-Fri; 10am-noon Sat, Sun; *rest of year* 10am-noon Sat, Sun.

St-Etienne-de-Tinée
Maison du Tourisme, 1 rue des Communes de France (04.93.02.41.96/fax 04.93.02.48.50). **Open** 9am-12.30pm, 3-6.30pm daily.
Guided tours of the chapel frescos (20F, 15F children) leave at 4pm from Monday to Friday. Book half an hour in advance. Weekend tours by arrangement.

Auron
Maison du Tourisme, Grange Cossa (04.93.23.02.66/fax 04.93.23.07.39). **Open** 8.30am-12.30pm, 1.30-6.30pm Mon-Fri; 8.30am 6.30pm Sat, Sun.

The Parc National du Mercantour

Created in 1979, the Mercantour National Park covers 68,500 hectares of high mountain land, from the Roya-Vésubie watershed just north of Sospel north to the Italian border and the 3,143-metre Cime du Gélas, and then west as far as the high peaks around the Col de la Cayolle and the Col de la Bonette. Even on the tamest walk (and there are over 600 kilometres of waymarked paths), you are likely to see a few chamoix and at least hear a marmot – a sort of huge furry hamster that emits a high-pitched warning whistle whenever potential predators get too close. Among the birds you might catch a glimpse of are imperial eagles, eagle owls, snow grouse and the recently reintroduced lammergeyer, a bearded vulture that lives mainly on bones, dropped onto the rocks from a great height in order to get the marrow out. Another recent success story is the Alpine ibex (*bouquetin*), which until the 1930s was confined to a tiny enclave of the

Gran Paradiso reserve in Italy. Now over a thousand roam, Schengen-like, between the Mercantour and the adjacent Parco Naturale delle Alpi Marittime in Italy (which has been officially twinned with its French cousin since 1987). Less welcome to some locals are the wolves that have made their way back over the border from Italy in recent years; not long ago, a dead one was left on the doorstep of the park office in Tende. Endemic flora include saxifrage and the rare vanilla orchid. The park is efficiently and even aggressively run, with strictly enforced bans on dogs, camping, firearms, gathering of plants, fires and off-road driving.

Parc National du Mercantour
Information office, 23 rue d'Italie, Nice (04.93.16.78.88).
There are also local information offices at Tende, St-Martin-Vésubie, St-Sauveur-sur-Tinée, St-Etienne- de-Tinée, Valberg, Entraunes, Allos and Barcelonnette.

Directory

Getting There   **282**
Getting Around   **283**
Accommodation   **286**
The South by Season   **288**
Resources A-Z   **292**
Essential Vocabulary   **306**
Further Reading   **307**

Feature boxes

Santons & Christmas traditions   291
Top ten choices for children   294
Emergencies   296
Tourist information   302
Provence on the Web   305

Directory

Getting There

By air

Air France *(UK 0845 084 5111/ USA 1-800 237 2747/France 08.02.80.28.02/www.airfrance.com)* operates flights from Paris to Nice, Marseille, Avignon and Nîmes. There are no direct Air France flights to the South from the UK.

British Airways *(UK 0345 222111/US 1-800 247 9297/France 08.02.80.29.02/ www.britishairways.com)* flies to Marseille and Montpellier from Gatwick, and Nice from Heathrow and Manchester.

British Midland *(UK 0870 607 0555/France 08.00.05.01.42/ www.britishmidland.com)* flies direct to Nice from Heathrow and East Midlands, and via either of these two airports from Aberdeen, Belfast, Edinburgh, Glasgow, Leeds, Manchester and Teeside.

Low-cost flights to Nice are operated by **Easyjet** *(UK 0870 600 0000/ Nice 04.93.21.48.33/ www.easyjet.com)* from Luton and Liverpool.

Ryanair *(UK 0870 156 9569/ www.ryanair.com)* has two daily low-cost flights from Stansted to Nîmes (starting 1 July 2000).

From the United States, most flights involve a Paris connection. **Delta** *(US 1-800 241 4141/France 08.00.35.40.80/ www.delta.air.com)* have a daily flight from JFK New York to Nice, and another to Lyon, 200km north of Avignon.

From Paris, **Air Inter** *(France 08.02.80.28.02)* runs hourly *navettes* (shuttle flights) from Orly to Marseille, Nice, Avignon and Nîmes. **TAT** *(France 08.03.80.58.05)* flies from Paris Orly to Toulon-Hyères. **Air Liberté** *(France 08.03.09.09.09)* flies from Paris Orly to Nice. **AOM French Airlines** *(France 08.03.00.12.34)* has flights from Paris Orly to Nice, Marseilles and Toulon-Hyères.

Major airports

Nice International Airport

(04.93.21.30.30/recorded flight times 08.36.69.55.55/www.nice.aeroport.fr). Seven kilometres west of the centre, Nice International Airport is the second largest in France. Most flights arrive and depart from Terminal 1; Air France (Paris flights), Air Liberté and AOM use Terminal 2.
Bureaux de Change Terminal 1 *(04.93.21.39.51).* **Open** 8am-10pm daily. Terminal 2 *(04.93.21.33.72)* **Open** 10.45am-1.15pm, 2-6pm daily. For transport from the airport to central Nice and other towns, *see chapter* **Nice**.

Marseille-Provence

(04.42.14.14.14/ www.marseille.aeroport.fr). Situated in Marignane, 20km north-west of the centre. For transport from the airport, *see chapter* **Marseille**.
Bureau de change *(04.42.14.21.35).* **Open** 6am-8.30pm daily.

By train

There are international train connections from Spain, Italy, Switzerland, Germany and the Benelux countries. From the UK, Eurostar trains run to Lille and Paris Gare du Nord. Services for the South depart from the Gare de Lyon (two stops on RER line D), where they connect with the French TGV (high-speed train) network. The line runs south from Paris to Avignon, where it splits west to Montpellier and east to Marseille and Nice; note, however, that the track is only truly high-speed as far as Avignon; by the summer of 2001, the high-speed track will reach Marseille and Montpellier. Nine TGVs per day depart from Paris Gare de Lyon for Nice (journey time approximately 6 hours 30 minutes), 10-12 a day for Marseille (approx 4 hours 15 minutes) and 15 a day for Avignon (approx 3 hours 30 minutes). All these stations connect with the local train network (*see page 284* **Getting Around**).

SLEEPERS

For long-distance journeys you can travel overnight by *couchette* (sleeping car shared with up to six others) or *voiture-lit* (more comfortable sleeping car for up to three people). Both services are available for first- and second-class travellers, and must be reserved in advance.

TICKETS

You can book tickets for through journeys from outside France. In the UK, tickets can be booked from any mainline station or travel centre or the International Rail Centre, Victoria Station (020 7834 2345). You can also visit the Rail Europe Travel Shop (179 Piccadilly; 0870 584 8848) or book on line at **www.raileurope.co.uk** or **www.sncf.fr**. Note that you must have reservations and seats booked for the TGV, and you must *'compostez votre billet'* – date-stamp your ticket in the orange *composteur* machine on the platforms at the station – before starting your journey. SNCF central reservations and information is on 08.36.35.35.35, open 7am-10pm daily. If you reserve by phone or Minitel (3615 SNCF), you must pick up and pay for your ticket within 48 hours.

DISCOUNTS & PASSES

A Eurodomino pass allows unlimited travel on France's rail network for three- to eight-day duration within one month, but must be bought before travelling to France. Discounted rates are available for children aged between four and 11 and young people between the ages of 12 and 25.

Directory

Visitors from North America also have a wide choice of passes, including Eurailpass, Flexipass and Saver Pass, which can be purchased in the US (call 212 308 3103 for information and 1-800 223 636 for reservations).

For passes and discounts available within France, *see page 285* **Getting Around**.

BICYCLES
For long-distance train travel bicycles need to be transported separately, and must be registered and insured. They can be delivered to your destination, though this may take several days. On Eurostar services you need to check your bike in at least 24 hours before you travel or wait 24 hours at the other end.

By bus

Long-distance buses are the cheapest way, bar hitching, to get to the South. Eurolines (UK 01582 404511/France 08.36.69.52.52) has regular services from London to Avignon, Marseilles and Nice.

For local bus information, *see page 285* **Getting Around**.

By car

Taking your own car from the UK can be an option, especially if you plan a stopover; remember that most of France heads south in the summer. The school holidays take up July and August, and the roads are at their worst around 15 August, a national holiday.

Special scenic diversions attempt to reduce summer traffic; look out for the small green BIS (*Bison Futé*) signs.

From Calais to Nice is 1,167 kilometres, from Caen to Nice 1,161 kilometres. Dieppe to Avignon is 854 kilometres, Calais to Avignon 965 kilometres. Journey times depend on routes; for Provence, the quickest route from Calais is via Paris (though avoid the Périphérique ring road at rush hour) and on the A6 Autoroute du Soleil to Lyon and the Rhône Valley. A less-trafficked route to western Provence is the A10-A71-A75 via Bourges and Clermont-Ferrand. All autoroutes have *péage* toll-booths, where payment can be made by cash or credit card. From Calais to Menton, expect to spend around 500F on tolls. Websites: **www.iti.fr** (route planner); **www.autoroutes.fr** (motorway info).

MOTORAIL
A comfortable though pricey option is the Motorail; put your car on the train in Calais or Paris and travel overnight down to the coast. *Couchettes* are obligatory. For UK bookings, contact Rail Europe (0870 584 8848).

CAR HIRE
Hiring a car in France is expensive. Consider fly-drive packages, or arranging car hire before leaving home, which can work out a lot cheaper. Most airlines offer fly-drive packages and SNCF offers a train/car rental scheme.

To hire a car you must normally be 25 or over and have held a licence for at least a year. Some hire companies will accept drivers aged 21-24, but a supplement of 50F-100F per day is usual. Take your licence and passport with you. Ensure you have all the relevant information about what to do in case of an accident or a breakdown and arm yourself with the relevant telephone numbers. (*See also box page 296*).

There are often good weekend offers (Fri evening to Mon morning). Week-long deals are better at the bigger hire companies – with Avis or Budget, for example, it's around 1,600F a week for a small car with insurance and 1,700 kilometres included. Members of auto clubs may get a discount.

Most of the international hire companies will allow the return of a car in other French cities and even other countries. Be warned that low-cost operators may have an extremely high excess charge for dents or damage.

Hire companies
ADA *01.55.46.19.99*
Website: www.net-on-line.net/ada
Avis *01.55.38.68.60*
Website: www.avis.com
Budget *08.00.10.00.01*
Website: www.budget.com
Europcar *08.03.352.352*
Website: www.europcar.com
Hertz *01.39.38.38.38*
Website: www.hertz.com
Rent A Car *08.36.69.46.95*
Website: www.rentacar.fr

Getting Around

By car or motorbike

Driving in Provence is mostly a pleasure. However, coast roads, especially between Cannes and Menton, can

become heavily congested in summer, though you only have to drive a few miles inland to find peace and quiet again (except at major beauty spots). It's worth remembering that the hallowed French lunch break is still widely observed,

so it's a good time to get to the beach – or pretty much anywhere.

French school holidays last through July and August, and the roads are at their worst around 15 August, which is a major national holiday.

Directory

PAPERWORK

If you bring your car to France, you will need to bring the relevant registration and insurance documents, and, of course, your driving licence. New drivers need to have held a licence for at least a year.

ROADS & TOLLS

French roads are divided into *autoroutes* (motorways, marked A8, A51, etc), *routes nationales* (national 'N' roads, marked N222, etc), *routes départementales* (local 'D' roads) and tiny, often unpaved rural *routes communales* ('C' roads). Autoroutes are toll (*péage*) roads, although some sections – especially around major cities – are free. There are service stations (*aires*) with 24-hour petrol service approximately every 20 kilometres and, more frequently, well-designed parking and picnic areas, with toilets and sometimes showers. The tolls can work out quite expensive: Nice to Monaco costs 25F, Aix to Nice 90F.

SPEED LIMITS

In normal conditions, speed limits are 130 kilometres (80 miles) per hour on autoroutes, 110 kilometres (69 miles) per hour on dual carriageways, and 90 kilometres (56 miles) per hour on *routes nationales*. In heavy rain and fog, these limits are reduced by 20 kilometres on autoroutes, by 10 kilometres on other roads.

BREAKDOWN SERVICES

The AA or RAC do not have reciprocal arrangements with French organisations, so it's best to take out additional breakdown insurance cover, for example with Europ Assistance (in the UK 01444 442211). Local 24-hour breakdown services include Dépannage Côte d'Azur, which offers a 24-hour service (*04.93.29.87.87*). Autoroutes and *routes nationales* have emergency telephones every

two kilometres. Police stations and *gendarmeries* can give information about the nearest breakdown service or garage. For what to do in the case of an accident, *see page 296* **Emergencies**.

DRIVING TIPS

● At intersections where no signposts indicate the right of way, the car coming from the right has priority. Roundabouts follow the same rule, though many now give priority to those on the roundabout: this will be indicated either by stop markings on the road or by the message '*Vous n'avez pas la priorité*'. A yellow diamond sign indicates that you have priority; the diamond sign with a diagonal black line indicates that you do *not* have priority.

● Drivers and all passengers must wear seat belts.

● Children under ten are not allowed to travel in the front of a car, except in special baby seats facing backwards.

● You should not stop on an open road; pull off to the side.

● When drivers flash their lights at you, this means that they will not slow down and are warning you to keep out of the way. Oncoming drivers may also flash their lights to warn you when there are *gendarmes* lurking on the other side of the hill.

● Carry change, as it's quicker to head for the exact-money line on *péages*; but cashiers do give change and *péages* accept credit cards.

● Motorbikes must have headlights on while in motion, and cars must have their headlights on in poor visibility. All vehicles have to carry a full spare set of light bulbs and drivers who wear spectacles or contact lenses must carry a spare pair with them.

● The French drink-driving limit is 50mg alcohol per 100ml of blood, about the equivalent of two glasses of wine.

● *Cédez le passage* = give way.
● *Vous n'avez pas la priorité* = you do not have right of way.
● *Passage protégé* = no right of way.
● *Rappel* = remember. This reminds drivers of a restriction previously signposted.

FUEL

Since January 2000, French petrol stations have no longer sold leaded petrol. It has been replaced by a substitute unleaded petrol that can be used in leaded fuel vehicles. Petrol on autoroutes is the most expensive; most French drivers fill up at supermarkets.

PARKING

Parking along the coast in high season is difficult; you'll have to get up very early to get a parking space at the beach. In most small French towns it is pretty difficult, too, especially in medieval town centres with narrow streets. In most towns, parking meters have now been replaced by *horodateurs*, pay-and-display machines, which take either coins or cards (100F or 200F, available from *tabacs*). Many towns now have marked blue zones where you can park free for an hour.

CAR HIRE

See page 283 **Getting There**.

By train

There is a reasonably good SNCF rail network in the South, especially in the Rhône Valley and along the coast. You can buy regional rail maps and timetables from *tabacs* and pick up free timetables from stations. Services range from high-speed limited-stop TGV lines to the local Omnibus services that stop everywhere. Out-of-town stations usually – but not always – have a connecting *navette* or bus to the town centre. Sometimes SNCF runs a connecting bus service (indicated as *Autocar* in timetables) to stations where the train no longer stops or along disused lines; rail tickets and passes are valid on these. The Metrazur runs along the coast, stopping at all stations between Marseille and Ventimiglia in Italy. Two mountain lines depart from Nice: the Roya Valley line via Sospel, and the private Train des Pignes (*see box page 270*).

FARES & DEALS

Fares vary according to whether you travel on a peak 'white' day or a cheaper, less busy 'blue' day; stations have leaflets with the calendar. You can save on TGV fares by purchasing special discount cards. Carte 12/25 gives 12- to 25-year-olds a 50 per cent reduction. Pensioners benefit from similar terms with a *Carte Vermeil*. A *Carte Enfant* entitles a child under 12 and up to three accompanying adults to travel at a 50 per cent reduction, or 25 per cent on 'white' days. Couples are entitled to a '*Decouverte a deux*' 25 per cent reduction for return journeys on 'blue' days. There are also advance purchase discounts available. Children under four travel free.

SNCF

(08.36.35.35.35/www.sncf.fr). **Open** 7am-10pm daily. Call the above number for national reservations and information. For rail information in English call 08.36.35.35.39. You can buy tickets in stations from automatic ticket machines; some travel agents also sell tickets. If you reserve on Minitel 3615 SNCF or over the phone, you must pick up and pay for the ticket within 48 hours. The TGV must be booked in advance, and can be reserved up to two months in advance or, if there are seats available, up until the time of departure. Before you board any train, be sure to validate your ticket in the orange *composteur* machines.

By bus

The coastal area is reasonably well served by buses, especially around the main

towns and cities, and city centres have good regular services. Out in the country, things can get difficult, as services are run by a galaxy of small local companies. Most towns of any size have a bus station or *gare routière*, which is usually near the train station. In remote rural areas buses are often linked to the needs of schools and working people, so often there may be only one bus in the morning and one in the evening. Local tourist offices can advise on timetables. When boarding a bus tickets should be punched in the machine.

By taxi

Nice

Centrale de Taxi *(04.93.13.78.78)*. There are 29 taxi ranks in the city but you can also hail cabs in the street. Cost 10F per km.

Marseille

Eurotaxi *(04.91.02.20.20/ 04.91.97.12.12 for driver with foreign languages)*. There are eight ranks, but you can also hail taxis in the street. Cost 7.60F per km.

By air

Air St-Tropez

(04.94.97.15.12). Flies between Nice and La Môle, St-Tropez. Cost 8,000F for five people.

Héli Air Monaco

(00.377.92.05.00.50). Return Nice-Monaco 750F-785F.

Nice Hélicoptères

(04.93.21.34.32). Cannes-Nice return approx 780F.

By bicycle

Cycling is an excellent way to see Provence at the right pace. You'll get plenty of support, from hotels and repair shops, but if you have a foreign-made bike, be sure to bring spare tyres with you, as French sizes are different. You can travel with your bike on many local trains; look out for the bicycle symbol in timetables. For bike

transport on long-distance trains, *see page 283* **Getting There**. Bikes can be rented from many SNCF stations, at a rate of around 70F a day, plus a 1,000F deposit, and returned to any of the stations in the scheme. Rental is subject to availability and you can reserve in advance; see the SNCF brochure *Guide Train + Vélo*. For cycling tours and specialist holidays, *see page 301* **Sport & activity holidays**.

On foot

Provence is a wonderful place to explore on foot. It is crossed by several well-signposted *sentiers de grande randonnée* (GR), long-distance footpaths – numbers 4, 5, 6 and 9 are the main ones – which are described in the excellent Topo Guides, available from bookshops and newsagents. Walking along the coast can be more difficult since it is either built up or too rocky; in some areas, such as the *calanques*, walking gives access to spectacular scenery and unspoilt beaches that are inaccessible to cars. The best times for walking are spring and autumn. At all times, make sure you have plenty of water and sun protection. For walking holidays, *see page 301* **Sport & activity holidays**.

Hitch-hiking

People do hitch-hike (*faire l'autostop*) in France, but it's safer and more reliable to arrange lifts with an agency.

Allô-Stop

8 rue Rochambeau, Paris (01.53.20.42.42). **Open** 9am-6.30pm Mon-Fri; 9am-1pm, 2-6pm Sat. **Credit** MC, V.
Call several days ahead to be put in touch with drivers. There's a flat agency fee of between 30F and 70F depending on distance; you then pay 22 centimes per kilometre to the driver. A one-way journey from Paris to Nice would cost around 205F.

Directory

Accommodation

There is a huge variety of accommodation available in the South, from the grandest seafront Palace hotel to the simplest mountain refuge, all priced accordingly. In between you can rent villas or *gîtes*, camp, or stay in a wide range of small-town hotels, country *auberges* and *chambres d'hôtes*. During the summer it is obviously advisable to book, and essential if you want to stay on the coast, but outside the peak holiday period between mid-July and mid-August, when the French head south en masse, you should not have too much trouble finding accommodation. Many hotels close between November and February, and most campsites will be closed in the winter months. Tourist offices in many areas offer a free booking service.

Hotels

Hotels in France are very reasonably priced; you can usually get a decent room with an adequate bathroom for around 250F-300F. Prices are usually given per room rather than per person, and will be posted on the back of the door. Breakfast is not normally included in the price, and is often expensive; generally, you are better off going out to a bar or café for coffee and croissants, which is all you'll get from the hotel anyway. On the coast and in popular tourist areas such as the Alpilles or the Luberon, prices will be higher. There are five grades of hotels, from no stars to four, graded according to standard factors such as room size, lifts and services, but the star system does not necessarily reflect quality or atmosphere, or indeed the prices charged: an old building may lack a lift

but be otherwise charming. All hotels charge an additional room tax (*taxe de séjour*) of 1F-7F per person per night.

When booking direct with a hotel you may be asked for a deposit, though most will accept a credit card number; some may be satisfied with a confirming fax. When booking a room, it is normal to look at it first; if it doesn't suit, ask to be shown another (rooms can vary enormously within the same hotel). Supplements may be charged for an additional bed or a cot (*lit bébé*).

Lists of hotels can be obtained from the French Government Tourist office or from regional tourist offices.

HOTEL GUIDES

Various guides can be obtained from the French Government Tourist Office (in person or by sending £1 in stamps towards P&P; for address *see below*). These include *Châteaux & Hotels de France* (hotels and B&Bs in private chateaux) and *Relais du Silence* (hotels in chateaux or grand houses, in peaceful settings.)

Relais & Châteaux is a consortium of fine hotels and restaurants throughout France. A free copy of the guide can be picked up from French Tourist Offices (UK 178 Piccadilly, London W1; 0891 244123/US 444 Madison Avenue, NY NY 10022; 212 838 7800) or send a £5 cheque or postal order to Relais & Châteaux, 35-37 Grosvenor Gardens, London SW1W OBS (020 7630 7667).

Logis de France is France's biggest hotel network: it acts as a sort of quality-control stamp for over 5,000 private hotels in the French countryside, most of them one or two star. Contact the Fédération Nationale des Logis et Auberges de France (83 av

d'Italie, 75013 Paris; 01.45.84.70.00), or the French Government Tourist office for a Logis de France handbook.

Bon Weekend en Villes is a tourist office promotion that has been going for nine years, offering two nights (either Fri-Sat or Sat-Sun) for the price of one. Aix, Nîmes and Marseille qualify all year, Arles, Draguignan and Gap from November to March (in 2000). The offer is usually valid between November and March, and all year round in some towns. You need to book at least eight days in advance. Contact the French Government Tourist Office for further information.

Résidences de tourisme

Holiday accommodation within a purpose-built complex, offering fully equipped flats for rent by the day, week or month. A free guide is available from French Government Tourist Offices.

Chambres d'hôtes

Chambres d'hôtes are the French equivalent of bed and breakfast, in private homes. Sometimes lunch or dinner *en famille* is also offered. Note that Gîtes de France (*see below*) has some *chambres d'hôtes* on its books as well as self-catering accommodation.

The following guides provide listings, and most tourist offices will have a local list, but it is also worth simply looking out for roadside signs, especially in rural areas. Note, however, that standards are not as strict as hotels, and they may not be especially cheap; some chateaux offer luxury *chambres d'hôte*.

The following guides are available from French Government Tourist Offices:
Chambres et tables d'hôtes – listings for all 14,000 French B&Bs.
Chambres d'hôtes Prestige – a selection of 400 luxury B&Bs, plus 100 luxury *gîtes*.
Châteaux Accueil – a selection of B&B in private chateaux.
Thomas Cook Welcome Guide to Selected Bed & Breakfasts in France – 500 personally inspected B&Bs.

B&B Abroad
5 Worlds End Lane, Orpington, Kent BR6 6AA (01689 857838/fax 01689 850931).
B&B Abroad offers a straight-forward B&B booking service, which can include ferry bookings if desired. They will book accommodation at either a single destination or various stops around the region.

Gîtes

The Fédération des Gîtes Ruraux de France was set up 40-odd years ago with the aim of offering grants to owners to restore rural properties and let them out as holiday homes. These *gîtes* (literally: places to lay one's head) are an inexpensive way of enjoying a rural holiday in regional France. The properties range from very simple farm cottages to grand manor houses and even the odd chateau.

Properties are inspected by the Relais Départemental (the county office of the national federation) and given an *épi* (ear of corn) classification according to level of comfort. *Gîtes* are completely self-catering (in some cases you will be expected to supply your own bedlinen), but most have owners living nearby who will tell you where to buy local produce (or even provide it).

Note that some of these properties will be off the beaten track and the use of a car, or at the very least a bicycle, is usually essential. Bicycles can often be hired locally and occasionally from *gîte* owners. Prices average 1,200F-1,800F per week in

August for a two- to four-person *gîte*.

Brittany Ferries is the UK agent for Gîtes de France; bookings can be made through The Brittany Centre, Wharf Road, Portsmouth PO2 8RU (0870 536 0360). In France, contact the Maison de Gîtes de France, 59 rue St-Lazare, 75009 Paris (01.49.70.75.85/fax 01.42.81.28.53).

Note that the list of *gîtes* in the Brittany Ferries brochure is only a selection. The Gîtes de France brochure *Gîtes Accessible à Tous* lists *gîte* accommodation with disabled access and services.

Gîte d'Etape accommodation – which is often found in mountain areas, or along long-distance footpaths – is intended for overnight stays by hikers, cyclists, skiers or horse-riders. These *gîtes* are often run by the local village and tend to be spartan, with bunks and basic facilities. Reservations are recommended, especially in busy periods. *Gîte de neige*, *Gîte de pêche* and *Gîte équestre* are all variations on the *Gîte d'étape*, for skiers, anglers and horse riders respectively.

Mountain *réfuges* (refuges) range from large and solid stone houses to basic huts. All have bunk beds; many offer food – often of surprisingly high quality. Many are open only June-September; they should always be booked in advance. Prices vary between 40F and 90F per person. Lists of *réfuges* are available from local tourist offices.

Camping

Camping is a very popular option in France: campsites (*les campings*) can be surprisingly luxurious, and many are run by local councils. Prices range from 40F to around 100F per night for a family of four, with car, caravan or tent. Note that in summer, campsites can get

crowded, especially on the coast. Camping rough (*camping sauvage*) is discouraged but you may be given permission if you ask. Be very careful camping in areas that may have a fire risk.

FACILITIES
Campsites are graded from one-star (minimal comfort, water points, showers and sinks) to four-star luxury sites that allow more space for each pitch and offer above-average facilities. The majority of sites are two-star. To get back to nature look out for campsites designated *Aire naturelle de camping* where facilities will be absolutely minimal, with prices to match. Some farms offer camping pitches under the auspices of the Fédération Nationale des Gîtes Ruraux – these are designated *Camping à la ferme*, and again facilities are usually limited.

INFORMATION
The *Guide Officiel* of the French Federation of Camping and Caravanning (FFCC), available from French Government Tourist Offices, lists 11,600 sites nationwide, and indicates those that have facilities for disabled campers. The *Michelin Green Guide – Camping/Caravanning France* is informative, and lists sites with facilities for the disabled.

Youth hostels

To stay in most youth hostels (*auberges de jeunesse*) you need to be a member of the International YHA – join via your country's organisation – or join the Fédération Unie des Auberges de Jeunesse.

Fédération Unie des Auberges de Jeunesse (FUAJ)
27 rue Pajol, 75018 Paris (01.44.89.87.27/fax 01.44.89.87.10). Affiliated to the International Youth Hostel Federation.

The South by Season

In summer, the South of France becomes one big festival. Alongside internationally renowned cultural events, every village seems to put on its own festival (sometimes no more than an outdoor concert or two), not to mention fireworks displays, exhibitions in wine chateaux, open-air cinema seasons at resorts along the coast and age-old pagan rituals involving sacrificial oxen.

Tourist offices are good sources for concert leaflets. The useful booklet, *Terre de Festivals* (available from main tourist offices in the region), covers summer arts festivals in the Provence-Alpes-Côtes d'Azur region; it can also be found online at **www. festival.cr-paca.fr**.

Festival tickets can often be bought directly at Offices de Tourisme or at branches of FNAC (**www.fnac.fr**) and Virgin, or via France Billet (04.42.31.31.31).

Spring

The Rhône Delta

Féria Pascale
Arles. Information Office de Tourisme (04.90.18.41.20). **Date** Easter.
Three days (Sat to Easter Mon) of corridas, bull-running and brass bands. *See box p79.*

Fête des Gardians
Roman arena, Arles, and around town. Information Office de Tourisme (04.90.18.41.20). **Date** 1 May.
A parade of Camargue *gardians* and equine bravado in the Roman arena. *See box p79.*

Féria de Pentecôte
Nîmes. Information/box office (04.66.67.28.02). **Date** Pentecost (seven weeks after Easter).
A reminder that bullfighting culture extends well into southern France. Two smaller *férias* take place in September and February. *See box p63.*

Pélerinage de Mai
Les Stes-Maries-de-la-Mer. **Date** 23- 25 May.
France's biggest gypsy festival, in honour of Black Sarah and the two apocryphal Marys, whose servant she may or may not have been. *See box p86.*

Avignon & the Vaucluse

Transhumance
Information from local tourist offices. **Date** May/June.
Transhumance – the traditional moving of flocks of sheep between winter and summer pastures – is still a living tradition in Provence; the key weekend is usually around Whitsun. In Jonquières, 8km east of Orange (tourist information 04.90.70.59.04), 1,500 sheep accompanied by dogs and donkeys cross the village to the sound of tambourines; similar celebrations (backed up by copious amounts of food and drink) take place in Riez, St-Etienne-de-Tinée and St-Rémy-de-Provence.

Ascension Day
Cavaillon. Information Office de Tourisme (04.90.71.32.01). **Date** May.
A parade of bands and carnival floats along the streets of Cavaillon; similar *corsos* (processions) are also held in Apt and Pertuis, each with its own distinctive technique of float decoration.

The Western Côte

La Bravade
St-Tropez. Information Office de Tourisme (04.94.97.45.21). **Date** mid-May.
Harking back to the days when St-Tropez was just a simple fishing village, the colourful Bravade procession evokes the arrival of headless Christian martyr Torpes (alias Tropez) in a barge in AD 68.

The Riviera

Carnaval de Nice
Nice. Information Office de Tourisme (04.92.14.48.00). Box office 5 promenade des Anglais (04.93.92.80.73). **Tickets** 50F-120F; free *charivari* serenades. **Date** month before Lent.
For almost a month in the traditional period of excess before Lent, carnival

floats and street performers parade through Nice each weekend behind a giant carnival king and queen, with illuminated parades and the *bataille des fleurs* (floral floats) along the promenade des Anglais. In 2000, the medieval tradition of *charivari* – noisy serenaders who beat on cauldrons and blow trumpets – was revived for the last five days of *Carnaval*, culminating in the grand parade, fireworks and burning of the carnival king on Mardi Gras. Smaller *Carnavals* take place in Aix-en-Provence and Marseille.

Monte-Carlo Tennis Open
Monte-Carlo Country Club. Information 04.93.41.72.00. Box office fax 04.93.78.12.04 (book in writing by fax). **Tickets** 90F-500F. **Date** mid-Apr.
International men's hard-court tournament.
Website: www.mcopen.org

Cannes Film Festival
Cannes. **Date** mid-May.
See box p31.

Art Jonction
Jardins Albert 1er, Nice. Information 04.93.96.01.00. **Tickets** 40F. **Date** end May.
Nice's growing contemporary art fair gives an overview of the European scene. Expect around 60 galleries, half-French, half-foreign; most present one artist each in a solo show.

Grand Prix de Monaco
Monaco. Information/box office 00.377.93.15.26.00. **Tickets** 1,000F-2,000F (on sale from 1 Feb). **Date** May or June.
Formula One racing cars charge around the narrow bends of Monte-Carlo, usually crushing a few spectators on the way. Note that you need tickets for the stands and they usually sell out within days.

Summer

Fête de la Musique
Throughout France. **Date** 21 June.
The longest day of the year sees free concerts all over France of every conceivable type of music, from string quartets and Johnny Hallyday covers to hip hop and accordions.

Bastille Day
Throughout France. **Date** 14 July.
The French national holiday commemorates the storming of the Bastille prison in Paris in 1789 and

the start of the French Revolution. There are usually dances and fireworks displays on the evening of 13 and/or 14 July.

The Rhône Delta

Festival de la Nouvelle Danse

Jardin de l'Archevêque, le parc du Duché and other venues, Uzès. Information 04.66.22.51.51. Box office (from mid-May) Office de Tourisme (04.66.22.68.88). **Tickets** 30F-150F. **Date** June.
The Uzès festival puts the emphasis on introducing unknown dance talents from Europe. Recent years have seen companies visiting from Germany, Austria, Switzerland and Scandinavia.

La Foire à l'Ail

Uzès. Information Office de Tourisme (04.66.22.68.88). **Date** 24 June.
The Uzès garlic fair has been held on this date ever since it received its letters patent from Charles IX in 1571. Garlic growers display their produce along the boulevards, and in the evening a flame carried from village to village to Mont Ventoux for the Fête de la St-Jean marks the solstice and the arrival of summer.

Fête de la Tarasque

Tarascon. Information Office de Tourisme (04.90.91.03.52). **Date** last weekend in June.
Tarascon celebrates St Marthe's miraculous victory over the amphibious Rhône-dwelling beast, which supposedly once terrorised the area. A model of the monster is paraded, costumes are worn, there are bullfights and tributes to Good King René (who founded the fête in 1474) and Daudet's fictional adventurer, Tartarin of Tarascon.

Rencontres Internationales de la Photographie

Espace Van Gogh, Musée Réattu, Cloître St-Trophime and other venues, Arles. Information 04.90.96.76.06. **Tickets** *exhibitions* 20F-35F; *soirées* 80F. **Date** early July to mid-Aug.
Over the course of three decades, the RIP has become a major gathering for the world of contemporary art photography. Themed shows, individual retrospectives and specially commissioned works are complemented by an opening week of debates, meetings, films and workshops. There's also an alternative event.
Website: www.r.i.p-arles.org

Suds à Arles

Théâtre Antique and other venues, Arles. Information 04.90.96.06.27. **Tickets** up to 140F. **Date** July.
World music festival from Latin America and Africa to the Balkans. As well as concerts in the Théâtre Antique, look out for free concerts, brass bands, dance classes, outdoor film screenings and mint tea.
Website: www.suds-arles.com

Nuits Musicales d'Uzès

Uzès. Information Office de Tourisme (04.66.22.68.88). **Tickets** 70F-240F. **Date** July.
Concerts take place in historic buildings and squares, from international baroque ensembles such as Musica Antiqua Köln and the Ensemble Baroque de Limoges.

La Féria Provençale

St-Rémy-de-Provence. Information Office de Tourisme (04.90.92.74.92). **Date** mid-Aug.
Three days of bull races, parades and the traditional mounted *abrivado* (rounding up the bulls and herding them into the ring) and *bandido* (taking them back again).

Avignon & the Vaucluse

Fête de la Vigne et du Vin

Châteauneuf-du-Pape, Gigondas and other villages. Information 04.90.22.65.65 or local tourist offices. **Date** end May/early June.
On the Saturday after Ascension, the wine-producing communes in the *département* organise a day of tastings and competitions.

Festival d'Avignon

Avignon. Information Bureau du Festival d'Avignon (04.90.27.66.50). **Date** July.
The theatre festival to end them all, worth scheduling a visit around. *See box p94.*

Festival Provençal

Palais du Roure and other venues, Avignon. Information 04.90.86.27.76. **Date** July.
This festival in Avignon and nearby villages (including Cabrières d'Avignon, Cavaillon and Valréas) promotes the cause of Provençal language and folklore with plays, readings and debates.

Festival de la Sorgue

L'Isle-sur-la-Sorgue. Information Office de Tourisme (04.90.38.04.78). **Date** July.

Folklore, street theatre, exhibitions, a floating market and a *corso nautique*, in which flower-laden punts battle it out on the canals of this Provençal Venice, plus concerts in L'Isle and in neighbouring Fontaine-de-Vaucluse.

L'Eté de Vaison

Théâtre Antique, Vaison-la-Romaine. Information/box office 04.90.28.84.49. **Tickets** 120F-220F. **Date** July.
Dance works by the likes of Béjart, Decouflé and Pietragalla.

Les Estivales de Carpentras

Théâtre de Plein Air, Carpentras. Information/box office 04.90.63.46.35. **Tickets** 170F. **Date** July.
A multidisciplinary array of music, dance and theatre staged in an open-air theatre.

Les Chorégies

Orange. **Date** July-Aug.
The Ancient Roman amphitheatre provides a sublime setting for lyric opera. *See box p104.*

Festival International de Quatuors à Cordes

Luberon. Information 04.90.75.89.60. **Tickets** 120F. **Date** July-Sept.
Some of Europe's best string quartets perform in the Abbaye de Silvacane, and churches at Cabrières d'Avignon, Fontaine-de-Vaucluse, Goult, L'Isle-sur-la-Sorgue and Roussillon. Tickets on the door only.

Les Musicales du Château d'Ansouis

Ansouis. Information/box office tel & fax 04.90.09.80.00. **Tickets** 100F-150F. **Date** Aug.
Classy vocal and chamber music on the terrace of the Renaissance chateau of this Luberon village.

Marseille & Aix

Fête de la St-Pierre

Martigues. Information Office de Tourisme (04.42.42.31.10). **Date** end June.
A statue of St Pierre, patron saint of fishermen, is carried from the Musée Ziem to the port for a nautical parade and blessing of boats. Events also take place in La Ciotat, Cassis and Marseille.

Fêtes de la Céramique Aubagne

Aubagne. Information Office de Tourisme (04.42.03.49.98). **Date** mid-Aug.

Every two years (the next event is scheduled for 2001), the biggest ceramics market in France puts the emphasis on art pottery for a two-day show.

Festival International d'Art Lyrique
Aix-en-Provence. Box office (04.42.17.34.34). **Tickets** 150F-1,200F. **Date** July.
One of two big opera fests in the South (*the other is Les Chorégies; see above p289*). See box p146.
Website: www.aix-en-provence.com/festartlyrique

Festival Danse à Aix
Aix-en-Provence. Information/box office 04.42.96.05.01/from June 04.42.23.41.24. **Tickets** 70F-150F. **Date** July-Aug.
Contemporary dance performances from the movers and shakers of the French scene.

Festival International de Piano
Parc du Château de Florans, La Roque d'Antheron. Information/box office 04.42.50.51.15. **Tickets** 70F-270F. **Date** July-Aug.
Top concert pianists perform from the classical repertoire in this increasingly high-profile festival, which is held mainly in the gardens of this pretty Renaissance chateau in La Roque d'Antheron, 30km north-west of Aix-en-Provence.

Musique à l'Empéri
Château de l'Empéri, Salon-de-Provence. Box office 04.42.92.73.88. **Tickets** 60F-110F. **Date** early Aug.
The courtyard of the castle that dominates Salon-de-Provence is the setting for chamber music from Mozart to Dusapin.

The Western Côte

Festival Medieval
pl de la République, Hyères. Information Office de Tourisme (04.94.01.84.50). **Date** July.
Jugglers, fire eaters, musicians, acrobats, storytellers and locals in tights carouse in ye olde town of Hyères, inspired by Louis IX's landing in 1254.

Inland Var

Draguifolies
Draguignan. Information Office de Tourisme (04.98.10.51.05). **Date** July-Aug.
Free concerts, theatre and dance performances in numerous open-air sites around town.

The Riviera

Jazz à Juan
Juan-les-Pins. Information 04.92.90.53.00. **Date** July.
Major beachside jazz festival.
Website: www.antibes-juanlespins.com

Nice Jazz Festival
Jardins de Cimiez, Nice. Information Office de Tourisme (04.92.14.48.00). **Date** July.
The line-up is less serious than at Jazz à Juan, but the Roman amphitheatre of Cimiez is still a great place to take in a classy international soul, blues or jazz concert.

Musiques au Coeur
Chantier Naval Opéra, Port Vauban, Antibes. Information/box office 04.92.90.54.60. **Tickets** 90F-350F. **Date** early July.
A small but glossy open-air opera festival, with one or two fully staged operas backed up by a series of concerts and solo recitals.

Les Nuits de la Danse
Monaco. Information 00.377.92.16.24.20. **Tickets** 160F-200F. **Date** mid-July.
A selection of works from the previous season of the Ballets de Monte-Carlo are performed on the casino terrace.

Biennale de Céramique Contemporaine
Château-Musée Magnelli and Musée de la Céramique, Vallauris. Information 04.93.64.16.05. **Tickets** 17F, 8.50F children. **Date** July-Oct.
Every two years (the next two will be 2000 and 2002), the potters' mecca features contemporary ceramics by the new generation from Spain, Italy, France and Portugal.

Festival de Musique
Parvis St-Michel, Menton. Information 04.92.41.76.95. **Tickets** 60F-400F. **Date** Aug.
One of the oldest Riviera festivals, the Festival de Musique has worthy concerts (Barbara Hendricks, Jean-Pierre Rampal, Yuri Bashmet in 1999) in a pretty church square overlooking the old port.

Inland Alpes-Maritimes

Les Baroquiales
Sospel and other places in the Roya and Bévéra valleys. Information/box office 04.93.04.92.05. **Tickets** 50F-120F. **Date** July.

Baroque music ensembles play in churches in these Alpine valleys.

Fête du Jasmin
Grasse. Information Office de Tourisme (04.93.36.66.66). **Date** early Aug.
For four days during the jasmine harvest, the streets of Grasse are even more than usually scent-laden as the jasmine queen heads a *corso* (procession) of floral floats.

Autumn

Journées du Patrimoine
Throughout France. **Date** third weekend in Sept.
Architectural heritage weekend, when historic and official buildings around France open to the public.

The Rhône Delta

Fêtes des Prémices du Riz
Arles. Information 04.90.93.19.55. **Date** mid-Sept.
The start of the Camargue rice harvest is marked by a *corso* (procession) of decorated floats illustrating episodes of Provençal history, led by the *Ambassadrice du riz* on a Camargue pony.

Marseille & Aix

Fiesta des Suds
Docks des Suds, bd Paris, Marseille. Information 04.91.99.00.00. **Tickets** 30F-150F. **Date** Oct.
A musical melting pot from a collection of 'Souths', reflecting Marseille's multiracial culture. You might find salsa violinist Alfredo de la Fe alongside Cape Verdean Césaria Evora or local ragga boys Massilia Sound System.

Winter

La Pastorale
Throughout Provence. **Date** Dec-Jan.
La Pastorale, a ritualised theatrical representation of the announcement to the shepherds of the birth of Christ, interspersed with carols, is performed in numerous villages.

The Rhône Delta

Salon International des Santonniers
Cloître St-Trophime, Arles. Information 04.90.96.47.00. **Date** Nov-Jan.

Santons & Christmas traditions

Christmas in Provence, as in most of France, was a non-event until well into the eighteenth century. The Revolution forced piety into the home, encouraging cribs and seasonal cuisine. Elaborate church cribs – a tradition imported from Italy – had already begun to appear in the seventeenth century. But it was only after 1789 that the most distinctively Provençal form of crib began to appear, a simple table-top nativity scene populated by brightly coloured clay *santons* figures.

As in Naples, the regulation Biblical personages were soon joined by a vast array of local characters – the miller, the tavern keeper, the village idiot, and so on. Today, *santons* from the golden age of the craft, in the early nineteenth century, fetch high prices among collectors. But their mass-produced modern equivalents – mostly produced in Aubagne, east of Marseille – are still in great demand from local families, who crowd the region's big *santon* fairs in Aix, Arles and Marseille.

The tradition of a living crèche of villagers and animals, and the ceremony of *pastrage* (a lamb offered by shepherds to the priest),

also remains alive in many Provençal villages, most notably at Les Baux-de-Provence, Manosque, St-Rémy-de-Provence, Séguret and Valréas.

On the Provençal table, the *gros souper* – the family meal eaten on Christmas Eve – culminates in 13 traditional desserts. These are supposed to symbolise Christ and the 12 apostles, but are in effect a gathering together of the region's fruits and sweets: the *pompe à l'huile* (a form of sweet biscuit made with olive oil and orange flower water); white nougat; dark nougat; *les quatres mendiants* (the four mendicant orders – hazelnuts for Augustine friars, figs for Franciscans, almonds for Carmelites, raisins for Dominicans); and fresh fruits: dates, oranges, mandarins, apples, pears and grapes. Local specialities, such as *calissons d'Aix* (almond sweetmeats), melon or candied fruits are sometimes substituted for one or other element.

Dinner is traditionally followed by midnight mass in the church, with carols sung in Provençal and accompanied by the *galoubet* (a type of flute) and tambourines.

A fair of Provençal *santons* (traditional Christmas crib figures), in the beautiful cathedral cloisters. The other big *santons* fair in the region (which is held at the same time) is the Foire aux Santons in Marseille. *See box above.*

Avignon & the Vaucluse

Les Hivernales

L'Opéra, l'Auditorium de Vaucluse, Théâtre Cavaillon, Salle Benoît XII, Chapelle des Penitents Blancs, Avignon. Information/box office (04.90.82.33.12). **Tickets** 40F-120F. **Date** Feb.
Contemporary dance performances and workshops.

Marseille & Aix

Marché aux Truffes

Rognes. Information Office de Tourisme (04.42.50.13.36). **Date** mid-Dec.
The 'black diamond' is serious business at the region's most important truffle market in Rognes, 19km north-west of Aix, which

features minstrels and costumed truffle fraternities. Restaurants contribute special menus.

La Chandeleur

Basilique St-Victor, Marseille. Information 04.96.11.22.60. **Date** 2 Feb.
A candlelit procession around the church behind the black virgin of the Basilique St-Victor marks the end of Christmas.

The Riviera

Festival International de la Danse

Palais des Festivals and other venues, Cannes. Information 04.93.39.01.01. **Tickets** 110F-170F. **Date** Nov.
Now biennial (next in 2001), Cannes' dance festival reflects the dynamic contemporary dance scene in Europe and the Mediterranean basin. Rwo or three performances a day in the Palais des Festivals and other theatres.

Rallye Automobile Monte-Carlo

Monaco. Information Office de Tourisme (00.377.92.16.61.16). **Date** Jan.

Since 1911, drivers have careered over snow-bound passes and down into the principality in the big date on the world rally calendar. Mind you, there are so many sports cars in Monte-Carlo anyway, you'd hardly know the difference.

Festival International du Cirque de Monte-Carlo

Espace Fontvieille, Monaco. Information 00.377.92.05.23.45. **Tickets** 100F-300F. **Date** Jan.
The cream of international circus artistes compete in avant-garde acrobatics and daredevil stunts.

Fête du Citron

Menton. Information Office de Tourisme (04.92.41.76.76). **Date** Feb.
How many kitsch things can you do with a lemon? Find out by watching the floats parade through Menton each Sunday during the lemon festival. The tangy yellow ovals are arranged in giant sculptures according to the year's theme. In 2000, it was the fables of La Fontaine: the Fox and the Lemon, the Lemon and the Frog, and so on. Highly fruity stuff.

Directory

Resources A-Z

Banks & money

Since 1 January 1999 there have been two currencies in France: the franc and the Euro. One franc is made up of 100 centimes; the smallest coin in circulation is five centimes. There are coins for five, ten, 20 and 50 centimes, one, two and five francs; the heavier ten and 20 franc coins are silver-centred with a copper rim. There are banknotes of 20F, 50F, 100F, 200F and 500F.

The beginning of 1999 saw the start of the transition to the Euro, when it became the official currency in France (and ten other nations of the European Union). Shops and businesses are increasingly indicating prices in both currencies. You can open Euro accounts, and some places will accept payment in Euros by cheque or credit card, although Euro coins and notes will not be circulated until 2002. Beware high bank charges for cashing cheques for Euros from other countries. Travellers' cheques are also available in Euros.

Bureaux de change

Nice

Change Opéra *1 rue St-François-de-Paule (04.93.80.86.00)*. **Open** 9am-6pm Mon-Sat.

Thomas Cook *Gare de Nice, 12 av Thiers (04.93.82.13.00)*. **Open** *May-Oct* 7am-10pm daily; *Nov-Apr* 8am-8pm daily.

American Express *11 promenade des Anglais (04.93.16.53.53)*. **Open** 9am-6pm daily.

Marseille

Comptoir de Change Méditerranéen *Gare St-Charles (04.91.54.93.94)*. **Open** *June-Sept* 9am-7pm Mon-Sat; *Oct-Apr* 9am-6pm Mon-Sat.

American Express *39 La Canabière (04.91.13.71.21)*. **Open** 8am-noon, 2-5pm Mon-Fri; 8am-noon, 2-4.30pm Sat. Closed Jan, Feb.

Avignon

Compagnie Avignonais de Change *19 rue de la République (04.90.16.04.04)*. **Open** *Nov-Mar* 9am-5.45pm Mon-Fri; *Apr-Oct* 9am-5.45pm Mon-Sat.

Cannes

Office Provençal *17 av Maréchal-Foch (04.93.39.34.37)*. **Open** *Nov-Apr* 8am-8pm Mon-Sat; *May-Oct* 8am-8pm daily.

Thomas Cook *8 rue d'Antibes (04.93.39.41.45)*. **Open** *May-Oct* 9am-10pm Mon-Sat; *Nov-Apr* 9am-6.30pm Mon-Sat.

Monaco

Bureau de Change *35 bd Princesse Charlotte (00.377.97.70.77.59)*. **Open** 9am-noon, 2-6pm Mon-Fri.

Hours & rates

French banks usually open 9am-5pm Mon-Fri (some close for lunch 12.30-2.30pm); some banks also open on Saturday. All are closed on public holidays (actually closing at noon on the previous day). Note that not all banks have foreign exchange counters. Commission rates vary between banks. The state Banque de France usually offers good rates. Most banks accept travellers' cheques, but may be reluctant to accept personal cheques with the Eurocheque guarantee card, which is not widely used in France. Eurocheques are increasingly frowned on due to fraud, and will no longer be accepted anywhere after 31 December 2000.

Bank accounts

To open an account (*ouvrir un compte*), you need proof of identity, address and your income. You'll probably have to show your passport or *Carte de Séjour*, a utility bill in your name and possibly a payslip or a letter from your employer. Students need a student card and may need a letter from their parents.

Most banks don't hand out a *Carte Bleue*/Visa until several weeks after you've opened an account. A chequebook (*chéquier*) is usually issued in about a week. *Carte Bleue* transactions are debited directly from your current account, but you can choose for purchases to be debited at the end of every month. French banks are tough on overdrafts, so try to anticipate any cash crisis in advance and work out a deal for an authorised overdraft

(*découvert autorisé*) or you risk being blacklisted as *interdit bancaire* – forbidden from having a current account – for up to ten years. Depositing foreign-currency cheques is slow, so use wire transfer or a bank draft in francs to receive funds from abroad.

Credit cards & cash machines

Major international credit cards are widely used in France. Visa is the most readily accepted; American Express coverage is more patchy. French-issued cards have a security microchip (*puce*) in each card. The card is slotted into a card reader; the holder keys in a PIN to authorise the transaction. Occasionally, UK/US cards with magnetic strips cannot be read by French machines. Most retailers understand the problem. If you come across one who doesn't, explain that the card is valid and that you would be grateful if the transaction could be confirmed by phone, by saying: '*Les cartes internationales ne sont pas des cartes à puce, mais à bande magnétique. Ma carte est valable et je vous serais reconnaissant d'en demander la confirmation auprès de votre banque ou de votre centre de traitement.*'

In case of credit card loss or theft, call the following 24-hour services, which have English-speaking staff:

● **American Express** *01.47.77.72.00*
● **Diners' Club** *01.49.06.17.17*
● **MasterCard** *01.45.67.84.84*
● **Visa** *08.36.69.08.80*

If your cash withdrawal card carries the European Cirrus symbol, withdrawals in francs can be made from bank and post office cash machines bearing the same symbol by using your card's PIN. The specific cards accepted are marked on each machine, and most give instructions in English. Credit card companies charge a fee for cash advances, but rates are often better than bank rates.

Beauty spas

Seawater spas are popular with the French, who will spend an entire vacation seeking thalassotherapy – therapeutic water massage and seaweed treatment. Six days is the recommended stay, though you can usually just visit for the day. The atmosphere is seriously health-focused, and children are not encouraged. Most will cost around 300F to 500F per day depending on treatments and facilities.

Hôtel Aquabella
2 rue des Etuves, Aix-en-Provence (04.42.99.15.00). Special spa treatment packages available in modern luxury hotel.

Thalassa Hyères
allée de la Mer à la Capte (04.94.58.00.94).

Thalazur Antibes
770 chemin des Moyennes Bréguières, 6600 Antibes (04.92.91.82.00).

Thermes Marins de Monte-Carlo
2 av de Monte Carlo (00.377.92.16.40.40).
Grape Cures are also available in the Vaucluse wine region (contact Avignon Office de Tourisme on 04.90.82.65.11).

Business

The most important thing to know about doing business in France, especially in the South, is that people will invariably prefer to meet you in person. You will often be expected to go in and see someone, even if it's to discuss something that could easily have been dealt with over the phone.

Most major banks can refer you to lawyers, accountants and tax consultants; several US and British banks provide expatriate services, in Paris and locally. For business and financial news, the French dailies *La Tribune* and *Les Echos*, and the weekly *Investir*, are the tried and trusted sources. *Capital*, its sister magazine *Management* and the weightier *L'Expansion* are worthwhile monthlies. *Défis* has tips for the entrepreneur, *Initiatives* is for the self-employed. BFM on 96.4 FM is an all-news business radio station. *Les Echos* gives stock quotes on

www.lesechos.com; Minitel service 3615 CD offers real-time stock quotes. Business directories *Kompass France* and *Kompass Régional* also give company details and detailed French market profiles on 3617 KOMPASS.

The standard English-language reference is *The French Company Handbook*, a list of all companies in the 120 Index of the Paris Bourse, published by the *International Herald Tribune* (01.41.43.93.00). It can be ordered for £50 from Paul Baker Publishing, 37 Lambton Road, London SW20 0LW (020 8946 0590).

Institutions

Banque Populaire de la Cote d'Azur
International Branch, 22 bdVictor Hugo, 06000 Nice (04.93.82.81.81/fax 04.93.82.25.49). Banking advice in English.

British Chamber of Commerce
22 av Notre Dame, Nice 06000 (04.93.62.94.95/fax 04.93.62.95.96). By appointment only.

Centre de Ressources Côte d'Azur
Chambre de Commerce et d'Industrie Nice Côte d'Azur, 20 bd Carabacel, Nice 06000 (04.93.13.74.36/fax 04.93.13.75.71/ www.fr-rrc.com).
Information centre for business resources and facilities across the Côte d'Azur region.

Conference centres

The Acropolis
1 esplanade Kennedy, Nice (93.92.83.00).

Centre de Congrès Auditorium
bd Louis II, Monte-Carlo, Monaco (00.377.93.10.84.00).

Centre de Rencontre Internationale
13 bd Princesse Charlotte, Monte-Carlo (00.377.93.25.53.07).

Palais des Festivals
La Croisette, Cannes (04.93.39.01.01).

Miscellaneous

Accents
Pauline Beaumont, 120 chemin des Serres, 06510 Gattières (04.93.08.38.38/fax 04.93.08.39.30/ pauline.beaumont@worldonline.fr). Translation service.

DHL
Freephone 0800.20.25.25.25.

DK Express
06.09.88.51.71. Parcel taxi service, document delivery, small local removals.

FedEx
Freephone 0800.12.38.00.

Gale Force
13 av St-Michel, Monte-Carlo (00377.93.50.20.92/ fax 00377.93.50.45.26/ www.galeforce.com). Computer sales and servicing in English.

Children

The beach and the sea are the easiest way to amuse children and private beach concessions with sunloungers and parasols are the easiest of all; just book your parasol close to the shore and watch the kids make sandcastles. Inflatables are often provided and there are sometimes bouncy castles, too. Sightseeing is only likely to be difficult in steep hill villages, which can be hard to negotiate with a pushchair.

Eating out is easy, especially during the day: just choose a restaurant with a terrace and they can run around while you have another glass of wine. Many restaurants offer a children's menu or will split a *prix-fixe* menu between two children or even give you an extra plate to share your own meal. Most hotels have family rooms so children do not have to be separated from parents and a cot (*lit bébé*) can often be provided for a supplement, although it is a good idea to check availability in advance.

Disposable nappies (*couches à jeter*) are easy to find, and

Directory

Choices for children

Marineland, Antibes

Attractions include Aquasplash (with giant water slides), a Provençal-style farm, a butterfly farm, crazy golf and performing sea life. See page 213.

Musée Océanographique, Monaco

One of the world's great aquariums, containing some of nature's most bizarre creatures, dead and alive. See page 245.

Luge run, Valberg

Plus-nines will love careering down the run at Valberg (see page 278), open in July and August only (04.93.02.55.68.

Submarine tour, Nice

Trans Côte d'Azur (Quai Lunel; 04.92.00.42.30; open year round) and **Visiobulle** (Embarcadère Courbet; 04.93.67.02.11; open April to September) run undersea creature-watching tours.

Village des Tortues, Gonfaron

2,500 tortoises live, breed and frolic in this park in Gonfaron, near Vidauban, and there's not a hare in sight. Open between March and November; call 04.94.78.26.41 for details. See also page 166.

Course Camarguaise

Bullfighting in the Roman arenas of Arles or Nîmes. Make sure it is not a *mise à mort* (fight to the death) and they'll enjoy watching the bulls chase the men.

Parc Ornithologique de Pont de Gau, Camargue

Aviaries and birding trails on the Ginès lagoon. See page 85.

Le Vieux Mas, near Beaucaire

A reconstruction of an early twentieth-century Provençal farmhouse, chickens and all. See page 70.

Fêtes & festivals

They're everywhere in summer, and children love them. See chapter **By Season**.

French baby food is often of gourmet standard, especially the puréed artichoke – though watch out for added sugar.

When hiring a car, be sure to book baby seats in advance – though larger hire companies usually have a few ready to go.

Customs

There are no limits on the quantity of goods you can take into France from another EU country for personal use, provided tax has been paid on them in the country of origin. However, Customs still has the right to question visitors. Quantities accepted as being for personal use are:

● up to 800 cigarettes, 400 small cigars, 200 cigars or 1kg loose tobacco.

● 10 litres of spirits (over 22% alcohol), 90 litres of wine (under 22% alcohol) or 110 litres of beer.

For goods from outside the EU:

● 200 cigarettes or 100 small cigars, 50 cigars or 250g loose tobacco.

● 1 litre of spirits (over 22% alcohol) and 2 litres of wine and beer (under 22% alcohol).

● 50g perfume.

Visitors can carry up to 50,000F in currency.

See also **Tax refunds** *below.*

Disabled travellers

Le Shuttle (UK 0990 353 353) – the Channel Tunnel car-on-a-train service – is good for disabled passengers travelling to France as you may stay in your vehicle. **Eurostar** trains (UK special requests number 020 7928 0660) give wheelchair passengers first-class travel for second-class fares. Most **ferry companies** will offer facilities if contacted beforehand. Cars fitted to accommodate disabled people pay reduced tolls on autoroutes.

But once you get there, France in general, and the South in particular, is not as sensitive to the needs of disabled travellers as it might be. In small hill villages with cobbled streets, wheelchairs are simply not feasible. In bigger cities there is usually reasonably good provision – especially in newer museums – and in small towns and cities disabled parking is provided and indicated with a blue wheelchair sign; the international orange disabled parking disc scheme is also recognised in France. (Don't forget to bring the disc with you.) Even if places claim to have disabled access, it's wise to check beforehand. Many places are accessible to wheelchair users but do not have accessible toilets. If you need to hire a wheelchair or other equipment, enquire at the local pharmacy.

TAXIS

If you are disabled, a taxi driver cannot refuse to take you. They must help you into a taxi and transport a guide dog for the blind.

An autoroute guide for disabled travellers (*Guides des Autoroutes à l'usage des Personnes à Mobilité Réduite*) is available free from:

Ministère des Transports *Direction des Routes, Service du Contrôle des Autoroutes, La Défense, 92055 Cedex, Paris (01.40.81.21.22).*

CAR HIRE

Europcar has specially adapted cars for disabled drivers available from its Nice airport office (04.93.21.42.53). Hire charges are approximately 630F per day. Apply in advance.

HOLIDAYS & ACCOMMODATION

Gîtes Accessible à Tous lists *gîte* accommodation equipped for the disabled. It's available from Maison de Gîtes de France, 59 rue St-Lazare, 75009 Paris (01.49.70.75.85/fax 01.42.81.28.53).

The *French Federation of Camping and Caravanning Guide* indicates which campsites have facilities for disabled campers. It's available from Deneway Guides, Chesil Lodge, West Bexington, Dorchester DT2 9DG (0130 889 7809), price £8.95. The *Michelin Green Guide – Camping/Caravanning France* lists sites with facilities for the disabled.

Useful addresses

Association des paralysés de France *17-19 bd Auguste-Blanqui, 75013 Paris (01.40.78.69.00).* **Open** 9am-12.30pm, 2-6pm Mon-Fri).

Comité national de liaison pour la réadaptation des handicapés (CNRH) *236 bis rue de Tolbiac, 75013 Paris (01.53.80.66.85/ www.handitel.org).* Publishes *Paris Ile-de-France Pour Tous*, an all-purpose tourist guide for the disabled (60F in Paris; 80F from abroad).

RADAR (Royal Association for Disability & Rehabilitation) *Unit 12, City Forum, 250 City Road, London EC1V 8AF (020 250 3222/fax 020 7250 0212).* Information department can give specialist advice (lines open 10am-4pm Mon-Fri), and sell *Getting There*, a guide to facilities in airports. Price £5; send an SAE.

Local information

Office de Tourisme *4 La Canebière, Marseille (04.91.38.89.00).* Can provide a list of sights and areas accessible to the disabled, and a list of suitable hotels. For disabled transport call 04.91.11.41.02.

Ulysse *23 bd Carlone, 06200 Nice (04.93.96.09.99).* **Open** 24 hours

daily. Will organise transport from airport, tourist visits, find accommodation and provide general assistance.

Drugs

Possession of drugs is illegal in France, and even a small amount of marijuana for personal use could land you in jail and incur a large fine.

Electricity & gas

Electricity in France runs on 220V, so visitors with British 240V appliances can simply change the plug or use a converter (*adaptateur*), available at better hardware shops. For US 110V appliances, you will need to use a transformer (*transformateur*), available at the FNAC and Darty chains.

Gas and electricity are supplied by the state-owned EDF-GDF (Electricité de France-Gaz de France). Contact them about supply, bills, or in case of power failures or gas leaks. Look under *Urgences* in the phone book for a local number.

Note that Butane gas is widely used for cooking (and sometimes water and heating) in towns and villages without mains gas supply. If you stay in rented accommodation, you may need to change the cylinder and buy new ones, from a garage or local shop.

Remember that in rural areas electricity sometimes flickers or cuts out altogether; you will need a good supply of candles and torches. You also need computer back-up and some form of surge control.

Embassies & consulates

Before going to an embassy or consulate, phone and check opening hours. You may need to make an appointment. Otherwise, the answerphone

will usually give an emergency contact number. There's a full list of embassies and consulates in the *Pages Jaunes* under *Ambassades et Consulats*. For general enquiries or problems with passports or visas, it is usually the consulate you need. You are advised to contact the consulate in the first instance and staff will advise you whether your problem can be dealt with by them, or if you need the embassy in Paris, or if it can be dealt with by a local honorary consul.

Paris embassies & consulates

Australian Embassy
4 rue Jean-Rey, 15th (01.40.59.33.00). M° Bir-Hakeim. **Open** 9am-6pm Mon-Fri; *visas* 9.15am-12.15pm Mon-Fri.

British Embassy
35 rue du Fbg-St-Honoré, 8th (01.44.51.31.00). M° Concorde. **Open** 9.30am-1pm, 2.30-6pm Mon-Fri. **Consulate** *16 rue d'Anjou, 8th (01.44.51.33.01/01.44.51.33.03). M° Concorde.* **Open** 2.30-5.30pm Mon-Fri.

Canadian Embassy
35 av Montaigne, 8th (01.44.43.29.00). M° Franklin D Roosevelt. **Open** 9am-noon, 2-5pm Mon-Fri. *Visas 37 av Montaigne (01.44.43.29.16).* **Open** 8.30-11am Mon-Fri.

Irish Embassy
12 av Foch, 16th. **Consulate** *4 rue Rude, 16th (01.44.17.67.00). M° Charles de Gaulle-Etoile.* **Open** *for visits* 9.30am-noon Mon-Fri; *by phone* 9.30am-1pm, 2.30-5.30pm Mon-Fri.

New Zealand Embassy
7ter rue Léonard de Vinci, 16th (01.45.00.24.11). M° Victor-Hugo. **Open** *visas* 9am-1pm Mon-Fri.

South African Embassy
59 quai d'Orsay, 7th (01.53.59.23.23). M° Invalides. **Open** 8.30am-5.15pm Mon-Fri, by appointment. **Consulate** 9am-noon.

US Embassy
2 av Gabriel, 8th (01.43.12.22.22). M° Concorde. **Open** 9am-6pm Mon-Fri, by appointment. **Consulate/** *visas 2 rue St-Florentin, 1st*

Directory

Emergencies

Most of the following services operate 24 hours daily.

Police *17*

Fire (Sapeurs-Pompiers) *18*

Ambulance (SAMU) *15*

In the case of a serious accident or medical emergency, phone either the police (17) or the Sapeurs-Pompiers (18). Though primarily a fire brigade, the latter are also trained paramedics, and both they and the police have medical back-up and work in close contact with SAMU. In rural areas, the local taxi service often doubles as an ambulance, so it can be worth finding out the number, from the tourist office or *mairie* (town hall).

What to do in a car accident

There is no need to call the police if no one has been hurt. The usual procedure is for each driver to fill out a *'constat amiable'* form and for each to sign the other's copy. Forms are provided with hire cars.

If you are involved in a serious road accident phone the police-secours (17). This is a free number but in a public phone box you will have to insert a coin in order to make a connection (this will be returned to you after the call). There will be a number and address in the telephone box if you are not sure where you are. You may be asked the name of the nearest town or city so that the operator can identify which *departement* you are in. Alternatively you may find the number of the local police-secours in the general information on the inside of the phone box.

There are free SOS call boxes on autoroutes and some other roads, and in cities there are also emergency telephone boxes at major intersections. These are marked Services Médicaux and have direct lines to emergency services.

(01.43.12.22.22). Mº Concorde.
Open 8.45-11am Mon-Fri. *Passport service* 9am-3pm Mon-Fri.

Consulates in the South

British *24 av Prado, 13006 Marseille (04.91.15.72.10/fax 04.01.37.47.06).*

US *12 bd Paul Peytral, 13286 Marseille (04.91.54. 92.00). 31 rue du Maréchal Joffre, 06000 Nice (04.93.88.89.55).*

Canadian *10 rue Lamartine, 06000 Nice (04.93.92.93.22).*

Irish *152 bd JF Kennedy, 06160 Cap d'Antibes (04.93.61.50.63/fax 04.93.67.96.08).*

Gay d'Azur

The Riviera has long been a stamping ground for pink people – plenty of beach cruising, sun to soak up and same-sex action. Your first pick-up, however, should be a copy of local free gay listings magazine *Ibiza*.

Despite a large gay population, the Côte d'Azur lacks a gay infrastructure to match. Bars and saunas abound in Nice, Toulon, Marseille and Montpellier, but other aspects of gay culture, including helplines, self-help groups and drop-in centres, struggle by despite the largest HIV/AIDS infection rates in France outside Paris.

The high temperatures and Latin temperament mean that bars and community groups are not favoured for socialising. Terraces, meanwhile, are always busy with wandering eyes, and the boardwalks and beaches are a mecca for Mediterranean man. Gay beaches are eye-popping day-trip destinations. Reaching the designated area can resemble a Famous Five adventure along winding cliff paths or hopping across rocks, as is the case at the 24-hour Nice cruising point, **Coco Beach**. Ritziest of Riviera gay beaches is the **Plage de St-Laurent-d'Eze**.

Further along the coast at Fréjus is **St-Aygulf** on the road to St-Tropez, and heading west past Marseille are the gay beaches of Montpellier, notably **Grand Travers**, the locals of **Nîmes l'Spiguette**... just head for the lighthouse on the edge of the Camargue, book in the car park then walk west.

Considered the capital of the gay South, **Montpellier** has the region's largest gay disco, **La Villa-Rouge** (rte de Palavas Commune de Lattes). Also in town is a gay superstore, **Le Village**, also the jumping-off point for the most developed gay beach, which has its own gay resto/bar. The beach and some serious club action make this a favoured gay destination for the French.

Gay institutions on the Côte d'Azur include the **Blue Boy** (9 rue Spinetta; 04.93.44.68.24), Nice's downsized answer to Heaven, and friendly bar restaurant **Le Santiago** (28 rue de Lepante; 04.93.13.83.01), which offers a very particular brand of humour from local drag act Miss James. Otherwise, try a relative newcomer, cruise bar **Traxx**

(11 av de Maréchal-Foch; 04.93.80.98.10).

Cannes offers a trip down memory lane at the **Zanzi Bar** (85 rue Félix Faure; 04.93.39.30.75), one of the oldest gay bars in France, where Noël Coward used to repair for colourful inspiration. Just round the corner is **Disco 7**, with kitsch drag (7 rue Rouquière; 04.93.39.10.36).

Naval port **Toulon** offers a rougher hew of diamond and has a number of saunas. Try **Sauna Club les Mouettes** (87 chemin de la Pinède; 04.94.42.38.73), which has a swimming pool and garden. Plus, macho Toulon is home to long-running lesbian club **Pussy Cat** (655 av de Claret; 04.94.92.76.91).

Big-city **Marseille** is home to **Entrepôt** (7 rue Moustier; 04.91.33.51.70), France's biggest sex club.

Lesbians are almost invisible on the Côte d'Azur, though in St-Tropez live the high-profile gay girl couple Amélie Mauresmo and Sylvie, to be found of a summer evening singing songs in **Le Gorille**, St-Tropez.

Health

All EU nationals staying in France are entitled to use of the French Social Security system, which refunds up to 70 per cent of medical expenses (but sometimes much less, for example for dental treatment). To get a refund, British nationals should obtain form E111 before leaving the UK (or E112 for those already in treatment). The form E111 is open-ended; you don't need a new one every time you travel. Nationals of non-EU countries should take out insurance before leaving home. Consultations and prescriptions have to be paid for in full, and are reimbursed, in part, on receipt of a completed fiche.

If you undergo treatment in France, the doctor will give you a prescription and a *feuille de soins* (statement of treatment). The medication will carry *vignettes* (stickers) that you must stick on to your *feuille de soins*. Send this, the prescription and form E111 to the local Caisse Primaire d'Assurance Maladie (in the phone book under *Sécurité Sociale*). Refunds can take over a month to come through.

Contraception & abortion

For the pill, a diaphragm or a morning-after pill you will need a prescription. Visit a GP (*médecin généraliste*) – look in the *Pages Jaunes* or ask at a pharmacy for a recommendation. In France, women usually go direct to specialists for contraception and help with gynaecological problems. You can buy condoms and spermicides from pharmacies. If you need an abortion, either consult a gynaecologist or look for the local *Planning Familial* centre in the telephone directory.

Doctors & dentists

A complete list of practitioners is in the *Pages Jaunes* under *Médecins Qualifiés*. To get a Social Security refund, choose a doctor or dentist registered with the state system; look for *Médecin Conventionné* after the name. Consultations cost at least 115F, of which a proportion can be reimbursed.

Local helplines & house calls

● In cases of medical emergency, dial 15 to call an ambulance or ring the Service d'Aide Médicale d'Urgence (SAMU), which exists in most large towns and cities – the numbers will be given at the front of telephone directories.

Alcoholics Anonymous South of France

(04.93.82.91.10). Local contacts and meetings.

Centre Hospitalier H-Duffaut

305 rue Raoul-Follereau, Avignon (04.90.80.33.33). Casualty hospital.

Hôpitaux La Conception

144 rue St-Pierre, Marseille (04.91.38.30.00). Casualty.

Médecins de Garde Avignon

(04.90.87.75.00). Hospital.

Nice Médecins

(04.93.52.42.42). The local doctor service for home visits.

SIDA Info Service

(08.00.84.08.00). **Open** 24 hours daily. Confidential AIDS information in French (some bilingual counsellors).

SOS Médecins

(04.93.85.01.01). Covers the whole region and will give another number for another locality if necessary. Can send a doctor on a house call. A home visit before 7pm starts at 250F if you don't have French Social Security, 145F if you do; fee rises after 7pm.

SOS Médecins Marseilles

(04.91.52.91.52). 24-hour casualty.

Hospitals

For a complete list, consult the *Pages Blanches* under *Hôpital Assistance Publique*.

Pharmacies

Pharmacies sport a green neon cross. They have a monopoly on issuing medication, and also sell sanitary products. Most open from 9am or 10am to 7pm or 8pm. Staff can provide basic medical services such as disinfecting and bandaging wounds, attending to snake or insect bites (for a small fee) and will indicate the nearest doctor on duty. French pharmacists are highly trained; you can often avoid visiting a doctor by describing your symptoms and seeing what they suggest. They are also qualified to identify mushrooms, so you can take in anything you aren't sure about. Towns have a rota system of *pharmacies de garde* at night and on Sundays. Any closed pharmacy will have a sign indicating the nearest open pharmacy. Otherwise, you can enquire from the *Gendarmerie*. Toiletries and cosmetics are usually cheaper in supermarkets.

Opticians

Any optician will be able to supply new glasses, but remember to bring

Directory

your prescription. Also remember that drivers are required by law to carry a spare pair.

Complementary medicine

Most pharmacies also sell homeopathic medicines and can advise on their use. For alternative medicine practitioners, ask in the pharmacy, or look them up in the *Pages Jaunes*.

Legal advice

Mairies (town halls) may be able to answer legal enquiries. Phone for details and times of free *consultations juridiques*. Or they will be able to recommend a local *notaire*. (lawyer). Note that lawyers are always addressed as *'Maître'*.

Living & working in the South

Anyone from abroad coming to live in France should be prepared for a long and tiring struggle with bureaucracy, whether acquiring a *Carte de Séjour* (resident's permit), opening a bank account, reclaiming medical expenses or getting married. Among documents regularly required are a *Fiche d'Etat Civil* (a sort of identity card consisting of essential details translated from your passport by an embassy/consulate) and a legally approved translation of your birth certificate (embassies will provide lists of approved legal translators). You will need to be able to prove your identity to the police at all times, so keep your passport/*Carte de Séjour* or a photocopy with you.

RESIDENCE

Officially, all foreigners, both EU citizens and non-Europeans in France for more than three months, must apply at the local *mairie* (town hall) for a *Carte de Séjour*, valid for one year. Those who have had a *Carte de Séjour* (*see above*) for at least three years, have been paying

French income tax, can show proof of income and/or are married to a French national can apply for a *Carte de Résident*, which is valid for ten years.

WORK

All EU nationals can work legally in France, but must apply for a *Carte de Séjour* (*see above*) and a French social security number from the nearest social security office (*Caisse Primaire d'Assurance Maladie*). Some job ads can be found at branches of the *Agence National Pour l'Emploi* (ANPE), the French national employment bureau. This is also the place to sign up as a *demandeur d'emploi*, to be placed on file as available for work and to qualify for French unemployment benefits. Britons can only claim unemployment benefit if they were signed on before leaving the UK. If you also have a *Carte de Séjour*, you can get free French lessons (*perfectionnement de la langue française*), although these are not aimed at complete beginners.

Offices are listed under *Administration du Travail et de l'Emploi* in the *Pages Jaunes*, or get a list from ANPE (113 rue Jean-Marin Nauden, 92220 Bagneux; 01.46.64.58.58). There is also a European Employment Service (EURES) network, which aims to put job seekers in touch with job offers (details available in local employment offices in member countries). In the UK, the Employment Service (Overseas Placing Unit, Level 2, Rockingham House, 123 West Street, Sheffield S1 4ER; 0114 259 6051) publishes information on working in France.

The South is part of the expanding Mediterranean high-tech sunbelt, focused on the technopark of **Sophia-Antipolis** near Valbonne, where a number of international high-tech companies are based. Seasonal work is available mainly in the tourist industry, though this is notoriously badly paid. The main openings are in hotels, restaurants, bars, ski resorts and outdoor activity centres. You will need to speak decent French and ensure you have the correct papers. Other possibilities are gardening, house-sitting and teaching English. Foreign students in France can get a temporary work permit (*autorisation provisoire de travail*) for part-time work in the holidays.

PGL Young Adventure Ltd (Alton Court, Penyard Lane, Ross-on-Wye; 01989 764211) has activity centres in France and recruits temporary chalet staff and sports instructors.

Grape and fruit picking is another possibility, but very difficult to set up in advance.

ACCOMMODATION

Rented accommodation is plentiful in France. For short-term rentals, tourist accommodation can often be found at very reduced rates out of season (Oct-Mar). As always in France, contacts are the thing, as well as rental agencies, which can be found under *Agences de Location et de Propriétés* in the *Pages Jaunes*. Other sources include local newspapers and English-language magazines (eg the *Riviera Reporter* – see **Media** *below*), advertisments in shop windows, supermarkets and colleges and club, church and expatriate newsletters.

Those intending to buy should survey the market carefully; there will be great variations in price between small inland villages and coastal resorts. As always, get good legal advice. There are several English-language magazines devoted to French property-buying including *Property France* and *French Property News*, which are good sources of information, advice and properties for sale.

RENTAL LAWS

The legal minimum period for a rental lease (*bail de location*) is three years for an unfurnished apartment and one year for a furnished flat. Both are renewable. During this period the landlord can only raise the rent in line with the official construction inflation index. At the end of the lease the rent can be readjusted to any level, but tenants can object before a rent board if it seems exorbitant. Tenants can be evicted for non-payment, or if the landlord wishes to sell the property or use it for his own residence.

Before accepting you as a tenant, agencies or landlords will probably require you to present a dossier with pay slips (*fiches de paie/bulletins de salaire*) showing three to four times the amount of the monthly rent; foreigners may also be required to furnish a financial surety. When taking out a lease, payments usually include the first month's rent, a deposit (*une caution*) equal to two months' rent and an agency fee, if applicable. It is customary for an inspection of the premises (*état des lieux*) by a bailiff (*huissier*) at the start and end of the rental to assess the flat's condition; the cost of this inspection (around 1,000F) should be shared equally between landlord and tenant. Landlords may try to rent their flats *non-declaré*, without a written lease, and get rent in cash. This can make it difficult for the tenant to establish their rights. Note that all important communications to one's landlord must be sent by registered letter.

Useful addresses

Riviera Insurance Brokers

rue de la Paroisse, Valbonne (04.93.12.36.10/fax 04.93.12.36.11).

Union Nationale des Accueils des Villes Françaises

Relations Internationales, Secretariat Administratif, 3 rue de Paradis, 75010 Paris (01.47.70.45.85). This national volunteer organisation welcomes and supports new arrivals with free advice and information. Consult them for local addresses.

Lost & stolen property

To report a crime or loss of belongings, visit the local *gendarmerie* or *commissariat de police.* If you want to make an insurance claim, you will need a police report anyway. Telephone numbers are given at the front of local directories; in an emergency dial 17. If you lose a passport, report it first to the police, then to the nearest consulate (*see above* **Embassies & consulates**).

Maps

Tourist offices can usually provide free town maps. The large-format Michelin Atlases or sheet maps are good for driving. For walking or cycling, the Institut Géographique National (IGN) maps are invaluable. The Top 100 (1:100,000, 1cm to 1km) and Top 50 (1:50,000, 2cm to 1km) maps have all roads and most footpaths marked. For even greater detail, go for the IGN blue series 1:25,000 maps.

Good map sources in the UK include:

Stanfords International Map Centre *12-14 Long Acre, London WC2E 9LP (020 7730 1354).*

The Travel Bookshop *13 Blenheim Crescent, London W11 2EE (020 7229 5260/ www.thetravelbookshop.co.uk).*

World Leisure Marketing *11 Newmarket Court, Derby DE24 8NW*

(freephone 0800 83 80 80/fax 01332 573399). IGN agent, offers a mail order service.

Opening times

The sacred lunch hour is still largely observed in the South, which means that most shops and offices will close at midday and may not reopen till 2 or 2.30pm.

Hypermarkets (*grands surfaces*) usually stay open through lunch and till 7pm or 8pm. Many shops may also close in the morning or all day Monday or Wednesday. Opening hours for food shops, hardware stores and other useful shops are generally 8.30am-1pm and 2.30pm-7pm; fashion shops often open later but may skip lunch. Most shops close on Sundays, though *bureaux de tabac* (cigarettes, stamps) and *maisons de la presse* (newspapers, magazines) are often open Sunday mornings.

Banks are usually open 9am-noon and 1.30-5pm Mon-Fri, though these times can vary.

For post offices, *see* **Post & fax** *below.*

Boulangeries are open daily, though some small villages may have a closing day. Usual hours are 9am to 7pm, closed for lunch noon-2pm or 3pm, plus Sunday morning; some open earlier in the morning.

Petrol stations usually open at 8.30 am, close for lunch noon-2pm or 2.30pm and close around 9pm except on motorways; those attached to supermarkets may stay open for credit card sales only.

Museums: except during July and August, most museums close for lunch from noon to 2pm. They also close on certain public holidays, notably 1 January, 1 May and 25 December. Municipal museums are usually closed on Monday, national museums on Tuesday.

Public offices usually open 8.30-noon, then 2-6pm. *Mairies*

(town halls) will also close for lunch and in smaller places may only open in the morning from 9am to noon.

Post & fax

Postes or PTTs (post offices) are generally open 9am-noon, 2-6pm Monday-Friday, and 9am-noon Saturday, though main post offices in major towns don't usually close for lunch. In small villages, they generally open only in the morning. Inside major post offices, individual counters are marked according to the services they provide; if you just need stamps, go to the window marked *Timbres*. If you need to send an urgent letter overseas, ask for it to be sent *par exprès*, or through the Chronopost system, which is faster but much more expensive. Chronopost is also the fastest way to send letters and parcels inside France; packages up to 25g are guaranteed to be delivered within 24 hours.

For a small fee, you can arrange for mail to be kept *poste restante* (general delivery) at any post office, addressed to *Poste Restante, Poste Centrale* (for main post office), then the town postcode and name. You will need to present your passport when collecting mail.

Stamps are also available at tobacconists (*bureaux de tabac*) and other shops selling postcards and greetings cards. For standard-weight letters within France and most of the EU, a 3F stamp is needed.

Telegrams can be sent during post office hours or by telephone (24-hours); to send a telegram abroad, dial 08.00.33.44.11.

Fax and photocopying facilities are often available at major post offices and *maisons de la presse* (newsagents). Many supermarkets now have coin-operated photocopiers.

Directory

Minitel is being superseded by the Internet, and is no longer always available in French post offices.

Main post offices

Marseille

Bureau de Poste, rue Henri Barbusse (04.91.15.47.00). **Open** 8am-7pm Mon-Fri, 8am-noon Sat.

Nice

Bureau de Poste, 35 av Thiers (04.93.82.65.00). **Open** 8am-7pm Mon-Fri 8am-noon Sat.
Bureau de Poste, pl Wilson (04.93.13.64.26). **Open** 8am-7pm Mon-Fri, 8am-noon Sat.

Most of the major British and a few American papers can be picked up from newsagents (*maisons de la presse*) in the centre of the major towns, at train stations and airports, and along most of the coast in summer. Supply goes with demand; even in tiny Luberon villages, one can normally find one or two British papers, albeit in their weekly editions. The Paris edition of the *International Herald Tribune* is widely available.

The French are attached to their local papers: *Nice Matin, La Provence, Var-Matin, Le Dauphiné Vaucluse* and the left-wing *La Marseillaise* cover most of Provence.

The *Riviera Reporter*, an English-language magazine aimed at local foreign residents, is a mine of local information, news and small ads; it can be picked up at English-language bookshops and other outlets. If you can't find a copy easily, call it for your nearest outlet: *Riviera Reporter*, 56 chemin de Provence, 06250 Mougins (04.93.45.77.19/fax 04.93.45.49.23). It also has a website with events listings, an archive of past stories and good links: www.riviera-reporter.com.

Public holidays

On public holidays, banks, post offices and public offices will be closed. Food shops – in particular *boulangeries* (bread shops) – will still open, even on Christmas Day. It is common practice, if a public holiday falls on a Thursday or Tuesday, for French businesses to *faire le pont* (bridge the gap) and have the Friday or Monday as a holiday, too. Details of closures should be posted outside banks a few days before the event but it is easy to be caught out, especially on days such as 15 August (Assumption), which is the climax of the summer and the biggest holiday of the year. And while the shops may be shut there will almost certainly be a *fête* in every town and village. Note that foreign embassies and consulates observe French public holidays as well as their own.

1 January New Year's Day (Nouvel an).
Easter Monday (Lundi de Pâques)
1 May Labour Day (Fête du Travail)
May Ascension Day (Ascension), on a Thursday 40 days after Easter.
8 May Victory Day (Fête de la Libération) to commemorate the end of World War II.
May/June Pentecost (Pentecôte), ten days after Ascension.
14 July Bastille Day (Quatorze Juillet).
15 August Assumption Day (Fête de l'Assomption)
1 November All Saints' Day (Toussaint).
11 November Armistice Day (Fête de l'Armistice).
25 December Christmas Day (Noël).

Radio

The French have a passion for radio; many prefer it to the television. However, a recent quota law requiring a minimum of 40 per cent French music has led to overplay of Gallic oldies and local groups mixing French and English lyrics.

AM radio

Wavelengths are in MHz.

87.8 France Inter State-run, MOR music and international news.
90.9 Chante France 100% French chanson.
91.7/92.1 France Musique State classical music channel with concerts and jazz.
93.5/93.9 France Culture Highbrow state culture station; literature, poetry, history, cinema and music.
96.4 BFM Business and economics. Wall Street in English every evening.
98.2 Radio FG 98.2 Gay station, music and explicit lonely hearts.
101.5 Radio Nova Hip hop, trip hop, world, jazz.
104.3 RTL Most popular French station mixing music and talk.
104.7 Europe 1 News, press reviews, sports, business and good weekday breakfast news broadcast.
105.5 France Info 24-hour news, economic updates and sports. Repeated every 15 minutes, so good for learning French.

Local FM stations

98.8 FM Radio Monte Carlo.
106.3 & 106.5 FM Riviera Radio parochial English-language radio with small ads and local gossip.

BBC World Service

Between **6.195** and **12.095** MHz shortwave.

Religion

The presence of so many English people in the South of France means there are a number of English churches. For more information on churches and chaplains in France, including seasonal chaplaincies that operate only during the holiday season, contact:

Intercontinental Church Society *1 Athena Drive, Tachbrook Park, Warwick CV34 6NL (0192 643 0347/fax 01926 330238/www.ics-uk.org)*.
Holy Trinity Church *rue du Canada, Cannes (04.93.94.54.61)*. **Services** 10.30am Sun.
Monaco Christian Fellowship *9 rue Louis Notari, Monaco (00.377.93.30.60.72)*. **Services** 11am Sun.
St Mark's Anglican/ Episcopalian International Church *Sophia-Antipolis, Mougins*

School (04.93.33.64.39). **Services**
10.15am Sun.

St Michael's Church *11 chemin des
Myrtes, Beaulieu (04.93.01.45.61).*
Services 10am Sun.

Removals/ relocation

For international removals you
should use a company that is a
member of the International
Federation of Furniture
Removers (FIDI) or the
Overseas Moving Network
with experience in France.
They will advise on the
customs formalities and
documentation required.

Overs International *Unit 4, Abro
Development, Government Road,
Aldershot GU11 2DA (01252
343646/fax 01252 354861).*
Weekly service to Côte D'Azur.

Tooth Removals *107 rte de Plan,
06130 Le Plan de Grasse
(04.93.77.90.15/fax 04.93.77.90.21/
UK 01784 251 252/UK fax 01784
248 183).*
From London to the Côte d'Azur.

Smoking

Despite health campaigns and
a 1991 law that insists
restaurants provide non-
smoking areas (*zones non-
fumeurs*), the French remain
enthusiastic smokers and
happily ignore rules against
smoking on public transport.
Airports can be particularly
unpleasant for non-smokers.

Sport & activity holidays

Not everyone goes to the South
of France to lie on the beach;
there is a huge range of sports
and activities to choose from.
Even beach bums can indulge
in windsurfing, water-skiing
and jet-skiing.

The sea is usually warm
enough for swimming from
June to September. Almost
every town also has a
municipal pool, though it may
only be open during school
holidays. Even small villages

often have a tennis court,
though you may have to
become a temporary member
to use it – enquire at the local
tourist office or *mairie* (town
hall), which will also provide
details of all other local
sporting activities.

Inland Provence and the
mountains offer walking,
riding, cycling and climbing,
river rafting and canoeing, and
skiing in the winter months. At
certain times of the year it is
possible to fulfill that urban
dream of sunbathing on the
beach in the morning and
going for a ski after lunch (or
vica versa).

Information on sports and
activities can be had from
local tourist offices, national
organisations or from the
Centre Régional Information
Jeunesse Côte d'Azur (19 rue
Gioffredo, Nice; 04.93.80.93.93/
fax 04.93.80.30.33). Many UK
tour operators offer holidays
tailored to specific activities.

Climbing

The Conseil Général des Alpes-
Maritimes publishes several excellent
guides for climbers and trekkers, *Les
Guides Randoxygène* (available from
main tourist offices), with detailed
trails in the region. Dozens of
climbing clubs provide beginners'
courses, plus guides and monitors for
day outings. There are also a few
voies ferrés (climbing routes with
pitons and wire handrails) in the
Alpes-Maritimes.

For climbing information contact
the Club Alpin Français at 14 av
Mirabeau, Nice (04.93.53.37.95) or
7 rue St Michel, Avignon
(04.90.82.34.82).

Canoeing & kayaking

Options include sea-kayaking or
canoeing in the Gorges du Verdon.
Some clubs organise day outings
accompanied by guides.

**Fédération Française de Canoe-
Kayak et des Sports Associés
en Eau-Vive** *87 quai de la Marne,
94340 Joinville-le-Pont
(01.45.11.08.50/fax 01.48.86.13.25).*

**Ligue Régionale Alpes-
Provence** *14 av Vincent Auriol,
30200 Bagnols-sur-Cèze
(04.66.89.47.71).*

Cycling

Taking your own bike (*vélo*) to
France is relatively easy (*see*
Getting There); once there, they
can be carried free on most ferries
and trains (*see* **Getting Around**).
Once there, you'll be well treated on
the roads. Some youth hostels rent
out cycles and arrange tours with
accommodation in hostels or under
canvas. For more info, contact the
YHA (*see page 287*).

Package cycling holidays are
offered by various organisations,
with campsite or hotel
accommodation; luggage is normally
transported each day to your next
destination.

It is advisable to take out insurance
before you go. Obviously, the normal
rules of the road apply to cyclists (*see*
Getting Around). The IGN 906
Cycling France map gives details of
routes, cycling clubs and places to
stay (*see above* **Maps** for stockists).

Advice and information can be
obtained from the Touring
Department, **Cyclists Touring
Club** (Cotterell House, 69 Meadrow,
Godalming, Surrey GU7 3HS; 01483
417217). Its service to members
includes competitive cycle and travel
insurance, free detailed touring
itineraries and general information
sheets about France, while its tours
brochure lists trips to the region,
organised by members. The club's
French counterpart, **Fédération
Française de Cyclotourisme**, is
at 8 rue Jean-Marie-Jégo, 75013 Paris
(01.44.16.88.88).

Golf

Provence has some excellent golf
courses, and the weather means golf
can be played all year round. Most
clubs provide lessons with resident
experts. **Cordon Rouge Villas**
(01253 739749) and **French Golf
Holidays** (01277 824100/www.golf-
france.co.uk) offer golf holiday
packages out of the UK. For more
information, contact either of the
following:

Fédération Française de Golfe
*68 rue Anatole France, Le Vallois,
Perret 92306 (01.41.49.77.00/fax
01.41.49.77.01).*

**Ligue de Golf Provence-Alpes-
Côte d'Azur** *Domaine de Riquetti,
Chemin départemental 9, 13290 Les
Milles (04.42.39.86.83).*

Golf courses

Golf de la Grande Bastide
*Châteauneuf de Grasse
(04.93.77.70.08).* **Open** all year
round. **Holes** 18.

Directory

Golf de Nîmes *Vacquerolles (04.66.23.33.33)*. **Open** all year round. **Holes** 18.

Golf Opio-Valbonne *Opio (04.93.12.00.08)*. **Open** all year round. **Holes** 18.

Pont Royal Golf et Country Club de France *Mallemort (04.90.57.40.79)*. **Open** all year round. **Holes** 18.

Horse riding

Horse riding and pony trekking are popular activities, with *centres équestres* all over the region, in rural areas, the mountains, less inhabited parts of the coast, and the Camargue. **Equestrian Travellers Club** (0208 3878076) and **Foxcroft Travel** (01509 813252) offer French equestrian tours and holidays out of the UK. For further information, contact:

Ligue Régionale de Provence de Sports Equestres *298 av du club Hippique, 13090 Aix-en-Provence (04.42.20.88.02)*.

Skiing

There are several large ski resorts in the Maritime Alps within a few hours of the coast; the three with the best facilities are Auron, Valberg and Isola 2000. For more information see the relevant chapter for the tourist officecontact:

Fédération Française de Ski *50 av des Marquisats, 74000 Annecy (04.50.51.40.34/www.ffs.fr)*.

Watersports

All along the coast you can water-ski, windsurf or scuba dive; surfing, too, is possible on certain beaches when the mistral is blowing. Antibes and Cannes are major watersports centres, and the Iles de Lerins, the Iles de Hyères and the *calanques* offer some of the best diving in the Med. For detailed listings pick up the *Watersports Côte d'Azur* brochure from main tourist offices or go online to www.france-nautisme.com.

Comité Régional de Voile Alpes-Provence *6 promenade Georges Pompidou, 13008 Marseille (04.91.77.19.38/fax 04.91.77.20.14)*.

Comité Régional de Voile Côte d'Azur *Espace Antibes, 2208 rte de Grasse, 06600 Antibes (04.93.74.77.05/fax 04.93.74.68.87)*.

Fédération Française d'Etudes et de Sports Sous-Marins *24 quai Rive-Neuve, 13007 Marseille (04.91.33.99.31/fax 04.91.54.77.43)*.

Walking

Walking holidays are popular in France, and there is an extensive, well-signposted network of *sentiers de grande randonnée* (long-distance footpaths). For more detailed information *see* **Getting Around**. For information on maps *see* **Maps**. Each *département* has its own ramblers' organisation that arranges guided walks of a day or more, as well as walks to see local flowers or wildlife. For local

information contact the relevant tourist office, or:

Comité Départemental de la Randonnée Pédestre *4 av de Verdun, Cagnes-sur-Mer (tel/fax 04.93.20.74.73)*.

Fédération Française de Randonnée Pédestre *14 rue Riquet, 75009 Paris (01.44.89.93.90/fax 01.40.35.85.48)*.

Study & students

Foreign students or would-be students can get information on courses, grants and accommodation from:

Centre Régional des Oeuvres Universitaires et Scolaires (CROUS) *69 Quai d'Orsay, 75007 Paris (01.44.18.53.00)*.

Cultural exchange & language courses

Alliance Française
101 bd Raspail, Paris (01.45.44.38.28).
Non-profit, highly regarded French language school, with beginners' and specialist courses. Centres throughout France.

Central Bureau for Educational Visits & Exchanges
Seymour Mews House, Seymour Mews, London W1H 9PE (020 7486 5101).

Tourist information

Every town and city, and almost every small village, will have its own *office de tourisme*, sometimes also referred to as the *maison* or *bureau de tourisme*, or the *Syndicat d'Initiatif*. They can supply information about local sights, accommodation, festivals and events. If there is no tourist office, you can get a wide range of help and information from the local *mairie* (town hall). Note, though, that especially in small places the offices close at midday, and may not open again in the afternoon.

Comité Régional du Tourisme Riviera Côte d'Azur *55 promenade des Anglais, BP 602, 06011 Nice (04.93.37.78.78/fax 04.93.86.01.06//www.crt-riviera.fr)*.

Comité Regional du Tourisme de Provence-Alpes-Côte d'Azur *Les Docks, Atrium 10.5,*

BP 46214, 10 place de la Joliette, 13567 Marseille Cedex 2 (04.91.56.47.00/fax 04.91.56.47.01).

Comité Régional du Tourisme Languedoc-Roussillon *20 rue de la Republique, 34000 Montpellier (04.67.22.81.00/fax 04.67.58.06.10/www.cr-languedoc.fr/tourisme)*.

Maison de France *French Government Tourist Office, 178 Piccadilly, London W1V 0AL (0891 244123/fax 020 7493 6594/www.franceguide.com)*. A French Travel Centre for information, books and guides.

Office de Tourisme et des Congrès de la Principauté de Monaco *2A bd des Moulins, 9800 Monaco (00377 92.16.61.16/ fax 00377 92.16.60.00/ www.monaco-congrès.com)*.

Centre des Échanges Internationaux

1 rue Jolzen, 75006 Paris (01.40.51.11.71). Sporting and cultural holidays and educational tours for 15-30-year-olds. Non-profit-making organisation.

Socrates-Erasmus Programme

In Britain *UK Socrates-Erasmus Council, RND Building, The University, Canterbury, Kent CT2 7PD (0122 776 2712).* **In France** *Agence Erasmus, 10 pl de la Bourse, 33081 Bordeaux Cedex (05.56.79.44.02/ mj.bio.ndini@ socrates-fr.org).* This scheme enables EU students with a reasonable standard of written and spoken French to spend a year of their degree following appropriate courses in the French university system. The UK office publishes a brochure and helps with general enquiries, but applications must be made through the Erasmus co-ordinator at your home university.

Souffle

BP 133, 83957 La Garde Cedex (04.94.21.20.92/fax 04.94.21.22.17). An umbrella organisation for courses in French as a foreign language.

Local language courses

International School of Nice *15 av Claude Debussy, 06200 Nice (04.93.21.04.00).*

Actilangue *2 rue Alexis Mossa, 06000 Nice (04.93.96.33.84/fax 04.93.44.37.16).* French courses and cultural activities.

Azurlingua *25 bd Raimbaldi, 06000 Nice (04.93.62.01.11/fax 04.93.62.22.56/www.azurlingua.com).* Language holidays.

Centre International d'Antibes *38 bd d'Aguillon, Antibes (04.92.90.71.70/fax 04.92.90.71.71/ www.cia-France.com).* French tuition.

ELFCA (Institut d'Enseignement de la Langue Française sur la Côte d'Azur) *66 av de Toulon, 83400 Hyères (04.94.65.03.31/fax 04.94.65.81.22/ www.elfca.com).* French tuition.

Universities

For the **University of Marseille**, contact CROUS (Centre Régional des Oeuvres Universitaires et Scolaires) on 04.91.62.83.60. For the **University of Nice**, contact CROUS on 04.92.15.50.50.

Discounts

A wide range of student discounts are on offer in France. To claim discounts in museums, cinemas and theatres you need an **International Student Identity Card** from **CROUS** (*see above*) or from travel agents specialising in student travel. ISICs are only valid in France if you are under 26. Under-26s can also get discounts of up to 50% on certain trains with the **Carte 12/25** (*see* **Getting Around**) or buy the **Carte Jeune** (120F from FNAC), which gives discounts on museums, cinema, theatre, travel, sports clubs, restuarants, insurance and some shops.

Tax refunds (Détaxe)

Non-EU residents can claim a refund (average 13 per cent) on value added tax (TVA) if they spend over 1,200F in any one shop. At the shop ask for a *détaxe* form and when you leave France have it stamped by customs. Then send a stamped copy back to the shop, which will refund the tax, either by bank transfer or by crediting your credit card. *Détaxe* does not cover food, drink, antiques or works of art.

Telephones

The French telephone system, the third largest network in the world, is now very efficient, and you can usually find operational telephone boxes (*cabines publiques*). Telephone numbers have been rationalised to ten figures, always written and spoken in sets of two – 01.23.45.67.89.

Regional telephone numbers are prefixed as follows **Paris, Ile de France region** 01; **North-west** 02; **North-east** 03; **South-east and Corsica** 04; and **South-west** 05.

When dialling from outside the country, omit the zero. If you want numbers to be given singly rather in pairs as is customary, ask for them *chiffre par chiffre*.

Public phones

Coin-operated phones take most coins and card phones are now very common and simple to use. It is worth purchasing a phone card (*une télécarte*) if you are likely to need to use a public call box, as most have now been converted to cards. Cards are available from post offices, stationers, stations, some cafés and *bureaux de tabac*.

Calls from metred cabins in cafés, shops or restuarants are generally more expensive.

To make a call from a public phone box, lift the receiver, insert card or coin, then dial the number. When you replace the receiver, unused coins will be returned to you. If you wish to make a follow-on call and have coin credit left, do not replace the receiver but press the '*appel suivant*' button and dial the new number.

If you need to make a phone call in rural areas, or villages with no public phone, look out for the blue *téléphone publique* plaque on private houses. This means the owner is officially appointed to allow you to use the phone and charge the normal amount for the call.

You cannot reverse charges within France but you can to countries that will accept such calls. Go through the operator and ask to make a pcv ('pay-say-vay') call. Incoming calls can only be received at boxes displaying the blue bell sign.

International calls

Dial 00 followed by the country's international call number, found in the front of the *Pages Jaunes* section of the *annuaire* or on the information section in a phone box.

Free calls

When dialling free numbers (*numéros verts*, which generally begin with 08.00), you must insert your card or money first in order to make the connection (coins will be returned immediately after the call, units will not be registered against cards). 08.36 numbers are premium-rate.

Cheap rates

The cheapest times to telephone are weekdays 7pm to 8am and at weekends.

Phone directories

Phone directories are found in post offices and in most cafés. The *Pages Blanches* (*White Pages*) lists names of people and businesses alphabetically. *Pages Jaunes* (*Yellow Pages*) lists businesses and services by category. *Pages Jaunes* are available on the Internet at www.pagesjaunes.fr.

24-hour services

French directory enquiries (*renseignements*) **12**.
International directory enquiries **00 33 12** then country code (44 for UK).
Telephone engineer **13**.
International news (French recorded message, France Inter) dial **08.36.10.33** (2.23F/min).
To send a telegram (all languages): international **08.00.33.44.11**, within France **36.55**.
Speaking clock **36.99**.

International codes

Australia *00 61*
Canada *00 1*
Ireland *00 353*
Monaco *00 377*
New Zealand *00 64*
South Africa *00 27*
UK *00 44*
US *00 1*

Minitel

Minitel is the computer-based videotext information system linked to the telephone, pioneered by the French long before the Internet. Most homes and hotels have a

terminal and most post offices offer use of the Minitel as a telephone directory (on 3611) and information resource. It is rapidly being superseded, however, by the Internet. For directory information dial 3611 on the keyboard, wait for the beep, and press *connexion*. Then type in the name and address you are looking for, and press *envoi*.

Television

France has six channels. **TF1** is the biggest, privatised since 1987, featuring movies, game shows, dubbed soaps, audience debates and the main news at 8pm with star anchors Patrick Poivre d'Arvor and Claire Chazal. **France 2** is a state-owned station mixing game shows, documentaries and cultural chat such as Bernard Pivot's literary *Bouillon de Culture*. **F3R** is more of a heavyweight with local news, sports, wildlife documentaries and late-night Sunday *Cinema Minuit* with classic films in the original language (VO *Version Originale*) and a news and documentary programme, *Continentales*, broadcast five days a week with broadcasts from around Europe in the original language with French subtitles.

Canal+ offers a roster of subscription channels with recent movies (sometimes VO), exclusive sport and late-night porn. **Arte** is a Franco-German hybrid specialising in intelligent arts coverage and films in VO. Wavelength shared with educational channel, **La Cinquième**. (5.45am-7pm). **M6** is a daytime base of music videos, plus magazine programmes such as *Culture Pub* about advertising.

Time

France is one hour ahead of Greenwich Mean Time (GMT) and six hours ahead of New

York. The 24-hour clock is frequently used in France when giving times: 8am is 8 heures, noon (midi) is 12 heures, 8pm is 20 heures, and midnight (minuit) is 0 heure.

Tipping

Service of 10 per cent is usually included in restaurants as part of the bill; leave an extra small tip if you are particularly pleased. *Service compris* is generally indicated at the foot of the *carte*. If in doubt, ask: *Est-ce que le service est compris?* Service is also usually included in taxi fares, though an extra 5 to 10F tip will be appreciated. The same amount is also appropriate for doormen, porters, guides and hairdressers. In bars and cafés you will be charged more for service at a table, and less at the bar. It is usual just to leave small change as a tip.

Toilets

Anyone may use the toilet in a bar or café whether they are a customer or not. (Ask for *les toilettes* or *le WC* – pronouced 'vay say'.) Public toilets vary considerably and some are still old-fashioned squat jobs. Men and women sometimes use the same facilities.

Videos

Due to the difference in transmission standards, British and American TVs and video recorders won't work in France, so videos on the PAL system won't work unless you have a multi-standard TV and video, which most of the French now do.

Visas

To visit France, you need a valid passport, and all visitors to France require a visa except for citizens of EU countries.

USA, Canada, Australia or New Zealand citizens do not need a visa for stays of up to three months. If in any doubt, check with the French consulate in your country, as the situation may change. If you intend to stay in France for more than 90 days, then you are supposed to apply for a *carte de séjour*.

Weather

Most of the South of France is hot and dry, except for spring, when there may be heavy rainfall, and November, which can be blustery, cold and wet. The coast has a gentle Mediterranean climate with mild winters, daytime temperatures rarely lower than 10°C/50°F degrees, and hot summers with temperatures often rising above 30°C/86°F. Average sunshine on the French Riviera is six hours in January and 12 hours in July. Late January and February can be a wonderful time to visit, when there are few other tourists, but most museums are open and the cafés have tables outside.

Inland Provence has similar conditions mitigated by the dreaded mistral, a harsh, cold wind that blows down the Rhône Valley. It howls through the streets of Arles, Avignon and Marseille, bringing the temperatures down dramatically. It usually lasts three or four days, but can go on as long as ten days. The mistral, however, clears the air, giving it the exceptional luminosity that has attracted so many artists to the area. The area has also seen dramatic storms in recent years, causing major floods and damage. The high mountains usually have snow from November to March.

Information

English 08.36.70.1.2.3. For local forecasts dial 08.36.68.12.34 followed by the *département* number. Minitel 3615 METEO.

Women

Women need feel no more threatened in the South of France than in any other European country. Indeed, you are likely to feel more comfortable alone than in many places. Women often go to the beach alone, and you will be welcomed graciously in restaurants. What better thing for a woman alone to do than eat well? The usual safety precautions should be taken in big cities at night and dodgy neighbourhoods. Be careful on trains especially sleepers, where the rates of assault have risen, and always lock car doors when driving alone.

For contraception and abortion, *see page 297* **Health**.

International Women's Club of the Riviera
04.93.12.10.03.
Coffee mornings for newcomers.

Service des Droits des Femmes
31 rue Le Peletier, 75009 Paris (01.47.70.41.58/fax 01.42.46.99.69). Sponsored by the Minstère de l'Emploi et de la Solidarité, this is a service to promote women's rights and implement equal opportunity legislation. In each region contact the Préfecture for a local representative.

SOS Viol Informations
08.00.05.95.95. Freephone in French dealing with rape.

Provence on the Web

www.provence-beyond.com Excellent independent website in English run by Riviera resident Russ Collins, with in-depth descriptions of the whole area, from large towns to tiny villages, plus info on transport, folklore and much else; personalised tours can also be arranged. A true labour of love.

www.provenceweb.fr French site listing several hundred villages and towns, with hotels, restaurants and brief descriptions. Good links to all main towns and cities.

www.visitprovence.com Official government tourist website (French and English) with lots of info on sights to visit, tours, walks, practical information, hotels and restaurants.

www.riviera-reporter.com Well-connected expat magazine site, in English, with archive of practical and political subjects and good links to travel, government and advice sites.

www.cr-languedocroussillon.fr/tourisme/ Government tourist site that lists local sights, hotels and camping, and connects to the other regional sites. You can order brochures on line.

http://luberon-news.com Local Luberon newspaper site with listings of restaurants and hotels, links to their sites, info on local markets, property, events, museums, sports and leisure facilities.

www.crt-riviera.fr Government tourist site with information on museums, transport hotels etc, still under development, so info sometimes limited.

www.sncf.fr Information, timetables and booking online for French Railways.

www.tourisme.fr/annu/index.htm A database for finding tourist office details throughout France. In French, but very straightforward.

Directory

Essential Vocabulary

In French, as in other Latin languages, the second person singular (you) has two forms. Phrases here are given in the more polite *vous* form. The *tu* form is used with family, friends, young children and pets; you should be careful not to use it with people you do not know sufficiently well, as it is considered rude. You will also find that courtesies such as *monsieur, madame* and *mademoiselle* are used much more than their English equivalents. *See page 302* for information on language courses and *page 50* for Provençal menu terms.

General expressions

good morning/good afternoon, hello *bonjour*
good evening *bonsoir;* **goodbye** *au revoir*
hi (familiar) *salut;* **OK** *d'accord;* **yes** *oui;* **no** *non*
How are you? *Comment allez vous?/vous allez bien?*
How's it going? *Comment ça va?/ça va?* (familiar)
Sir/Mr *monsieur (M);* **Madam/Mrs** *madame (Mme)*
Miss *mademoiselle (Mlle)*
please *s'il vous plaît;* **thank you** *merci;* **thank you very much** *merci beaucoup*
sorry *pardon;* **excuse me** *excusez-moi*
Do you speak English? *Parlez-vous anglais?*
I don't speak French *Je ne parle pas français*
I don't understand *Je ne comprends pas*
Speak more slowly, please *Parlez plus lentement, s'il vous plaît*
Leave me alone *Laissez-moi tranquille*
how much?/how many? *combien?*
Have you got change? *Avez-vous de la monnaie?*
I would like... *Je voudrais...*
I am going *Je vais;* **I am going to pay** *Je vais payer*
it is *c'est;* **it isn't** *ce n'est pas*
good *bon/bonne;* **bad** *mauvais/mauvaise*
small *petit/petite;* **big** *grand/grande*
beautiful *beau/belle;* **well** *bien;*
badly *mal*
expensive *cher;* **cheap** *pas cher*

a bit *un peu;* **a lot** *beaucoup;* **very** *très;* **with** *avec;* **without** *sans;* **and** *et;* **or** *ou;* **because** *parce que*
who? *qui?;* **when?** *quand?;* **which?** *quel?;* **where?** *où?;* **why?** *pourquoi?;* **how?** *comment?*
at what time/when? *à quelle heure?*
forbidden *interdit/défendu*
out of order *hors service/en panne*
daily *tous les jours (tlj)*

On the phone

hello (telephone) *allô;* **Who's calling?** *C'est de la part de qui?/Qui est à l'appareil?*
Hold the line *Ne quittez pas/Patientez s'il vous plaît*

Getting around

When is the next train for...? *C'est quand le prochain train pour...?*
ticket *un billet;* **station** *la gare;*
platform *le quai*
bus/coach station *gare routière*
entrance *entrée;* **exit** *sortie*
left *gauche;* **right** *droite;*
interchange *correspondence*
straight on *tout droit;* **far** *loin;*
near *pas loin/près d'ici*
street *la rue;* **street map** *le plan;*
road map *la carte*
bank *la banque;* **is there a bank near here?** *est-ce qu'il y a une banque près d'ici?*
post office *La Poste;* **a stamp** *un timbre*

Sightseeing

museum *un musée;* **church** *une église*
exhibition *une exposition;* **ticket** (for museum) *un billet;* (for theatre, concert) *une place*
open *ouvert;* **closed** *fermé*
free *gratuit;* **reduced price** *un tarif réduit*
except Sunday *sauf le dimanche*

Accommodation

Do you have a room (for this evening/for two people)? *Avez-vous une chambre (pour ce soir/pour deux personnes)?*
full *complet;* **room** *une chambre*
bed *un lit;* **double bed** *un grand lit;* (a room with) **twin beds** *(une chambre) à deux lits*
with bath(room)/shower *avec (salle de) bain/douche*
breakfast *le petit déjeuner;*
included *compris*
lift *un ascenseur*
air-conditioned *climatisé*

At the café or restaurant

I'd like to book a table (for three/at 8pm) *Je voudrais réserver une table (pour trois personnes/à vingt heures)*
lunch *le déjeuner;* **dinner** *le dîner*
coffee (espresso) *un café;* **white coffee** *un café au lait/café crème;*
tea *le thé;* **wine** *le vin;* **beer** *la bière*
mineral water *eau minérale;* **fizzy** *gazeuse;* **still** *plate*
tap water *eau du robinet/une carafe d'eau*
the bill, please *l'addition, s'il vous plaît*

Behind the wheel

give way *céder le passage*
it's not your right of way *vous n'avez pas la priorité;* **no parking** *stationnement interdit/stationnement gênant;* **deliveries** *livraisons*
toll *péage;* **speed limit 40** *rappel 40*
petrol *essence;* **unleaded** *sans plomb*
traffic jam *embouteillage/bouchon;*
speed *vitesse*
dangerous bends *attention virages*

Numbers

0 *zéro;* **1** *un, une;* **2** *deux;* **3** *trois;* **4** *quatre;* **5** *cinq;* **6** *six;* **7** *sept;* **8** *huit;* **9** *neuf;* **10** *dix;* **11** *onze;* **12** *douze;* **13** *treize;* **14** *quatorze;* **15** *quinze;* **16** *seize;* **17** *dix-sept;* **18** *dix-huit;* **19** *dix-neuf;* **20** *vingt;* **21** *vingt-et-un;* **22** *vingt-deux;* **30** *trente;* **40** *quarante;* **50** *cinquante;* **60** *soixante;* **70** *soixante-dix;* **80** *quatre-vingts;* **90** *quatre-vingt-dix;* **100** *cent;* **1,000** *mille;* **1,000,000** *un million.*

Days, months & seasons

Monday *lundi;* **Tuesday** *mardi;* **Wednesday** *mercredi;* **Thursday** *jeudi;* **Friday** *vendredi;* **Saturday** *samedi;* **Sunday** *dimanche.*
January *janvier;* **February** *février;* **March** *mars;* **April** *avril;* **May** *mai;* **June** *juin;* **July** *juillet;* **August** *août;* **September** *septembre;* **October** *octobre;* **November** *novembre;* **December** *décembre.* **Spring** *printemps;* **summer** *été;* **autumn** *automne;* **winter** *hiver.*

Further Reading

History & archaeology

Histoire de la Provence
Raoul Busquet, VL Bourrilly & M Agulhon
The definitive, scholarly account of the region, in French. Jeanne Laffitte, 1972.

The Roman Remains of Southern France
James Bromwich
Leaves no stone unturned in its tour of Roman Provence. Routledge, 1996.

The World of the Troubadours
Linda Paterson
Puts those courtly singer-songwriters in their historical context. Medieval Occitan Society, Cambridge UP, 1995.

Provençal identity

Letters from my Windmill
Alphonse Daudet
French nineteenth-century version of *A Year in Provence*, for escapist Parisians. Penguin (out of print).

Memoirs
Frédéric Mistral, tr George Wickes
The ninteenth-century prophet of Provençal regionalism relives the events that inspired his passion for the region. Alyscamps Press, 1994.

Village in the Vaucluse
Laurence Wylie
A readable sociological account of life in the village of Roussillon in the 1950s. Harvard UP, 1976.

France in the New Century
John Ardagh
Few journalists writing in English know France as well as Ardagh. Written with an insider's understanding, this book updates Ardagh's earlier *France in the 1980s* to take in the rapid changes of the last two decades. Penguin, 2000.

Eileen Gray
Eileen Gray
Memoirs of the Irish architect and furniture designer Eileen Gray. Her two Modernist houses on the Riviera near Menton – the only buildings she ever designed – earned her a cult following. Thames & Hudson, 1998.

Art & architecture

Van Gogh in Provence and Auvers
Bogomila Welsh-Ovcharov
Well-documented study of the earless one's Provençal jaunt. Hugh Lauter Levin, 1999.

Letters of Van Gogh
ed Ronald de Leeuw
Van Gogh is often pigeon-holed as art's mad genius, but his letters show a perceptive, engaged and engaging observer. Penguin, 1997.

La Côte d'Azur et la Modernité
This French exhibition catalogue offers an excellent, well-illustrated account of the South's crucial place in modern art. RMN, 1997.

The Sorcerer's Apprentice: Picasso, Provence and Douglas Cooper
John Richardson
Gossipy, first-hand account of the Riviera lifestyle of Picasso and his main dealer, the exuberant Douglas Cooper, from the artist's multi-volume biographer. Cape, 1999.

Emigrés

Caesar's Vast Ghost
Lawrence Durrell
Durrell's last work is a dithering mélange of historical essay and earnest reflection, interspersed with some fairly bad poetry. Faber & Faber, 1990.

J'Accuse: the Dark Side of Nice
Graham Greene
Impassioned exposé of corruption in the regime of former Nice mayor Jacques Médecin. Penguin, 1982 (out of print).

A Year in Provence
Peter Mayle
Surprisingly readable advertising copy with a few insights among the clichés. And you have to admire the royalties. Penguin, 1989.

Côte d'Azur – Inventing the French Riviera
Mary Blume
An entertaining, informed account of the decline and fall of the Riviera myth, and the emigrés who fuelled it. Thames & Hudson, 1992.

Poetry & fiction

The Count of Monte Cristo
Alexandre Dumas
A ripping yarn of prison, buried treasure and revenge in the post-Napoleonic South. Various editions.

The Water of the Hills: Jean de Florette & Manon of the Springs
Marcel Pagnol
Dour Provençal peasants bicker with incomers about the water supply. As a special bonus, the book comes *sans* Gérard Depardieu. Picador, 1989.

The Man who Planted Trees
Jean Giono
Eco-fable for grown-ups: a good introduction to the work of this gritty, chthonic Southern writer. Harvill, 1992.

Perfume
Patrick Süskind
If a mysterious character asks if they can kill you to extract your scent, Just Say No. A smelly thriller set in the eighteenth-century Grasse perfume trade. Picador, 1989.

Food & wine

Flavours of France
Alain Ducasse
The seven-star chef's classic first cookbook. Artisan, 1998.

Touring in Wine Country: Provence
ed Hugh Johnson
Essential companion for those serious fact-finding tours of Southern vineyards. Mitchell Beazley, 1993.

The Markets of Provence
Dixon Long
Seven produce markets in the *départements* of Vaucluse and Bouches-du-Rhône, with recipes and lavish photos. Collins US, 1996.

Olives
Mort Rosenblum
US newsman buys a farm in Provence, saves its olive trees and gets hooked on the little green fruit. Absolute Press, 1997.

Directory

Page numbers in italics indicate illustrations.

a

abbeys (abbaye)
de Lérins 199
de Montmajour 73-74
Notre-Dame-de-Sénanque, Gordes 121
St-André, Villeneuve-lès-Avignon 100, 101
de St-Michel-de-Frigolet, nr Châteaurenard 68
St-Roman, nr Beaucaire 69, 70
de St-Victor, Marseille 129
de Silvacane, Cadenet 115
du Thoronet, nr Cotignac *184*, 184-185
abortion 297
accommodation 286-287
b&b/chambres d'hôtes 286-287
disabled travellers 295
camping 287
essential vocabulary 306
gîtes 287
hotels 286
rented/self-catering 298;
Authentiques Cabanes de Gardian de la Grand Mar 85, the Camargue; Cannes 205; St-Tropez, Le Pré de la Mer 172
youth hostels *see* youth hostels
Agay 178, 180
AIDS (SIDA) 297
airlines & airports 282, 285
Aix-en-Provence 139-148
festivals 290
map 140
Almanarre 161
the Alps 256-280
Alpes-Maritimes 271-280
the Alpilles 72-74; museum 71
Les Alyscamps 77, *77*
ambulance 296
American War Cemetery, Draguignan 189
Ancienne cathédrale, Vence 265
Ancienne Cathédrale Ste-Anne, Apt 120
Anjou dynasty 2, 6, 10
Ansouis 115; music festival 289
Anthéon 178
Antibes 210-214, *210*
Musiques au Coeur 290
antiques
Isle-sur-la-Sorgue 116

Nice, Marché de la Brocante 231, Village Ségurane 232
Apt 120-121
aquariums
Musée Océanographique, Monaco 245
archaeology
further reading 307
architecture
cubism & Modernists 22-23;
Villa Noailles, Hyères 161, 163, *164*
further reading 307
see also specific architects
Les Arcs 189, 190
Les Arènes
Arles 77-78, *78*, 80
Fréjus 177
Nîmes 58, *58*, 59, 63
Argens Valley 189-190
Arles 75-82
festivals & events 289, 290
map 75
the Arrière-pays 268-270
art in the South 19-23
contemporary 29-32
Cubists 20
L'Estaque 137
festivals 288-291
further reading 307
Impressionists 19-20
museums *see* museums
medieval 10
naïve Musée International d'Art Naïf Anatole Jakovsky, Nice 224
photography *see* photography
St-Paul-de-Vence 263
see also specific artists
Art Jonction, Nice 288
arts & entertainment 29-37
see also dance; festivals & events; music; opera; theatre
Aubagne 138
ceramics fair 289-299
Aups 185, 186
Aups-Ste-Baume 148
Auron 278, 280
Avignon 88-100
bureaux de change 292
festival 35-36; 94; 289, 291
map 89

b

Bagnols-sur-Cèze 102, 107
Bandol 154

banks 292
Bargème 190-191
Bargemon 190-191
Barjols 183, 185
Baroncelli, Folco 84, 90; Palais du Roure, Avignon 95
Le Barroux 112
Le Bar-sur-Loup 261
bars & nightlife *see* music in the South
gay & lesbian *see* gay & lesbian travellers
the Basse Corniche 235-239
Basses Gorges du Verdon 196
Basilique Ste-Marie-Madeleine, St-Maximin-la-Ste-Baume, *147*, 148
Les Baux-de-Provence 72-73
b&b/chambres d'hôtes 286-287
beaches, top ten 203
Basse Corniche 238-239
Carry-le-Rouet 137
Cassis 152
gay & lesbian 296; La Batterie, Cannes 203
Hyères 161-163
Les Lecques 153
Nice 220-221
nudist beaches La Batterie, Cannes 203; Ile du Levant 163-164
Le Pradet 160
St-Raphaël 175
St-Tropez 170-171
Six-Fours-les-Plages 157
Beaucaire 70, 71
Beaulieu 237-239
Beaumes-de-Venise 112
Le Beausset 154
beauty spas 292-293; *see also* thalassotherapy
Bédoin 111
Ben 31-32; Le Centre du Monde, Nice 231
Bévéra Valley 271-275
Biot 216-217
birdwatching
Parc Ornithologique de Pont de Gau 83, 85
Bonnard, Pierre 20
Bonnieux 114, 116, 117
Bories, Village des *4*, 121
Bormes-les-Mimosas 164, 166
boules & pétanque 35
St-Paul-de-Vence 263
bouillabaisse 43
Braque, Georges 20
Brayer, Yves

Musée Yves Brayer, Les Baux-de-Provence 73, 74
Breil-sur-Roya 273-275
Brignoles 182
La Brigue 274-275
Le Brusc 157
bullfighting
  Arles, Les Arènes 80; Féria Pascale 288
  course Camarguaise 79
  Musée Baroncelli 84, 85
  Nîmes 63; Les Arènes 59; Féria de Pentecôte 288
  St-Rémy-de-Provence 289; Féria Provençale 289
bungee jumping
  Gorges du Verdon 194
Buoux 114
bureaux de change 292
buses 283, 285
business 293

C

Cabasson 165
Cabris 259, 260
Cadenet 115
Cagnes 214-216
Les calanques 153
Callas 190, 191, 192
Callian 192
the Camargue 83-86
  course Camarguaise 79; Fêtes des Prémices du Riz, Arles 290
camping 287
Camus, Albert
  Lourmarin 115
canals
  Isle-sur-la-Sorgue 117-119
  Port Grimaud 173-174
Cannes 198-206
  film festival 30
  bureaux de change 292
  dance festival 291
  gay Cannes 297
  map 200-201
Le Cannet, Cannes 199
canoeing 301
  Fontaine-de-Vaucluse 118
  Pont du Gard 67
Cap d'Antibes 210, 212
Cap Eden-Roc, Hôtel du 210
Cap-Ferrat 236-237
Cap Lardier 167
car hire 283; disabled travellers 295; *see also* driving
Carlton Hôtel, Cannes *204*, 205
carnival, Nice 288
Carro 137
Carpentras 108-109
  festival 289
cash machines 292

casinos
  Beaulieu 237, 239
  Monaco & Monte-Carlo 245, 247
  Nice 225
Cassis 152, *152*
Castellane 193, 194, 195, 196
Castellar 254
Le Castellet 154
Castillon 254
Castillon-du-Gard 67
Cathédrale St-Nicholas, Nice 221
Cathédrale St-Sauveur, Aix-en-Provence 141
Cathédrale St Siffrein, Carpentras 108, 109
Carry-le-Rouet 137
Catalans 9-10
Cavaillon 119-120
Cavalaire-sur-Mer 167
cave paintings
  Calanques de Cassis 158
cave systems
  Souterroscope de Baume Obscure 259, 260
La Celle 182
Celts & Ligurians 5
  Oppidum d'Entremont, Aix-en-Provence 143
Centre d'Art VAAS 265
Centre Atomique de Marcoule 107
Centre Jean Giono 122
Le Centre du Monde, Nice 231
ceramics *see* pottery & ceramics
Cézanne, Paul 19-20, 142
  Atelier, Aix-en-Provence 143
  L'Estaque 137
Chagall, Marc
  Musée National Message Biblique Marc-Chagall, Nice 225
chambres d'hôtes 286-287
Chapelle du Rosaire, Vence 265, *266*
Chartreuse de Valbonne 107
Châteaudouble 188
Château d'If 134
Châteauneuf-du-Pape 104-106
Châteaurenard 68, 69
Le Chêne Noir, Avignon 96
children 293-294
  Aquatica, Fréjus 177
  Aquavallée, Isola 278
  La Colmiane *275*, 276
  Eze Astrorama, La Turbie 241
  Marineland, Antibes 212, 213
  Zoo de la Barben, Salon-de-Provence 150
  Zoo du Cap-Ferrat 237
Chorégies d'Orange 103, 104
Christmas traditions 291

La Ciotat 152-154
circus festival 291
Cité Episcopale, Fréjus 177
Cité Radieuse, Marseille 129
Clans 277
Claviers 190, 191, 192
Clement V, Pope 91
climate 305
Clews, Henry and Marie 28
  Fondation Henry Clews, La Napoule 179, *179*
cloths & fabrics
  L'Arlésienne, Arles 82;
  Le Chandelier, Nice 231;
  Les Olivades, Avignon 98
Club Alpin de Provence 112
Coaraze 268
Cocteau, Jean
  Chapelle de St-Pierre-des-Pêcheurs, Villefranche-sur-Mer 235, 236, *236*
  Musée Jean Cocteau 250-251
Cogolin 173, 174
Col de la Bonette 278
Collection Lambert, Avignon 92
Collégiale Notre-Dame-des-Anges, L'Isle-sur-la-Sorgue *117*, 118
Les Collettes, Cagnes-sur-Mer 214-215
Collias 65, 66
La Colmiane 276
computer sales Gale Force, Monte-Carlo 293
Comtat Venaissin 10, 108
conference centres 293
consulates 295-296
Contes 268, 269
contraception 297
cookery courses *see* food & drink
Corniche de l'Estérel 178-180
Corniche des Maures 164
the Corniches 235-241
cosmetics & soaps Compagnie de Provence, Marseille 135;
  Occitane, Manosque 122
Côte d'Azur identity vi
Côtes du Ventoux 111
Cotignac 183, *183*, 185
course Camarguaise 79
Cours Mirabeau, Aix-en-Provence 144
Courthezon 106
credit cards 292
La Croisette, Cannes 198
La Croix-Valmer 167
Cros-de-Cagne 214
cubism *see* architecture; art
Cucuron 115, 117
Customs 294
cycling 283, 285, 301

d

dance in the South 37
  Danse à Aix 146
  festivals 288-291
Daudet, Alphonse
  Moulin de Daudet, Fontvieille
  73, 74, *74*
Les Dentelles de Montmirail 111-
  112, *111*
dentists 297
dialects *see* language & dialects
disabled travellers 294-295
diving
  Calanques de Cassis 158
  Musée Frédéric-Dumas,
  Sanary-sur-Mer 157
doctors 297
Draguignan 187-188, 290
drink 41-42; *see also* wine
driving 283-284
  breakdown services 284
  car accidents 296
  car hire 283; disabled
  travellers 295
  essential vocabulary 306
  scenic routes Corniches de
  l'Estérel 178-180; the Corniches
  235-241; Gorges de
  Châteaudouble 187-188;
  Gorges du Verdon 193; Route
  de Gineste 137; routes des
  Crêtes 152
drugs 295
Ducasse, Alain 44-45; book 307
Duché d'Uzès 65, 66

e

E111/E112 forms 297
Eglise Collégiale, St-Paul-de-
  Vence 263
electricity 295
embassies & consulates 295-296
emergencies 296
emigrés 24-28
English in the South 24-28
Entrecasteaux 184, 185
Entrevaux 270
épeautre 111
Ephrussi-de-Rothschild, Villa,
  Cap-Ferrat 236, 237
L'Escarène 268-269
Escoffier, Auguste
  Musée de l'Art Culinaire,
  Villeneuve-Loubet 214, 215
Espace 13, Aix-en-Provence
  144
Espace de l'Art Concret 262
L'Estaque 128, 129
Les Estivales, Carpentras 289
L'Eté de Vaison 113

Eygalières 71
Eze 239-240

f

fashion & designers
  Agnès B, Nice 230
  Christian Lacroix, Arles 82
  Claire l'Insolite, St-Tropez 171
  Façonnable, Nice 231
  Movida, Nice 231
  La Thuberie, Marseille 136
fax services 299
La Favière 165
Fayence 192
the Félibrige school 72
férias *see* bullfighting
Ferrières 137
Festival d'Avignon 35-36, 94
Festival International d'Art
  Lyrique, Aix-en-Provence 146
Festival International de Danse à
  Cannes 291
festivals & events 288-289;
  Avignon 35-36, 94
  dance *see* dance festivals
  folklore Fête de la
  Transhumance, St-Etienne-de-
  Tinée 278
  film *see* film
  opera *see* opera
  theatre *see* theatre
La Figueirette 178
film in the South 32-33
  Espace Lumière & Eden
  cinema, La Ciotat 153
  Festival International de
  Cinéma, Cannes 31, 198, 199
  cinemas Avignon Utopia 96;
  Nice Cinémathèque 227; Nîmes
  Le Sémaphore 61
  Pagnol, Marcel *see* Pagnol,
  Marcel
fire service 296
fishing trips, Bendor 155
Fondation Maeght 263
Fondation Van Gogh 77, 78
Fondation Vasarely 143
Fontaine-de-Vaucluse 118-119
Fontvieille 73
food & drink 38-54
  bakeries, confiseries & sweets
  Aptunion, Apt 120; Boitel,
  Arles 82; Confiserie Florian, Le
  Pont-du-Loup 261; Four des
  Navettes, Marseille 135
  bouillabaisse 43
  chefs see Ducasse, Alain;
  Escoffier, Auguste; *see also*
  restaurants
  chocolate Bernard Castellain,
  Chateauneuf-du-Pape 106

  coffee Torrefaction Noailles,
  Marseille 136
  cookery courses Ecole de
  Cuisine de Soleil, Mougins 207
  further reading 307
  garlic La Foire à l'Ail, Uzès 289
  lemons Fête du Citron, Menton
  291
  melons Cavaillon 119-120
  menu glossary 50-53
  museums Musée de l'Art
  Culinaire, Villeneuve-Loubet,
  214, 215
  rice Fêtes des Prémices du Riz
  290, Arles; Musée de Riz, Le
  Sambuc 84, 85
  truffles Aups 185, 186; Marché
  aux Truffes, Rognes 291
  see also olive oil, wine
football
  Olympique de Marseille 17,
  133
Foreign Legion
  Musée du Képi Blanc,
  Aubagne 138
Fox-Amphoux 184
Fragonard, perfumery 240, 259
Fragonard, Villa-Musée, Grasse
  256, 257
Fréjus 177-178
La Friche la Belle de Mai,
  Marseille 131

g

La Galère 178-179
Galerie Beaubourg 265, 266
Galerie Roger Pailhas, Marseille
  131
Gallimard, perfumery 259
gardians 84
Gardon *see* Gorges du Gardon
garrigues 65
gas 295
Gassin 172, 173
La Gaude 266-267
Gauls *see* Celts & Ligurians
gay & lesbian travellers 296-297
  venues
  Avignon, L'Esclave 98
  Cannes, Zanzibar 204
  Marseille, The New Cancan
  135
  Nice, Blue Boy Enterprise &
  Cherry's Café 230
  Nîmes, Lulu Club 63
Giens 161, 162
Gigondas 112
Giono, Jean 122; works 307
gîtes 287
glass factory Biot *215*, 217
go-karting

Fun Kart, Gorges du Loup 261
Golfe-Juan 209
golfing 300-301
    Monte-Carlo Golf Club 241
Gorbio 253-254
Gordes 121, 122
gorges
    de Châteaudouble 187
    du Gardon 65
    du Loup 261
    du Verdon 193-196
    de la Vésubie 275
Gourdon 261
the Grande Crau 72-74
Grand Prix, Monaco 288
Grasse 256-259; Fête du Jasmin
290
Grand Canyon see Gorges du
Verdon
the Grande Corniche 240-241
Graveson 68, 69
Gray, Eileen 22
the Great Schism 91
Greek civilisation 5
    towns & remains Marseille
    124, 130; St-Rémy-de-Provence
    70-72
    Villa Kerylos, Beaulieu 237,
    238, 239
Greene, Graham 16
Grimaldi family 242
Grimaud 173, 174
Grottes des Audides 259, 260
Grottes de St-Cézaire 259, 260
gypsies 86

Haut-de-Cagnes 215
health 297-298
hiking see walking & hiking
history 4-28
    further reading 307
    Le Midi today 15-18, 25
hitch-hiking 285
Les Hivernales, Avignon 291
horse riding & pony trekking 302
    Authentiques Cabanes de
    Gardian de la Grand Mar 85
    La Ferme d'Anais, Cannes 204
hospitals 297
Hôtel du Cap Eden-Roc, Cap
d'Antibes 210
Hôtel Dieu, Carpentras 109
Hôtel Donadeï de Campredon,
    Isle-sur-la-Sorgue 118
Hôtel Negresco, Nice 232, 234
Hôtel Windsor, Nice 233
hotels 286
Huguenots 11
Hyères 161-164
    Festival Medieval 290

IAM, Marseille
ibn Tibbon dynasty 5
Ile de Bendor 154, 155
Iles des Embiez 157, 158
Iles d'Hyères 163-164
Ile de Lérins 199
Ile du Levant 163-164
Ile d'Or 178
Ile de Porquerolles 163-164
Ile de Port-Cros 163-164
immigration in the South 25
    living & working in the South
    298-299
the Impressionists 19-20
internet cafés & points
    Avignon, Cyberdrome 96
    Draguignan, Les Milles
    Colonnes 188
    Grasse, Le Petit Caboulet 257
    Nice, Webstore 234
    Nîmes, Le Pluggin 64
islands see Ile, Iles
L'Isle-sur-la-Sorgue 116, 117-119
    Festival de la Sorgue 289
Isola 278, 280
Isola 2000 278

Jardin Medieval, Uzès 65, 66
jazz in the South 34-35
    festivals Aix 146; Juan-les-Pins
    212, 290; Nice 290
Jeu de Paume, Aix-en-Provence
144
Jews in the South 108; see also
synagogues
Jonquières 137
Juan-les-Pins 210-214

kayaking see rafting & kayaking;
see also canoeing
Kelly, Grace 235, 242

Lacoste 114
Lac St-Cassien 192
Lambesc 150
language & dialects
    courses 302-303
    essential vocabulary 306
    menu glossary 50-53
    Nissart 225
    Provençal (Occitan) 9-10, 11, 72
lavender Riez 196
Le Corbusier 23
    Le Cabanon & memorial,

Roquebrune-Cap-Martin 252,
253
Cité Radieuse, Marseille 129
Le Lavandou 164-166
Les Lecques 153
legal advice 298
Léger, Fernand
    Musée National Fernand
    Léger, Biot 216, 217
lemon festival 291
Ligurians see Celts & Ligurians
literary Provence
    festival Cité du Livre, Aix-en-
    Provence 144
    émigrés 24-28
    see also specific authors
La Londe-les-Maures 164
lost property 299
Lourmarin 114-115, 117
the Luberon 114-122; festivals 289
Lucéram 269
Lumière brothers
    Espace Lumière & Eden
    cinema, La Ciotat 153

Madone de Fenestre 276, 277
Maeght, Fondation 263
Maillane 68, 69
Maison Carrée, Nîmes 58, 59
Malaucène 112
Mallet-Stevens, Robert 22
    Villa Noailles, Hyères 161, 163
Manosque 122
maps 299
Marcoule nuclear waste plant 102
Marie 277, 278
marine parks
    Antibes 212, 213
markets, further reading 307
Marseille 124-137
    bureaux de change 292
    gay & lesbian 297; The New
    Cancan 135
    maps 126-127
    Olympique de Marseille 17,
    133
Martigues 137, 138; Fête de la St-
Pierre 289
Massif de l'Estérel 179
Massif des Maures 166
Massif de la Ste-Baume 148
Matisse, Henri 20-21
    Musée Matisse, Nice 225
Mayle, Peter & A Year in
Provence 307
Ménerbes 114
Médecin, Jacques 16
Ménerbes 114
Menton 250-252
    Festival de la Musique 290

Fête du Citron 291
menu glossary 50-53
Merveilles, Vallée des 272
minitel 304
Miramar 178
Mistral, Frédéric *13*, 72, 90
  memoirs 307
  Museon Arlaten 77, 78-79
  Museon Mistral 68, 69
Modernism *see* Art in the South
Monaco & Monte-Carlo 242-249
  bureau de change 292
  Festival International du Cirque de Monte-Carlo 291
  Grand Prix *245*, 288
  map 243
  Rallye Automobile Monte-Carlo 291
  Tennis Open 288
money 292
Montagne du Luberon 114-117
La Montagnette 68
Montagne Ste-Victoire 142
Montauroux 192
Monte-Carlo *see* Monaco & Monte-Carlo 242-249
Montmajour 73-74
Montmirail 112
Mont Ventoux 110-111, *111*
mountaineering & rock-climbing 301
  Cassis 152
  Club Alpin de Provence 112
  Les Dentelles de Montmirail 111-112
  Vallon Sourn 182
Mouans-Sartoux 262
Mougins 206
Mourre Nègre 115
Moustiers-Ste-Marie *193*, 194, 195, 196
the Moyenne Corniche 239-240
Mur de la Peste 118
Musée de l'Annociade, St-Tropez 169
Musée d'Art Contemporain (MAC), Marseille 130; Nîmes 58, 59-60
Musée d'Art Modern et d'Art Contemporain (MAMAC), Nice 224, *227*
Musée Camarguais 83, 85
Musée Cantini 130
Musée Matisse 225
Musée du Petit Palais, Avignon 90, 93
Musée Réattu 77, 78
Museon Arlaten 77, 78-79
museums, opening times 299
  anthropology & archaeology

Musée d'Archéologie, Nice 224, Nîmes 59; d'Archéologie Léon Alègre, Bagnols-sur-Cèze 107; d'Histoire et d'Archéologie, Antibes 212, 213; de l'Hôtel Dieu, Cavaillon 119; Lapidaire, Avignon 93; des Merveilles, Tende 273, 274; de Taureontum, Les Lecques 153; La Vieille-Charity, Marseille 131
art Collection Lambert, Avignon 92; Angladon-Dubrujeaud, Avignon 92; Musée Albert André, Bagnols-sur-Cèze 107; de l'Annonciade, St-Tropez 169; d'Art Contemporain (MAC), Marseille 130, Nîmes 58, 59-60; d'Art Modern et d'Art Contemporain (MAMAC), Nice 224, *227*; d'Art Naïf Anatole Jakovsky, Nice 224; des Beaux Arts Marseille 130, Menton 250, 251; Nice 224, Nîmes 60; Calvet, Avignon 92-93; Cantini, Marseille 130; Mediterranéen d'Art Moderne, Haut-de-Cagnes 215; Pierre du Luxembourg, Villeneuve-lès-Avignon 101; Réattu, Arles 77, 78; Villa Ephrussi-de-Rothschild, Cap-Ferrat 236, 237; *see also* art in the South
artists & writers Yves Brayer, Les Baux-de-Provence 73, 74; Marc Chagall, Nice 225; Jean Cocteau, Menton 250-251; Fragonard, Grasse 256, *257*; Jean Giono, Manosque 122; Fernand Léger, Biot *216*, 217; Matisse, Nice 225; Petrarch, Fontaine-de-Vaucluse 118; Picasso, Antibes 212-213, Vallauris 208-209; Van Gogh, Arles 77, 78
basketmaking Musée de la Vannerie, Cadenet 115, 116
bullfighting Musée Baroncelli, Stes-Maries-de-la-Mer 84, 85
cars Collection des Voitures Anciennes, Monaco 244; Musée de l'Automobiliste, Mougins 207
corkscrews Musée du Tirebouchon, Ménerbes 114, 116
diving Musée Frédéric-Dumas, Sanary-sur-Mer 157
folklore & local history Musée Camarguais, Stes-Maries-de-la-Mer 83, 85; Castellane 193, 194;

Comtadin & Duplessis, Carpentras 108, 109; du Pays Brignolais, Brignoles 182; des Traditions Provençales, Draguignan 187, 188; de Vieux Nîmes 60; Museon Arlaten, Arles 77, 78-79
food Musée de l'Art Culinaire, Villeneuve-Loubet, 214, 215
maritime & marine life Fondation Océanographique Paul Ricard, Isles des Embiez 157; Musée de la Marine, Toulon 159, 160; de la Marine et de l'Economie de Marseille 131; Naval et Napoléonien, Antibes 212, 213; Océanographique, Monaco 245
mining Musée de la Mine du Cap Garonne, Le Pradet 160
photography Musée de la Photographie, Mougins 207
pottery & ceramics Musée de la Faïence, Marseille 130; des Faïences, La Tour-d'Aigues 115, 116; de la Potterie Meditérannéenne, Uzès 65, 66
religious art & artefacts Pont-St-Esprit 106; Musée Juif Comtadin, Cavaillon 119
rice Musée de Riz, Le Sambuc 84, 85
Romans Musée d'Archéologie de Nîmes 59; de L'Arles Antique 77, 78; Municipal, Orange 102; Quartier de Puymin & Villasse, Vaison-la-Romaine 112
textiles, costume & jewellery Musée de la Mode, Marseille 131; Provençal du Costume et du Bijou, Grasse 256, 257; Souleiado, Tarascon 69, 70
World War II Musée de la Libération, Le Muy 189, 190; Musée-mémorial du Débarquement, Toulon 160
see also perfumes, wines
music in the South 33-35
  English-language, Nice 230-231
  festivals & events 288-291
  lessons Cité de la Musique, Marseille 131

Napoléon Bonaparte 12
  Golfe-Juan 209
  Musée des Souvenirs Napoléoniens, Monaco 245
nature reserves

the Camarge 83-86
Cap Lardier 167
Gorges du Verdon 193
the Luberon 114-122
Parc National du Mercantour
268, 271
Negresco, Hôtel 232, *234*
newspapers 300
Nîmes 56-64
map 57
Nice 218, 218-234
bureaux de change 292
carnival 288
jazz festival 290
map 219; Vieux Nice 221
Les Moulins 15
politics 16
taxis 285
Nietzsche, Friedrich 239
nightlife *see* music in the South
Nissart 225
Nostradamus, Maison de 148-149
Notre-Dame-de-la-Garde,
Marseille 130
Notre-Dame-du-Puy, Grasse 256
nuclear plants 102; 107
Nuits de la Danse, Monaco 290

o

Occitan *see* language
Le Off, Avignon 36, 94
olive oil, local production
The Arrière-pays 268-269
Beaumes-de-Venise 112
Cucuron 115
Moulin du Flayosquet &
Lorgues 188
Nice, Alziari 230-231
Ollioules 155-158
opera in the South 33-34
festivals 288-291; Aix-en-
Provence 146; Orange 103, 104
opera houses Marseille 131;
Nice 227
Oppède-le-Vieux 114
opticians 297-298
Orange 102-104

p

Pagnol, Marcel 14, 32; works 307
Château d'Astros 190
Aubagne 138
Palais Episcopal, Uzès 65, 66
Palais des Festivals, Cannes 198,
199
Palais/Salle Garnier, Monte-Carlo
casino 245
Palais Longchamp, Marseille 125
Palais des Papes, Avignon *9*, *90*,
93-95

La Palud-sur-Verdon 195, 196
papacy in Avignon 91
Parc Naturel Regional *see* nature
reserves & parks
parascending
Antibes 213
parks & gardens
country estates Domaine du
Rayol, Corniche des Maures
166, 167
town parks Antibes 212, 213;
Avignon 90; Hyères 161;
Menton 250-251; Monaco 244;
Nice 219; Nîmes 57, 59, *61*;
Uzès 65
Peille 268
Peillon 268
perfumes 258-259; Annick Goutal,
Avignon 98; Parfumerie
Fragonard, Beaulieu 240;
Parfumerie Gallimard 259
books 307
museums Musée des Aromes
de Provence, St-Rémy-de-
Provence 71, 72; International
de la Parfumerie, Grasse 259;
Grasse d'Antan 257
Pernes-les-Fontaines 109-110
pétanque *see* boules & pétanque
Petite Crau 68
Petit Palais, Musée du, Avignon
90, 93
Petrarch 92, 118
pharmacies 297
photocopying 299
photography
Musée de la Photographie,
Mougins 207
Rencontres Internationals de la
Photographie, Arles 289
Théâtre de la Photographie et
de l'Image, Nice 227
Picabia, Francis 20
Picasso 22-23
Mougins 206
Musée National Picasso,
Musée Magnelli, Musée de la
Céramique, Vallauris 208-209
Musée Picasso, Antibes 212,
213
Musée Réattu, Arles 77, 78
Vallauris 208-209
pilgrimage routes and towns
Pont-St-Esprit 106
St-Gilles-du-Gard 84, 86
Plateau de Vaucluse 121-122
police 296
politics in the South 15-18
Pont d'Artuby 194, *194*
Pont du Gard *7*, 67
Pontevès 183
Pont-St-Esprit 102, 106-107

Port Grimaud 173-174
post offices 299-300
pottery & ceramics
fairs Biennale de Céramique
Contemporaine, Vallauris 290;
Fête de la Céramique,
Aubagne 289-290
museums see museums
shops & galleries Faïence d'Apt
120; Faïence Figuères,
Marseille 135; Fayences de
Moustiers, Nice 231; Uzès 65-66
tiles Salernes 185, 186
Poulx 65
Le Pradet 160
press 300
Promenade des Anglais, Nice 218,
220
Protestantism in the South 11
Provençal identity 4-18
language *see* language
prehistory 4-5
La Vallée des Merveilles 272
public holidays 300
Puget-Théniers 270

r

racism & Front National 17-18, 24
Radio 300
rafting & kayaking 301
Breil-sur-Roya 273-275
Vallon Sourn 182
Ramatuelle 172-173
rape 305
Réal 183-184
La Redonne 137
religion 91; 300-301
Jews *see* Jews; synagogues
museums *see* museums
Wars of Religion 11
Remoulins 67
removals 301
Rencontres Internationals de la
Photographie, Arles 289
René of Anjou 2
Anjou dynasty 6, 10
Renoir, Auguste 20
Les Collettes, Cagnes-sur-Mer
214-215
restaurants
food & drink 38-54
menu glossary 50-53
regional highlights 42-54
top ten 39
the Rhône 55-86
Riez 196
the Riviera 197-254
emigrés & tourism 24-28
politics 15-18
by train 270
rock-climbing *see* mountaineering

& rock-climbing
Rognes, Marché aux Truffes 291
Romans in the South 5-7
  towns & remains Antibes 210-
  212; Arles 75-79; Fréjus 177;
  Orange 102-103; Nîmes 56-59;
  Nice Musée d'Archéologie 22;
  Pont du Gard 67; Riez 196; St-
  Raphaël 175; St-Rémy-de-
  Provence 71-72; Sillans 192;
  Trophée des Alpes 6, 241;
  Vaison-la-Romaine 112-113
  see also museums
La Roque d'Anthéron 115
  Festival International de Piano
  290
La Roque-sur-Cèze 107
Roquebrune 252-253
Roquebrune-Cap-Martin 252-253
Roquebrune-sur-Argens 177
La Roquebrussane 182
Roseline de Villeneuve, St 189
Roussillon 121, 121, 122
Roya Valley 271-275
Russians in the South 26-27
  church Cathédrale St-Nicolas,
  Nice 221

S

Saignon 114, 116-117
St-Bonnet-du-Gard 67
St-Cézaire-sur-Siagne 259, 260,
261
St-Cyr-sur-Mer 153-154
St-Dalmas-de-Valdeblore 276
St-Dalmas-le-Selvage 278, 279
Ste-Agnès 254
Ste-Anne-d'Evenos 154, 155
St-Etienne-de-Tinée 278, 280
Ste-Maxime 174
Stes-Maries-de-la-Mer 83, 84-86
St-Gilles-du-Gard 84, 86
St-Jean-Cap-Ferrat 237
St-Jeannet 266, 267
St-Quentin-la-Potterie 65, 66
St-Martin-Vésubie 275-277
St-Maximin 66
St-Maximin-la-Ste-Baume 148
St-Paul-de-Vence 263-264
St-Quentin-la-Potterie 65, 66
St-Raphaël 175-177
St-Rémy-de-Provence 70-72
St-Sauveur 278
St-Théodorit, Uzès 65, 66
St-Tropez 168-172
  festival La Bravade 288
  gay & lesbian 297
St-Trophime, Arles 8, 77, 79, 80
St-Vallier-de-Thiey 259, 260, 261
Salernes 185, 186
Salin-de-Giraud 83-84

Salon-de-Provence 148-150
  Musique à l'Empéri 290
Sanary-sur-Mer 157-158
santons & Christmas traditions
291
  workshops Arterra, Marseille
  135; Aubagne 138
Saorge 273-275
Savoy, House of 10, 12
Séguret 112
Seillans 192
Sernhac 67
shipping services 293; removals
301
shopping 299
  Arles 81-82
  Avignon 98
  Cannes 204
  Marseille 135-136
  Monaco & Monte-Carlo 249
  Nice 220, 230-232
  Nîmes 63
  St-Tropez 171
  see also cloths & fabrics;
  cosmetics & soaps; fashion;
  food & drink; perfumes;
  pottery & ceramics
Sillans-la-Cascade 184, 185
Six-Fours-les-Plages 157-158
skiing 302
  Auron 278, 280; Isola 2000 278;
  Mont Ventoux 111
smoking 301
Sophia-Antipolis 262
Souterroscope de Baume Obscure
259, 260
sport & activity holidays 301
soaps Compagnie de Provence,
  Marseille 135
Sospel 271-275
study & students 302-303
Le Suquet, Cannes 199
surfing
  Six-Fours-les-Plages 157
Surrealists in the South 23
swimming
  rivers & lakes Basses Gorge du
  Verdon 196; Gorges du Verdon
  194; Pont du Gard 67
  fun pools Aquavallée, Isola 278
  swimming pools Avignon 96;
  Monaco & Monte-Carlo 246;
  Nice 227; Orange 103
  see also beaches
synagogues Carpentras 108;
  Cavaillon 119

T

Tapie, Bernard 16-17, 133
Tarascon 69-70; Fête de la
Tarasque 289

tax refunds 303
taxis 285; disabled travellers 294
telegrams 299
telephones 1, 303-304
television 304
Tende 273-275
tennis
  Antibes 214
  Beaulieu 237
  Cannes 204
  Monte-Carlo Tennis Open 288
thalassotherapy 292-293; Les
Thermes Marins de Monte-Carlo
246
theatre in the South 35l; festivals
288-291
  Aix-en-Provence 144
  Arles 80
  Avignon 96
  Marseille 132
  Nice 227
  Nîmes 61
Théâtre de la Criée, Marseille 132
Théâtre du Gymnase, Marseille
132
Théâtre de Nice 227
Théâtre Antique, Arles, 77, 79
Théâtre Antique, Orange 102,
102-103
theft 299
Thermes de Constantin, Arles 77,
79
time 304
Tinée Valley 277-280, 279
tipping 304
Tour Fenestrelle, Uzès 65, 66
tourist information 302;
  websites 305
Tour Magne, Nîmes 57, 60
Tourrettes 192
Tourrettes-sur-Loup 266, 266, 267
Tourtour 185-186
trains 282-283, 284-285; Train des
Pignes 270
transhumance 288
  Fête de la Transhumance, St-
  Etienne-de-Tinée 278
translation service 293
transport 282-285
Le Trayas 178
Trophée des Alpes 241
troubadours 9-10; see also
Provençal identity
truffles
  Aups 185, 186
  Marché aux Truffes, Rognes
  291
La Turbie 241

La Tour 277
La Tour-d'Aigues 115, 117

Utelle 275, 276
Uzès 65-67; festivals 289

Vaison-la-Romaine 112-113
  festival 289
Valbonne 261-262
Vallauris 208-209, *209*
  Biennale de Céramique
  Contemporaine 290
La Vallée des Merveilles 272
Vallon Sourn 182
Van Gogh 20, 81
  Fondation Van Gogh, Arles 77,
  78
  Monastère St-Paul-de-Mausole,
  St-Rémy-de-Provence 71
Var
  Central & Eastern Var 187-192
  Var Valley 268
  Western Var 182-186
Vasarely, Victor 143
the Vaucluse 87-122
  festivals 289
Venanson 276
Vence 265-266
Verdon *see* Gorges du Verdon
Vers-Pont-du-Gard 67
Vésubie Valley 275-277
Vidauban 189-190
videos 304
Vieux Port, Marseille 125
Vieux Port, St-Tropez *168*, 169
Villa Ephrussi-de-Rothschild,
  Cap-Ferrat 236, 237
Village des Bories 121
Villa Arson, Nice 225

Villa-Musée Fragonard, Grasse
  256, 257
Villars-sur-Var 270
Villecroze 185, 186, *186*
Villefranche-sur-Mer 235-236
Villeneuve-lès-Avignon 100-101
Villeneuve-Loubet 214-216
visas 304-305
vocabulary *see* language

walking & hiking 285, 302
  Calanques de Cassis 153
  Cap-Ferrat 236
  Corniche de l'Estérel 178
  Gorges du Gardon 65
  Gorges du Verdon 195
  long-distance footpaths 285;
  GR6 65, 67; GR9 166, 182;
  GR49 179, 191; GR51 157, 179;
  GR98 153; GR90 166; GR99 182
  Massif de l'Estérel 179
  Massif des Maures 166
  Mercantour national park &
  Vallée des Merveilles 272-277
  Mont Ventoux 111
  Ollioules 157
  St-Cyr-sur-Mer & Les Lecques
  153
  Sillans-la-Cascade 184
  Uzès 65
  Vence (La Gaude) 267
waterfalls
  Sillans-la-Cascade 184
watersports 302
  Antibes 214
  Cannes 204
  Cassis 152
  Lac St-Cassien 192

Le Lavandou 165-166
weather 305
wildlife
  Camargue 83-86
  St-Raphaël 175
wine 41-42
  books 307
  festivals Fête du Millésime,
  Bandol 155; Fête de la Vigne et
  du Vin, around Chateauneuf-
  du-Pape 289
  museums Châteauneuf-du-
  Pape 105-106; Contes 268, 269;
  Ile de Bendor 154
  Roman production Mas des
  Tourelles, nr Beaucaire 69, 70
  towns, villages & regions
  Bandol 154-155; Baux-de-
  Provence 73; Beaumes-de-
  Venise 112; Cassis 152;
  Châteauneuf-du-Pape 104-106;
  Coteaux Varois 182; Côtes de
  Provence 172-173, 187-190;
  Côtes du Ventoux 111;
  Gigondas 112; St-Jeannet 266,
  267; Séguret 112
  isolated wineries Chartreuse de
  Valbonne, La Roque-sur-Cèze
  107; Domaine de la Citadelle,
  Ménerbes 114
women travellers 305
working in the South 298-299

youth hostels 287
  Corniche de l'Estérel 179-180
  Marseille 136
  La Palud-sur-Verdon 195
  St-Raphaël 175

Advertisers' Index

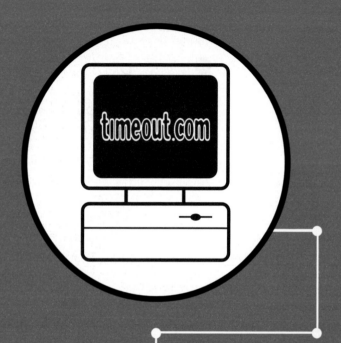

timeout.com

Amsterdam•Barcelona•Berlin•Boston
Brussels•Budapest•Chicago
Dublin•Edinburgh•Florence•Glasgow
Hong Kong•Johannesburg
Las Vegas•Lisbon•London
Los Angeles•Madrid•Miami
Moscow•New Orleans•New York
Paris•Philadelphia•Prague
Rome•San Francisco
Shanghai•Sydney•Tokyo•Vienna
Washington DC

www.timeout.com

Maps

The South of France   318
The Rhône Delta   320
Avignon & the Vaucluse   322
Marseille &
 Aix-en-Provence   324
Inland Var & the
 Western Côte   326
Inland Alpes-Maritimes   328
The Riviera   330

The South of France

Annonay

Yssingeaux

Le Puy

Tournon

Romans

Valence

Clelles

Privas

Crest

Die

Langogne

F   R   A

Vals

Aubenas

Montélimar

Dieulefit

Largentière

Villefort

Joyeu

Valréas

Nyons

Séderon

Pont-
St-Esprit

Vaison

Alés

Orange

Sault

Banon

Lédignan

Uzès

Carpentras

Ganges

Remoulins

Avignon

Avignon &
the Vaucluse
(pages 322-3)

Quissac

Nîmes

Cavaillon

Apt

St Rémy

Les Baux

Pertius

Montpellier

The Rhône Delta
(pages 320-1)

Arles

Salon

Aix-en-
Provence

Aigues-
Mortes

Miramas

Marseille &
Aix-en-Provence
(pages 324-5)

Sète

Stes-Maries-
de-la-Mer

Istres

Golfe
du Lion

Marseille

Aubagne

_M E D I T E R R A N E A N   S E A_

Grenoble
Vizille
Le-Bourg-
d'Oisans
La-Mure

Briançon

Aiguilles

Pinerolo

Torino
Montcalier

A 4
A21
A32

I T A L Y

N   C   E   Guillestre

Aspres
Serres

Gap

Embrun

Fossano

Sisteron

Peyruis

Barcelonnette

Colmars

St Etienne-
de-Tinée

Cuneo   Mondovi

Digne

Barrême

Entrevaux

St-Martin-
Vésubie

Tende

A 8

Inland Alpes-
Maritimes
(pages 328-9)

Sospel

Manosque

Castellane

Vence

Menton   San
Remo

A51

Grasse

Nice

Monaco

MONACO

Aups

Salernes   Draguignan

Barjols

The Riviera
(page 330)

Brignoles

Le-Luc

Vidauban

Cannes
Antibes

A 8

Inland Var
(pages 326-7)

St Raphael

A57

The Western Côte
(pages 326-7)

Cuers

St-Tropez

Toulon

Hyères

Le-Lavandou

La Seyne-
sur-Mer

0   30 miles

0   50 km

© Copyright Time Out Group 2000

Time Out South of France Guide **319**

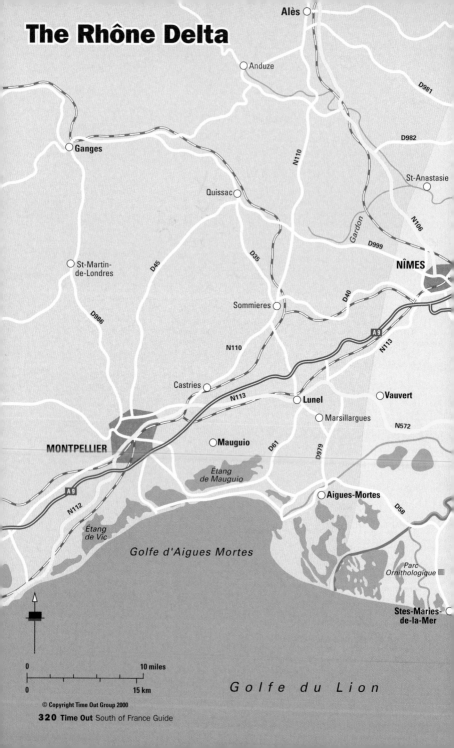

The Rhône Delta

Alès

Anduze

D981

D982

Ganges

St-Anastasie

Quissac

N110

N106

St-Martin-
de-Londres

D45

D35

Gardon

D999

NÎMES

D986

Sommieres

D40

N110

A9

N113

Castries

N113

Lunel

Vauvert

Mauguio

Marsillargues

N572

MONTPELLIER

D61

D979

Étang
de Mauguio

Aigues-Mortes

D58

A9

N112

Étang
de Vic

Golfe d'Aigues Mortes

Parc
Ornithologique

Stes-Maries-
de-la-Mer

0   10 miles

0   15 km

© Copyright Time Out Group 2000

Golfe du Lion

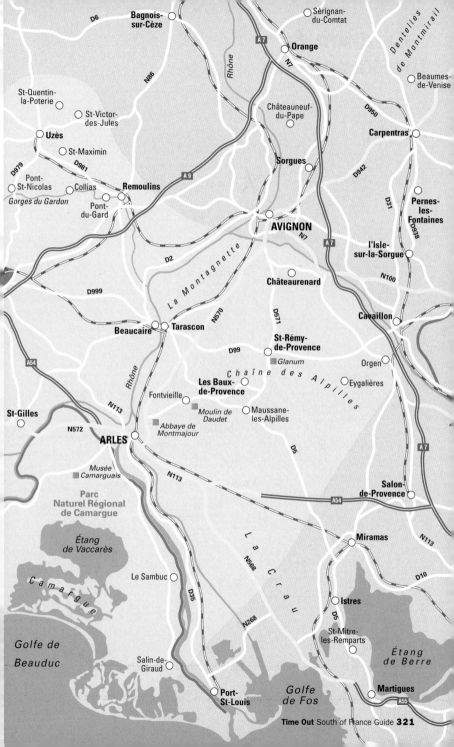

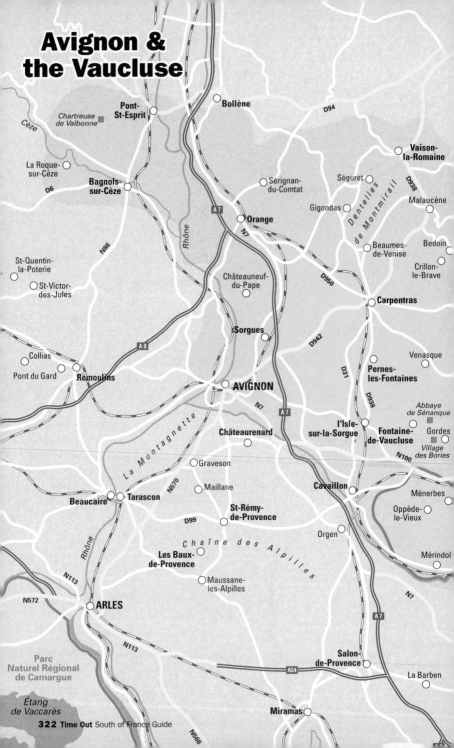

Avignon & the Vaucluse

Cèze

Chartreuse
de Valbonne

Pont-
St-Esprit

Bollène

D94

La Roque-
sur-Cèze

D6

Bagnols-
sur-Cèze

Vaison-
la-Romaine

Séguret

Sérignan-
du-Comtat

Gigondas

Malaucène

N86

Orange

N7

Beaumes-
de-Venise

Bedoin

Crillon-
le-Brave

St-Quentin-
la-Poterie

St-Victor-
des-Jules

Châteauneuf-
du-Pape

Rhône

D950

Carpentras

Dentelles de Montmirail

A7

Sorgues

D942

Venasque

A9

Collias

Pont du Gard

Rémoulins

D31

Pernes-
les-Fontaines

D938

AVIGNON

N7

A7

l'Isle-
sur-la-Sorgue

Abbaye
de Sénanque

Fontaine-
de-Vaucluse

Gordes

Village
des Bories

Châteaurenard

N100

Graveson

La Montagnette

Maillane

N570

Cavaillon

Ménerbes

Beaucaire

Tarascon

D99

St-Rémy-
de-Provence

Orgen

Oppède-
le-Vieux

Rhône

Chaîne des Alpilles

Les Baux-
de-Provence

Mérindol

N113

Maussane-
les-Alpilles

N7

N572

ARLES

N113

A7

Parc
Naturel Régional
de Camargue

Salon-
de-Provence

A54

La Barben

Étang
de Vaccarès

Miramas

N568

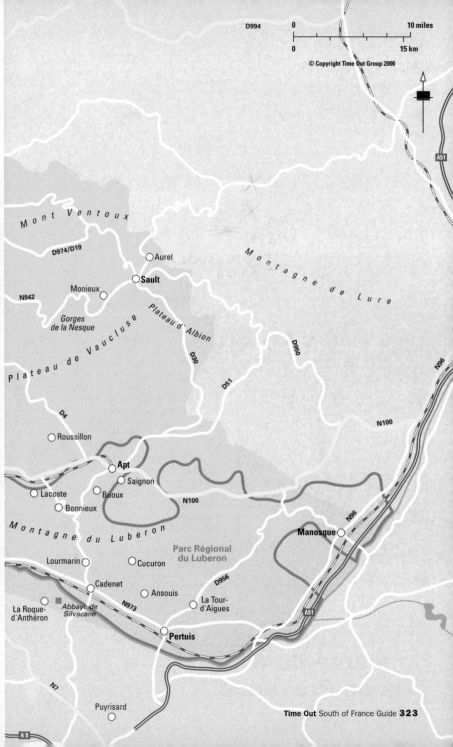

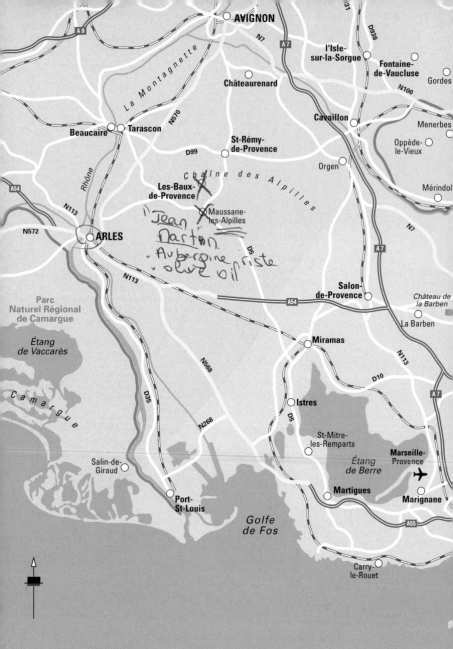

Marseille &
Aix-en-Provence

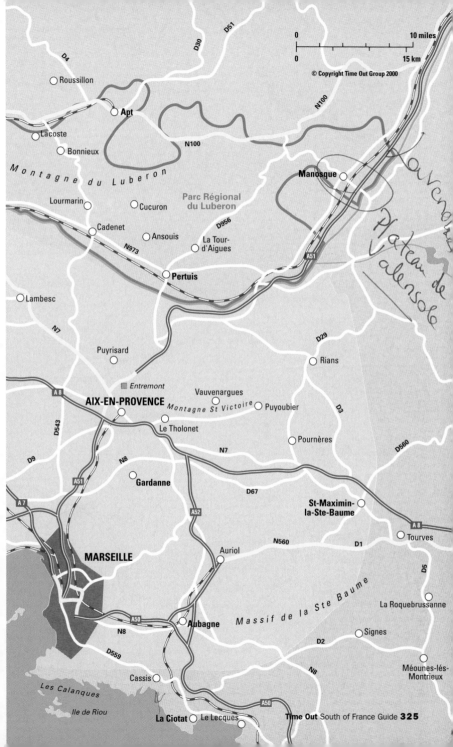

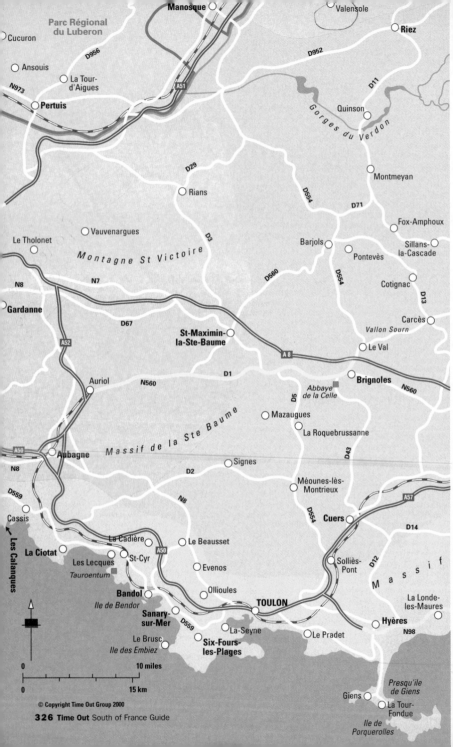

Manosque

Valensole

Parc Régional
du Luberon

Cucuron

Riez

Ansouis

D956

La Tour-
d'Aigues

D952

N973

Pertuis

D11

Quinson

Gorges du Verdon

A51

D29

Montmeyan

Rians

D554

D71

Vauvenargues

Fox-Amphoux

Le Tholonet

Montagne St Victoire

Barjols

Sillans-
la-Cascade

D3

Pontevès

N8

N7

D560

D554

Cotignac

Gardanne

D67

Carcès

D13

A52

St-Maximin-
la-Ste-Baume

A 8

Vallon Sourn

Le Val

Auriol

N560

D1

Brignoles

N560

D5

Abbaye
de la Celle

Mazaugues

A50

Massif de la Ste Baume

La Roquebrussanne

Aubagne

D43

N8

Signes

D2

Méounes-lès-
Montrieux

A57

D559

N8

D554

Cuers

Cassis

D14

La Cadière

Le Beausset

A50

Massif

Les Calanques

La Ciotat

St-Cyr

Solliès-
Pont

D12

Les Lecques

Evenos

Tauroentum

Ollioules

La Londe-
les-Maures

Bandol

TOULON

Ile de Bendor

D559

Sanary-
sur-Mer

La-Seyne

Le Pradet

Hyères

N98

Le Brusc

Six-Fours-
les-Plages

Ile des Embiez

0   10 miles

0   15 km

Presqu'île
de Giens

Giens

© Copyright Time Out Group 2000

La Tour-
Fondue

326 **Time Out** South of France Guide

Ile de
Porquerolles

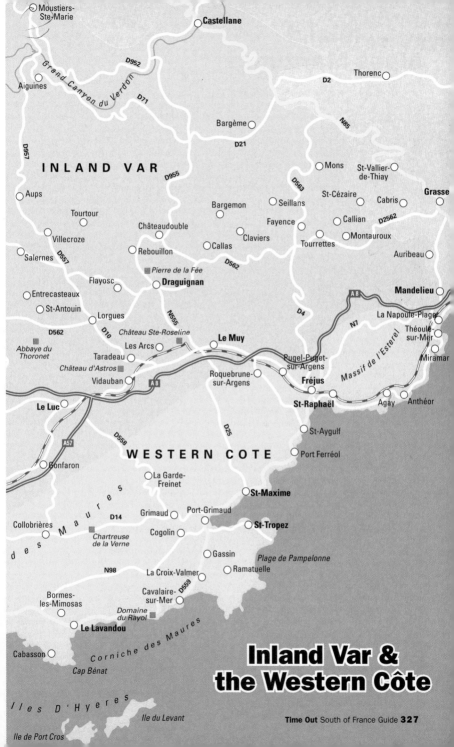

Moustiers-Ste-Marie

Castellane

Aiguines

Thorenc

Grand Canyon du Verdon

D952

D71

D2

N85

Bargème

D21

INLAND VAR

D957

D955

Mons

St-Vallier-de-Thiay

St-Cézaire

Cabris

Grasse

Aups

Tourtour

Bargemon

Seillans

Fayence

Callian

D2562

Châteaudouble

Villecroze

Rebouillon

Callas

Claviers

Montauroux

Tourrettes

Auribeau

Salernes

D557

D563

Flayosc

Pierre de la Fée

Draguignan

D562

Mandelieu

Entrecasteaux

St-Antouin

Lorgues

D10

N555

Château Ste-Roseline

Le Muy

D4

La Napoule-Plage

Théoule-sur-Mer

A8

N7

D562

Abbaye du Thoronet

Les Arcs

Taradeau

Château d'Astros

Vidauban

A8

Roquebrune-sur-Argens

Pugel-Puget-sur-Argens

Fréjus

Massif de l'Esterel

Miramar

Le Luc

A57

D558

WESTERN COTE

D25

St-Raphaël

Agay

Anthéor

Bonfaron

La Garde-Freinet

St-Aygulf

Port Ferréol

Collobrières

D14

Grimaud

Port-Grimaud

St-Maxime

Chartreuse de la Verne

Cogolin

St-Tropez

Gassin

Plage de Pampelonne

N98

Ramatuelle

La Croix-Valmer

Bormes-les-Mimosas

Cavalaire-sur-Mer

D559

Domaine du Rayol

des Maures

Le Lavandou

Cabasson

Corniche des Maures

Cap Bénat

Iles D'Hyeres

Ile du Levant

Ile de Port Cros

Inland Var &
the Western Côte

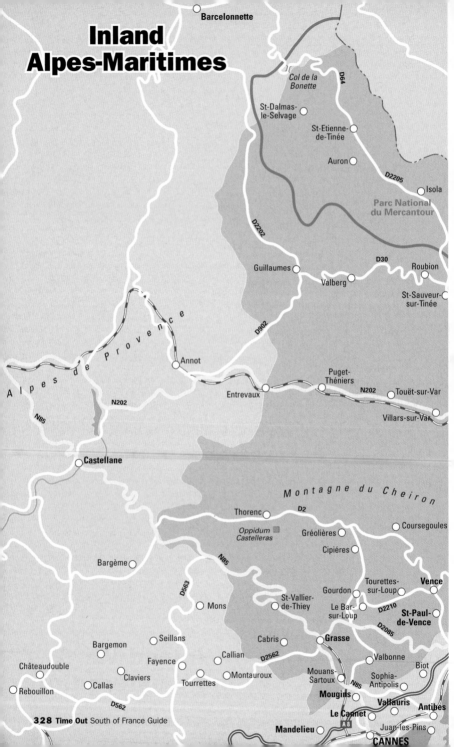

Inland
Alpes-Maritimes

Barcelonnette

Col de la Bonette

St-Dalmas-le-Selvage

St-Etienne-de-Tinée

Auron

D64

D2205

Isola

Parc National du Mercantour

D2202

Guillaumes

Valberg

Roubion

D30

St-Sauveur-sur-Tinée

D902

Alpes de Provence

Annot

Puget-Théniers

Entrevaux

N202

Touët-sur-Var

Villars-sur-Var

N202

N85

Castellane

Montagne du Cheiron

Thorenc

D2

Coursegoules

Oppidum Castelleras

Gréolières

Cipières

Bargème

N85

St-Vallier-de-Thiey

Gourdon

Tourettes-sur-Loup

Vence

D563

Mons

Le Bar-sur-Loup

D2210

St-Paul-de-Vence

D2085

Bargemon

Seillans

Cabris

Grasse

Fayence

Callian

Valbonne

Biot

Châteaudouble

Claviers

Montauroux

D2562

Mouans-Sartoux

Sophia-Antipolis

N85

Rebouillon

Callas

Tourrettes

Mougins

Vallauris

Antibes

D562

Le Cannet

A8

Juan-les-Pins

Mandelieu

CANNES

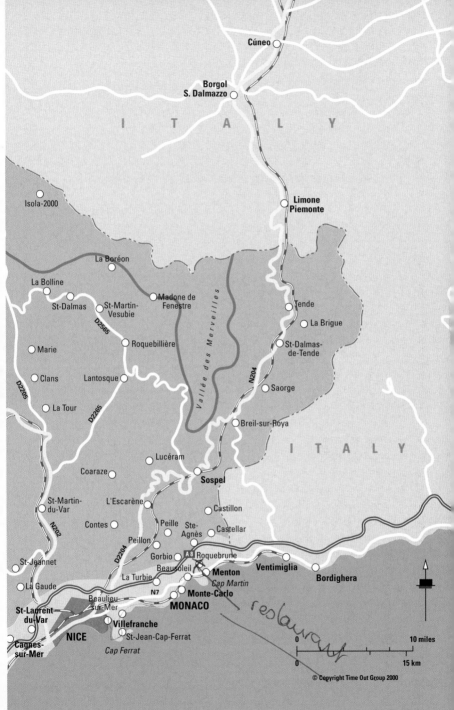

Isola-2000

La Boréon

La Bolline
St-Dalmas   St-Martin-
            Vesubie
D2565
Marie
Clans   Roquebillière
Lantosque
D2205
La Tour
D2265

St-Martin-
du-Var
Contes
N202
St-Jeannet
La Gaude
Beaulieu-
sur-Mer
St-Laurent-
du-Var
Cagnes-
sur-Mer   NICE
               Villefranche
               St-Jean-Cap-Ferrat
               Cap Ferrat

Coaraze
L'Escarène
Peille
Peillon
Gorbio
D2204
La Turbie
N7
Beausoleil
MONACO

Lucéram
Sospel
Castillon
Ste-
Agnès
Castellar
A8 Roquebrune
Menton
Cap Martin
Monte-Carlo

Madone de
Fenestre

Vallée des Merveilles

Tende
La Brigue
St-Dalmas-
de-Tende
Saorge
N204
Breil-sur-Roya

Ventimiglia
Bordighera

Cúneo

Borgol
S. Dalmazzo

ITALY

Limone
Piemonte

ITALY

restaurant

0   10 miles
0   15 km

© Copyright Time Out Group 2000

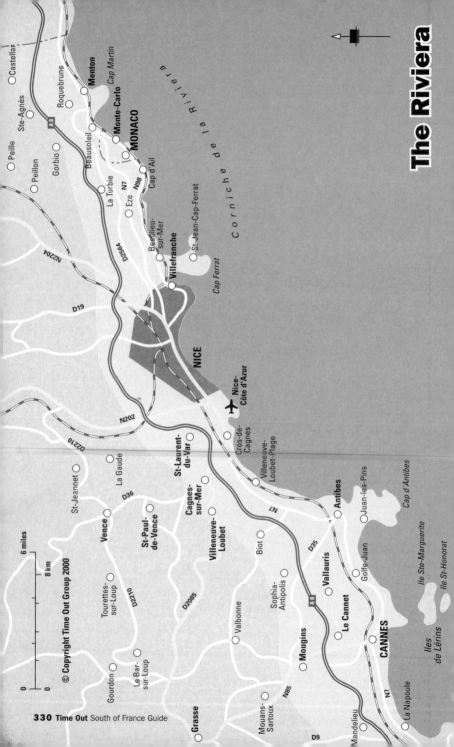

The Riviera

© Copyright Time Out Group 2000

6 miles

8 km

Castellar
Ste-Agnès
Peille
Peillon
Gorbio
Roquebrune
Menton
Cap Martin
Monte-Carlo
Beausoleil
MONACO
La Turbie
Eze
Cap d'Ail
N98
N7
Corniche de la Riviera
Beaulieu-sur-Mer
Villefranche
St-Jean-Cap-Ferrat
Cap Ferrat
NICE
Nice-Côte d'Azur
Cros-de-Cagnes
Villeneuve-Loubet-Plage
St-Jeannet
La Gaude
St-Laurent-du-Var
Cagnes-sur-Mer
Vence
St-Paul-de-Vence
Villeneuve-Loubet
Biot
Antibes
Juan-les-Pins
Cap d'Antibes
Tourettes-sur-Loup
Sophia-Antipolis
Vallauris
Golfe-Juan
Ile Ste-Marguerite
Ile St-Honorat
Valbonne
Le Cannet
CANNES
Iles de Lérins
Gourdon
Le Bar-sur-Loup
Mougins
Mandelieu
La Napoule
Grasse
Mouans-Sartoux

A8
N204
D2564
D19
N2204
D2210
N202
D36
D2210
D2085
N85
D35
A8
N7
D9

South of France Please let us know what you think

(FIRST EDITION)

About this guide…

1. How useful did you find the following sections?

	Very	Fairly	Not very
In Context	☐☐☐	☐☐☐	☐☐☐
The Rhône Delta	☐☐☐	☐☐☐	☐☐☐
Avignon & the Vaucluse	☐☐☐	☐☐☐	☐☐☐
Marseille & Aix	☐☐☐	☐☐☐	☐☐☐
The Western Côte	☐☐☐	☐☐☐	☐☐☐
Inland Var	☐☐☐	☐☐☐	☐☐☐
The Riviera	☐☐☐	☐☐☐	☐☐☐
Inland Alpes-Maritimes	☐☐☐	☐☐☐	☐☐☐
Directory	☐☐☐	☐☐☐	☐☐☐
Maps	☐☐☐	☐☐☐	☐☐☐

2. Did you travel to the South of France…?

Alone ☐
As part of a group ☐
On business ☐
With a partner ☐

With children ☐
On vacation ☐
To study ☐
I live here. ☐

3. How long was your trip to the South of France? (write in)

_____ days

4. Where did you book your trip?

Time Out Classifieds ☐
On the Internet ☐
With a travel agent ☐
Other (write in) ☐

5. Where did you first hear about this guide?

Advertising in *Time Out* magazine ☐
On the Internet ☐
From a travel agent ☐
Other (write in) ☐
_____

6. Is there anything you'd like us to cover in greater depth?

_____
_____
_____

7. Are there any places that should/ should not* be included in the guide? (*delete as necessary)

_____
_____
_____
_____
_____
_____
_____

8. How many other people have used this guide?

none ☐   1 ☐   2 ☐   3 ☐   4 ☐   5+ ☐

9. What city or country would you like to visit next? (write in)

_____
_____

About other Time Out publications…

10. Have you ever bought/used other *Time Out* magazine?

Yes ☐.   No ☐

11. Have you ever bought/used any other *Time Out City Guides?*

Yes ☐   No ☐

If yes, which ones?
_____
_____

12. Have you ever bought/used other *Time Out* publications?

Yes ☐   No ☐

If yes, which ones?
_____
_____

About you…

13. Title (Mr, Ms etc):
First name:
Surname:
Address:

Postcode:
Email:
Nationality:

14. Date of birth   ☐☐/☐☐/☐☐

15. Sex: male ☐   female ☐

16. Are you…?
Single ☐☐
Married/Living with partner

17. What is your occupation?
_____

18. At the moment do you earn…?

under £15,000 ☐
over £15,000 and up to £19,999 ☐
over £20,000 and up to £24,999 ☐
over £25,000 and up to £39,999 ☐
over £40,000 and up to £49,999 ☐
over £50,000 ☐

☐ Please tick here if you'd like to hear about offers and discounts from *Time Out* products and relevant companies.

Time Out Guides

FREEPOST 20 (WC3187)
LONDON
W1E 0DQ

City Guides are available from all **good bookshops** or through **Penguin Direct.**

Simply call 020 8757 4036 (9am-5pm) or fill out the form below, affix a stamp and return.

ISBN	title	retail price	quantity	total
0140289445	Time Out Guide to **Amsterdam**	£9.99		
0140289410	Time Out Guide to **Barcelona**	£10.99		
0140289399	Time Out Guide to **Berlin**	£10.99		
0140284052	Time Out Guide to **Boston**	£10.99		
0140289429	Time Out Guide to **Brussels**	£9.99		
0140286330	Time Out Guide to **Budapest**	£10.99		
0140281738	Time Out Guide to **Dublin**	£10.99		
0140289453	Time Out Guide to **Edinburgh**	£9.99		
0140293930	Time Out Guide to **Florence & Tuscany**	£10.99		
0140289402	Time Out Guide to **Las Vegas**	£10.99		
0140273158	Time Out Guide to **Lisbon**	£9.99		
0140289372	Time Out Guide to **London**	£10.99		
0140274456	Time Out Guide to **Los Angeles**	£9.99		
014027443X	Time Out Guide to **Madrid**	£9.99		
0140266852	Time Out Guide to **Miami**	£9.99		
014027314X	Time Out Guide to **Moscow**	£9.99		
0140274480	Time Out Guide to **New Orleans**	£9.99		
0140274529	Time Out Guide to **New York**	£9.99		
0140289380	Time Out Guide to **Paris**	£10.99		
0140274448	Time Out Guide to **Prague**	£9.99		
0140287558	Time Out Guide to **Rome**	£10.99		
0140289364	Time Out Guide to **San Francisco**	£10.99		
014029077X	Time Out Guide to **The South of France**	£10.99		
0140274464	Time Out Guide to **Sydney**	£10.99		
0140284605	Time Out Guide to **Tokyo**	£10.99		
0140284060	Time Out Guide to **Venice**	£10.99		
0140284677	Time Out Guide to **Vienna**	£10.99		
0140284591	Time Out Guide to **Washington**	£10.99		
		+ postage & packing		£1.50
		Total Payment		

(Please use block capitals)

Cardholder's Name

Address

Town   Postcode

Daytime Telephone Number

Method of Payment (UK Credit cards only)

Barclaycard/Visa

Access Card/Mastercard

Signature (if paying by credit card) _____

Expiry date

Cheque
I enclose a cheque £ _____ made payable to 'Penguin Direct'

Delivery will normally be within 14 working days. The availability and published prices quoted are correct at time of going to press but are subject to alteration without prior notice. Order form valid until May 2001. **Please note that this service is only available in the UK.** Please note your order may be delayed if payment details are incorrect.

Penguin Direct
Penguin Books Ltd
Bath Road
Harmondsworth
West Drayton
Middlesex
UB7 0DA